CW00821437

Johann Joseph Ignaz von Döllinger

The Church and the Churches

or - thepapacy and the temporal power - an historical and political review translated with the

author's permission

Johann Joseph Ignaz von Döllinger

The Church and the Churches
or - thepapacy and the temporal power - an historical and political review translated with the author's permission

ISBN/EAN: 9783337816087

Printed in Europe, USA, Canada, Australia, Japan

Cover: Foto ©Lupo / pixelio.de

More available books at **www.hansebooks.com**

THE CHURCH AND THE CHURCHES;

OR,

THE PAPACY AND THE TEMPORAL POWER.

An Historical and Political Review.

BY

DR. DÖLLINGER.

TRANSLATED, WITH THE AUTHOR'S PERMISSION,

BY

WILLIAM BERNARD MAC CABE.

IN ONE VOLUME.

LONDON:
HURST AND BLACKETT, PUBLISHERS,
SUCCESSORS TO HENRY COLBURN,
13, GREAT MARLBOROUGH STREET.
1862.

The right of Translation is reserved.

LONDON:
PRINTED BY R. BORN, GLOUCESTER STREET,
REGENT'S PARK.

BIOGRAPHICAL PREFACE.

BY THE TRANSLATOR.

As it is possible this book may fall into the hands of many but little acquainted with the claim which the Author has upon the attention of the learned in every country, it has been deemed advisable to collect some materials respecting his antecedent biography. The life of an author is to be found in his works; and it will be seen by the subjoined narrative that the years of Dr. Döllinger have been crowded with events; and that each of these reflects honour upon him as a theologian, a scholar, and an historian, as a man of deep research and of original thought.

Dr. Döllinger was born at Bamberg, on the 28th February, 1799, and educated at Würzburg. After several years passed, first at a curacy in Franconia, and as Professor at the Ecclesiastical Seminary of Aschaffenberg, he was, in 1826, appointed one of the Faculty of Theology in the new University of Munich. The results of the French Revolution were felt in the youth and early manhood of Dr. Döllinger. Rationalism was everywhere predominant. There was no master-mind amongst the Roman Catholics of Germany; and the young and ardent student was thrown upon his own resources, and compelled

to rely on his own independent research for the acquisition
of knowledge and the formation of his judgment. The
results of such a course are apparent in the writings of Dr.
Döllinger; for all exhibit profound and extensive learning,
a judgment free from personal and partial influences, the
habit of penetrating directly to original sources, and a
critical method to which the works of the patristic, the
scholastic, and modern writers are indifferently subjected.

Dr. Döllinger's earliest work was on "The Doctrine of
the Eucharist in the three first Centuries," 1826. Two
years later appeared a "History of the Reformation," forming the third volume of "The Ecclesiastical History" of
Hortig. He then undertook to re-write the whole work,
and published in 1833 the first, and in 1835 the second volume
of that "Church History" by which his name first became
widely known for his learned and able defence of the
Catholic idea, and for the confidence with which many
views, so often repeated as to be believed unquestionable
and essential, were abandoned as untenable. Four more
volumes which had been announced were never written;
but an elaborate treatise on "The History, Character, and
Influence of Islamism," appeared in 1838; and a Com-
pendium of the History of the Church down to the
Reformation, was published in the years 1836-1843. The
history of the six first centuries is given with extreme
brevity; but the history of the Middle Ages, though much
compressed, displays even more copious erudition than the
account of the earlier period in the larger work. In the
English translation, these two histories have been unskil-
fully combined. Between the years 1846 and 1848, Dr.
Döllinger published three large volumes on the history of
German Lutheranism, "The Reformation, its Internal Development and its Effects." The original design was too
extensive to be completed; the work remains a fragment,
and the innumerable extracts from the writings of the period,
many of them rare, and some unpublished, whilst they confer
on these volumes a value they will never lose, yet render
them difficult to be read with pleasure. But the immense

research with which the ideas of the Reformers and their contemporaries, on the doctrine and the condition of their Church, are exposed, make this by far the most instructive account of the German Reformation.

During this period Dr. Döllinger delivered courses of lectures on several other branches of Divinity besides that which specially belonged to his chair; " on the Philosophy of Religion," "on Canon Law," "on Symbolism," and on "the Literature of the Patristic Age." Having ceded, for some years, his professorship of ecclesiastical history to Möhler, whose lesser writings he afterwards collected, he took that of dogmatic theology, which in his hands was transformed into a history of revelation and of the development of doctrine. None of these lectures have been printed, but the author has published from time to time a large number of occasional writings. Among the earliest were "An Essay on the Religion of Shakespeare," and a lecture "on the Introduction of Christianity among the Germans." A "Commentary on the Paradise of Dante," accompanied by the designs of Cornelius in 1830; "Mixed Marriages—a Voice for Peace," came out in 1838, during the conflict between the Prussian Government and the Archbishop of Cologne. In the following years articles on "The Tractarian Movement," "John Huss and the Council of Constance," "The Albigenses," appeared in the "Historisch-politische Blätter," over which, though very rarely a contributor, he presided for many years. A dissertation on "The Position of the Church towards those who die out of Her Communion," was written in 1842, on the occasion of the death of the Dowager Queen of Bavaria; a lecture on "Error, Doubt, and Truth," was originally delivered by Dr. Döllinger before the students, as Rector of the University; a speech on "The Freedom of the Church," one of his most excellent publications, at Ratisbon, in 1849. "Martin Luther, a Sketch," was reprinted in the year 1852, from a theological Encyclopædia to which he also contributed articles on "Bossuet," and on "Duns Scotus." A pamphlet on "Coronation by the Pope," was produced in 1853, when it was feared that Pius IX. would be induced to crown the Emperor of the French; and described the different instances in which it had been done, and the error committed on the last occasion.

From 1845 to 1847 Dr. Döllinger represented the University of Munich in the Bavarian Chamber, where he was regarded as one of the leaders of the Ultramontanes. Several of his speeches have been published. In the latter year he was deprived of his professorship, and consequently of his seat in the Chamber, where the ministers who had been raised to power by Lola Montez dreaded the influence of his eloquence and character. Having been elected a deputy to the National Parliament in 1848, he spoke and wrote with great effect in favour of religious liberty, and the definition of "the relations between Church and State," which was carried at Frankfort, and was afterwards nominally adopted both at Vienna and Berlin, is said to have been his work. The same spirit and the same principles which made him in religion the keenest of controversial writers, and the most earnest advocate of reforms, guided him in political life, and made him the exponent of the highest Catholic views, and the champion of ecclesiastical freedom. He regarded the oppression of the Church as the safeguard of absolutism in the State, and the faults and errors of Catholics as a fruitful source of the divisions and disputes among Christians. In his desire to reconcile religion with society, and Protestantism with Rome, Dr. Döllinger admitted no compromise, but, acknowledging the just claims and real progress of the modern world, and the evils that afflict the Church, he sought to distinguish *that which is essential and true* from those things with which, from ignorance or superstition, interest or unbelief, it had been surrounded.

In the spring of 1849, he returned to Munich and was restored to his professorship, and also to his seat in the Chamber, which he, however, resigned two years later, in order to devote himself to the completion of his literary plans. Three principal works have since appeared, each complete in itself, and superior, both in style and matter, to those by which they had been preceded. The publication of the "Philosophumena," by Miller, in 1851, gave rise to a prolonged discussion, in which many Catholics sought to weaken the testimony of the author, whilst Protestant writers endeavoured to use his authority for the purpose of throwing discredit on the Church of Rome. In answer to both parties—especially to Gieseler, Baur, Bunsen, Wordsworth, and Lenormant—Dr. Döllinger published, in 1853, "Hippolytus and Callistus—The Roman Church in the Third Century,"—perhaps, of all his writings, the one in which his ingenuity of combination, his skill as a logician, and his lofty tone in handling the interests of his Church, are most conspicuous. The classical learning shown in this work was more abundantly displayed in the introduction to the history of Christianity, which appeared in 1857, under the title of "Paganism and Judaism." In 1860 appeared a volume entitled "Christianity and the Church in the period of their Foundation," which is the author's masterpiece. It is understood to be Dr. Döllinger's intention to continue this work down to the present time. The newspapers have also announced a volume on the thirteenth century, and a rumour has long circulated that a work on the Mediæval Heresies, founded on very extensive researches in Rome, Florence, Paris, and Bologna, was in preparation. These labours were interrupted by the course of events which called forth the present volume. Of the value to be attached to this work, it would not be becoming in the Translator to express an opinion; but a few words he cannot refrain from adding with reference to the spirit in which the translation has been executed.

In our Courts of Justice, when a witness speaking a foreign language is called upon to give his evidence, there is at the same time sworn an interpreter, to whom an oath to the following effect is administered:

"You shall well and truly interpret to the Court and Jury, and to the best of your skill and knowledge, the evidence of the Witness in this Cause."

When undertaking to convey to English readers the opinions and statements of the most distinguished of living

German scholars and writers, upon topics of paramount interest, the translator felt himself under an obligation somewhat similar to that which binds the sworn interpreter. He has, "to the best of his skill and knowledge," given as close an English representation of Dr. Döllinger's German words as the genius of the two languages would permit.

In accordance with such a desire, he has adopted, verbatim, or, with only a few alterations, passages of Dr. Döllinger's work, which he found translated in "The Rambler," vol. vi., part 16.

The Author has, in the second part of this book—"The Papacy and the Papal States"—made frequent reference to the favoured bureaucratic class in Rome, the "Prelatura." A literal translation of the word "Prälaten" into English, as "Prelates," might lead to a gross misapprehension. In England, Ireland, and Scotland, the universal signification given to the word "prelate," corresponds precisely with Johnson's definition of it—"an Ecclesiastic of the highest order and dignity." Our "Prelates" are either archbishops or bishops; but it will be seen by the annexed account given of the *Roman* "Prelates," that they are far different, in every respect, from members of the Episcopal order.

"The 'Prelatura,'" (observes Mr. Lyons, in his letter to the Marquis of Normanby, No. xxxi.,) "is essentially an Ecclesiastical Body: its members, whether they actually take orders or not, are looked upon as belonging to the clergy. They wear the ecclesiastical habit; they are expected to act, think, and speak as Churchmen. They form a body apart from the rest of the community. They have ecclesiastical privileges. It is true that *they have not all of them irrevocably taken a vow of celibacy;* nay, I believe there are even *some rare instances of prelates actually married.* But if a prelate marry, his career is almost inevitably closed —his hopes of high office and of the cardinalates are at an end."*

To prevent misunderstanding, whenever this class of

---

* Despatches from Mr. Lyons, respecting the condition and administration of the Papal States. London, 1860, p. 50.

officials is referred to in the following pages, they will be found designated with the name by which they are known in Rome, that is, as " *Prelati.*"

W. B. M.

Mill Hill Lodge, Hastings.
    April, 1862.

CONTENTS.

THE CHURCH AND THE CHURCHES.

INTRODUCTION.

THIS work has arisen out of two lectures which were delivered in the month of April of the present year. I feel myself bound to explain how I came to speak, before a very mixed auditory, upon the most difficult and complicated question of our time; and that, too, in a manner decidedly different from what is usually adopted. I had at first determined, when the request to deliver some lectures reached me, simply to speak of the present state of religion in general, with a comprehensive view extending over all mankind. It happened, however, that by those very circles (from which the impulse to the delivery of the lectures had come) the question was frequently put to me—"How was the position of the Papal See—the partly consummated, partly threatened loss of its temporal sovereignty—to be explained?" "What"—I was repeatedly asked—"what was one to say in reply to those non-churchmen who pointed, with triumphant scorn, to the numerous episcopal manifestoes in which the States of the Church are declared essential and necessary to her existence, even though the events of the last thirty years appear with unerring distinctness to announce their downfall?"

I had, too, in newspapers, periodicals, and books, fre-

B

quently found the hope expressed, that with the downfall of
the temporal sovereignty of the Pope, the Church itself
would not escape the doom of dissolution. At the same time,
I was struck by finding, in the Memoirs of Châteaubriand,
this expression of Cardinal Bernetti, Secretary of State to
Leo XII.: "That if he lived a long time, there was the
prospect before him of yet beholding the fall of the temporal
power of the Papacy."[1] I had also read in the communication of a Paris correspondent, whose name has been
mentioned to me as that of a well-informed and trustworthy
person, "that the Archbishop of Rheims, on his return from
Rome, had recounted what Pope Pius had said to him: 'I
yield to no illusions; the temporal power must fall. Goyon
will abandon me ; I shall then disband my remaining troops.
I shall, as the King enters, excommunicate him, and calmly
await my death.'"[2]

I already believed, in April, I could perceive that which is
still more plainly exhibited in October, that the enemies of
the temporal Papal-Sovereignty are resolute, united, predominant, and that nowhere is there to be found a protecting
power which possesses at the same time the will and the
ability of averting the catastrophe. I considered it, therefore, probable that an interruption of the temporal dominion
would ensue—an interruption which, like to others that had
preceded it, would again cease, and be followed by a restoration. I resolved, therefore, to avail myself of the opportunity
which the lectures afforded me to prepare the public for those
coming events the shadows of which had been cast into the
present time, and thus to prevent the scandals, the doubts,
and the offence which must inevitably arise if the States of
the Church should pass into other hands, although episcopal
pastorals had hitherto energetically asserted that they belonged to the integrity of the Church. I meant, therefore,
to say :—That the Church can exist by and for herself, and
that she did exist for seven centuries without the territorial

---

[1] "Mémoires d'Outretombe," viii. 136. Ed. de Berlin.
[2] Such is the statement in the London Catholic weekly journal, the
Weekly Register, March 2, 1861, p. 4.

possessions of the Popes; but that at a later period this property, through the condition of the world, became necessary, and, in spite of great changes and vicissitudes, has discharged in most cases its function of serving as a foundation for the independence and freedom of the Popes. As long as the present state and arrangement of Europe endures, we can discover no other means to secure to the Papal See its freedom, and, through it, general confidence. But God's knowledge and power reach further than ours, and we must not presume to set bounds to the Divine Wisdom and Omnipotence, and cry out to it—"This way, and not otherwise." Should, however, the event which now threatens to occur actually take place, and the Pope be despoiled of his landed possessions, one of three eventualities will assuredly come to pass:—Either the loss of the Papal States is only temporary, and the territory will revert, after some intervening casualties, in its entirety or in part, to its rightful sovereign; or Providence will bring about, by ways unknown to us, and combinations which we cannot divine, a state of things in which the object—namely, the independence and free action of the Papal See, without those means which have hitherto sufficed for it; or, lastly, we are approaching great catastrophes in Europe—a collapse of the whole edifice of existing social order—events of which the downfall of the Papal States is only the precursor, or, as it may be said, "the Job's-messenger."

I have developed, in this book, the grounds upon which I think of these three possibilities, the first the most probable. As to the second possibility, there is nothing to be said but this—that it is an unknown, and consequently indescribable $=x$—it is only good for this much: we must retain it against certain over-confident assertions, which profess to know the secret things to come, and trespassing on the Divine Domain, wish to subject the Future absolutely to the laws of the immediate Past. That the third possibility must also be admitted, few of those who studiously observe the signs of the times will dispute. One of the shrewdest historians and statesmen, Niebuhr, had, so long ago as the 5th October,

1830, written these words: "If God does not marvellously help, there is impending over us a destruction such as occurred to the Roman world in the middle of the third century—the annihilation of prosperity, freedom, civilization, and literature." And we have proceeded much further on the inclined plane since then. The Powers of Europe have overturned, or permitted to be overturned, the two main pillars of their edifice—the principles of Legitimacy and public international Law. Those monarchs who have made themselves, like to slaves, the tools of revolution, are now active performers in the world's historical drama—the others conduct themselves as quiet spectators, and are, in their hopes, smiling heirs, like Prussia and Russia; or they are bestowing applause and giving help, like England; or they are as passive invalids, like Austria, or the hectic-fever-stricken Turkey. But the Revolution is a permanent chronic disease, breaking out now in one place, now in another, and then attacking several members at the same time. The Pentarchy is dissolved; the Holy Alliance, even though a defective and misused form of European political order, is buried. The right of the strongest alone now prevails in Europe. Is it a process of renovation, or a process of dissolution, in which European society is plunged? I still believe it to be the former; but I must, as I have said, admit the possibility of the other alternative. If it occurs—then, when the powers of destruction have done their work, it will be the business of the Church at once to co-operate actively in the reconstruction of social order out of the ruins, both as a connecting civilizing power and as the preserver and dispenser of moral and religious tradition. And for this, too, the Papacy has, with or without territory, its own function and its own mission.

Such, then, were the ideas from which I started; and it may be supposed that my language concerning the immediate fate of the temporal power of the Pope necessarily sounded ambiguous—that I could not, with the confidence that is given to others, perhaps more keen-sighted men—come before my auditors, and say: "Rely upon this—the States of the Church—the land from Radicofani to Caperano, from Ravenna to Civita Vecchia, shall and must and will remain with the Popes—heaven and earth shall pass away, before the States of the Church pass away!" I could not do this, because I had not then any such conviction, nor do I now, in the slightest degree, entertain it; but of this I am alone confident, that the Papal See will not be permanently deprived of the conditions necessary for the fulfilment of its mission. Hence, the substance of my words was this, "Let no one lose faith in the Church, if the temporal principality of the Papacy should disappear, whether it be for a season, or for ever. It is not essence, but accident; not end, but means; it began late; it was formerly something quite different from what it is now. It now justly appears to us to be indispensable; and so long as the existing order lasts in Europe, it must, at all cost, be maintained; or, if it is violently interrupted, it must be restored. But it is possible to suppose a political condition of Europe in which it would be superfluous, and then it would be only a clogging burden." At the same time, I wished to defend Pope Pius IX., and his government, against numerous accusations, and to show that the inward infirmities and deficiences which undeniably exist in the country, and through which the State has been reduced to such an astounding condition of weakness and helplessness, are not attributable to him; that, on the contrary, he has, both before and since 1848, shewn the best will to reform; and that, actually by him, and under him, many things are now much better than they had been.

The reports in the newspapers, written out at home from memory, gave but an inaccurate representation of a discourse which did not attempt to cut the knot in the usual way, but which, with *buts* and *ifs*, and referring to certain elements—to critical and decisive events, for the most part left out of the calculation—alluded to an uncertain future and manifold contingencies. This was unavoidable. Every report, not absolutely verbal, must, despite of the best intentions of the reporter, give rise to a distorted apprehension. When, therefore, one of the most widely circulated journals reported the first lecture, without any intentional falsification, but with omissions, which altered the sense and tendency of my words, I immediately proposed to the editor to print my manuscript; but this was declined. In other reports of the daily organs I was often unable to recognize my own ideas; whilst expressions were put into my mouth to which I was altogether a stranger.

And here I will admit that, when I gave the lectures, I did not think that they would be discussed by the press; but I expected that, like others of the same kind, they would at most be mentioned in a couple of words, *in futuram oblivionem.* Of the controversy which sprang up at once in separate works, and in newspaper articles—in Germany, France, England, Italy, and even in America—I shall not speak. Much of it I have not read—the writers often did not even ask themselves whether the report which accident put into their hands, and which they carelessly adopted, was at all accurate. But I must refer to an account in one of the most widely read of English periodicals, because I am there brought into a society to which I do not belong. In the July number of the *Edinburgh Review,* there is an article, written, as it is reported, by Mr. H. Cartwright, and entitled "Church Reformation in Italy." The author first analyses Rosmini's treatise, " Le cinque piaghe della chiesa ;" he then speaks of what is congenial to it, of the existing change of circumstances in Italy favourable to the views of Rosmini, of the Dominican of St. Mark in Florence, of the Capuchins, of a writing by the Oratorian Capecelatro of Naples, which takes an unfavourable view of the Temporal Sovereignty of the Pope—and then, misapprehending the tendency of my expressions, and under the erroneous notion that I had already published an apology of my ortho-doxy, he appeals to me—and then comes a detailed descrip-tion of the sentiments and sufferings of Passaglia and Tosti. A sharp attack upon me in the *Dublin Review* I know only from extracts in the English papers, but I can see, from the vehemence with which the writer pronounces himself against "liberal" institutions, that, even after the appearance of this book, I cannot reckon on coming to an understanding with him.

Upon this matter every one now can judge for himself. To fulfil a promise that I had given, I have had both lectures printed as an appendix, just as they were originally composed, merely omitting the introduction, it not touching upon the general Church and State question, and being nothing more than casual reflections. As a matter of course, in revision, many things that were introduced extempore are left out, although not in the slightest degree at variance with the sense of what is here published.

The excitement which was caused by my lectures, or rather by the reports of them in the daily press, had this advantage, that it brought to light, in a way which to many was unexpected, in what wide circles, how deeply and how firmly rooted is the attachment of the people to the See of St. Peter. · For the sake of this, I was glad to accept all the attacks and animosity which fell on me in consequence. But wherefore—it will be asked, and I have been asked innumerable times—wherefore not cut short misunderstandings by the immediate publication of the lectures, which must, as a whole, have been written previous to delivery? Why wait for five months? For this I had two reasons. First, it was not merely a question of misunderstanding. Much of what I had actually said had made an unpleasant impression in many quarters, especially among our optimists. I should, therefore, with my bare statements, have become involved in an agitating newspaper and pamphlet squabble, and that was not an attractive prospect. My second reason was—I expected that the further development of circumstances in Italy, the irresistible logic of facts, would dispose many minds to receive certain truths. I hoped that people would learn by degrees, in the school of events, that it is not enough always to be reckoning with the figures "Revolution," "Secret Societies," "Mazziniism," "Atheism," or to estimate things only by the standard supplied in "The Jew of Verona," but that other factors must be admitted into the calculation; for instance—the condition of the Italian clergy, and their position towards the laity. I wished, therefore, to let a few months pass away, previous to my appearing before the public. Whether I calculated rightly, the reception of this book will show.

I thoroughly understand those who think it censurable that I should have spoken in detail of circumstances and facts that are willingly ignored, or that are skipped over with a light and fleeting foot, and that, too, especially at the present crisis. I myself was restrained for two years by these considerations, in spite of the feeling that urged me to speak on the question of the Papal States ; and it required the circumstances I have described, I may almost say, to compel me to speak publicly on the subject. I beg, then, of those persons to reflect on the following points. First, when an author openly exposes a state of things already abundantly discussed in the press ; if he draws away the necessarily very transparent covering from the gaping wounds which are not in the Church herself, but on an Institution nearly connected with her, and whose infirmities she is made to feel —it may fairly be supposed that he does it, in accordance with the example of earlier friends, and great men of the Church, only to show the possibility and necessity of the cure, in order, so far as in him lies, to weaken the reproach that the defenders of the Church see only "the mote" in the eyes of others, not "the beam" in their own ; and, with narrow-hearted prejudice, endeavour to soften, or to dissimulate, or to deny every fact which is, or which appears to be, unfavourable to their cause. He does it in order that it may be understood that where the impotency of man to effect a cure becomes manifest, God interposes, in order to sift on His threshing-floor the chaff from the wheat, and to consume it with the fire-glow of catastrophes which are only His judgments and His remedies. Secondly, I could not, as an historian, present results without going back to their causes ; and it was, therefore, my duty, as it is that of every religious inquirer and observer, to try and contribute something to the Theodicea. He that undertakes to write on such lofty interests, which nearly affect the weal and woe of the Church, cannot avoid examining and displaying the wisdom and justice of God in the conduct of terrestrial events. The fate which has overtaken the States of the Church must, before all things, be considered in the light of a Divine Ordinance for the advantage of the Church. So considered, it presents itself as a trial which will endure until the object is attained, and the welfare of the Church, so far, secured.

It seemed evident to me that, as a new order of things in Europe lies in the design of Providence, so the disease through which, for the last half century, the States of the Church unquestionably have passed, might be the transition to a new form. To describe this malady, without overlooking or concealing any of the symptoms, was, therefore, an undertaking I could not avoid. The disease has its source in the inward contradiction and discord of institutions and of circumstances; for the modern French institutions stand there in close and constant contact with a mediæval hierarchy; and neither of these two elements is strong enough to expel the other; and either of them would, if it were the sole predominant power, be in itself a form of disease. Yet, in the history of the last few years, I recognise symptoms of convalescence, however feeble, obscure, and equivocal its traces may appear. What we behold is not death or hopeless decay; it is a purifying process—painful, consuming, and penetrating bone and marrow—such as God is wont to inflict upon His chosen persons and institutions. There is no lack of dross, and time is required before the gold can come pure out of the furnace. In the course of this process, it may happen that the territorial dominion will be interrupted— that the State may be broken up, or pass into other hands; but it will revive, though, perhaps, in another form, and with a different kind of government. In a word, *sanabilibus laboramus malis*; that is what I wished to show, and that, I believe, I have shown.

Now, and for the last forty years, the condition of the States of the Churth is the heel of Achilles to the Catholic Church; the standing reproach with opponents in every part of the world—in America as in Europe ; and a stumbling-block for numbers. Not as though the objections which are founded on the fact of this transitory disturbance and discord in the social sphere possessed any weight in a theological point of view. But still it is not to be denied that they are of incalculable influence on the disposition of the whole world external to the Church.

Whenever a state of disease has appeared in the Church, there has been but one method of cure—that of an awakened, renovated, healthy consciousness ; and of an enlightened public opinion in the Church. The very best will on the part of ecclesiastical rulers and heads has not been able to effect a cure, unless sustained by the general sense and conviction of the clergy and of the laity. The healing of the great malady of the sixteenth century, the true internal reformation of the Church, only became possible when people ceased to disguise or to deny the evil, and to pass it by in silence and with concealment ; and when so powerful and irresistible a public opinion had formed itself in the Church, that its commanding influence could no longer be evaded. At the present day, what we want, before all things, is the truth—the whole truth—not merely the acknowledgment that the Temporal Power of the Pope is required by the Church—for that is obvious to everybody, at least out of Italy ; and everything has been said about it that can be said—but what there must be also is—an acknowledgment *upon what conditions* this power is possible for the future. The history of the Popes is full of examples, shewing how their best intentions remained unaccomplished, and how their most firm resolutions had been baffled, because persons in inferior circles were adverse to them, and because the interests of a firmly-compacted class, like an impenetrable hedge of thorns, resisted them. Adrian VI. was fully resolved to set about a reformation in earnest ; and yet he achieved virtually nothing ; and felt himself, though in possession of supreme power, utterly impotent when he came into contact with the passive resistance of all those who should have served as instruments in the work. Only when public opinion—even in Italy, and in

Rome itself—had been awakened, purified, and strengthened; and when the cry for reform resounded imperatively on every side, then only was it possible for the Popes to overcome resistance in the inferior spheres, and gradually, and step by step, to open the way for a more healthy state. May, therefore, a powerful, salubrious, unanimous public opinion in Catholic Europe come to the aid of Pius IX.!

Here I must justify myself upon one point. Fault has been found with me that I have appealed to the "Reports" of Mr. Lyons, which had been printed by order of the English Parliament. English "Reports," it is said, are undisguisedly partial and unreliable. I have referred to them in proof that the Pope, with the best-intended reforms, was not in a position to content his dissatisfied subjects; and that every concession made by him was instantly perverted into an instrument for undermining his government. Now, the Count de Montalembert made use of the same "Reports" in his celebrated second Letter to Count Cavour; and he did so with this remark: " *M. Lyons le seul diplomate honnête que l'Angleterre ait envoyé en Italie.*" I subscribe to this eulogy; but, remembering Lord Normanby and Mr. Sheil, of whom my friend did not think in writing, I would strike out the word " *seul.*"

Concerning another part of this book, I have still a few words to say. I have given a survey of all the churches and ecclesiastical communities now existing. The necessity of attempting this task presented itself to me, because I had to make clear both the universal importance of the Papacy as a world-power, and the things that it actually performs. This could not be done fully without exhibiting the internal condition of the churches which have rejected it, and withdrawn from its influence. It is true that the plan increased under my hands, and I endeavoured to give as clear a picture as possible of the development which has accomplished itself in the separated churches since the Reformation; and, through it, in consequence of the views and principles which then had been once for all adopted. I have, therefore, admitted into my description no feature which is not, according to my conviction, an effect, a result, however remote, of those principles and doctrines. There is doubtless room for discussion in detail upon this point, and there will unavoidably be a decided opposition to this book, if it should be noticed beyond the limits of the Church to which I belong. I hope that there also the justice will be done me of believing that I was far from having any intention of offending; that I have only said what must be said, if we would go to the bottom of these questions; that I had to do with institutions which, because of the dogmas and principles from which they spring, must, like a tree that is nailed to a wall, remain in one position, however unnatural it may be. I am quite ready to admit that, on the opposite side, men are often better than the system to which they are, or deem themselves, attached; and that, on the contrary, in the Church, individuals are, on the average, inferior in theory and in practice to the system under which they live.

And here is the proper place for me briefly to explain myself with reference to the Erfurt Conference, and the hopes connected with it, and especially as regards the relative positions of the Confessions (different creeds or religions) in Germany. I believe I am the more bound to do this, because some expressions of mine addressed in a letter to a friend, and bearing upon this subject, have been printed, although my name was not published. The following points may, perhaps, contribute in throwing some light upon the state of affairs:—

1. The re-union of the Catholic and Protestant Confessions in Germany would, if it were now, or a short time hence, effected, be, in a religious, political, and social sense, a most salutary circumstance, both for Germany and Europe.

2. There is not the smallest probability that this union can be immediately carried into effect.

3. It is not possible at present, first, because the greater, more active, and more influential portion of German Protestants do not desire it, for political or religious reasons, in any form, or under any practicable conditions.

4. It is impossible, secondly, because negotiations con-

erning the mode and the conditions of Union can no longer be carried on. For this purpose plenipotentiaries on both sides are required; and these only the Catholic Church is able to appoint, by virtue of her ecclesiastical organization— not so the Protestants. Upon that side there is now no common basis, no one single starting-point (not even the Augsburg Confession), and every decree, and every dogmatic canon is underlaid with principles evoking the veto of individuals, as well as of entire Schools and Parties.

5. The Catholic Church could, without the slightest difficulty, enter into a negotiation with the separated Greek and Russian Churches in reference to a re-union; and this negotiation, if not opposed by foreign interests, and the stolid ignorance of the clergy and people of those churches, might hold out a hope of the most favourable results. There, both parties stand on the same ground, in so far as they have both taken the same views as to the Church, its authority, and its uninterrupted continuity. This view is wanting on the Protestant side, and with it fails a common basis, without which, negotiations and attempts at coming to a common understanding are not possible. Isolated points are not here to be taken into consideration.

6. To take the Holy Scriptures as a common basis, upon which Catholics and Protestants should make the attempt to come to an understanding would be purely illusory; for,

Primarily, so long as there have been Christians they never by such means came to be unanimous. A striking example of this is the dispute upon the Eucharistal consecration between the Lutherans and Reformers (Calvinists), which—after countless colloquies, and thousands of books published for three hundred years—has never progressed a single step.

Secondly, the great advances that have undoubtedly been made, within the last thirty years, in expositions of the Bible, have in no way produced, on the Protestant side, a larger amount of faith or unity in doctrine—so far from that, the very contrary is perceivable.

7. Nevertheless, Protestants and Catholics have, *theologically*, come nearer to each other; for that main doctrine—those "articles with which the Church was to stand or fall," and for the sake of which the Reformers declared separation from the Catholic Church to be necessary, are now confuted and given up by Protestant theology, or are retained only nominally, whilst other notions are connected with the words.

8. The *Augsburg Confession* is not only "the fundamental creed of the Reformation," but it is also the only one which the great majority of Christ-believing Protestants now acknowledge. Were this acknowledgment based upon a perfectly serious, clear recognition and right understanding of what it contains, then would the union of the separated Churches be proportionably attainable. "But," as Heinrich Leo[1] has lately observed, "everyone has this Confession in his mouth, but there is scarcely one who knows what it is, and no one seeks to embrace it in its *original* meaning. It is declared to be the corner-stone of Protestantism, and great festivals have been celebrated in its honour; it is yearly lauded in every Protestant School, and scarcely one individual knows what is contained in it."

9. The *Augsburg Confession*, in its seventh article, declares, "that there is, and must continue to be at all times, *one holy* Catholic Church, which is an assembly of all the faithful, and by which the pure Gospel is preached, and the holy sacraments, in accordance with the Gospel, administered." If language has not been invented for the purpose of concealing men's thoughts, then this is affirming that, before the birth of the Protestant doctrine, there was already in existence a church, "one," "holy," with "pure doctrine," and "real sacraments." Can there be along with "one holy Church" also a second and a third? Has the Church, which in the year 1517 was still "one," "holy," suddenly ceased to be, because since then new Associations, by separating from her, have arisen—which Associations instantly began to accuse her of false teaching, and of

[1] "Neue Preuss. Ztg.," 26th September.

having untrue sacraments—without there being, according to the Separatists' own avowal, any essential changes in her? Could the authors of, and subscribers to, this article have so understood its signification, that the "one holy Church" was to consist of an undefined number of churchmen, separated in doctrine, sacraments, order, and mutually accusing one another of vital errors? Can the authority or symbolical value of the *Augsburg Confession* be seriously spoken of when this weighty and conclusive article is treated as non-existent, and when science ignores, or strongly disputes, or gives to it a directly contrary signification? An affirmative logical answer to these questions is an indispensable preliminary to every Confessional understanding, and this, too, it must, moreover, be in the interest of all laymen who are struggling after religious purity and certainty.

10. So far as one can judge from literature, there appears to be the wish amongst theologians and clergymen on the Protestant side, that there should be a union amongst the Germans, now separated by religious distinctions. How it is to be effected some do not show—some put it in the form of a request that the Catholics should at once turn Protestants —whilst with others there is manifested the inclination, with a complete dimness as to the ways and the mode. Seldom, at least, has the author, in real life, met with a religious-minded Protestant layman who did not feel a desire for this union, and who also, for the most part, entertained the opinion that the time for it is come, as the duration of the separation has done much more evil than good.

11. Protestant theology is, at the present day, less hostile, so to speak, than the theologians. For whilst theology has levelled the strongest bulwarks and doctrinal barriers which the Reformation had set up to confirm the separation—the theologians, instead of viewing favorably the consequent facilities for union, often labour, on the contrary, to conceal the fact, or to create new points of difference. Many of them may participate in the opinion of Stahl of Berlin, who, shortly before his death, said, "Far from allowing that the breach of the sixteenth century can be healed, we ought, if

it had not already occurred, to make it now."[1] This, however, will not continue, and a future generation—perhaps even that which is now growing up—will rather adopt the recent declaration of Heinrich Leo: "In the Roman Catholic Church a process of purification has taken place since Luther's time; and if the Church had been in the days of Luther what the Roman Catholic Church in Germany is at present, it would never have occurred to him to assert his opposition so energetically as to bring about a separation."[2] Those who think thus will then be the right men and the chosen instruments for the acceptable work of the reconciliation of the Churches, and of the *true* unity of Germany.

12. Upon the day when, on both sides, the conviction shall arise, vivid and strong, that Christ really desires the unity of His Church, that the division of Christendom, the multiplicity of Churches, is displeasing to God—that he who helps to prolong this situation must answer for it to the Lord—on that day four-fifths of the traditional polemics of Protestants against the Catholic Church will, with one blow, be cast aside, like chaff and rubbish; for four-fifths of it consists of misunderstandings, logomachies, and wilful falsifications; or relate to personal, and therefore accidental, things, which are utterly insignificant, where only principles and dogmas are at stake.

13. On that day, also, much will be changed on the Catholic side. Thenceforward the personal character of Luther and of the Reformers will be no more dragged forward in the pulpit. The clergy, mindful of the words, "*Interficite errores, diligite homines*," will ever conduct themselves towards members of other Churches in conformity with the rules of charity, and will therefore assume, in all cases where there are no clear proofs to the contrary, the *bona fides* of opponents.[3] They will never forget that no man is convinced

[1] Address at the opening of the Berlin Pastoral Conference, in the "Evang. Kirchen-Ztg.," June, 1861, p. 564.

[2] "N. Preuss. Ztg.," 27th September.

[3] After the example of one of the best prelates of our time, Cardinal

and won over by bitter words and violent attacks, but that everyone is rather repelled by them. Warned by the words of the Epistle to the Romans (xiv., 13), they will be more careful than heretofore to give to their separated brethren no scandal, no grounds of accusation against the Church. In popular instruction and in religious life they will accordingly make the great truths of salvation the centre of all their teaching: they will not treat secondary things in life and doctrine as though they were of the first importance, but, on the contrary, they will keep alive in the people the consciousness that such things are but means to an end, and are only of inferior consequence and subsidiary value.

14. Until that day shall dawn upon Germany, it is our duty as Catholics, in the words of Cardinal Diepenbrock, "to bear the religious separation in a spirit of penance, for guilt incurred in common." We must acknowledge that here also God has caused much good, as well as much evil, to proceed from the errors of men, from the contests and passions of the sixteenth century; we must, too, admit that the anxiety of the German nation to see the intolerable abuses and scandals in the Church removed was fully justified; and that it sprang from the better qualities of our people, and from their moral indignation at the desecration and corruption of holy things, which were degraded to selfish and hypocritical purposes. We do not refuse to admit that the great separation, and the storms and sufferings connected with it, were an awful judgment upon Catholic Christendom, which clergy and laity had but too well deserved—a judgment which has had an improving and salutary effect. The great intellectual conflict has purified the European atmosphere, has impelled the human mind on to new courses, and has promoted a rich, scientific, and literary life. Protestant theology, with its

de Cheverus, who, when he was Bishop of Boston in America, declared, from his intercourse with Protestants, converted by him to the Catholic faith: " Que plusieurs Protestans pouvaient être dans la bonne foi ou ignorance invincible qui excuse l'erreur devant Dieu. Il en conclut qu'il falloit être très—indulgent pour ceux qui se trompent, et très reservé à les condamner."—Vie du Cardinal de Cheverus, 2d edit., p. 140.

c

restless spirit of inquiry, has gone along by the side of the Catholic, exciting and awakening, warning and vivifying; whilst every exalted Catholic theologian will readily admit that he owes much to the writings of Protestant scholars.

15. We have also to acknowledge that in the Church the rust of abuses, and of a mechanical superstition, is always forming afresh; that the servants of the Church sometimes, through indolence and incapacity, and the people through ignorance, brutify the spiritual in religion, and so degrade and deform and misemploy it to their own injury. The right reforming spirit must therefore never depart from the Church, but, on the contrary, must periodically break out with renovating strength, and penetrate the conscience and the will of the clergy. In this sense we do not refuse to admit the justice of a call to penance, when it proceeds from those who are not of us,—that is, of a warning carefully to examine our religious life and pastoral conduct, and to remedy what is found defective.

16. And yet it never must be forgotten that the separation did not ensue in consequence of abuses in the Church. For the duty and necessity of removing those abuses has always been recognised; and only the difficulty of the thing, the not always unjustifiable fear lest " the wheat" should be pulled up with " the tares," prevented, for a time, the reformation which was accomplished in the Church, and through her. Separation on account of mere abuses in ecclesiastical life, when the doctrine is the same, is rejected as criminal by the Protestant Church, as well as by us. It was therefore for the sake of *doctrine* that the separation occurred; and the general discontent of the people, the weakening of ecclesiastical authority by the existence of abuses, only facilitated the adoption of the new doctrines. But now, upon the one side, some of these defects and evils in the life of the Church have disappeared, and more have greatly diminished since the reforming movement. And, on the other side, the principal doctrines for which men separated, and on the truth of which, and their necessity for salvation, the right and duty of secession had been based, are given up by Protestant

science, deprived of their Scriptural basis by exegesis, or, at least, made very uncertain by the opposition of the most eminent Protestant theologians.

17. Meanwhile, we live in hope; comforting ourselves with the conviction that history, or that process of development in Europe which is being accomplished before our eyes (as well in society and politics as in religion), is the powerful ally of the friends of ecclesiastical union ; and we hold out our hands to Christians on the other side, for a combined war of resistance against the destructive movements of the age. For this—to use the words of Von Radowitz—is the state of affairs: " We plainly perceive that the minds of men are ranging themselves under two banners—upon one of which is inscribed the name of 'Christ, the Son of God ;' and beneath the other are incorporated all to whom That Name is Foolishness and a Reproach."

Munich, 12th October, 1861.

THE CHURCH AND THE NATIONS.

In all time, antecedent to Christ, there were none other than National and State religions. The populations had each their own divinities, and their peculiar form of worship. Their religions essentially contributed to keep the peoples more widely apart and more distinctly separated from one another. One nation might derive its divinities and take its form of worship from another; but a religious bond, embracing both, and drawing them closer together, was not thereby formed. The Christian religion, whose very existence from the beginning rested upon the disruption of Jewish national-religious individuality, was the first that appeared amongst mankind with a claim to Catholicity. It declared itself to be a universal religion; one that did not belong to any people in particular, but, on the contrary, whose calling and innate qualification were to extend itself over the surface of the globe; to receive into its bosom every variety of population; to satisfy their real religious wants, and, regardless of national or geographical boundaries, to establish a great kingdom of God on earth—to found a Church for humanity!

The Roman Empire, through whose means the political, lingual, and conventional boundaries and bulwarks of conquered nations had been broken down and levelled, had thus prepared the way, and smoothened a path for the Christian Church. And then, after a battle of three hundred years—

a battle in which there were suffering and confession on the one side, of persecution and of slaughter on the other—this empire was conquered by the Church, which had, at the same time, through the three principal languages of the period—the Greek, Latin, and Syrian—produced a triple literature, extended itself far beyond the limits of the Roman boundaries, penetrated far into Persia, and travelled away to the North, and amongst the German nations. The central point of Church life was Rome—the world-city— " the sink of nations" —where Egyptians, Syrians, Asiatics, Armenians, Greeks, Jews, Gauls, Spaniards, met and mixed together—were mutually attracted towards one another, or repelled. Next to Rome, Alexandria—the great emporium of commerce, the seat of Greek and Oriental science and literature—served to nurture and develope the cosmopolitan character of Christianity.

And so was the Church nationally colourless. No one could then, or at any subsequent period, ever affirm that any one nation more than another had impressed the stamp of individuality upon the Church. After the fall of the Western Roman Empire the Church became the instructress and the foster-mother of new States. In its bosom were developed the ruling nationalities of the West, and all were penetrated with the consciousness of forming one mighty Christian folk-family; a European commonwealth, under the spiritual supremacy of the Papal See, and the temporal headship of the newly created Roman-Germanic Imperial Power. If France was proud to be called "the first-born son of the Church," it thereby recognized the fraternal relations in which it stood as regarded the other sons of the one mighty mother—that is, to the people and states of the South, the North, and the East. Wars between brothers could be no more than a transitory phenomenon; whilst a permanent state of hostilities between members of the same great family was in reality to be no longer conceivable. The Church Councils were also national Congresses. If a heathen people became Christian, and began to mould its customs, both socially and politically, in accordance with the Christian model, its chief or duke was raised to the kingly dignity by the Pope, was solemnly consecrated and crowned by the Church, and the people were enrolled as members of the Christian folk-family, as the equals of all in birth, and like to the rest in their rights.

In this manner was a problem solved, and a thought realised, which would have been declared by both Greeks and Romans to be alike absurd and impossible; that is a multitude of nationalities, through a community in faith, and of religious worship, as well as by the bonds of an all-embracing ecclesiastical organization, united into one great whole. That there should not be wanting a vigorous reaction on the part of particular nationalities was a thing to be expected. The long and sanguinary persecution which was carried on amongst the Persians, under the kings of the Sassanides dynasty, was a reaction of this description. The new strange religion was hated and feared as being "un-Persian," as an intrusive "Roman-Empire religion," as coming to them from the territory of their hereditary foe; and hence they wished to exterminate its confessors, as men who had, at the same time, abandoned the national religion of Persia, and with their religion—Persian patriotism!

An element of nationality speedily mixed itself up with the schism of the Donatists. The separation from the Church, and its central point at Rome, which was effected in North Africa, although it was an act repudiated by all the rest of the Christian world, was, in point of fact, an outburst of the North African spirit of nationality, which sought to establish for itself its own thoroughly pure national Church, in opposition to all others, which were assumed to have become corrupt and decayed. In the same manner was Egyptian nationality urged to take a part, ever since the fifth century, in the great Christological battle of the Monophysite doctrine, that brought it to its having its own national Coptic Church, which still remains separated from the Catholic world, and the fragments of which, in a truly lamentable condition, subsist to the present day. In Armenia like causes produced like effects.

At a later period—that is, since the twelfth century—the separation and isolation of the Church of the Byzantine Empire has been gradually completed. Two Powers ruled there, to whom a union with the Universal Church, and with Rome, was incommodious, because with that union were conjoined dependence and restraint: these two Powers were the Emperor, and the Patriarch at Constantinople.[1] The latter (the Patriarch) sought to extend his spiritual dominion —so as that it might be an absolute despotism—over every inhabitant of the empire. The Emperor, for his part, wished to have in his hands the Church, and the Patriarch especially, as a useable political tool at his uncontrolled disposal. Under such circumstances was developed *Byzantinism*, that is, the national political spirit of the Greek Empire, and whose two factors were the absolutism of Imperialism over the State and the Church ; and ignorance, combined with the arrogant self-exultation of the people. The Byzantines regarded their emperor as the successor of the old Roman Cæsars. Each Greek emperor was a new Constantine, entitled to reign over the East and the West—to the utmost limits to which the old imperial power had extended ! The establishment of the Western Empire, the separation of Italy, the independence of the Pope, who, moreover, neither would nor could be the subject of the Emperor at Constantinople —all these circumstances were, in the eyes of the Greeks, insurrections, usurpations, attempts against the œcumenical power of the Emperor, who had been instituted by God as the head of all Christendom ! And then, the people, who, as they said, had, with the language, also inherited classic Greek literature and civilization—they haughtily and self-complacently looked down upon all who were not Greeks, as mere barbarians !

In the complete control over the Church in their Empire,

---

[1] The general notion, that Photius and Cerularius were the originators of the separation, is not quite correct. In the twelfth century, there is still to be found frequent community in the Divine Services between the Greek and Latin Churches ; as, for instance, in the year 1147, when King Louis VII., of France, arrived at Constantinople.

the Greek Emperors, especially after the exaltation of the
Comnenes dynasty, went much further than the Russian Czar
at a later period ever did. They willingly permitted the
Patriarch to have unlimited power over bishops and clergy;
but then, according to their own pleasure, they appointed,
and they deposed him. Every Emperor was a born theologian,[1]; he was above the canons of the Church, and he was
above the laws of the State.[2] Through their anointment and
by their imperial dignity they had, as Isaac Angelus (who
came to the throne in 1185),[3] declares, obtained a supreme
superintendence in all matters of ecclesiastical doctrine and
discipline. In short, they were, with the exception of the
administration of the sacraments, in possession of all Church,
official, and governmental rights. And the new Byzantine
State and Court-Church laws had reduced all this to a
regular, systematic theory.

Contrasted with the active life, the juvenile freshness,
and expansive vigour of the West, the Byzantine exhibited
naught but that senile torpidity and haughty obstinacy which
are no longer capable of learning; and are as sterile as they
are incompetent of improvement, or of expelling that which
is internally corrupting. As dethroned rulers, or as a person
who has been despoiled of his property, the Byzantine looked
at Rome and the restless movements of the Latin—that is,
the half or wholly barbaric world. The great massacre, by
which, in the year 1182, such numbers of the Latins were
destroyed in the capital, was an outbreak of that national
hatred which had struck such deep and ineradicable roots,
from the moment that those foreigners had, with their army,
overthrown the Greek throne, and established a Latin
Emperor in Constantinople. In such a disposition, and in
such a state of affairs, all—even the most trivial differences

---

[1] So says the historian, CINNAMUS, p. 521. It is permitted to no one
to investigate into the nature of God, but doctors, bishops, and—the
Emperor!

[2] BALSAMON, ap. "Bevereg. Cod. Canon," i. 338.

[3] Κοινὸς τῶν ἰκκλησιῶν ἐπιστημονάρχης καὶ ὢν καὶ ὀνομαζόμενος, says
DEMETRIUS CHOMATERUS, ap. "Leunclav. Jur. Gr. Rom.," p. 317.

—in dogmatic expressions, in rites, and in church life, were carefully sought out, nurtured, and widened. It had formally become a question of national honour to possess the capability of accusing the Latins of heresy; and ritual forms. were invented, for the purpose of tangibly expressing the pollution which any contact with the Latins must occasion. In their common conversation, they contrasted "Christians"—that is, Byzantines—with the "Latins;" and in the capital, even women, workpeople, and schoolboys chattered about "the procession of the Holy Ghost;" and upon this abstruse (and only to practised theologians in some measure comprehensible) question, finally turned the controversy between the two Churches. The later Emperors, rendered by their necessities more prudent than their predecessors, yet found themselves incapable of repairing this breach: they were unable to contend against the national sentiment, which, though impotent in all other matters, was, upon this one point of anti-Latinism, obdurate and invincible. The union of Florence was again torn asunder—the Church of St. Sophia was doomed to become a mosque !¹

The destructive schism which took place towards the end of the fourteenth century, in consequence of the election of a French anti-pope, and then convulsed the Church for more than forty years, had, too, its origin in purely national interests. For that which was really intended to be effected by it was to have the Papal See and court, as the exclusive possession of the French nation, located upon French soil, and under the predominating influence of the French government. And

¹ Some felt strongly what injury must accrue to the Church through the operation of an Imperial Popedom; but those entertaining such a conviction appear to be but few. The strongest expression of opinion I have met with is that of the Archbishop Simeon of Thessalonica (ap. "Morin. de Ordin.," p. 138. Ed. Amstd.). He affirms that the perversion of the Church order, through the assumptions and assaults of the temporal power, is the cause of the decay both of the Empire and the nation. "And hence it is," he observes, "that we have become impotent and contemptible in the estimation of all nations; and hence, too, it is that our foes scorn us, consume our harvests before our eyes, and possess themselves of our sacred relics and consecrated places," &c., &c., &c.

scarcely had this wound been healed, when the Hussite movement took place—that, too, was an attempt at a national separation, and the formation of a particular peoples' church. The Czechish antipathy against the Germans had from the commencement a large share in their essay at a new Ecclesiastical Structure, which was to be limited to the race of Czechs.

When, with the appearance of Luther, began that powerful movement which split asunder Western Christendom, until then whole and united; and when new churches, with doctrines and constitutions entirely different from the old, were formed, there was not at its commencement to be found the impulse of the supreme interests of a nationality pushing onward reformation, and inciting insurrection against the Pope and the Church. The German people had, for a series of centuries, with a deep and complete devotion, been absorbed by the spirit of the Catholic religion; they had made their churches the most nobly-endowed of any in the world: they had created a literature that was purely Catholic, and yet was the genuine production of the German mind. But in the beginning of the sixteenth century there was spread far and wide in Germany a strong repugnance against the Popedom, as it was then; and no unrightful indignation with reference to abuses in the Church, and the moral depravity of a much too numerous and far too wealthy clergy. The national feeling of the German people had been for a considerable time offended by the treatment which German persons, things, and interests had experienced in Rome; and by the part which had been played, since the fourteenth century, by German kings and emperors, as opposed to the See of Rome. It was when this state of feeling prevailed, that the mightiest democrat and most popular character that Germany has ever possessed—the Augustinian monk of Wittenberg—presented himself as a leader and eloquent orator. At the same time, he, with his newly-invented doctrine of "Justification," had discovered a lever of wonderful strength, by means of which he might destroy the still great attachment of the people to the Catholic religion. He tendered a compensation—eagerly and joyfully to be sought for—in repayment for what they had lost.

Luther well understood how to draw into the service of his cause the German national feeling, which then exhibited itself in a decided manner, by its dislike of the Italian nation. He shews this by his frequent expressions in reference to the " *Whalen,*" as the Italians were then called. There is scarcely a single vice that he does not attribute to them; and he purposely descants upon their assumed " haughtiness, and their contempt for the Germans, who, in their eyes, are not even human beings."[1]

When the separation had been completed, the new Church system established, and the violent movement brought to a stand-still and a conclusion, it was found that only the half of Germany had submitted itself to the Lutheran doctrine. The other half remained as it had been, or it had again become Catholic. The Protestant portion was split up anew, for Calvinism was introduced into some territories previously Lutheran. Upon the whole, however, the Germans—that is, such of them as had broken off their communion with the old Church—were attached to the Lutheran doctrine; for Calvinism was in their estimation un-German and outlandish, and did not satisfy their religious feelings; whilst Lutheranism, in the two first centuries of its existence, was felt and comprehended as the most accurate product of the German mind, in matters of religion. Outside of Germany, the kindred Scandinavians were the only states that introduced amongst them the Lutheran form of Protestantism; whilst, on the other hand, the Calvinistic form owed its existence and diffusion on the German soil, for the most part, to the constraint exercised by individual princes.

A Lutheran national Church was not established in Germany. The whole ecclesiastical power—such power as in the Catholic Church had been exercised by primate and episcopacy—was systematically intrusted to the temporal princes, and (in the imperial cities) to the municipal authorities,

---

[1] See " Luther's Werke," Walch, Ausg., xiv. 273; xix. 1155; xxii. 2365; ii. 1429.

so that there were just as many churches as there were states and territories. Every prince and every Germanic-Empire titled noble was now both Pope and Bishop in his land or little holding. He was, in fact, something more ; for he could alter the religion of his subjects according to his own pleasure ; and the Palatine Electoral princes did actually, in a single generation, and through the instrumentality of depositions and banishments, four times violently change the religion of their country. And, then, so weakened has been the Church impulse in Protestant Germany, under the influence of the Lutheran doctrine, that, in three hundred years, there never has been one serious attempt made for the establishment of one all-embracing Lutheran Church-like band, having one common Church action.

They content themselves with the conviction that they are in the exclusive possession of the pure doctrine, in which is, beyond all other things, to be understood " self-attributed righteousness," and upon which is founded unconditional personal " salvation." This is called "the Gospel !" Besides this, they console themselves for this lamentable condition, dismemberment, and territorial servitude of Church affairs, with thoughts of the assumed glory of the invisible Church, which possesses in richer abundance and more fanciful perfection all that is wanting to the visible.

In the rest of Europe, the Lutheran doctrine was a decided failure. It was either rejected, or it had to give way to the Calvinistic reform doctrine. It devolved upon the Saxons in Transylvania, after the German inhabitants of the cities amongst Hungarians and Poles had paved the way for it. But even so, it was plainly nothing more than the creed of a small minority, which saw itself on all sides overridden and pressed down by the logical, and (on that which is the main point) still more consolatory Calvinism. It was the same in the Netherlands and France. It was, therefore, correctly (even though but lately) said :—" That the Lutheran Church was so absolutely modified, and so thoroughly animated with the *German* character, that, in another country, and under different national conditions, it could never exist. The

Scotch, for instance, could never be Lutherans, so long as they are Scotchmen."[1]   According to Schaff's remark, "Lutheranism loses more or less of its original features, and imperceptibly assimilates itself to the Reform Confession, so soon as it, through emigration, is transplanted to French, English, or American soil.   This," he adds, "is to be seen very plainly in the United States, if we compare the Anglicised portion of the Lutheran denominations with the foreign German Synods of Missouri and Buffalo."[2]

Calvin was as decidedly the creator of the so-called "reform" doctrine, as Luther was the originator of that which has been called after him.   Calvin had only Zwinglius as a predecessor, whilst Luther was dependent on no one, and indebted to no one for anything.   Calvin was not able, however, in his own country, France, to obtain the success and the high position which accrued to the German Reformer at home.   The great majority of his countrymen still continue to see in him only the founder of erroneous doctrines, and of a false Church; but as regards other nations, which, either wholly or partially, have accepted his system, he remains still a foreigner; and their national feelings will not tolerate the Church in their own land to be called by his name, and so be made known as the work of a stranger.   They would have, therefore, their Church only known as being *reformed*; whilst the German Protestants, with the conviction that Luther is flesh of their flesh, and bone of their bone, that he is the nation-born prophet of Germans — name with satisfaction themselves " Lutherans," and their church " Lutheran."

Upon the whole, the Calvinistic Church-form, which had not at its commencement the stamp of a particular nationality upon it, has had a wider expansion than the Lutheran. Scotland, as regards the great majority of its inhabitants, became Calvinistic; whilst in the Netherlands and in Switzerland the larger portion of the population that adopted

---

[1] " Allgemeine Kirchenzeitung," 15th May, 1855.

[2] " Germany ; its Universities, Theology, and Religion."   Edinburgh, 1857, p. 168.

Protestantism accepted it in that form.   In Germany Calvinism attained an entrance into the Palatinate, Anhalt, Hesse, Bremen, and finally (since the conversion of Sigismond in 1614) into the Brandenburg territory.   In Hungary the Magyars, so far as they fell off from the old Church, did so, for the most part, to become Calvinists.   In France, up to the time of the incorporation of Alsace, " Calvinist " and " Protestant " were synonymous terms.   The churches of this confession, however, remained separated according to the territories in which they were placed; and in Switzerland, according to the Cantons in which they were located.   Only once was there found to take place one common action, and one general confederation of all—or the most of the communities conforming to the Calvinistic doctrine.   It was at the Dordrecht Synod, in the year 1618, when it was desired to defend and confirm genuine Calvinism in its practical doctrines, and such as they were most wished for by the masses, against the alterations of the Arminians.   This was also the culminating point of Calvinistic Church development. From that time began its internal dogmatic and Church decomposition.

As a third chief form of Protestantism, and with a complete national colouring and exclusiveness, the Episcopal *State-Church in England* instituted itself.   Wholly differing from Lutheranism, it was, at the beginning, in its dogma superabounding with Calvinism.   It is, in its constitution, a mixture of Catholicity and Protestantism; it is territorially Protestant, or imperially papistical, in its principles and institutions ; it is, in its Liturgy, more Catholic than Protestant, and in its creed—" the 39 Articles "—more Protestant than Catholic.   It suffers from its internal contradictions; and resembles a building which, erected out of heterogeneous materials, can only be prevented from falling to pieces by the strong hand of the State.   The struggle with the Calvinistic elements contending for the supreme power, and which had been carried on for a long time in its bosom, gradually led to the separation of the Puritans, and to the great civil and religious war of the seventeenth century.   At last the

more logical Protestant parties—the Presbyterians, Congregationalists, and Baptists—gave to themselves a constitution of
their own, and placed themselves in opposition to the State
Church as independent Churches. It then shut out all the
Protestant communities on the Continent so completely, that
an ordained Lutheran or Calvinist preacher in England passes
simply as a layman; and, in order to enter into the service
of the Anglican Church, has to submit himself once more to
Episcopal ordination.

When we look over the whole course of the Reformation-
century, at the result of the great movement, and the state
of the newly-formed religious communities, we find everywhere
the victorious principle of national distinct Churches manifesting itself. "Principle" is not, perhaps, the right expression to make use of; for this state of things was by no
means systematically brought about — it should rather be
said that it was self-formed—it was the inevitable consequence
of the opposite principle—that is, of Catholicity, of a Church
for the entire world having been, with deliberate design,
renounced. To the Temporal Power, to Princes, and their
officials, in Protestant lands, was assigned, in its fulness,
ecclesiastical power, with a supremacy in spiritual matters.
The Reformers had willed that it should be so,[1] and
therewith must necessarily cease every religious tie between
different nationalities. In Germany there were as many
Protestant Churches as there were distinct territories; and

---

[1] This has been frequently denied, but let any one confront the denial
with the Wittenberg Consistorial Ordinance of the year 1542, in Richter's
"Sammlung der Kirchen-Ordnungen," p. 371, which was either composed or approved of by Luther and Melancthon. With reference to it
Professor Schenkel says: "In this manner, with a single stroke of the
pen, was the important matter of Church discipline placed wholly in the
hands of the heads of the State, and this, too, without any reservation of
ecclesiastical rights; so that *affairs of conscience* were, from this time,
treated precisely like worldly matters, and were to be settled altogether
according to the form of temporal legal proceedings. The subjection of
the Church to the State was therewith completed, and the gate thrown
wide open for boundless tyranny by the State over men's consciences."
—"Studien und Kriticken," 1850, p. 459.

each lord of the land was invested with the highest ecclesiastical power.   If a general " Lutheran " Church, or an " Evangelical " Church, were mentioned, this expression, in reality, meant no more than an aggregate of National Churches, each one of which was limited by the frontiers of its own country ; and, in no point of view, representing a living whole—an organically associated unity.   In the same manner there were, and there still are, in " reformed " Switzerland only Cantonal Churches.   It is, however, as a Protestant theologian correctly remarks, untrue and perplexing to speak of a " unity," when it only represents " something present in one's thoughts ;" and where we can point to nothing in which this assumed unity manifests itself. "Unity" and "similarity," or " relationship," are very different ideas.[1]

Nationalities are certainly not the products of accident ; they are not the children of a blindly-ruling force of nature. On the contrary, in the great world-plan of Divine Providence, every distinct people have their own peculiar problem to solve, their own assigned mission to fulfil.   They may mistake it, and, by a perverted course, wander away from it, or, by their sloth and moral depravity, leave it unperformed— and of such we have examples before our eyes. This mission is determined by the character of the people themselves, by the boundaries within which nature and circumstances confine them, and by their own peculiar endowments.   The manner in which a nation undertakes to solve the problem re-acts, again, upon its position and character, determines its welfare, and decides the place it shall occupy in history.   Each distinct people forms an organically connected limb of the great body of humanity—it may be a more noble and distinguished limb—it may be a people destined to be the guide and educator of other nations—or it may be an inferior and a subservient limb ; but, then, each nationality has an original right (within easily-recognised limits, and without interference on the part of any other equally privileged nation) to vindicate and freely develope itself. The suppression of a nationality, or of a manifestation of its existence within its natural

---

[1] LECHLER, " Lehre vom heiligen Amte.," 1857, p. 139.

and legitimate limits, is a crime against the order decreed by God, and which sooner or later brings its own punishment along with it.

Higher, however, than associated nationalities, stands that Community which unites the multiplicity of nationalities into one God-connected totality, which binds them together in one brotherly relation, and forms them into one great peoples' family; the Community that does this is—the Church of Christ. It is the will of its Founder that it should be just with every national peculiarity; "one shepherd and one flock." It must, therefore, in its views, in its institutions, and in its customs, bear no peculiar national colour. It must neither be prominently German, nor Italian, nor French, nor English, nor to any of those nations show a preference; and still less must it desire to impress upon any one people the stamp of a foreign nationality. The thought will never occur to it to despoil or injure one people for the advantage of another; nor to molest them, as regards their rights and properties. The Church takes a nationality as it finds it, and bestows upon it a higher sanctity. The Church is far from desiring that all the nationalities received into its bosom, should bend down beneath the yoke of a monotonous uniformity, much less does it wish to annihilate the differences of races, or to put an end to historical customs. As the firmest, and at the same time the most pliable of all institutions, it is able to become "all things to all men," and to educate every people, without doing violence to their nature. The Church enters into every nationality, purifies it, and only overcomes it, when assimilating it to itself. The Church overcomes it when it struggles against excrescences upon national character, and when it removes from the popular traits whatever had previously been intractable. It is like to the house of the father, in which, to use the words of Christ, "there are many mansions." The Pole, the Sicilian, the Irishman, and the Maronite, have each their national character—a character not in common with each other—whilst still each of these is, in his own way, a good Catholic. Should there, however, be nationalities or races

D

so deeply degraded, and so thoroughly corrupt, that the Church, with all its appliances, can do nothing with them, then they must gradually die out, and give place to others.

There is a reciprocal gain. As each new and vigorous population enters into the circle of the Church, the Church becomes not merely numerically, locally, and externally strong, but also inwardly and dynamically enriched. Every people, in whatever way gifted, gradually contributes its share in religious experiences, in peculiar ecclesiastical customs and arrangements, in its interpretation of Christian doctrine, in its impress upon life and science. It adds all these to the great Church capital—to that which is the product of former times and older nationalities. Every Catholic people can learn from another, and may borrow from foreign nations institutions worthy of being imitated. This has often already happened. It has occurred, too, even in the most recent times, and mostly with an evident blessing; and it will for the future (with the advantage of rapidly increasing communication, and the greater means for reciprocal knowledge) take place to a much greater extent. In this sense, populations long since degenerated have continued to exercise a beneficial influence. Even still the Church feels the operations of the old African and Egyptian Churches of the first century.

The course which the history of Christianity has taken from the beginning, even to the present day, may be thus measured:

With the first issuing forth of the Christian Church, from the maternal bosom of the Jewish, there developed itself, as a fundamental law of Church life, the principle of Catholicity, that is, of a world-religion, of a world-Church, of one that has space and air, laws and liberty, for all nations; which summons all, and receives into itself all who obey its call. This principle is, however, in reality superhuman; and it can only be maintained among men by institutions to which strength from above is given, and with which a permanent blessing abides. It will always elicit the most violent resistance on the part of natural humanity. The centrifugal forces and tendencies of individual nations are aroused; they tear themselves loose ; they make for themselves a creed, and manage themselves, ecclesiastically, according to their own plan and fancy ; and then have to experience what is to be their own special history, which is found to be dependent on the fact of original separation from the Church, modified by the character of the nation, and of the doctrine it has accepted.   As to the Church, it proceeds on its path ; the majority remains faithful to it ; new members replace those that have fallen off; and it approaches slowly, yet with a firm step (for with its great losses there are still great com-pensations and advantages), and so it at last arrives at its goal—absolute Catholicity.   That goal is still far distant; and the Church will only have reached it when it shall have an abiding place in every part of the earth, and when the words of Malachi (i. 11,) shall be completely fulfilled.[1]

So singular is the position of the Catholic Church, both in the past and the present, that no other religion, or religious society can, even in the most remote manner, be compared with it.   There are, indeed, besides the Catholic, two other religions, which, since they have passed beyond the bound-aries of one nation or state, may make a claim to the title of being " a world-religion :" these are the Mahommedan and the Bhuddist.[2]   If we look to Islaminism, we find it never

---

[1] " For from the rising of the sun even to the going down, my name is great among the Gentiles, and in every place there is sacrifice, and there is offered to my name a clean oblation."

[2] Bhuddism is usually mentioned as the most numerous of all religions ; and counting the entire of China as being Bhuddist, it is said to have five hundred millions. This, however, is incorrect. The Bhuddist religion in China is, in fact, only tolerated ; and to ask a Chinese whether he is a Bhuddist or not, would be, as Wassiliew (in the " Abhandlungen der Petersburger Akademie," xi. 356) observes, absurd.   The three religions of China are those of Confucius, Taosse, and Bhudda.   They subsist not only by the side of one another, but they mingle with each other, and the Chinese occasionally take a part in all.   It can therefore only be said that there are in China many Bhuddist confraternities, and that a great number of the people regularly, or from time to time, observe some Bhuddist rites.   Hence it becomes indispensable, if we wish to compare the religions of mankind, with reference to the numbers of their disciples, to pass over that of the Bhuddists.

has exhibited the organic unity and brotherhood of a Church, and that it is split right asunder. The Sunnites are opposed to the Shiites; the head of the Sunnites, the Turkish, is hostile to the Shiite head, the Persian. Bhuddism is confined to Eastern Asia. It is in fact only a religion of the clergy. It knows only "brotherhoods," and has no congregations—there is no organic relation between the clergy and the laity; no Church powers, and no ceremonies of reception.

Thus, then, is there the Catholic religion, which counts more disciples than all the other Christian communities taken together—nearly two hundred millions—and it is the only world-religion in the true sense of the word; and, as there was formerly only given but one world-religion, so is it at present, and so it will remain for ever!

THE PAPACY.

THAT a Church of nations is not able to maintain itself without a primate, without one supreme head, must be evident to every one; and history has demonstrated it.

Every living totality requires a central point of union, a chief head, which shall hold its parts together. In the nature and structure of the Church it is established that this central point shall be a determined personality; the chosen bearer of an office corresponding to the nature of the thing and the requirements of the Church.

He who declares: "I do not recognize the Pope—I, or the Church to which I belong, will stand for itself, the Pope is for us a stranger, his Church is not ours,"—he who declares this thereupon says: "We separate ourselves from the Universal Church, we will be no longer members of that body."

Or, if it is theologically maintained: "That there may be, and shall be no primacy in the Church; that the Papacy is an institution in contradiction with the will of Christ, that it is a usurpation,"—then that is only saying, in other words, that one Universal Church, comprehending a variety of nations, should not exist; that it ought to fall to pieces, and that the normal state of religion ought to be—that there should be as many various churches as there are nations or states. But that the state of this one Church should be that of one composed of the scattered multitudinous fragments of several national or political churches, is such a church as cannot afford a shadow of claim either from higher authority, or be based upon a Biblical foundation; and, it may be added, there has not even the attempt been made to establish it theologically, as approved of by God.

It lies in the nature of things, that a State Church, in its isolation, can no longer inspire piety, or evoke veneration; that it appears as something conventional, from which, as soon as the political constraint that maintains it is withdrawn or crippled, one may separate with ease, and without any scruple of conscience. Thus the principle and law of Church-dismemberment being once for all sanctioned, new Church communites arise, the Sectarian system flourishes, and theologians, reflecting upon the article of faith which speaks of "one Universal Church," in despair, betake themselves to an abstraction, an idea, which they call "the invisible Church." And so there must be euphonious sounding inanities of a hidden, holy community, a silent band of spirits—there must be fine phrases, that are culled but to cover over the abyss caused by the loss of the Church ! [1]

---

[1] Julius Müller makes use of such phrases in his remarkable essay, " The Universal Church," in " The German Journal of Christian Science," 1850, p. 14. It is naturally easy for him to show what is untenable and erroneous in the recent efforts of Lutheran theologians to make out a visible Church confined to the professors of the pure Lutheran doctrine ; and he is able also to demonstrate that the Reformation had forced them out of a " visible," and compelled them to the conception of an " invisible Church." But when he wishes to establish this idea he can give to his readers nothing more than solemn sounding and hollow phraseology. He tells us of " a silent band of spirits, independent of space and time ; conscious of itself, but free from all guildship with external institutions ; as distant and yet near, as scattered and yet gathered together, as unknown and yet known, permeating the variety of Church confessions and constitutions, and *in all places, wherever it is*, carrying with it the consciousness that this Band is the highest that has been formed on earth," and so forth ! So then " this silent spirit band " has really been formed upon this earth, and is " conscious of itself," and so forth. When or where was it then formed ? By what signs can one know the members of " the band," or can they recognize each other ? Soberly and pro-

The more distracted and forlorn is the actual condition of a Church, so much the more poetical and enthusiastic becomes the talk of unity and love in mysterious undiscoverable regions, where the invisible Church is said to be at home!

saically expressed, the matter will stand thus : " It may be assumed that in every one of the various Christian communities some well-meaning pious souls are to be found, earnestly seeking for salvation, and for them we must hope that, with God's grace, they will find it." But no man of common sense can, for that world-institution, the one Universal Church, with its settled doctrines, and its means of Salvation, find a compensation in the fancy that has been feigned about "a band of spirits," and which may be compared to the stone that Rhea presented to her husband in place of a child—a false notion, enveloped in the swaddling clothes of rhetoric! By Jean Paul (Richter) the advice was once given to a Swedish pastor in winter, to walk up and down in his room and eat barley sugar, and thus have on his tongue, and before all his senses, a notion of lovely Italy and its gardens. H. Müller thus advises his followers to take his " still spirit band " into their mouths, and then to fancy they have with them " the Church." That the visible Church has also its invisible portion—and precisely that which is best and holiest in it is invisible—that is a fact which may be taken as understood. But it is indeed something very different to rend asunder the soul and body of the one Church, and oppose them to each other as two Churches, in order to be able to withdraw into this " silent band of spirits ; " that so it happens when one has quarrelled with the Universal Church, and made . the unpleasant discovery that the branch to which he adheres is rent away, that it no longer belongs to the tree, and is suffering for want of the living sap. The sharp-sighted Richard Rothe (" Anfänge der Christl. Kirche," p. 100) has openly said, " An invisible Church is a *contradictio in adjecto*. In no way can it be made a substantiality. It suffers from one of two evils—either the expression is quite unsuitable to it, or it has in itself no real existence. The idea was first formed when it was sought to give a factitious notion of a Church in its full development, and that idea was acted upon when the idea of leaving the Catholic Church was carried into effect." That the whole theory of an invisible Church is self-destructive for the community which desires seriously to adopt it, is a fact that becomes more and more generally acknowledged. It is said in the " Gottin. Gel. Anzeigen," 1848, p. 224, " With this theory of an invisible Church something truly sectarian has found its way into Protestantism ; something that has shown itself as *self-destructive ;* and it is only to the circumstance that it has never come to a general recognition, we are indebted for finding limits set to its self-destructiveness."

"The silent spirit band" has, in sooth, neither hand nor foot ; it speaks not, hears not ; it gives forth neither doctrine, nor discipline, nor the administration of Ecclesiastical means of grace. All these being matters that may, indeed, be dispensed with, since not one of "the spirits" knows anything of the other, nor can act upon another, either for good or for evil.

It is well known that, in order to escape from subjection to the Papal authority, the following phrase was adopted at the time of the Reformation, and has again been recently brought into vogue : "We who have separated ourselves recognize only Christ as the head of our Church." And with this it has been intended openly to declare, or such, at least, as an inevitable consequence is to be said : "There may be, and there shall be no earthly office, which shall confer upon its possessor the supreme guidance of the Church," or, "No one is entitled to guide the common affairs of many particular churches connected together, and forming one Whole. For the guidance of individual communities or local churches, and for the conduct of some ecclesiastical departments, there may be offices, and earthly bearers for them ; but as regards the guidance of the whole Church, there shall be no office, and no bearer of such an office. That is a place which must always remain empty." A suitable symbol of this theory (in accordance with which the head of the Church can only be in Heaven, and never must come too near it on earth, lest His presence might be an inconvenience) may be found in that stately empty arm-chair which is still to be seen in the magnificent ancient Gothic cathedral of Glasgow, and that, to the inexpressible disappointment of the spectator, is placed upon the very spot where formerly stood the high altar. Thus had the Manicheans, in their halls of assembly, "the Bema"—a pulpit always empty—and for them the representative of their invisible Lord and Master, and before which their believing members prostrated themselves on the earth.

When a community says: "Christ alone is the head of our Church," it is at the same time, in other words, saying:

" Separation and isolation constitute a principle of the Church
—such is its normal condition." When, in common life, a
person says, " I leave that to God, He may provide for it,"
the meaning of such words is at once appreciated. It is to
the effect, " I will trouble myself no more about the matter, it
does not concern me." When, for example, the Church of
Greece declared, " No one shall be the head of the Church,
but Christ alone," the declaration ultimately resulted in this,
" We provide only for ourselves, and do not trouble ourselves
about other Churches. Christ may see to them, and do with
them as He pleases." And so, under the mask of piously
sounding phrases, we find the most common-place national
selfishness.

Church communities have, in this respect, moved upon a
declining path. At first, it was said by the Byzantines,
" We recognize only Patriarchs, and each of these governing
a portion merely of the Church ; but no Pope, no head of
the Patriarchs." Then came the English Church, and it
said, " Neither Pope nor Patriarchs, but merely Bishops."
Upon their side, the Protestants of the Continent declared,
" No Bishops either, but merely pastors, and above them the
sovereign of the country." Subsequently came the new
Protestant sects of England, with the declaration, " We
have no need of pastors, but only preachers." Finally
appeared " the Friends " (the Quakers), and many more new
communities who had made the discovery " that preachers,
also, are only an evil, and that every man should be his
own prophet, teacher, and priest." One step still further
downward has to be made. It has not yet come to pass, but
already in the United States they are considering about it.

Let us now approach somewhat nearer to the institution
of the Papacy, which is comparable with no other; and let
us cast a glance at its history. Like to all living things,
like to the Church itself of which it is the crown and the
corner-stone, the Papacy has passed through an historical
development full of the most manifold and surprising
vicissitudes. But in this its history is the law which lies at
the foundation of the Church—the law of continual develop-

ment—of a growth from within outwards. The Papacy had to pass through all the changes and circumstances of the Church, and to enter with it into every process of construction. Its birth begins with two mighty, significant, and far-extending words of the Lord. He to whom these words were addressed, realised them in his own person and actions, and planted the institution of the infant Church in the central point—at Rome. There it silently grew, *occulto velut arbor aevo ;* and in the oldest time it only showed itself forth on peculiar occasions: but the outlines of the power and the ecclesiastical authority of the Roman Bishops were ever constantly becoming more evident, and more prominent. The Popes were, even in the time of the Roman Emperors, the guardians of the whole Church, exhorting and warning in all directions, disposing and judging, "binding and loosing." Complaints were not seldom expressed of the use which, in particular cases, Rome had made of its power. Resistance was offered, because the Pope was supposed to have been deceived; an appeal was preferred to him, when it was believed he had been better informed; but there was no refusal to obey his commands. In general, his interference in Church affairs was less necessary; and the reins of Church discipline needed less to be drawn tightly, so long as the general Church, with few exceptions, was found within the limits of the Roman Empire, when it was so firmly kept together by the strong bands of the civil order, that there could neither be occasion nor prospect of success to any reaction on the part of various nationalities, which, on the whole, were broken and kept down by Roman domination.

Out of the chaos of the great Northern migrations, and the ruins of the Roman Empire, there gradually arose a new order of states, whose central point was the Papal See. Therefrom inevitably resulted a position not only new, but very different from the former. The new Christian Empire of the West was created and upheld by the Pope. The Pope became constantly more and more (by the state of affairs, with the will of the princes and of the people, and through the power of public opinion) the Chief Moderator at the head of the European commonwealth—and, as such, he had to proclaim and defend the Christian law of nations, to settle international disputes, to mediate between princes and people, and to make peace between belligerent states. The Curia became a great spiritual and temporal tribunal. In short, the whole of Western Christendom, formed, in a certain sense, a kingdom, at whose head stood the Pope and the Emperor—the former, however, with continually increasing and far preponderating authority. The efforts of the Hohenstaufen Emperors to subject Italy, and with Italy also the Papal See, led to a prolonged conflict, from which both powers, the imperial and the papal, come forth weakened and wounded; for ever since then the position of the Papacy, in its political relations, has been more difficult and unfavourable. The Papacy saw itself compelled to lean more and more upon France, and, when the aspiring plans of Boniface VIII. were frustrated, it naturally passed into French hands, and upon French soil; and a resistance on the part of other nations was then inevitable; its high position over peoples and princes could no longer be successfully maintained. The authority of the Papal See sank still lower through the Franco-Italian schism. Then followed the reformatory efforts of the Councils, in the fifteenth century, which were mainly directed against the oppression of the Curia; and, subsequently, the Popes became entangled in the devious path of Italian politics. The former social-political, universal power led, when it was attempted to be realised, to troubles and disputes, and then it went utterly to wreck in the storms of the age of the Reformation.

From that time forth the whole of Europe assumed a new form. Powerful and internally united political bodies, each having a special interest, and pursuing a fixed policy of its own, came into the foreground, and a new system of "a balance of power" was formed amidst severe struggles. The Papal See could no longer be the regulator of a European Commonwealth, and the centre of a general polity. It could not be so, amid the confusion of merely political interests, and changes of Catholic and Protestant states—sometimes in alliance, and sometimes hostilely opposed to each other. The popes withdrew themselves more and more to their purely ecclesiastical domain. They could stand in no other relation to the new principles (the Territorial system, and such like), which had found their way, through Protestantism, into the laws of European states and peoples. Thus has the matter stood to the present time. On ecclesiastical grounds the Papal See is, at present, as strong and powerful as ever, and as free in its action as it ever had been. Dangers and perplexities await it in temporal affairs—in the position of Italy, and in the possession of the States of the Church.

What is now, and in point of fact, the actual function and vocation of the Papacy, and why is the whole existence of the Church at this time, and in future, so inseparably bound up with the existence of the papal authority, and with its free exercise?

The Catholic Church is a most opulent, and, at the same time, a most multifarious organism. Its mission is nothing less than to be the teacher and moulder of all nations; and however much it may find itself hampered in this task; however limited may be the sphere of action allowed to it, by this or that government, its task always remains the same, and the Church requires and possesses an abundance of power to attain its purpose: it has a great number of various institutions, all directed to the same end; and with these it is continually creating new. All these powers, these institutions, these spiritual communities, stand in need of a supreme guidance, with a firm and strong hand, in order that they may work harmoniously together; that they may not degenerate, and may not lose sight of their destination; that they may not suicidally turn their capabilities, one against the other, or against the unity and welfare of the Church. It is only an ecclesiastical primacy can fulfil this mission—it is the Papacy alone that is in a position to keep every member in its own sphere, and to pacify every disturbance that may arise.

Besides this, there is another task, just as difficult as it is important, which it lies upon the Papal See to fulfil.

It is the duty, namely, of the Pope to represent and to defend the rights of individual Churches against the domination of states and monarchs; to watch that the Church be not altered in its character, nor crippled in its power, by becoming interwoven with the State. For this purpose, with the voice and action of the church immediately concerned, the intervention of the Supreme Church authority becomes indispensable; since this stands above and outside of the conflicts, which may possibly arise between any one church and the state; and it solely is capable, in its high and inaccessible position, and in possession of the richest experiences, won in centuries of ecclesiastical government, to specify accurately the claims of both parties, and to serve as a stay and support to the weaker—to the one which otherwise must inevitably succumb before the manifold means of compulsion and seduction which lie at the command of modern states.

It is, moreover, a beautiful, sublime, but certainly difficult mission of the Papal See—a mission only to be fulfilled by the strength of an enlightened wisdom and a comprehensive knowledge of mankind—and that is, to be just to the claims of individual nations in the Church; to comprehend their necessities, and restrain their desires within the limits required by the unity of the Church.

For all this there is wanted a power opulently endowed with manifold views and prerogatives. If there were a primacy of dignity and honour, without any real power, the Church would be but badly served. This is not the place to enumerate all the particular rights which the Pope exercises in the ordinary course of his administration over the Church. They may be found in every hand-book of ecclesiastical law. But concerning the measure and extent, the limitation or illimitability of the Papal power, a few words, amid the prevailing confusion of ideas on the subject, cannot be considered as superfluous.

Outside of the Catholic Church it has become almost a

common form of speech—to brand the Papal power as being
boundless, as being absolutist, as one which recognizes no
law capable of controlling it.   There is a great deal of talk
of " Romish omnipotence," or of one at least with a never
unceasing pretension to universal dominion.   Persons maintain that " Rome never foregoes a claim which she has once
put forward; that she keeps such constantly in view, and
upon every favourable opportunity strives to enforce it." All
these representations and accusations are untrue and unjust.
The Papal power is in one respect the most restricted that
can be imagined, for its determinate purpose is manifest to
all persons; and as the Popes themselves have innumerable
times openly declared that purpose, " to maintain the laws and
ordinances of the Church, and to prevent any infringement
of them."   The Church has long since had its established
ordinances, and its legislation determined on, even to the
most minute points.   The Papal See is thus, then, before all
others, called upon to give an example of the most rigid adherence to Church tenets ; and it is only upon this condition
that it can rely upon obedience to itself on the part of individual churches, or calculate upon the respect of the faithful.
Hence every one thoroughly well grounded in a knowledge
of ecclesiastical legislation can, in most cases, with certainty
anticipate what the Papal decision will be. · Besides this, a
considerable portion of Church ordinances rests, according to
the views of Catholics, on the Divine Commandment, and
are consequently for every one, and of course for the Papal
power also, not to be tampered with.   The Pope cannot dispense with things which are commanded by Divine Law.
This is universally acknowledged.   What then can restrain
the Pope?   De Maistre says, " Everything—canons, laws,
national customs, monarchs, tribunals, national assemblies,
prescription, remonstrances, negotiations, duty, fear, prudence, and especially public opinion, the Queen of the
World."

In another respect, the Papal authority is certainly truly
sovereign and free, one, too, which, according to its nature
and purpose for extraordinary accidents and exigencies,

must be endowed with an altogether extraordinary power to control every mere human right, and to permit or ordain exceptions to general rules. It may occur that serious embarrassments, new situations of things, may be placed before the Church; and to which existing ecclesiastical ordinances do not extend, and in which a solution can be found only by overstepping the regulations in force. If the necessity of the case requires it, "the Pope," as Bossuet says, "can do all,"[1] of course with the exception of what is contrary to the Divine Law.

The most conspicuous instance of an extraordinary application of the highest Church power, because the weal of the Church urgently required it, was the step taken by Pius VII., on the conclusion of the French Concordat, in the year 1801. With a stroke of the pen (by his Bull of the 29th November of the same year), he deprived of their dignity thirty-seven French bishops who had refused to resign. He, too, abolished all the episcopal churches for ever, with their Chapters and privileges; and he erected, at the same time, ten Metropolitan sees and fifty Bishoprics. A proceeding so unprecedented, such an abolition of well-founded rights, was only to be justified by the most extreme necessity—by the imperative duty of creating a new system of order out of the deeply-convulsed Church of France. Pius himself declared to individuals in whom he reposed his confidence, that, of all the circumstances in his eventful life, "the act which he then found himself compelled to perform was that which had cost him the greatest effort, and caused him the deepest pain"; but the necessity of the measure he had taken was so obvious, that everyone in the Church, with the exception of those affected by it, had approved of his conduct.

The delusion that the Papal See has arrogated to itself a despotic and absolute power, and exercised it wherever it was not restrained by fear, is so generally diffused, especially in Germany and England—it is so customary to proclaim the boundlessness of that power, and the defencelessness in

[1] "Defens. Declar.," 2, 20; "Oeuvres," vol. xxxiii. p. 354.

which individual Churches and persons find themselves· when opposed to it, that I cannot refrain from exposing the error by a few decisive testimonies. Let us hear on this matter one who was a pope himself—Pius VII. :—

"The Pope," he says, in an official document drawn up in his name, and having reference to Germany[1]—"The Pope is bound by the nature and the institutions of the Catholic Church, whose head he is, within certain limits, which he dare not overstep, without violating his conscience, and abusing that supreme power which Jesus Christ has confided to him to employ for the building up, and not the destruction, of His Church. Inviolable limits for the head of the Church are the dogmas of the Catholic faith, which the Roman bishops may, neither directly nor indirectly, violate; and although in the Catholic Church faith has always been regarded as unalterable, but discipline as alterable, yet the Roman Bishops have, with respect even to discipline, in their actual conduct, always held certain limits sacred, although by this means they acknowledge the obligation never to undertake any novelty in certain things, and also not to subject other parts of discipline to alterations, unless upon the most important and irrepugnable grounds. With respect to such principles, the Roman Bishops have never thought that they could admit any change in those parts of discipline which are directly ordained of Jesus Christ Himself; or of those which, by their nature, enter into a connection with dogmas; or of those which may have been attacked by erroneous believers to sustain these innovations; or also in those parts on which the Roman Bishops, on account of the consequences that might result to the disparagement of religion and of Catholic principles, do not think themselves entitled to admit a change, whatever the advantages might be offered, or whatever the amount of evils might be threatened.

"So far as concerns other parts of Church discipline,

---

[1] " Esposizione dei sentimenti de Sua Santita," in the treatise, "Die Neuesten Grundlagen der Deutsch-Katholischen Kirchenvervassung." Stuttgard, 1821, p. 334.

which are not comprehended in the classes above-mentioned, the Roman Bishops have felt no hesitation in making many changes; but they have always been grounded on the principles on which every well-ordered society rests; and they have only given their consent to such changes when the need or the welfare of the Church required them."

I will here quote the words of an individual, who, to a certain extent, speaks in the name of the whole Church of a country, which is, in point of fact, the youngest member of the Universal Church. He is the first prelate of the American Church—the present Archbishop of Baltimore, Father Patrick Kenrick. "The power of the Pope," he says, "is chiefly employed in maintaining the general laws already established, regulating the mutual relations of the clergy, and mitigating the strictness of disciplinary observance, whensoever local or individual causes demand it. The faithful are sufficiently protected against the abuse of power, by the freedom of their own conscience, which is not bound to yield obedience to authority when flagrantly abused. The Pope only addresses conscience: his laws and censures are only powerful inasmuch as they are acknowledged to be passed under a divine sanction. No armies or civil officers are employed to give them effect; and in case of flagrant abuse of authority, he loses the only influence by which they can become effectual."[1]

The work of the Archbishop is, even for Europe, a remarkable phenomenon. It shows how the two millions of Catholics who live in the free states of America regard their relations both to the Pope and the Republic. "The obedience," says Kenrick, "which we owe to the Pope has regard only to matters in which the salvation of souls is concerned—it has nothing to do with the loyalty and allegiance which belong to the civil government. The Church is indifferent as to the various forms of political administration. The acknowledgment of the primacy of the Bishop of Rome

[1] "The Primacy of the Apostolic See Vindicated." Philadelphia, 1845, p. 358.

E

cannot have the most remote connexion with any danger to our republican institutions, but will much more serve to render them stronger and more lasting, since they will moderate the enjoyment of civil liberty by moral restraints, and so prevent the evils of licentiousness and anarchy.[1]

There is now lying before me the most recent production of a very respectable individual, who stands at the head of an important party in Holland—this is Groen van Prinsterer. He declares against Stahl, who had maintained, "that the temporal sovereignty of the Pope, and the persecution of heretics by the temporal power, were not dogmas, or articles of faith, with respect to which Rome could assert its claim to infallibility." Groen will not admit this; he says, "Rome must, in principle, acknowledge the independence and sanctity of the temporal powers; it must no longer claim the right of disposing of heretical kingdoms, or of altering the law of succession, et cetera: it must, too, acknowledge that the Bull of Boniface VIII., with the assertion as to the two swords at the command of the Church—the spiritual and temporal—no longer affords an authentic resumé of the long sought for Roman omnipotence; and, finally, it must recall its protest against the Peace of Westphalia. And when all this has been done," he adds, "Rome will have spoken its own condemnation."[2]

My first reason for selecting Herr Groen van Prinsterer, out of a whole troop of persons entertaining similar opinions, is, that his is one of the most recent declarations on the same subject which I have been able to find; and next, because, in point of fact, there are hundreds of our literati who do not know that of which he also is either actually ignorant, or which he intentionally ignores.

In the first place, the matter is put thus: "Rome must acknowledge the independence of the Temporal Power, and renounce the right of deposing non-Catholic monarchs." But this has been done long since. Cardinal Antonelli,

[1] "Kenrick's Primacy," p. 475.
[2] "Le Parti Anti-revolutionnaire et Confessionel." Amsterdam, 1860.

Prefect of the Propaganda (under whom the Irish Bishops are placed), addressed, on the 23d June, 1791, a Rescript to the Archbishops and Bishops of Ireland, wherein it was said:— " We must very carefully distinguish between the real rights of the Apostolic See, and what have been, with an inimical intention, in modern times imputed to it. The Roman See has never taught that faith was not to be kept with heretics; or, " that an oath of allegiance made to kings, in a state of separation from the Catholic Community, could be broken ;" or, " *that it was allowable for a Pope to interfere with their temporal rights and possessions.*" This Rescript has been often enough printed, and I do not know what could be said more clearly or distinctly.[1]

Some years ago, the Bishops of the United States, in North America, when assembled in their fifth council, prepared an address to the Pope, in which, when complaining of their numerous "calumniators" in the country, they expressed themselves in the following terms:—"They (the calumniators) strive to cast suspicion and bring the odium of Government on us, their Catholic fellow-citizens, although our fathers poured out their blood like water in defence of liberty, against a sectarian oppressor ; and falsely assert that we are enslaved to a foreign prince—namely, under the political and civil authority of the Roman Pontiff; and that we are faithless to the Government."[2] We see here the same things alleged which have been a thousand times before stated in Germany, and that still continue to be repeated. The Archbishop of Baltimore, who communicates this fact, adds : " This disclaimer of all civil power in the Pontiff, which many of us have made on our oaths, was graciously received by Gregory XVI. Can any further evidence be required that the authority which we recognise in him is spiritual, and nowise inconsistent with the most unqualified allegiance to the civil Government ? "

Four and seventy French Bishops, with two Cardinals at

[1] See " Ami de la Religion," vol. xviii. ; also in the works of Archbishop Affre of Paris, " Essai sur la Suprematie temp. du Pape," p. 508.
[2] KENRICK, p. 434, where he appends the Latin text of the Council.

their head, presented, on the 10th April, 1826, a memorial to the King, in which they declared that they held fast to the old doctrine of the French Church upon the rights of their monarchs; and of their full and absolute independence in temporal matters of any authority, direct or indirect, on the part of every spiritual power. Archbishop Affre has reprinted this document.[1]

A short time before this, on the 25th January, 1826, the Archbishops and Bishops of Ireland put forth a similar declaration, in which they renounced, in the strongest terms, any jurisdiction or power in the Pope to interfere in temporal matters within the British Kingdom.[2] As a matter of course, both these Declarations were made with the consent of the Papal See.

Secondly, it is briefly to be observed, with respect to the Bull of Boniface VIII., and the theory therein put forward, as to the Spiritual and Temporal Power, that the retractation or abrogation of the same had been made a few years after its assertion; and that, too, by Pope Clement V.[3] Archbishop Affre of Paris, who, in the discharge of his pastoral functions, afterwards died an heroic death at "the barricades," has, in reply to La Mennais, clearly shewn that the Bull of Clement could recall nothing else than the assertion made in the Bull of Boniface—viz., that the exercise of the Temporal was subject to the correction of the Spiritual.[4]

Thirdly, and finally, "Rome is to recall its Protest against the Peace of Westphalia." This Protest is, in fact, a favourite theme, which is regularly discussed whenever an attack is to be made upon the Pope, or the Catholic Church in Germany. In the year 1846, this Protest was brought forward as a powerful argument against me in the Bavarian Chambers. Not long since, in the Prussian Chambers, Herr von Gerlach resisted a proposal of the Catholic Deputies (the justice of which, as well as I recollect, he was obliged himself to

[1] AFFRE, "Essai," p. 505.
[2] Unam Sanctam, so it stands in the Lib. vi. Decretal.
[3] The Bull "Meruit," in the Collection of Decretal.
[4] AFFRE, "Essai," p. 340.

admit), by a reference to this very Protest. It will, therefore, be allowable for me to go a little further back, and to
enter somewhat more minutely into the true state of the case.
I must here make what at first sight may be regarded as a
paradoxical confession, when I say that I rejoice that there
should have been, at that time, one man found in Europe,
who, in the name of God and of Christian conscience, entered
a Protest against the Peace of Westphalia; and that this
man should have been precisely the one who was the bearer
of the highest ecclesiastical office upon earth. The Pope,
indeed, did not protest for the reason that he would not
admit that there could be any peace between Catholics and
Protestants—the whole course of subsequent history has
proved the contrary—but he protested because it was for
him a sacred duty to resist the deeply immoral and unchristian principles that lay at the foundation of the religious
stipulations of that entire Treaty of Peace. I allude to the
territorial system—to the principle "that to whomsoever
the country belongs, to him also belongs its religion."[1] Un-
happily! they were German Theologians and German Jurists
who first brought forward this doctrine, hitherto unheard of
in the Christian world—namely, that it was a right of
princes to alter the religion of their subjects, as it seemed
good to them; and to change Catholics into Protestants, and
to make Calvinists out of Lutherans! It is well known
how willingly princes made use of this new doctrine. In the
states of the Middle Ages there certainly was religious compulsion; but how completely different were the ideas and
practice of former times when compared with the new! In
those times people and princes were members of the Catholic Church, by the side of which none other existed. All
were agreed that the State, by its close connection with the
Church, could tolerate no falling off from it; could allow no
new religion to be introduced; and that every attempt of the
kind was an attempt against existing social order. Every
heretical doctrine which broke out in the Middle Ages, either
had distinctly avowed, or bore, as its inevitable consequence,

---

[1] "Cujus est regio, illius est religio."

a revolutionary character. It must, in proportion as it attained influence and authority, bring with it a dissolution of the existing condition of the State, and effect a political and social revolution. The sects of the Gnostics, the Cathari, and the Albigenses, which especially elicited the harsh and relentless legislation of the Middle Ages against heresy, and that had to be resisted in sanguinary wars, were the Socialists and Communists of that time. They attacked marriage, family, and property. Had they been triumphant, the consequences would have been general ruin—a collapse into barbarism and heathenish licentiousness. As to the Waldenses, it is well known to every one acquainted with history that their principles concerning oaths, and the right of the State to inflict punishments, were such as could find no place in the European world at that time.

In the Middle Ages the laws and rights in religious matters were the same for all. It was everywhere taught that not only every bishop, but the Pope himself, must, should he have fallen into erroneous doctrines, be deposed; and, in case of his perseverance in error, he must, like every other, be condemned. The King knew that a separation from the Church would inevitably cost him his crown, and that he would cease to be sovereign over a Catholic people. Never, during the thousand years before Luther, was an attempt even made by a monarch to introduce into his states a new religion, or a new doctrine, or in any form to separate himself from the Church. If there ever was one, like the Emperor Frederick II., who was, in fact, an unbeliever, yet he had it publicly denied, and got a testimony of his orthodoxy made out for him by bishops and theologians.

All this was changed with the Reformation. The Reformers committed to temporal princes from the beginning "the authority"—that is to say, power over the religion of their country and their subjects. It was the duty and the right of "the authority" to plant the new Church and the new Gospel, to root out Popery, and to allow no strange doctrine to spring up. This was at every opportunity impressed upon temporal sovereigns. There resulted, indeed, from this an irreconcileable contradiction; for Luther at the same time represented it as a sacred duty for every individual to please himself in religious matters—to place himself above every authority, and, before all things, above the Church, and even to disregard princes! "Notwithstanding every human command," he says, "each one must determine his own faith for himself. Even a miller's wench, or a child nine years of age, who decides according to the Gospel" (that is to say, according to the new dogma of Justification), "may understand the Scriptures better than Pope, and Councils, and all scholars collected together!" In another place he says: "You must decide for yourself; your own life is at stake" —and so forth.[1] Luther never attempted to reconcile this contradiction. In practice he adhered to it; and it became the religious Protestant doctrine, that princes had the highest juridical office over religious doctrines and the Church; and that it was their right and their vocation to suppress every opinion in matters of faith that should differ from their own. In this opinion Lutherans and Reformers were consentaneous. In the *Augsburg Confession* Melancthon, who was at that time inclined to uphold Episcopal authority, or to help in re-establishing it, reckons it as the office of the Bishop to judge of doctrine; but he had already, in his "Apology,"[2] declared that it is to kings and princes that the protection and maintenance of the pure doctrine is, as an office, committed by God. The Lutheran princes assumed, then, to themselves expressly this right in the Preface to the Concordian-Book; and have, since then, exercised it to the widest extent. The Calvinistic writings upon the creed give to "the authority" the right of opposing false doctrine, and defending the true.[3] Luther himself reckons it as a matter

[1] LUTHER's Werke, Walch's Ausgabe, xii., Sermon, v. 3, 1522; xi. 1887.

[2] At the end of the 9th Article.

[3] The Swiss Confession in the 30th, the English in the 37th, the Scotch in the 24th, and the Belgic in the 36th Articles. In the Brandenburg Electorate this is placed at the head of the Confession of Faith. In the Confession of Basle it is said: "Hoc officium gentili magistratui commendatum esse debet, *ut vero Dei vicario.*" For this reference is made to the example of the Jewish kings, who had abolished idolatry.

to his especial credit, that he had, in this respect, benefited the temporal Powers, who, in the Catholic Church, had been robbed of their good right ; and thus, by him, those in supreme authority were " exalted, enlightened, and adorned."[1] The Danish Court-preacher, Masius, mentions it as a particular advantage of the Lutheran religion, that, according to it, princes are "the highest vicegerents of God upon earth;"[2] that they may at their pleasure appoint and depose the servants of the Church, and freely govern the whole territory of ecclesiastical rites and ceremonies.[2] This doctrine was long the prevailing one, and it still has its defenders ; for example, Petersen, who, after having assured us that the German people are the specific people of the New Testament, then proceeds to declare its "lords of the land" as the only possessors of power over the whole Christian world, and as those " in whom the Evangelical Church reverences the delegates of Christ."[3]

And so arose a despotism, the equal of which has never before been seen.[4]   The new system, as it was expounded by

[1] Walch's Ausg., xiv. 520 ; xix. 2287 : "If any gratitude," he says, "from this scandalous and accursed world were to be gained, and I, Doctor Martin Luther, had taught and done nothing else than this, that I have enlightened and adorned the temporal rule or ' authority'—and for this thing alone should men be favourable and thankful to me, since even my worst enemies well knew that a like understanding as to the temporal authority was completely concealed under the Papacy," &c., &c., &c.   The favour of princes was, in truth, not wanting to him.   He gives another reason why princes and authorities ought to be especially grateful to him.   Formerly, that is in Catholic times, they had felt great anxiety about executions.   Many princes had, from religious scruples, and under the influence of their confessors, avoided signing numerous sentences of death ; but now, by Luther's doctrine, they were perfectly tranquillized.—See " Colloquia et Meditationes Lutheri."   Ed. Rebenstock, i. 147.

[2] " Interesse principum circa religionem evangelicam." — Hafn, 1687, p. 31.

[3] " Die Idee der Christlichen Kirche," vol. iii., pp. 224-227.

[4] To mention only one example : At the Westphalian Peace Congress, Wolfgang von Gemmingen, a deputy of the Imperial Equestrian Order, stated that the city of Oppenheim, pawned to the Palatinate, had, since the Reformation, been forced to change its religion ten times ! —PFANNERI, " Hist. pacis Westph.," i., p. 42.

theologians and jurists, was worse than the Byzantine practice; for there no attempt had ever been made to change the religion of the people. The Protestant princes were not merely Popes in their own country, but they were much more; and were able to do what no Pope had ever dreamed of attempting. Every Pope knew that the power he possessed was a conservative one—that he held it to maintain the doctrine that had been transmitted to him, and that an attempt on his part to alter the teaching of the Church would infallibly be frustrated by a universal resistance. To the Protestant princes, however, it had been said—and they themselves believed and declared it—that their power in religious matters was entirely unlimited; and that, in the use of it, they need attend to no other standard than their own consciences. They also, as a matter of course, declared that they were subject to " the Gospel," or the Holy Scriptures; but then it was to the Scriptures according to their own interpretation of them, or that of the court-preachers of their selection. The Reformers had naturally so understood the matter, that the princes should proceed according to the advice of theologians, and that they would especially allow themselves to be guided in all questions of doctrine by the theological faculties of the universities of their country. But these changed, or were changed; and as often as it pleased the sovereign to alter the religion of his territory the old professors were dismissed, and new professors were summoned.

With this new system of ecclesiastical and political power united in the person of the prince, was introduced a change of incalculable gravity in the condition of the entire German people. The distinction and the contrast between the two Powers, which, on the whole, had acted beneficently for the people, and which, through collisions and counterpoises, had aroused and maintained intellectual activity and political freedom, were now completely put an end to. The Church became altogether incorporated in the State, and was regarded as a wheel in the great state machine. He who can exercise an absolute power over that which is noblest and,

for the most part, invisible—he who can so rule over religion
and conscience—is also one who, if he chooses, can have at his
disposal everything which the State can bestow or the people
yield.   With the establishment of the Consistories, as
sovereign authorities ruling ecclesiastical affairs, began the
development of Bureaucracy—of monarchical and political
omnipotence—of Administrative Centralisation.   As soon as
ecclesiastical and religious affairs were placed in the hands
of Government officers, a mechanical, clerk-like-scribbling
system, and the benumbing spirit of a mere administrative
machine, whose functions were to command and issue ordinances, took the place of a living organism—of an authority
acting through moral motives.   It went on then as it goes
on still ; the Bureaucratic system became a polypus, perpetually putting out new branches, and swallowing up more
materials.[1]

An inevitable consequence followed—a still more onerous
system of despotism weighed down upon the greater part of
Germany.   The Protestant people were oppressed by a
slavery such as had never before existed, through their
monarchical supreme Bishops.   Pecuniary fines, imprison-
ments, and banishments, were inflicted for non-appearance in
church on Sunday, for not attending regularly at Communion,
and for a few persons meeting together for the purpose of
private edification.

Upon this system of princely dominion over religion and
conscience the Westphalian Peace had put its seal.   This

[1] So remarks the well-known jurist, LEYSER ("Medit. ad Pandect.,"
vol. vii., p. 292) : "In former times, and far even into the seventeenth
century, the governmental business of the German princes was so
limited that it could be disposed of by a few Councillors and a single
College.   But afterwards, and when, by the Peace of Westphalia, the
territorial authority became so very widely extended, the business of the
Administration had multiplied tenfold, and a crowd of Colleges, Courts,
and official persons became necessary.   It was then seen what influence
must have upon the Government the committing into its hands the whole
of the Church business and religious affairs."   The same Leyser also
reminds us (vol. vi., p. 49), that "the Protestant Consistories conducted
themselves in a much more tyrannical manner than the Pope."

Reformation law was only limited by the fixed normal year —1624. But, beyond the right of quiescent continuance guaranteed for that year, every Catholic might be compelled by his Protestant sovereign, and every Protestant by his Catholic sovereign, either to change his religion or to quit his country. The Protest of the Pope was, therefore, a solemn declaration that the fact of his envoy taking part in the Congress must not be regarded as an assent to its articles, which had, as their inevitable consequence,- the compulsory secession of a number of Catholics from the Church.[1] It is true that the Pope in his Bull places himself in this exclusive stand-point, that every cession of Catholic bishoprics and Church property to Protestant princes, and every further extension of Protestantism, were things to which he could not give his approval, and against which he must endeavour to guard. This, under the circumstances of the times, was a course which the Supreme Pastor of the Church could not avoid taking. He stood there opposed to a system which, at the same time with a denial of the Church and its authority (and in consequence of that denial), had exalted into a principle of religious doctrine the arbitrary power of the Prince in ecclesiastical affairs, and the boundless dominion of the Prince over the consciences of mankind. With such a system a substantial peace was, in reality, not possible; it was nothing more than an armistice. Every advance of such a system, into countries hitherto Catholic, must be regarded as a calamity to be prevented at any cost. The terrible territorial system must first be moderated, and, in some measure, its destructive consequences obviated by custom, by public opinion, and by experience, before there could be expected a friendly, neighbourly feeling between Catholics and Protestants. In Rome, as in Germany, it was known right well that in purely Lutheran countries, like Sweden and Denmark, the punishment of death had been affixed to the exercise of the Catholic religion, and had, only a few years previously, been

[1] Instr. P. O., 5, 30: " Cum statibus immediatis cum jure territorii et superioritatis —etiam *jus reformandi exercitium religionis* competat."

carried into execution, by Gustavus Adolphus, on several young persons.[1] It was known also that, in the symbolical books of the German Protestants, it was said to princes and kings: " You are the lords and rulers over religion and the Church in your countries, and you have to regard in this matter no other limits than the Bible, as interpreted by yourselves, or by your chosen theologians." It was, finally, also known that the authority of princes over religion was declared by Protestant theologians and jurists to be a real and essential constituent part of the sovereign power; and, therefore, that every prince must regard persons adhering to a religion different from his own, as in a state of permanent revolt against his lawful authority—as half-subjects, who perversely refused to acknowledge and yield obedience to the nobler and more perfect part of his governmental authority.[2] This position of affairs must be taken into consideration when reference is made to a treaty by which so many Catholics, and so many territories and possessions formerly Catholic, were ceded to Protestant powers, and with scanty or very feeble security for freedom of conscience. At that time the Chief Pastor of the Church could, in reality, do nothing else than enter his Protest against partitions and concessions, the consequence of which must be a considerable number of souls being lost to the Church. Had the Pope taken up his former position—that which through the circumstances of the Middle Ages, and since the great emigration of the Northern nations had been occupied by him—his rejection of this Treaty would have been equi-

---

[1] BAAZ, " Inventar. Eccl. Suegoth." Lincop. 1642, p. 739.

[2] The *jus circa sacra*, and the *jurisdictio Ecclesiastica* constituted, it was said, the most costly and precious jewel of territorial superiority. See SHAUROTH, " Sammlung d. Concl. Corp. Evang.," ii. 39. The statesman and historian, Lord Clarendon, designates the Church supremacy of the Kings of England " the better moiety of their sovereignty."—" Edinburgh Review," vol. xix., p. 435. In point of fact, " this better moiety" of the sovereignty has, since the Revolution of 1688, become partly a dead letter, and has partly passed away from the Crown to the Prime Minister for the time being, and a Parliamentary majority.

valent to a demand that war should break out anew, and that
the whole work of the Peace negotiation should be gone over
again from the very beginning. It was now far otherwise.
The Papacy, since the Reformation, no longer stood at the
head of the European commonwealth—was no longer the
general acknowledged mediator of peace: the protector and
interpreter of international law. The Papal rejection of
the articles of Peace had, therefore, only this effect—it was
to be regarded as a disapproval and a censure, taken from
the ecclesiastical point of view. No prince has ever called
into question the validity of the Peace of Westphalia by an
appeal to the judgment of Rome, and theologians have
always taught that a Papal Dispensation from its obligation
would not be admissible.[1]

It is certain that in Catholic countries compulsion was
exercised to eject Protestantism, which had found its way
into them, and to restore the unanimity of the Church; and
Catholic princes willingly appealed to a right invented at
the Reformation by the Protestants, in order thus to overcome it in their own territories, with a weapon offered to
them by their adversaries, and which was declared by them
to be legitimate. In order, however, that a just judgment
should be formed upon this point, the following matters
are to be taken into consideration:

First, On the Catholic side they had to do with a theory
and a practice whose founders and adherents had declared,
at the celebrated Protestation of Spire, in the year 1529,
that they would not tolerate the Catholic religion by the
side of the new one; and they, in fact, had everywhere
begun to destroy all traces of the old religion, and they
likewise had devised a system which, by committing the
ecclesiastical power to temporal princes, had degraded every
religion, even that of Luther and Calvin, into a mere
question of power, or the will and pleasure of the sovereign.
Where the Catholic prince recognised above him and his

---

[1] LAYMAN, "Theol. Moral," lib. ii., tr. 3, c. 12. "Si Catholici
cum acatholicis publicum fœdus ineunt, non potest per auctoritatem
Pontificiam solvi aut relaxari."

people the firm and always equable authority of the Church,
and desired to be only a member, a faithful and obedient
member, of that great organism, the world-Church—there was
(on the other side) the Protestant prince; and this prince,
according to the supposition of his being invested with a supreme religious judgeship in religious affairs, both for himself
and his subordinates, knew of no authority higher than his own.
So had they constructed in England an Episcopal church,
out of an unnatural combination of Catholic and Protestant
elements—and this had so happened because the king had so
willed it.   Then there were Denmark, Sweden, and Norway,
which became and remained Lutheran, because their kings
regarded that doctrine as the most convenient, and also as
the most favourable to the extension of their power.   In
Holland there reigned a pure Calvinism, because it was professed by the more numerous and powerful party, who,
as soon as they felt themselves strong enough, violated the
agreement they had made with the Catholics of the
country,[1] and annihilated their religious freedom.   In the
German principalities no one could know whether the
country the next year would be Lutheran, or Calvinist, or
half-Calvinistic, according to the pattern that had been
introduced into Brandenburg.   It depended upon the person
of the monarch and his varying views, or on the death of
one and the succession of another of a different opinion.

Secondly, The theory of the supreme episcopal authority
of the Sovereign, and his obligation to allow no other religion than his own, was distinctly a part of the Protestant
system, and had become an article of faith.   When a prince,
hitherto Lutheran, suppressed Lutheranism in his territory,
and forced Calvinism upon it, the Lutheran theologians na-

[1] Namely, the Union-Treaty of Utrecht, in the year 1579, and by
which the still preponderating Catholic provinces and cities joined the
League.   Four years afterwards William of Orange issued a new edict,
which, without the slightest pretext, broke the promise that had been
given to the Catholics, and permitted only the exercise of the Calvinist
religion.   Compare on this point STOUPE, " La Religion des Hollandais,"
1672, p. 12 ; and " Oeuvres," D'ANT. ARNAULD, xiv. 509.

turally said, " Your Calvinist conscience is in error;" but at the same time they were obliged to admit that, since the prince considered the Calvinist doctrine as the Biblical one, he was certainly entitled—nay, bound—to "reform" his country in that direction. The Catholic Church found itself in quite a different position. Here, the two Powers were completely separated; the prince and the authorities had not to be the rulers and bishops of the Church, but merely its protectors. The Church had already passed through various stages with respect to its position as regarded persons differing from it in faith. Under the Christian Emperors it had been, taking it on the whole, the ruling or most favoured corporation in the Roman Empire; but the conduct of the Emperors towards those outside of the pale of the Church, towards heathens, Jews, heretics, and schismatics, was very unequal. Amongst the great variety of sects it was observed that, whilst some had an extremely immoral character, others were distinguished by the severity of their manners, so that general rules could not be applicable to both. On the whole, amongst the bishops of that time the prevailing view was, that a departure from the faith of the Church, if no other offence were conjoined with it, could not be severely punished by the State. "The mildness of the Church," declares Pope Leo the Great, "contents itself with the sacerdotal judgment, and desires no blood-stained vengeance." Therefore was the action of two Spanish bishops, who appeared before the Imperial tribunal as accusers of the Priscillianists, visited with the severest reprehension by the most illustrious men of the Church—by an Ambrose and a Martin. For a long period of time during the Middle Ages there was no separation from the Church on the ground of varying doctrines. In the eleventh century first began that gloomy, morally destructive sect, with Gnostic doctrines, and which had come hither from the East, and in secret extended itself. Against the adherents of that sect the ruling authorities acted with great severity, and not one obdurate member of it was permitted to live. Gradually it became the rule that a falling off from the faith, and the diffusion of un-ecclesiastical

doctrines, should be regarded as a crime worthy of death.
The idea that by the side of the Church, by which the whole
political and social life of the time was penetrated and supported, there should also be other religious communities with
a doctrine of their own, and that such might exist in the
State, was a conception of a condition of circumstances such as
no one at that time regarded as a possibility, and to which no
one had ever given expression. Where sects did exist they
retreated into the deepest obscurity, and the decrees of Popes
and Councils, with respect to heresies, were naturally based
upon the views generally prevailing at the time. But the
regulations and commands therein contained do not fall within
the domain of faith—of received and unchangeable doctrine;
they appertain to discipline, which is changeable and capable
of modification by peculiar and transitory circumstances.

The insurrection of Protestantism against the Church
assumed, in a very short space of time, the character of a
conflict of life and death. Already in the writings of Luther,
in the years 1520-1521, there was opened between the new
doctrine and the old Church an abyss that could never more
be bridged over. The rejection of all ecclesiastical tradition
and of every Church authority—the setting up of a dogma
concerning the relations of God to man, of which the
originator confessed that it had remained unknown to
the whole Church from the time of the Apostles to himself. Such were the principles now undisguisedly brought
forward and maintained. The demand was no longer merely
this: "that the Church should reform itself thoroughly, in
its head and in its limbs," but that "it should be dissolved,
and that the judgment of self-destruction should be executed
by itself." Its Primacy and Episcopacy were to be abolished;
the organism which had kept nations together was to be rent
asunder, and in the place of its worship, prayer, and Sacrifice,
there were to be preachers appointed, and the Church must
break with the entire past, in doctrine, in sacraments, and
institutions. Upon a common understanding, upon a mere
half-candid reunion, could only the person think who neither

comprehended the nature of the Protestant doctrine nor the bearing of the Reformation movement.

For a long time there was no question as to mutual toleration, or an attempt at a friendly communion together. Such a thought was utterly foreign to that entire age. On the Protestant side the theory of absolute ecclesiastical power being vested in the temporal sovereign, rendered a system of toleration an impossibility. Historically, nothing is more untrue than the assertion that " the Reformation was a movement for freedom of conscience." The fact is that it was precisely the very opposite. Both Lutherans and Calvinists, as well as all men at all times, desired freedom of conscience; but then, to grant it to others when they were themselves the stronger party, was a thought that did not even occur to them. The Reformers all regarded the complete suppression and extirpation of the Catholic Church as a matter of course. From the very· beginning they called upon princes and the political authorities to abolish by main force the worship of the Ancient Church. In England, Ireland, Scotland, Denmark, and Sweden, they went so far as to affix the punishment of death to the practice of the Catholic religion. Towards other sects, that arose about the same period, they proceeded with no less severity. That the Anabaptists should atone for their doctrine with their lives, was required even by him who was renowned as the mildest of the Reformers, Melancthon.[1] The same man desired that corporal punishment should be inflicted on the Catholics, because it was the duty of the temporal power to proclaim and defend the Divine Law![2] Calvin also besought of the Duke of Somerset, as the Regent-Protector of England, that he should destroy with the sword all—namely, the Catholics—who opposed the new Protestant Constitution of the Church.[3] Kings, states-

[1] See " Corpus Ref." Ed. Bretschneider, ii. 18, 711, 713.

[2] " Corp. Ref.," ix. 77.

[3] " Epistolæ Genev.," 1579, p. 40. It is remarkable that he also brought forward, as a ground why the punishment of death should be inflicted, that an attempt against the monarchy, appointed by God, was involved in the refusal to submit to its ecclesiastical authority. IIis

F

men, theologians, and philosophers were all agreed that
neither the Catholics, nor any one of the sects who differed
from the dominant Church, were entitled to claim toleration.
To have two or several religions in a country, they said, was
dangerous, and enfeebled the Government![1] Even the Lord
Chancellor, Bacon, considered that the extreme limit of toleration to which a Government could venture to go would
be attained when it should content itself with a mere external conformity to the established religion, and should make
no attempt to penetrate into men's consciences and secret
convictions.[2]

Thus, the Catholic princes, clergy, and people knew with
perfect certainty that they themselves would be oppressed so
soon as the party of the new religion felt itself strong enough
to work out its will against them.   They carried on a war of
self-defence, when they endeavoured by all means to prevent
the entrance of Protestantism into their territory, or to expel
it if it had already penetrated.   All the Reformers and the
theologians of the New Church expressed in their writings
not the slightest doubt upon the principle—"that the Catholic religion must be exterminated wherever men had the
power to do so."   In Germany, in the Scandinavian countries, in England, in Switzerland—in short, everywhere that
the Protestant religion predominated—its practice was soon
found in correspondence with its theory.   And as Reformers
at the same time held firmly to the doctrine that princes and
the civil authorities were the possessors of supreme religious
authority, it was resolved, by the Coryphæi of the reformed
faith, that they should refuse to princes, who did not conform

---

friend Beza even urged that anti-Trinitarians should also be put to death,
and this, too, even though they recanted!—" Crenii Animadversiones,"
xi. 90.

[1] As, for example, Lord Burghley, minister of Queen Elizabeth. His
fixed principle was that the State could never be secure in which two
religions were tolerated, for there was no stronger feeling of animosity
than that on account of religion —See "Life of Lord Burghley," in
Peck's "Desiderata Curiosa," p. 33.

[2] "Certain Observations made upon a Libel, 1592,"—Works;
London, 1846, i. 382.

to Calvinistic principles, the right to govern, and declare their deposition as permissible and necessary. It is well known how far Knox and others went in this way, and what share such men had in the dethronement of Charles I. of England. In Sweden, Sigismund was despoiled of his crown because he was a Catholic.

Bayle supposes that the Reformers and their followers must have felt themselves in a very embarrassing position, because they had always, when opposed to the old Church, insisted upon "freedom of conscience," and declared that the compulsion exercised towards them was criminal; whilst they themselves, nevertheless, exhorted the authorities to suppress every other doctrine and religious community. Such a circumstance, however, took place so universally, and it was so much in accordance with the spirit of the times, that it was not felt to be self-contradictory.[1] The French Protestants, although they formed but a poor minority, and only found protection from the Edict of Nantes, yet refused, in the places of security that had been granted to them, to allow any Catholic, or the practice of the Catholic religion, to be where they were. The same scene was enacted in all parts of Protestantised Europe. The prevailing maxim was: "Freedom for ourselves, and oppression for every other party!"

The first who were in earnest about religious freedom, and who really placed the two religions on an equality, were the Catholic Englishmen who, towards the middle of the seventeenth century, founded the colony of Maryland, under the leadership of Lord Baltimore. That little State, under a Catholic administration for a few years, was in the enjoyment of perfect tranquillity and the most complete freedom. But barely two decades had been completed, when the more numerous Protestants, protected by the government of the mother country, overthrew the existing regulations,

[1] We need only see how the well-known Marnix de Saint-Aldegonde defends himself in his "Réponse Apologétique," 1598, against the reproach made to him in the piece entitled "Antidote ou Contrepoison contre les Conseils Sanguinaires, de M. S. A."

brought in the Church of England as the established religion, and passed severe penal laws against the practice of the Catholic faith.[1]

For a long time, the Netherlands had the reputation of being the only country in Europe where freedom of faith, although very limited, existed. Here Calvinism was the State Church, but a very considerable part of the population remained Catholic; and there were, besides, Arminians, Lutherans, Mennonites, and other sects from foreign countries. These the States-General allowed to live in peace, so that many settled down in Holland on account of this freedom. The Catholics alone lay under severe oppressions.[2] Since the middle of the seventeenth century, various isolated Protestant voices had been raised in favour of the concession of religious freedom. The first of these was the Dutchman, Koornheert, a predecessor of the Arminians; but he stood quite alone in his views concerning toleration. After the middle, and towards the close of the seventeenth century, some defenders of the principle of toleration came forward: Milton, Richard Baxter, Bayle, Locke. But Locke alone discussed the question thoroughly and candidly, without falling into glaring contradictions, or taking refuge

[1] The facts are given in detail in MACMAHON's "Historical View of the Government of Maryland," Baltimore, 1831, pp. 198-250; and in BANCROFT's "History of the United States." Boston, 1834. It is interesting to have the opinion of a living Protestant theologian, Thomas Coit, of Newrochelle, on this point. He says—(in his work, "Puritanism, or a Churchman's Defence;" New York, 1855)—"In Maryland, as the Roman Catholics claim, the rights of conscience were *first* fully acknowledged in this country. This is a fact I never knew disputed by good authority, and though a Protestant with all my heart, I accord them the full praise of it with the frankest sincerity," &c.

[2] This is noticed by Sir William Temple, in 1670, in his "Observations upon the United Provinces."—WORKS; London, 1720, i. 58. The preacher Brun, in his treatise—("La Veritable Religion des Hollandois;" Amsterd. 1675, p. 171)—adduces, as a proof of the commendable piety of the Netherlands Government, that they had not only taken from the Catholics their churches, schools, and institutions, as well as excluding them from any office, but also continually interfered with and disturbed them in their religious worship! &c., &c.

in prevarication. The others required, in accordance with the precedent given by the Netherlands, that all Protestant parties and sects should reciprocally afford to each other liberty; but the Catholic Church, as their common antagonist, was still to be oppressed and persecuted. As grounds for thus dealing with Catholics, they stated, first, that the Catholics alone acknowledged an Ecclesiastical head in a foreign country; and next, that the Catholics would, if their side ever became again the stronger, oppress the Protestants.[1] Subsequent experience has, indeed, proved that this Protestant possibility has long since been worked out by them into an actual reality; because, for two hundred years after the rise of Protestantism, no religious freedom was granted to Catholics, in any country or district where Protestants had gained the upper hand. In some towns and villages of Germany alone, there was a prescriptive parity in pursuance of the provisions of the Peace of Westphalia.

How deeply-seated was the principle of religious persecution in the very blood of the professors of the new doctrine, is shown in a striking manner by the conduct of the Anglo-Saxon race. In England, after the Restoration, executions were no longer numerous, and these fell only upon Catholic clergymen; but the prisons there did the work of the executioner—for they were so unhealthy, that human beings died in them by thousands. The Quaker, William Penn, reckoned that, in a short space of time, about 5000, who had been incarcerated on account of their religion, had perished in the English jails.[2] This was also the fate of numerous Protestant Dissenters, as well as of Catholics—and especially so of the new sects of Baptists and Quakers.

Puritans and Presbyterians were, by turns, oppressors and oppressed; but they were also theoretically convinced that it was a matter of conscience to tolerate no other religion than

[1] BAYLE, "Oeuvres," ii. 412.
[2] MACKINTOSH, "History of the English Revolution," pp. 158-160. According to the calculation of this historical investigator, there were in England, from 1660 to 1685, about 25,000 persons imprisoned on account of their religion, and 15,000 families utterly ruined.

their own, the moment that they should possess the means of exercising compulsion. So soon as the very men who had escaped from persecution in the mother country founded new States on the soil of North America, they devised a body of laws unequalled for their severity and intolerance.[1] Catholic priests were put to death, if they were but seen in the country; Quakers were hanged; the mildest punishments of the new Code, for them and other heterodox persons, were branding, banishment, and piercing through the tongue with a red-hot iron. In that land which, since the Declaration of Independence, in the year 1776, has carried out to its widest extent a separation between the Church and the State, there was, in the seventeenth century, a theocracy established that so mingled together religion and civil life as to destroy all freedom; and, for the like of which, a second example is not to be found in history. The state of things in Lutheran Sweden, came the nearest to that of the Calvinists in America. There it was a law of the State, that whoever remained a year under the ban of the Church should be expelled from the kingdom; that a person under excommunication should be excluded from all social intercourse; and further, it was ordained that whosoever, in theological matters, should use even an objectionable mode of speech, and would not recant it, should be dispossessed, and transported out of the country.[2] As a matter of course, in such a state of affairs, and with such a restrictive system of laws, a theological literature, and scientific culture of the sacerdotal order in Sweden, must come to naught.

Mackintosh has strikingly remarked what an incalculable amount of despotic power Protestantism placed in the hands of princes, for, by committing to them the chief authority over religion, it armed them with powers whose

[1] The so-styled "Blue Laws" of New England. Dr. Spalding, Bishop of Louisville, in North America, has given an elaborate analysis of them in his "Miscellanea: comprising Reviews, Lectures, and Essays." Louisville, 1855, pp. 355-380.

[2] "Kirchengesetz und Ordnung Karls XI." Stockholm, 1687, pp. 7-33.

exercise was not restrained either by law or custom, of regulated by experience, and whose limits were undefined.[1] This notion, however, became so intertwined with Protestant views, that theologians, when they were urging persons to conformity with the Church of the country, and writing against Separatists, made loyalty towards the sovereign, and veneration for the law and authorities, their most weighty arguments. It is thus Archbishop Tillotson expatiates on this theme: "That whosoever cannot, like the Apostles, show a directly Divine mission, is committing an offence against authority and the law, by proclaiming any other doctrine than that approved of by them."[2]

Even in a Catholic country, in France, the theory that the religion of the king should be also that of all good subjects, had, in the seventeenth century, met with general acceptance. To it especially is to be attributed the revocation of the Edict of Nantes, by Louis XIV., and the attempt to change Protestants into Catholics, by all means, gentle and coercive, allowable and unallowable. It is a fact that the Intendants and Magistrates were accustomed to bring forward, as a decisive argument to Protestants, that it was "the command of the King;" and the reproach which Bayle makes to the Catholic clergy is, that they suffered this to be done, and did not loudly protest against it, although such a proceeding was contrary to the Catholic religion. The reproach was not unjust;[3] and the French clergy had, one hundred years afterwards, to wipe away, in streams of

[1] "History of the Revolution." Ed. Paris, i. 230. "The execution of the prerogative, of which neither law nor experience had defined the limits."

[2] See his treatise or discourse, "The Protestant Religion Vindicated from Novelty."—WORKS, London, 1751, ii. 247. In later times has DAUBENY ("Appendix to the Guide to the Church," ii. 434) put in a very prominent light a separation from the National Church as a crime of disobedience against the highest authority in the State. Every one acquainted with the state of affairs in England is aware that the same motive has still a considerable influence with certain classes of the population.

[3] "Oeuvres," ii. 348.

their best blood, this fault of their predecessors. The same
Bayle remarks that "the Royal Edicts which suppressed
Protestantism' were referred to in books and pastoral
writings, as if they had been 'Sacraments.'"[1]   A precedent
Protestant author, Brueys, endeavours, in a work of his, upon
the obedience which Christians owe to the temporal power,
to show that the Protestants were bound in conscience to
obey the Royal Edicts which forbade their assembling for
Divine worship!   Instead of an Ecclesiastical repudiation
of his work, it obtained praise and commendation![2]

From the excess of the evil—out of the paroxysm of the
malady—there arose gradually the recovery.   It required a
long time.   Several circumstances concurred together to
bring ultimately about a more endurable state of things.
There was, in the first place, the internal languor of the
Protestant State Church—namely, of the most powerful of
them all, the English, which was severely damaged by the
consequences of its own victory—the Revolution of 1688.
With the eighteenth century had appeared such a wide and
deeply-penetrating decay of religion, and such a temper of

---

[1] " Oeuvres," ii. 33.

[2] In a note appended to the Introduction in this book, the author remarks,
with reference to the persecution of the French Protestants by Louis
XIV., that in writing the above paragraph he would have wished to have
called attention to the fact that " Pope Innocent was greatly displeased
at the oppression of the Protestants in France, and took steps to have
them treated with more lenity."   The author, however, adds, he could
not at the moment discover the authorities upon which this statement
rested ; but whilst his work was passing through the press he had discovered, and therefore cites them.   They are MAZURES, "Histoire de la
Révolution de 1688," Paris, 1825, ii. 126 ; and MACAULAY's well-
known work (Tauchnitz Edit., ii. 250).   The author adds : " It is
notorious that the relations between the Pope (Innocent) and the King
(Louis XIV.) were not merely unsatisfactory, but actually hostile, and
the Pope was therefore under the necessity of seeking to attain his object
not by a direct appeal to the French King, but through another channel.
He therefore commissioned his Nuncio, D'Adda, in London, to pray of
King James II. of England that he might intercede with Louis XIV. in
favour of the persecuted Protestants.   James declined complying with
this request, although he himself did a good deal for an alleviation of
their sufferings."

indifferentism had become dominant, that in the upper classes there was not so much of that kind of zeal which is necessary for the persecution of people for a different opinion. Indifferentism had gone so far, that strangers, like Montesquieu, received in England the impression that there existed no religion any more; and serious men, like Gibson and Butler, expressed their anxiety lest the whole nation should fall into demoralization and infidelity.[1] The sects of dissenters were left to act as they pleased, because their doings were regarded as mere folly, or harmless fanaticism; and as to the Catholics in England, they had shrivelled up into a small, quiescent, scarcely perceptible group; and persons were ashamed to put in motion the heavy hammer of the Penal Laws for the purpose of crushing a feeble and scarcely visible antagonist. The state of affairs in Ireland was, however, far different. There the interests of the Protestant party still required that the majority of the nation should be kept in a state of Helotism. But in England, to the feeling of indifferentism, which allowed things to go on as they might, was added that disposition in favour of right and freedom peculiar to the Anglo-Saxon race; and which served to arouse still more and more an inclination towards religious toleration

Germany, during the seventeenth, and at the beginning of the eighteenth, adhered constantly to the track of the sixteenth century. The yoke of the ecclesiastical princes' dominion — " the Cæsaro-Papism," as people called it — weighed with undiminished and suffocating force upon the Protestant Church system. Almost every well-disposed man complained of it; and, forgetful that it was the fathers and reformers of the New Church who had put this bandage upon their child in its cradle, at its birth, they said, with Valentin Andrea, " that Satan had been the inventor of Cæsaro-Papism."[2] Executions, too, on account of religion, still continued.[3] The reaction against Pietism led to new

[1] " Quarterly Review," vol. cii. p. 463.

[2] ANTON BOHME's " Schriften," ii. 986.

[3] In Sweden, Banier of Stargard was executed, because he did not think as a true Lutheran concerning the doctrine of " Justification." At

and endless religious oppressions and vexations. No one was allowed to meet with others for religious purposes.[1] There was soon added to this the hostility of the authorities against the disciples of Zinzendorf. It was forbidden, under pain of banishment, to circulate the books of the Moravians.[2] In the Prussian States Lutherans were taken to task, and the Government prohibited religious practices that were distasteful to the Calvinists. People were so accustomed to religious despotism, and to the interference of the authorities in private life, under religious pretexts, that persons of the world, in their writings, urged the authorities to bring before the tribunals and severely punish expressions used in social intercourse which did not sound as being quite orthodox![3]

In the meantime—by the middle of the last century— Germany had become thoroughly weary of the theology of the sixteenth century. The dogmatic system of the Concordian-Book and the Heidelberg Catechism, with their internal contradictions and their social-political consequences, lay like a mountain upon the German mind. The two chief supports of the old Protestant system—the authority of the University Professors and the Church Government of Princes —were worn out and decayed. The Professors became Rationalists; and, on the throne of the principal Protestant State, there sat a Supreme Bishop of the Church of his country, who, as he said, "never lived under the one roof

Königsberg, John Adelgreiff was, in 1636, beheaded and burned. At Lubech, Gunther was beheaded on account of his Socinian views in 1687, on the recommendation of the Jurist faculty of Kiel, and of the theological faculty of Wittenberg.—ARNOLDS, "Kirchenhist.," ii. 643.

[1] John James Moser reports in his Biography, p. 191, that in Auspach-isch, for a few persons singing a hymn together in their own homes they were thrust into the tower! Whole volumes are filled with Penal edicts against Pietists and Conventicles.

[2] MEUSELS, "Hist. Lit. Magazin," 1790, ii. 26.

[3] This is required, for example, by Bernard von Röhr, in his introduction to "Staats-klugheit," (Leipsic, 1718, p. 292,) with respect to the then often-repeated expression, "that a way to salvation was to be found in all religions."

with religion," and whose favourite occupation it was to mock
the clergy, who, in his eyes, were only a heap of blockheads,
sluggards, and profitless bread-consumers![1] With wonderful
rapidity a flood of rationalism and infidelity, under the mask
of theology, poured over Germany; and everywhere theologians and preachers were the first to yield to it. Frederick
the Second's expression—"That in his States everyone might
become blessed (work out his salvation) after his own fashion"
—portrayed the revolution that had taken place. By the
want of faith in the princes and theologians (a sentiment
which soon communicated itself to the upper classes in
Germany), persons showed themselves well content with the
temporal and police-like treatment of ecclesiastical affairs;
but it also indisposed them to the application of compulsory
measures, upon religious grounds. The liberty of taking
part in, or withdrawing from, a particular form of worship,
was generally desired and conceded. This led further; it
appeared to be natural and reasonable that confessional
restrictions and the civil inequalities of various religions
should be done away with. Then, the separation hitherto
existing between Lutherans and Calvinists had also lost
much of its significance since the diffusion of the Rationalistic mode of thinking. The old opposition between the
Catholic Church and that of the Protestants remained,
however, as strongly marked as before. Denmark, which, in
respect to religion, was accustomed to follow the German
current, did, however, in the years 1777 and 1779, issue
ordinances by which the regular (Catholic) clergy were
prohibited, upon pain of death, from entering the country.[2]

In France, the violent and hateful proceedings against
Protestants, and the consequences of these proceedings—the
emigration of so many thousands, which had inflicted a deep
wound upon the prosperity of the country—had also aroused
a strong and long-continued reaction. The emigrants,
amongst whom were many men of scientific attainments,

[1] "Für die protestantische Kirche und deren Geistlichkeit, ein
Journal," 1810, ii. 84.
[2] REUTER's "Theolog. Repertorium," 702, vol. lxx. p. 168.

got hold of a great part of the foreign press, and filled all
Europe with their complaints. The "*dragonnades*" and the
persecuting tyranny of the French Government passed into a
proverb. People began in France to feel ashamed and
humbled before foreigners. The "halo" of the monarchy,
which had made every measure of Louis XIV. appear in a
favourable light to Frenchmen, had been extinguished by
the Regency, and the despicable government of Louis XV.
The story of Calas afforded an occasion for popular, warm,
and eloquently-written treatises concerning "the advantage
and rationality of religious freedom;" and then the deistical
and indifferentist mode of thought, which had got possession
of the upper classes, did the rest. Every turn in the views
and disposition of the French people is accustomed to exercise a decisive influence upon the mode of thought and
condition of all Europe. At that time it was considered in
France, as elsewhere, that persecution and restraint only
made hypocrites; that the fact of suffering for the faith,
and being able to show martyrs, exalted the self-complacency
and the confidence, as well as the authority, of a religious community. It was felt and said that a Church which called for
the arm of temporal power to sustain it, and that closed the
mouth of its antagonists by compulsion and punishments,
did, by so acting, make out a certificate of its own spiritual
impotency. In all Europe the idea became more and more
prevalent that Churches only needed spiritual weapons for
their protection; and that it was the duty of the temporal
power to refrain from all constraint in matters of religion.
The old legislation, which rested on the opposite principle,
existed certainly for a long time—indeed, it still exists, particularly in Sweden and Spain; but the aversion to put its
enactments into execution, with all their exclusive severity,
has, for a long time, restrained the temporal power, and has
made an alteration in the still existing Penal Laws appear,
even to the Governments themselves, desirable. Catholic
Bishops also endeavoured now to show that the principle of
persecuting and oppressing persons of a different opinion had
never been a dogma of the Church; and if Catholics in former

times practised persecution, their so doing was not to be
regarded as a consequence of a Church dogma.[1]

The Catholic Church could, in fact, always, without difficulty and without scruple, enter into the new direction of
the times, and contribute to the sustainment of public
opinion, now becoming continually stronger and more
unanimous in disapproving of constraint being employed in
matters of religion. It had never put forward the assertion
"that sovereigns were to be rulers over the religion of their
people." Its whole doctrine of the princely power, and of the
relations between governments and their subjects, was limited
to the Apostolic demand of "obedience in things lawful."
It had always left the most ample room for the most
manifold political combinations. It had, remembering what
were its own boundaries, never undertaken to decide what
should be the amount or the form of political authority, and
how much should be left to the mass of the people, or
how much to the ruler and his organs — it has never determined what things should be reserved as matters for
the administrative, and what, on the contrary, should be left
to the decision of the people, nor what should be dependent
upon the consent of the Estates: all these were subjects
that did not concern the Church. Freedom of movement in
its own spiritual sphere is what it had always demanded.
Thus there could not only exist in its bosom states with the
most various institutions, as regarded their religious relations, but monarchs also could, without experiencing the
disapproval of the Church, make the strongest concessions to
persons of another belief in their dominions, as the French
King had already done by the Edict of Nantes, and that, too,
without any contradiction on the part of the French Episcopacy and the Papal See. On the part of the Church, it was
considered to be reasonable and right that King James II.
of England, although a Catholic, should bind himself to
maintain the freedom and the possessions of the Anglican

---

[1] So speaks Bishop SPALDING in the "Introductory Address" to his
"Miscellanea," p. xxx.

Church, and to urge on Parliament a general freedom of religion. He, indeed, did not keep his promise, and thereby brought about his own downfall. It was then to be generally expected that the Church, in its altered situation, and in the revolution that had taken place in the views of nations, should occupy a position where it might show, as it had already done, with what tranquillity it could bear independent and fully-developed religious communities to exist by its side, whether with equal or with lesser rights.

At present there reigns in all Europe the most decided dislike to make use of religion as a political instrument, and just as generally and decidedly do men protest against compulsion in religious affairs by the State or the police. As often as, in any part of Europe (with the exception of Russia, which is herein regarded as privileged), any act of religious restraint takes place, there arises a general sensation—an agitation and a demonstration in the opposite direction—and that, too, is almost always so well-managed, and so perseveringly carried out, that it finally gains its point.

And yet there is another side to this question. Let us especially consider the position of a State, and a popular Church still in the possession of the entire nation—that unity still exists in the country, and that this unity and this religious peace can only be disturbed through the diffusion of a new doctrine by intruders from abroad. If we place ourselves in that which is the general Christian point of view (and abstractedly from the differences prevailing among Christians), we may certainly say " that the religion and morality of a people are, in every state, inseparably connected with one another, and that an attack upon the one inevitably involves an injury to the other. It is, then, the business of a government to provide for the public weal —for the maintenance of those principles and views by which general morality is sustained, and to prevent all threatened violations of it."[1] From this follows the duty also of protecting the religion of the country. It might here be

---

[1] Compare the opinion of Bossuet with Mazure, " Histoire de la Révolution de 1688." Paris, 1825, iii. 386.

objected that the Christian Church is strong enough, or ought to be strong enough, to protect itself and overcome attacks from heresy or infidelity; but, as a matter of fact, it is not strong enough to do so. It is not so, in the first place, because the attack allies itself with the passions and strongest inclinations of the natural man, and also finds a fellow-combatant in the breast of every individual abandoned to his own impulses, and who is thus arrayed against a religion felt to be burdensome, and requiring so many difficult things for him to do. In the second place, religion is not equal to the struggle, for this reason—that is, when its opponents are completely unrestrained, because Christianity is one connected whole of doctrines, precepts, counsels, and historical facts, in which each is supported and responsible for the other. There are, however, very few who are competent, at one commanding view, to take into contemplation this connexion, and still fewer, perhaps, who are able to keep it clearly and constantly present before their mind. Its antagonists direct their attacks always upon isolated points, taken away from their connexion with the whole; and so the attack seems to be stronger and more plausible than the defence. On this account the weight of the power of the State must be thrown into the scale in favour of the assailed religion.

Furthermore, no advocate for the freedom of attack on existing religion has ever yet succeeded in determining exactly the limits within which that freedom is to be permissible. Logically has this freedom never yet been carried out in the world—not even in England, nor in North America. On the other hand, it may indeed be replied that the defenders of protection to be afforded by the State to religion, and for compulsion—for, without such, protection cannot be made effective—are, on their side, not in a position to point out any rational limits, up to which the repression of new doctrines and the defence of the State Church may proceed. In times of religious excitement such a repression, if severely and thoroughly carried into execution, becomes an awful tyranny, which revolts all minds against it; and the reaction from which is far more destructive to the Church than a state of defencelessness would have been.

This, then, at the end, is the only thing to be said : That, since the great divisions of the sixteenth century, a condition of circumstances has come to pass in the cultivated states of Europe, and the intercourse and the intermingling of nations, (with the facility of communication,) have so increased, and the reciprocal influence of populations has become so incalculable, and public opinion exercises such an irresistible power, that Governments, in their own interests, as well as in that of the various churches, find themselves placed under the necessity of refraining, so far as it is possible, from any interference with religious entanglements, and of preserving for the members of various religious creeds, so long as they really can be called Christian, equal duties and also equal civil rights. And then these Governments, looking tranquilly on at the spiritual struggle of the Churches, must still be careful to provide for the preservation of the public law, of civil order, and the perfect freedom of all. For one hundred years past the whole course of development in Europe has led to this—and we may see in it the hand of Divine Providence—that Protestants and Catholics have been approaching each other more and more —have been brought into closer, more frequent, and more intimate civil relations with one another—and have been placed under the necessity of a common action and a common understanding. The old confessional bulwarks and walls of separation have fallen down more and more, and become untenable. We can no longer withdraw from one another—we can no longer retire back to the old distance and separation, however troublesome and painful the consequences of the present state of things may be. And many problems and puzzles which have sprung from this intermingling, however insoluble they now appear to us, may yet with time find a solution ; or, at least, it is to be hoped they will. Our posterity will one day perceive that this intertwining and mingling has yet had preponderating beneficial consequences ; that it—

" Like the toad, ugly and venomous,
    Wears yet a precious jewel in its head. "

At the same time, however, the State can and must (if it will not abandon its cause altogether and yield itself, as captured, to the destructive forces and tendencies of the age) preserve and defend its character as *a Christian State.* It may not put off and give up what is common to all Christian Churches, because it must, in the existing equality of creeds, do so with what is peculiar as to individual religious church communities, and does not afford to their doctrines or institutions a governmental guarantee. The Christian social elements and principles are those by which marriage, the family, childhood, the foundations of civil order, are fortified and consecrated; the social virtues of neighbourly love, industry, chastity, and moderation have become Christian duties; and with them is bound up the relation between the civil power and its subjects. These are all built upon one sanctified basis. This whole Christian social order, and its sureties in doctrine and in life, must be maintained at all cost, by every State which desires to continue in existence. And every State, too, must be prepared with a negation if there is required from it, as is now frequently done, by an appeal to " the freedom of science," to yield up such things to the assaults of "the scientific," and of their destructive doctrines, whether couched under the name of a "materialist theory of nature," or of a "critical, analytical treatment of history." The State must be prepared to refuse permission to do mischief — it must act precisely as if one were to say of a tree, that it might still hope to bloom, if permission were once given to destroy its roots through which hitherto it had imbibed sap, and strength, and life.

82

THE CHURCH AND CIVIL FREEDOM.

A few years ago, the "Privy Councillor of Justice," Professor Stahl of Berlin, in some printed lectures of his,[1] made a sharp attack upon the social and political character, as well as influence of the Catholic Church. With respect to what he says on the point of religious toleration, I shall not subject it to any further examination. The description which I have already given of the historical development of this question will, when compared with that of Herr Stahl, be sufficient for forming a judgment upon it. Herr Stahl, however, goes much further. According to his theory, Protestantism gives, by its "justification from faith, a higher degree of *inward* (moral) *freedom* to man, and carries him forward thereby ("to a certain extent," he cautiously adds) "also to a degree of *external* (political) freedom." According to this, he assumes that the States which have become Protestant have attained, by their change of religion, to greater freedom than the Catholic. I cannot refrain from a brief historical examination of this assertion.

Stahl points out the chief doctrine, from which he deduces

[1] "Der Protestantismus als politisches Princip." Berlin, 1853. I confess that I had not paid any particular attention to this work. I only lately read it, when I wished to write upon the subject. I have perused it with astonishment. I really had no idea that one in the position of the author could possibly have indulged in such notions and treatment of history.

such great political blessings, more precisely as the doctrine of *imputed righteousness;* and he is quite correct when he, in this "article of the standing and falling Church," as well as the same in the Concordian-Formulas, and of the whole old Protestant theology, recognises the dogma in which the contrast between the Catholic Church and Protestantism, in its old form, is most sharply marked out. I must, however, remark, that he with this, his favourite doctrine, as the mother of political freedom, stands somewhat isolated. All, or almost all, learned theologians of his own faith in Germany, as well as elsewhere, have renounced it. Exegetists acknowledge that it is foreign to the New Testament, and that Luther had only introduced it into one of the Epistles of St. Paul by a false translation; and dogmatic theologians have repudiated the attempt to establish it on speculative or biblical grounds. I, for myself, undertake to point out to him for every single one who adopts it, fifteen who have given it up as untenable.[1]

Let us now see how it stands with the greater measure of political freedom which the "imputation" doctrine is said to have brought to the people. We will begin with *the Scandinavian States,* as those in which Lutheranism has developed itself most purely, without any foreign interference, and has been able to unfold its social and political consequences without any obstacle.

The Englishman, Lord Molesworth, who made himself thoroughly acquainted with the Protestant North, remarks in the year 1692, "In the Roman Catholic religion, with the head of the Church in Rome, is a principle of resistance

---

[1] Stahl refers to p. 98 of Baxter's ascetic writings, which he far prefers to the "Exercises of St. Ignatius." He appears not to know that this certainly distinguished theologian made it the peculiar task of his whole life to contend against the Protestant doctrine of "Justification," and especially the "imputation" dogma, as an un-Biblical and soul-destructive error; and this, too, as well in his practical-ascetic as in his dogmatic writings. For forty long years did Baxter oppose this doctrine which Herr Stahl regards as the innermost mystery of the Christian religion. Baxter pursued it in all its windings, and hunted it out of every corner in which it sought refuge.

against unlimited civil power; but in the North, the Lutheran Church is entirely subject and subservient to the civil power, and the whole northern population of Protestant countries have lost their freedom since they exchanged their religion for a better." The cause for this he seeks in the absolute and sole dependence of the clergy upon the monarch. "The Lutheran clergy," he says, "protect their political power in a chamber of their own at the Diet, although at the same time they are dependent on the Crown, as their temporal and spiritual head."[1]

In *Denmark* the Lutheran doctrine obtained as complete a victory as possibly could be desired. Its influence and its strength are neither disturbed nor lamed by the existence of sects, nor by any remnants of the old religion. Denmark and Sweden are still purely Lutheran countries. The social and political consequences of the victory over the Catholic Church in Denmark are described by Barthold in a very few words:[2] "A dog-like servitude weighs down again upon the Danish peasant; and the citizens, deprived of all representative power, groan under oppressive burdens, and the quartering of soldiers upon them. The North has become *Lutheran*, but *the King* and *the nobility* share the dominion between them, and even the children of preachers and sacristans continue to be *serfs*."

The nobility at once made use of the Reformation to appropriate to themselves not only the greatest part of the Church property, but also that belonging to the free peasants. At the same moment (in 1569) by the increased severity of the Religious Article, the non-reception of which was punishable with death, they drove strangers out of the country.[3] From 1536 to 1660 the nobility had become rich and power-

[1] "Account of Denmark," p. 236.

[2] "Geschichte von Rügen und Pommern," iv. 2, 294.

[3] This and the following facts are taken from ALLEN's "History of the Kingdom of Denmark," translated into German by Falck, 1846, pp. 287, 296, 304, 309. The Copenhagen Society assigned to this book a prize, as the best work of its kind published. See "Berliner Polit. Wochenblatt," 1832, p. 224.

ful by the oppression of the other orders, and the monopoly of all state privileges in their own hands. To the wants of the State they contributed nothing. The oppressive taxes had to be borne by the poorer classes. "The impoverishment and degradation of the peasant class, in consequence of the strong and stern rule of the nobility, operated most disadvantageously for the State." "The dwellers upon the great estates of the Church were now obliged," says Allen, "to exchange the mild rule of the clergy for the oppressive yoke of the nobility. Forced labours were arbitrarily multiplied, and the peasantry were treated as thralls."[1] "Agriculture sank to a much lower degree than it had been in the Middle Ages; the population declined, and the country was overspread with untenanted farms." Through new nobility privileges, by the cruelty of the Game Laws,[2] introduced directly after the Reformation, and by forced compacts, was the servitude, the spoliation, and the degradation of the once free peasant class completed. Not only were the peasantry, but also the citizens and the clergy—in short, the whole nation was trampled under foot by a nobility comprising from eight to nine hundred individuals.[3] Christian IV. (1588-1648) made an attempt to procure some alleviation of this oppression; but his attempt was frustrated by the resistance of the nobility, whose power proved to be greater than that of the monarch. The slavery of the peasantry continued. King and citizens were in reality the bondmen of the nobles.

By the Revolution of 1660, the power of the nobility was broken; but then, on the other hand, King Frederick III. and his successors were declared to be absolute monarchs. The Royal Law of 1665 decreed that the King of Denmark was bound to take no oath, and need impose on himself no duties of any kind, but, with uncontrolled and boundless power, do as he pleased. By this means was lost an interest

---

[1] "ALLEN," pp. 310-11.

[2] In 1537, by pulling out the eyes. Even the punishment of death was inflicted for keeping a hunting dog.—ALLEN, 313.

[3] ALLEN, p. 319.

in public affairs, and the public spirit and co-operation of the people with the government was annihilated.[1] The peasantry remained in the same slavery as before, and the nobility retained a great part of their privileges. The wretchedness of the peasantry was still further aggravated, after the year 1687, by new despotic laws; "so that one-fifth part of the farms on the crown-lands lay waste, and things appeared to be still worse on private estates."[2] In the year 1702, Frederick IV. abolished slavery; but another yoke—attachment to the soil—was soon put in its place; so that the position of the peasantry, by a regulation of 1764, was little, or not at all, different from their former thraldom. The result was, that the population of the country in the eighteenth century diminished from year to year, innumerable peasant farms were abolished, and even whole villages destroyed to make room for manors.[3] Schools were wanting. The education of the people still stood, in 1766, at the very lowest grade. It was not until 1804 that personal freedom was conferred on twenty thousand families, who had been in a state of servitude.[4]

The Provincial Estates, introduced by Frederick VI., did not restrain the absolutism of the Danish monarch. An observer, favourable to the Danes, Mr. Laing, a Scotchman, remarked in the year 1839—that since the Danes are, politically, quite passive, and had no voice in their own affairs, they had found themselves, in spite of many good regulations of the government, merely in the same state in which they had been in 1660, and had remained two hundred years behind the Scotch, Dutch, and Belgians, with whom, according to their population and position, they best could be compared.[5]

---

[1] ALLEN, p. 336.   [2] ALLEN, pp. 389, 431.

[3] ALLEN, p. 438. Out of 600 landed proprietors in "Holland" before the year 1660, there were no more than 100 remaining in 1766.

[4] How much remained to be done for "the Danish peasantry," is shown by a frightful description of their situation in WEGENER's "Chronik Friedrichs VI.," in the "Gegenwart." Leipz., 1853, vol. viii. p. 473.

[5] "Tour in Sweden." London, 1839, p. 12.

In March, 1848, "after a hundred years of legalised and systematic despotism," Denmark had its revolution; and the government of Frederick VII. was brought, by frequent changes of ministry, into relations with a Diet, in which (in most striking contrast to the former state of things) the peasant-order preponderated. To this must be added a press, which in boundless licentiousness equalled that of the French, in 1793.[1] A new institution—a national convocation—(a Reichsrath), two-thirds of which were elected by the people, was created; and now the fate of the greatly enfeebled monarchy will very speedily be decided.

In *Sweden*, Gustavus Vasa had introduced the Lutheran religion, and by robbing an immoderately wealthy Church, had founded a strong monarchy and kingdom. The people were, in fact, cheated out of their religion; for Gustavus had always denied that he had introduced any new doctrine; and fifty years afterwards, notwithstanding the changes that had been made, a great part of the people were not at all aware that they were not Catholics![2] By degrees, however, Sweden became a thoroughly Lutheran country.

Three results now followed. The first we will permit to be described by the classical historian of Sweden—Geijer. After the great religious wars, he says, the share of the Commons, in Ecclesiastical affairs, was suspended, and in the same degree that of the princely power was confirmed. Thus the Church lost more and more its connection with the people, and soon became merely a monarchical or aristocratical external form—a clerical addition to the military and civil officers of the State.[3]

The second result which followed the subjugation and spoliation of the Church by the monarch was, a new public law. Gustavus declared that the commonage lands of the villages and hamlets, and even also the rivers, weirs, and mining districts—finally, even all uncultivated lands, were

[1] "Allgemeine Zeitung," 1859, p. 5932.
[2] GEIJER's "Geschichte Schwedens," ii. 218.
[3] "Ueber die innern gesellschaftlichen Verhältnisse unsere Zeit mit besonderer Rücksicht auf Schweden." Stockholm, 1845, p. 47.

the property of the Crown.   Therewith was, as Geijer says,
an arbitrary power given into the hands of the King, which
was extremely perilous to the rights of private property
belonging to individuals.[1]   Gustavus unhesitatingly persevered in his spoliations ; and, since he looked upon himself
as the universal heir to Church property, he took also the
farms wherever he pleased.[2]   He could not, however, keep
the whole inheritance of the Church to himself : the nobility,
whose support he much needed, had to be adopted as co-heirs ;
and, in the end, obtained an equal, or still larger share of
profit than the monarchy, from the change in religion.

As a third result of the Reformation, came that dislocation
of the national relations of the Estates, that discord into civil
order which has given to the history of Sweden for three
hundred years its changeful character, and has occasioned
a series of revolutions, such as never occurred in any
European state until 1789; and which has also elicited
revengeful feelings, party spirit, intrigues, a violent disposition, corruption, and caprice, as prominent national characteristics.[3]   Three of their kings have the Swedes (namely
the nobles) murdered—Erick IV., Charles XII. and Gustavus III ; two of them have been deposed, Sigismund and
Gustavus IV ; and finally, they have driven out their native,
hereditary dynasty, and presented or sold their crown to a
foreign officer, one of Napoleon's generals.

Here, too, as well as in Denmark, there has arisen out of
the Reformation an oppressive and pettifogging domination
on the part of the nobility ; and it was only because " the
laws and customs of Sweden in its early rude state had been
so excellent," as Arndt says, " that Sweden was saved from
the fate of Russia and Poland.[4]   There was wanting, the
dignified, independent position, and the regulating influence
of the Church.   The Lutheran clergy were always too
dependent on the possessors of power."   Arndt further
remarks, " that the priests " (for the clergy there are called
priests) " have always been accused of never having originated

---

[1] GEIJER, ii. 101.   [2] GEIJER, ii. 110.   [3] See ARNDT, pp. 29, 31.
[4] " Schwedische Geschichten."   Leipsic, 1839, p. 30.

an important movement; and, also, that they, more than any other of the Estates, have been the most subservient to those possessed of power.[1] The Reformation had given over the clergy completely into the hands of the king and the nobility. Every nobleman residing in a parish had the right of choosing the pastor, whom he paid whatever he chose to give.[2]

The four Estates were represented at the Diet; but the nobility, who possessed almost all the public offices of the kingdom, were the only real Estate of the monarchy, and dared not be outvoted by the other Estates. As to the peasantry—being under the control of the nobility—they were only indirectly subjects of the kingdom.[3] As the nobility had, already, on the change of religion, and at the division of the Church plunder, gained immensely in possessions, privileges, power, and influence, so was their gain still further increased, when the government was compelled to alienate its domains, and could only alienate them to nobles.[4]

There were, indeed, after the death of Gustavus, attempts occasionally made on the part of the clergy to withdraw themselves from the domination of the nobility. They desired that the admissibility to office should be made possible for the sons of preachers; but the nobility were too strong for them, and the hopes that were held out to Bishops, Superintendents, and Doctors of Theology, of being themselves ennobled, sufficed to separate the higher from the lower clergy.[5] That a married clergy cannot attain to a resolute corporate position, or cannot maintain it, lies in the nature of things. Under the yoke of a nobility-mastership the peasant class had been impoverished and degraded, and the people had become feeble, wretched, and oppressed.[6] To free themselves from this yoke, they endeavoured in Sweden, as well as in Denmark, to make the King's power unlimited. Thus, in the year 1680, the Estates declared, "That the King was bound to no special form of government"; and in the

---

[1] ARNDT, p. 47.   [2] GEIJER, iii. 400.   [3] GEIJER, iii. 18.
[4] GEIJER, " Ueber die innern gesellsch. Verhältnisse," p. 65.
[5] GEIJER, " Verhältnisse," p. 110.   [6] ARNDT, p. 80.

year 1682, " the Estates held it as absolutely unreasonable
that the King should be compelled, by statutes or ordinances,
first to hear the Estates ;" and from this time was adopted the
maxim, "That *the King's will is law*," and everything, as
Geijer says, was now interpreted to the advantage of an
Autocracy. The Estates were no longer called *the Estates
of the Kingdom*, but *of his Royal Majesty*; and in the year
1693 the monarchy was declared to be fully absolute. "The
King," it was said, " could, without any responsibility, govern according to his own will.[1]

This led to the pernicious reign of Charles XII., who had,
in answer to the Diet, told them " he would send one of his
boots to preside over them." His reign plunged the country
into the greatest misery, and brought it to the very brink of
destruction.

After his murder kingly absolute power was condemned,
and what is called "Swedish freedom," that is to say, the
mastership of the nobility, was re-established. All power
and official administration, all great privileges and superior
rights, fell again into the hands of the nobility. In the acts
of the Diet, from 1720 till 1772, "aristocratic ignorance and
arrogance were" (according to Arndt's remark) "expressed
in the most shameless terms against what were called the
lower Estates." The monarchy was a mere misty shadow—
despicable and impotent. At the same time, two factions of
the nobility contended fiercely for dominion. These were the
" hats" and the "caps," or the French and Russian parties.
At length Gustavus III. brought about the bloodless revolution of 1772 : the Council was dissolved, and the King again
ruled as lord. But he was not long a match for the nobility.
The officers of his own army betrayed him, and he fell at last,
in 1792, the victim of a conspiracy of the nobility.[2]

"Until now," says Geijer, in the year 1845, "no change
in the representation has ever taken place in Sweden, unless
in and by a revolution ; and of revolutions, after our own
fashion, we have had too many."[3] Since the assassination of

---

[1] GEIJER, pp. 113, 115.   [2] ARNDT, p. 92.
[3] " Ueber die innern gesellsch. Verhältnisse," p. 128.

Gustavus, Sweden has become the hotbed of intrigue and corruption. Finland was parted with to Russia—lost by the treacherous sale of the fortresses—Gustavus IV. was dethroned—even his posterity were excluded, and a foreign officer, unknown in Sweden, was preferred, to be the founder of a new dynasty, to the descendants of Vasa. The acquisition of Norway—continuing independent—was no compensation for the loss of Finland. Sweden now stands powerless before the mighty Northern Colossus, whose cannons can almost reach its capital; and it can but now abide whatever Russia may be pleased to decide concerning its destiny.

Mr. Laing, the Scotchman, who has occupied himself much with the political and moral condition of the Swedish people, and both in the one respect and the other, assigns to Sweden the lowest place amongst the nations of Europe, has, although himself a decided Protestant, come to the conclusion that the Reformation has injured more than it has benefited the moral and social state of the Swedish nation; and that the Lutheran Church has shown itself to be completely powerless in its influence on the people; whilst the Catholic Church, on the contrary, had been in its time, as he affirms, an effective system of moral discipline.[1]

In Germany it was a natural result of the Reformation that the power of the prince and of the imperial cities (of their magistrates namely) should be increased, and the freedom of the lower order of nobles, the rural classes, and the peasantry diminished.[2] The German clergy had previously been (unfortunately for themselves) the richest and most powerful in the world, and the change was now so complete, that their Protestant successors became, according to Menzel, the mere serviceable tools of political power, and within a very short time the most insignificant link in the chain with which the new order of things had bound the nation.[3]

A brief survey of the position of affairs in particular German states will serve to show more clearly the great change

---

[1] "Tour in Sweden," p. 125.
[2] LEO's "Universalgeschichte," iii. 208. 3d Edit.
[3] "Neuere Geschichte der Deutschen," v. 5, 6.

that the Reformation had effected in the political and social condition of the nations.

In *Mecklenburg* the first effect was, that the order of prelates disappeared from the Diet. Since the year 1552, only two orders had appeared there—the *Ritterschaft*, or Equestrian Order; and the *Landschaft*, or Provincial Estates.

The nobles as well as the dukes had carried off their share of the Church property; and there now began a system of subjugation and plunder of the peasantry, whose rights, since the suppression of the Church, no one any longer represented. The plan was to appropriate the labour of the peasantry for the benefit of the nobles, and to drive them from their farms by the process called " Legan," or laying. At the Diet of Güstrow, in the year 1607, the peasants were declared to be mere colonists, who were bound to give up possession of their lands, even of those that they might have held from time immemorial, at the desire of their landlords. In the year 1621, the unlimited disposal of the farm lands was secured to the landlords; and subsequently, by the ordinances of 1633, 1646, and 1654, the personal freedom of the peasantry was completely annihilated, and all persons of this class declared to be serfs.[1] As the peasants frequently endeavoured to escape from this slavery by flight into other countries, they were punished, when they were caught, by flogging, and other severe penalties were inflicted upon them, and occasionally even they were put to death. In the year 1660, indeed, the punishment of death was openly affixed to the crime of leaving the principality. " Then," says Boll, " was forged the slave-chain which our peasantry had to drag within a few decades of the present time. Their lot was only in so far better than that of negro slaves, that it was forbidden to sell them singly, like so many head of cattle, by public auction, to the highest bidder, but it happened nevertheless often enough that people traded underhand with their serfs, precisely as they did with their horses and cows.

About the middle of the eighteenth century it is observed

[1] Boll's " Geschichte Mecklenburgs." New Brandenburg, 1855, i. p. 352; ii. 142-147-48.

the peasantry of Mecklenburg were treated by the nobles like the most abject slaves,[1] and they attempted, whenever they could, to make their escape, even to Russia. To prevent this, they were again threatened with condemnation to forced labour in the prisons or fortresses ; and " there was," according to the ordinance, "a complete depopulation of our generally thinly-populated country, and the ruin of all the landed estates was greatly to be feared."[2] In the year 1820 serfage was abolished.

In *Pomerania*, which, down to 1637, had its own Duke, though it was afterwards united with the Margravate of Brandenburg, Protestantism had won the victory so early as 1534. Duke Philip had well weighed the project that the new doctrine would bring him "in the wealth of the clergy —the numerous prerogatives and the supreme headship of the National Church."[3] The citizens, say the historians of Pomerania, having attained the spiritual goal (of the Reformation), renounced mere earthly freedom ; and in Stralsund and Stettin all representation of the Commons ceased. The lower population of the towns became " painfully sobered from its dream of civil freedom, and looked with contented resignation to heaven."[4] The confiscated Church property was squandered here, as in many other places, in luxury, drink, and gormandizing. The fate of the peasantry in Pomerania was what it had been in Mecklenburg. Since the Reformation the "laying" of the villages had been carried on with great earnestness and success, and sheep pastures and manors took their place. Sometimes the nobles would lay waste the peasants' farms, inclose them in their estates, and by that means make them free from taxation.[5] The oppression of the peasantry became so atrocious, that even those who still held farms fled the country.[6] But

---

[1] FRANKE's " Altes und neues Mecklenburg," i. 102.

[2] BOLL, ii. 569.

[3] BARTHOLD's " Geschichte von Pommern," iv. 2, 259.

[4] BARTHOLD, 297-299.

[5] ARNDT, " Gesch. der Leibeigenshaft in Pommern und Rügen," 1803, p. 143.   [6] ARNDT, 159, 211 ; BARTHOLD, 365.

it was, according to Barthold, the principle of the Roman law that first brought down the full curse of slavery upon Pomerania. In the Peasant Ordinance of 1616,[1] they were declared to be "serfs without any civil rights," and preachers were compelled to proclaim fugitive peasants from the pulpit. The peasants whose farms were seized by the nobles were in general completely plundered; and the Pomeranian jurist and noble, Balthazar, confessed, in the year 1779, whilst in Germany the original serfs had become almost free, in Pomerania the ancient methods of establishing serfdom had increased. And down to the present century complaints were made of the desolation of the country, and the thinness of the population.

In the territories of *Brunswick* and *Hanover* it is very evident how the new absolute ecclesiastical power of the princes, simultaneously with the substitution of the Roman law for the German, which took place subsequently to the Reformation, undermined the ancient liberties of the nation, and paved the way for the bureaucratic mode of government and arbitrary power. The judges and magistrates, taken from the rural districts, were gradually supplanted by lawyers, salaried as princely counsellors; and cases formerly decided by precedent and the law of the country, were now settled by Roman law.[2] The towns lost the independence they had inherited (Brunswick alone retained it for some time longer), "and the rulers, supported by learned disciples of the Roman law, exercised an arbitrary authority before unknown." The confiscated Church property sufficed, at least for some time, for a luxurious and extravagant mode of life in the palaces, and a great increase in the number of attendants. In the courts of law, for the speedy verbal method of transacting business, was substituted a tedious, long-winded written process.[3] Down to the middle of the seventeenth

---

[1] DAHNERT, "Urkunden-Sammlung," iii. 835.

[2] HAVEMANN, "Geschichte der Lande Braunschweig und Lüneburg," 1855, ii. 479.—"With all these complaints of the state of the country," says SPITTLER ("Gesch. von Hannover," i. 347), "the Roman law obtained a complete victory." [3] HAVEMANN, ii. 515.

century, the cities and the knightly order offered some resistance to the measureless extravagance, oppressive taxes, and demands of the Court; but the old beneficent institution of Administrative Councils chosen from various orders—nobles, prelates, and others, who had mediated between sovereigns and their subjects, and whose decisions in cases of dispute were binding also on the princes—now fell to decay through the absence of the spiritual members, consequent on the Reformation, and became gradually supplanted by a Princely College.[1] The habits of extravagance engendered and encouraged by the robbery of the Church property occasioned a complete disorder in the finances of the Principalities; the princes took to debasing the coinage, and other immoral means. The nuisance and scandal of "money-clipping," combined with the general luxury and passion for gormandizing and drinking, completed the ruin of thousands.[2] In place of the decisions of the Administrative Councils came ordinances of the governments (first, in the Principality of Calenberg, in 1651); and soon after this the last traces of the ancient freedom and independence of the Estates was annihilated. "The clergy," says Havemann, "had been long (that is, since the Reformation) sunk into dependence, and the nobles had entered into the service of the Court. The cities were languishing for want of public spirit; and in the after-pains of the great German War, as well as of corrupt internal government, the 'free' princely power of modern States was unfolding itself over the sad remains of the ancient life and liberty of the Estates."[3]

In the *Brandenburg* and *Prussian* territories the condition of the Estates, even after the Reformation, remained for a time strong and unbroken. Duke Albert of Prussia was a man feeble in character, and had, in the consciousness of his very doubtful title, been fearful in his dealings with the Estates; and the Elector Joachim was, by his own extravagance and that of his paramour, rendered constantly

---

[1] HAVEMANN, iii. 112.   [2] SPITTLER, i. 380.
[3] " Geschichte der Lande Braunschw. und Lüneburg," iii. 172.

dependent on them for the payment of his debts.[1] His son, John George, found himself (1571 to 1598) in the same pecuniary dependence. The condition of the peasants had become more and more miserable[2] since the Church had fallen ; and the nobles and princes were the only powers in the country. After the seventeenth century, the princely power, by the impoverishment of the nobles and cities, continually struggled onwards to unrestrained dominion. Military executions, formerly quite unknown in Germany, became frequent, especially for non-payment of imposts. The Estates were not summoned to meet, and the prince imposed taxes by his own authority. Stenzil has not allowed it to pass unobserved, how, in Prussia also, the princely power being above that of the Church, led to the practice, that affairs of the higher police and the administration, which were formerly discussed and determined by the Estates, should be more constantly decided by princes on their own authority, and settled in the cabinet,[3] so that the Estates became continually more insignificant, and the government in an increasing ratio more despotic and bureaucratic.

After the reign of the Elector Frederick-William (1640-1688), the absolute arbitrary power of the government was developed more systematically. A General Diet was not called after 1656 ; and the oppressive taxes imposed not only without the consent, but against the protest of the Estates, were extorted by the Elector with military violence—so that the peasants left their farms by troops, and turned robbers. Peasants and nobles fled to Poland, twelve thousand farms lay uncultivated, and the taxes of many thousands of acres were greater than their produce. The Estates of the Dukedom of Prussia, who had imagined themselves still protected by the treaties with Poland, asserted that all that was left them of their ancient freedom was "the right of complaining of their ruin;" and they threatened to emigrate. In the Markgravate, the Estates were degraded into a mere credit institution.[4]

[1] GALLUS, " Gesch. der Mark Brandenburg," iii. 94.
[2] STENZEL, " Gesch. d. Preuss. Staats.," i. 347.
[3] " Gesch. des Preuss. Staats." i. 359.
[4] STENZEL, ii. 422.

It was an unexampled tyranny, and deeds worse than those of the French, when laying waste the Palatinate, were perpetrated by a prince whom persons afterwards agreed—and in his dominions, too—to call "the Great!"

Prussia was, according to Stenzel's expression, on the way to a complete Asiatic despotism, which would stifle everything noble and beautiful. To maintain soldiers, and to gratify a passion for the chase (for which the Elector kept three thousand people in his pay),[1] were the objects for which the country was exhausted, and many thousands brought to beggary, whilst, at the same time, the subjection and serfdom of the peasants was maintained in all its severity.

Frederick I., the parade-loving first king of Prussia, continued the system of his father; and the Estates, where they still subsisted, had no other function than, willingly or unwillingly, to vote taxes and guarantee loans.[2]   Frederick William I., however, (1713—1740) surpassed even his grandfather; and with his accession began in Prussia the reign of a petty, capricious, and often cruel despot;[3] a harsh, narrow-minded man, filled with the notion of his own unlimited power, and eager only for money and soldiers, who beat his judges with sticks, to compel them to alter their decisions according to his wishes; who had men hanged "without prolix law-suits," and who decreed, that if a deserter should be harboured in any hamlet or place too poor for a pecuniary fine, the chief inhabitants should be made "to drag carts" for some months.[4]   Under this king, the Lutheran clergy had to drink to the very dregs the bitter cup of monarchical Church supremacy.   The king himself undertook reforms, in ecclesiastical as well as worldly affairs, in an equally ignorant and arbitrary spirit.   He dictated to the Lutheran clergy, as their spiritual head, what subjects they were to treat upon in their pulpits, and what they were to be silent about; as well

---

[1] STENZEL, ii. 456.   [2] STENZEL, iii. 196.
[3] " Il faut donner une victime au bourreau," said the nobles, speaking of him. —MORJENSTERN, "Ueber Fr. Wilh. den Ersten." Brunswick, 1793, p. 140.   [4] FÖRSTER's "Friedrich Wilhelm I.," ii. 202.

H

as what ceremonies were to be observed at divine service, and what to be omitted. Thus, for instance, in 1729, he forbid the Lutherans to carry a crucifix or a cross before the body, at funerals, as the custom was known to bear a vexatious relic of Papistry." [1]

His son, Frederick II., was enabled, by his own genius, and the utmost exertion of all the energies of his people, and all the resources of the country, to raise Prussia into the rank of a powerful state of European importance. His government, also, was a pure despotism; but it was, in the French sense of the word, "an enlightened, philosophical despotism," and the despot was a man of powerful mind—a born ruler of men—who knew how to inspire his people with a spirit not so much national as devoted to the Prussian state. The most numerous portion of the population remained, however, in the same oppressed, miserable condition as before. The greater part of the rural inhabitants were so entirely without personal freedom, that Buchholtz compares their condition to that of a West Indian colony.[2] Frederick decreed, not only that discharged soldiers should again become subject to their former landlords, but even that their wives, widows, and children should be submitted to the same destiny.[3] Dietereci, the Prussian government statist, describing in 1848 the state of the country in 1806, exclaims, at the conclusion of his portraiture, " How many restraints are there on the freedom of the individual! How many difficulties are thrown in the way of a man wishing to exercise his energies—to improve his condition, and earn as much as possible! How much personal dependence is there of one on another. What arbitrary authority!—what violence on the part of the privileged towards the unprivileged or oppressed! What heavy taxes and personal burdens are laid on the lower classes![4] One kind of liberty, however,

[1] Stenzel, iii. 474. See also p. 475, the description of the so-called " Priest Review" in Berlin.

[2] " Gemälde des gesellch. Lebens im Königr. Preussen," i. 19.

[3] Verordnung Vom., 7th April, 1777.

[4] " Ueber Preussische Zustände." Berlin, 1848, p. 13.

Frederick had left the people. Every one was allowed to seek salvation in his own way; and every one might, if he pleased, after the example of the sovereign, announce himself as a mocker of religion.

In the Electorate of *Saxony*, it is very evident how, after the Reformation, the princely power over the whole Church went hand-in-hand with the increase of taxation—the oppression of the lower classes, the extinction of ancient liberties, and the ever-growing vice of over-government. The struggle between the Lutherans and Calvinists, which broke out twice under Augustus and Christian I., led to a long series of acts of violence, to depositions and banishments, to the dungeon, the rack, and the scaffold. The government intruded itself into every sphere of life, in order to root out more effectually Calvinism, which had got into the land, and to insure the strictest observance of Lutheranism, which was further secured by a new book of Faith, and an oath to be taken upon it. People became accustomed to violent modes of proceeding, and to a severe and unmerciful treatment of those who were subjects. The cities lost their former independence, the Estates had to submit to the most oppressive laws of the chase,[1] and even, in 1612, the introduction of a secret police;[2] and they were obliged more and more to limit their functions to the granting of taxes, and in undertaking the payment of the Prince's debts. At the Diet of Torgau, in 1555, the Estates declared, "it was not possible for them to pay the new excise on liquor—their lands would become waste, and they would be utterly ruined." But it was maintained, nevertheless, and, in 1582, with the addition of a greatly increased land-tax.[3] The results were such, that even one of the Court preachers declared "that the people were so destitute, that they had scarcely the means of keeping themselves alive;" and a contemporary reports "that in 1580 the people were so steeped in poverty and hunger, that they

---

[1] All dogs, not belonging to persons whose occupation is the chace, were to have a fore-foot cut off.—BÖTTICHER, ii. 67.

[2] BÖTTICHER, ii. 141.

[3] GRETSCHEL, "Gesch. des Sächs. Volkes und Staates," ii. 70.

had eaten the husks in brewhouses."[1] "It is not to be denied," says Arnold, "that tyranny, injustice, and extortions had risen to the highest point since the Reformation."[2]

I refrain from entering into any further consideration of the state of affairs in Germany—in Hesse, Würtemberg, and still smaller states. It is sufficient to quote Stenzel's remark: "Whilst the unlimited power of the princes advanced in many other German countries, no less rapidly than in Prussia, the produce of the subject's toil was, in that country, lavished upon mistresses, favourites, courtiers, chamberlains, opera singers, dancers, and other objects of princely caprice, and ministrants to princely pleasure, without any of it being expended on the higher purposes of a government.[3]

Let us now turn to those countries which accepted Protestantism in its Calvinistic form, amongst which the *Netherlands* and *Scotland* appear the most prominent. England, with its Church like to none other, is to be considered by itself. We will not speak of Switzerland, since there Catholic and Protestant cantons subsist together, and no one will maintain that civil liberty has flourished more in the latter than in the former.

The *Netherlands*, that dismembered portion of Germany which came forth from the struggle with Spain, in the form of a Republic, but had barely maintained itself as such, through the internal contests and factions of two hundred years, and had vacillated between the "republican" constitution desired and represented by the city aristocracy, and the "monarchical," represented by the Stadtholder-General and the House of Orange. Had Calvinism become generally prevalent in the country, the power of that house would have been developed, and confirmed as a stable religious or political despotism. "The Dutch Reformed Church," says Niebuhr, "has always, wherever it was free, become coarsely tyrannical, and has never, either for the spirit it manifested, or the good dispositions of its teachers, deserved any great esteem. The Calvinistic religion has everywhere, in England,

---

[1] "Jenisii Annal. Annæberg," p. 45.   [2] "Kirchenhistorie," i. 792.
[3] "Geschichte des Preuss. Staates," ii. 4.

in Holland, as in Geneva, set up its blood-stained scaffold as
well as the Inquisition, without its possessing a single one of
the merits of the Catholic.[1]

The uncontrolled rule of Calvinism, and with it that of the
House of Orange, was prevented, partly by the formation of
new sects, partly by the continued adherence to Catholicity
of a considerable portion of the population, which was,
indeed, robbed of every civil and ecclesiastical right; but
being, by that very means, withdrawn from the influence of
party spirit, threw its weight—as far as it had any—into the
scale of the Orange party and the Stadtholdership, and
strengthened the opposition to the domination of the Calvinistic preacher-party. The new Arminian doctrine, which
opposed the Calvinistic, brought about the first politico-
ecclesiastical struggle. With the execution of Olden-Bar-
neveldt, the imprisonment of the Arminians, and the holding
of the Dordrecht Synod, the United Calvinist and Orange
party obtained a complete victory; but the party of the
States, the chiefs of which were disposed to Arminianism,
or at all events friendly to the Arminians, rose again
after the death of Maurice. And then, when Holland declared
the Provincial Estates the sovereigns of the country,
William II. took up arms; and it seemed to him that he
would be able to succeed in subjecting the republic to monarchical dominion; but his bold plan was frustrated, in 1650,
by death. The States-party now obtained a transitory
preponderance, and attempted, by its " Perpetual Edict," to
get rid of the Orange party and their Stadtholdership.
The contest led to a bloody conflict. Young William III.,
of Orange, was brought forward by the Calvinistic preachers,
and the populace under their guidance; and the murder of
the brothers De Witt, which William had sanctioned and
turned to account, confirmed his authority.[2] When, however, he became King of England, and governed the Netherlands from thence, there arose in Zeeland and elsewhere an
energetic resistance.

[1] " Nachgelassene Schriften." Hamburg, 1842, p. 288.
[2] VAN KAMPEN, " Geschichte d. Niederlande," ii. 322.

Their great, and, on the whole, their successful wars, their naval supremacy, their foreign conquests—all those things turned the energy and the attention of the nation to external affairs, and domestic dissensions were thereby checked. But with the eighteenth century decay set in. The selfishness of the provinces asserted itself against the country at large, and that of the cities against the provinces. Eagerness for money, a narrow, shopkeeping greed, and party spirit, remained to the end of the century the chief motive powers of the people. There were no longer any men of weighty character; there was only a crowd of little tyrants, and at the same time, as Niebuhr observes, " not only the ruin of the States but the decline of the nation was hastened by the madness of party spirit." Towards the end of the century even foreign aid was called in, and the Netherlanders saw without shame Prussians, French and English in the heart of their country. The Prussians in 1787 conquered Amsterdam, and procured for " the Orangemen " the triumph they had desired. The " patriots" fled to France, and in 1795, without striking a blow, took possession of the whole country. From this time forth, the French revolutionary doings—with clubs, Jacobinism, and all their appurtenances—were mimicked by a people who had now lost all character of their own. The Netherlands became the Batavian Republic, after that a French kingdom, next a French province, and finally— but by the aid of foreign powers — again an independent kingdom.

The freedom enjoyed in the Netherlands was essentially determined by the circumstance that Calvinism had lost its great authority; and we see in *Scotland*, where Calvinism in its most genuine form had been introduced by Knox, a simi-lar result. Up to the end of the sixteenth century the civil condition of the country was very unsettled. It had long been the prey of feudal violence and private feuds, which James I., towards the end of his reign in 1624, boasted of having suppressed. Then came the period of the struggle against the " episcopal constitution" and " the Liturgy," which Charles I. wished to force upon the Scots. With the victory obtained by Scotch Calvinism, was that state of Protestant power and supremacy restored, which the Reformation in Scotland, according to the intentions of its founder, had established, since the Reformer Knox declared that the " ordering and reformation of religion specially appertains to the civil magistrate,"[1] and the punishment of death was on two different occasions affixed to the celebration of mass. And now began such a system of spiritual tyranny, and such merciless meddling in private and family life, as has never been seen anywhere else, except in North America.

The Presbyteries extended their power so far, and wielded the terrible weapon of excommunication, which amounted almost to complete expulsion and banishment from society, with such effect, that no one could feel himself secure, and that almost every action of life might be brought before the Presbyterian forum.[2] As a matter of course, every attempt in a spiritual direction to break through the narrow limits of Calvinistic views was crushed in the germ.

It has often been maintained that the Calvinistic Church Constitution was, before all others, popular and favourable to freedom, because it afforded so much room to the lay element in the Presbyteries, and gave it so much influence even in higher matters. Experience has shown, however, that no other Church form ever led to so potent and intolerable a tyranny, or irritated men everywhere to such strong opposition ; for which reason, wherever it came, it sowed bitterness and discord, and was unable to maintain itself long. The institution of the Presbytery, as a tribunal of morals, has never been effectively introduced except in small towns and villages, where everyone knows the domestic circumstances of every other, and stands connected with many others by ties of kindred, and everyone is influenced by motives of friendship or hos-

---

[1] "To the civil magistrate specially appertains the ordering and reformation of religion."—" Westminster Review," vol. liv., p. 453.

[2] A striking picture of this state of things has been lately given by ROBERT CHAMBERS, in his " Domestic Annals of Scotland, from the Reformation to the Revolution." Edinburgh, 1858.

tility. When individuals are chosen in such cases as " lay
elders " to sit in judgment on their fellow-townsmen, then
three evils are unavoidably incurred. In the first place, these
men are exposed to the strongest temptation to abuse such a
completely discretionary and vaguely defined power to private purposes of personal advantage, or for the satisfaction
of personal dislike or vengeance. In the second place, a
system of espionage is established in every such community,
of meddling intrusion into the secrets of private life. De-
nunciations, tale-bearing, malice, and hatred are all veiled
under the appearance of religious zeal. In the third place,
persons invested with such power become the objects of general displeasure, suspicion, and hatred. Their externally
religious life, which had determined their election, appears
now as hypocrisy, as a calculated means of advancing themselves. People will consent to allow a certain amount of moral
and religious authority to a man who has received the seal of
a special vocation, and occupies a position apart from the
business of every-day life ; but they will not consent to subject themselves in religious affairs to one who is entirely their
equal, and who like themselves is engaged in worldly business
and the care of their families. That in the age when these
religions and churches were constructed, there should have
been devised an institution like the Presbytery, with lay
elders and tribunals of morals, is one of the many instances
of short-sightedness, and want of practical sagacity and
knowledge of human nature, that were then exhibited by the
Reformers.

This state of things had not, however, a lengthened duration ; for, from 1660 to 1688, the Calvinist Church of Scotland was compelled, by the renewed efforts of the English
Government, to introduce the Anglican form of worship; and to
put forth its utmost energies for the preservation of its own
existence. Calvinism was, indeed, again victorious with the
Revolution of 1688 ; but an Act of Parliament of 1712, by
which the assistance of the temporal arm was refused to
Presbyterian tribunals, made the re-establishment of the
former tyranny impossible, and at the same time the

Calvinists were compelled to tolerate the establishment of an Episcopal Church by the side of their own in Scotland.

England had in its Catholic days, and with the powerful assistance of the Church, laid the foundations of its political freedom, and carried the edifice far towards completion. It was the Church that the nation had to thank for the Magna Charta of 1215; for the gradual amalgamation and equalization of the conqueror and the conquered, of the Norman and Anglo-Saxon races, and also for the abolition of " villenage." The first sparks of the religious conflagration that had broken out in Germany had just kindled on the British island, when Henry VIII. conceived the plan of opening the way for himself to unlimited monarchy, by the complete subjugation of the Church. How he succeeded in this is well known. He and the succeeding princes of the House of Tudor, or those who ruled in their name, could manage the National Church as seemed good to them—and they made abundant use of their power. It was not till the reign of Edward VI. that complete Protestantism, as it had developed itself on the Continent, was introduced into England. Elizabeth restored the work of her brother, or rather of his guardians and advisers (after it had been interrupted by Mary), but with some important modifications. The Protestant doctrine was so foreign to the nation, that no Englishman in the sixteenth century originated a single idea on the subject, nor added anything to the doctrine as it was brought from the Continent. Nothing more was done than that the ready-made doctrine, as it had been stamped in Geneva and Zurich, was imposed on the people by those above them. By force, and with the assistance of the arms of foreign mercenaries, were the people compelled to renounce the Catholic religion, and submit to the creed of Bullinger and Calvin. Even such a laudatory historian of the English Reformation as Bishop Burnet, confesses that all the efforts of the Government to overcome the dislike of the people to Protestantism had been in vain, and that a troop of German mercenaries had to be brought over from Calais, in 1549, to con-

quer their resistance.[1] " With eleven-twelfths of the people,"
said at that time Paget to the Duke of Somerset, the Protector, "the new religion has found no entrance." [2]

The resistance of the Catholic people was indeed overcome, under Edward VI. as well as under Elizabeth, but it
was found still more difficult, or rather impossible, to establish
the unity of the Protestant Church, or prevent separations,
on the basis of the Reformation.

The new State Church, with its peculiar character and heterogeneous elements, was of no party, and belonged to no one
of the systems then present; but owed its existence, on the one
hand, to the exertions to afford to the still preponderating
Catholics, by the retention of some externals—the priestly
vestments and certain customs—an appearance of what was
traditional and Catholic; and on the other hand, to the personal inclinations of the Queen, who, being a Protestant,
more from policy than from any preference for the doctrine,
desired to retain as many elements of the old religion as
possible, at least in the liturgy and the administration of the
sacraments. The men who stood at the head of the new
Church, however, Parker, Grindal, Jewell, Nowell, and
others, were all decided Calvinists, as well as Puritans,
though they were at the same time very obedient palace
theologians. In the nation they had no genuine support;
the portion of the people disposed to Catholicity, which was
now constantly decreasing, saw in the new Court and State
Church a less evil than the yoke of hated Calvinism; whilst
zealous Protestants were all at heart puritanically disposed—
that is, they reasoned logically that the exterior of a Church
should express its inner life, and that a Calvinistic doctrine
required a Calvinistic constitution and a Calvinistic form of

[1] " History of the English Reformation."   London, 1681, fol., iii.
190-196.   " In Cornwall an insurrection broke out in 1547 against the
Protector, who wished to make England Protestant.   The people
sought to be allowed to obey the decisions of the General Councils
of the Church."—" Quarterly Review," 1857, vol. cii. p. 319.   In 1569
there followed in the North a great rising against the yoke of Protestantism.   It was only crushed by wholesale executions.
[2] STRYPE's " Ecclesiastical Memorials," ii.   Appendix II. II.

divine worship. The State Church had therefore for fifty years no theological literature of its own, but subsisted entirely on the productions of the Schools of Zurich, Strasburg, and Geneva. It was not till 1594, when Richard Hooker came forward with his celebrated book on the constitution of the Church, that any attempt was made to afford it a dogmatic foundation; and here, in a necessary contradistinction to Calvinism, he endeavoured to make the breach with the old Church as trifling as possible, and so found himself irresistibly impelled into a path leading back to Catholicity.

Another extremely important point of dispute now came into discussion. The Court reformers of the Tudors, Cranmer at their head, had not kept to the theory of other Protestants (Lutherans as well as Calvinists)—that the civil authorities had also the right of deciding on matters of religion, of ordering Church affairs, and, if need were, of reforming the Church. They had gone further, and, according to them, the King was the representative of God upon earth, in the sense that, as High Priest, he was the chief teacher of Church doctrine, and the source of every power relating to Church service.[1] The archbishops Cranmer and Parker maintained that princes could make as good priests as bishops, and that a person once nominated a priest by the king stood in need of no further ordination. They were accustomed, indeed, to except from the functions of their royal priesthood the performance of divine service and the administration of the sacraments. It was said the King or the Queen made no claim to these functions; but it is evident, as a living theologian of the Anglican Church has correctly remarked, that this was the only exception the Court reformers wished to make, and that they claimed for the monarch every other ecclesiastical power.[2] In accordance with these principles was the reformation of

---

[1] " The vicar of God, the expositor of Catholic verity, the channel of sacramental graces "—thus does Macaulay quite correctly express this theory in his " History of England."—Tauchnitz Ed., i. 54.

[2] PRETYMAN, " The Church of England and Erastianism and the Reformation." London, 1854, p. 34.

the English Church carried through; the bishops consented
to receive from the Crown every kind of spiritual power, and
allowed those powers to be limited or extended at the pleasure of the Crown; and as such powers were supposed to
expire with the death of the bestower, they had to be renewed at every new accession to the throne.[1]

Elizabeth would not indeed appear, as her father and
brother had done, as possessor of the high priestly dignity;
but she and the Parliament together confirmed the principle
of the boundless power of the monarchy of England over
the collective Church, and that all jurisdiction concerning the
doctrine, discipline, or reformation of the Church should be
vested in the Crown for ever.[2]   When James I. was on the
point of ascending the English throne, and was informed for
the first time of the full extent of the inheritance left him
by his predecessors, and of the greatness of his royal prerogative, exclaimed, "I do what I please, then.   I make the
Law and the Gospel!"[3]

The new Protestant Church became in this way, for a
hundred and fifty years, the slavish servant of the monarchy,
the persistent enemy of public liberty.[4]   The character of the
English people seems to have undergone a complete meta-
morphosis.   In the fourteenth and fifteenth centuries, two
foreign historians, Froissart and Comines, had described
them as the freest and proudest nation in Europe, the one
that would least endure oppression.   And what had now
this nation become?   Its Parliament subjected its holiest

---

[1] David Lewis has, in his "Notes on the nature and extent of the
Royal Supremacy in the Anglican Church," given from original sources
abundant proofs of this fact.   London, 1847.   See p. 29 especially.

[2] "Yet it was not in fact the Queen or her successors, but the Parliament, which formally claimed for itself infallibility, by adding to the Act
concerning the Royal Supremacy a clause to the effect, that no act or
decision of the present Parliament on religious matters shall ever be
altered or regarded as erroneous."—See the passage in " Lewis," p. 37.

[3] Literally, in his Scotch dialect, "Do I mak the judges?   Do I mak
the Bishops?   Then God's Wauns!   I mak what likes me—law and
Gospel."—"Hist. Essays," by JOHN FORSTER.   London, 1858, i. 227.

[4] MACAULAY'S " Essays."   Paris, 1843, p. 73.

interests, the most solemn rights of conscience, to the arbitrary authority of a woman; its Church lay humbly at the feet of the monarchy, preaching the absolute power of the Crown, and unconditional passive obedience to the will of kings. If it is remembered, too, that the Government had at the time no standing army in the country, the matter will appear still more striking; but the condition of affairs and the state of parties well explain all. The Government, by supporting itself on two, or in fact on three parties, could with their help overpower, first, the adherents of the old religion, and then one of the factions which had lent their help for that purpose. The State Church had of course in its favour all those who had carried off a portion of the spoils of the convents, and of the ancient Church—namely, the court nobility, and a large proportion of the rural gentry; and as long as the object was to destroy the Catholic Church, and to oppress its adherents, it had all the Protestants for its friends and helpers. United, they would have been strong enough to effect a complete Reformation, according to the Swiss view, and erect a Calvinistic Church establishment; but by means of the bait of Church dignities and benefices, the Court succeeded in dividing them. The majority of the theologians accepted, along with the Calvinistic dogma, the liturgical and sacramental constituents that had been retained from the old Church, partly in the hope that if once this dogma should take root in the minds of the people, these papistical remains would fall away of themselves, or could be easily stript off. The genuine Calvinists found too late that they had given their assistance to the erection of an absolute and oppressive Church and State power, and that the rope they had helped to put round the necks of the Catholics was now pressing on their own throats; and then resistance was broken, under Elizabeth, by the dungeon, the rack, and the scaffold. In the Lower House sat only Protestants, since the Catholics had been excluded; but amongst these were not a few zealous Puritans, and yet laws were passed which affixed the most oppressive and cruel punishments to the slightest deviation from Elizabeth's

Church —even the mere absence from Divine service. It was, indeed, a great advantage to the Government that the Calvinists were united among themselves, for whilst Cartwright and his followers were developing the Presbyterian system, the more thorough-going Brownists became the harbingers of the subsequent Congregationalists. On the whole, the state of things was such that, according to Macaulay's expression, had it lasted, the Reformation would have been the greatest curse, in a political point of view, that had ever fallen upon England.[1] The English people, says another historian, had sunk to the lowest degree of civil and political degradation to which it is possible to press down the moral and physical energy of the Anglo-Saxon race.[2]

The Queen had established her court of Inquisition,[3] which decided upon heresy and orthodoxy, and imposed pecuniary fines, the dungeon, and the rack, at its pleasure. From this, her favourite tribunal, she decreed suspensions or removals over the third part of the whole clergy, on account of nonconformity. She made it an offence for several persons to meet together to read the Holy Scriptures. "No one shall be allowed," she said, in a letter addressed to the Archbishop of Canterbury, "to depart, in the smallest degree, to the right or the left of the line drawn by my ordinances."[4] Her statesmen and lawyers maintained, and the House of Commons readily admitted, that she might exalt herself above all laws; could restrain all rights and liberties; that, by means of her Dispensing Power, she could set aside every Act of Parliament; and that her prerogative had no limits.[5] According to these doctrines she reigned; but tyrannical as were many of her proceedings, she was, and remained, in a high degree, a popular sovereign. Her subjects did homage to her intellectual superiority; they knew that under her England was powerful and respected in Europe; that it stood

[1] "Essays," p. 153.

[2] MACGREGOR, "History of the British Empire." London, 1852, i., p. cclxx.   [3] Court of High Commission.

[4] MACGREGOR, i., cccl. xxi.   [5] Dr. EWES, p. 649.

at the head of Protestant states and Protestant interests throughout the world; and they bore from her what a feebler or more narrow-minded monarch would not have dared to attempt.

One circumstance of the highest importance prevented the English people from sinking into the condition of the Protestant continent. The country had retained in constant use its old Germanic laws. The Roman law could never gain an entrance into England; no class of Roman jurists, no officials trained in the views of Roman jurisprudence, could ever be formed there. England received no Consistorium, after the German pattern; it never became a bureaucratically-governed country; and it kept clear of the continental bureaucracy, with its ever-increasing numbers of government officers and places. Notwithstanding the exceptional courts created in consequence of the Reformation, England had, on the whole, maintained the German independence of its courts of law against the power of the Crown.

Under the first Stuarts—James I. and Charles I.—the seeds scattered in two opposite directions ripened to their harvest. In the State Church, though it took part in the Dordrecht Synod, the aversion to Calvinism was constantly on the increase; and in the same degree arose the wish and the effort to return towards the ancient Church. The anti-Calvinistic doctrine, the ecclesiastical-political regulations, the theory of an Episcopacy of divine institution, and of the Apostolic succession—all this gave to the Anglican Church a more Catholic colouring. The Church of England was no longer to pass for one of the various Protestant communities, but for an improved and purified branch of the Catholic Church; and on this account the wrath of the Calvinists against all this Arminianism and Papistry in the State Church burned the more fiercely.

The royal supremacy over the Church, now no longer maintained by a powerful, respected, and dreaded woman, but by a petty, pedantic, and generally despised king, like James I., who was always talking of his divine right and his unlimited prerogatives, sank very low in public opinion.

It was also felt that the Church was destined to serve as the protecting bulwark to the absolute power of the monarchs, and to act as its pliant tool. Charles the First actually declared that he regarded the Episcopacy as a stronger support of the monarchical power than even the army;[1] and thus did the political struggle against royalty become likewise a struggle against the State Church. The Puritans of Elizabeth's time were now, for the most part, Presbyterians; and they sought, in the overthrow of the Episcopal order, the establishment of the Calvinistic doctrine, united with stricter Church discipline; the extermination of the Arminianism and Papistry that had made their way into the Church; the abolition of a liturgy, which had been the source of these evils; and, finally, they desired to make the Church independent of the Crown. Their influence in the Lower House was strengthened by the "doctrinal Puritans"—that is to say, the Calvinistically-disposed members of the State Church.[2] The Independents wished for no further ecclesiastical organisation, but the independence of the several congregations; and though they were subsequently the most dangerous enemies of the Presbyterians, yet they at first made common cause with them against their common enemies —monarchy striving for absolute power, and its subservient implement, the State Church.

The vicissitudes of the great politico-ecclesiastical struggle are well known. Strafford, Archbishop Laud, King Charles, the three representatives of ecclesiastico-political absolutism, died on the scaffold. The Church fell with the monarchy; but the hopes of the Presbyterians, that they would be able to overpower all other churches and parties, as in Scotland, and bow the whole English nation under the yoke of genuine Calvinism, were frustrated. Their brief triumph was followed by defeat, under Cromwell's dictatorship; the Independents rose again, and with them the sects of Baptists and Quakers; and all sects (with the exception, perhaps, of the Quakers)

---

[1] MACAULAY's "Essays," p. 86.

[2] See SANDFORD's "Studies and Illustrations of the great Rebellion." London, 1858, p. 77.

desired to rule, and to persecute, and oppress the rest. Of the State Church it could hardly be said that it had been crushed into a sect, for it had ceased to exist.

With the Restoration, however, it revived; it rose into full glory as a National and Parliamentary Church, with a royal head-bishop, and once more it was able to plant its foot on the neck of its enemies. So violent was the re-action against the intolerable oppression Calvinism, in its various forms, had then recently exercised, that King Charles II. was compelled to retract his promise of religious toleration. The removal of 2000 preachers, the Conventicle Act, the laws that annihilated the hopes of the anti-Episcopalians, followed rapidly, blow after blow. The Parliament seemed desirous of finally settling ecclesiastical affairs, and of securing the Episcopal Church, not only in the possession of its ancient rights and privileges, but the exclusive possession of the nation. In 1673, the Test Oath—a solemn declaration upon oath of belonging to the Anglican Church, and an acknowledgment of the Royal Supremacy—was imposed on all civil and military officers. This measure, however, was directed especially against the Catholics. Since the heir to the throne, the Duke of York, had become a Catholic, fears—certainly not unfounded—were entertained, that the future king would use his supremacy over the Church to bring it back, step by step, to Catholicity. Such apprehensions prevailed among all statesmen and zealous Protestants, and formed, with them, the strongest motive of political action. The Catholics, as a party, could not then cause the slightest anxiety. They were lost in the mass of the population, and it was only on account of the names of some distinguished families that the little group retained any significance at all. They would be perfectly content to have, in peace and quietness, toleration, and the permission to worship God in the chapels attached to their own homes. It was not on them that James II. founded his hopes, but upon the religious distractions of England; on the unconditional devotion of the State Church to its royal head-bishop; and the fidelity with which, as he imagined, they would act up

I

to their favourite doctrine of "passive obedience," and show an example to all others; and, finally, he trusted to the Catholic elements and tendencies in the Church itself. The most important theologians had, then, for fifty years, been combating most of the chief doctrines of the Reformation —the very foundations of Protestantism — with acuteness and learning, and had declared the old Church doctrine to be, in many and important points, the only tenable one. The great Protestant doctrine of "Justification" had been so thoroughly demolished by Ball, Hammond, Thorndyke, and others, in the Church, and by Baxter outside of the Church —its contradictions and destructive consequences were shown to be so glaring, that, in spite of its assertion in the 39 Articles, it had never been able to maintain itself in the Episcopal Church, and no one scientifically-cultivated theologian continued to defend it.[1]

The amalgamation of the political king's power with that of the State Church had generated the doctrine of *passive obedience;* and the Anglican bishops and theologians had maintained that, according to Christian principles, the people and the Parliament were bound, even in the most extreme cases of defence of life, or of the ruin of the social order, not to resist the will of the sovereign, but to obey unconditionally; and, in case the thing commanded were a sin, to remain entirely passive. They appear to have been considering the origin of their religion and Church, which was really the will of a king, by whom it had been forced on a reluctant people. This duty of passive obedience was, it was said, the doctrine of all Protestant Churches, but especially of the English, in contradistinction to that of the Catholic, which maintained that in certain cases there was a right of resistance, and even (according to the principles of the middle ages) of deposition of princes in extraordinary circumstances.[2] This

---

[1] The so-called Evangelicals at the end of the preceding century, Toplady, Venn, Newton, James Hervey, and others, cannot be reckoned among learned theologians.

[2] In fact, even under the reign of Philip II., the doctrine put forward by a Spanish preacher in Madrid, that kings had an absolute power over the persons and property of their subjects, had been condemned by

doctrine of passive obedience was not merely taught in books and pamphlets,[1] but it sounded from all pulpits, and was declared to be a doctrine necessary to salvation.[2] It was practically applied to all the measures of Charles II. and James II., and both monarchs were thus encouraged and assured in their efforts for absolute power by the Church, whose Head they were. Defoe bitterly reproached the bishops and Church clergy for having flattered James II. with assurances of his unlimited power, and thus led him on to the brink of ruin, and then overthrown him. When William III. landed, the whole Anglican clergy, in mockery of its own teachings, went over to the usurper, and only 400 Nonjurors had so much of conscience as to refuse the new oath.[3]

James II. had been mistaken in his calculation; for the attachment to Protestantism was then deeply rooted in the feelings of the great majority of the people. All parties, Calvinists as well as Anglicans, were united in their fear of, and aversion to, the Catholic religion, or what was represented to them as inseparably connected with it — political and ecclesiastical despotism, persecution, Smithfield fires, subjection under a foreign Italian prince, or, as the zealots said, "the Romish Antichrist," and a drain of English gold towards Rome! All these terrific phantoms hovered before the English fancy, in connection with the words "Catholic Church." That it was precisely the Catholic period in England which had been that of increasing civil freedom,

the Inquisition. The preacher was compelled to revoke his assertion from the very pulpit where he had made it, and declare that "kings had over their subjects no other power than such as was afforded by Divine and human law; and by no means any power proceeding only from their own free and absolute will." This is reported by ANTONIO PEREZ in his Relations.—"Université Cath.," xxii. 76.

[1] A rich fund of material concerning this matter, so important to England, is contained in the work of an unknown person (Abr. Seller). —"History of Passive Obedience since the Reformation." Amsterdam (London), 1689.

[2] "Edinburgh Review," vol. lv., pp. 32-34. See there the answer of James II. to Burnet's Remonstrances.

[3] WILSON's "Life of Defoe," i. 160.

and that of the Reformation the time of slavery, absolutism, and the loss of individual rights, perhaps not one in a thousand of the English knew, and that one took good care to say nothing concerning it. It is doing no injustice to James II. to say that, as a true Stuart, and as an admirer of Louis XIV., he did aim at absolute power, and would have used the Church of England, when restored to Catholicity, as a serviceable implement to this end.

The short reign of James, and the preceding years of fear as to what he might attempt, served to give a powerful impulse to Protestantism, and occasioned an approximation, though certainly only a transitory one, amongst all Protestant sects and parties. Even the toleration offered by James was rejected by them, with the exception of the Quakers. He had offered it, persons supposed, merely for the sake of procuring a more tolerable position in the country for his hated fellow-believers. With the fall of James II. and the Stuart dynasty, and the elevation of William III., the Protestant succession was secured, and the movement which had begun with the Reformation completed as to its main features. The most important acquisition of recent times was the Habeas Corpus Act, the guarantee of personal freedom against arbitrary power, which passed in 1679, under Charles II., and wherewith the rights secured by the ancient Magna Charta were thus then confirmed and secured against the ambiguous interpretations of Crown lawyers.[1] The " birth-rights," or fundamental rights, of the English nation, as it was expressed when William ascended the throne in 1689, contained, with the exception of the limitation of the succession to the Crown, only the ancient rights and franchises. Two powers, however, or rather one power regarded in two different points of view, were for ever destroyed—these were an arbitrary monarchy, and the royal supremacy over the State Church. William himself was not able, even by the threat of an abdication, to overcome the opposition of the Parliament; and since his death, and the accession of the Hanoverian dynasty, no King of England has ever been able to govern in his own

---

[1] HALLAM's " Constitutional History." London, 1832, iii. 17.

person.[1]   The kings of this dynasty continued to be strangers, unloved by the nation.   And whilst the monarchy withdrew from the eyes of the nation into the background, and lost more and more of its dignity, the power and authority of Parliaments were considerably on the increase ; and during nearly sixty years the administration of the Whig party, the political centre of gravity, was moved entirely into the Lower House.

With this enfeeblement of the monarchical element in England, the ecclesiastical supremacy of the Crown could not but gradually receive a different interpretation, and produce different results.   Queen Anne had, in 1707, declared her supremacy to be a fundamental element of the constitution of the Church of England;[2] and George I., who, shortly before, had been a Lutheran, issued, as early as 1714, certain ordinances concerning things connected with the liturgy, that went very much into detail.[3]   But the political advantage and importance of the supremacy now fell to the Prime Minister for the time being, and ecclesiastical patronage was used in the interests of the Whig party, and as a means of gaining over the more powerful families, and obtaining their influence in the elections and in Parliament ; but the Church,

---

[1] It may be objected that George III., from his accession to the dissolution of the Cabinet under Lord North (1761-1782), exercised great influence on the course of Government and the decision of political questions, and that by means of a party formed outside the Cabinet, and in opposition to it.   But that was an abnormal, unnatural state, which awakened great discontent in the nation, as BURKE has shown in his " Thoughts on the Causes of the Present Discontent."   (Works, London, 1834, i. 127, &c.) "The power of the Crown," he says, " 'almost dead and rotten as prerogative,' has grown up anew, with much more strength and far less odium, under the name of influence."   He then goes on to describe this plan as a system of favouritism, the invention of a double Cabinet, &c. It was exercised through the corruption of a great number of the members of the Lower House, to which purpose a portion of the Civil List was applied.   The matter proves, in the most striking manner, that henceforward there was to be no such thing as a legitimate exercise of personal power on the part of the king.

[2] See WILKINS's " Concilia Britanniæ," iv. 685.

[3] DAVID LEWIS, p. 41.

in which Jacobite and Tory tendencies prevailed, was robbed
even of what had remained to it of the power of free movement, and for this purpose the royal supremacy did excellent
service. The Convocations were no longer allowed to meet;
and the Church was more and more temporalized, and
degraded into an institution for the advantage of the sons and
cousins of influential families.

As soon as the Constitution of the Estates of England
entered into its new *Stadium* of Parliamentary government,
that which was formerly called in England *Erastianism*,
namely, the control and depression of the Church, and
" turning it to account" by the laity, became a regular practice, as if belonging to the natural order of things. The
Government has had since then greater power over the
Church, and in the Church, than in the State, both in
theory and in practice.[1] If ever a statesman employed this
supremacy for the good of the Church, it was a mere lucky
accident.

Since the Nonconformists, or Dissenters, were friends of
the Hanoverian dynasty, and of the Whig party, the government, which was glad of their support, set aside the restraint
under which they had lain in Anne's reign, though this
certainly was only effected by an Indemnity Act yearly renewed; still it granted them access to public affairs, whilst
the State Church was not only unable to make any aggres-
sion on the Dissenters, but was incapable of protecting itself
against heterodoxy and infidelity in its own bosom. The
penal laws remained in force against the Catholics alone.

Thus there was presented in England the remarkable
phenomenon of one State (since Scotland had become by
the Union a province of the British Empire), with two
entirely different and mutually hostile State Churches—a
Calvinistic Presbyterian in the North, and an Episcopal
Church in the South; and further, the English Church,
deprived of all power of free action, lay bound and helplessly
dependent on the State; whilst all the sects and religious
societies that had arisen, or were to arise out of it, whatever

---

[1] PRETYMAN, " The Church of England and Erastianism," p. 215.

their doctrines or institutions might be, could govern themselves in perfect autonomy and freedom.   An Englishman
thinks this quite in the regular order of things!

The supremacy is, according to Hallam, who expresses the
prevalent view on the subject, the dog's collar which the
State puts on the Church that it has endowed, in return for
food and shelter.[1]

If we now ask what has been gained in almost one hundred
years of an embittered struggle between parties and Churches?
—what can be shown as the actual result?—it appears to
amount, in the first place, to this: that religious freedom, or
rather the liberty of *not* belonging to the State Church, but
of forming an independent community, has been won after
a contest of about a hundred and seventy years, and after
thousands of Englishmen have lost their lives; and this, too,
has been won in direct contradiction to the original principles
of Protestantism.

Secondly, the civil liberties that the English possessed
in Catholic times, had been essentially enervated, and in
some cases destroyed, by the Reformation and the spirit of
State-Churchship.   They had primarily to be reconquered,
and then confirmed and extended, in the sanguinary war
which the partisans of the sects, in alliance with the political
champions of freedom, carried on against the monarchy and
the dependent State Church.   In so far as all these sects
proceeded from the principle of the Reformation, and all
called themselves Protestant, it may be said that Protestantism in England, after having been, in its first form, the most
dangerous enemy and destroyer of civil freedom, did, in all
subsequent forms, or through the consequences of Church
dismemberment involved in it, contribute to the re-establishment and extension of political liberty.   Every one of these
Protestant communities oppressed every other when it could,
or was prepared and resolved to do so; every one wished to
lay on the nation the yoke of its own views and institutions.
The Presbyterians, Prynne and Edwards, as soon as their

---

[1] " Constitutional History of England," iii. 444.   " The supremacy of
the Legislature is like the collar of the watch-dog," &c., &c.

sect had obtained a momentary pre-eminence, endeavoured
to prove that the authorities were entitled and bound to
wield the sword against all erroneous doctrines—that is to say,
against all that were not Calvinistic.[1] Ultimately, all
religious parties came forth from the long contest weakened
and shaken. The Presbyterians disappeared in England,
and were replaced by other sects. The State Church had
become so powerless; there was such an uncertainty in all its
doctrines, and such a dissolution of all ecclesiastical bonds had
taken place within it, that even bishops declared the English
clergy to be the worst in all Europe ; and in the eighteenth
century England was distinguished above all other nations
for its general contempt of the Church, and a wide-spread
infidelity, even among the female sex.

The fall of James II., and the summoning of a new
dynasty, did not, in fact, bring any accession to English
popular liberty, for such had been, as to all essential particulars, already won; but it brought with it two changes,
pregnant with important consequences, viz: the degradation
of the monarchy into a mere powerless phantom, and the
system of parliamentary government by majorities of the
lower house, whose views and aims had to be modified by
the limitation or extension of the suffrage. Upon the value
of these two acquisitions the future must decide.

Since the passing of the Reform Bill, England has been
treading a downward path ; and, upon the question whether
it can be arrested in its decline—whether it is in a position
to recoil from the increasingly democratic tendencies of the
House of Commons and of the constitution—will depend the
future prospects of this kingdom, and, to a certain extent,
of the world also.

On the whole, it appears, as a fitting inference from the domestic history of each country, that wherever the Reformation
produced one united State Church, it acted prejudicially on
civil liberty ; that such States retrograded on the political
path in the sixteenth and seventeenth centuries; and that it is

[1] See the expressions of Burnet, Lady Mary Wortley, and others, in
the "Quarterly Review," vol. ccli., p. 462.

only where Protestantism did not attain to absolute supremacy, in the form of a State Church, but where a considerable
portion of the population remained Catholic, while another
formed various religious communities, that there arose, from
the collisions and limitations thereby occasioned, a greater
measure both of civil and political freedom.

THE CHURCHES WITHOUT THE PAPACY—
A PANORAMIC SURVEY.

IF we wish to understand all that must stand or fall with the Papal See, and how inextricably interwoven it is with the innermost being of the Church, we must cast a glance upon those religious bodies which have separated themselves from Rome, or have arranged their constitution so as to have no place for a Primate. I here, then, enter so much the more willingly on a survey of the Churches, since it is my object to make clear the condition of the present time, with respect to ecclesiastical affairs; and I also do so because such a survey is indispensable for a comprehension of the question concerning the States of the Church.

THE CHURCH OF THE PATRIARCHATE OF CONSTANTINOPLE.

We will begin with the oldest of the dismembered Churches, the Oriental, or "Orthodox Anatolian Church," which recognises the Patriarch of Constantinople as its head. It embraced, formerly, all the countries of the Greek Empire, but has been for some time past continually crumbling away, by ecclesiastical resistance to, and separation from it of particular portions. The separations have been based on the antagonism of various nationalities, and on the decay of the Turkish Empire, which, in the day of its power, upheld, for the sake of its own interest, the authority of the Pàtriarch. The Hellenic Church, that of the kingdom of Greece, has declared itself independent; the Metropolitan of Carlowitz, in Austria, with his eleven bishops, has done the same, and his Church is now an independent Patriarchate. The Churches of Cyprus, of Montenegro, and of Mount Sinai, have declared their independence. In the Danubian Principalities a similar attempt has been made to form an independent Romaic Church. Almost all the organs of the press there demand a solemn declaration of the independence of the " Moldavo-Wallachian Church," and the formation of a Moldavo-Wallachian Synod. A separation of the Bulgarians has taken place, but they have joined the Catholics. That the Ionian Islands have not gained the Hellenic Church, but still acknowledge the Patriarch as their ecclesiastical head, is probably to be ascribed to English influence or compulsion.[1]

The Patriarch, whose sway still extends over about nine millions of persons, has in some respects more than a Papal power. He can appoint or remove, on his own irresponsible authority, all archbishops, bishops, and priests, and, with exception of four prelates belonging to the standing synod, can relegate them all to their dioceses. He possesses at the same time an extensive civil jurisdiction, the right of punishment, and an unlimited power of taxation. His whole administration has now been for hundreds of years connected with an unexampled system of extortion, corruption, and simony. Every Patriarch attains by these means to his dignity. According to long-established precedent, the patriarch is usually changed every two or three years; he is, namely (the custom originates in Turkish despotism and Greek corruption), deposed by the synod, for bad administration, or he is compelled to resign.

The cases in which a Patriarch dies in possession of his dignity are extremely rare, for those who make a profit by bargains for the patriarchate take care that they shall be transacted as often

[1] In Roumelia and the Herzegovina, separations from the Patriarchate are expected.—" Neue Evang. Kirch.-Zeitung von Messner," 1860, p. 400.

as possible.[1]   When the Patriarch has purchased the dignity
of his deposed predecessor for hard cash, he gets his money
back again by the sale of archbishoprics and bishoprics, and the
purchasers of these, in their turn, make amends by extortions on
the inferior clergy and the people. The most important part in
these intrigues and bargainings about the patriarchate is played
by a temporal official, the Logothetes, who at the same time, as
an ecclesiastical dignitary for the patriarch, stands by the side
of the executive and mediates between him and the Porte.
Only a year ago the Patriarch Kyrillos was deposed on
account of simony and waste of the patriarchal finances, and,
after a regular election contest, Joachim, Bishop of Cyzikus,
was chosen in his place. The clergy attached to Greek nationality have been hitherto the instruments by whose means
the Turks have ruled over not only the Greek, but also the
Sclavonian population of the empire, and in so doing exercise
a despotic power that the Sclavonians are more and more
revolting against. The eight dignitaries of the Synod (they
bear the name of metropolitan, but six of their number are
mere villages), are the ruling powers, in subordination to the
patriarch, but when united against him are more powerful
than he can be. The temporal power that has been committed or left to the Greek-Church-princes is a source of
innumerable outrages, and the means of enriching immoderately their families, as well as those upon whom they feel
themselves to be dependent.

The great Sclavonian party, relying on "the Hatti-Humayun" of the Turkish monarch, and in alliance with a
portion of the Greek laity, is endeavouring to break through
these ecclesiastical and political fetters. The Greek oligarchy, however—namely, the seven first prelates of the
Synod, in union with the national Hellenic party, which dreads
the Sclavonic preponderance — is ever contending against
them, and a struggle for life or death is carried on, in which
national hostility, strengthened by indignation at a state of

---

[1] EICHMANN, "Die Reformen des Osmanischen Reiches." Berlin, 1858,
p. 27-28.—PITZIPIOS, "L'Eglise Orientale," Rome, 1825, ii. 82.—
GELZER's "Monatsblätter," vii. 224.

things so intolerably corrupt, leaves apparently no room for reconciliation.   Thus the patriarchate of Constantinople has already entered on the stage of approaching dissolution. The three other patriarchates, which, according to the Anatolian schismatic theory, exercise, in conjunction with that of Constantinople, the supreme authority in matters of faith, are scarcely more than titular dignitaries, for the patriarchate of Alexandria has but 5,000, that of Antioch 50,000, and of Jerusalem 25,000 souls.   The Patriarch of Jerusalem has his regular summer residence on the Prince's Island, near the capital; and the two others reside, with his permission and that of the Synod, in the capital itself.

The Greek Patriarchate is in the most shameful and perishing condition to which an ancient and venerable Church has ever yet been reduced; but that does not prevent the youngest prophet of Slavism, which is to be called to the dominion of the world, from founding on that See the most splendid hopes.   " When the Turkish dominion is destroyed," says Pogodin, " the Patriarchate of Constantinople will arise again in all its glory, and the Church of the East will again attain its world-wide importance.   Then " (according to Pogodin) " will the worn-out West be rejuvenated, namely, by the Slave and his Church, for all the future belongs to the Sclavonic race."[1]

This Church certainly lies under the most pressing necessity of reforming itself and of becoming re-vivified; for simony in its widest sense, veniality, corruption of the clergy both high and low, the employment of all imaginable means, both religious and superstitious, for the extortion of gifts— all these features of the Byzantine Church system have been authenticated by all observers.   To this must be added the gross ignorance of the clergy, the majority of whom in many districts cannot write, and sometimes not even read.   Laskarato, the author of a work that appeared in 1856, on the state of Cephalonia, declares, in his letters to the archbishop of that place, that it might happen to any one to dismiss a servant one day for misconduct, and meet him on the mor-

[1] " Politische Briefe aus Russland."   Leipsic, 1860, p. 17.

row as a priest; people that you have known as petty
chandlers, day labourers, or boatmen, you may see in a few
days appear on the altar or in the pulpit.[1]

Devotion to the civil power is so completely the lot of all
special churches that have been rent away from the one universal World-Church, that the Greeks will even acknowledge
their Turkish ruler as a supreme judge in ecclesiastical questions. As incredible as this appears, it has been stated in the
most decided terms, and in the most official form, in quite
recent times. Pius IX., in his evangelical letter to the prelates of the East, in the year 1848, reminded them of their
want of religious unity; and thereupon the Patriarch answered, in his own name and that of his Synod, "In disputed
or difficult questions, the three Patriarchs discuss the matter
with the Patriarch of Constantinople, because that city is
the seat of empire, and because he is the president of the
Synod. If they cannot agree the affair is, according to
ancient precedent and usage, referred for decision to the head
of the (Turkish) Government."[2] The Greek who makes
known this communication, mentions also a case in which a
decision was really given. The Armenian clergy had a dispute with the Greek priests concerning the custom of mixing
water with the sacramental wine; and the dispute was finally
brought before the Turkish Reis-Effendi, who accordingly
gave his decision. "Wine is an impure drink, condemned
by the Koran; pure water only, therefore, should be made
use of."

And yet it is undeniable that a splendid prospect lies
before the Church of the Turkish Empire, if it should be
able to raise itself only in some measure from its present
degraded condition, and to comprehend the greatness of its
mission. For the days of the Turkish dominion are numbered. Not only can the Empire not continue in its present

---

[1] Τὰ μυστήρια τῆς Κεφαλονίας, 1856. This work entailed on its author
the punishment of excommunication.

[2] Διαγγέλλεται τὸ πρᾶγμα καὶ εἰς τὴν Διοίκησιν κατὰ τὰ καθεστῶτα.
PITZIPIOS, l. c. l., 140.

form, but the power of Mohammedanism in Europe must also fall. The Turks will be compelled to emigrate and to return to Asia, or they will die out—and in fact they are actually dying out at the present moment. The Christians are already four times more numerous than the Turks, and the latter already begin to fear that if the Hatti-Humayun were truly and honestly carried out, they (the Turks) would within five years' time be driven across the Bosphorus. They themselves are absolutely unimprovable and stationary: the hatred of every kind of reform is as much an article of faith with them as the hatred of all non-Mahommedans. Their polygamy, their frequent divorces, the seclusion and unnatural mode of life of their women, the criminal methods employed to prevent the increase of families, the want of an aristocracy, as well as of a genuine middle class—their entire social position, as a slothful, parasitical race, living on the impoverishment and plunder of the Christian population—all these things make the elevation of the Turkish race an impossibility.

They themselves are filled with the idea that their time is coming to an end. They are continually declining in numbers, in morals, in courage, and in hope.[1] Their slothfulness nourishes their fatalism; and, again, their fatalism serves as a pretext to their slothfulness, and disinclination to every kind of exertion. The Christian stands towards the Turk in the

[1] "All is dying around the Christian populations," says RAOUL DE MALHERBE (" L'Orient.," 1718-1845. "Histoire, Politique, Religion, Mœurs." Paris, 1846, ii. 157.), " All is perishing, under that hard law of fatalism—all is becoming extinguished in polygamy, vice, and debauchery; beyond these the East has no other prospect than depopulation and the desert." See also the communications of so excellent an observer as NASSAU W. SENIOR, in his "Journal kept in Turkey and Greece." London, 1859, pp. 28, 32, 147, 212. The British Consul, Mr. Finn, lately said, " The Mohammedan population of Syria is dying out, and I cannot even say that it is dying slowly."—" Allg. Zeitung," 1861, p. 1144; 11th March.—" Even Asia Minor, which, in 350 years, the Turks have changed from a rich and prosperous country into a desert, shows the same phenomenon. A Pacha himself reports that, in his Pachalik, the deaths exceeded the births by six per cent."—SENIOR, p. 183.

same relation as if a living man were bound to a corpse; but the Christians are evidently increasing in numbers, in prosperity, in intelligence, and in courage. The Turks themselves say that it will soon be necessary to fill all offices with Christians; and then some day the ministers will say to the Sultan that he must become a Christian, and—so it will happen.[1] The future belongs, then, to Christianity, and not to Islam; and the same thing is true of a great part of Asia, for the Persian Empire also is in a state of hopeless internal distraction, and the population is very thin and constantly decreasing. At the beginning of the present century it was estimated at twelve millions, it is now said not to exceed eight. Almost all Persian cities, with the exception of Tabris, Teheran, and Schiras, are in ruins,[2] and must fall more and more under the Russian dominion. Mohammedanism also, though it has in recent times made some progress among the Malays of Borneo and the negroes of Soudan and Madagascar,[3] has, on the whole, entered into the stage of decay, and must fall back whenever the superior energy of the Christian nations advances against it. Apart from the question of truth, Islam bears within itself the germ of dissolution, since it is a religion of fixed definite precepts, embracing every department of life, and in their nature destructive of all progress. As the production of an individual nation, and of a decidedly low degree of culture, it could not, when transferred to other nationalities, be otherwise than injurious and inadequate, and must ultimately fall before the internal contradictions it occasions, and the necessities of life; whilst Christianity, as a religion of ideas, and of an institution adapted to the whole world, and limited neither by time nor locality, is capable of doing justice to every really human requirement—of promoting and encouraging the onward progress of the human race.[4]

---

[1] " Diary in Turkish and Greek Waters," by the EARL OF CARLISLE. London, 1864, p. 78.

[2] " Allg. Zeitung," 1st March, 1857, p. 956.

[3] " Edinburgh Review," vol. c. (1854), p. 412.

[4] This contrast of the two religions has lately been noticed by a very

THE HELLENIC CHURCH.

The Church of the *Kingdom of Greece* has dissolved its connection with the Patriarch and Synod of Constantinople. On the motion of thirty-five bishops assembled in Nauplia, the Regency, in the year 1833, declared the " Orthodox Oriental Church of Hellas" independent of every foreign authority. The government of the Church is to be vested in a Synod, consisting of five ecclesiastical members, to be appointed by the king, and two laymen, of whom one is to be the Attorney-General (*Staats Procurator*). A Concordat had been previously agreed upon (the *Tomos*), by which greater freedom had been granted to the Church with respect to the constitution of the Synods. The Government, however, altered this arrangement, and arrogated to itself the right of appointing the members, in accordance with the precedent given by Russia. In fact, the whole new Constitution was an imitation of the Russian; whilst the remarkable provision, that the members of the Synods should only be appointed by the State authorities for a year at a time, went far beyond the Russian model. But the Patriarch of Byzantium nevertheless, in the year 1850, acknowledged this peculiar kind of Church constitution, merely with the reservation of certain acts of homage.

The clergy of the newly constituted Church are taken from the lowest classes of the people, and are so parsimoniously paid that they are obliged to carry on some mechanical trade or rural occupation in addition to their priestly functions. They are mostly men utterly uneducated, and have no influence whatever amongst the cultivated classes, amongst whom a species of Voltairianism has made great progress.[1] In the powerful, and, in fact, wonderful intel-

acute observer, the COUNT D'ESCAYRAC DE LAUTURE, in " Le Désert et le Soudan." Paris, 1853, p. 135. The remarks made by him were the result of his close attention to the condition of the Mohammedan population. The author is the person who, a short time since, was taken prisoner by the Chinese, and frightfully mutilated.

[1] W. SENIOR, " Journal kept in Turkey and Greece." London, 1859,

lectual movement that has taken place of late years among
the Greeks, the clergy have not participated.   An attachment
to the National Church, a preference for the peculiarities of
the Anatolian doctrine and rites are found, to some extent,
among the Greeks, but such attachment is more political
than religious.   The ecclesiastical peculiarities were regarded
as the bulwarks of Greek nationality, as things connected
with the great superiority of the Hellenes over other nations.

For this Church of Hellas, also, there is a hopeful prospect;
because, in proportion as the kingdom extends—of which, in
the rapid decay of the Turkish Empire, there is every likeli-
hood—the Church also will be enlarged at the cost of the
Patriarchal See of Constantinople.   The inhabitants of the
Ionian Islands would doubtless join the Church of Hellas on
the first opportunity; and Thessaly also, where the Greek
race is preponderant, desires greatly a union with the kingdom
of Greece; and the subjects of King Otto look to this event
with eagerness;[1] and no sooner should the incorporation take
place than the province would certainly separate itself from
the Patriarchate of Stamboul, and enter the Synodical Church.
The politico-ecclesiastical hopes of the Hellenes of the kingdom, however, are well known to extend much further—even
to Little Asia.

THE RUSSIAN CHURCH.

The Church of the great European-Asiatic Empire, if we

---

p. 330.—GELZER's "Monatsblätter," vii. 251.   The author of the Essays
called "The Cross and the Crescent," in the latter publication mentions
(vii. 226) that he visited a great number of bishops and metropolitans in
the islands of the Archipelago, in Asia Minor, and in Syria, and sometimes enjoyed their hospitality; and that in conversation with them he
frequently alluded to the religious apathy of the people, whose worship
appeared to him as if they were rather troublesome ceremonies of polite-
ness, *in which the heart had no share.*   The answer he got was, " What
can we do?   How can we think of devoting ourselves to quiet study and
the instruction of others, *when we have our own wives and children to
provide for,* and are scarcely able to procure the means of existence?"

[1] SENIOR, p. 35.

include the sects of which the State does not recognize the existence, numbers more than fifty millions of persons, and is also a daughter of the Byzantine ; and though, towards the end of the sixteenth century, it declared itself separate from the Patriarchate, it has retained, with perfect fidelity, the Church system, with its doctrines and ritual, as it was received from Byzantium. According to theory, it recognizes in matters of faith the four Anatolian Patriarchs as a supreme authority ; and if the decision of a point of doctrine is in question, it is laid before them, that is to say, in fact before the Patriarch of Constantinople, with his Synod—for the three others no longer represent any great ecclesiastical body, but are merely titular, and must be regarded as members of the higher Byzantine clergy. The Catholic Church passes for heretical, on account of the doctrine of the procession of the Holy Ghost; and even in Russia for heretical and for schismatic, on account of the claims of the Papal See. But with respect to the third point of difference, the intermediate state after death, it would be easy to come to an understanding. It is only put forward when there is a desire to multiply the pretexts for separation, and to widen the chasm.

The Russian Church has been, since the separation from the Patriarchate of Constantinople (1587), a completely isolated National Church, without any connection with the rest of the Christian world. At its head stood the Patriarch, resident at Kiev, who was the Metropolitan for all Russia, and, in power, almost the equal of the Czar—for the Church was still independent, and represented the rights of the people, in opposition to the imperial power, and that of the Boyars—so that the remonstrances of the Patriarchs were almost equivalent to a veto. Peter I., who was early initiated, by his Genevese tutor, into Protestant views, and who was determined to get the mighty influence of the Church into his own hands, abolished the Patriarchal dignity, because "the people would otherwise think more of the Chief Pastor than of the Chief Ruler," and appointed (1721) a "Holy Synod," appointed by himself—a permanent Council, in the eyes of the Bishops, and an Upper Consistory, in the Pro-

testant sense, in the eyes of the Czar. When the clergy
petitioned for the re-appointment of a Patriarch, Peter
replied, angrily striking his breast—" Here is your Patriarch."[1] This overthrow of the ancient ecclesiastical constitution was acknowledged by the Patriarch Jeremiah of
Constantinople. "The Synod appointed by the Czar Peter,"
he declared, " is, and is to be called, our brother in Christ."
It has the power to transact and to decree, like the four
sacred Apostolic Patriarchal Sees.[2]

These Synods, with their permanent Procurator, taken
from the laity (and occasionally from the army), form a kind of
State Council and Ecclesiastical Tribunal, an administrative
machine for the Church, which is placed by the State on a
level with other administrative authorities. Being in itself
a body without a soul, it receives the principle of life from
the Czar, through the Procurator, without whose signature
none of its proceedings are valid, and none of its words have
any power. It cannot even itself appoint its secretary and
subordinate officials ; but they are all nominated and displaced
by the Czar. It subsists only by the will of the Emperor,
and merely to fulfil his commands.

On the whole Russian religious system, therefore, is impressed the stamp of Imperial State Churchship. The entire
property of the Church was attached by Catherine II. to the
estates of the Crown, in order, as it was said, to relieve the
clergy from the burden of their administration.[3] The Church
bears this supremacy as a yoke that has been laid upon it; but
it bears the burden willingly—it undeniably serves the State as
a political instrument, and assists in confirming the absolute
power of the Czar. The slightest movement towards independence in the Bishops, leads to threats of imprisonment
and exile; and although the three Metropolitans of Petersburg, Kiev, and Moscow, are permanent members of the
governing Synod, the latter, when he on one occasion pre-

---

[1] HERMANN's " Geschichte des Russ. Staats," iv. 350.
[2] MURAWIJEW's " Geschichte der Russischen Kirche." Carlsruhe,
1857, p. 252.
[3] DOLGOROUKOW's " La Vérité sur la Russie." Paris, 1860, p. 344.

sumed to differ in opinion from the Emperor Nicholas, was immediately dismissed to his diocese, by which he was prevented from taking any further part in the proceedings of the Synod.[1]

Notwithstanding this, the Protestant idea, that the sovereign, as such, must be the chief Bishop or head of the National Church, is really foreign to the Russians, and to the Sclavonic nation in general. A religious Russian would not admit, even now, that the Czar was the head of his Church, or that it belonged to his office to decide on questions concerning faith and doctrine, divine service, and the Sacraments. In fact, no Czar has ever taken on himself to do, what, in Protestant countries, is regarded as among the ordinary, and, what may be called, the normal proceedings of the government—to make enactments concerning faith and divine service, or impose any changes on the Church.

What, however, the Russian Czar, with all his power, declines to do, with respect to his own Church, that he arrogates to himself, according to the Protestant system, with respect to the Lutheran Church of the Baltic provinces.[2] This archiepiscopal power, too, has even been exercised in a somewhat hostile spirit, not only by the extension of the laws concerning mixed marriages to the Protestant provinces, according to which all the children of such marriages belong to the Russian Church,[3] but also by prohibiting Protestant clergymen from baptizing heathens, Jews, and Mohammedans. Authority in dogmatic or liturgical questions has never been ascribed to the Emperor in his own Church, but he has assumed it over that of the Protestants, for the Edict

[1] DOLGOROUKOW, p. 343.

[2] By a Rescript of the year 1817. HENGSTENBERG's "Kirchen-Zeitung," vol. xxxi., pp. 569-567.

[3] Concerning the consequences that have already resulted, see "Russland und die Gegenwart." Leipsig, 1851, i. 163 ; and HENGSTENBERG, "K.-Zeitung," i., p. 575.—Both witnesses maintain that, by this law, the Protestant Church of those countries must gradually pass into the Russian-Greek Church.

of 1817 commands the General Consistory to refer all such matters to the Czar.

There is, therefore, no question of an Imperial Papacy or Caliphate in Russia; but, nevertheless, in the " Order of Succession," which the Emperor Paul read aloud in the Cathedral at Moscow, and then laid on the altar, the Emperor is styled the " Head of the Church." In the Book of Laws he is called merely the " Divinely annointed Protector" of the Church of God; and at his coronation he is treated as the " first-born son" of the Church. Prince Dolgoroukow remarks that the Emperor Nicholas never regarded himself as head of the Church, though he certainly acted as if he was;[1] and, as a matter of fact, the Church of Russia is more completely in the power of the monarch than any other religious community in the Christian world.

It is wanting, to a degree, of which there is scarcely another example in Christian history, in every capacity of free action. There are no Councils, no conferences of the clergy, no co-operation of the clergy and their parishioners, no centre of ecclesiastical knowledge and culture, no exchange of views through literary organs, or an ecclesiastical literature. No such things exist in Russia, nor may they exist; and thence it follows that there is in the Church no such thing as public opinion or public feeling; and it cannot be said that the Russian clergy have before them any purpose clearly defined or recognised, or even instinctively felt, or that it has any indwelling organic life. The Bishop and his clergy are separated by a broad and impassable chasm. The Bishop is mostly an aged monk, who, after a life passed in his cell, in total ignorance of temporal affairs and administrative business, sees himself suddenly elevated by the Imperial will to an Episcopal throne, the choice being made with special reference to personal qualifications—a lofty stature, a majestic beard, a generally imposing appearance. He has two main duties: first, devotion to the Emperor, and unconditional obedience to his will; and, secondly, a watchful attention to the pomp of liturgical ceremonies. The serious business,

[1] " La Vérité sur la Russie." Paris, 1860, p. 341.

and the cares of Catholic Bishops, are unknown to him; for
these the Bishop leaves, partly to the Imperial Synod (since
the Emperor has withdrawn from the Episcopacy the greater
part of its spiritual power and jurisdiction), and partly to
the Consistories, which are notorious for their venality and
simony. Among the Bishops themselves there is no hierarchical organization, no internal connection, and no reciprocal
action. All these the Czars have annihilated; and thus the
Russian Church is found in glaring contradiction to a
fundamental law acknowledged by itself — namely, the 33d
Apostolic Canon, by which "every national Church is to
recognise one bishop as its first and its head." The secular
clergy, who are mostly the sons of clergymen—for the clergy
here form an hereditary class—have usually, even before the
time of their ordination—that is, from their early youth—to
maintain in a church that the Czars have robbed of its
property, a constant struggle against poverty and destitution. They are mostly married to priests' daughters, and
the fathers of a numerous progeny, and they have to till
their fields with their own hands: they are in general, as
may be supposed, extremely ignorant—indeed, are merely
taught to read and to sing, and but too often addicted to the
national vice of drunkenness. They are entirely defenceless
against the bishops, who sometimes treat them like slaves;
they cringe before them with trembling humility; and as it is
impossible for them to live with their families on the income
allowed them by the Church, they are compelled to descend
to the most supple pliancy of demeanour, both towards those
above them (their Bishops and patrons), as well as towards
the people below them.[1]

The Russian Church is a dumb one: there is no singing
by the congregation, and there is no sermon—only occasionally, and especially on Imperial fête-days, does the Pope or
Bishop say a few words, to impress on the people the duty
and great merit of unconditional obedience towards the
Czar, and to point out that they cannot better show their

---

[1] See the description given by an eye-witness in the "Correspondant,"
vol. xxii. (1826), p. 316.

love to God than by a faithful subjection to the Imperial will.[1] Amid such a want of all instruction and of spiritual renovation (for there are neither prayer-books nor ascetic writings in the hands of the people), the individual remains completely confined within the circle of his own thoughts, and there are no remedies against the overwhelming mass of superstition which cannot fail to be engendered by a purely ceremonial religion in the absence of doctrine and of the living Word.

Spiritual culture, and even a smattering of theological knowledge, can only be found in the monasteries, and with a few monks. Very unfavourable opinions are, nevertheless, given of the monastic orders: "They are," says Dolgoroukow, "idle and demoralized, and, with the exception of the Bureaucracy, the most mischievous class of men in Russia. At the same time, the secular priest stands so much lower in the social scale, and in public opinion, that he can, if he pleases, again become a layman, or be, by degradation, restored to the laity, and may then even be placed in the ranks as a soldier."[2]

The Russian is, however, unconditionally devoted to his Church; it is for him the firm citadel of his nationality, in which, and through which, he feels himself invincible; and the Slavonian Liturgy, which so completely expresses the manners and the tendencies of the people, gives to the clergy

---

[1] Intelligent Russians now acknowledge that it is a perverse practice, in their Church, to make marriage compulsory on the clergy, and to admit no man to ordination who is living in celibacy. See upon the subject Dolgoroukow, p. 350. The difficulty is not to be got rid of, as the Prince thinks, by leaving them free on this point—for a married clergy, and one living in voluntary celibacy, could not well subsist together. The former would sink too low in public opinion by the contrast: the confidence—and, as a natural consequence, the contributions—of the people would be bestowed upon the latter. In the appointments to livings, the parishes would certainly petition for a wifeless pastor, that is, if they were allowed to express their wishes. There have been, very lately, complaints from Galicia, of the injurious consequences that have followed from the compulsory early marriages of the Greek clergy there.—See "Kleine Beyträge zu grossen Fragen in Oesterreich." Leipsig, 1860, p. 81.

[2] Léouzon le Duc, p. 224, et seq.

a great power over their minds. The Russian is far from feeling that moral indignation at the low moral state of his "Popes," which to the Germanic and Romanic nations made the corruption of their clergy ultimately intolerable.[1]

The Russians believe in themselves, and in a great futurity for themselves, and this confidence especially applies to their Church. The extension of their empire and of their Church are jointly regarded as great national objects; and as their Church stands alone in the world, the government can always stamp every war as a religious one—as, indeed, Nicholas, in the recent great war, actually did. All who are not Russians are, in accordance with the opinion officially inculcated on the people, either heterodox or infidels. According to this view, an Appeal of the Holy Directing Synod of Petersburg summoned the people, in 1855, to devote their lives and fortunes to the cause of their country and their holy religion. And the proclamation of the year 1848 closed with the words, "Hear, ye heathens, and humble yourselves, for God is with us!"

Russia is, for the people, the "*Holy* Land"—Moscow, the "*Holy* City"—the monarch, the "*Holy* Czar"—God is the "Russian God." In the prayers of the Church supplication is made for the extension of the dominion of the Czar and of the orthodox Church on earth, and many a Russian hopes to see the day when the Greek cross will be planted on St. Peter's at Rome. The Government only acts in accordance with the spirit of the nation when it meditates preparing the other nations of the same confession, Greeks and South Slavonians, for the reception at some period into the Russian Imperial and ecclesiastical body. Before all things,

---

[1] The Russian author of the work called "Vom anderen Ufer" (Hamburg, 1850), p. 167, says, indeed, of the Russian peasant, "He despises the clergy as slothful, covetous fellows, who live at his cost, and in all street ballads and popular ribaldry, the priest, the deacon, and their wives, are always brought in as examples of the absurd and the despicable." Even if that should be the case, yet that the clergy occasionally exercise great power over the country people would not be contradictory to the fact, but would rather afford a psychological explanation of it.

however, the Russians look longingly towards Constantinople —the Emperor-city (Zargrad), as they call it. They believe that God has given them a right to possess that city —the mother of their Church—and that they are to have the church of Saint Sophia. It is their mission to restore this great church of Anatolian Christianity, after its desecration into a mosque, once more to its original destination.

One great Slavonian Empire, extending from Archangel to the Adriatic, and, by means of this empire, a dominion over the world, which, as the pious say, is to serve for the diffusion and the glorification of the orthodox Church—this is the ideal that, more or less consciously, hovers before every Russian. As early as 1619, in an original document of the Holy Synod at Moscow, the Czar is solemnly assured of the dominion of the world, and it is promised that there shall be continual prayer offered up that "he may be the only sovereign over the whole earth!"[1] It is well known how this expectation, and the devotion to the great Protector of their Church, has been awakened and cherished among the Slavonian populations belonging to the separated Anatolian Church. For this purpose are church-books, with "obligate" prayers for the orthodox Czar, furnished gratuitously from Russia, to both priests and parishes, and with the same object pecuniary assistance is secretly afforded to the clergy. The most insignificant priest in Albania, Corfu, Zante, and Cephalonia receives a little yearly income from the ecclesiastical treasury at Nischnei-Novgorod.[2] Even amongst the Slavonians of Austria, the Wallachians in Hungary and Transylvania, the Russian influence is actively maintained.[3]

To plant this Emperor-worship in the minds of the young,

[1] KOPITAR, in the "Wiener Jahrb. d. Lit.," vol. xxviii. p. 247.

[2] "Allg.-Zeitung," 29th Febr., 1860, p. 983.

[3] DE GERONDO, "La Transylvanie," Paris, 1845, recounts this fact: "An Hungarian officer pointed to a troop of Wallachian soldiers that he commanded, and said, 'Ces hommes m'aiment, ils m'obéissent aveuglement, mais le Pope s'est laissé gagner par les moines Russes; qu'un seul cosaque paraisse a la frontière, et ils me passeront sur le corps pour aller où le pretre les conduira.'"

and to cherish and strengthen it in those of the old, is, according to their views of the government and the Synod, the main business of the Russian clergy. The power of the Emperor, according to their catechism, comes immediately from God; the veneration due to him must be expressed by the most complete submission in words, bearing, and actions; the obedience must in every respect be unlimited and passive.[1]

The police-like character, the mechanical constraint of a church system degraded into a mere machine of government, strikes the observer everywhere in Russia. Even for confessions and absolutions a fee is fixed by Imperial ordonnance. Every Russian is bound to confess and communicate once a-year, and get a certificate made out for him to that effect. Without this confession and communion certificate he can neither take an oath nor bear witness. It is required for everything, and is, therefore, frequently bought, so that a regular trade is carried on in these documents. It is generally maintained that priests are instructed to report to the governmental authorities anything that may appear of political significance from the confessional, and that in general they have no scruple in obeying this instruction. The Civil Code, "the Swod," prescribes that people are not to change their places in church, and so forth. The Emperor reserves to himself the decision concerning divorces,[2] and the canonization of saints takes place by Imperial ukase.

The greater part of the Russian clergy do not, nevertheless, feel the imperial supremacy as a burden and a deformity in the Church. They have grown up in this view, and know no other—the Bible and the history of the Church are sealed books to them; and they feel like the Russian populace, who take a pride in the fact that the Czar is the sole lord and ruler in the empire, and who find their nationality involved in it. "If we were to unite ourselves to Rome," said a Russian priest to a Frenchman a short time ago, " our Emperor would no longer be the sole ruler in his States. He

[1] " Protest. Kirchen-Zeitung," 1854, p. 354.
[2] " Allg.-Zeitung," 1858, 12th Decr., p. 5607.

would have to be accountable to a foreign sovereign, and that would be humiliating. We cannot understand how you Frenchmen, who usually possess a pretty good share of national pride, should allow your bishops to receive the confirmation of their appointments from Rome !"[1]

Churches are, like individuals, punished by that wherein they have sinned. How carefully did this Church cherish the bad heritage it had received from the spiritually impoverished Byzantium, a mechanical ritualism; and how carefully did it exclude itself from every breath of spiritual religion and of deeper feeling! How it has allowed its clergy to sink into a mass of rude, mindless machines; how it has left its people, without the spiritual nourishment of the tidings of salvation, to languish and perish in the dreary monotony of a barren ceremonial and empty religious etiquette! Amidst endless crossings and prostrations, and genuflexions, the body is kept so hard at work, and so constantly occupied in the Church, that the mind has not a moment for thought.[2] Only in Russia could sects arise, founded on a difference as to whether the sign of the Cross was to be made with two fingers or three, or whether a fast was to be kept on Wednesday or Friday, if either of these days should happen to be a holiday. Russia is the true home of a sect which would consider its salvation endangered by a revision of the faulty text of the liturgical books, or by a variation of images from the ancient pattern.

The temporalization of the Church by the supremacy of the Czar has, on the whole, had a great part in the formation of the numerous sects and Separatist communities, which form in Russia an evil not to be remedied by ecclesiastical means, and appear to threaten danger to the State, since they only need skilful leaders to give them a politically revolutionary direction. On the other hand, however, the existence of these sects has been put forward as a reason why

---

[1] "Correspondant," May, 1861, p. 189.

[2] See LÉOUZON LE DUC's "La Russie Contemporaine." Paris, 1854, p. 228.

the supreme power of the Emperor over the entire ecclesiastical territory must be maintained unaltered.[1]

The *Raskolnikes*, or Apostates, as they are called by the State Church, or the *Staroverzes* (old Believers, as they call themselves) are very widely spread among the lower orders. They represent old Russia, as it was before Peter I., and ostensibly protest against the alterations made in the Church books by the Patriarch Nikon, but really also against the dominion of the Czar over the Church. This sect is extending every year more and more; and, according to a recent statement, it has increased, since 1840, from nine millions[2] to thirteen millions. Throughout Siberia, the Ural mountains, among the Cossack tribes, and in Northern Russia, the population belongs chiefly to the Staroverzes. The Government will not consent to tolerate them; but they know how to manage with the Government officers;[3] whilst the bishops and Popes of the State Church, who are sent by the Synod to Siberia, are regarded very much in the same light as the Protestant clergymen of Ireland in purely Catholic districts.[4] Through a bishop of their own Church, who, since 1845, has taken up his residence in a Galician village, they have been arranged into six large dioceses, and have obtained bishops and ordained priests of their own. Besides these Separatists, a considerable number of heretical sects have issued from the fruitful womb of the State Church. One of the youngest of these sects is that of the *Molokaner*, who profess to be strictly Biblical in their faith; but it is according to an arbitrary and mystical interpretation of the Bible. They have already spread throughout Russia, and number a million of disciples.[5]

To this increasing estrangement of the lower classes may be now added the complete indifference of the educated and higher orders.[6] " There is perhaps no country in the world,"

[1] See the Russian Memorial in "The Rambler," Nov., 1857, p. 313-55.

[2] GOLOWINE, "Autocratie Russe," Leip., 1860.

[3] DOLGOROUKOW shows (p. 366) what a lucrative branch of income the Staroverzes form for the venal police.

[4] MESSNER's "N. Ev. Kirchen-Zeitung," 1860, p. 367.

[5] "N. Preuss.-Zeitung," 21st Dec., 1859.

[6] "La Russie—sera-t-elle Catholique?" p. 66.

says Gagarin, " that counts so many Voltairians as Russia."

The Russian Church maintains that in its creed and administration of the Sacraments, it is completely in harmony with the Church of Constantinople; but this, in reality, is not the case—on the contrary, a very striking difference has lately appeared. Both Churches—namely, the Russian and the Greek—are accustomed to administer baptism by three complete immersions; whilst the Catholic Church and the Protestants (Baptists excepted) content themselves with pouring water on the head of a person to be baptized; or, as in England and elsewhere, with a mere sprinkling of water. The form of baptism, by pouring on the head, was declared by the Greek Church, in a Synod assembled at Constantinople in the year 1484, and with consent of the four Patriarchs, to be effectual; and the same thing was done for Russia by a mixed Synod of Greek and Russian bishops in the year 1667; but in the year 1756, the Greeks, in a Constitution signed by three Patriarchs, overthrew the former decisions,[1] and resolved that, for the future, all proselytes from any one of the Western Churches should be immersed.

This custom has since continued in all the churches belonging to the Patriarchate of Constantinople, and is now declared by the Hellenic Church to be indispensable. The Russian Church, however, with its comprehensive projects for obtaining Catholic and Lutheran converts, rightfully considered that the necessity for a new baptism might prove a stumbling-block to such proselytes, and would, therefore, not accept this new decision; so that, in the eyes of the Greeks, not only the Russian Empresses, but many of the priests, and a considerable number of laymen, are not baptized at all. From 150,000 to 180,000 of the latter, for example, of Lutherans of the Baltic provinces, who have become " orthodox," and the thousands of converts received every year, and for all of whom the anointing with the *Chrism* has been thought sufficient.[2] Such a profound difference

---

[1] As a pretext, the incorrect assertion was made, that the Latins baptized by mere sprinkling ῥαντισμός.

[2] The Patriarch of that time, Cyrillus of Constantinople, approved,

would certainly, under other circumstances, have led to a complete dissolution of ecclesiastical association; but in the Turkish East, as well as in Hellas, there are the most pressing reasons for keeping up a good understanding with the Czar and the Czar's Church; and it has therefore been resolved, with very cautious "prudence," to pass over in silence the crime of which, according to Anatolian principles, the Russian Church has been guilty, by admitting whole troops of unbaptized persons to all Christian rights and means of salvation, and by having also allowed the whole Church to be ruled by (Catherine II.) an unbaptized Empress.

THE CHURCH OF ENGLAND AND THE DISSENTERS.

The Church of England cannot properly be called a National Church, since at least the half—in fact, a much larger number —of the population, do not belong to the Anglican Church. The Catholics of England (without reckoning Scotland and Ireland) amount to a million and a half; the Dissenters of various denominations are much more numerous; and there is a mass of the poor population, factory workers and others, who are, for the most part, attached to no Church at all, and about whom the Anglican Church does not trouble itself—and partly for this reason, that in its stiff and narrow organization, and all want of pastoral elasticity, it feels itself powerless against the masses; whilst they, on their side, never think of reckoning themselves members of the Church, or asking from it any assistance.

The Anglican, however, is still the State Church; it is the only one politically-privileged; its Bishops sit in Parliament, though only in the Upper House—whilst in the Lower House, which is the real centre of power and government,

and made public, in the year 1756, the book of EUSTRATIUS ARGENTES, Στηλίτευσις τοῦ 'Ραντισμοῦ, which is intended to show that the whole of Western Christendom is unbaptized. See also the detailed discussion of this subject by WILLIAM PALMER, in his "Dissertations on subjects relating to the Orthodox, or Eastern Catholic Communion." London, 1853, p. 163-203.

the Church is only casually represented by some few members, especially regarded as friends of the Church. It is most closely connected with the civil power; the King or Queen is its head in the fullest sense, and the State provides before all things for the Church and its wants. The intellectual classes belong almost exclusively to the State Church, and it scarcely ever happens that a man of eminence professes himself a member of any Dissenting body.[1] In England the upper ranks of society are in so far religious, that scarcely one of them would acknowledge himself an unbeliever, and the majority attend Divine service on a Sunday. It is, then, the rich and distinguished who go to Church, the poor and low who remain away. The clergy of the Episcopal Church themselves proceed from the higher classes, and are by relationship or marriage intimately connected with them; it is only very seldom that clergymen of the Church have sprung from the lower orders; and whoever does not belong by birth and connection to the privileged classes, generally finds the door of ecclesiastical preferment closed against him. The patronage is mostly in the hands of the nobility and gentry, who regard the Church as a means of provision for their younger sons, sons-in-law, and cousins. Its patronage partly belongs to the Crown, the bishops, and the universities, who also usually provide for their own. Besides the rich beneficed clergy, however, there is a subordinate poor class of clergymen (an auxiliary clergy), the curates, who perform service for the more numerous classes of sinecurists and pluralists, and very commonly do this for very slender emoluments. The son of a family of the lower order might perhaps attain to the position of a curate, but there is no Christian country where the poor and humble are so much excluded from the higher schools and educational establishments—and thereby of course from the Church and the service of the State—as in England.

Nowhere else is the chasm between the rich and the poor so great—nowhere else so little intercourse between these classes, so little community of thought and feeling, as in

[1] The celebrated chemist, Faraday, seems a rare exception.

England. The aristocratically born and educated clergy of
the State Church belong to the higher orders—they understand them, and are understood by them—they think and
feel with them—and from the people they are separated by a
chasm that their pastoral zeal is seldom able to bridge over.[1]
The Anglican Church clergyman does not preach—he reads
a speech or an essay; he reads the lengthy Sunday liturgy,
and he visits the boys' school; but the people are not specially
fond of these lectures in the churches; and, with the prevailing system of hired seats and pews, they cannot even find
room inside the churches. Of the confessional, which, in the
Catholic, the Greek, and the Russian churches, brings the
priest into immediate communication with the individual,
there is of course no question. The liturgy directs indeed
that the sick man, if he feels confession necessary for the
easing of his conscience, may resort to it; but no practical
use is ever made of this permission, since persons who have
never confessed in their whole lives do not think of it when
on a sick bed. The English clergyman is therefore a lec-
turer, and in general nothing more; whilst to the lower classes
his manners and his modes of expression are strange, unintelligible, and repulsive.

There is no Church that is so completely and thoroughly
as the Anglican the product and expression of the wants
and wishes, the modes of thought and cast of character, not
of a certain nationality, but of a fragment of a nation, namely,
the rich, fashionable, and cultivated classes. It is the religion
of deportment, of gentility, of clerical reserve. Religion and
the Church are then required to be, above all things, not
troublesome, not intrusive, not presuming, not importunate.
What specially recommends it is its freedom from pretension—
that it claims no high authority, is no inconvenient disturber
of the conscience, but keeps within the limits of general
morality; and whilst retaining some Christian doctrines, seldom wounds the hearts of the hearers by an application of

---

[1] LYTTON BULWER has made some excellent remarks on this "cause
of weakness in the Established Church" in his "England and the
English." Paris, 1833, p. 210.

L

them. As to what it once possessed of positive ecclesiastical tenets, it has gradually allowed them to become obsolete. It is content with taking up just so much space in life as commerce, the enjoyment of riches, and the habitude of a class, desirous before all things of "comfort," may have left to it. Of the numerous pious practices by which formerly the lives of Englishmen, during their whole course, were attached to the Christian faith, there are few that this Church has not broken, or allowed to be broken; and the few that remain are those which possess the smallest restraining power. The Confession of sins, Fasting, everything that falls within the limits of the ascetic, the average Englishman reckons as "superstition," an idea that is for him a very comprehensive one. His Church, and it is that for which he specially admires it, requires of him nothing "superstitious." Its insulated character, also, its separation from every other Christian community, suits the national taste, and is a popular feature of the Anglican Church. The Englishman, especially of the higher ranks, finds it quite in the proper order of things that he should have a Church exclusively to himself, in which no other nation has any share; a Church, too, which, while it has all the accommodating spirit, the reserve, and the exclusiveness of Continental Protestantism, on the other assumes, by means of its episcopacy and its more liturgical character, an aspect of more dignity and importance.[1]

[1] It is necessary to have been in England, to see, and to observe, this self-complacent feeling with regard to the National Church, before one can have anything like an exact idea of its strength, intensity, and peculiarity. In Catholic countries the case does not occur; since Catholics—except those who live scattered amongst nations of other creeds—are little, if at all, aware of the contrast between their own Church and that of others. From their youth upwards they have heard only of one Universal Church—they have breathed only its air—they have moved only within the circle of its ideas—and they know that their nation is only one among many—one branch of the great tree of the Church, and has no peculiar advantage over any other branch. The Englishman, on the contrary, has sucked in, with his mother's milk, the idea of an *English* religion, an *English* Church, to which all others stand related only as degenerate—as bastard Churches—as superstition does to faith —and he enjoys the agreeable conviction of belonging to the chosen

The Episcopal State Church has, since the Revolution of 1688, and especially since 1770, suffered enormous losses. In the year 1676, that is, only seventeen years after its re-establishment, it was calculated that Catholics and Dissenters together only made up a twentieth part of the population. At present, at least one-half of the nation is estranged from it. What makes it pleasing and acceptable to the higher classes repels the lower. They see in the Anglican clergyman only the elegant gentleman, who has no mission to them ; he is not a friend, not a messenger of God, and, what is worse, he has no fixed doctrine to proclaim to them, for the Church he serves has none. What he teaches is only the opinions of the party or school to which he belongs, by the accidents of birth, of education, or of society.

It may be conceived that a great part of the people prefer belonging to one of the sects which have a definite form of doctrine, and leave little or nothing to the whim of a preacher.

Clergymen of the Established Church assert[1] that, since the Reformation, the Church has never been so much the religion of the people, has never been able to win so much of their confidence, as their Catholic predecessor. But as the Church of the richest country in the world, and of the richest classes in that country, it has the disposal of larger pecuniary means than any other; and, during the last thirty years, it has done more in the way of the restoration of old, and the

---

people of a new Church—the modern favourite of the Godhead ! It is this very Jewish mode of thought that has also found so much satisfaction in the Jew-like observance of the Sabbath. The one true Church, thinks the average Englishman, is physically and morally an Insular Church. Where the firm British soil ceases, and the *sea begins*, there ceases also the firm ground, ecclesiastical—outside of it are the heaving billows of superstition, and of false or defective Churches. Admirably, and from the very hearts of his countrymen, has the " Saturday Review" (1859, ii. 104) portrayed this state of feeling. "There is no feeling so pleasant as the assurance that you are yourself right, and everybody else wrong—that your Church and nation are the very perfection of Churches and nations—and that, by implication, you are yourself the most perfect specimen of both temporal and spiritual society."

[1] " Christian Remembrancer," vol. xxvii. (1854), p. 385.

building of handsome new churches, than had previously
been done in the present century.

There is little prospect, nevertheless, that it will ever
succeed in becoming what its Catholic predecessor was, or in
doing what that effected; that is, of becoming the Church of the
lower classes and of the poor, and winning both their confidence
and their attachment. Every one who observes the effects
that the change of religion has had upon this portion of
the population, and the relation in which the present Established Church stands with respect to the poor, will admit that,
as regards both, there can be little room for doubt.

The depression, detriment, and spoliation of the lower
classes, have everywhere followed on the revolutionary change called "The Reformation." In England, the
robbery of the Catholic Church—the transference of its
property, in enormous masses, into the hands of the laity
—left thousands of the poor destitute, and transformed
thousands of peasant proprietors into helpless paupers.
Expenditure upon the poor, in Catholic times, ceased at
the Reformation, with the marriages of the clergy, and the
enrichment of the nobility, from the property of the Church.
"In places where formerly twenty pounds sterling were
given away to the poor every year," says a contemporary,
"the poor do not now get so much as a handful of meal."[1]
The churches and monasteries, as well as the parish priests,
had hitherto chiefly provided for the poor: they had on
their lands a dense population of farmers and tenants. Leslie
and Kennett[2] describe the conduct of the Catholic clergy to
the poor. They did not, it is said, merely give them alms;
they procured work for them; they put their children to
trades and handicrafts; the poor, when they were travelling,
found shelter in the monasteries and parsonages, and the
pastors kept lists of the poor, that they might give alms to
those who most needed them.[3]

But by the sudden abolition of the monasteries, and by the

[1] Selden's Works, iii. 1339.
[2] "Divine Right of Tithes," Works, ii. 873.
[3] "Lease of Impropriations," 1704, p. 16.

bestowal of the Church and monastic estates on the courtiers and nobles, not only were countless numbers of the people rendered all at once destitute, but the new proprietors found it advantageous to turn fields into pastures, and so depopulate large tracts of land, on which, hitherto, an agricultural population had lived under the protection of the Church; so that at last "the sheep devoured men."[1]   It appears (under Edward VI.), says Burnet,[2] to have been the general intention and plan of the nobility to press down the country people into the same state of degradation and slavery in which they languished in other countries.   Thus, with the very first steps that Edward's government made towards the introduction of Calvinism into England, a regular state of slavery was established by law.   Such pitiless and un-Christian severity of legislation as was now adopted (after 1548) had never, hitherto, been heard of.   Idle persons —(and for confirmation of the fact of idleness, it was sufficient to show that they had not been at work for three days)— as well as vagrant beggars, were to be branded on the breast, and to be made slaves—to be fed on nothing but bread and water, thrown into irons, put to forced labour, and attempts to escape were to be punished with death.[3]   Thus a helpless

---

[1] This was said in a political work that appeared in 1581.   ("A Compendious or Briefe Examination of Certayne Ordinary Complaints," f. 5.")   "The sheep are to blame for all this mischief: they have driven agriculture from the country," &c., &c., ap. EDEN, p. 115.   HARRISON's " Description of England," p. 206, speaks of whole hamlets, or towns, that have been pulled down, and the ground turned into pastures. BECON, SANDYS, and other reformers, theologians, and Protestant bishops, of the time of Edward and Elizabeth, speak of cold covetousness, and rude, pitiless oppression of the poor, as prevailing characteristics of the titled and opulent classes, and confess that in the Catholic times they were much more charitable and merciful.   Another Protestant theologian traces this change to the doctrines of Faith and Justification. —STUBBES, " Motives to Good Works."   London, 1596, p. 42.

[2] " History of the Reformation," fol. ed., ii. 114.

[3] Sir FRED. M. EDEN, "State of the Poor."   London, 1797, i. 100-101.   PASHLEY, " Pauperism and Poor Laws."   London, 1852, p. 180.   This writer calls it "a statute characterized by a barbarous and ruthless severity, wholly unworthy of the legislation of any Christian people."

pauper population was first created — for England was not at that time an industrial country; and its poor were treated worse than the beasts of burden.

Under Elizabeth these laws were renewed, and even boys of fourteen or fifteen years old were to be branded if they begged for alms.[1] If they were beyond eighteen, they might, on being arrested for the second time, be put to death.[2] In the year 1597, severe whipping, or condemnation to the galleys, was substituted for branding. At the same time, however, under Elizabeth, the burden of the poor-rates was first imposed, by which free Christian charity was degraded into a legal obligation, and a compulsory oppressive tax substituted for a willing gift.[3] In more recent times, the poor, or workhouses have been added, whose arrangements, by the separation of husband and wife, parents and children, are completely un-Christian, and even, according to English judgment, in their present state a disgrace to the country,[4] since there is nothing like them to be found throughout the rest of Europe. In England—at an expense of six millions sterling a-year—this much is attained, that the working classes will endure the greatest privation, and live in the most disgusting filth, rather than go voluntarily into "the workhouse." It is the Reformation, as it is now acknowledged, that has brought upon the English people, as its permanent consequence, a legally existing and officially established pauperism.[5]

By the abolition of the Catholic holidays, and the transformation of the Christian Sunday into a Jewish Sabbath,

---

[1] STOWE'S " Chronicles of England." London, 1630, ad. an. 1564, 1568, 1572.

[2] EDEN, p. 128.

[3] See the remarks of the " Edinburgh Review," vol. xc., 507. " The Poor Law," it is said, " poisons the springs of Christian love to our neighbour, by making, on the one side an irresistible claim, and on the other a tax, from which there is no escape," &c. At the beginning of the last century, LESLIE represented the heavy Poor-Rates (ii. 873) as a just punishment for having " robbed God, the Church, and the poor of their patrimony."

[4] PASHLEY, p. 364.   [5] " Dublin Review," xx. 208.

a further oppressive yoke has been laid on the poor. All the cheering and enlivening Church festivals that had been allowed to the people in Catholic times—processions, rustic fêtes, pilgrimages, dramatic representations and ceremonies—were, as a matter of course, abolished, and nothing remained but the sermon, read out of a book—the Liturgy, read out of a book—and with this the grim Calvinistic suppression of every social sport, and every public amusement, on the Sunday. By these means the whole character of the English people was changed.[1] Formerly known throughout Europe as a people full of genial humour—as cheerful " merry England "—they assumed, after the Reformation, a sullen, discontented aspect ![2]

Music and dancing, once the favourite amusements of the

[1] Literally thus (LORD JOHN MANNERS in his " Pleas for National Holidays ;" London, 1843, p. 7), " The English people, who were of yore, famous all over Europe for their love of manly sports and their sturdy good humour, have, year after year, been losing that cheerful character, and acquiring habits of discontent and moroseness." The extensive spread of drinking among the lower classes is certainly connected with this ; and experience everywhere shows that when individuals are dissatisfied with their lot, and their lives are gloomy, they become disposed to fall into intemperance. It is only after the middle of the sixteenth century that this immoderate drinking is mentioned. In the old Catholic times the English people were so free from this vice that their country was regarded as the most sober of all the northern nations. It was entirely changed under Elizabeth, according to the report of two contemporaries, the historian CAMDEN (" Annals of Queen Elizabeth," p. 263), and Bishop GODFREY GOODMAN (" The Fall of Man ;" London, 1616, p. 366). The military men, who returned home from the wars of the Netherlands, are said to have specially contributed to the spread of this vice, and the first laws against it were made under James, in 1606. At present, the working classes of Great Britain drink every year, in brandy and spirits, as much as the revenue of the kingdom, namely (counting also what is spent on tobacco), more than fifty-three millions sterling.—PORTER, " On the Self-imposed Taxation of the Working Classes," vol. xiii. of the " Journal of the Statistical Society."

[2] The English proverb, " All work and no play makes Jack a dull boy," is specially true of the working classes in England. They are overburdened with work, and the Church does nothing for them. Lord John is perfectly right in designating their general condition as the " all work and no play system."

people, have disappeared. An Englishman of the humbler
ranks is unmusical, and neither will nor can dance.   All the
enjoyments of life, all the means of making the Puritan monotony of an English sabbath more tolerable, are reserved to
the higher classes.   To the working classes nothing is left
but—drink! Since the authority and intervention of the
Church, which protected all classes equally in the enjoyment
of their holidays, has been abolished, the people cannot any
longer allow themselves any time for rest ; for amidst a general
breathless competition, days of rest—nay, hours of rest—
would be the forerunners of want, misery, and death.   At
the aspect of such a state of things, even so ardent a Protestant as Robert Southey could not refrain from casting
longing glances on Catholic countries like Spain, where religion favours and consecrates the innocent pleasures of the
people.   He complained of the Calvinism of his country,
which, with its gloomy, joyless sanctimoniousness, its Jewish
observance of the Sabbath, and its suppression of all holidays,
had crushed down and brutalized the working classes.[1]

English sovereigns have long recognised this evil.   Charles
I. wished to protect the freedom of the population against
the Puritanism of the Parliament, but was defeated ; and the
"keeping holy the Sabbath day" became an effective war-
cry against the King, who was unfortunate even in his best-
intended measures.[2]   A hundred years later the first king of
the House of Hanover had to content himself with the barren wish, "that the amusements and games of which his
people had been deprived by Puritanical bigotry, and presumptuous latitudinarianism, might be restored to them."[3]
But to do anything effectual in this direction is for the existing shadow of monarchy impossible.[4]

Down to the time of the Reformation, there were in
almost every parish in England several chapels and oratories,

[1] Espriella's " Letters."   London, 1814, p. 147.

[2] J. D'Israeli's " Commentaries on the Life of Charles I."   London,
1839, ii. 29.

[3] Lord John Manners, p. 21.

[4] See, amongst others, Polwhele's " Letter to the Bishop of Exeter."
Truro, 1833, p. 23.

which were doubly desirable for the poorer classes and the country people, in a land were there were few actual villages, but so many of the rural population lived in scattered farms and cottages, and the parish church was at a great distance from a considerable part of the congregation. All these chapels and religious places Protestantism has destroyed, and left no more than the parish church.

But even this was not thought enough. The church is the house of the poor, in which—if it is anything more than a lecture-room—they feel themselves happy, for this reason, that they find there what is wanting in their confined and mostly cheerless homes—the adornment of pictures; symbols; —ample space; the solemn influence of architectural beauty and proportion; tranquillity and silence inspiring devotion; an atmosphere and the example of prayer. Protestantism has not only robbed the churches it permitted to remain of every ornament, but it has even locked and bolted them up, so that during the week no one can pay a visit to the church.

Before the Reformation no closed pews were allowed in the churches; the space belonged to the whole congregation, and high and low were mingled together when they prayed.[1] With Protestantism, however, pews, or boxes, obtained an entrance—pews furnished with all comforts, in which the rich and great can remain completely apart and separated from the common people.

Thus all things have combined together to exclude the poor from the Churches of England, or induce them voluntarily to keep away : the listless form of a service consisting almost wholly of readings; the space taken up by the pews of the rich, the feelings of the humbler as to the wretchedness of their attire by the side of the elegant costumes of the opulent; and then—the widening separation and estrangement between these different classes.

To the Dissenting sects the utterly poor cannot turn, since these sects are supported entirely by the payments of their members; and the consequence is, that the masses have sunk

[1] This is remarked by Bishop KENNETT in his " Parochial Antiquities,". new ed., by Bandford. Oxford, 1818, ii. 282.

into such a state of complete religious and moral barbarism, that a "numerous nation of heathens" has grown up in the country,[1] or rather, according to the confession of one of the bishops, something worse than heathenism, for a fierce hatred against the Christian faith rages in many parts of England.[2] According to a statistical statement, only a fifth part of the population of London, and that even of the opulent classes, goes to church. "The poor," says one of the city missionaries, "absent themselves almost wholly from religious worship."[3] He found that in the parish of Clerkenwell, containing 50,000 souls, only one in fifty goes occasionally to church.[4] The consequences have not failed to follow; Worsley, a clergyman of the Established Church, maintains that among the poor in the manufacturing towns the last remains of modesty between the sexes have almost disappeared; and, what is still more significant, that even in the country villages chastity and continence have almost entirely disappeared from among the labouring classes.[5]

Along with the churches the schools also were abstracted

[1] An expression of PUSEY's, in his sermon, "Christ the Source and Rule of Christian Love," pp. 5, 11.

[2] "Charge of the Bishop of Exeter," p. 56. German observers also certify to this fact. "The poor in England find no other way of avoiding complete religious and moral destitution than that of going to Rome. It is not, alas! to be doubted, that the great majority of the poor who, in the widest extent of the word, may be called the *mass* of the lower orders of the people, have passed away without having had any part in its moral and religious life."—B. A. HUBER, "Hengstenberg Kirchen-Zeitung," 1858, p. 345.

[3] VANDER KISTE, "Notes and Narrations of a Six Years' Mission, principally among the Dens of London," 1853. He says, (p. 14), "Heathenism is the poor man's religion in the metropolis."

[4] According to the Census of 1851, it appears, that if we take the number of persons capable of attending Church at fifty-eight per cent. of the population, six and a half millions belong to the Established Church, six millions to the Free communities, Catholics and Dissenters, and five and a half millions to no Church at all. In the towns the number of Established Church people is less than that of the Dissenters, and in Wales and Monmouth not one third of the population belongs to the Established Church.

[5] "Prize Essay on Juvenile Depravity." London, p. 68-82.

from the poor.   In the year 1563, the Speaker of the Lower House declared that, in consequence of the robbery and plundering of the foundations at the Reformation, the education of youth had been prevented, and a fresh supply of teachers cut off.   That there were a hundred less schools now than had formerly existed, and that many of those that remained were very poorly attended.   This was the cause of a glaring diminution in the number of learned men.[1]   Several grammar-schools were afterwards founded, but the poor were excluded from these also, and the case was the same at the two universities.   Among the numerous colleges several had been founded in Catholic times expressly for poor students, but after the Reformation these also were made aristocratic.

Even an organ of the Established Church cannot help confessing, in the face of these facts, that the Reformation in its results was, without doubt, a triumph of the rich over the poor, and of money over the rights of labour.[2]

The laws from the time of the three Tudors, Henry, Edward, and Elizabeth, declare the supremacy over the Church to be an inalienable prerogative of the Crown.   These statutes still exist in full force.   The king or the reigning queen is in possession of the Church ecclesiastical power, and that of the bishops, is only an emanation of the royal authority.   The wearer of the crown is consequently in one respect the most unfree person in his dominions; for if he were to enter into communion with the Papal See, become a Catholic, or even take a Catholic wife, he would thereby incur an abdication or loss of his throne.   According to the statute of 1689, the nation would be in that case released from the oath of fealty and allegiance.[3]   At the same time, he must

[1] COLLIER's "Ecclesiastical History of Great Britain," ii. 480 ; also HALLAM's "Introduction to the Literature of Europe," ii. 39, Paris ed., mentions the poverty and insignificance of English literature in the time of Elizabeth, and remarks that Spain, at that time, stood higher than England in this respect.

[2] "British Critic," vol. xxxiii., p. 419.

[3] See upon this the remarks of PUSEY in "Patience and Confidence the Strength of the Church." Oxford, 1841, p. 30.   He cites the words of the statute: "The people are, in such case, absolved from their allegiance."

be, in fact, by turns the religious head of two Churches, and of two opposite, and sometimes mutually hostile religions; for in Scotland, Presbyterian Calvinistic Protestantism is the Established Church.

The present Queen, therefore, is accustomed to be in winter an English Episcopalian, and in summer a Scotch Presbyterian; in winter she attends the Anglican Liturgy, and has the sacrament administered to her by the hand of a bishop, or an Episcopally ordained clergyman—and during her summer residence in Balmoral, or any other part of Scotland, she hears a Calvinistic sermon, and receives the Communion from a clergyman who would not in England be admitted to a pulpit of the Establishment, and that a great part of the clergy and laity would not regard as a regularly ordained clergyman.

Besides the Ministers and the Parliament, "the Privy Council," since 1833, exercises a supremacy over religion and the Church. It was appointed by Parliament to be the Supreme Court of Appeal in ecclesiastical disputes, whether concerning doctrine or discipline, and consists wholly or chiefly of laymen, who are in part not even members of the Established Church.

A ministerial daily paper, the "Globe," published, a few years ago, a declaration upon the nature and position of the National Church, which even Bishop Wilberforce, of Oxford, publicly adduced as the expression of the views of the Government. "The State Church, by law established," it is stated, "is, in fact, a creation of this world; it is a machine for the employment of the spiritual element in the variable public opinion of the day. Its government is managed by the Prime Minister; its characteristics are passive immobility, persevering silence, an absolute nullity in its censures—and, then, the thousands of its declared adherents, who laugh aloud, whenever its ministers overstep their humble sphere, as officers of a national institution— all these things are signs and tokens of a servitude which the lowest sect of Jumpers would not subject itself to, but which, in our department of public worship, is both natural and appropriate."

When, about the same time, a desire for a certain independent Synodical action arose, the "Times" said—It ought
to be considered that this Church, to which the Parliament
had given its present form, "possesses every attribute, every
advantage, and every disadvantage of a compromise. Her
Articles and authorised formularies are so drawn as to
admit within her pale persons differing as widely as it is
possible for the professors of the Christian religion to differ
from each other. Unity was neither sought nor obtained;
but comprehension was aimed at and accomplished. Therefore we have within the Church of England persons differing
not merely in their particular tenets, but in the rule and
ground of their belief—the one party seeking religion in the
Bible, with the help of the Spirit, the other in the Church,
by the means of tradition. The same power of freely meeting and deliberating, of discussing and altering, which is
essential to the existence of a voluntary Church, is destructive to a compromise entered into and carried out under the
sanction and authority of the state."[1]

The Bishops are, on the whole, powerless concerning
doctrine and discipline; and, for fear of a long and expensive
lawsuit, they seldom venture to proceed against a beneficed
clergyman. They have greater power over the curates,
who, also, are mostly very poor; whilst Cathedral institutions
have no place in the organization of the Church, and consist
of sinecures. The numerous Ecclesiastical Courts have also
a crowd of sinecure places attached to them. Of the 11,728
benefices of England and Wales, the Crown has the disposal
of only 1,144, and private persons, 6,092, which they may
give away by mere favour, without any conditions concerning
examination to be passed, or years of service. The Bishops
dispose of 1853 livings, with the widest opening for nepotism,
which has become proverbial among them. Plurality, or
the simultaneous possession of several benefices, and the
consequent inevitable absenteeism, although somewhat restrained by recent enactments, is still of frequent occur-

[1] "Times," 5th August, 1852. The article may also be seen in the
"Christian Remembrancer," vol. xxiv., p. 382.

rence. In Ireland, in the year 1834, out of 1385 church
livings, 157 had no divine service, and 339 no resident clergyman.

Thus, according to the confession of serious and conscientious men in the English Church, it is an intensely worldly
institution. The ecclesiastical offices have been, for 150
years, disposed of by the civil power, chiefly according to
political views, and regarded and treated according to their
lucrative value. The Bishoprics, and other rich preferments,
have been employed to procure for the ministry the support
of influential families. At present they are chiefly bestowed
on men of the Evangelical party, as these are most agreeable
to powerful dissenters, and to great numbers of similarly-
disposed Anglicans of the middle class. The designation of
a church benefice as a *living* is very characteristic. It is
regarded entirely as a piece of private property—as a mere
ware, that may be bought, and sold, and bargained for, as
one pleases. The most open simony is an everyday occurrence in England, and meets with no remonstrance on the
part of the Bishops. It creates no surprise when the next
presentation to a living is publicly offered for sale ; and it
is quite usual for a father to buy for one of his sons a
commission in the army; and for the other, the next presentation to a church living.[1] And yet, every clergyman, upon
entering on his living, has to take an oath that he has not
obtained it through simony ! A thoroughly mercantile spirit
has taken possession of this part of the Church system. The
office of preacher to a church or chapel, built on speculation, is
publicly advertised, with the remark, that a free and complete
" preaching of the Gospel (that is, according to the convenient Calvinistic doctrine of Justification) is expected."
Not unfrequently clergymen offer themselves, and mention
their recommendations—their powerful voice, their impressive
manner, their pure Protestant principles, or their attachment
to the " moderate and liberal" views of the Establishment.[2]

[1] " British Critic," vol. xxx., p. 281.

[2] A great number of such tenders of their services are to be found in
the " Ecclesiastical Gazette."

Others profess " decidedly Evangelical principles," and very generally "extreme religious views are disclaimed," and moderation and sobriety announced. Others, again, state that they have " Anglo-Catholic principles," or an agreement with the theologians of the seventeenth century.

There is probably no Church journal in the world in which there is so much talk of "views," and such a choice of opinions to suit every taste, as the publication in which the clergy of the Established Church, so to speak, sit in the market, and offer themselves for hire. In a country like England, one would suppose that nothing would be more intolerable to the freeborn Briton, usually so great a stickler for his rights, than the state of so many congregations—the being obliged to allow themselves to be sold to the first purchaser who may present himself. "There is nothing," said the "Times" lately, " to prevent any one from going into the market, and buying a living for any silly, fanatical, extravagant, or incapable booby of a son, and installing him forthwith as the spiritual mediator between the Almighty and one or two thousand of his creatures."[1] And yet there has never yet been, as far as I know, any agitation against this enormous abuse, which can hardly be equalled out of Turkey.

The inextricable contradiction between the 39 Articles, which are essentially Calvinistic, and the strongly Catholicized Liturgy, originated in the circumstance of the age of the Reformation. The Articles were to be the dogmatic fetters, binding the clergy to Calvinism, and were only laid before them for signature. But the Liturgy, with its prayers and sacramental forms, was intended to prove to the people, who were still more Catholic than Protestant, and who had to be threatened with pecuniary fines before they would attend the service, that their religion had not been essentially altered, and that the old Catholic Church still really existed.[2]

The Anglican Church is, therefore, distinguished from all

[1] See " Weekly Register," May 11th, 1861.
[2] This must be openly admitted even on the Protestant side.—See

other Protestant Churches in this, that they possess in their symbolic books at least the possibility of unity of doctrine, and a corresponding ecclesiastical life—as, for example, the Lutherans, by keeping seriously and closely to their Concordian-Book, might effect a unity of life and doctrine, provided they got rid of theology. But the English Church has the germ of discord and ecclesiastical dissolution in its normal condition, and in its Confessions of Faith. It is a collection of heterogeneous theological propositions, tied together by the Act of Uniformity ; but which, in a logical mind, cannot exist by the side of one another, and whose effect upon the English Churchman is, that he finds himself involved in continual contradictions and disingenuousness, and can only escape the painful consciousness by sophistical reasoning.

Each of the two great parties in the Church cast on each other an aspersion of hypocrisy and disingenuousness, with equal right : for the one cannot sign the Calvinistic articles with inward conviction ; and the others can only accept the liturgy, to which they have an antipathy, for the sake of the benefices they receive, and are obliged to wrest the meaning of liturgical forms in the most violent manner. Many feel the contradiction involved in the rule that the doctrinal articles are to be binding on the conscience, whilst there is no authority to be found that might guarantee the truth of these articles. No such authority is, in fact, recognised. One of the articles declares, indeed, that the Church has authority in matters of faith, but no one is able to say what and where this Church is. It cannot be the English State-Church, for this has no organ, and, since the Reformation, has never had one ; unless, indeed, it be the political supremacy of the prime minister for the time being, and his privy-council of laymen.

The present distracted state of the Established Church, in

WILL. GOODE's " Defence of the thirty-nine Articles." London, 1848, p. 10.—The " Christian Remembrancer" (vol. xvi., p. 472) thinks, indeed, that Mr. Goode has herein manifested an extremely presumptuous contempt of the Church, of which he is the servant. But the matter is familiar to every reader of history.

which there are not so many various Schools, as parties with extremely various and contradictory views, is the consequence of the measures adopted at the Reformation, and of its subsequent historical course. The old contrast between genuine Protestant, and old Church or Catholic views, has manifested itself from time to time, under various forms, in the bosom of the Church itself.

After the Revolution of 1688, arose that class of theologians and clergymen who were the forerunners of rationalism—the so-called Latitudinarians. Archbishop Wake said, in 1710, that "the English Church was only preserved from destruction by her hands being bound (by the civil power), so that she could not destroy herself."[1]

During the long period of perfect languor and indifference which followed, the contrast between the two parties died away. Towards the end of the last century, there arose the elder Evangelical school; and through its means, and the struggle with Methodism, some symptoms of life began to re-appear in the hitherto benumbed limbs of the English Church. This was a re-action against the spiritless mechanism and the half-veiled infidelity of the English Church; a religious movement proceeding from the re-awakened Calvinism of the Church doctrine, which had been so long dormant. To this earlier generation of Evangelicals, the English owe the abolition of slavery, and the establishment of several useful societies, which are still, in fact, financially prosperous. But the present race of Evangelicals may, in comparison with the former, be called a declining one. As the party is at present constituted, it represents within the Established Church, continental Protestantism, but without any Lutheran feature; on the contrary, with a preponderating Calvinism—for example, it has the Calvinist feature of a degradation of the sacraments into mere symbols. Its favourite doctrine, and most effective instrument, is the dogma of "Justification by imputation," which is so popular in England and America; and, when proclaimed with fluent oratory, fills both chapels and churches. This party is

[1] CALAMY's "Life of Baxter," i. 405.

M

mostly deficient in university culture, and there is no question
of theological science among its adherents ; their literature
consists almost wholly of sermons and writings " for edification ;" they also occupy themselves and their hearers much
with Apocalyptic and Chiliastic theories and prophecies ;
with "the approaching fall of the Man of Sin," and "the
Beast," or with "the discovery of the ten lost tribes," and so
forth. A narrow understanding, a defective education, and un-
acquaintance with the world are, according to Arnold's definition, the signs of an Evangelical. The party is internally
much nearer to the Methodists, the Congregationalists, and
Baptists, than to the High Church and the "Tractarians,"
whom they fervently hate, though both belong to the same
Church.

Since this party is entirely deficient in everything that
could be called theology, it is hard to say how the various
fractions into which it has now fallen are to be distinguished
one from another. Besides the characteristics above-mentioned, their most prominent features are the rejection of the
whole body of Church tradition—the denial of the visible
Church as a divine institution—the treatment of the Bible
according to a theory of literal inspiration which would make
every theology impossible—the transformation of the Christian Sunday into a Jewish Sabbath, and in accordance with
which the lower classes of the people are prohibited from all
recreation, and even children are forbidden to laugh and play.
The sacramental system is, in their eyes, only Popery in
disguise. Of the decided Calvinist Record-party, Cony-
beare[1] says, "The religion of many of its members seems to
consist only of love to the Jews, and hatred of the Papists."
On the whole, the Evangelicals may be regarded as sons
and descendants of the old Puritans, but without their deep
earnestness, or their hatred against the Episcopal constitution of the Church ; which, indeed, in the absence of all
authority, is but the shadow of a Hierarchical order. In
the year 1660, when matters came to a rupture between the

[1] In his description of the English Church parties in the "Edinburgh
Review," vol. xcviii. p. 274, et seq.

Puritans and the Episcopalians, the present Evangelicals would have left the Church, or been driven from it. It is at bottom only the Liturgy—the Prayer Book—to which they submit, though unwillingly. They scornfully call their opponents "Prayer-Book clergymen," but the State supremacy they are not willing to part with, especially since the government has bestowed many bishoprics on men of their school.[1]

The true Anglicans, or High-Church men, take a middle position between the Evangelicals and Tractarians. They reject, as a rule, the Protestant doctrine of Justification, and the Calvinistic degradation of baptism to a ceremony. They value the professed apostolic succession of the Anglican episcopacy—they maintain the existence of a Church endowed with doctrinal authority; but they defend themselves against every logical conclusion that must be drawn from such premises. The English Established Church is not only in their eyes the only true one, but it is the purest, the best constituted, the most free from all exaggerations. They are really the best sons and the truest representatives of this Church, and are most content with its existing state; and since, also, they are by no means exacting in their claims on the Christian lives of their congregations, they are much in favour with those classes which give the tone to society. That they should form so considerable a part of the English clergy, is only explicable with a nation to whose peculiarities it belongs, that, even according to the judgment

---

[1] What motives often determine a clergyman to join the party of the Evangelicals, and how much their teaching is in favour with the circles of the rich and fashionable world, is strikingly exhibited in the "Tales by a Barrister." London, 1844, iii. 174-183. The clergyman, above all things, finds that the Anglo-Saxon School requires too much devotion to the Church, and provides too little for the interest and personal importance of the individual. He remarks that the position of the "Evangelical" preacher is a far more favourable one. And then the doctrine is so admirably adapted to the taste of the polite world. Such consolatory views of the utter depravity of our nature!—such sweet assurance deduced from the tranquillizing doctrines of Election and Grace! &c., &c.

M 2

of Englishmen themselves, they do not see the logical consequences of their own doctrines.[1]   As these Anglicans
formerly found the continual profanation of the Lord's
Supper, in consequence of the Test Act, to be quite a
matter of course; so they now feel no repugnance at the
Burial Service;[2] and the clergy of the Established Church,
Evangelicals, and High-Church men, are certainly the
only clergy in the world who "give every deceased person
to the grave," let him have lived how he may—let him be
even a Catholic or a Dissenter—in the "sure and certain hope
of a blessed resurrection."[3]   There can hardly be a more
distinct declaration that, after all, belonging to the Church,
taking part in her services, and using her means of salvation,
can be a matter of no consequence.

Public opinion has borne so much the harder for this
reason on the *Tractarians.*   This school arose thirty years
ago at Oxford, chiefly in the view of awakening the Church
from its lethargic slumber, when its safety seemed endangered by the suppression of ten Irish bishoprics; and it then
attempted to revive the theology and the Church principles of the Carolan age (that is, from 1625 to 1680), and
to inspire them with new vigour.   But the experience of a
few years rendered it evident that the re-establishment of a

---

[1] "The peculiar incapacity of the English mind for perceiving the
sequence of doctrine," is the observation of the "Christian Remembrancer," vol. xxxvi., p. 247.

[2] And yet I find that in the year 1852, 4000 clergymen did present
to the Archbishop of Canterbury, a remonstrance against the compulsory
use of the "Burial Service." The Archbishop, with a number of his
bishops, considered the matter; but decided that every attempt at an
alteration would meet with insuperable difficulties.—"Christian Remembrancer," vol. xxiv., p. 254.

[3] "Every Dissenter who is to be buried in a parish graveyard must
be committed to the grave with the Church Service, and by an Established Church clergyman: that is to say, he must, as the phrase is, return
at his death into the bosom of the Established Church.   In the April of
the present year, Sir M. Peto moved, in the Lower House, 'That Dissenters be allowed to bury their dead in the parish churchyards, according to the forms of their own confessional ritual,' but the bill was thrown
out by a majority of eighty-one."—"Allg.-Zeitung," May 1, 1861, p. 1976.

theological and ecclesiastical position that had long since passed away was a sheer impossibility, and that the fragments of a system which, in the seventeenth century, was a mere arbitrary one, intended to meet a peculiar condition of circumstances, could not be made to suffice for the nineteenth. Men still believed, indeed, and not without reason, that in the Prayer Book they possessed a memorial and a guarantee of old-church, anti-Protestant views; but the greater part of the members of the Established Church had come to a tacit agreement to regard these things as a mere dead letter. The originators of the movement, and the men of most note, of the same way of thinking, entered the Catholic Church; whilst many others, when they were made aware, by this event, of the consequences of their own principles, turned back, and, from being "Anglo-Catholics," became again mere ordinary Anglicans.

Many have remained true to their principles, and have therefore necessarily been carried further—in fact, to the extreme limits of the Established Church, or even over them, into the Catholic territory. They are those (the number of the clergy is estimated at 1,200) whose organ is the paper called the "Union." They belong, fundamentally, quite to the Catholic Church—they recognize the necessity of an infallible authority in the Church, and they find it in the Catholic—they remain for the present in the English Church, only in the hope of coming events. Catholic doctrines and modes of thought have, they flatter themselves, gained so firm a footing, and made, in silence, such progress, that the Catholicizing of the Established English Church is now only a question of time;[1] but then it must indeed cease to be—in the sense in which it has hitherto been—a State Institution. Events are not favourable to this view: the clergy and laity have the current of public opinion in the upper and middle classes against them; and in the lower the influence of the Anglicans is very small.

Finally, a school or party of the clergy has been distin-

[1] See the declaration in the work called "Church Parties." London, 1857, p. 87.

guished as the "*Broad Church.*" The designation of "party" is not quite appropriate, since those included in it have
nothing positive in common.   Their entity is in negation:
they can only be described by saying, they are not Anglicans, they are not Evangelicals, and so on.   They are all
under the influence of German literature and theology; they
are opponents of a fixed form of doctrine, and they endeavour to make the contradictions of the Anglican Church
formularies more tolerable, by assigning to dogma in general
only a relative and temporary value; and declare a sort of
general Christianity, levelled and smoothed on rationalistic
principles, to be all that is essential;[1] though they are well
content with the Established Church, or a decorous institution the best embodiment of the national will in matters
ecclesiastical, and well adapted to the real state of things.

    For the more serious Anglo-Catholics, or Tractarians,
"the yoke" of the State Supremacy may in truth be named
one of "iron."   All the powers are against them—public
opinion is altogether hostile to them; the higher and middle
classes are decidedly Protestant, that is, they are opposed to
all that is Catholic in doctrine, rites, and discipline.   Every
attempt to introduce or re-animate an old-church element in
the Establishment has been frustrated by the resistance of
the government, the bishops, and of the people—every question has been decided to their disadvantage.   They have
been defeated in the struggle with theological rationalism in
the Hampden controversy; they have suffered in the
Gorham dispute a two-fold defeat—first, that the question
has been decided according to the opinion, and in favour of
the Calvinists;[2] and that lay state officials, acting in the
name of the Queen, have been recognised by almost the
whole clergy, and of course by the people, as the highest

    [1] The " Semi-Infidelity of the Broad Church School" is the expression
of the " Union," Jan. 4, 1861.

    [2] The Church doctrine as to the effect of baptism was, nominally, not
rejected; but the Calvinistic was declared permissible; and this, in fact,
amounted to a declaration that the English Church has no doctrine concerning baptism, and that every one may think and teach what he pleases
about it.

tribunal, indeed the only organ of the otherwise completely dumb English Church — an event to which there can be found no parallel in the whole history of the Church previous to 1517. At the same time, the first prelate of England, the Archbishop of Canterbury, when publicly questioned by a clergyman on the subject, answered, that in such things he had no more power than any other man—that everyone who could read, and who took the Bible into his hand, was as capable of deciding the question, and as much entitled to decide it, as he was. Every member of the Church must, therefore, be under the necessity of renouncing the hope of any authoritative decision —of any announcement of doctrine on the part of the Church; and however bitter it might be, they must adopt the view of the Evangelicals, that in England the Church is no more than a religious club, which the civil power superintends, and takes charge of and keeps in order: the same civil power which in England supports the Episcopal Church, and by which in Scotland and Ulster Presbyterians, in India Brahminism, in Ceylon Buddhism, are paid and supported.[1]   In fact, if the validity of Church principles is to be really asserted, the Church standard must be applied, and the Establishment declared to be an institution, infected through and through with heretical principles, corrupt to the very core, and the Erastianism of which makes every attempt at cure almost hopeless. At every step the lay supremacy comes in the way. The Church would gladly, for example, restore the Eucharistic Sacrifice, in the Catholic sense, and make it a ceremony of divine service for the congregation; but the ministry, or the Privy Council, has declared that no "altar" shall be erected in a church, but only a "communion-table"—that no lights

---

[1] How little fixed and secure are the prospects of the British Established Church will become clear, if we consider that in Scotland it includes rather less than a third of the population, in Ireland a seventh, in Wales a tenth, in England the half. Since the English and Irish Church are legally joined as "the United Church of England and Ireland," it results that this exclusive Established Church includes only a third of the population of both countries.

shall be burnt upon the altar during divine service, and so forth.[1]

A new defeat for the seriously-disposed among the clergy is the law of 1858, which declared that marriages could be dissolved, and at the same time erected a divorce court. The question had formerly been disputed in the Anglican Church. Burnet relates that, as early as 1694, a division had taken place among the clergy concerning it—that all the older bishops, those appointed under Charles II. and James II., declared themselves against the dissolution of marriage on account of adultery; but the new ones, those appointed since the Revolution, had pronounced in favour of second marriages in such cases.[2]

At this time there were not even two parties amongst the Bishops. Not one of them declared himself decidedly for the indissolubility. Bishop Wilberforce, of Oxford, indeed, was inclined to do so, but contented himself with setting up a general claim for the Church to decide the question, and complained of the wrong done by a body like the Parliament, a great part of which did not even belong to the Church, arrogating to itself the power to decide upon God's law with respect to marriage. With the same right, he said, they might decide concerning baptism, the communion, and the confession of faith.

The Bishop seems to have forgotten that this had already actually been done—namely, in the Gorham case, where they did decide concerning baptism and confession of faith. Whether the Parliament or the Privy Council does this is a matter of indifference, since the Privy Council really only exists by the will of Parliament. To the question, whether a clergyman was bound to solemnise the marriage of a couple separated by a divorce, the Attorney-General declared that it was the duty of a clergyman, as a minister of the National Church, to do whatever the State ordered him. This the Bishop of Oxford found rather too hard. It gave the idea of a thoroughly degraded, demoralized, and, for religion, impotent Church—its bitterest enemies could have

[1] HENGSTENBERG's " Kirchen-Zeitung," 1858, p. 791.

[2] " History of his own Times," ed. 1838, p. 601.

said nothing stronger upon its disgraceful condition.[1] At the same time, if we accept what the English Constitution says of the Supremacy of the State, it is impossible to arrive, logically and juridically, at a different conclusion from that of the Attorney-General. If the English clergy find this position dishonourable, it does but remind one of the fable of the watch-dog, who, in return for the comforts of his life, and the caresses of his master, had to allow himself to be chained.

Lord Chatham said, in his time, that the English Church had Calvinistic Articles, a Papistical Service, and an Arminian clergy. The saying has become a general opinion, but the designation of the dogmatic sentiments of the clergy is only now in so far correct, that the great majority of the clergy agree with the Arminians in rejecting the favourite doctrines of the Reformation age—"Justification by imputed right-eousness," and Calvinistic "Predestination." The fact, however, that the Established Church has not so much as the semblance of unity of doctrine and character, is well known to every educated Englishman, and appears as something quite natural, and as a matter of course. It has the effect that, even to the religious-minded Englishman, doctrine appears as something relatively unimportant and subordinate, which one need not be too exact about ; and it has also the further effect, that in questions of doctrine very little confidence is placed in clergymen of the Established Church, when it is seen that, with the most contradictory views, they are able to accommodate themselves to the same formularies.[2]

From this circumstance we may explain the fact, that, in general, there reigns among the clergy a certain fear of theology, and a disinclination to theological studies. Pro-fessor Hussey, in his last discourse at Oxford, shortly before his death, complained that the study of theology was dying

---

[1] See " Charge of the Bishop of Oxford," 1858.—" Christian Remem-brancer," vol. xxv., p. 258.

[2] " The result is, that the preachers of truth, in their own place and office, are the very last persons in the nation to be believed ; that the pulpit is as little trusted for sincerity as that appointed resort of hired advocacy—the bar."—" Westminster Review," vol. liv., p. 485.

out in England.[1] In a theological periodical it has lately
been maintained that there were not now in Oxford six
clergymen left who occupied themselves with the study of
theology.[2] That is comprehensible. The most important
theological works of recent times have been written by men
who soon after became Catholics.[3] Since then, the works of
the Germanized Rationalists, or Broad Church men, have
been the theological writings most esteemed.[4] The Evangelicals are struck with sterility, and all the better intellects
of the younger generation are turning with dislike and
contempt from this degenerate school, whose average amount
of culture does not attain to the degree of a good German
schoolmaster. The Anglican, or High Church school, has
never, even in its most flourishing time, produced a systematic
and comprehensive theology. They furnish nothing more
than essays and fragments; and it is very characteristic, that
the whole Anglican Church has not a single system or hand-
book of doctrine to show.[5] This Church, as the excellent
Alexander Knox has complained, is wanting in all settled
dogmatic principles.[6] A theological system—a dogmatic
divinity—presupposes a knowledge of what the Church
really teaches; but in England no one knows that, or can
know it—not even the Prime Minister and his Privy Council.
If, for example, a hand-book of Anglican Theology had been
issued before the decision of the Gorham controversy, it must
have been—after that decision—entirely remodelled, since the
principle thereby disavowed, and the one thereby established,
govern the entire organism of doctrine—for the question that
was answered in the negative by the celebrated decision of
the Privy Council was, whether the dogma of the sacramental

---

[1] "Christian Remembrancer," October, 1860, p. 325.

[2] "Ecclesiastic and Theologian," December, 1860, p. 547. The article
is entitled, "Intellectual Declension of the Clergy."

[3] Newman, Wilberforce, Manning, William Palmer, Allier, and others.

[4] Jowett, Maurice, the authors of "Essays and Reviews," &c.

[5] Pearson's "Exposition of the Creed," which is given to the young
as a book of instruction in doctrine, cannot satisfy even the scantiest
requirements.

[6] "Remains." London, 1837, iv. 233.

effect of baptism was a doctrine of the Anglican Church. The view of the Evangelicals, according to which baptism is a mere rite of consecration, has hereby obtained its franchise in the Anglican Church; and that is, even according to the Lutheran theology, "a heresy which alone would make every union of the Lutherans and Calvinists for ever impossible."[1]

It may be said of the English Church, that it is like an Indian idol, with many heads (and every one with different "views"), but very few hands. The want of freedom in the English Church—its being bound to the chariot-wheels of the State, and dragged after it through thick and thin, acts so much the more injuriously, as it affords to the feebleness, slothfulness, and indecision of the English clergy a welcome pretext for doing nothing. A large portion of them are quite satisfied with their Sunday reading exercises, and pass the remainder of their time with their wives and children, or in paying visits;[2] and in the meantime there exist in England millions of persons, who, according to the fiction of "a general national religion," are members of the Established Church,

---

[1] KAHNIS "Die Sache der lutherischen Kirche gegenüber der Union." Leipsig, 1854, p. 17.

[2] Only a few months ago an Established Church periodical made the remark, "Perhaps no men in any other profession under the sun spend so much time with their wives and children."—"Ecclesiastic and Theologian," Dec., 1859, p. 553. Thus there are in England two modern heresies, which have helped to bring about the deplorable state of the English Church. The first is, the "gentleman heresy," of which the deceased Froude so frequently complained—that is, the idea that a clergyman must be and appear before all things a "gentleman." Edward Lytton Bulwer (in his "England and the English," p. 214) says: "The vulgar notion that clergymen must be *gentlemen born*, is both an upstart and an insular opinion." In the second place, the "domestic heresy," in accordance with which, for the sake of family life, the congregation goes away empty. The marriage of the English clergy is, nevertheless, according to the remark of a celebrated English dignitary, the solid basis upon which the Church of England rests, and by which it is kept together. But for that, Englishmen, so accustomed to freedom and self-government, would not have borne so tamely and patiently the yoke of ministerial supremacy.

but of whom no clergyman of this Church ever takes the slightest notice, and thousands of whom have never heard the name of the Saviour mentioned.

The warmest adherents of the State Church complain of its want of influence on the people—of its moral and spiritual impotence. Alexander Knox thinks that, interiorally, the English Church is the most excellent of all, but practically, indeed, the most inefficient.[1] "If the whole Episcopal constitution were done away with," says Hallam, "it would make no perceptible difference in the religion of the people."[2] The Catholic idea, that the Church is the guardian of divine truth, the divinely-appointed teacher, is foreign to the Englishman :—"The true Church," says Carlyle, not unfairly, "consists now of the publishers of those political newspapers, which preach to the people daily and weekly, with an authority formerly only possessed by the reformers or popes."[3]

The Church of England declares pure doctrine, the right use of the Sacraments, and the maintenance of discipline to be the three signs of a true Church. The Church itself, however, has no fixed doctrine; its formulas contradict each other; and what one part of its servants teach is rejected by the other as a soul-destroying error. It is also dumb, and incapable of making known, in any form, its true sentiments, even when it has them. Concerning the proper administration of the Sacraments, there exist within its bosom the same contradictions as with respect to doctrine; and as to discipline, it has lost even the semblance of unity. How can there be even a talk of any correctional discipline in a Church that declares every one at his burial in a state of grace— whatever chain of sin he may have dragged through his whole life, and without his ever having given any sign of repentance, and who has not even externally or nominally belonged to its communion? How fatal is the effect of this general beatification at the grave prescribed by the Liturgy, and

[1] " Remains." London, 1832, i. 51.
[2] " Constitutional History of England," ii. 238.
[3] " Miscellanies," ii. 165.

into what false security it lulls the mind, has been described by Englishmen themselves with terrible severity.[1]

But even in this case the Church is helpless, from the fear that any change in the liturgy would be used by the Evangelicals as a breach through which greater changes might be effected.

On the whole, the entire existence of the Established Church is seriously threatened, and its dissolution only a question of time. It is completely in the power of the House of Commons, and of the Cabinet constituted by the majority of that House, which already counts among its members a considerable number of Dissenters, who are all enemies of the State Church, as well as Catholics, and, it is not necessary to mention, the Jews. In the proportion in which, through new Reform Bills, extending the suffrage, the democratically-disposed middle classes attain to dominion, the Church will be damaged by the combined hostility of the sectarians and of the professors of no religion, who are increasing every year in numbers and influence. Perhaps it will, like the Church of the Vaudois, be bound more and more closely in the bonds of State authority and the will of the majority. The dissolution of this ill-connected organism will then follow; the profounder and more earnest minds will withdraw from a Church in which the double yoke of governmental authority and compulsory communion with a foreign doctrine will not allow them in honour and conscience any longer to remain.

THE ENGLISH DISSENTING SECTS.

The *Protestant sects* of England, taken as a whole, appear flourishing and vigorous. They have, in the course of 200 years, won for themselves a broad territory; they have taken away millions of Englishmen from the State Church, and they afford a splendid proof of the power of association, of the gift of organization, instinctive in the Anglo-Saxon race.

[1] See, for example, THORN's "Fifty Tracts on the State Church." Tract xii. p. 3.

They enjoy the most perfect freedom, they arrange their
affairs quite as may seem good to themselves. The State
does not ever exercise any superintendence over them, and
they look down with no unjustifiable feeling of contempt on
the helplessness and slavery of the Established Church,
which, in its rent and divided condition, its want of fixed
doctrine and ecclesiastical discipline—in its incapability of
manifesting an activity corresponding to the wants of the
nation, and enlarging its sphere of action—can hardly do
otherwise than shun a comparison with a free religious community. With some who have left the Church, the wish to
do so has no doubt been influenced by the determination to be
no longer members of an institution so humiliated, so shackled,
and so trammeled in the fulfilment of the first and simplest
duties of a Church.   But there is usually another motive
which has led the trading middle classes out of the Church
to one of the Dissenting sects.   The practical Englishman
desires a doctrine that shall be accommodating, intelligible,
consolatory, and tranquillizing, and which shall flatter his
self-complacency and his prevailing tendencies.   All this he
finds in Calvinism, as it is conceived and taught by the
Dissenting sects.   A man is there taught that, by an act of
mere imputation of the righteousness of another, one may
pass into a state of perfect security and certainty of salvation.
He believes as firmly as he can believe that he is "elect,"
that by being clothed with the merits of the Saviour, he may
be received by God as righteous, though inwardly he is not
so; and that he can never forfeit this state of grace—this
crown of everlasting glory.   He knows no better than that
all depends on his having a completely favourable opinion of
his own state.   This is the "Assurance"[1] that plays so im-

---

[1] "Zuversicht." JONATHAN EDWARDS, the most renowned of the
American theologians, remarks that he scarcely knew a single instance of
a man who, in consequence of an easy and common self-delusion, had
arrived at a false conviction of his own " state of grace," ever being unde-
ceived. For with the natural tendency to self-flattery and self-exalta-
tion, there was united in almost all the entire absence of due caution and
fear of self-deception.—WORKS, London, 1839, i. 257.

portant a part in the religious life of England and America.
Preachers in public places, as well as in churches and
chapels, announce to their hearers the immediate and certain
forgiveness of all sins and assurance of salvation—as the
price of a momentary excitement and concentration of feeling. This is called "preaching the Gospel in its fulness
and freedom."

The internal history of these sects, therefore, turns essentially on the doctrine of "Justification" and what is connected with it; and it may be said that they cannot exist
and flourish either without this doctrine or with it. Not
without this doctrine—for, were it renounced, the talisman
would be broken by which men have been attracted to the
sect and kept in it—and the decay of the congregation,
where the favourite doctrine was no longer heard—or even
of the whole denomination—would soon follow.[1] But even
with this doctrine the sects cannot prosper, for its moral
and religious effect has always been very injurious. The
crop of fancies which have been regularly brought forth by
the preaching of the doctrine of "Justification" has been
generally called in England by the name of Antinomianism;
but the most distinguished theologians—Baxter, Williams,
Bull, and others—showed, as early as the seventeenth century, that what was so called was nothing else than genuine
Calvinism, followed out into its clearest and most irrefragable
consequences. In the history and literature of these Churches
and sects, we accordingly meet with perpetually renewed
complaints of the plague of Antinomianism,[2] or, what was
in fact the same thing, of a Calvinism which hardens the
conscience and lulls men into a false security.[3] The society
of Baptists was, according to the strong expression of their

---

[1] J. BOGUE and BENNETT's " History of the Dissenters," iii. 318.

[2] BOGUE and BENNETT, iv. 390.

[3] Strong admissions are made on this subject by ROBERT HALL, the
most distinguished of the Baptist preachers. " Difference between
Christian Baptism and that of John," p. 58 ; and also in his collected
Works, 1839. iii. 123.

preacher Fuller, very near becoming, with its Calvinism, a moral dunghill.[1]

If we wish to understand rightly the nature of these *made* religions, we must study the English and American sects and dissenters. Christianity is a dough that in their hands is kneaded into the most convenient form. The first requisite is a doctrine easy to be understood; and that may be compressed into a few ideas and feelings, which may be found pleasantly accommodating to the ruling inclinations and course of life among the middle classes—to the trading and artisan community. Fixed and accurately expressed Confessions of Faith are regarded as a burdensome yoke, to which neither preachers nor congregations would like to submit. Of their own society, Dissenters in general have a poor opinion; they are very far from regarding it as the Catholics do their Church—as a divine institution, endowed with power and authority from above. They know very well that their sect, or church system, is only a very recent production, contrived for a specific purpose,[2] and they reserve the right of altering its arrangements as may seem good to them. That objective certainty, affording security against all error in doctrine, which the Church claims for herself, appears to the practical middle-class Englishman of no value.

The only thing he is anxious about is his own subjective infallibility; he requires a system that may afford him an easy certainty of his own election, justification, and salvation. If he has this, he is not very uneasy about dogmatic scruples and biblical obscurities. He has a decided aversion

---

[1] Morris's "Life of A. Fuller;" London, 1816, p. 267. "Baptists would have become a perfect dunghill in society."

[2] "What shop do you go to?" (Welchen Kramladen besuchen sie?) the middle-class Englishman will say, when he wishes to inquire to what Church or Dissenting community any one belongs. Of a preacher, they say, "He *works* that chapel," as they might say, "He *works* that factory." Churches and chapels are, indeed, frequently "shops." They are built upon speculation, and the proprietor is accustomed, when he finds that the preacher he has engaged does not possess sufficient power of attraction to fill the chapel properly, to dismiss him, and employ another.

to religious practices, symbols, and exercises; to the worship of God in humble prayer, and to kneeling. Almost everything in religion, which is not a sermon, falls, with him, under the general head of "superstition," and its empire is in his regard illimitable. But he likes to keep the "Sabbath;" that is to say, he does not work on that day, and he listens to preaching; and it suits him much better to sit in judgment upon the form and contents of the sermon, than to cast himself down in humble adoration before God.

How little, on the whole, is done by the free or Dissenting congregations for the millions of poor, is evident from the remark made by Dr. Hume, before a Committee of the House of Lords—"That when a district became impoverished, the Dissenting congregations generally moved off, and met elsewhere."[1] The preachers are, except among the Methodists, entirely dependent on the congregation; they are mostly scantily paid, and in constant fear of losing a part even of their trifling income, through the discontent, or from the increased parsimony, of their congregations. The hearers of the preacher are his judges and his masters; they decide whether his sermons are, according to the standard of the sect, orthodox, evangelical, and edifying or not, and upon this decision depends his existence. Before all things, the congregation desires to hear repeated its favourite doctrine, that man need do nothing himself for his salvation, but only lay hold of the merits of Christ, and firmly believe in his own election and justification;[2] that the little community is the elect, that it alone is in possession of the pure unadulterated Gospel, and is the most genuine and the best of all Churches.[3] Were the preacher incautious

---

[1] "Christian Remembrancer," 1860, ii. 97.

[2] See "British Critic," vii. 232. Spurgeon, the greatest favourite among the preachers of the day, proclaims the purest Calvinism, and is fond of telling his numerous hearers how infallibly certain he is of his salvation—so that, in fact, there are only two things he need do—sing hymns, and sleep.—SPURGEON's "Gems." London, 1859; and the "Saturday Review" thereupon, 1859, i. 340.

[3] See the striking description of the position of a Dissenting preacher, in the "Christian Remembrancer," 1860, ii. 86.

enough to touch on the failings and sins to which his congregation, especially the richer portion of it, might seem most liable, he would be ruined. "As soon," says Thomas Scott, one of the most considerable theologians among the Evangelicals, "as a preacher begins to appeal in an earnest, practical manner to the consciences of his hearers, a party is formed against him to censure, intimidate, humiliate, resist, and finally eject him."[1] But, even without having given any such offence, he must be prepared, after a few years, to receive a hint to resign, when he has preached himself out, or the congregation is tired of seeing the same man and hearing the same phrases ; or even if his wife or his daughter has displeased the feminine part of the congregation by dressing too well; or if, at a political election, he has not voted for the candidate favoured by the majority of his hearers.

The old *Presbyterian* community, once the most powerful and influential among non-episcopal connexions, has, in the course of the last century, fallen completely into decay in England, and therewith genuine Presbyterianism has died out. The cause of this is to be found chiefly in the change of doctrine. The most distinguished theologians of the party—Richard Baxter and Daniel Williams—had demonstrated so clearly and convincingly the contradictions in the Calvinistic doctrine of Justification, and its inevitable moral consequences, that most of the congregations renounced this doctrine, and became, according to the customary mode of expression, Arminian.[2] By that means, however, the spiritual bond which had held these communities together was loosened; and in the latter part of the seventeenth, and the beginning of the eighteenth century, an internal dissolution of the Presbyterian congregations commenced. Several of them turned to Arianism, at that time recommended by some theologians even of the Established Church, and they, in a short time, naturally passed into Socinianism. Thus have

---

[1] John Scott, "Life of the Rev. Thomas Scott ;" London, 1836, p. 136. The whole description is instructive.

[2] Bogue and Bennett, ii. 303. New ed.

arisen the present Unitarian congregations, which, rejecting almost all the chief doctrines of Christianity, stand at something like the same grade that is occupied in Germany by the " Free Congregations." Of the 229 Unitarian chapels which existed in the year 1851, 170 had been originally Presbyterian. The Presbyterians who remained Calvinists became amalgamated with "the Independents." There are at present, in England, 160 Presbyterian congregations with a Calvinistic doctrine; but most of these are of Scottish origin, or consist of immigrant Scotchmen, and are connected with Scotch sects.[1]

The *Methodists*, or *Wesleyans*, who have now subsisted for a hundred years, may promise themselves a longer life than was appointed to the Presbyterians. John Wesley, next to Baxter, certainly the most important man whom Protestant England has produced, did not really wish to establish a new religious community in addition to the Established Church, but only an auxiliary society. Under his successors, however, and especially by means of Bunting, who first gave the connexion its firm organization, the auxiliary became a rival, and the Wesleyans have now for twenty-five years called their "connexion" a Church, though they still constantly maintain that they are one in doctrine with the Establishment.

In Wesley's community, also, the Justification doctrine forms the turning-point, and runs like the thread of destiny through the whole history of the sect. Wesley himself fell, with respect to this doctrine, into the most flagrant contradictions, and made great leaps from one dogma to its very opposite. For ten years, he said, he had been really a Papist without knowing it, and had taught Justification by Faith and Works, that most destructive of all the errors of Rome, in comparison with which the other errors of "the mother of all horrors" were mere insignificant trifles.[2] But his zeal for the favourite doctrine of Luther and Calvin did not last long. The experience of some years convinced him,

[1] MANN's "Census of Religious Worship," p. l. lxviii.
[2] SOUTHEY's "Life of Wesley," i. 287-288.

N 2

as well as his brother and assistant, Charles Wesley, that Protestant Justification by Faith, and Calvinistic Predestination, were the utter ruin of all serious religious life. Antinomianism, he said, had been a greater hindrance to the success of his work than all other obstacles together, and had destroyed the seed he had been scattering for many years.[1] " We must all fall," he wrote to his brother, " through Solifidianism, if we do not summon James to our help."[2] In the year 1770, John Wesley gave his community the signal for a doctrinal revolution ; and it shows strikingly the personal greatness of the man, and his wonderful gift for controlling the minds of his followers, that he could, without forfeiting anything of his authority, make so public and undisguised a confession of an error in a fundamental doctrine of Christianity, and that he was able to make his whole sect alter their creed, and, from Calvinists, to become Arminians.[3]

A hundred other founders of sects would have failed in such an attempt. He obtained an effective support in his friend Fletcher, of Madely, whose writings against the Protestant system are the most important that the theological literature of England has to show. It was the fear of Calvinistic infection that ultimately induced Wesley to take unwillingly the step he had so long delayed, and separate his community from the Established Church.[4] His success in this was, indeed, only partial—a breach occurred, and Whitfield, who had hitherto been his friend, with a troop of Calvinistically-disposed members of the society, separated themselves from Wesley, and from those who had remained faithful to him. A . Calvinistic community of Methodists was formed, whose prophet was Whitfield, and its mother in

---

[1] SOUTHEY, ii. 318.

[2] FLETCHER's " Works."   London, 1836, i. 105.

[3] The proclamation (Minutes) of Wesley is given in Southey, ii. 366 ; and more completely in the work called " Life and Times of Selina, Countess of Huntingdon."   London, 1841, ii. 236.

[4] " Correspondence of J. Jebb and A. Knox," ed. by FORSTER.   London, 1836, ii. 472.

the Church, the Countess of Huntingdon, a gifted woman, who considered it her appointed vocation to rule over the Church, and appointed and displaced at her pleasure the preachers of the "Connexion."[1] This sect, which in 1794 had 100,000 followers, had, in spite of its pure Calvinism, sunk down, in 1851, to 19,159, with about 109 chapels.

The great body of the Wesleyans continued for some time in complete prosperity, and, until lately, in increasing growth, and such success they owe to their firm, well-calculated organisation. But a Protestant community, with Arminian doctrines, and which has renounced the imputation doctrine, is not generally able, (as the example of the Remonstrants, in the Netherlands, shows,) to maintain itself long, at least in such a community as is desired by the mass of the people. The Methodists are gradually passing back to a conception of the process of conversion and justification more suited to Protestant ideas, and they are accustomed to place the essence of religion in the strongest possible excitement of feeling, and an imaginary certainty of grace and salvation. With this notion, Wesley's favourite doctrine of a perfect state of sanctification, to which it is possible to attain in this life, will not agree; and, at the same time, the idea of immediate justification by feeling opens the door to the most dangerous illusions and self-flattery. This opening is still further widened by the institutions of the society. The members are divided into Bands and Classes, and in their meetings they have reciprocally to inquire into the state of each other's consciences; they are to question each other publicly as to their inward feelings and "experiences"—a practice which has this inevitable result, that they confess not their sins, but their virtues, and their imaginary assurances of grace; and whilst they call themselves the most miserable sinners, always declare that they have the assurance of salvation. Probably no institution has ever been invented that makes it easier for spiritual pride to clothe itself in the garb of humility, and to induce persons to deceive first themselves, and then others.

[1] MARSDEN's "History of Christian Churches and Sects," ii. 8.

It has been stated, to the honour of the Methodists, that they had a special gift for alarming, by their preaching, the consciences of hardened, unrepentant sinners. Their mode of preaching is, above all things, calculated to heat the imagination, and the bodily sensations it awakens are then regarded as inspirations and effects of the Spirit. They have, like certain physicians, only one medicine for all ages, sexes, and classes, without any distinction. Their uniform method is to frighten people, and agitate them to the brink of insanity—to make them at first completely disconsolate, as it is stated in their writings, and then to lead them to absolute certainty of being in a state of grace, for which one act of faith alone is sufficient.[1] A man is desired to feel that it is God who has justified him, and thenceforth he is justified. Whatever aversion Methodists may usually feel to the Calvinistic doctrine, on this point it comes very close to it.[2] The effect of it is such, that in districts where Methodism is very prevalent, an actual change takes place in the physiognomy of the people, and you meet an unusual number of hard, coarse, and gloomy faces.[3]

The often-admired strength of the Methodist Church constitution has not been able to prevent continued separations, and a decay that is becoming more and more visible. The first separation (by Kilham) took place in 1796, and twenty years afterwards the introduction of an organ led to a second separation. In 1835 came the third great secession, and the new association of Warren was founded. In the meantime, discontent was increasing at the boundless and arbitrary power of the Conference, which was self-renewing, and had the entire direction of the society's affairs. This oligarchy of preachers was accused of permitting itself to be ruled by a clique, so that in 1850

---

[1] It is "a distinct and indubitable internal witness which tells the believer of his certain acceptance."—"British Critic," xvi. 12.

[2] Thus it was remarked lately (1857) that in Cornwall Methodism was altogether Antinomian, that is to say, deeply Calvinistic in its colour."—"Quarterly Review," vol. cii., p. 323.

[3] "Quarterly Review," iv. 503.

violent internal disputes broke out, and the whole society was thrown into a state of confusion and raging insurrection. The Reformers wished to render the constitution of the society more democratic, and give the lay element more influence. The Conference resisted with unyielding rigidity, and the result was, that within three or four years there was a further separation of 100,000 members, that is to say, nearly one-third of the entire society.

After the Methodists, the sect of *Congregationalists,* or *Independents,* is the most influential from its numbers, and the opulence of its members. It has in England 1401 preachers, and some hundreds of congregations without preachers. They separated themselves from the Presbyterians in the seventeenth century, on the principle of complete independence of individual congregations, and to carry out the plan of a mere association among themselves. Formerly they were strictly Calvinistic in doctrine, and were, therefore, strengthened by the accession of the followers of Whitfield,[1] who felt more nearly related to them than to the Arminian Wesleyans; whilst in Wales, the Calvinistic Methodists form an independent and tolerably numerous sect. The Independents, in 1833, published a Confession of Faith,[2] which is wide enough, and vague enough, to admit of very different views, and, moreover, all authority and binding power are expressly renounced. It is, therefore, signed by no one, and there cannot be, consequently, any question of a definite doctrine among the Congregationalists. The preachers are, therefore, free to preach this or that doctrine at their pleasure; or, rather, they have to accommodate their preaching to the views and expectations of their congregations, and especially of the more opulent and influential members. In order to maintain their position they must continually keep their finger on the mental pulse of their hearers, and see that their lectures are in harmony with it.

[1] MARSDEN, ii. 22.

[2] It is to be found in MANN's " Causes of Religious Worship," 1853, p. liv.

The *Baptists* also are, in general, decided Calvinists in their views of the dogmas of Election and Justification; they are distinguished, from the other parties of the same way of thinking, by their principle of performing baptism only on adults, and by complete immersion, since any other form is, in their opinion, no baptism at all. They arose in England about the year 1608, but never formed any connection with the Mennonites of Holland and Germany, and did not attain to any importance till 1688. Towards the end of the last century, their Calvinism, or Antinomianism, was so fully developed, that most of their preachers would only speak of and to the elect, and would have nothing to do with sinners in their congregations.[1] The absence of a confession of faith, laxity of Church constitution, and the complete dependence of the preachers on the congregations, belong to their character as a sect. From the chief party, called "Particular Baptists," five smaller sects have diverged, partly from aversion to Calvinism, partly on account of certain differences. In 1851, the Particular Baptists numbered 1947 congregations.

The *Quakers*, or *Friends*, who, being convinced that the immediate inspiration of the Holy Ghost is attainable by everyone, have neither sacraments nor ordained preachers, but edify themselves by the discourses of spiritually-awakened men and women. These are now a declining sect, and, since the beginning of this century, have decreased considerably in England. The *Moravian Brethren* vegetate in England, with their little community of thirty-two chapels, as a quiescent, scarcely noticeable little household; and the *Swedenborgian* Church of the New Jerusalem, since its doctrines have no especial comfort in them, cannot infuse any greater animation into their fifty congregations; for such was the number in 1851. More sensation has been caused by the still young *Irvingites*. Agreeing with the Plymouth Brethren, that immediately after the Apostles the Church began to decline, they have undertaken, by means of a new

---

[1] This is mentioned by OLINTHUS GREGORY, in the Biography of the celebrated Baptist Preacher, Robert Hall.—See MARSDEN, i. 83.

gift of the Holy Ghost to them, to re-establish the true
Church (long since fallen into fragments and ruins) with its
four essential offices—those of Apostles, Prophets, Evangelists,
and Shepherds. They reject entirely Protestantism, with its
assumption of sovereign judgment for every individual in
matters of faith—its revolutionary method of proceeding
"from below upward"—and in the Justification doctrine;
whilst in the Sacraments, and in the sacrificial character of
their service, they approach nearly to the Catholic Church.
The personal visible appearance of the Saviour, the first
resurrection, and the commencement of the Millennium, are
expected speedily. But the community of the Apostolic
Church has nothing especially attractive to the English; its
doctrine is not, like that of other sects, consoling and flatter-
ing to self-love—it is wanting in the talisman of the Imputation dogma, and the cheap certainty of salvation—it has too
much that is Catholic, Liturgical, and Sacramental. It has,
therefore, only a few small congregations in England, and
has no prospect of increasing them. On the other hand,
Mormonism, with its Christian mask, which has been introduced from America, has obtained within a few years nearly
20,000 adherents.

The *Plymouth Brethren*, or Darbyites, as they are called,
from their still living founder, may be said to exist on the real
or assumed decrease of all other Churches. For in consequence
of an apostacy of the first Church, which took place, they say,
in the Apostolic time itself, there is no true Church nor any
spiritual office any more existent, but all Churches are under
the Divine curse. No one must presume to build up again
this fallen Church; but the Holy Spirit, with its gifts, has remained to the faithful, and the Brethren edify one another by
means of these gifts present among them. The sect is a rejuvenated and modified Quakerdom: it is distinguished
chiefly by negations; it will have no confession-formula—no
liturgy, no church organisation, no sabbath according to the
English fashion, no sacraments, and only two symbols or
testimonies—baptism and the breaking of bread. This, like
most English sects, occupies itself much with the expecta-

tion of the approaching thousand years of Christ's kingdom. In the year 1851 its places of meeting amounted to 132.[1]

THE CHURCH IN SCOTLAND.

In Scotland, John Knox, Calvin's most devoted son, triumphantly succeeded in establishing the Calvinistic-Presbyterian doctrine and church form, after the pattern of Geneva. The people have become completely imbued with this system. Under Charles II. Presbyterianism was indeed defeated; four hundred preachers had to withdraw, and the Episcopal Constitution appeared to be victorious. The Cameronians alone maintained themselves in remote districts. The change was nevertheless merely external. Doctrine, Church customs and observances, were not touched, and Calvinism continued to be in accordance with the general mode of thought. In this long struggle of the Scotch Church, and its resistance against the Royal power, the opposition of the Scotch was strengthened by the republican constitution of their Church, which associated together both clergy and laity in one common action. The result has been, that this Church, among all Protestant communities, became distinguished by its independence and freedom, and for its never having sunk into the notorious servitude of the English Church.

With the Revolution of 1688, and the elevation of William (himself a Calvinist and Presbyterian), there commenced a complete and absolute change of circumstances. The "parsons," so were the Episcopal clergy called, were in a popular insurrection ill-treated, plundered, and driven away, and "ministers" (for the Scotch will not hear of "parsons," or "priests," or "clergymen," but only "servants,") and these, the "ministers," immediately placed themselves in possession of the parsonages and churches. The Presbyterian National Church, being now also favoured by the Government, presented itself as the sole established Church of the country, and was able to plant its foot on the neck of its enemy, the Episcopalian Church. It is, in truth, one of the most extra-

---

[1] REUTER's "Repertorium," vol. l., p. 276, and vol. li., p. 82.

ordinary but significant facts in the history of Protestantism, that after the last rising of the Highlanders in favour of the Stuarts, in 1745, the British Parliament—which at that time, of the 526 members in the Lower House, could count 513 as belonging to the Episcopalian Church—should yet have passed a series of Penal Laws against the self-same Church, on the other side of the Tweed—laws which threw its clergy completely within the power of their bitter enemies the Presbyterians,[1] and brought down upon them a harsh persecution.

Upon the whole, Calvinism, after a rule of one hundred and fifty years, exercised no favourable influence on the social condition of the Scotch nation. The Scotch patriot, Andrew Fletcher, of Saltoun, describes its situation at the close of the seventeenth century in the gloomiest colours: "One-fifth of the population then consisted of wandering beggars, and many of these were dying of starvation; there were one hundred thousand vagabonds living by theft and robbery in the country, and one-half of the whole landed property was in the hands of an idle, worthless, violent gang of robbers."[2] Fletcher knew of no other remedy to be proposed for such a state of barbarism than—the introduction of slavery!

It is a very significant fact, that the Scotch people, who on many occasions exhibited a fiery zeal for Calvinism, and who could be easily roused by their preachers to a religious insurrection, should yet, for centuries together, have done nothing as regards their churches. The Reformation had nowhere awakened a more wild desire for destruction than in Scotland; it had left only a few ruins of the beautiful and spacious churches of the country in the times of Catholicity. Since then the people made shift with wretched hovels, with damp unhealthy cabins, which often had more the appearance of stalls for cattle than God's houses; and during the whole of the eighteenth century not one single church had been

---

[1] STEPHENS's "History of the Church of Scotland." London, 1848, iv. 327.

[2] TYTLER's "Memoir of Lord Kames." Edinburgh, 1814, ii. 227.

built by a people who regarded themselves as the most religious in Europe. Many parishes had no church at all, and the people listened to their preachers in the open air.[1]

As regards the present time, what surprises one at the first glance is, that the people who are regarded by Englishmen as the most theological amongst all European nations, should be also persons with whom there is a universal passion for drink. "It is a fact," says the "Saturday Review,"[2] "that Scotland presents the spectacle of the most Puritanized and most drunken community on the face of the earth. New York is about the most profligate city in the world. In Geneva, religion is all but unknown; and in Glasgow the sons of the Covenanters are the most drunken population on the face of the earth."[3]

If the Church of the Netherlands and of Scotland are compared with one another, the contrast is striking. Both Churches have, in the main, a like faith, and the one doctrine, founded on the fifth Dordrecht article; they have, too, a similar Constitution; and yet, how great is the difference between them! Whilst Protestantism in the Netherlands has produced so abundantly a theological literature, Scotch Calvinism—although, by similarity of language, brought under the operation of rich English literature—has yet remained sterile; and has, in its spiritual poverty and lethargy, contented itself with very few, and very poor, productions—a fact the more surprising, when occurring amongst a people so intellectually gifted. Gross ignorance in theolo-

[1] CUNNINGHAM's "Church History of Scotland." Edinburgh, 1860, ii. 586-587.

[2] October 8, 1859, p. 421.

[3] "Scotland is now, by its increased consumption of spirits, the country most given to drink in all Europe. Since 1825, the consumption of spirits has quintupled. In a similar proportion have crime, diseases, and deaths increased." —"Neue Preuss. Ztg.," 21st Feb., 1854. The Scotchman LAING ("Observations on the Social and Political state of the European People," London, 1850, p. 284,) says, that his countrymen must not boast of their morality, so long as, according to statistical returns, they exceed England in their enormous consumption of spirits, and drink about four times as much as Ireland.

gical matters had always been a striking feature of the Scotch preachers. Burnet, even in his time, makes the remark.[1] Since the Reformation, Scotland has had, in fact, only two important theologians—Robert Leighton and Forbes; and both belonged to the Episcopal Church, and were themselves bishops. Theological instruction has been very negligently carried on: "the students were for the greatest portion—or, at the least—partly a very large portion of each year discharged from the strictly scientific course," and, in the intermediate time, occupied themselves with the teaching of children.[2] If we put aside a period of prevailing moderatism, but which was merely scepticism as to dogma,[3] we find that original thought, and variety in opinion and teaching, were unheard of in Scotland among the clergy, as well as the laity, although the official Catechism makes it the duty of every Scotch Christian to examine what he has heard in sermons by the Holy Scriptures.[4] Had this "duty" really been performed, by only a small number, ecclesiastical divisions would naturally have become much greater than they have been. The spirit of the nation remained bound up in the Calvinistic system. Only questions of Church constitution, and, before all things, that of patronage, have agitated the Scotch. The sect-system did not originate in the Scotch soil, but was rather dragged in upon it from England. The great secession of the preceding century took place, not on account of doctrines, but by reason of the constitution and position of the civil power.

A glance at the dogma of the Scotch Church, as it has found expression in the Westminster Confession, and which still passes as its valid confession of faith, enables us to learn what is the chief cause of the Scotch dislike to theology.

[1] "History of his own Time," p. 103.

[2] Köstlin in "Der deutschen Zeitschrift für Christl. Wissenschaft," i. 190.

[3] To this time and disposition belongs the only important Exegist the Scotch Church has produced—MACKNIGHT—who, however, according to the standard of the Westminster Confession, was very heterodox.

[4] "Confession of Faith," &c., p. 318.

There is, in fact, a solid chain of belief, with which the Calvinistic system, as it is fixed in the Westminster Confession, has encircled the minds of men. Ever since the people have been taught to measure the value of a religion according to the amount of confidence it affords, it is but natural that the Calvinist should be still more firmly convinced of the excellence of his dogma than the Lutheran, since the problem as to which affords the higher degree of tranquillizing confidence is here solved. Man—so this system teaches—receives, by the hearing of preaching, the soul-saving faith that he is, from all eternity, one of the elect; and that God will attribute to him, as if he himself had yielded it, the obedience of Christ. This faith, and the unfailing assurance of his election, of his state of grace, or his righteousness, and his future salvation, are never again lost by him, although a transitory doubt or obscurity may intrude upon him.[1] He now knows that he is under the irresistible power of the grace of God; and that all that he does, or neglects doing, is in accordance with God's will, and by God's grace. If he sins, he remains, nevertheless, one of the elect, and irrevocably in a state of grace; and he knows this will be his state, even though, like David, he commit murder and adultery. By such sins, the certainty of salvation may, indeed, be shaken, diminished, obscured, says the Confession; but the seed of God, and the life of faith, are never quite lost to the believer. And since, according to the doctrine of the Confession, he is unfree, and a merely passive instrument of the Divine Will—and that the best deed has in it a mixture of evil, so that the good in it is the action of God, through man, but the evil man's own addition to it—so persons can pretty well tranquillize themselves, even concerning sins that are, according to human judgment, heavy and grievous.[2]

[1] "The Confession of Faith. &c., of Public Authority in the Church of Scotland." Glasgow, 1756, p. 98.

[2] Concerning the practical effects which this system produces, there is an article in the " Quarterly Review," vol. lxxxix., p. 307, entitled " Puritanism in the Highlands." The writer observes: " It is held that

With such a doctrine, it is easily explained, as Köstlin remarks, why there is so little mention, in their sermons, of the Revelation of the Son of God in the flesh, and the human history of the Saviour; and that " Scotch theology possesses no system of pure Christian ethics."[1]   He adds, further, that in this system the real meaning of Evangelical faith never comes to light.

What Köstlin here remarks of the Scotch Church, is also shown, elsewhere, as the natural consequence of the Protestant doctrine of " Justification."   It was not possible to bring a tolerable scientific moral theology into harmony with this doctrine; and, therefore, so long as the mastership of the system built upon " Imputation" lasted, there too was renounced the study of Christian morals.

This has been already remarked by Staudlin[2]—that, in consequence of the Lutheran doctrine of faith, no one, during the whole of the sixteenth century (and up to 1634), in the whole German Evangelical Church, had ever thought of treating " Christian morals" as a special science, or even in their dogmatic system entering into its doctrine in any detail.   The first who undertook to do so was Calixtus, but he immediately departed from the Lutheran dogma.   The historians of the Netherland Church, Ypey and Dermout, confirmed this fact with respect to the Calvinistic theology.   Theological, Biblical ethics had, neither in the university lectures nor in literature, any place.   Every one feared an inevitable collision with the dogma, and dreaded

a person of great faith, according to his own account, and of extraordinary attainments, as his neighbours believe, in praying and prophesying, and generally of high devotional repute, may indulge in various sins without endangering his everlasting safety, or, of course, weakening his position *as a man*," (so are called here those deemed especially sacred and pious).   I have been assured in Scotland, that the example of David was regarded by the people as particularly consolatory and tranquillizing.   The writer of the above-quoted article remarks (p. 325), that the preachers frequently cherish such notions, and—according to the Westminster Confession—they are justified in doing so.

[1] " Deutsche Zeitschrift," i. 187-8.

[2] " Geschichte der Christl. Moral."   Göttingen, 1808, p. 235.

that he might get into bad odour as " a law-teacher."[1]   All
the later Protestant moral theologians, therefore—men like
Baxter, Hammond, Taylor, Mastricht, La Placette, and Arnold—were decided opponents to the Protestant doctrine of
" Justification."   But wherever that doctrine has remained
predominant, there also has there been no moral theology.

The fear of the morally destructive effects of the Calvinistic
system, and a perception of the actual consequences following
from it, essentially contributed, about the middle of the last
century, to create what is called Moderatism—a mode of
thought corresponding to German " Rationalism ";[2] although
here again, as almost always in Scotland, ecclesiastical antagonism, between patronage and congregational election,
became most prominent.   According to their theological
tendencies, the most of the Moderatist preachers were " Pe-
lagian," or even " Socinian," in their views; but yet they
did not usually attack the received doctrine : they endeavoured, by confining their preaching to moral subjects only,
to avoid it—and so made the yoke of the Calvinistic confession light for themselves.   The leaders of this school passed
for unbelievers amongst the people, and at their divine service
scarcely a tenth of the congregation were accustomed to be
present.[3]

Against this long-predominant Moderatism arose, in the
present century, the reaction of " the Evangelical party,"
whose spiritual leader was Thomas Chalmers.   This party
has passed into the Free Church.   But the genuine old Dordrecht Calvinism is now no longer preached by the majority
of the clergy of both Churches—the State Church and the
Free Church.   Only among the " reformed " and " United
Presbyterian " does it still reign.[4]   According to the statement of Maurice, the mechanical, fatalistic doctrine of the

---

[1] " Geschiedenes van de hervormde Kerk in Nederland."   Breda, 1822,
ii. 409.

[2] KÖSTLIN in " Herzogs Encyklop.," xiii. 720.

[3] See the picture given of them in " Hamilton's Autobiography " in
the " Quarterly Review," vol. xcviii., p. 362.

[4] See the newspaper, the " Union," 7th June, 1861, p. 356.

American, Jonathan Edwards (a doctrine which relegates all human freedom and self-determination to the sole will of God as affecting all things), has gained great influence in Scotland. This influence, according to Maurice, is connected with Materialism, which is very widely spread in that country. That the old Calvinistic faith is, however, lost to the Scotch Church, is, according to his testimony, the view of every intelligent man in the country.[1] In such a state of things a scientific theology in Scotland is not to be thought of. With it the most irreconcileable contradictions would come to light immediately; and the preachers would forfeit all authority among a people so watchful over all things connected with the Church. It is only by an entire absence of theology that the three Presbyterian communities can maintain their existence.

In a Jewish rigidity of the observance of the Sabbath, the Scotch Calvinists endeavour to surpass even their English co-religionists—so much so, that even a little walk for recreation on the Sunday is not permissible. And so, on the other hand, there is on that day a much greater consumption of spirituous liquors. In their churches there is no organ, no altar, no cross, no pictures, no light.[2] In God's service no symbol, no liturgical action. Calvinism has nowhere—and certainly not in Scotland—been able to produce a religious poetry. Of devout hymns that might be sung in church, no one has ever even mentioned them, for a psalm is the only thing that can be sung there. That there had been a deficiency of religious compositions suitable for popular perusal was a want already felt in England; whilst, as regards Scotland, such a deficiency is strikingly apparent. Hence it is that they are so much the more dependent upon the words of their preachers—for by them alone are the people provided with religious ideas and feelings. The complete preponderance of the sermon in a divine service, stripped of every liturgical element, the people are well content with, since this passivity of mere hearing and receiving, instead of

[1] "Kingdom of Christ." London. 1842, i. 157-60.
[2] "Hengstenberg's Kirchen-Zeitung," vol. xlix., p. 962.

O

the religious activity which is calculated upon in the Catholic worship, agrees with their mode of thought.   For
the same interest of convenience and passivity are the
long prayers (commonly lasting for half-an-hour), introduced
into every service by the clergyman, and into which he
huddles all the notions that occur to him.   Ever since there
have been Christians, the complete spiritual dependence of
the laity upon the clergy and their religious tutorship has
never been carried so far as it now is in Scotland.   Instead
of speaking to God himself, from his own personal position
and character, the Scotchman willingly leaves it to the
preacher to tell him, for half-an hour together, how he can,
or should, pray.   This plan is, at least, according to the
feeling of all educated persons, so much the more perverse,
since the clergyman, in the absolute absence of the confessional, has very little precise knowledge of the state of the
soul and spiritual wants of the laity.   A very animated and
well-written work of a celebrated and seriously religious
Scotch lawyer, Home, Lord Kames,[1] presents a picture of the
endless abuses, absurdities, and blasphemies connected with
this practice.   The necessity of the long public prayer naturally causes this prayer to be frequently nothing more than a
sermon—a sermon disguised as being addressed to God—or
it degenerates into empty gossip and hollow phrases ; or the
preacher may intrude his own petty passions and prejudices
upon his hearers in the form of a prayer.   The Duke of
Argyle has, in his defence of Scotch Presbyterianism, admitted that it is a great defect of this Church system that
the entire devotion of the congregation is dependent
upon the will of the preacher.[2]   The consequences of such a
system have not failed to follow it.   The Presbyterian
Churches are losing more and more the higher and educated
classes of the country.   The whole of the nobility, with the
exception of two families, have gradually passed to the
Episcopal Church, which, as well as the Catholic, is continu-

[1] "A Letter from a Blacksmith to the Ministers and Elders of the
Church of Scotland."   Dublin, 1757.

[2] "Presbytery Examined."   London, 1848, p. 302.

ally increasing. A great number, too, of the educated classes, though they have not formally left the State Church, yet rent seats in the Episcopal Chapel, in order that they may attend on the Sunday to the dignified forms of an Episcopal liturgy, instead of listening to declamation offensive to every refined feeling, and phrases (purporting to be prayers) of an uneducated, or half-educated, clerical speaker.[1]

Further, it is to be observed that the unfrequent and undignified celebration of Communion is felt as a repulsive evil. It is converted into a theatrical display-piece of performance, in which a long preparation, when several clergymen speak in turns one after another, is the main-piece of action. The crowding of the guests, the coming and going of those who are to sit at the long tables, whilst bread and wine are handed about in dishes and goblets—the numerous lookers-on filling the church; the noise and confusion that prevail—are all circumstances portrayed by Lord Kames in harsh colours. The low notion which the Scotch as well as English Calvinists are accustomed to entertain respecting the purport of Communion compels them to supply the meagreness of the ceremony by high-flown pathos on the part of preachers, in their raging excitement, trying to out-top one another.

The mode of burial, also, in Scotland, manifests a ritual poverty and disdain of everything symbolical. The Duke of Argyle complains of this. When Wesley was in Scotland he was greatly struck by the contrast between the English and the Scotch mode of interment. When, he said, the coffin was shovelled into the earth without a single word being spoken, it reminded him of the words of Scripture concerning "the ass's burial" of Jehoakim.[2]

The Free Church, the separation of which from the State Church began in the year 1843, and that now comprise one-third of the population, has developed a wonderful

[1] See, upon this subject, an article, "John Knox's Liturgy," in the "Edinburgh Review," vol. xcv., p. 477, et seq.

[2] SOUTHEY's "Life of Wesley," ii. 248.

amount of strength and activity. It has, in seventeen years, built above 800 churches, and a corresponding number of parsonages and schools, out of voluntary contributions; and it has, too, assigned to its preachers a considerable income. The former Secessionists have, for the most part, united among themselves, so that there are now three Presbyterian Churches—the State Church, the Free Church, and the United, subsisting by the side of one another. To these are to be added the Independents, who have about 100, although mostly small congregations. In narrower dimensions exist Baptists, Methodists of two descriptions, Glassites, Unitarians, and Quakers. Lately, there has been rather a widely diffused sect—the Morisonians—which, in opposition to Calvinism, teaches the universality of the Redemption.[1] Thus, then, is Scotland, ecclesiastically the most divided nation in Europe, and in this respect only surpassed by another country, America.

The Episcopal has, it will be thus seen, favourable prospects in Scotland. Formerly, it and its service passed for nothing better than a " modified idolatry ;" and, in order that they might exterminate it by the sword, the Scotch set up their Covenant. When negotiations were going on for the political union of Scotland with England, the Scotch Church addressed a petition to the Parliament in Edinburgh, declaring it would bring down heavy guilt upon itself and the nation, if it consented that the constitution and ceremonies of the Church of England should obtain a legal footing in England itself;[2] and still less could it, of course, endure the thought of a toleration of that Church on Scottish soil. Upon the news of the death of Queen Anne, in 1714, the Episcopal Chapel in Glasgow was, on the instant, destroyed. Since then, this Church has obtained perfect freedom, and has, of late years, by the erection of some good schools, and the college of Glenalmond, as well as by the building of the cathedral of Perth, given signs of its vigour. But lately, however, party spirit, dogmatic contradictions,

---

[1] " Union," 14th Dec., 1860, p. 188.

[2] " Edinburgh Review," vol. xxvi. p. 55.

and discord have broken out in its bosom, so that now, as a periodical recently said, persons in this Church are engaged, with all their means and all their strength, in tearing down what they ought to build up.[1]

Lord Clarendon said in his time (1660) of the Scotch: " that their whole religion consisted in a hatred of Popery."[2] That " the Pope is the Antichrist, the Man of Sin, and the Child of Perdition ;"—and that, consequently, all who attach themselves to him are lost—has always been, where genuine Calvinism prevailed, received as an article of faith, and it stands as such in the Westminster Confession. All classes and authorities, ecclesiastical as well as temporal, have, since the victory of the Reformation, always zealously co-operated to destroy the Catholic religion. But in this they have not succeeded. In the year 1700, every priest who returned from banishment was condemned to death ; and old men of seventy years of age, who had ventured to give their religious services to poor Catholic Highlanders, languished away their lives in pestiferous dungeons.[3] The old Church stands, nevertheless ; and it has in recent times— namely, through Irish immigration—considerably increased, and its churches and chapels have arisen from 87 in the year 1848, up to 183 in the year 1859.

THE CHURCHES IN HOLLAND.

The reformed Church in Holland comprehends about one-half of the population. It counted in the year 1856, 1,668,443 members. (The total population, in the year 1859, amounted to 3,348,747 souls.) After this comes the Catholic Church, with 1,164,142 souls. Then there are the Lutherans, about 600,000 (divided into two sects) ; and then the Mennonites, 38,000 ; Separatists, 42,000 ; and 5,000 Remonstrants. Thus two-fifths of the population are Catho-

---

[1] " Ecclesiastic," February, 1860. p. 50.

[2] The Oxford edition has modified this expression into—" a great part of their religion." See " Edinburgh Review," vol. xliv. p. 38.

[3] CHAMBERS's " Domestic Annals of Scotland," iii. 205.

lic.   Two out of the eleven provinces are almost entirely
Catholic, and three almost wholly Protestant.   In the meantime, Calvinism retains the tradition of its former domination.   And although the Calvinist dogma, the Dordrecht
orthodoxy, has vanished from the minds of the great majority, still the Calvinist antipathy to the Catholic Church
has maintained itself—so that the two creeds are thus more
sharply separated, and more inimically opposed to each other,
than is the case in Germany.

The new organization of the Reformed Church, in the year
1816, had (in contradiction to the old Calvinist doctrine)
principles introduced by the King, which allowed to the
State great influence, and, according to the views of many
persons, much too great influence in Church affairs.

But, by the Constitution of 1852, the greatest freedom
and independence of movement has been secured to the
Reformed Church.   The chief power rests with the freely-
elected Synod, and its decisions are subject to no royal
placet.   The only thing, almost, that there can be found to
object to is, that the Professors of Theology are nominated by the Government, without the co-operation of the
Church.[1]

Calvinism, in Holland, has the advantage of being intimately interwoven with historical recollections, of which the
Netherlanders are especially very proud.   The struggle against
the Spanish dominion was, at the same time, a struggle for
the Protestant cause ; and with the establishment of the
Dutch Republic also ensued the establishment of the
Reformed Church.

Holland was, for a long time, the classic land of genuine
Calvinism.   The struggle between Lutheranism and Calvinism in Germany exercised little or no influence upon the
internal development of the Reformed Churches; but the
ejection of Arminianism, and the decision and fixing of the
Calvinist doctrine, as to Grace, Election, and Justification,
through that dispute, is to be regarded as the most important

---

[1] " Exposé Historique de l'état de l'Eglise ref. des Pays-bas."   Amsterdam, 1855, p. 23.

event in the whole early history of Reformed Protestantism. The Dordrecht Synod is the culminating point in this history, and it is in the bosom of the Dutch Church, and with its forces, that those battles were fought and those possessions won.[1]

But from this height of Calvinistic renown the Dutch Church has long since descended. In England, Scotland, and North America, there are still adherents to the Five Articles; but in their native home, the race of Dordrecht confessors among the clergy, if it has not entirely died out, has certainly shrunk up into a very small party.

Three or four sections may be distinguished amongst the clergy; and every one of them, in its views of Christianity, widely differs from the others.

The Gröninger school, whose theological head is Hofstede de Groot, was a short time ago the most numerous. It might be named, according to the German designation, "Rationalist," only that the title of Rationalist would pass in Holland as an offensive expression.[2] With this school, Christ is but a mere potential Socrates, Who wisely adapted Himself to existing ideas, and can make no claim to absolute truth in His doctrine. All the chief doctrines of Christianity are, therefore, resolved into the transitory ideas of the time. A Church with a settled doctrine, binding on the clergy, is to this party—a horror.[3]

For the present, however, the Leyden school, with Professor Scholten at its head, is the one which has the greatest preponderance among the clergy, or promises to retain it. With that section most of the younger theologians may be

[1] So lately. MERLE D'AUBIGNE. "Quand est-ce que l'Eglise de Hollande a été triomphante et glorieuse? Quand a-t-elle marché à la tête de toutes les églises de la Chrétienté? C'est lorsqu'il lui fut donné de porter dans les murs de Dordrecht le plus complet, le plus magnifique témoinage, qu'ait jamais été permis aux hommes de rendre à la grâce de Jesus-Christ." Compare GROEN DE PRINSTERER, "Le Parti Anti-révol. et Confessionnel," p. 18.

[2] Messner's "Kirchen-Zeitung," 1861, p. 163.

[3] CHANTEPIE DE LA SAUSSAYE in the German "Zeitschrift für Christl. Wissenschaft," 1855, p. 200.

reckoned.   Many deem its spirit as much more injurious than
that of the Gröninger theology : because the veiled rationalism and heathenism of the Leyden school assumes the authority of being a deeper speculative establishment of the Calvinistic system of unconditional predestination ; whilst, in
point of fact, the whole theology of this same school leads
ultimately to a dispersion and dissolution of individual
personality—Divine as well as human.

Of the theologians of Utrecht, and their disciples, it is
said, to their honour, that if they are not Calvinistically orthodox, they are more Christianly conservative than the
two other schools.   The religious party under Groen van
Prinsterer, and not represented in the universities, calls itself
the "Christian Historical," and personifies the genuine Calvinism that is so intimately interwoven with the history of the
country.   It desires of the civil power that it will maintain
by compulsion the old creed ; and of the Church authorities,
that they will tolerate no variation from it in preachers ;
but at the same time it complains of its weakness, and of
the failure of all attempts that have been recently made, and
of the falling off of friends, and dispiritingly admits that it
is, at all events for the present, impossible to discover a cure
for the confusion now prevailing amongst Protestants.[1]   What
Groen will not, but which others, nevertheless, see clearly
enough is, that the dogmatic Calvinism of the sixteenth and
seventeenth centuries has in Holland, as elsewhere, died of
theology, and that every attempt at its reanimation must
begin with the suppression of theology.

The Netherlands clergy have therefrom made the yoke of
their Confessional Declarations as light as possible.   The most
important announcement on this subject is that which is
stated at the conclusion of the General Synod in 1854 :
"Since it is impossible, even in the shortest Confession of
Faith, to unite all opinions and desires, so the Church allows
variations from the symbolical writings, only excepting what
is essential, namely, veneration for the Holy Scriptures, and

---

[1] GROEN, "Le Parti Anti-révol.," p. 108.   Compare Preface, p. 1.

faith in the Redeemer of sinners. These must be held fast."[1]

With this, then, excellent care has been taken of the freedom of the pastors to teach as they please; but the freedom of congregations, on the other hand, not to allow any unbelieving or erroneous-believing preacher to be forced upon them, is absolutely illusory; and in cases occurring within the last few years, in which congregations have preferred a protest against the pastor, the latter has always conquered.[2] "The congregations," says Chantepie, "were treated as if they were sheep;" and this tyranny is complete! Besides this, the obligation, until recently in force, to preach upon the Heidelberg Catechism has been done away with by the Synod, and so has the last confessional ligature been torn to pieces.

"At present," says Molenaar, "everyone preaches and teaches what he likes." At the same time the Synod, in its yearly meetings, and the Synodal Commission, speak of "the doctrine of our Church;" whilst the general Synod gives to all questions, concerning the doctrine of the Church and the confession of faith, evasive or equivocatory answers.[3] The unity of the Netherlands Church consists, according to Groen's expression, only in this, that all its preachers are paid out of the same treasury; and "this chaos," he adds, "should not any longer be called a Church."[4]

Dissatisfaction with the existing Church, its want of a creed, its general falling off from the doctrines of the age of the Reformation, and its entire absence of discipline, have led, since the year 1838, to the formation of a separate Church, under the guidance of the preachers Cock and Scholte. It is scattered in small congregations over the whole country. In the year 1853 its number was estimated

[1] "Berl. protest. Kirchen-Zeitung." 1854, p. 846.
[2] CHANTEPIE DE LA SAUSSAYE, "Le Crise relig. en Hollande." Leyden, 1860, p. 67.
[3] "Beknopte Opgaaf van de verschillen Gevoelens." Gravenhage, 1856, pp. 88-92.
[4] "Le Parti Anti-révolutionnaire," p. 106.

at 42,000; but even amongst these a division has already taken place, concerning a prime Calvinistic doctrine, upon " the perfect consciousness of one's own faith, as an essential sign of election."[1]   Other differences also prevail amongst them. Apart from the " Cockyanys" (Coccianern) as they are called, as well as from the State Church, there exists a little religious community of perhaps thirty, called " Congregations under the Cross."

In Holland, also, almost the whole of the Divine service consists in exceedingly long sermons, which are very frequently read.   The Communion is, as in other Calvinist Churches, administered only four times in the year; and the religious instruction of youth is, through the idleness of the preachers, left to " catechism-masters," persons who are also accustomed to carry on a trade.   As in Scotland, so is it in the Netherlands, at least in several of the provinces—burial is not a religious act, so that cases of death are not even notified to the clergyman.[2]   The custom of hiring seats in the church has also here had, as in other places, the effect of excluding the poor from the church, but so much the more here because the number of churches is strikingly small.   Rotterdam, for example, with 104,000 inhabitants, has only four churches.   If, in these circumstances, a want of religious feeling is manifested, still, on the other hand, Protestant consciousness, on its negative side, is so much the more lively and vigorous.   Even the English Bishop Burnet had remarked it in his time : " The chief thing which the preachers in Holland inculcate upon their people is a detestation against Arminianism.   They seem much more anxious about this than about other most important subjects."[3]   At present the Arminians have shrunk up into a small, weak group, whilst the great majority of the clergy of the Reformed Church think Arminian, but in some respects go far beyond the old Arminianism.   The very numerous Catholics who, after their long depression, have been placed on a level with

[1] REUTER's " Repertorium," vol. lxxxvi. p. 147.
[2] GÖBEL's " Ref. Kirchen-Zeitung," 1855, p. 266.
[3] " History of his own Time," fol. ed., i. 689.

the Protestants, are, however, the object of most attacks.
Niebuhr had already remarked that an "orthodox" Calvinist,
in his conviction of his own personal election (and of the rejection of those of a different opinion), was a most irreconcileable enemy. "One does not," he says, in the year 1808, "so
much as mention the great poet Vondel, the only poet who
does honour to the nation, and, indeed, immortal honour; but
he must not be spoken of, because he had become a Catholic."[1]

Since then this aversion has naturally increased—especially since the organization of the Catholic Episcopacy, in
the year 1853, which, in the same manner as in England,
two years previously, had evoked a storm of indignation,
that was sedulously cherished from the pulpits, and before
which the ministry had to give way; and Groen and his
followers flattered themselves with a great Protestant
revival in the country. Ultimately, however, nothing was
effected beyond the formation of five societies, partly to
convert the Catholics to Protestantism, and partly to keep
them down as much as possible, both as citizens and subjects. The religious life of Protestantism has derived no
advantage from the great agitation, and the rent in its
Church is as wide as it had previously been.

Thus, then, the opinion entertained concerning the present
state and future prospects of the Reformed Church in
Holland, must be gloomy and disconsolate enough. Of its
1500 preachers, it was a short time since publicly mentioned
that 1400 were Unitarians or Socinians.[2] "If the present
state of things continues," says the preacher, Chantepie, "it
is impossible for the Reformed Church to fulfil its mission
(that of being the chief dam against revolutionary principles),
for being itself in a state of dissolution, it must leave a free
course to decomposing and destructive forces."[3] Not less
gloomy is the most recent description given of this state of
things, which closes with these words: "The death-waters

---

[1] "Nachgelassene Schriften," p. 289. See his startling description of
Dutch fanaticism, p. 266.

[2] Messner's "Kirchen-Zeitung," 1860, p. 541.

[3] "Deutsche Zeitschrift," 1855, p. 206.

of Unbelief, Rationalism, Pantheism, and Materialism are in
Holland, as in Germany, filtering through, and wasting
away those protecting dykes—the Family, the State, and the
Church.[1] No one knows what advice to offer, nor what aid
to give. The disease has its seat even more in the clergy
than the people. The bond of a common faith, and of a
fixed doctrine, is wanting, and we may sum up the state of
affairs in three short sentences :—

1. Without a code of doctrine laid down in authoritative
Confessions of Faith, a Church cannot long endure.

2. The old confessional writings cannot be maintained,
and are universally given up.

3. To make a new Confession of Faith is impossible.

PROTESTANT CHURCHES IN FRANCE.

The Reformed, and (according to its origin) Calvinistic
Church, in France, enjoys important advantages. In every
thing which concerns its doctrine and ecclesiastical life, it
moves with the most complete freedom that can be wished
for; and it enjoys, too, the prestige of nearly one hundred
years' endurance of oppression (down to the time of Louis
XVI.), and of a severe and sometimes bloody persecution.
By the Revolution of 1789, it was much less injured than the
Catholic Church, which, for a long time, did not recover the
heavy blows inflicted on it, or rather, it may be said that it
is still bleeding from some of the wounds it then received.
In comparison with it, Protestantism was treated very for-
bearingly at the Revolution, and sometimes favoured as an
ally.

With a community so small, so scattered, and so inun-
dated by a great mass of Catholicity, one point has been
always vigilantly attended to, namely : that exclusively
Protestant ideas, and a sharp contest against all that is
Catholic in doctrine and in practice, should be a principle of
existence in this Church, which, if not firmly adhered to, the
small religion must, inevitably, be absorbed in the greater.

[1] In MESSNER'S " Kirchen-Zeitung," 1861, 16th March.

That the " French" spirit is a " Catholic" one, is said in
France even by Protestants themselves. " The feeling that
it is so, prevails in the Evangelical Church of France,"
writes a German correspondent, from Paris; " it feels itself
to be an exception to the general rule."[1] But so much the
more certainly might one expect all that is Protestant to
gather around its banner, and close together its ranks, not
merely maintaining a negative position, but advancing with
a positive creed against the Catholic Church.

The natural consequences of this position are, in so far,
not to be mistaken, that among the French Protestants there
is not to be found the slightest trace of an approximation
towards Catholic doctrine, ideas, institutions, or observances
—there is not a single French theologian, or preacher, has
ever, so far as I know, fallen under the suspicion of having
his thoughts turned in the same direction as numbers of the
Tractarians and Anglo-Catholics in England. In France,
they all are, in this sense, " extremely good and staunch
Protestants." The variation in tendencies, and the manifold
conflicts within the heart of their own community, have not
the slightest effect in preventing them from making war, with
all their combined forces, upon their Catholic rivals. To no
Protestant, believing in Christ, if he is a preacher, has the
thought ever occurred that the believing Catholic stands
nearer to him than the unbelieving or rationalistic member
of his own Church.

Internal want of unity, and distraction, among French
Protestants are, at the same time, strikingly great; whilst a
common dogmatic position, and a settled doctrine, are here
as little to be looked for as in Holland. The causes for this
state of things are, for the most part, to be found in the
precedent history of this Church. Among all Protestant
communities, Calvinistic as well as Lutheran—of the English
Church we do not here speak—the French was the first in
which the process of decomposition in the chief Protestant
doctrines was completed. Previous even to 1685, and,
therefore, before the great Protestant emigration commenced,

[1] HENGSTENBERG's " Kirchen-Zeitung," 1851, p. 866.

the most important theologians, men like Cameron, Drelin-
court, Mestrezat, Daillé, Testard, Amyrault, Leblanc de
Beaulieu, Jurieu, La Placette, had given up the old doctrine
of "Justification," and the Dordrecht Articles (which had
been at first accepted by their Church), as untenable; and,
in Holland also, where, after the revocation of the Edict of
Nantes, many of them had found an asylum, they contributed essentially to the undermining the Calvinism there
existing.   Thus the old Calvinist tradition of French Protestantism was broken through towards the end of the seventeenth
century, and never has there taken place any re-animation of
original Calvinism.   The more modern French Protestantism,
as it has shaped itself within the last fifty years, has never
attempted any dogmatic alliance with the historical past; and
Adolf Monod, who was removed on the complaint of his
consistory at Lyons, remained the only one who maintained
the permanent validity of the old Confession of La Rochelle.
The great majority of the clergy declared, in the year 1849,
against this Confession, and would have, in fact, no Confession, as the whole Reformed Church of France has no
theology.   The works of the older theologians are quite
forgotten—a new theological literature has not been formed,
and the theological writings of German Protestants have
only obtained a very small influence.

Since the year 1819, a "revival" has taken place; but it
did not spring up in French soil—it was introduced from
England and Switzerland, and partly by Methodist missionaries—by these called "the awakened" Methodists, and to
whom, in French Switzerland, is given the designation of
the "Momiers."   The Methodism which has found its way
into the French Protestant Church, through the "awakening," is described as being the chief cause of the weakness
and wretched state of this Church.   It is a dogma-destroy-
ing sect.   Under the pretext that a Church confession-of-
faith is a mere form, which genuine Christianity ought to do
without, it has abolished Confessions, it has set aside
holidays, it has degraded the Communion into a mere love-
feast, and it has cut out a pattern for "a new faith," in

accordance with the history of each person's individual conversion. Methodism undermines all the bonds of political as well as social life in the community.[1] Such are the accusations which the friends of French Protestantism are found to prefer against "the Evangelical party," as it likes to call itself.

Since then the French Reformers have fallen into two unequal divisions: those of "the believers," or "the awakened," and the unbelieving, or the "indifferent." The preachers are educated in some one of the three theological schools—at Geneva, Strasburg, and Montauban; of these, the two first are chiefly Rationalists, and the latter is so mixed that almost every professor represents a different opinion.

There is, however, an older and a younger Rationalism in France,.to be distinguished from one another. The older, whose representative may be taken to be Athanasius Coquerel in Paris, leaves to the Holy Scriptures the importance of being a Divine revelation, but breaks down or denies particular dogmas, and, before all things, will allow no settled, binding doctrine to be established. It will either not meddle with decided dogmas, or it places them altogether within the territory of individual selection. The negation of all authority is, with it, the essence of Protestantism. The more modern Rationalism is, on the other hand, essentially the historic-critical of the German school; or, as the believing Protestants say — "the destructive which has obtained its entrance into France through the theological faculty of Strasburg." This particular division of Rationalism is represented by the periodical published by Colani and Scherer, and is the only real theological periodical of French Protestantism. It is stated that in general a sceptical tendency is gaining more and more adherents among the younger clergy.[2] Even Grandpierre was compelled to confess, before the Berlin Assembly, that the Rationalistic or

---

[1] PRESSEL, " Zustände des Protestantismus in Frankreich." Tubingen, 1848, p. 66, *et seq.*

[2] MESSNER's " Kirchen-Zeitung," 1860, p. 48.

latitudinarian element prevailed above the orthodox, and
that most of the pastors and their congregations are going to
sleep.[1]

In the circle of "the awakened" a dissidence has gradually grown up, and especially since 1848. This separation of a number of preachers with their congregations has
not had any origin in the relations that exist between the
State Church and the power of the State. Freedom with
respect to the State is certainly not wanting to the French
Reformed Church. Its freedom is rather more complete
than that of the Scotch Church. The ground of separation
lay in the dogmatic indifferentism or latitudinarianism of the
great majority of clergy and laymen. This came to light in
a very striking manner, when the Protestants, immediately
after the February Revolution of 1848, met together in a
Synod, without the assent, and also without any prohibition
from the government. They there found that a community
which desired to lay claim to the name of a Church, must,
before all things, possess a common doctrine, or be able to
show a document of Confession of Faith. At the same time,
the result of the debate was that the whole assembly acknowledged the impossibility of putting forth a Confession,
and were obliged to come to the humiliating admission that
their Church had, in fact, no common doctrine any more.[2]
The old confessional declarations were abandoned, and the
putting forth of a new form was evaded with the phrase—
"that they would not diminish the liberty of the children
of God by setting up any other authority than that of God's
own words."

This appeared to several preachers and laymen, amongst
whom the Count Gasparin was distinguished, as an intolerable state of things, and they determined to leave the State
Church, and to erect a "Free Evangelical" Church. Three
and twenty small congregations now form "the Union of the

---

[1] "Verhandlung der Versammlung Evangelischer Christen." Berlin,
1857, p. 123.

[2] See the detailed report in HENGSTENBERG'S "K.-Z.," 1849, p. 98,
et seq.

Evangelical Church of France."[1] These dissidents, who are, altogether, about three thousand, or a little more, are supplied with pecuniary means from England and Switzerland. They have nothing in common with one another but a dislike to the State Church, and a belief which assumes various colours and forms; and they are in so far inclined towards the Baptists, that they allow children to be left unchristened at the will of the parents, whilst declared Baptists are willingly received amongst them. It stands with this " Union " very much as with the Evangelical Alliance. They are kept together—although an organization comprehending within it each individual does not substantially exist—yet they are united, not by what is positive, nor by one common Confession, but by that which is negative. Since, however, the State bears the cost of the Reform Church, and pays the clergy of the State Church, the Secession which is limited to foreign resources is very weak in its supplies, as English and Swiss donors care much more for having their money laid out in the purchase of Catholic proselytes than in the formation of Dissenting congregations.

It has almost excited astonishment that Adolf Monod, who, according to Vinet, is the most important man belonging to French Protestantism,[2] should have declared, notwithstanding his Calvinism, the intention of remaining in the Established Church. He has, indeed, animadverted severely on the " organized chaos " of this Church, in which, under the pretext of toleration, and freedom of thinking, not only the obligation, but even the very existence, of a positive doctrine is denied.[3]

By the new Constitution which Napoleon III. gave to the Protestant Church of the Empire, the Reformers obtained their wished-for Presbyterian Council, and the Consistories emanating from it—at the same time, however, a Central

---

[1] They are enumerated in the " Annuaire Protestant." Paris, 1858. p. 107.

[2] That is, if we omit the statesman, M. Guizot.

[3] See the pamphlet, " Pourquoi je demeure dans l'église établie." Paris, 1849.

P

Council as the chief authority was established, that which
was not desired by the majority. Again, since then, as
formerly, a desire has arisen for a General Synod, from which
they promise themselves great things. But the influential
Protestants of Paris are exerting themselves to prevent the
calling of a Synod; for, they say, the Consistories already
disagree,[1] and in a General Assembly discord would at once
flame out amongst them; and all that would be done would
be to present to Catholics the scandalous spectacle of a
multiplicity and variety in Protestant opinions, whilst not a
single important question would obtain a satisfactory determination by an imposing majority.

It is natural that such circumstances should provoke the
bitterest complaints from seriously disposed men. In the
most recent times it has been said, "That the present state
of things has become intolerable[2]—that there exists no
authority which might watch over clergymen, so that they
should not preach unchristian doctrines." It is admitted,
"That the community of the Reformers in France, in its
entire want of a Confession of Faith, and of every kind of
discipline, is, in fact, no Church, but only 'an Institution for
the edification of non-Catholic Christians, founded by the first
Napoleon.'" "The Church," says an organ of still-believing
Protestants,[3] "is on the path to individualism—it is all
breaking and crumbling up into the opinions and views of
individuals." Every Consistory ordains preachers as it
pleases,[4] and the person to be ordained is not even obliged to
signify his agreement with the doctrines of the Church, for
the Church has no doctrines; but he presents to the Consistory a Confession drawn up by himself, and so, if the
authorities approve of this Confession, he is ordained." Of
the Consistories themselves Link had heard that only one
fourth of them were Christian, since wherever there was an

[1] LINK, p. 14.

[2] MESSNER's "Kirchen-Zeitung," 1860, p. 48. See also HENGSTEN-
BERG's "Kirch.-Ztg.," 1851, p. 984.

[3] The "Espérance," edited by GRANDPIERRE.

[4] LINK, "Kirkliche Skizzen aus dem Evangelischen Frankreich."
Gottingen, 1855, p. 22.

unbelieving pastor, the elders all joined him.[1]   And every
Consistory forms a Church of its own, completely independent of others—it is, in fact, "keeping house" for itself.[2]

Thus, then, it may be seen that State pay and the negation
of Catholicity are the strongest bands that hold together the
Reformed Church in France.   This Church has no doctrine,
no confession, no theology, no discipline ; and its divine
service is a cold performance, limited to a sermon, to some
prelections by a clerk, and a psalm.[3] No one can be excluded
from it.   No one can specify what are the principles by which
it is governed, or how it governs itself.   A German observer
of these circumstances remarks concerning them : "It is,
alas ! but too true the reproach which the enemies of our
Church are incessantly making with respect to it, viz., that
there is nothing active in it but the spirit of dissension, and
of individual caprice; and no other links than those of Pro-

---

[1] At the "Alliance" meeting in Berlin, in 1857, the preacher Grandpierre, of Paris, endeavoured to give the most favourable possible representation, and he declared, "One may certainly maintain that of the
thousand Protestant pastors in France, of which there are 600 Reformed,
300 Lutherans, 100 Independents, at least from 500 to 600 were
orthodox" (the words are, of course, to be taken in the sense of the
Alliance).   But the official (and by the Protestant authorities themselves
published) "Annuaire" of the year 1858, contained a very different statement from the above.   According to this authority there are 530 Reformed,
253 Lutherans, and about 23 Independent preachers—altogether 806
preachers.   According to this may be judged whether the official statistics
are correct.   The last census gives the following numbers of the population : 480,507 Reformed, 267,825 Lutherans, making altogether 748,332
Protestants.   Kolb ("Handbuch der vergl. Statistik ;" 2 Edit., p. 51)
thinks that this statement is, by more than one-half, too small, and "is
inclined" to give the numbers as 1,300,000 Reformed, and 700,000
Lutherans.   That would be, on the average, more than 2,000 souls to
each preacher, whilst in France it is notorious that a great number of
the congregations do not, at the utmost, count more than from 200 to
300 members.   The "Annuaire," whose publisher, from the completeness
of its statistical notices, must be well informed as to the number of his
co-religionists, is silent, and therefore confirms the accuracy of the
Government returns.

[2] Pressel, p. 36.

[3] Kienlen, in "Herzogs Encyclopädie," iv. 561.

test and Negation cement together this mass of 'malcontents.'"[1] Since then two other phenomena have occurred, which indicate the continuation of the process of decomposition. The Darbyite sect, which rejects every ecclesiastical office, and every remnant of Church order, and believes in nothing but the private edification of the individual, or of a few, has found entrance among the French Protestants. In the South, and in Cevennes—as Gelzer had already perceived—a fragmentary sectarian spirit had gained the upper hand. Quakers, Wesleyans, "Inspired," or the so-called "Convertites," or "Strict Predestinarians," and other sects, had found followers. In the congregational "congenies," for example, near Nismes, there were reckoned, a few years since, six sects. "If," said a German reporter, " we look steadily at the matter, as regards the future of the Church, the aspect of the French Protestant Church is such that it is as difficult to obtain a clear idea of it, as it is not to allow every hope respecting it to be depressed.[2]

THE PROTESTANT CHURCHES IN SWITZERLAND.

In Switzerland the Protestant population stands in about the same relation to the Catholic as in the Netherlands. To about one million of Catholics there are about one million and a half of Protestants (in the year 1850, 1,417,916). Lutheranism is here unknown. The whole of Protestant Switzerland is "reformed"—it is, or was at least, Calvinist; its confession of faith, and standard of doctrine, were of the Helvetic Confession of the Heidelberg Catechism, the Dordrecht Decisions, and the Consensus-formula—altogether genuine Calvinist documents. Berne, with 403,000; Zurich, with 243,000; Vaud, with 192,000 Protestants,[3] must, when attention is devoted to ecclesiastical circumstances, come most into consideration. With the advantage of having given existence to the second chief form of Protestantism—

[1] PRESSEL, p. 35.

[2] "Protestantische Briefe aus Südfrankreich und Italien." Zurich, 1852, p. 51.

[3] According to the calculation for 1850, in FINSLER's " Kirch. Statistik der. ref. Schweiz." Zurich, 1854, p. 1.

of having shaped it out, and afforded it a dwelling-place, Switzerland ranks next to Germany as the classic ground and home of Protestantism. Berne and Zurich are, in respect to religion, as important as Wittenberg. From the plague of princely domination, which is so frequently to be regarded as the chief source of ecclesiastical corruption, the Swiss Church has, of course, remained free. It has had, in its political relations, only to do with republican, and, formerly, with aristocratic authorities chiefly. Notwithstanding the similarity of doctrine, no attempt has ever been made to establish a collective Protestant Church in Switzerland. The clergy and the people felt no impulse to pass, in Church affairs, beyond the cantonal frontier limits, and the several governments did not like to have their ecclesiastical sovereignty diminished.

As elsewhere, so too in Switzerland, the Reformation placed the new Church under the control of the civil power. The Government seated themselves in the chairs of the Bishops. Zwinglius himself had given the administration of the Church to the Council of Zurich. In Berne the State domination over the Church was completely carried out. It was regarded as a branch of the public service; and the Bernese senators decided upon doctrine and rites, and determined theological disputes, according to their own good pleasure, even though they did previously have the advice of theologians. Of a defined legal position of the Church towards the State there was no question;[1] and so early as the year 1837, the Professor Zyro, in Berne, made the accusation against the State: "That it had temporalized, and almost annihilated, the Church; and that the clergy had become the servants of the rich and the powerful.[2]

Thus, domination over the Church was inherited by the new governments that arose out of the storms of the year of revolutions. Frequently, under the influence of radicalism, so powerful in Switzerland, they maintained, in the most

[1] ROMANG, in "Gelzers Mon.-Blättern," v. 90.
[2] "Die Evangelisch ref. Kirche," besonders im Kanton Bern., 1837, pp. 81-82.

favourable circumstances, an attitude of indifference towards the Church, which they treated as a police institution.

Geneva, the old metropolis of Calvinism, would now be scarcely recognized by Calvin himself. It is becoming more and more a Catholic city.[1] "The faith of our fathers," said, lately, Merle d'Aubigné, "now counts but a small group of adherents amongst us." Calvin's Church, with its definite doctrine and constitution, exists no more: it fell in the political revolutions of 1841 and 1846; and the new one is governed by a lay consistory, elected by an absolute majority of all Protestants. Confessions of Faith are abolished,[2] and the Church "grounds its belief on the Bible, and allows to every one the right of free inquiry."[3] Among the clergy "prevails the most absolute confusion with respect to doctrine."[4] Under the influence of Methodism, which has found its way hence from England, Geneva has established, since 1816, an "Evangelical Sect," and out of this a "Free Church," which rejoices in the consciousness of being a little band of "the elect," in the midst of a universal decadence. Still more serious have been the proceedings in the Canton de Vaud. Here, where the Government has always been, since the Reformation, and through it, in possession of a complete domination over the Church, the majority of the clergy, when power passed into democratic hands, found the yoke quite too oppressive; and especially so when the State Council, at one and the same moment, dispossessed forty-three preachers. Encouraged by Vinet, 180 clergymen, out of about 250, left the State Church. They were replaced by others, and the secessionists erected a "Free Church," which is inimically regarded by the population, and in twenty years has only obtained about 3,000 members, divided into forty little congregations.

---

[1] Of the 83,845 inhabitants of the Canton of Geneva, there are now 42,355 Catholics, and 42,266 Protestants. In the year 1850 there were 64,146 inhabitants, of whom 34,412 were Protestants, and 29,764 Catholics.   [2] MESSNER's "K.-Ztg.," 1861, p. 202.

[3] GENF's "Kirchliche und Christliche Zustände," in "Der Deutschen Zeitschrift," i. 248.   [4] *Ibid.*, i. 253.

The Heidelberg Catechism, with its eighty questions, has always been so carefully inculcated upon the Bernese people, that, according to the testimony of Romang, the pastor, "There is scarcely anywhere so decidedly an anti-Catholic people as the Bernese;"[1] and so much the easier was it, therefore, in the year 1847, to inflame the agitation against the Catholic "Sonderbund" into a religious war. The object was attained. The Sonderbund has been annihilated; but the re-action had not been well calculated upon. It struck their own Church. Romang describes the immediate consequences: "Zeller's call; the increased indifference of the people towards religion; the falling off in attendance upon the churches; the impotency of the clergy, without corporate strength or authority, and whose main thought is to provide for themselves and their families; and then, the great evil, beyond all others—the entire want of an ecclesiastical authority, which formerly its Governments, and they only, exercised, but which the present Democratic Government neither can claim, nor has claimed."

Adherents to the Calvinistic doctrine no longer exist among the clergy of German Switzerland; and even amongst the French they form, at the most, nothing more than a little clique. Of Confessional writings, or of a doctrine in accordance with them, there is no longer a word said. A Swiss theologian boastingly declares that "even believers now ask very little about a confession of faith, and seldom trouble themselves concerning the institutes of the Church."[2] In the Cantons of Zurich, Glarus, St. Gall, Aargau, Geneva, Vaud, Thurgau, Appenzell, Basle, and Neuenburg, there is not a single old Protestant creed any longer in force. In the Canton of Vaud the abolition of the Helvetic Confession, in 1839, was the inevitable consequence of a decision, by which it was shown that only 9,000 citizens wished to retain it, whilst 12,000 desired its abolition. In Berne, the Grisons, and Schafthausen, the clergy are under an obligation to regulate themselves according to the *principles*, or *funda-*

[1] GELZER's "M.-Bl.," v. 194.
[2] GUDER, in Gelzer's "Monats-Blättern," vi. 121.

mental doctrine, contained in the Helvetic Confession; and by it their freedom of teaching is very little limited. In St. Gall they promise to preach according to the Bible, in the spirit of the Reformed Church. It is, however, only in the city of Basle that the obligation is really acted upon. The two theological faculties in Zurich and Berne follow chiefly a creedless and destructive tendency. The school at Basle alone possesses, and still teaches, a positive theology; but it is, according to the estimate of it in Wette's and Hagenbach's writings, nothing better than an "accommodating theology."

The position of the Swiss Protestant Church is worse than that of other countries. It suffers from two severe maladies—from Radicalism in the people, and from the unbelief, the spiritual unsteadfastness and shattered condition of the preachers. Among the clergy the influence of German literature and theology, and a decomposing process of Church doctrine, with its consequences, have become complete, so that every preacher is accustomed to preach what pleases himself, or what may be pleasing to his congregation. The more ancient Nationalism is no longer in possession of authority;[1] and as to old positive Protestantism, it can only find a place for itself amongst "a knot of the congregation."[2] The majority of the clergy naturally keep to what had been taught to themselves in Berne, or Zurich, or Basle. In the canton of Berne most of the clergy and of the Church authorities have openly taken part with the unbelieving Faculty. In the synod and other assemblies the believing clergy generally find themselves in a minority.[3] On the other hand, Radicalism, which, for thirty years past, had sometimes by starts, through revolutions, and sometimes silently and gradually, by the diffusion of its destructive principles, obtained the mastery, has, beyond all other things, used and exercised its power in laying waste the

---

[1] PFEIFFER, "Ueber die Zukunft der evangelischen Kirche in der Schweiz." St. Gall, 1854, p. 21.

[2] "Gemeindlein in der Gemeinde." *Ibid.,* p. 23.

[3] HENGSTENBERG's "Kirch-Ztg.," 1856, pp. 598-599.

Church territory. It has made itself felt in the desolation of Churches, in the alienation of schools, in the extinction of the influence formerly possessed by the clergy. Unbelief has penetrated so deeply amongst the population, that, according to the report of the elders of a congregation in the town of Berne, " of every ten householders there is scarcely to be met one who now believes in God and Christ, or makes any use of the Scriptures."[1] "It is only a Church with a Catholic organization (unless by some extraordinary descent of the Holy Ghost) that could," says the preacher Güder, "maintain itself against the attacks which Radicalism and a Radical Democracy have made upon it since they entered the lists to encounter it upon a soil that was already rotten."[2]

In the general report of the Berne Synod of the year 1854, it is said :—" We cannot any longer conceal from ourselves that some great thing is wanting to our public Divine service to meet the indispensable requirements of the present generation." To recognise " this great something which is wanting," there is no need, as the Report considers, of " another new Pentecost." It suffices to look steadily at the picture which another Swiss preacher has drawn of Divine service in that country. " Our worship," he says, " is that of a mere teaching school—our churches are lecture-halls, with naked walls, and destitute of a sanctuary; and these churches are constantly closed, with the exception of a few hours on the Sundays; and yet they are the only public memorials still left us of our religion ! Preaching is, in fine, the one thing, and everything in our Divine service. The rest has been abbreviated as much as possible, and limited to a few verses of a hymn and some formal prayers. It is from the pulpit only that the clergyman can speak before or to his congregation. There he remains during the whole of the Divine service; and the congregation are always sitting or standing, but never kneeling : they have nothing to do but to listen, and allow themselves to be talked to."[3]

[1] GELZER'S " Mon.-Bl.," iv. 149. [2] GELZER'S " Mon.-Bl.," iv. 124.
[3] VÖGELIN, " Welche Veränderungen und Verbesserungen sollten in unserm Cultus vorgenommen werden?" Frauenfeld, 1837, p. 34, et seq.

This picture is completed by another of the same class and country. "The clergy," he says, "are mostly mere orators in the pulpit, and not shepherds in the midst of their congregation. The weekly Divine service is dying out. In many districts not one-eighth, and sometimes not a tenth of the population any longer go to Church."[1] It must be admitted that for some time back it has been with the Church and religion "all down hill," ("bergab"). And yet, so early as the year 1837, a distinguished theologian and public teacher pronounced upon the clergy of his country this judgment: "The clergy appear to present in themselves the image of our Protestant Church, the image of a predominant, one-sided, selfish capacity, which only rejoices in itself, will alone know itself, and solely seeks for what is its own self-interest," &c.[2]

When the Swiss clergy in their meetings have expressed their opinions respecting the state of their Church, they have done so in a tone not alone disconsolate, but also accusatory against the Church itself. Thus Güder confesses, at the Paris Assembly of the Evangelical Alliance in the year 1856: "Our religious position is very humiliating, and very well suited to urge us to repentance.[3] The pastor Meyer declares in his Report made at the meeting of "the Preachers' Society," at St. Gall, in 1859: "The tendency of the time is no longer towards the Church, but to pass by the Church; and the fault of this lies on the Church, and upon its own contradictory conduct. To-day, for example, it contends against the Baptists, and to-morrow it will offer them its hand in the 'Alliance.' The Protestant Church is so great, and the Protestant spirit is so small."[4]

In the year 1849, Professor Ebrard, who had been engaged several years in Switzerland, wrote concerning this country: "The state of the Church in Switzerland is a melancholy one; it is a Cæsaro-Popedom of the sovereign people, who

[1] GELZER's "Monats-Blätter," iv. 160.

[2] ZYRO, "Die Kirche im Canton Bern.," p. 102.

[3] "Conférence de Chrétiens Evang." Paris, 1856, p. 300.

[4] HENGSTENBERG's "Kirchen-Zeitung," 1859, p. 917.

will have their religion made just what pleases them. In the Vaudois there are oppression and persecution of the Free Church—a total corruption of the State-Preaching Establishment. In the other cantons, as a young Christian friend lately wrote to me, "there are merely two trifling things wanting to the Free Church—flocks and shepherds; of dogs and wolves there is a superfluity."[1]

The position of the clergy of Protestant Switzerland, French as well as German, is, in such a state of affairs, not enviable. To religious indifference and the materialistic tendency of mind in the people, is added the plague of sects. New Baptists, New Believers, or Böhmists, Antonians, for whom there is no law and no sin any more, Mormonites, Irvingites, Darbyites have found entrance; and yet the character of the people, and the prevailing tendency, is not favourable to sects. It is so much the worse for the clergy, that in some cantons the clergy hold their appointment only during pleasure; or they must, after a few years, subject themselves to a new election; so that, like the Dissenting preachers, they are wholly dependent on the favour of the more influential members of the congregation. There are also complaints of a continual deterioration in their worldly position, which is so bad, that lately in the daily papers the question was discussed whether it was proper that clergymen's daughters should be publicly advertised for as housemaids.[2]

PROTESTANT DENOMINATIONS IN THE UNITED STATES OF AMERICA.

No State or National Church, and nevertheless a general profession of Christianity. Such is the first fact that strikes us with reference to religion in the Eastern States of North America. No one would in that country venture openly to proclaim himself an infidel. It belongs, among the higher and middle classes, to the tone of good society, and to the de-

---

[1] SCHAFF's "Deutscher Kirchenfreund." Mercersburg, 1849, p. 272.
[2] "Protestantische Kirchen-Zeitung," 1856, p. 138.

corous conduct of life, to be a Christian. There does not,
therefore—or there did not till very lately—exist such a thing
as a literature of Atheism, Pantheism, or Materialism. A
religious atmosphere is diffused over the whole country, from
which no one can venture to withdraw himself; and this manifests itself especially in the strict observance of the Sunday, in the extraordinary number of churches[1] and meeting-
houses, and in a diligent attendance at them; in the energetic, emulous activity of the various religious parties, in
their efforts for missions, and in the number of religious
periodicals. Irreligion, or contempt of religion, is there only
displayed by the Germans, and contributes much to the con-
temptuous manner in which the Anglo-American looks down
upon Germans.

In the West, indeed, over which the great stream of emigration from Europe and the Eastern States is pouring itself
in a full flood, the case is quite different. There are, in the
West, regions where nine-tenths of the population belong to
no Church at all, who are not even christened, and do not
get their children baptized or instructed in the Christian religion.[2] Many there will answer to the question, as to what
Church they belong to, by saying, "I belong to the big
Church,"—that is to say, "I, as a free American, believe as
much or as little as I like; and I can get on very well myself with my Bible, and do not need the crutches of any religious society, nor the sectarian coloured glasses through
which they compel their readers to read it." For, as a rule,
every American holds the Bible in respect, and in the West,
also, the Germans are the only prophets of unbelief. The
name of the "big Church" is indeed Legion, for, in a population of twenty-nine millions, the number of recognisable
Christians, who, by taking part in the Communion, show
themselves to be really members of a Church, can be estimated at the utmost at not more than five millions.[3]

---

[1] Which, indeed, according to LÖHER, all look like private chapels.

[2] RAUSCHENBUSCH, "Die Nacht des Westens." Barmen, 1847, p. 45.

[3] SCHAFF'S "Bericht in den Verhandlungen der Versammlung-
Evang." Christen. in Berlin, 1857, p. 234.

Each of the larger sects is divided, namely, into two classes —into the majority, who outwardly profess to belong to it— or, as it is said there "stand under its influence," and who attend divine service regularly, or tolerably so—and into the minority, who are really full members. If we subtract from these the Catholics, of 2,400,000 souls, there remain about 2,600,000 Protestants, of about seventy sects and denominations, who make full use of the means of religion offered by their respective sects.[1]

According to this there are about twenty-four millions, a part of whom are entirely without religion, and a part who attend the meetings of a sect regularly or occasionally. Of these, many are not christened, and all naturally refrain from Communion, which they may do much the more easily that the views of Zwinglius respecting it prevail over the whole of Protestant America. It has been calculated, indeed, that there is one preacher for every thousand persons, but the proportion is quite differently arranged; most of the preachers have very small congregations; 1239 congregations of Old Presbyterians have not above fifty members each—1907 between 50 and 100, and only 736 above 100. Of the Congregationalists, 696 have fifty, 1219 up to 100, and 750 above 100, and that in the great towns.[2]

The consequence of this is, great poverty of the preachers and their families; and the complaint that the clergy are worse paid in America than in any other country, cannot excite any surprise. How great is the number of those who keep aloof from every religious exercise may be gathered from the fact, that in all the churches of New York only 205,580 persons find room, and 638,131 are excluded.[3] The most moderate estimate is, that above the half of all the poorer people in America belong to no religious community.[4]

[1] The author has corrected this statement He mentions. in a note to his Introduction, that, misled by an estimate in SCHAFF's book upon "North America," he had calculated the church-going members of the different Protestant sects much below what they must be ; and is, upon reflection, disposed to double the number which he had, at first, supposed them to be.   [2] KRAUSE's "Kirchen-Zeitung," 1856, p. 430.

[3] MESSNER's "Kirchen-Zeitung," 1861, p. 238.

[4] MARSHALL's "Notes on the Episcopal Polity," London, 1844, p. 501.

These are the consequences of "the voluntary principle;" thus does the want of a National Church avenge itself. This is and must be the result of the rule of the sectarian system; for if millions receive the impression that they may choose their Church and their religion freely, out of a variegated crowd of denominations, some will allow their choice to be determined by some one accidental circumstance. The majority, however, will put an end to the painful condition of uncertain hesitation by indifferent neutrality, and tranquillize their conscience with the reflection that among so many assumed brides there is really no lawful spouse; that they are, in fact, all only concubines, who can make no real claim to the fidelity and devotion of a free man.[1]

The state of Christianity in America is an awful and serious warning, and will in future become still more so. The want of a people's Church which receives everyone in his infancy, incorporates him with itself by baptism, and draws him into one common life-giving atmosphere, is a want that cannot be supplied by anything else. The condition which Europe would not like to realise for herself she has transplanted to America; for America has become the rendezvous of all the sects and divisions of Protestant Europe.

One of the worst consequences of this want is seen in the American school system, from which every kind of religious instruction is excluded. The Bible may be used as a reading

[1] Thus H. SEYMOUR TREMENHEERE, in his "Notes on Public Subjects made during a Tour in the United States" (London, 1852, p. 51), relates, on the authority of the Protestant clergyman, Edson, at Lowell: "The young people who stream into Lowell, as workers from the neighbouring States, are usually without the slightest knowledge of Christian doctrine, and utterly indifferent as to what sect they shall belong to, since they think all religions really pretty much alike. In other respects they are generally well instructed, though very lax in their ideas of morals and duty. Among the children who had received some religious instruction, Edson found that there was seldom any point inculcated as resting on authority; but that all doctrines were treated rather as the results of individual views, and to a great extent left to the child to decide. It is evident that the Americans have a faculty for logic." Edson adds, however, that this want of all authority in the education of children is now universally acknowledged to be a great evil.

book, but no word of explanation added to it by the teacher and no prayer be uttered.[1] If Sectarianism had brought on America no other curse than such a school system, which accustoms the youth of the country to regard life and knowledge on the one side, and religion on the other, as two completely separate and independent territories—such teaching must suffice to render it one of the greatest calamities of the New World. The bitter discovery is now being made in America, that an education destitute of a Christian spirit is not merely defective; it is positively injurious, and trains up men to make them cold, calculating scoundrels.[2] The Sunday schools that have been introduced are no sufficient substitutes for the absence of Christian parish schools. May Europe be terrified by the melancholy fruits that this system has borne in America, and which it will at a future time bring forth yet more abundantly, by following in the same path.

The separation of Church and State was really effected by the unbelieving Jefferson and his followers, who coincided with his views; and it was effected by a man who flattered himself that in the course of another generation all America would be Unitarian. By this separation it is forbidden to the Government and its officers to interfere in any way in the affairs of religious communities.

They have gone further, however. The constitution pro-

[1] Religious-minded Americans express the greatest dissatisfaction and indignation at this godless system of education. The "Mercersburg Review" calls it "Our ten-times helpless, wretched, and ruinous Common School system" (v., p. 41). A work by COLWELL on the subject, "The Position of Christianity in the United States" (Philadelphia, 1854, p. 98) says. "The exclusion of Christianity from the public education of this country is a suicidal arrangement—the worst enemy of humanity could think of nothing more destructive to the Republican institutions of the country," &c., &c. The same arrangement, as it is well known, exists in Holland, and is there also most bitterly complained of; for example, by the Baron v. Lynden, at the meeting of the Evangelical Alliance at Berlin, 1857. As long, however, as in both countries the same cause, namely, excessive Church dissensions exists, complaints and mutual recriminations will remain fruitless.

[2] See the energetic words of an American theological periodical, the Presbyterian "Bibliotheca Sacra," 1851, p. 763.

vides, that no profession of religious faith shall be made by
any candidate for a public office;[1] that the Congress shall
make no law respecting the protection of any religion,[2] or to
prohibit the free exercise of any. The whole document
ignores the existence of Christianity. Story, the American
Blackstone, states it as his opinion, in his Commentary, that
it is doubtless the duty of every government to cherish and
encourage Christianity by all means; but that by those regulations it was intended to prevent all rivalry between
Christian sects, and the rise of a national Church which
should turn the patronage of the Government to the exclusive benefit of its hierarchy.[3] On the other hand, in individual States—for instance in Pennsylvania—-the Bible
and the Sabbath are placed formally under the protection of
the law, and people may be brought before a magistrate for
using blasphemous expressions. In Massachusetts it has
even been decided by a court of justice that, according to the
laws, the murder of an unbeliever (an infidel) was no crime.[4]

All are of the religious parties and communities of England
that, since the seventeenth century, have taken root here—
partly to escape oppression at home, and partly in the natural
progress of colonisation. As the Anglo-Saxon race is the
prevailing one, so is also the Anglo-Saxon religious system,
the product of the long mutual struggle and contest between Calvinism and Episcopalianism—between the Association Church and the State Church; and it is the preponderating
element which has extended its influence over the other immigrant nationalities, and the forms of faith and church discipline they brought with them. One only—the Catholic
Church—has kept itself aloof from all such influence, in so
far as it might have suffered any change from it.

All Churches, or religious communities, have, therefore,
complete equal rights. Every person can join any sect he
pleases, or belong to none, or found a new sect for himself.

1 " Mercersburg Review," iii. 329.
2 " Respecting an establishment of Religion "
3 " Mercersburg Review," iii. 331.
4 " Atlantiische Studien," iii. 65.

As in politics, in trade, and in all other occupations, so also in the domain of religion, the freest competition prevails, and produces energetic action and elasticity of Church organism, combined, however, with an indecorous grasping at, and hunting after, proselytes, which forcibly contrasts with the passive tranquillity and stagnation of State Church bodies. For their practical skill in spreading these nets, and drawing on the masses, the Methodists appear to excel all others; but so much the more are the others obliged to concentrate their forces, keep their followers together, and endeavour to procure new proselytes. The mere prospect of being supported in case of falling into distress, brings in troops of converts. The art of getting money for religious purposes is here carefully cultivated; and for their talent in making money out of everything, and therefore also out of religion, the Americans certainly surpass all other nations. By exercising a kind of moral pressure that gives no offence, and leaves the appearance of voluntary action, they know how to incite crowds of people to bestow religious contributions—these, too, being persons who, if left to themselves, would give nothing. Their success in this way is truly extraordinary.

Upon everything that is Christianly is laid a blessing, which, in its integrity and entirety, never is utterly lost, and never can be perverted into a curse. No matter how defective may be its form, nor with what manifold errors disfigured, nor how much by human passion and perversity deformed and degraded, still that which is Christian will accomplish an incalculable amount of good. Tocqueville has eloquently remarked how much America owes to the serious sense of religion, and the Church discipline, which the Puritans brought with them from England and naturalized in their new home. This was the merit of the three great Puritan parties—Presbyterians, Congregationalists, and Baptists—which, towards the end of the last century, had the spiritual control of North America. Since then the Methodists are to be added to the others; and as they have addressed themselves to the lowest and most forlorn of the community, have attained considerable success. These four chief forms of American

Q

Protestantism—and beside them the Episcopal Church, which has, in the most recent time, greatly increased in strength—are, accordingly, the main supports of the religious feeling which still exists among native Americans. Those chief parties themselves are, indeed, split up into a greater number of sects, though certain common features and tendencies have remained among them. The swarm of other sects, however (a short time ago a list, amounting to above seventy names, was made out of those in New York alone[1]), possesses small positive influence—at least among the higher and middle classes—whilst it must be considered as weighing heavily in the scale, when its effect is to weaken faith in one firm Christian truth, and to aid in the generation and nourishment of sceptical indifferentism.

The prevalent opinion in America is not unfavourable to sectarianism—on the contrary, it is regarded rather as an advantage. The idea of *a Church*, of belonging to a Church, or the duty of belonging to a Church, does not exist for the American. He knows that he is one of a sect, a member of a denomination, which does not exist anywhere else in the whole world—unless perhaps in England or Scotland. As a rule, he entertains the firm conviction that the Anglo-Saxon race is the chosen one of modern times—the conservator of true religion, appointed by God. Of the past history of Christianity, if he ever thinks of it all, he has the idea that there have always existed a great number of sects, a variegated assortment of ecclesiastical bodies; and that, therefore, a Church established by Christ either never existed, or has long since been dispersed into various sects. He thinks, therefore, naturally, that, in the absence of the whole still unbroken vessel, we must content ourselves with fragments; and that one of these pieces is not much better or much worse than another, but that every particle has still something of the original vase left in it; or Christianity is supposed to be like a forest, in which many different kinds of trees stand near to one another, and receive alike light and life.

[1] " Darmstadter K.-Zeitung," 1857, p. 1150.

According to the prevailing view, therefore, the government ought not to favour one religious Confession and discourage another; it must maintain an equally neutral and indifferent attitude with reference to all religious communities, as long as they do and teach nothing contrary to the laws of the country.

In the eyes of politicians, advocates, and literary men, the chief advantage of the present state of affairs consists in this, that "the sects, by their mutual jealousy, keep one another in check," as the "New York Observer" remarks. It appears to them a great gain that there is in America no National Church, and no religious authority. True religious freedom—to which belongs, before all things, the freedom to do altogether without religion—is, they think, best secured by the existence of many different sects.

In the meantime, there are still Bible readers in the country, and they happen sometimes to hit upon those passages in which Christ speaks so clearly and energetically of the one visible Church, and of the unity of his disciples; and the consequence is[1] that the formal justification of the sectarian system, such as used to be promulgated in former years, is now seldom heard. On the contrary, the most distinguished theologians and Christians agree in their condemnation of the sectarian system, and in the opinion that it is a disease which all ought to be anxious to cure. The sectarian system, says one of the best of American periodicals, is, in its very innermost nature, a horror. The whole world knows that the relation of our sects to each other is much more one of rivalry, opposition, and jealousy than of brotherly love and harmonious co-operation. It was said of the primitive Christians, "See how they love one another;" but of the modern American sects it might be said, "See how they hate one another."[2] And the worst is, that even those who condemn this disunion, are compelled by circumstances, and by

[1] SCHAFF's "Deutscher Kirchenfreund für die Amerikanisch-deutschen Kirchen." Mercersburg, 1848, p. 141-47.
[2] "Mercersburg Review," v. 584.

the law of self-preservation, to identify themselves more or less with the denominational and sectarian spirit.

"All depends upon sect there," says a German observer, "and a preacher can only make way as a sectarian. The enlargement of one's own sect is the grand business to which every other must give way.[1] A man will pay 500 dollars a year for the maintenance of his sect, which consists of five members and a preacher."[2] A travelling preacher, who has been converted in the Methodist fashion, will preach to the congregations in his circuit, against other preachers, who have not been converted in the same fashion.[3] Even the peace-loving Quakers, who continue united in England, are in America split up into parties. It seems as if in this country, of the freest political movement, men found it indispensable to have their religious feelings compressed into the tightest possible sectarian stays—and as if they inhaled the spirit of religious dispute in the very air. Scarcely has a German congregation been formed among a body of new Protestant emigrants, than they begin to wrangle and quarrel among themselves.[4]

The conviction has forced itself even on Protestant clergymen of America, that "the land of freedom" is, in fact, the most intolerant country of the world—that it is the spirit of intolerance that has multiplied divisions like a plague of locusts.[5] The religious history of our country, says Colton, "is characterised by a constant boasting of religious freedom, and an untiring effort to crush it."

A solid scientific theology is impossible for America in its present state. Every theologian, or every one who might have a vocation for the cultivation of theology, belongs to some special sect, and finds himself more or less subject to the tyranny, or at least to the influence, of his denomination. His sect is a kind of make-shift hovel, hammered together, by narrow-minded men, out of fragments of doctrine, and it will afford him neither space, nor light, nor air for a theological

---

[1] BÜTTNER "Die Vereinigten Staaten," i. 247-346.

[2] BÜTTNER, i. 283.   [3] BÜTTNER, i. 341.   [4] BÜTTNER, i. 357.

[5] COLTON'S "Thoughts on the Religious State of the Country," pp. 204-5.

flight. Nevin, the only living American theologian of any importance, confesses that American theology, with all its pretentious and pious-sounding phrases, is, for the most part, mere school-boy pedantry compared with the German.[1] The only man, besides Nevin, who had in him the material and the vocation to make an eminent theologian, was William Ellery Channing, a preacher of Boston. But his profound aversion to the Calvinistic system, that "libel on his Heavenly Father," as he called it, and the destructive effects of which he saw everywhere around him, filled him (who had had no opportunity of becoming acquainted with a better theology) with a hatred to the theology of his own time, and made him a Unitarian.[2]

A work on the religious parties of America, which appeared in 1844 (and was considerably amplified in 1848), gives an outline of each of the sects, drawn up by one of themselves.[3] It appears from these, that almost all, however narrow may be the enclosure within which they have hedged themselves, however deplorably small their fraction of Christianity, still each declares that the Bible, the whole Bible, and nothing but the Bible, is the source and standard of its doctrine and institutions. Every one boasts of having kept conscientiously to the New Testament, and carefully endeavoured to puff away from its garment every particle of Church tradition. This Biblical purism, then, whose first axiom is the absolute clearness and transparency of the Scriptures, and that can quote chapter and verse for every article of its sectarian faith, has already produced in America more than fifty different sects! And since, almost every year, one or more new "Churches" arise, their partisans always know how to point precisely to this or that Bible text, which makes it impossible for conscientious Christians to join any one of the fifty or sixty already existing "Churches," and renders it

---

[1] "Mercersburg Review," ii. 165.

[2] See the expressions used in the 2nd vol. of "Memoirs of W. E. Channing," and particularly pp. 134-135. London, 1850.

[3] D. RUPP, "Original History of the Religious Denominations." Harrisburg, 1848, 2nd edition.

imperatively necessary to found a new one. Creeds, symbolic books, are either entirely rejected, since with the Bible they are superfluous, and they do not well agree with it, as the "Campbell Baptists" say; or they must, as the Congregationalists declare, be themselves measured by the Bible.[1] Several of the modern sects proclaim that they have been founded for the express purpose of re-establishing the original unity of the Church, an object which can only be attained by raising the Bible to be the sole standard. Each one of the sister sects had, indeed, proposed to keep closely to the Bible, but had not, it is said, remained true to its principles. The new one alone is the one that is to do so in earnest. As often as a new party branches off from the old, the separation takes place according to their assurance; because the old sect, notwithstanding its exclusive devotion to the Bible, has submitted to unbiblical "traditions," and so has afforded an opportunity for inaccurate interpretations.

We find, therefore, in so far, an agreement among the American sects, that each one starts with the same proposition as to the all-sufficiency of the words of the Bible, and the denial of any ecclesiastical authority and continuity. Each one has inscribed upon its banner the motto, "The open Bible, and the sovereignty of private judgment." The Bible—this is the universal theory—is perfectly clear to every human being endowed with common understanding; special studies and previous knowledge are not necessary; a person reads, and he may and must believe that the sense he finds is the only true one, and that he has perceived it by help of the Holy Ghost. This right of private judgment is declared to be the Palladium of the Gospel, the only alternative if we do not wish to submit to an infallible authority.[2] In reality, however, no single one of these sects permits the individual to make use of this right. Every sect has its own system, and compels the Bible text to express its views; every one of them rejects from its bosom—at least, according to theory—any member who should prefer his own judgment on a passage

---

[1] Rupp, p. 224, 281.
[2] See, for instance, "Cumberland Presbyterians."—Rupp, p. 512.

of the Bible, to the interpretation accepted by the community to which he belongs.

Several of the American sects maintain that they have separated themselves from the older denomination, to escape the "scourge of a human Confession of Faith." In fact, however, these sects are all prisons of the mind; every one has its own—mostly very meagre and narrow-minded—tradition and observances.

A sect is, by its nature, the instinctive enemy of every scientific theology. It is conscious of being short-lived, of having no connecting current with the great river-stream of the Church, which has been pouring down through centuries of time; and the sect is, therefore, filled with aversion to the entire ecclesiastical past. Thus, for instance, the Baptists of six principles say, "A true member of their community does not trouble himself as to whether its doctrines are found to have existed in the various ages of the Church: it is sufficient for him that Christ has announced them."[1] The chief sect of Baptists even takes a pride in not troubling itself about the ancient doctrines of the Church. With respect to ecclesiastical tradition, the sects are accustomed to keep to these principles: that a tradition is so much the more worthless as it is older and more generally diffused—and worth so much the more as it is younger, and most peculiar to their sect. The brief past of their own sectarian life, with its inventions and arrangements of yesterday, becomes thenceforward a chain that binds every one under penalty of expulsion.

Another feature common to the more modern sects is, rejection of infant baptism. Some, like the Baptists of the Seventh Day, have discovered that the New Testament contains nothing about a transference of the Sabbath to. the Sunday, and, therefore, regard the observance of the Saturday as a Sabbath as absolutely necessary.[2] They and others see, also, in "the foot-washing," a sacrament appointed by Christ. Further, the sacraments are, with almost all American sects, not vehicles or operative means of grace, and pledges of what God bestows on us; but they are

[1] Rupp, p. 88.   [2] Rupp, p. 121.

lowered into symbols of what passes in man, or they are
mere signs, intended to remind men of a certain event, or to
awaken in them a certain feeling. Germanism (that is
German theology) and Popery are in general the two powers
especially dreaded, and alike hated, by the American sects.[1]

About twelve sects profess to be established, not merely
on the basis of the Bible, but also on that of the Westminster
Confession—so that this Confession, although the most complete and theologically definite among the Calvinistic creeds
—one, too, that far excels, for instance, the Augsburg Confession, in point of clearness and plain speaking, has nevertheless not been able to prevent a number of subdivisions taking
place, even within the narrow circle of American Calvinism.

In one article there is still very general unanimity. "Justification by Faith alone" has been inscribed on the banner
of all the "Evangelical" sects. Thus, the Campbellites, for
instance, declare that the one great condition of admission
to their community is a "perfect trust in the merits of
Christ alone for justification." Their sect has been established on the two fundamental doctrines of the Reformation
—rejection of all tradition, and a reliance on faith alone.[2]
With this solifidianism, by which the righteousness of Christ
is placed quite externally to the account of believers, another
proposition is connected, extremely important to sectarian life,
and on which rests the whole theory of "Revivals." The
man who is justified by mere faith, and the imputation of
the righteousness of Christ, is conscious of this fact with
infallible certainty. He has an "experience" of his conversion, or of being taken into a state of grace, and can point
out the precise moment of his passage from death to life.
The Americans have, therefore, arranged their "conversions"
in a very business-like manner. Several preachers and laymen
enter into an association, and begin to operate upon an
assembly of persons, who desire to be converted. By long-
continued exciting preaching, by stormy addresses to individuals, by hymns with lively rattling airs, by threats, with
dreadful descriptions of the torments of hell, by entreaties,

[1] "Mercersburg Review," i. 517.   [2] Rupp, p. 225.

supplications, and passionate apostrophes, men and women are so agitated and wrought upon that they are eventually broken down. The mental and bodily exhaustion to which men, and especially women, are reduced by such means, produces a passive state, in which they feel everything they are desired to feel. Attacks of bodily illness, involuntary exclamations, pass for pledges of grace, and certain signs of victory over "the old man." The state of complete relaxation and weakness which naturally follows these stormy emotions and spasmodic convulsions is considered as "peace of mind from assurance of salvation." When any one has been so far worked upon as to be induced to seat himself on the "penitential bench," the matter is decided; he has yielded himself up to grace, and immediately after that he must, according to the prescribed rule, feel himself completely and wonderfully refreshed and relieved; and he is then entered as a convert, and as a member of the society in the lists of the sect. The "penitential bench" is the sacrament at the revivals—the infallible means of new birth. As the whole machinery is really a strictly logical application of the old Protestant doctrine of justification, all the "evangelical" communities —even the German Lutherans and Calvinists—have introduced "Revivals;" and they are regarded in America as the most important and beneficial religious discovery of modern times. Besides the town revivals, there are also the Campmeetings, specially set on foot, by the Methodists, as the great lever of American religion. Even the sects of a Socinian character, which deny the Trinity and the Godhead of Jesus Christ—such as the Campbellites—make use of this plan of revivals with the greatest success,[1] and have, by means of

[1] FLAVEL S. MINES, "A Presbyterian Clergyman looking for the Church." New York, 1855, p. 81.—The Rev. J. Marsden, Methodist missionary, who had attended several of the American camp meetings, and who expresses his strong approval of them, gives the following evidence as to the results produced by "a powerful spirit of prayer and exhortation":—"I have not unfrequently seen three or four persons lying on the ground, crying for mercy, or motionless, without any apparent signs of life, except pulsation."—MARSDEN's "Narrative of a Mission to Nova Scotia, New Brunswick," quoted in EVANS's "Sketch of the Denominations of the Christian World." London, 1827, pp. 211, 212.

them, considerably increased their numbers during the last thirty years — though it is true that the congregations speedily got together by revivals are apt to melt away again just as rapidly as they were collected; and troops of those who have been so regenerated, are liable, in a very short time, to forget all about their regeneration.

Two circumstances have contributed powerfully to the importance of "Revivals" in America: first, the character of the Americans themselves, which, under the influence of the climate of the country, and the monotony of lives entirely devoted to business and money-getting, requires, from time to time, some excitement, and seeks it—if not in gaming or drink—in religion;[1] secondly, the meagre, cold, Puritanical service, which, abolishing all that is liturgical or symbolical, consists merely in preaching, and long prayers, spoken by the minister, and affords so much the more ready entrance and favourable reception for a theatrical method of conversion, producing literally the most striking effects, and overpowering the strongest nerves.

If we observe the present state of the chief religious parties of America, we shall find that, next to the Methodists, the *Baptists*, the youngest of the great communities,[2] now subdivided into seven sects, are the most numerous of all the Protestant denominations of America. Only the Methodists can dispute with them this precedence. From the year 1792 to 1852, their churches had risen from 1000 to 9584; and in 1856, they numbered 1,322,469 communicating members. They have no representation, no organization, and no confessions. According to their theory, all church government and church offices are an evil. Every congregation is a complete independent body. The particular Baptist sects are separated from each other by very strong differences of doctrine. The American Baptist, or Socinian Campbellite, has, with the exception of his practice in baptism, little in common with a Calvinist Baptist.

[1] OTTO, "Nordwestliche Bilder." Schwerin, 1854, p. 22.
[2] The first Baptist congregation was formed in New York in 1762. See GORRIE's "Churches and Sects of the United States." New York, 1850, p. 134.

The fact that the Baptists form so numerous—indeed the most numerous—of all religious parties of North America, deserves much attention. They would be still more numerous, if it were not that the rites of Baptism and the Lord's Supper, in their sacramental signification, are regarded by the whole Calvinistically-disposed world as such subordinate matters, that the question as to their original form appears to many a matter of such indifference that no one needs trouble himself much about it. The Baptists are, in fact, from the Protestant point of view, unassailable, since they have the Bible text in favour of the practice of baptism by "immersion;" whilst the authority of the Church and her testimony will be recognised neither by the one party nor the other.[1]

More important, in a spiritual point of view, is the influence of the *Presbyterians*, who, with the Congregationalists, are the descendants and heirs of the old Puritans, "the Pilgrim Fathers," the founders of New England. They are the originators and curators of American theology, as far as it can be said to exist. They carried the most genuine Calvinism with them from their English home, and for a long time clung firmly to a system that had cost them so many sacrifices. Their preachers were inexhaustible in their way of working out their theory of Predestination, and in descriptions of the damnation to which God had pre-ordained the majority of little children. Fatalism and Antinomianism bore their fruits in the moral and intellectual decline of their congregations. Edwards endeavoured to prop up Calvinism by means of Locke's philosophy; but Dwight, Lyman, Beecher, and Barnes have, in modern times, broken down the sway of the Calvinistic doctrine and the Westminster Confession. Here-

---

[1] Not even a Baptist translation of the Bible can therefore be used by the other parties. An English missionary of the Congregationalists writes from Calcutta: "The Baptists take the first place in translations into the Bengalee. We here mostly make use of the translation of Yates (Baptist), but since the Baptist Society, whose property the translation is, insist on translating βαπτίζειν only by 'to immerse,' 'to dip under,' all friends of Infant Baptism, as well as the Calcutta Bible Society, feel the want of a new translation."—REUTER's "Repertorium," vol. liii., p. 70. This is saying, in fact, "We must translate the Bible falsely, in order that the heathens, to be converted, may not discover our weak points."

upon there followed, in 1838, a complete division. Barnes, and 500 preachers, with about 60,000 laymen, were ejected by the General Assembly on account of heterodoxy; and they formed immediately the Presbyterian Church of the "New School."[1]

The genuine Puritans or *Congregationalists*, who are found principally in New England, have undergone much alteration in America. The old organic connexion, by which the individual congregations were subordinate to a superior assembly —a Convocation or Association—has been dissolved. Their Church has, in consequence of Unitarian and Universalist movements, become more democratic. There is no common symbol any more, but each congregation has its own. The clergyman is merely the dependent servant of the congregation, called and elected by them.[2] The Presbyterians have followed an opposite course of development. With them the subordination of the congregation to the elders, Presbyteries, and Synods has been confirmed and increased—and the result is that the two religious communities, which had been previously approaching at many points, are now mutually repugnant to one another.

The whole bearing of the Puritanical sects, with their "Revivals," has had the effect of leading to numerous secessions among the clergy, and especially among those of the Presbyterian parties, who are more theologically instructed than the Baptists and Methodists, the latter being generally very ignorant persons. Within a few years—up to 1855—300 Presbyterian clergymen have gone over to the Episcopalian Church, which rejects Revivals, resists Calvinism, and allows to individuals the liberty at least to inculcate notions respecting justification and grace in an anti-Calvinistic sense.[3]

One of these clergymen, Colton, formerly the panegyrist of Revivals,[4] in which he saw "a new Dispensation, destined to be diffused over the whole world," has gradually, in

[1] See "History of the Division of the Presbyterian Churches, by a Committee of the Synod," &c. New York, 1855.

[2] KRAUSE's "Kirch.-Zeitung," 1856, p. 129.

[3] MINES, "Looking for the Church." p. 11.

[4] In his Essay, "History and Character of American Revivals." London, 1832.

consequence of the experience he has had of them, been brought to the decided rejection of the whole institution. "The mind," he says, "is enslaved by them, a false conscience is created and encouraged, and the whole intellectual and moral character of the people destroyed."[1]

There is still more clear and emphatic evidence concerning the root of all this evil. What Protestant theologians of former times, Lutherans as well as the Reformed, report concerning the destructive consequences of the Justification doctrine, as it was moulded by the Reformation, is now confirmed in America, where the doctrine is still in high repute, and proclaimed from innumerable pulpits. The writings of American theologians contain remarkable confessions concerning it. The preacher Flavel S. Mines says that—"After a long and careful examination of the matter, it is his conviction that the doctrine of Justification by Faith, as it is preached, separate from sanctity of life, and consisting merely in a feeling, a reflective act of the soul (the certainty of being in a state of grace), is the most soul-destroying heresy of the age.[2] Nevin, the most thorough and profound of all living American theologians, maintains also that the doctrine leads, in America, to fearful delusions, and does indescribable mischief.[3]

The general depreciation of the Sacraments, and the Calvinistic dogma of "Election," have had the effect of inducing the Presbyterians and Congregationalists very frequently to leave their children unbaptized. The parents consider it unnecessary to get them baptized—and the preachers on their side will frequently, on account of the religious position of the parents, not admit the children to baptism; and since, also, the Baptists of all denominations reject Infant Baptism,

---

[1] COLTON's "Thoughts on the Religious State of the Country." New York, 1836, p. 178.

[2] "Looking for the Church," p. 492.

[3] "Mercersburg Review," iv. 615. Some years later (1858, "Mercersburg Review," x. 395) the same theologian remarks: "That in its customary Puritanical acceptation, this doctrine of Justification by Faith has been turned into a fiction which contradicts the Apostolic teaching, and gives to the Christian religion a form altogether different."

many thousands grow up, and many thousands of Presbyterians and Baptists—die unbaptized.[1]

In the history of Sects which are not sunk into an inert state of vegetation, it is common to find them proceeding by fits and starts from one extreme to the other; and it happens inevitably that the emanations of mere caprice, groping in the dark—or of individual narrow-mindedness—have to serve as substitutes for the necessary results of organic institutions. Thus it has happened that the two main branches of the American Puritans — the Presbyterians and Congregationalists—being dissatisfied with their Westminster Confession, have introduced into their various congregations or Synods a number of whimsical or extravagant Confessions of Faith—so that, according to the statement of the preacher, Colton, some hundreds of these formulæ may be found among the Presbyterians, and you can hardly go from one town to another without coming upon a new creed, notwithstanding the similarity of the sect.[2] Colton, who filled the most influential offices in the Presbyterian Church, relates that he himself has organized above fifteen Churches, and introduced into each of them a Confession of Faith drawn up by himself, but which had to be modified every time, according to the degree of his knowledge and the momentary character of his views.

Thus in the Puritan communities there prevails the most extreme laxity of opinion, combined with isolated, and mostly fruitless, attempts to establish an obligatory orthodoxy. To the old disputes and differences of the Puritans, new ones have now been added. These are Hopkinsonians, and followers of the " New Light," " Mode-

---

[1] "Mercersburg Review," vol. viii. 34-35 ; vol. x., p. 41. The same periodical maintains (vol. vii., 202) that at present baptism is denied to the children of one half of the professed Christians of America, and thought slightingly of by the great majority. FLAVEL S. MINES (p. 60) calculates, in the Presbyterian publication, the " Princeton Review," that in the last twenty years two thirds of the children of this denomination, namely 413,298, remained unbaptized.

[2] "Thoughts on the Religious State of the Country." New York, 1836, p. 63.

rate" and "Strict" Calvinists, "Destructionists and Re-
storationists," deniers of original sin, like Taylor and
Park; "Pre-existents," like Edward Beecher, who place
the Fall of Man in a former state of existence. The "rejection of original sin" has even become a prevailing
theory in New England, that is, in the six North-Eastern
States, which are the oldest of the Union, and the original
home of American Puritanism.[1]

In consequence of a process of doctrinal decomposition,
there arose in America, towards the end of the last century,
as there had previously arisen in England, without any
foreign influence, congregations of *Unitarians.* It was the
rude and mechanical Calvinistic conception of the Atone-
ment theory, the rending asunder of the Trinity, implied by
that conception, and the opposing of the Divine Persons,
Who, according to that same conception, militated against
one another, like parties in a law-suit; it was this distortion
and disfigurement of the Central Doctrine of Christianity
that, by a natural reaction, made Unitarians of the Puritan
theologians and preachers. In the State of Massachusetts,
and in Boston especially, those pulpits from which had
preached the oracles of American Calvinism, are now occupied by clergymen who deny the Trinity, and reject the
Divine Nature of the Son.

In the meantime, Unitarianism in America has already
entered its stage of decay. The preachers of the sect have
renounced Christianity and adopted Pantheistic views, as
the most gifted among them—Theodore Parker—did in the
year 1859—and partly they have gone over to the Episcopal
Church.[2] Gorrie reckons that in the year 1850 there were
244 Unitarian preachers, and about 30,000 members.[3]

Very close to the Unitarians stand the *Universalists,* who
in 1840 had only 83 preachers, but, in 1855, 700 preachers,
with about 1,100 congregations. Their doctrine of the
ultimate salvation of all men has led many of them to a

---

[1] "Mercersburg Review," viii. 219.
[2] MESSNER'S "Kirch.-Zeitung," 1860, p. 96.
[3] "Churches and Sects," p. 132.

Rationalistic rejection of all Christian mysteries. This sect also, however, is already going to decay.

It is in the religious world as in the world of vegetation. Those plants which most readily propagate themselves— spread most rapidly and shoot up most luxuriantly—are neither the healthiest nor precisely those that are most welcome to the gardener. In America it is especially the Methodists and Baptists who have spread most easily, and can boast of the most prodigious progress. This they owe to the skill with which they have made religion palpable and palatable, so that everyone can appropriate it easily, and get on well with it—and also that the doctrine and practice can be mastered in the shortest possible time, and then distributed from the pulpit.

But it is also to their zeal and unwearied activity that these two great communities owe their success. Among all sects the *Methodists* have in America developed the most comprehensive activity, and within ninety years have spread to an extent of which there are not many examples in history. They have indeed become divided amongst themselves. The most distinguished party is the Episcopal Methodist Church; but even in this the slavery question has produced a breach—namely, between the Northern and Southern Methodists—and has led to a long law-suit concerning the partition of Church property. The term "Episcopal" is not to be taken literally; but Wesley did for America what he could not do in England: he ordained an Anglican clergyman—Thomas Coke—to be a Superintendent; and since then his followers have had superintendents, who allow themselves to be called "Bishops." The laity are excluded from all share in the government of the society—the Conference rules alone; the congregations are not allowed to choose their preachers—who are appointed for them, and that only for a few years.

The greater part of the Methodist preachers are utterly destitute of scientific culture; and real Biblical knowledge is not to be thought of amongst them.[1] They are amply pro-

[1] See RAUSCHENBUSCH's " Die Nacht des Westens."—Barmen, 1847, p. 22.

vided for if they have a good number of texts at command.
Many have been previously mechanics, and as they happened
to show some fluency of speech, were first, after a short
training, made "exhorters," and then appointed to be
preachers. After this, frequent class and prayer meetings
leave them no time for Bible studies. The end they aim at
is not the tranquil instruction and harmonious education of
men to a Christian life—violent excitement and agitation
are the means best suited to attain the purpose which the
sect seeks for and is desirous to attain.[1] In their divine
services, the Methodists, as their preacher Rauschenbusch
reports,[2] frequently make so much noise, partly during the
sermon, but still more during the prayers, since they not
unfrequently all pray aloud together, one outscreaming the
other, that it is not possible to hear the sermon or prayer
uttered from the pulpit.

The constant changes of the preachers—the travelling
preachers—the hymns sung to the wildest popular tunes—
the mutual communication of "heart experiences," so destructive to humility and truthfulness—the alternation of
religious emotions, dependent on purely physical states and
corporeal affections—the artificial groaning produced by a
half-sensuous, half-moral epidemic—this entire apparatus of
means invented by the Methodists, and copied by other
sects, even by Germans, is supposed to produce in a few
hours results for which a year's sedulous religious exercises
and self-instruction would otherwise be required. All this
evokes a sort of intoxication of mind, that for the moment
appears to satisfy it, but afterwards leaves it so much the
more void and famished; and so all such violent excitement and enthusiasm is not unfrequently followed by the
dreariest indifference. Many of those "converted" fall off

---

[1] Christian knowledge is to the Methodists mostly a very subordinate
matter—superfluous, if not dangerous. The religious instruction of the
young is regulated—and, indeed, why should it not be so, since it is
what takes place on "the bench of sorrow" that the salvation of the
soul depends? A vague, confused emotion is the pledge of election!—
HENGSTENBERG, "Kirch.-Zeitung," 1847, p. 328.

[2] "Die Nacht des Westens," p. 43.

R

again very soon, and avoid a religion which has occasioned them such bitter delusions.   A false confidence in this method, nevertheless, goes so far, that among Methodists the whole religious education of children is often neglected, in the expectation that a " Revival," a " Camp-meeting," and a few hours probation on the stool of repentance, will, all at once, make amends for the neglect of years.[1]

The theology of America is expressed by the form and character of the churches, the number of which has been increased enormously by the growth of the population and the rivalship of the various sects.   The European standard must not be applied to these buildings.   The feeling of religious veneration for a consecrated spot does not seem to exist; and many of the churches bear a much stronger resemblance to a theatre than to a Gothic Cathedral.   As a matter of course, they have no altars, for an altar would be an abomination in the eyes of a Protestant American; he likes a building in which a pompous theatrical rostrum for the spiritual " orator" occupies the place of the altar, and in which every possible provision is made for the comfort of the audience.   Many of the city churches look like elegant reception-rooms of fashionable ladies.[2]

The *Episcopal Church* is here, as well as in England, the Church of " good society," and is perhaps so much the more agreeable to its highly respectable members, that they have the church all to themselves, and need not fear the intrusion of the poor and lowly.   Even the educated German, if he cares about a Church at all, usually keeps to this,[3] and does not trouble himself about either the Lutheran or the Calvinist sects; whilst, on the contrary, the English immigrants, though they have been at home members of the State Church, generally in America join one of the Puritan or Methodist sects.[4]   The American Episcopal Church, departing from the practice of the Mother Establishment, has introduced a Lay Repre-

---

[1] Schaff, " America," p. 129.

[2] See the description in " Mercersburg Review," iv. 214.

[3] Hengstenberg, " Kirch.-Zeitung," 1847, p. 340.

[4] Caswall, " The Western World Revisited."   Oxford, 1854, p. 296.

sentation. But the deep chasm between the Evangelicals and the Arminian High Church people, which here as well as in the mother country divides the Bishops into two parties with very dissimilar views, renders every vigorous co-operation in this Church impossible. In any other denomination such a contrast would have led to open separation and the formation of a new community; and whenever either the one or the other comes to be in earnest in its views it must end in a like result.

In England many people look with longing and envy towards the daughter of the Anglican State Church, whose lot it is to be free from the oppressive yoke of Government supremacy; and Bishop Wilberforce wrote its history in this sense a few years since: "the mother was to rejoice in the consciousness of having brought forth a daughter happier than herself." One of the American bishops, however, remarks that "the laity have, in all church affairs (according to the laws there), an overpowering influence, which is still further increased by the dependence of the clergy on the voluntary contributions of the laity."[1] And this lay yoke, as he says, "fell the more severely on the Church, as the laymen are altogether irresponsible in the exercise of their ecclesiastical functions, and can be judged by no tribunal, even on account of heresy and schism."

By the side of, and after the Anglo-Saxon race, the Germans form the most important nationality in North America, and the numerous Protestants of this nation have managed their church affairs quite according to their own pleasure. Before all others, the German *Lutherans* in America have, for a long time, awakened great attention and sympathy. There—namely, where Lutheranism, completely free from political tutorship and dominion, has been fully able to develop itself—it was hoped its church-constructive power

[1] SILLIMAN IVES, "The Trials of a Mind;" London, 1854, p. 143. The author has become a Catholic. PUSEY also says, in "The Councils of the Church" (London, 1858, p. 24), "The introduction of lay representatives into the American Church was an unfortunate example, set in bad times.

would have shown itself in the production of a united Free German Church. But this hope has proved to be utterly vain. The great majority of the Lutherans have renounced both the language and the Lutheran doctrine, and become partly Zwinglian, partly Methodistic, and have thrown aside the old confession of faith. American Lutheranism is, in fact, in one word, autochthonic, and a plant very different from the German religious form of that name. Even the preachers and congregations that have desired to retain the Lutheranism they brought from Germany have not been able to effect any union. It is precisely among these that the clergy are exposed to the most painfully vigilant watching on the part of the members of the congregation who desire to govern them. They are tutored, worried, hemmed in, and oppressed by all parties, and at the same time miserably paid.[1] No Church authority has ever been organized, and the congregations are almost all independent. "Every Church," says our German informant, "is cleft by hostile divisions; none are in a healthy state — none stable, candid, faithful, and impartial, in their tendency. The individual has to seek his path painfully through a thorny field—there is no one to show him the way." How every town where German Protestants amount but to a few hundreds is immediately possessed by the demon of Church discord, and cannot in any wise attain to the formation of a united congregation, has been strikingly described by the Preacher Büttner.[2] Many of these German congregations are only "disorderly rationalist communities," who engage a preacher as they would a servant, and exclude him from the council of the Church."[3]

The *German Reformed* community is regarded by the true American Calvinist as an heretical sect; "it is almost Arminian," they say; "and, since Nevin and his companions have arisen within its bosom, also Romanizing."[4]

[1] HENGSTENBERG's "Kirch.-Ztg.," 1847, p. 300. See also REUTER's "Repertoire," vol. lxxiv. p. 93.

[2] "Die Vereinigten Staaten von Nordamerika;" Hamburg, 1844, and "Briefe aus und über Nordamerika." Dresden, 1845.

[3] SCHAFF, p. 99.

[4] Thus the Presbyterian BLAKEY, in his "Philosophy of Sectarianism;"

Through the whole extent of German Protestantism the slavish dependence of the preachers on the congregations is felt as one of the worst results of the prevailing Church system. The feeling of this dependence has been, indeed, from the beginning, stronger in the mind of the preachers than in that of his auditory. The consciousness weighs upon him that he has no high mission, no office sustained and guaranteed by an ancient and sublime institution. He is but a delegate, who only dares to proclaim to his hearers that which they had previously determined should be preached.

Schaff, in his report to the Berlin Alliance Assembly, in which the most rose-coloured representation possible of the state of circumstances in America was expected, animadverted on the fact of the unbecoming dependence of the clergy upon their congregations. "The Americans," he says,[1] "expect a clergyman to do his duty, and, without fear of man, or anxiety to please, lay before them the whole counsel of godliness, and point as sharply and specially to human depravity, and to the consolatory promises that have been made to it "—that is to say, that, in America, as elsewhere, wherever the doctrines of the Reformation are still in authority, the congregation like their preachers to relieve them of moral responsibility, by preaching the three connected doctrines of absolute Divine Election, of total depravity and complete moral impotency, and of Free Grace by mere Imputation. To do this, there is not the slightest occasion for the minister to be fearless; on the contrary, he would show much more freedom from the fear of man if he preached the opposite old Church doctrine.

The fact, to which every stranger bears witness, that there are in no civilized country so few people having opinions of their own, and the courage to express those opinions, as in America, must be extremely unfavourable to the mental

London, 1854, p. 55. The book is instructive, for the knowledge of American Sectarianism it displays; but still more attractive, from the light that the author lets fall on his own community, the Presbyterian Church, than from what he says as regards others.

[1] " Amerika."   Berlin, 1854, p. 63.

freedom of their preachers. A well-informed and sharp-sighted observer has remarked, lately, " that, in everything not political, a tyrannically-ruling majority works upon all minds, and levels and crushes down all varieties, till they all resemble one another, as do the rounded pebbles in a brook."[1] It is known how this tyranny of public opinion has operated in the question of race; the whole Protestant clergy have yielded to the prevalent aversion of every community of whites to the coloured population; and in New Orleans, for example, the Catholic Churches are the only places in which white and coloured people pray by the side of one another.[2]

All Protestant theologians, whose writings I have seen, complain of the want of independence in the preachers, of their general deficiency in moral courage, and the oppressive yoke that the congregations have fastened upon them. Channing, Colton, Mines, often recur to the subject.[3] They describe the preachers as the victims of a tyranny exercised frequently by the low and ignorant, and that to an extent such as has never hitherto been known. As a rule, the confidence and presumption with which the representatives of the congregation bear themselves towards their preachers, stand in an inverse ratio to their amount of mental culture.[4] Every idea that passes beyond their narrow sphere of theological vision renders the orthodoxy of their preacher doubtful to them. They are liberal with their exhortations and remonstrances, which they bestow upon him *ex officio*. A few years ago there was, in New England, a regular Preacher Visitation Society, of self-appointed laymen, who travelled from place to place, made inquiries concerning clergymen, and bestowed counsel, censure, or warning as they thought fit. It is quite consistent with this state of things that the congregations often only engage their preachers for a time,

[1] "Skizzen aus Nordamerika."—" Allg.-Ztg.," June, 1861, p. 2646.

[2] "Christian Remembrancer," 1860, ii. 79.

[3] For example, CHANNING's " Works," v. 317 ; COLTON, 138; MINES, 291.

[4] See the vivid description in HENGSTENBERG's " Kirch.-Ztg.," xx. 132.

and with the reserve of a certain notice in case of dismissal.[1] It is not surprising, therefore, that clergymen are met with every day, who have renounced voluntarily, or on compulsion, the office of preacher, and now carry on some secular occupation.

The orthodox Churches, says the reformed preacher, Büttner (he includes all Calvinist, Lutheran, and German Reformed Denominations under this head), however hostile they may be to one another, as soon as ever the word " Roman Catholic " is pronounced, forget their mutual differences and hostilities, and stand against the Roman Catholics like a wall. Should a religious war ever break out in the United States, which is not improbable, for there is combustible material enough in readiness, the question will not be asked, " Are you a Presbyterian, or a Methodist, or a Baptist —a Lutheran, a Calvinist, or a Congregationalist—but, simply, Are you a Protestant or a Catholic ?"[2]

Schaff has described how the polemical contest is carried on, by the whole Protestant press of America,[3] against the Catholic Church: it is, he says, by fabricated lies, by gross calumnies, by the ignoring or falsification of history. This cannot excite surprise, if we consider the breadth and depth of the chasm that divides all these sects, but especially the puritanical, from the Church, and if we are able to realise the contrast of their position. " Whilst," writes a German Protestant, from America, " all the Protestant denominations are weakened by perpetual new divisions, and mostly at bitter enmity with one another, the Catholic Church, as one man—one organism, animated by one soul, pursuing, with firm, clear consciousness, one object—advances without noise, without even, until lately, uttering one word of defence against accusations and hostile attacks, but persevering with iron consistency, and from year to year gaining new ground."[4]

---

[1] " Atlantische Studien," ii. 130.
[2] " Kirchliche Viertel-Jahresschrift."   Berlin, 1845, i. 130.
[3] " Kirchenfreund," Sept. 1852.
[4] HENGSTENBERG'S " Kirch.-Zeitung," 1847, 341.

The whole existing condition of North America, in a religious point of view, is calculated to awaken great anxiety among all thinking men in the country. "The great majority of the rising generation is without any positive religion," said the before-mentioned preacher, Edson; "all the instruction they receive consists in, perhaps, some lessons of natural religion; and I greatly fear that we are advancing by certain, and by no means slow steps, in the direction of complete absence of religion and moral ruin."[1] In the whole daily press there prevails worthless radicalism, and, for some time past, unveiled irreligion.[2] The total want of a sentiment of veneration, is, as the American theologians mournfully confess, a predominant feature of the national character.[3] The entire spirit in which the religious press is carried on is a disgrace to the cause of Christianity.[4] "The number of professing Christians," says a Baptist preacher, "is diminishing in all our sects." The Churches are stationary from want of preachers, and the conduct of professing Christians is generally such that it would be almost an affront to a man of honour to suppose him willing to be converted, and to become as "one of them." If the present decline continues, in the course of twenty or thirty years "the candlestick" will be removed from its place. The Church makes no proselytes, and has no influence upon the masses.[5]

In an American periodical, "The Evangelist," it was lately maintained that, even in the Free States of the Union, the present time was more favourable to Catholicity than had been any period for centuries past; but this certainly must not be understood with respect to the prevailing state

[1] TREMENHEERE, p. 53.

[2] See the article, "Signs of the Times," in the "Mercersburg Review," vii. 290.

[3] COLTON, "Genius and Mission of the Protestant Episcopal Church." London, 1853, p. 260.

[4] "Mercersburg Review," vii. 293. It is scarcely possible to say anything worse of the character of the religious press of America than what we find in this periodical.

[5] See the work of the American HECKER, "Aspirations of Nature." New York, 1857.

of mind in North America, which is decidedly hostile to the Catholic religion.[1] It is natural, however, that many persons should feel oppressed and imprisoned within the narrow boundaries of sectarianism; that they should be dissatisfied with the poor and meagre remnants of Christian faith there offered to them, and sigh for a harmonious and inwardly connected system of Christian faith and life; that, before all things, they should desire to be relieved from the torment of a dreary subjectivity, and an unauthorised conventional interpretation of the Bible. To what results this tendency will lead in the future, time must determine.

[1] KRAUSE's "Kirch.-Zeitung," 1858, p. 551.

THE LUTHERAN CHURCH IN SCANDINAVIAN COUNTRIES.

THE Wittenberg doctrine was, on the whole, introduced into the North by violence; by the will of monarchs, with the assistance of nobles, longing to gain possession of Church property; and—against the wishes of the people. The people were, in fact, systematically cheated out of their religion, as in Sweden; and partly they were kept in profound ignorance —so much so that in Denmark, at the end of the sixteenth century, not one in twenty knew how to read. In Norway, Christian III. had degraded the people beneath a twofold yoke—that of the Danish nobles, and of the new Danish religion; whilst, for the real religious culture of the people, nothing whatever was effected. This state of things lasted till the eighteenth century. Catechetical instruction was not given; the sermons were unintelligible to the multitude, who were unprepared for them; "and there reigned in the land an almost heathen blindness."[1] In a petition presented by the Norwegian bishops, in the year 1714, to King Frederick IV., they felt compelled to make the avowal: "If some few children of God are excepted, there

[1] Thus Bishop PONTOPPIDAN describes the total neglect and increasing barbarism of the people down to the year 1714, in his "Pastoral Letter," translated into German by Schönfeldt. Rostock, 1756, pp. 129-30.

is no other difference between us and our heathen ancestors than that we bear the name of Christians."[1]

In Denmark, by means of the Reformation, the king had become, as chief bishop, the complete master of the Church. In the royal law of 1665, it is declared boldly, without the least circumvention, or mitigation of the fact, "that the king, as supreme judge and ruler upon earth, possesses unlimited power over the Church and religion, as well as over the State."[2] One only condition was made with him by the patent of 1648—he was not to tolerate the exercise of any other religion than the Lutheran. The kings governed the Church through their chancellors, and subsequently by the College of Chancery, which, with its judicial business, the care of the poor, and other functions, had also to administer the affairs of the Church. As to the nine or ten bishops of the country—who had nothing but the same name in common with bishops of the Catholic Church—they, with the Lutherans, of course, must abandon every idea of episcopal succession and transmitted authority, and were nothing more than government officers of the royal chief bishop. The Danish history, since the Reformation, contains no mention of any attempt or effort at ecclesiastical independence, or of any movement indicating life in the Church. All remained dumb and subservient, and the rulers, in thankful acknowledgment of that pliant subjection which they owed to the Lutheran spirit, carefully suppressed the slightest departure from the Lutheran dogma, and the doctrinal type of the theological faculty of Wittenberg. In the only university of the country, that of Copenhagen, there was "scarcely more than a scanty training establishment for the Church service,"[3] and it took care to provide a theology acceptable to the Court; whilst the disputes and divisions occasioned by Pietism were decided and put down by Royal Rescripts and Cabinet commands.[4]

---

[1] HENGSTENBERG's " Kirchen-Zeitung," 1843, p. 536.

[2] ENGELSTOFT, in "Herzog's Encyclopedia," iii. 610.

[3] See a detailed description in BRUN's and HÖFFNER's "Neues Repertorium," v. 101.

[4] The measureless ignorance of the theologians educated at Copenhagen,

By the new Fundamental Law of 1849, which has given an overwhelming democratic character to the Danish Government, the Lutheran Church is called "the Danish National Church," and the religious character of the Government is renounced, since full freedom of doctrine and worship is granted; and indeed liberty had been carried to such an extent lately as to do away with the obligation to baptism. The old dependence of the Church on the State has, however, remained. The King, the only man in all Denmark who is obliged to be a Lutheran, is still Supreme Bishop; it is not, however, the King personally, but the constitutional Minister of Divine Worship who rules the Church; and how much stability is afforded by this mode of government may be known from the fact that Denmark has had since 1848 five and forty such ministers! Of a regulated constitution of the Danish Church there can be no question; at times it finds itself, as Bishop Martensen observes, "in a floating medium state that can scarcely be called any form or order at all."[1] Its constitution is for the present only a "subject of consideration." Three different views are at present put forward. Some wish for an ecclesiastico-political position for the bishops, after the fashion of the English Church. The supremacy of the Ministers and of the Diet over spiritual affairs would then remain. Others wish for a Church representation by clergy and laity in synods, on the basis of universal suffrage. All thoughtful persons, however, are alarmed at the idea of universal suffrage in church affairs. The majority are of opinion that the Church should get on as well as it can for the present in its provisional state, without a constitution, since affairs are at "the moment too unsettled, and people's views not sufficiently clear."[2] It must be a bad case if the existing state is preferred to any attempt to form

to which must be added their moral stagnation, corresponded but too well with the dreadfully slavish condition of the rural population, and the petty pedantry and stupidity of the cities." Thus speaks the Danish reporter.—" Repert.," p. 103.

[1] The "Verfassungsfrage der Dänischen Volkskirche." Kiel, 1852, p. 7.

[2] " Deutsche Zeitschrift für Christl. Wiss.," 1859, p. 88.

a constitution—a state in which the Church is dependent on a Diet, whose members not only do not belong to the Lutheran community, but in general are not even professed Christians. That a change in the position of the Church is felt more and more as a necessity, has been maintained by the preacher Kalkar von Gladsaxe, of Copenhagen, in the Berlin Alliance Assembly.[1] "Christ," he adds, in an apologetic tone, "is not so openly rejected as in other places, but there is very little spiritual life in Denmark."

Under the influence of Rationalism, which made its way hither from Germany since the end of the last century, not only the people of the higher and middle classes but even the clergy in masses, became unbelievers. The candidates for the pastoral office made some hypocritical pretences to orthodoxy, but in the sermon preached immediately on ordination, and under the eyes of their bishops, they showed themselves decided Naturalists.[2] According to Danish accounts, the great majority of the clergy have fallen as completely into the infidel new theological views as their Lutheran brethren, the clergy of Germany; they have only hovered between mere frivolous unbelief, and Rationalism that assumes somewhat more of a scientific character.

At present, and for a considerable time past, the Danish clergy have been divided into two great parties—the Rationalist unbelieving, whose teacher and leader was Professor Clausen, and the followers of Grundtvig. The persevering struggle of this man (Grundtvig) against Rationalism, has led him to a theory, that the German Lutherans, on their side, designate as "in its inmost core anti-reforming and anti-Lutheran!"[3] Whilst Protestantism in America wholly rejects the Apostles' Creed, or casts it aside as valueless, Grundtvig, regarding it as a clear and firm confession of faith, and a manifest witness of the faith of the primitive Church, desires, in the same way as Lessing and Delbrück, to place it above the Bible, disfigured as that is by the caprice of private subjective interpretation. He

---

[1] " Verhandlungen," &c., p. 534.   [2] Brun's " Repert.," v. 105.
[3] Rudelbach, in " Die Zeitschrift für Luth. Theol.," 1857, p. 7.

and his party have, however, become more and more estranged
from Lutheranism, and urge the complete abolition of State
Supremacy and parochial connexion, and desire that every
one should be at liberty to join whatever preacher, this or
that, no matter which, but the one that he finds best suits
him.   The main point is, however, that the whole Grundtvig
school is inclined to break with German Protestantism, or in
some measure has already broken away from it.   They will
have nothing to do with German Protestant theology, nor
with German confessions of faith.   Rudelbach has ascribed
this tendency to a fanatical hatred against everything German; but Grundtvig's whole course of thought for many
years proves that the real cause lies much deeper, and that
it springs from a mode of thought nearly akin to that of the
English Tractarians.

For three hundred years was Denmark in its spiritual and
religious affairs entirely dependent on the German theology
and literature, and every movement made in it was but a
feeble echo of German movements and German productions.
But orthodox Protestantism, as it exists at present in Germany, has no existence in Denmark any longer.   "Orthodox
preaching," says Petersen, "occurs in Denmark only spo-
radically."[1]

A Danish clergyman—who in the Darmstadt *Allgemeine
Kirchenzeitung* has written a description of the ecclesiastical
condition of his country—gives, indeed, a very bad account
of it; but then he explains and adds his opinion, that "the
Lord has not altogether forsaken the Church of Denmark."
"Many laymen," he says, "have been awakened," and, in
confirmation of his statement, mentions that "a smith has
been converted from the evil of his ways, and is now travelling about the country"—that "a farmer has established a
home mission society"—and that "a baker is labouring for
the freedom of the Church, and a more active spiritual life."[2]
Of what the clergy are doing he says nothing.

It would be difficult, in fact, to paint a more deplorable
picture of the state of any religious system.   The people in

[1] RUDELBACH, p. 106.   [2] "Jahrgang," 1855, p. 1473, *et seq.*

the cities withdraw so commonly from Divine service, that in Copenhagen, out of 150,000 inhabitants, there are only 6,000 regular churchgoers.[1] In other cities the case seems still worse than in Copenhagen.[2] In Altona one single church is found sufficient for 45,000 inhabitants. The Church, chained to a Government now in the hands of a thorough democratically-constituted assembly, is in any important question altogether helpless. The Church itself is split into parties, and has no spiritual or moral authority upon which to lean; and the people, without guide or shepherd, have to seek for religious aliment among Baptists and Methodists, or to fall in the wilderness of barbarism.

In Schleswig, also, the churches stand empty, both in the parts of the country where German is spoken and where Danish is the prevailing language. One chief cause of this is said to be the character of the Danish clergy. "The Danish clergy," says the Schleswig preacher, Petersen, "inoculate the country with Danish levelling doctrines, Danish infidelity, and Danish immorality. The chief evil is not the oppressive enactments concerning the German language, but the irreligion that has been transplanted from Denmark to Schleswig, and the demoralisation that has accompanied it. Among the Danish clergy religious and moral conduct is the exception, not the rule."[3]

The Danish ill-treatment of the Church in Schleswig is, as it is now acknowledged, and bitterly complained of, a consequence of the Episcopal power having been placed by the Reformation in the hands of the sovereign. All Church arrangements—even those which concern its most inward life—have long been made on the sole authority of the Government. In the year 1834, even the administration of the Church affairs was taken from the Upper Consistory, and transferred to the Schleswig-Holstein Government.[4]

---

[1] KRAUSE'S "Kirch.-Ztg.," 1859, p. 968.

[2] " Allg. Lit.-Ztg.," 1841, ii. 491.

[3] " Erlebnisse eines Schleswig'schen Predigers." Frankfort, 1856, p. 337.

[4] SCHRADER, " Die Kirchenverfassungsfrage." Altona, 1849, p. 174.

The Lutheran State Church of *Sweden* has been, from the beginning, even more than that of Denmark, entirely dependent in its theological relations upon Germany. The small number of theological writings that Sweden possesses are nearly all nothing more than translations from the German. The theological Rationalism of Germany has indeed seldom found entrance into Sweden; the clergy had, at the end of the last and the beginning of the present century, almost ceased to occupy themselves with theology; and when a celebrated Swedish theologian of the present time, Wieselgren, remarked, "our Church constitution and legislation only hold together on paper, for all has been detached and loosened by Rationalism," he must have used the word "Rationalism" only in the sense of "practical indifferentism."

In England, a short time since, a glance was cast at the Swedish Church, in the hope of finding a certain kindred feeling and ecclesiastical sympathy with the state of the English Church and the efforts of Anglo-Catholics. But this hope has, upon closer inquiry, proved to be illusory. It was discovered that the Swedish Episcopacy had, precisely as little as the Danish, a claim to Apostolic Succession; that the Swedish Bishops were very far from regarding and estimating their office in the sense of the old Church—that they were, in fact, Lutheran superintendents, and nothing more! The Swedish Church is simply a Lutheran one, a community from which every Catholic idea has been cleansed out; completely devoid of what an Anglican would regard as a "Church spirit."[1]

At the same time, however, the Swedish cannot be refused the testimony of being "the most perfectly organised Protestant community in Europe,"[2] and in its love for Luther it perhaps exceeds even the old Lutherans of Germany itself.[3]

On the other hand, the preacher Trottet maintains that the country of Gustavus Adolphus is the least Protestant of all countries into which the Reformation has found admittance.

---

[1] "Christian Remembrancer," xiii. 425.

[2] "Chr. Rem.," xiii. 435.

[3] "Hubers Janus." Berlin, 1845, i. 232.

As a follower of Vinet, he turns away from the history of the Reformation, and all the new ecclesiastical conditions founded on it, and places the essence of Protestantism in "the freedom of religious life and the unshackled movements of the Church." The Swedish Church, therefore, in which religion and politics are so closely interwoven, could not but appear to him exceedingly unprotestant.

The king is in Sweden the "chief superintendent and earthly lord of the Church;" he unites in himself the highest spiritual and temporal power of the kingdom, and exercises his authority over the Church through the Royal Chancery, whose superior officer is the Minister for Foreign Affairs.[1] The Diet also shares with the king the control of the Church; and ecclesiastical affairs are discussed by its members. Thus this singular state of things has followed, that while the clergy possess completely the position of a privileged class, and through their representation in the Diet exercise great political influence, the Church itself remains in slavish dependence upon the State.[2] The king has even the power to demand from the Consistory letters of divorce for married couples who may desire to separate, and that for other causes than a violation of the marriage vow.[3] The occupations of the clergy are mostly of a secular character—they are the best financiers and men of business in Sweden, and "capable of everything except their spiritual duties."[4] The Church affairs are generally left to the curates. The sermons are read, as, it is said, the people themselves do not desire extempore preaching; and after the sermon the clergyman has often to act as beadle or crier, and make from his pulpit the most trivial announcements for half an hour together. When in an assembly of Bishops the abolition of this repulsive and troublesome custom was recently proposed, they almost all declared themselves to its retention, for the reason

[1] KLIPPEL, in "Herzog's Encyclopädie," vol. xiv. p. 83.

[2] TROTTET, "Prediger in Stockholm," in GELZER's "Monatsblättern," xi. 140.

[3] "Kirchliche Vierteljahrsschrift." Berlin, 1845, iv. 149.

[4] LIEBETRUT, HENGSTENBERG's "K.-Ztg.," vol. xxxiv., p. 119.

that if it were not for these announcements, they would often
have only old women and children as their auditors.[1] The
examinations carried on by preachers from house to house,
which formerly enabled a clergyman to judge individually
of the religious knowledge of his congregation, have declined
in most districts into a mere mode of filling up tax-lists and
making a census of the population.[2] German observers
report an almost incredible ignorance of the clergy, even up
to the highest; and it is a thing unheard of that any one
appointed by a patron to a cure should be rejected, let him
be ever so rude and uneducated.[3] His ignorance causes him
no difficulty or embarrassment in his office; for if he can but
merely read and write, he satisfies all demands that can be
made upon him. He has fulfilled his duties if, besides the
performance of the Church formalities and ceremonies, of
which more have been retained in Sweden than elsewhere,
he can on Sundays read out a written sermon. If to this
we add that the vice of brandy drinking,[4] constantly on the
increase in Sweden, has reached even the clergy, the state of
things there will be tolerably intelligible. On the whole, it
may nevertheless be said that the clerical body enjoys in no
other Protestant country at the present day such important
privileges, such great and manifold influence, as it does in
Sweden. To this influence is to be ascribed the severity of
the proceedings there against the "awakened" and the
"readers," as well as obstinate resistance to all reforms. According to Liebetrut's remark, a Swede who should touch on
the existing abuses would be scouted on all sides as a Sama-
ritan, who cared more for "life" than for "doctrine"—a blind
zealot concerning things for which there was no help.[5]

Liebetrut and other writers are accustomed to give the
Swedish Church and clergy the credit of orthodox Lutheranism, but they say there reigns a dead orthodoxy. "The

---

[1] LIEBETRUT, xxxiv. 172.
[2] "Kirchl. Vierteljahrsschrift," 1845, iv. 149.
[3] LIEBETRUT, 163.
[4] See hereupon "Allg.-Ztg.," 1847, p. 5475.
[5] HENGSTENBERG's "Kirch.-Ztg.," vol. xxxviii., p. 148.

Swedish Church," says Liebetrut, " is a Church desolate!—
dead!—lying under the anathema of God. The Church
unity is the unity and peace of the churchyard."[1] And in
the same tone the Swedish preacher, Cervin Steenhoff, says,
" It is now the time of the humiliation of the Church!—she
is dead!—all has become contentious, desolate, and void!"[2]

Sweden is now (besides Norway) the only country in
Europe where the genuine Lutheran doctrine reigns in the
pulpit. To this the profound ignorance of the majority
of the clergy found no obstacle; for the customary forms
and catchwords of the system can be taken up and used
by any one readily enough. " Nothing is easier here," says
Trottet, " than to become suspected of heresy;" and, according to him, this state of the Church in Sweden is one
of the chief causes of the moral corruption that prevails
in that country. A destructive formalism has gained the
upper hand; religious indifference has, by degrees, undermined the strictness of manners formerly existing, and public
opinion authorizes and protects, in many cases, the most
revolting immoralities.[3]

" Defunct orthodoxy" is just now one of the favourite
phrases in Sweden, and in Germany also ; for the bad religious condition of the seventeenth and eighteenth centuries
is often laid to its charge. But there is a great mistake in
saying this. The Lutheran orthodoxy was not dead in
Germany—on the contrary, as long as it existed it was
extremely lively, and for two centuries (1550-1750) it
maintained a struggle against Calvinism ; then against Arndt
and his followers ; then against Calixtus and the Helmstadt
school ; then against Spener, Pietism and the Halle school ;
and most vigorously and successfully did it defend itself
against all attempts to enfeeble it, until at length Rationalism
became master both of it and orthodoxy, its rivals—and
built its hut upon their ruins. What is in Germany considered the effect of " defunct orthodoxy," was much more the

[1] HENGSTENBERG's " Kirch.-Ztg.," vol. xxxiv., 172-151.
[2] KLIEFOTH's " Kirch.-Zeitschrift," 1856, p. 713, &c.
[3] GELZER's " Mon.-Blätter," xi. 143.

natural and inevitable psychological and ecclesiological consequence of the Lutheran system itself; and of which the
historical proof may easily be given.

If mention is made of this "defunct orthodoxy" in Sweden,
it should be remembered that it is nothing new in that
country, but has been its normal state since the Reformation.
The Swedish State Church has remained, down to the present time, in sole undisturbed possession, and has not
tolerated the smallest deviation from the strictest Lutheranism. Serious theological controversies do not occur in
Swedish history, with the exception of the liturgical dispute
occasioned by the efforts of King John to return towards
Catholicity; and the Swedish clergy have had no need of
theological knowledge to defend themselves against strange
doctrines. When Gustavus Vasa desired to convert the
inhabitants of Helsingland to Lutheranism, he did not send
to them distributors of Swedish Bibles, or preachers of the
new doctrine, but he wrote to them, "that if they did not
forthwith become Lutherans, he would have a hole made in
the ice on the Deele Lake, and they should all be drowned."[1]
Thus it has been ever. The sword, the dungeon, exile, or
in modern times pecuniary fines, have been the approved
methods of preventing religious disputes, or of settling them
if they had already broken out. And this appeared so much
the more necessary, since, as the celebrated Atterbom remarks, "the state of public instruction, and the education of
the clergy, were far below what they had been in the immediately preceding papal epoch."[2] Charles IX. and Gustavus
Adolphus adopted, with obstinate Catholics, the simple
method of cutting their heads off; and when, at the end of
the seventeenth and the beginning of the following century,
several Swedes—Ulstadius, Peter Schäfer, Ulhagius, and
Erik Molin, became perplexed with the Lutheran main doc-

---

[1] This fact is mentioned in the periodical called the "Frey," issued by
the Professor of Upsala. It occurs in an article on Wieselgren's work
concerning Gustavus Vasa. The article has been translated in the "Annales
de la Philosophie Chret.," published by Bonnetty. Paris, 1848, vol. xvii.
p. 282.   [2] The same, p. 291.

trine of "Imputation," and spoke of the necessity of " good works," Molin was banished—Ulstadius condemned to the house of correction for his life (and remained there for thirty years)—and Schäfer and Ulhagius were condemned to death![1] And in accordance with the same principle were the "Awakened," or "Readers," treated thirty years ago.

It seems to be difficult to assign the precise cause why, for a long time past, religious life has so much departed from Sweden, and all spiritual action has become so mechanical. Foreign German influence is not the cause; but the observer cannot fail to be immediately struck with the effects produced by the great secularizing of the clerical orders, as well as by their want of due culture and preparation. A brief training for a few months is deemed sufficient to qualify a man to assume the pastoral office, and any one may pass with the greatest ease from any employment or trade at once into the ranks of the clergy—a position rendered attractive by social distinctions and good emoluments; nay, he may even become a bishop, without possessing so much as a smattering of theological culture.[2] This was done by the poet Tegner, and also by a Professor of Botany. The care of providing for wives and children, and the quantity of civil business devolving upon the clergy, does the rest. It appears almost enigmatical that a people that has produced a Linnæus, Berzelius, Geijer, and Atterbom—that has a richly-endowed Church and two universities—a Church, too, which, like other Protestant Churches, has raised the postulate of general Bible investigation into a religious principle— it is truly enigmatical that such a people should have done nothing at all in theology. The former Professor of Theology, afterwards Bishop Reuterdahl says : " Theological instruction could hardly be less organized than it is in

---

[1] "Nordische Sammlungen," 1755, vol. i., pp. 44-51. See also the Berlin " Allg. Kirchen-Ztg." 1849, p. 752. The sentence of death, pronounced by the Spiritual Court at Abo, was commuted by the secular authorities into imprisonment.

[2] See the examples adduced by Liebetrut in HENGSTENBERG, vol. xxxiv. p. 163.

Sweden. Ignorance, the love of gain and want of under-standing in the clergy, are the causes why so many people in every parish think they can do without the Church."[1] The Swedes need only look over to Denmark, and its now wholly Rationalistic clergy, to see the consequences of the neglect of theological studies. They have only the choice of retaining their Lutheran orthodoxy and renouncing theology—or of admitting theology at the cost of the former. It was natural that, in a country where the power of the State had maintained with such severity the old penal laws concerning religion; where the clergy are so enslaved that the secular authorities dictate Church penances, and when these have been performed the pastor *must* at once absolve every offender—it was natural that under these circumstances they should renounce theology, and prefer remaining good Lutherans. Symbolic orthodoxy and scien-tific theology can no more subsist peacefully together in Sweden than in other Protestant countries. Since their great quarrel in a preceding century, no attempt at recon-ciliation has ever succeeded, and each party of the married pair has sued for, obtained, and is prepared to present to its *ci-devant* partner—a deed of separation!

The only movement that for many years has taken place in the stagnant waters of the Swedish Church, has been that made by the "Readers," who were in fact, at first, nothing more than zealous Lutherans. Their motto was, "Justi-fication by Faith alone," and the non-freedom of man's will; and they separated themselves from the Church because the clergy did not preach to them this favourite doctrine —either with sufficient distinctness or often enough.[2] When the Lutheran State Church attempted to crush these poor people under the whole weight of a brutal police-despotism, hundreds allowed themselves to be brought to ruin rather than submit, or they emigrated, and fled into the deserts of Lapland. When the "Readers" had already

[1] See the extracts from his writings in HENGSTENBERG'S "K.-Ztg.," vol xxxviii., p. 151.

[2] "Neue Preuss.-Zeitung," 18th Decemb., 1856.

begun to administer baptism and the communion by one of
their own number, they betook themselves to the English
and American Baptist Missionaries, and got themselves baptized anew. In the year 1853, the utter inefficiency of
dealing with sectarians by the infliction of punishments was
acknowledged. In despite of all such penal measures, the
sects of Baptists had been continually increasing in the once
purely Lutheran Sweden; and the "awakening" of which
we hear so much in the reports from Sweden, consists chiefly
in the progress made over the whole country by the Anglo-
American sects—the irreconcileable enemies of Lutheranism—
and the preachers sent out by the Independents, Baptists,
and Methodists.

The condition of the Swedish Church, in its relation to
the State, is to be again met with in *Norway*—with this
difference only, that, in consequence of the former connection
with Denmark, the dependence of the clergy is still greater
than in Sweden. Here, also, the power over the Church is
in the hands of the civil authorities. The sovereign rules
the Church through the Minister of Public Worship, and the
clergy are not represented at the Storthing; for which
reason it was found possible—in the year 1844—to introduce
religious freedom into Norway, which it was not in Sweden.
The desire for a more independent position of the Church is
frequently expressed here, especially among the clergy.

Norway had, formerly, through the connection with Denmark (which was broken in 1813), been inoculated with
Rationalism. It made rapid progress, and most of the
pulpits were soon in possession of unspiritual Rationalists,
who preached dry moral lectures, or treatises on political
economy.[1]

When the rustic, Nielsen Hauge, by his sermons and
writings, succeeded in awakening a great number of people
of the lower class to a feeling opposed to the infidelity of
the preachers, he had to atone for it by an enormous fine
and ten years imprisonment—from the consequences of which

[1] Thus says the report on the state of the Church of Norway in
HENGSTENBERG'S " K.-Ztg.," vol. xxxiii., p. 566.

he died, in 1824 ;[1] but his followers, the Haugeans, were
treated with indulgence. The people endeavoured to find in
the sermons of lay preachers a compensation for what they
failed to receive in the Church. At present, among the
younger generation of the clergy, a return to Lutheran orthodoxy is perceptible ; but it is said this tendency has no
support in the religious feelings of the people.[2]

On the whole, the latest German writer on the subject
describes the state of the Church as wretched, as one which
affords abundance of weapons for the attacks of invading
sectarians.[3]   In the rural districts of both Sweden and
Norway, the weekly divine services have fallen off universally.[4]   As to Confession, nothing remains of it but "the
Absolution," which here, as in Denmark, is given to every one
without any previous recapitulation of his sins ; without the
applicant having even to answer a single question with a "yes"
or "no." In like manner, the visitation of the sick is no
longer practised. The complete decay of Church discipline
is here also complained of.   There is said (by the same
German observer) to be but a small circle of religiously
awakened people, opposed to a great mass which is lax and
thoughtless.   There also the pews of the higher classes and
official persons frequently stand empty.[5]   The laity in
general complain of their preachers—their worldly-minded-
ness—their neglect of all care for souls.   The clergy plead,
in their defence, that they are overwhelmed with worldly
business,[6] and also the size of their parishes—their own
farming and family cares ; and the great distance from them
and each other of most of the members of their congregation.

The reference to this last-mentioned circumstance brings
us to a feature common to the whole Protestant North—I
mean the disproportion of the number of preachers to the

[1] Forester's "Norway," 1848 and 1849.   London, 1856, p. 308.
[2] Krause's "K.-Ztg.," 1859, p. 639.
[3] Hengstenberg's "K.-Ztg.," vol. lxiii., pp. 769-781.
[4] Sarwey, in his "Theological Studies and Criticisms," 1849, ii. 774.
[5] Hengstenberg's "K.-Z.," vol. lxii., p. 499.
[6] Sarwey, "Theol. Studien und Kritiken," ii. 780.

population, and the spiritual incapacity of the Church consequent on this disproportion. In Norway, there are only 485 clergymen to 1,500,000 souls; on an average, there are about 3,600 persons to every parish; and, notwithstanding the enormous extent of the parishes, several of them—as many as five—are often united in the hands of one pastor, in order that he, with his wife and children, may enjoy a more abundant income. Even the English visitor, Forester, expresses his astonishment at this pluralism on a large scale, and the neglect of the people for the benefit of rich priests' families.[1] There are many parishes of from 6000 to 12,000 inhabitants, and these scattered over immense districts, who have but one preacher, and but very rarely two.[2] Thus, Holstein has, for 544,419 almost exclusively Lutheran inhabitants, only 192 preachers, two or three of whom also belong to one and the same Church.[3] In all the Scandinavian countries taken together, the Protestant Church is, on the whole, very badly served; that is to say, the number of churches and preachers is quite inadequate, so that immense masses of persons have it not in their power to attend any religious service. In the Duchy of Schleswig, not a few livings have been abolished since the Reformation, because the clergyman, with his wife and children, found the income too small; so that there are parishes of 13,000 people, dispersed over a vast breadth of country, with only two preachers. In the same way, in Farther Pomerania, in 1850, thirty formerly independent parishes, with as many churches, with a population of 15,000, had, through combination with other districts, disappeared.[4] In all these Scandinavian countries, there are innumerable persons who have never in their lives entered the House of God.[5] In the Russian countries, especially in the Baltic provinces, the Lutherans, whose number in 1854 was 1,834,224, had 192 preachers;

---

[1] "Norway," p. 309.
[2] "Darmst. Allg. Kirch.-Ztg.," 1856, p. 1650.
[3] MESSNER's "K.-Ztg.," 1861, p. 282.
[4] MOSER's "Kirchenblatt.," 1856, p. 188.
[5] "Darmst. Allg. K.-Ztg.," 1856, p. 1650.

so that there was one for every 4394 souls.[1] Thus the people have to suffer, because clergymen deem it to be right, proper, and necessary that they should have and provide for wives and children !

[1] REUTER's " Repert.," vol. xciv., p. 168.

THE PROTESTANT CHURCHES IN GERMANY.

GERMANY is the birth-place of the Reformation. Within the mind of a German man, and that man the greatest of his age, did the Protestant doctrine spring up. Before the superiority and creative energy of that one mind did the aspiring, active portion of the nation humbly and trustingly bend the knee! In him — in that union of strength and intellect — they recognised their master; they lived in his thoughts—he appeared to them as the hero in whom the nation, with all its characteristics, was incorporated. They admired him; they gave themselves over to him because they perceived in him their country's most potential, powerful self; because it was their feelings that he expressed more clearly, more eloquently, and with greater power than they would themselves have been able to give utterance to them. Thus has Luther's name become for Germany not merely the name of a distinguished man—he is himself the very core and kernel of a period of national life—the centre of a new circle of ideas—the most condensed expression of that religious and ethical mode of thought peculiar to the German mind, and from whose mighty influence even those who resisted it could not themselves wholly withdraw. Luther's writings have long ceased to be popularly read; and are only now consulted by the learned for historical purposes; but the image of his personality is still vivid. His name, his heroic figure, still work with an enchanter's power upon the high and low; and from the magic of his name the Protestant doctrine still derives a portion of its vital power. In other countries, people feel an aversion to adopt the name of the originator of a predominant creed; but in Germany and in Sweden there are still thousands who are proud to call themselves "Lutherans."

Although Protestant Germany forms the smaller portion of the nation, yet this smaller portion is both politically and intellectually the stronger. Politically stronger, for the German dynasties are chiefly Protestant, and—what is very important in Germany—the administration, even in Catholic districts, is mostly entrusted to Protestant officials, who are zealous for their religion. It is intellectually stronger, for the great majority of the high schools are wholly, or chiefly, in Protestant hands; and the entire body of literature, which has formed for a hundred years the mental aliment of the higher and middle classes, is, in its widest sense, Protestant— that is to say, it has arisen out of the great rupture with the whole past history of Christianity, which the Reformation, in conjunction with the *humanism* so hostile to the Church had brought about, and which two centuries and a half have rendered permanent. Ever since Lessing extended the Protestant view of the development of Christianity, and of the Church, to the earliest ages, it has applied to the Apostolic times the same standard of motive and cha- racter by which Protestantism has learned to measure the following centuries. By the theory long prevalent (though not always entertained with a full consciousness of its effects, and mingled with much obscurity), viz: that the Christian Church, on the whole, was a failure, and had brought more mischief and falsehood than truth and blessing to the human race, the whole history of Christian nations and states had been rendered soulless and trivial. What had been left by the Reformation, in place of the old Church edifice, could not possibly claim the sympathy and veneration of the educated classes. It is now generally acknowledged, even by believing Protestants, that the whole state of the Church, and of the

Protestant theology of that time, had "estranged from Christianity many of the noblest and most gifted men of the nation;" and thus was formed that atmosphere of infidelity, of contempt of all that was Christian, and in which heathenism, or Islamism, appeared more human, more invigorating, and more poetical than the gloomy Galilean doctrine of self-abnegation and sanctification.

Gervinus has said, in his rough, reckless manner, "We still stand, on the average, much at the same point as Goethe and Schiller, Voss and Jean Paul, Winkelmann and Wieland, Forster and Lichtenberg—all of whom 'released themselves from the bonds of dogmatic Christianity.'"[1] Sixteen years have passed since then, and these words are just as true now as they were at that period. Aversion to Christianity, as soon as it attempts to assert itself in life or in science, is still general amongst educated persons, and it opposes itself at every step, as an obstacle, to orthodox Protestantism, as well as to the Catholic Church; only that the latter is for several reasons—and especially because of its firmer organisation and greater power of resistance—more energetic, active, and universal. A campaign against the Catholic Church will unite all that is Protestant, positive and negative, and troops of the most heterogeneous combatants, under one banner, and bring about a transitory reconciliation among them. The events in Germany and Switzerland, from 1845 to 1847, and lately again in Baden and Würtemberg, have proved this.

In other Protestant countries the internal want of harmony between the Protestant system and theological science, has mostly led, as we have seen, to the decay or ruin of the latter. In Germany, however, the theological impulse, united to the general intellectual current in the country, has always been too strong and irresistible. Lutheran orthodoxy has not indeed been able to extinguish it, but it has for nearly two hundred years reduced theology to the condition of a subservient handmaiden; and even though it be but a mutilated theology, deprived of its two eyes—Bible study and Church history—and limited to dogmatic and polemic discussion.

[1] "Die Mission der Deutschkatholiken." Heidelberg, 1845.

After Pietism had inflicted some severe wounds on orthodoxy, theology roused itself to the struggle for its emanci-
pation; and then was the former mistress soon overthrown,
and did not long survive.

This invasion and complete victory won by theological
Rationalism in Germany, almost without a battle, is a remarkable and unique event in history, and one of which the
causes have not yet been sufficiently explained. By the long
contest with the Helmstadt school, and subsequently with
that of Spener, and Pietism, Lutheran theology had been
internally and logically developed, but at the same time the
logical and moral antinomianism to which it led became
obvious to the most purblind sight. Towards the middle of
the eighteenth century came also the influence of the new
Biblical and historical studies. As long as the rule of the
Lutheran system maintained itself consistently within the
Concordien formula, the study of the Bible was, of course,
intentionally neglected. It evidently shrank from the inevitable conflict with the symbolic books. Professor Heinrich
Majus, of Giessen,[1] when he entered on his office, mentioned
with censure that with very few, if any, of the universities
of Germany, the interpretation of the " Holy Scriptures was
made an object of earnest study." Spener gives the same
testimony, and lately Tholuck and Lücke[2] have again alluded
to the fact that, through the whole seventeenth century, Exegesis had fallen completely into disuse and disfavour. In
the year 1742, also, Bengel complains, in the preface to his
" Gnomon," that " the manifold misuse—nay, malicious contempt of Scripture, had risen to the highest point, even
among those who thought themselves to be philosophical and
very spiritual persons." As soon as the study of the Bible
had come again into fashion, partly through means of Bengel himself, and partly as a reaction against the Pietistic
movement, the dissolution of the Lutheran doctrine began.
The tone of historical criticism, and especially the conception of Church History in Germany, contributed greatly to

[1] " Praxis Pietatis, sive Synopsis Theologiæ Moralis." Gissæ, 1697,
Pref.   [2] " Deutsche Zeitschrift," 1854, p. 178.

this dissolution.   The idea that the whole course of development of Christianity, from the time of the Apostles, had been a continual and ever-increasing malformation, until at last, at the Reformation, this utterly distorted and ruined religion was awakened to new life, had been the prevailing notion since the sixteenth century.   In this sense were all histories taught and written.   A man who deserves to be called the most profound and acute theologian, of the first period of Rationalism, describes this state of opinion :—

" Among Protestants, Church History is nothing else than the historical proof of the necessity of a Church Reformation, and of a perpetual increase of corruption, both in doctrine and life.   According to the Protestants, the Church had been—at least, since the eighth century—a sink of ignorance and corruption.   *All the heads* of the Church had been dreadfully false teachers, and the Church itself a complete madhouse."   He then remarks : " The extreme care with which, on the Protestant side, every fact has been collected which could be made to afford the smallest testimony for the former prevalence of corruption in the Church—the injustice with which all former chiefs and heads of the Church have been represented as tyrants, and all the members of it as mere heathens—and the carelessness with which the good that has always been present in the Church, notwithstanding the great abuses that had crept into it, is overlooked ; this defect in Church History, as treated by Protestants, has been eagerly employed by the enemies of Christianity for their own purposes.[1]

Töllner quotes an expression of Frederick II.[2] in one of his writings, in which the monarch states the customary Protestant account of Church History, namely, " that it was a great drama performed by rogues and hypocrites, at the expense of the deluded masses ;" and such histories he supposes

[1] Töllner's " Kurze Vermischte Aufsätze."   Frankfort, a. d. Oder, 1769, ii. 87, *et seq.*
[2] The Preface to " Abrégé de l'Histoire Ecclésiastique de Fleury."
—Berne.   Berlin, 1767.   The book is by De Prades.   That the Preface was written by the King, Töllner probably did not know.

had been the real cause of the King's contempt for Christianity.

This manner of regarding the history of Christianity completely coincided with the reigning mode of thought and literature of the time, and through it was developed that spiritual revolt from Christianity which was completed in Germany by the simultaneous and reciprocal action of the clergy and the educated classes upon one another. The theology of the Reformers and their followers established the notion that God had withdrawn Himself from the Church after the demise of the Apostles—that He had resigned His place to Satan, who thenceforward had undertaken the office which, according to the promises in the Gospel, the Holy Ghost should have fulfilled—and so established a diabolical millennium, which continued until the appearance of Luther.[1] When faith in the infallible truth of the symbolic books became in a few years extinct,[2] in consequence of the new Biblical studies—when, after the accession of Frederick II., Lutheran orthodoxy lost more and more the protection of the ecclesiastical power of the State—when the Theologians began more and more mercilessly to expose the defects and contradictions of the Lutheran reformation doctrine,[3] then all the supports of religious feeling at once were tumbled down and prostrated. The entire education of the people, the ideas they had imbibed with their mother's milk, all was calculated to make them regard the whole history of Christianity before the Reformation as a churchyard covered with decayed and sunken tombstones, and with mouldering bones, and where ghostly shadows alone were wandering.

[1] See also SEMLER's "Lebenbeschreibung." ii. 156, concerning the part in Church history assigned to the devil by the Protestant world.

[2] "In the year 1770 there existed not a single theologian in a Protestant university who would approve any work that did not confine itself within the systematic formulæ."—SACK's "Lebensbeschreibung," i. 252. What a change must have taken place in fifteen years !

[3] It is especially in TÖLLNER's writings (which, on dogmatic subjects, are far more important than those of Semler) that the decomposing process going on in Protestant theology and the Genesis of Rationalism may be perceived.

With the faith in the Divine Guidance of the Church fell also all faith in its divine origin. The root was judged by the stem; the beginning judged by the subsequent career —judged and condemned!

And thus, then, there remained for the men who held office under, and got their bread by Christianity, nothing else to fall back upon but that aggregate of empty, unsupported notions concerning God, morality, and immortality, to which the name of Rationalism has been given.

So much the more certain and powerful became the effect produced by the writings of Semler, Lessing, Reimarus; by the prestige of the example of Frederick II.; and by the philosophy of Immanuel Kant. In the course of a few years the whole class of German Protestant preachers—and the theologians at the universities the first amongst them—had fallen off from the old positive faith. The entire of the new generation of clergy grew up in Rationalism; and stone after stone was taken from the Temple, and carried away by its own priests. From the pulpits even of village churches the new " Rational" Christianity was preached; whilst only a few remote congregations remained in undisturbed possession of the old faith;[1] and in the cities the preachers were often Rationalists before the best educated among the middle classes had fallen victims to that wide-spread Deistical enlightenment, which had been so carefully cherished by the new and flourishing literature of Germany. A Mecklenburg preacher repeats what he has heard from the lips of an old clergyman: " That the rapidity with which the mockery of infidelity was effacing from language and manners the old forms of faith in that country, bordered upon the marvellous."[2]

In France, about the same time, frivolous infidelity had seized on the higher ranks of society, but the clergy remained, on the whole, untouched by it; and even amid the

---

[1] Thus it is said in the New Dorpat " Zeitschrift Theol.," i., 588: " In many out-of-the-way districts of Westphalia, the Rhine country, and Western Schleswig, there are parishes that have never been touched by the Rationalist poison."

[2] RHEINWALD's " Repert.," viii. 259.

storms of the Revolution, it was only a comparatively small number of priests that became apostates. The great majority remained, even under the most fearful persecutions, true to their faith. In Protestant Germany, on the contrary, it was theology especially which completed the work of destruction—it was the clerical class that introduced to congregations, both in town and country, their open or veiled Naturalism, and brought on that defection of the masses from Christianity before which men now stand wringing their hands and knowing not what to do.

Rationalism has not, on the whole, had any great influence on the relations of Church and State, or on the constitution of the Church. The Reformation had already here done all that was essential. Germany—Wittenberg, is the true birth-place of princely episcopal supremacy and territorialism. The princes received the supreme power from the hands of theologians, not "*although*," but "*because*" they were princes. It was their right and their duty, they were told, to undertake the government of the Church, as a branch and an efflux of their political sovereignty. When a man now living says, "Let the name of *Episcopacy* (of the prince) be left as a memorial of the disgrace of the Church until she shall repent and do penance," he expresses a thought that was totally foreign to the first and second generation of German Protestants—which is still foreign to the majority of preachers and Consistorial Councils, even though many laymen may be of the same way of thinking as Hommel.[1]

Since the Princes and Estates of the Empire in Germany have come into possession, to an unlimited extent, of Protestant ecclesiastical power, there have arisen in Germany as many Churches as there are principalities or territories. The attempt to establish a united German Protestant, Lutheran, or Calvinistic Reformed Church was never made. Every one was content with the existing state of things; that in every little territory there should be a different Evangelical Church; and that this crowd of Churches should

[1] HOMMEL, "Die wahre Gestalt der Bayerischen Landeskirche," 1850, p. 26.

have no one point of union except antagonism to the Catholic Church.   At the Diets the *Corpus Evangelicorum* formed a kind of representative body ; and there was, on the whole, much similarity of doctrine, although the individual Churches had their own symbolic books, and very various liturgies. And thus there was, in fact, only an aggregate of National Churches.   Before the dissolution of the German Empire, the number of independent separate Churches was much greater.   "Germany," says Ernest Solomon Cyprian,[1] "has, with its isolated Evangelical Churches, if we reckon the free Equestrian order (the *Ritterschaft*), more than a thousand independent rulers ; for each one can do with his own congregation all that the Pope can do in the Roman See. Who can expect that so many masters, of such various temperaments and inclinations, and exposed to such different temptations to sin and disorder, can ever be brought to harmonious agreement ?"   This state of things, Cyprian thinks, both explains and palliates the numerous faults and abominations of the German Church system.   The Church (he says) is only answerable for her doctrine, and that, fortunately, is everywhere good, sound Lutheranism !

There are now in Germany about thirty-eight Protestant Churches, each of which is independent of the other, and has its own organization ; and since in each of the States the Church has been degraded into a mere branch of the Administration—has been inserted as a wheel in the great State machine—it has come to pass that all the threads of ecclesiastical government come together, and are united in the hands of a single Government official, the Minister of Public Worship.   Thus, in Saxony, for instance, it depends entirely on the judgment of their Minister what amount of attention he will pay to the recommendation of the Consistory of the country in Church affairs ;[2] and, as a matter of fact, the destinies of the Saxon Church are wholly within his grasp.

[1] Preface to GROSCH, "Nothw. Vertheidigung der Evangelischen Kirche," 1745. p. 33.

[2] See hereupon LEHMANN, "Zur Frage der Neugestaltung der evang. luth. Kirche Sachsens."   Dresden, 1861, p. 6.

T 2

The case is the same in Hanover; the Minister acts in Church affairs without asking the advice or opinion of the Consistory, and the Consistory has really nothing more to do than to execute the commands of the Minister.[1]

If in some countries the institution of Synods has been added to that of the Consistory and Monarchial Episcopacy, it has imparted no especial dignity to the Constitutional structure; for the Synods are chiefly composed of theologians and preachers, and the lay element is very sparsely represented in them; whilst the decrees of Synods and of the Church government united, have proved impotent when opposed to the resistance of the laity in Bavaria, Baden, and the Palatinate.

The "*Union*" which was begun in Prussia, and imitated elsewhere, has, since 1817, amalgamated the Lutheran and Calvinist Reformed Churches, and given an essentially different form to German Protestantism. The new Church thus formed was to take the name of the " Evangelical Church ;" and it was the Prussian Government especially which insisted upon the introduction of this name, because " Protestant" was a party name, and did not sound so well as " Evangelical."[2] The members of the united Church have, therefore, ceased to be Lutherans or Calvinists, and have become "Evangelicals." The names of "Lutheran " and " Protestant" were to be omitted wherever it was possible ; and lately the Consistory of the Province of Pomerania has declared that the general term " Evangelical" does not any longer signify what it did in 1818. It has already passed into State documents—as, for example, into that of the Constitution of 1850. It does not there specially designate "the union," but is a collective term *to express opposition to Catholicism.* In official notifications the term " Evangelical" is, therefore, not to be discontinued.[3]

[1] Reuter's " Repert.," vol. lxiv., p. 277.

[2] See Haupt's " Hanbuch über die Religions-Angelegenheiten im K. Preussen," 1822, ii. 160. Kampz, " Annalen," 1821, p. 341.

[3] See Wilsing, " Die reformirte Kirche in Deutschland." Altona, 1853, p. 123.

In consequence of this "Union," then, there are now, theologically considered, three Churches, instead of the former two, in Germany—the Lutheran, the Reformed, and the United or Evangelical.   Genuine Calvinism, for which the Dordrecht decisions serve as a standard, has almost died out in Germany; for there is said to be left only one congregation professing it.   With the other, not united congregations, "Reformed" generally means nothing more than that the Lutheran doctrine of the Communion is rejected.   On the other hand, the old Lutheran Church has also vanished from the German soil.   The name can but be claimed by the 31,000 Prussian Lutherans who have remained as a separate body; but these are not recognised by the Lutherans of Saxony and elsewhere as true disciples of Luther—on the contrary, they are reproached with having made important and objectionable variations from his doctrine.   The former Lutheran congregations, which have joined the Union, can, however, scarcely be called Lutheran any longer, for the mode of celebrating the Communion has been accommodated to that of the "Reformed," or "United," and it is upon this point that the most decisive and distinguishing mark of a Church union lies.   There are also certain ceremonies and institutions in which Lutheranism formerly differed from Calvinism —these have been abandoned, as well as, and before all others, that of private confession.   When, therefore, Stahl complains (as he did lately), of a threatened approaching absorption of the Lutheran Church into that of the Union,[1] it may be answered that in Germany the German Lutheran Church now only exists in the wishes and yearnings of some few theologians, pastors, and jurists, and by no means is a reality or concrete church establishment.   There is only the difference of "more" or "less" between the united and non-united churches.

The "Union" was the personal act of the King of Prussia, effected by him under the influence of his dynastic interests, and with the view of producing an ecclesiastical reconciliation between the Royal House of Prussia (which, since 1613, had

---

[1] "Die lutherische Kirche und die Union."   Preface, p. viii.

renounced Lutheranism and adhered to the doctrine of
Calvin) and the preponderating Lutheran population of the
country. An Agenda, the work of the king himself, was to
serve as the chief cement of the Union; but it struck upon
greater difficulties than the Union itself, as the introduction
of liturgical elements into the service was regarded as a dangerous approximation to the practice of the Catholic Church.
On the whole, "the Union" was accepted with marvellous
ease and promptitude by both preachers and congregations;
people were pretty well agreed that the doctrines in which
they differed were of no special importance, and might be
properly left alone. It was the question of fees for confessions, and not upon any difference of doctrine, that
made Schleiermacher, for a short time, fear that the work of
peace would· be wrecked. It was considered, too, that a
united Church would be stronger and much more respectable
as opposed to Catholicity.

Throughout Protestant Germany the disposition of the
preachers and their congregations was alike favourable to the
"Union;" and it was established speedily, and without the
smallest resistance, in Nassau, the Bavarian Rhine provinces,
Baden, Anhalt, and Würtemberg; and if such was not also the
case in Saxony, Hanover, Mecklenburg, and Bavaria, the cause
was discoverable in the small number of Calvinists in those
countries.

The King of Prussia had declared that it was a
ritual merely, and not a doctrinal amalgamation, had been
proposed by "the Union"—but the two could not be separated. Several preachers and village congregations who felt
this to be the fact, and perceived that the Union would be
the annihilation of the Lutheran Confession, wished to hold
themselves aloof from it; but the Government determined to
treat them as "dangerous sectaries," according to the pre-
scriptions of the general law of the country[1]—that is to say,
to inflict punishments upon them, expatriation, imprisonment,
and military executions. In Berlin the Bishops Eylert and
Neander had come to a complete understanding. The
present General-Superintendent, Hahn, marched at the head

[1] EILER's "Meine Wanderung durch's Leben," iv. 204.

of a military force against the refractory congregations. The Minister Altenstein spoke in accordance to the theory of "the limited understanding of subjects." "It was the duty of the Government to protect the deluded people against the consequences of their own thoughtless actions."[1] Thousands were compelled to emigrate to America, and not one single voice was raised in all Protestant Germany on behalf of the sufferers, who had been treated with refined cruelty, and against whom the whole apparatus of bureaucratic methods of coercion had been employed. The entire liberal press approved and applauded what had been thus done.

The Lutherans had rightly judged that "the Union" would inevitably lean to two results: the dissolution of Lutheranism, and the spread of dogmatic indifferentism—that is to say, of infidelity. As soon as Frederick William IV. had set free the imprisoned preachers, they established, at a synod at Breslau in 1841, a separate Lutheran Church —at the head of which was the jurist Huschke, and which soon obtained from the Government recognition and toleration as a separate sectarian Church.

Theology, in the meanwhile, had begun again to raise itself from the slough of unspiritual, unbelieving Rationalism. The accession of Frederick William IV.—who, as a zealous friend of his church, immediately promised and afforded it the most powerful protection—gave a new impulse to a tendency towards the Positive, already awakened and encouraged by excellent teachers at the Universities. The believing theologians and preachers saw themselves everywhere preferred by the Government; the rising generation of students turned towards them; and then there came to divide the feelings of old and young the catastrophe of 1848, which struck terror into the whole Protestant clergy of North Germany, and showed them in the perspective the threatened rule of a multitude destitute of religion through the fault of the clergy themselves. In Prussia the reign of Hegel's Pantheism was at an end—the Pantheism to which the minister Altenstein had given up both schools and

[1] EILER's "Meine Wanderung durch's Leben," iv. 235.

pulpits. By degrees theological educational offices were all filled by believing professors. Jena and Giessen alone remained on the hands of the Rationalists. In the new and now orthodox theology a twofold direction was soon observed, proceeding from two different assumptions, and leading to very different results. Chiefly on the foundation laid by Schleiermacher and Neander, there was formed a " Union," or " reconcilement theology," represented by Nitzsch, Julius Müller, Dorner, Lücke, Rothe and others. By the side of this arose a Lutheran theology, encouraged especially in Erlangen, Dorpat, Leipsig, and Rostock. It declared itself at first as merely a Repristination theology, as the doctrine simply of the Concordian formula, translated from the language of the sixteenth into that of the nineteenth century. But this soon manifested itself to be a sheer impossibility for scientifically instructed and energetically disciplined men. This dreary undertaking was abandoned to a few pastors, at the head of whom was Rudelbach, who could now boast that, as "old Lutherans," they cultivated the only genuine Lutheran theology—so that if Luther should come back to earth he might recognise the contributors to the " Zeitschrift fur lutherische Theologie" as his own true sons and spiritual heirs. In the Universities, with scarcely a single exception, they declined having anything to do with this Lutheranism; and in them (the Universities) was formed the party of " the new Lutherans," represented by such men as Kahnis, Delitzsch, Kliefoth, Stahl, and others, with whom are also to be mentioned Harnack, Vilmar, Petri, and Münchmeyer. These theologians declare that they keep to the Lutheran doctrine of Justification, but will not be bound by the favourite Protestant dogma of " the invisibility of the Church," and a "universal priesthood." Since they maintain the idea of a divine institution of the office of the Church, in opposition to that of a mere transmission by the congregation, they are logically compelled to the acceptance of another divinely ordained transmission, namely, that of the Sacrament of Ordination. They profess, therefore, opinions concerning "office" and "ordination," "sacrament" and "sacrifice," which have brought on them from all sides the reproach of "Catholicity." "You are already," it is said, "close to the gates of Rome—a little further on, and you will find yourselves inside of the Eternal City."[1] That this German Lutheran Puseyism must, like the Anglican, lead to a union with the Papists, is the opinion expressed in the "Zeitschrift" of Guerike and Rudelbach.[2]

Of the preachers in Prussia who are dissatisfied with "the Union," only a small number has left the Church: the great majority has remained within it, partly because they could not rely on their congregations—partly because they did not like to renounce fixed incomes, to become dependent upon the will of their congregations.[3] But they would like to throw off the yoke of "the Union," and withdraw themselves as far as possible from a community with Calvinism in doctrine and worship. They will not, however, give up their position in "the Union Church," because it is "the State Church," and one does not like to forego its rights and advantages by separating from it; and, also, because one can contend against "the Union" much more effectually when within its precincts than from the outside. The Unionists declare that, were the Union dissolved, there would be at least five Churches in Prussia. It would be the most "un-Prussian act" that could be committed; and it is added, "that they who endeavour to bring about the abolition of the Union are the enemies of Prussia."[4]

The ordinances of Frederick William IV. sought to content the Lutheran or Confessional party—at the head of which stood Stahl and Hengstenberg—by various concessions, and, at the same time, to restrain it within certain limits, by a renewed proclamation of the principles of "the Union." Finally, in the year 1857, "the English Evangelical Alliance" was summoned to Berlin to strengthen the

---

[1] LEHMANN, pp. 2, 6.   [2] "Jahrgang," 1853, p. 163.
[3] See the declaration of LENZ, "Denkschrift über die neuesten kirchlichen Bewegungen in Pommern." Berlin, 1858, p. 43.
[4] The General-Superintendent HOFFMANN, "Verhandlungen der Berl. Kirchl. Conferenz.," 1857, p. 577.

cause of "the Union." Baptists, Methodists, Presbyterians, Congregationalists, Calvinist Anglicans, and other sects, impelled by their common hatred to the Catholic Church to fraternize (but reserving their differences), proclaimed that "they came to Berlin to bear testimony against the new Pharisees and Sadducees." And the heads of the United Lutherans very clearly perceived that the first designation was meant to apply to themselves. On the other hand, Hoffmann, Nitzsch, Schenkel, Krummacher, Heppe, Sack, Kapff, Plitt, Ledderhose, and a numerous band of German spiritual kindred, declared that these English-Scotch-American "Denominations" were "flesh of their flesh and bone of their bone," and welcome fellow-combatants in the battle against exclusive Lutheranism and—"Rome."[1] It ought to be considered, they cried out to these members of many creeds, that "the Alliance" consisted only of good Protestant denominations, and all professing the grand fundamental doctrine of Justification by imputed righteousness; and that only by such an "Alliance" could it be possible to represent, on the Protestant side, the essential unity of the Church of Christ.[2]

When the grand display was over, the Lutherans scornfully asked, "What permanent end had been attained by it?" By thus calling in foreigners, they had cast suspicion and raised accusations against their German fellow-believers, with whom they had hitherto lived in peace; and they had, by fraternizing with erroneous believers, confirmed them in their error.[3] In fact, the result of this "Communion of Saints" made visible in Berlin was that the general confusion was greatly increased, the doubts and uncertainties of the laity strengthened, and the people confirmed in the idea that theologians and preachers had themselves no fixed doctrines; and that, after all, perhaps doctrine was a matter of very little consequence. "The Union" had previously provided that the people should be much puzzled what to believe

[1] Stahl's speech in HENGSTENBERG's "K.-Ztg.," 1857, p. 553.
[2] LIEBETRUT, "Die Evangel. Allianz." Berlin, 1857, p. 27.
[3] WANGEMANN's "Preuss. Kirchengesch.," iii. 750.

concerning the Lord's Supper; and now, through "the Alliance," Baptism also was placed among the articles of which no one knew what was to be taught as certainly true.

The chief promoter of the Berlin Alliance Assembly was Von Bunsen, who, as Geheimrath Eilers[1] testifies, was possessed with the idea of uniting all non-Catholic Confessions and Sects into one grand Evangelical union against the Catholic Church. After the death of Frederick William III., it was expected and desired, in the higher official world of Berlin—where, in the words of the same statesman,[2] "hatred to Catholicity had awakened an interest for the Evangelicals"—that Bunsen would be appointed to the Ministry of Spiritual Affairs, and the demonstration of the Alliance in the German metropolis of Protestantism was welcomed in those circles for the same reason. The same men who, at the Church Assembly at Bremen in 1852, had declared the struggle against "Rome" to be the first and most pressing affair to be considered,[3] formed also the kernel of the Berlin Alliance gathering. Hatred to the Catholic Church, and joy at every injury, real or imaginary, to it, constituted the fundamental tone to the whole proceedings of the Assembly; but whatever else was of permanent consequence solely to the Protestant Church system, was regarded by the orthodox Lutherans and Confessionalists as a blow aimed at themselves.

Since the illness and retirement of King Frederick William IV. from the Government, which followed immediately

[1] "Wanderung durch's Leben," iv. 48.   [2] Ibid., iv. 41.
[3] Against HENGSTENBERG's speech concerning the relation of the Catholic Church, especially of its mission, arose a cloud of witnesses. ZANDER's speech closed with the words, "Let us attack the enemy where he is to be found, namely, in the heart of Rome," and after this, "the sluices were opened, and the waters rose high." "Babel must fall." "Rome is an offspring of hell." "The infernal system of the Papacy evokes hatred, and the Gospel must, as long as Rome is Rome, hold no fellowship with it." These were the fundamental chords that were struck. Thus reports the "Neue Preussiche Zeitung," Sept. 19, 1852.

the Alliance Assembly, there has been a kind of truce entered upon. Those disposed to Lutheranism shake from time to time indignantly the ecclesiastical chains that "the Union" has imposed upon them; but they do not talk any longer of leaving the State Church. Some have endeavoured to establish themselves in countries that have remained Lutheran, but the majority feel themselves weak, because they are, in fact, nothing more than a party of theologians and pastors, without any flocks to follow them. Göschel, one of the temporal leaders of Lutheranism, mournfully confessed, lately, "that the Lutheran Church of Germany was really in a dying state. It has lost for the most part its very name; in many countries it has already fallen to ruin, and the cause of its destruction is the prevailing indifferentism." A reaction has indeed been aroused against the absorption of Lutheranism by "the Union," but it is utterly wanting in energy—it is sick with all kinds of hesitations and scruples.[1] "Throughout Germany," says a Würtemberg theologian,[2] "the Lutheran Church is become a mere name to the people; and as to the educated classes and theologians, it has with them been cut down to the root. 'Lutheran' has become in Würtemberg an obnoxious and abusive sectarian epithet."

If we now proceed to the contemplation of the state of individual Churches in Protestant Germany, there is first to be noted—especially since 1846—a very active life, and an impulse to ecclesiastical construction and improvement among the clergy, and the laity friendly to them. Numerous discussions at Conferences and Church-days, provincial and general, have taken place; and a considerable number of institutions of an educational or ethical character, or for the physical welfare of the people, have been established through the "Home Mission." But all great and really religious problems await their solution; and very few people have even made an attempt to come to an understanding as to *how* the problem can be solved.——

---

[1] "Zeitschrift für luth. Theolog.," 1860, p. 310.

[2] In Schaff's " Kirchenfreund," 1857, p. 67.

The very first question—that of the *Church Constitution*—the retention or abolition of the Episcopacy of the temporal sovereign—is at the outset calculated to cause a division, and to discourage the friends of the Church. In most countries, it is thought that the Cæsaro-Papacy is a chief cause of the decay of the Church. "What really oppresses our Church" (the writer is speaking especially of Saxony) "is the bureaucracy and the temporalization of the Church in all its institutions, so that all is bureaucratically governed, and spiritual affairs are disposed of like any other common matter of business.[1]

It is now well known what was thought of his own Supremacy by the monarch who, among all the princes of modern times, was the wisest and most clear-sighted friend of the Protestant Church. The state of the German Churches, we find, was in his eyes "absurd and untenable." "The territorial system, and the supremacy of the sovereign," says Frederick William IV., "are of such a nature, that one alone would be sufficient to kill a church, were it mortal." He then mentions, as a highly characteristic fact, that the abolition of the Consistory (in the year 1808), and the transference of its business to the government authorities, had been allowed to pass as a purely indifferent administrative measure, in which "the Church" was by no means concerned. "With all his soul and with all his strength" the king said, "he longed for the moment in which he might resign his Church supremacy to Bishops, with whatever name it might be thought fit to bestow upon them."[2]

Every important change in the state of things previously existing is regarded, however, with fear and trembling, even though the subserviency of the Church, and its absorption into the organism of the State, are felt to be oppressive and degrading. "Take from the Church," it is said, "in its present shattered condition—a condition that has become much worse since 1848—the support and strength it receives

---

[1] HENGSTENBERG's "K.-Z.," 1851, p. 99.

[2] L. RICHTER's "König Friedrich-Wilhelm IV., und die Verfassung der evangel.-Kirche." Berlin, 1861, pp. 22, 38.

from having the sovereign as its head and guardian, and you will see that it will fall asunder so completely that no one will ever be able to re-unite the fragments."[1] Up to this time it has never appeared that the orthodox have anywhere shewn themselves at all in earnest with the principle of Church independence. "The majority" warns and threatens them with fatal consequences. The only country in which a really new Church constitution has been introduced is Baden; and this does, in fact, appear as a terrifying example, although its originators regard their modern constitution as "a model for the whole of Evangelical Germany." Their plan is a transference of "political constitutionalism" to the Church—a change even in the idea and essence of the Church—which is hereby transformed from "a community of all who think to be justified by faith in Christ" into "a community of those who," according to the expression of a government organ, " believe in the moral order of the world."[2]

High hopes were placed for many years in the institution of the Synods. In Prussia—in all Germany—great things were expected from these assemblies; but they were required —that was the first condition—to leave the Episcopacy of the sovereign untouched, and restrict themselves to a merely deliberative character ; and to play the part rather of a convocation of Church notables than of a modern constitutional representative assembly. The first attempts were not encouraging. Concerning the ecclesiastical conference of the Deputies from German Princes, held in 1845, in Berlin, it is said : " The first attempt was the last, and remained without any visible result."[3] Then came the splendidly-composed General Synod of 1846, including the very flower of theological intelligence, and of the religiously-disposed portion of the Government. It undertook the solution of the most difficult religious questions, and desired to set aside the

[1] MESSNER's " K.-Zeitung," 1860, p. 84.
[2] MESSNER's " K.-Ztg.," July, 1861.
[3] RICHTER's " Geschichte der evangel. Kirchenverfassung in Deutschland," p. 253.

confessional writings of the old Reformers, and introduce a
new formula. This, which was drawn up by Nitzsch, was,
however, made so vague and verbose, in order that it might
be acceptable to all parties, that, as the Lutherans said, "it did
not attribute too much faith to the unbelieving, nor too much
incredulity to the believing." Although approved by the Synod,
it became a jest to the public in general; and a few months after
the termination of the Synod, no one would have anything to do
with the resolutions that had been passed by great majorities.[1]

New attempts at Synods were made in Berlin in the years
1856 and 1857. The King desired to have them, but he
was warned "that, by calling them together, he made
obvious to all the world the imperfection and disorders of the
Church, which otherwise had been partly a secret of the
authorities, and were known in all their extent only to a few
of the initiated."[2] The impossibility of a Synod devising
anything tenable in the way of a Confession of Faith, and
steering a safe course between the claims of the Union and
of the Lutherans, but especially the anxiety as to the form
in which this Synodical system was likely to develope itself,
occasioned this plan to be again dropped. One thing was
dreaded and detested as the worst that could happen to the
Church—namely, the rule of "majorities," or that Church-
democracy so warmly recommended by Bunsen. "If," said
Rothe, "the majority of those who count themselves as
members of our Church is to decide concerning matters of
faith, and doctrine, and worship, the Church established
according to their notions will soon have little more of a
Christian Church left in it."[3]

If we now turn to the doctrinal-theological side of the
German Protestant Church, we shall acknowledge, that here
—even at the present time—is its chief strength and fame.
That only in Germany does there now exist a real Protestant

[1] HENGSTENBERG, in the "Aktenstücken der Evang. Oberkirchenraths," 1856, iii., ii., p. 25.
[2] HENGSTENBERG. 1856, iii., ii.
[3] "Ethik," iii. 1041. See HENGSTENBERG's "K.-Ztg.," 1856, p. 533.

theology, a science of theology, is generally acknowledged. All other Churches of the Reformation obtain their theological nutriment—as far as they feel the want of any—from the Germans. Julius Müller and Liebner are quite in the right —the former, when he designates theology, " with its restless spirit of inquiry, and its earnest desire to dig deep," as the actual *charisma* of German Protestantism ;[1] the latter, when he paints the contrast between the burden of ignorance which lies on the Protestant Church—so that the "city upon a hill is scarcely any more to be seen, or the eye is blinded to it,"—and the splendid efforts of the German theologians of the present day.[2]

The Protestant Church of Germany is, before all things, and essentially, *a Theological Church*. Theologians, *literati*, learned university men, created it, and fixed on it, ineffaceably, the stamp of their own thoughts and actions. Theologians form its only authority, and, through the advice they give to princes, may be called its rulers. Its "churches" are, consequently, "schools," or " lecture-halls ;" and its "pulpits," "professorial chairs." It began its existence with the theses of an academical dispu- tation. The " word," as its founder was accustomed to say (and he never really departed from his professorial character), is, in fact, all—first and last—and its only word. It lec- tures, makes its bow, and withdraws; it preaches, and it sings, but its "chaunts" are not "hymns ;" they are, for the most part, nothing more than "versified theological treatises," or " sermons in rhyme." It is a Church born of a connubial alliance between professors and princes; the features of both parents are discernible in its features, though not exactly in harmonious combination; and if it is frequently reproached with being "sicklied o'er with the pale cast of thought"—and that it is " temporalized "—and that it is to be regarded as an institution rather than a Church—why, that is but merely saying that "the child cannot deny its

[1] " Fortbildung · der Deutsch-protestantischen Kirchenverfassung," p. 4.

[2] " Zur Kirchlichen Prinzipienfrage der Gegenwart." Dresden, 1860, p. 24, *et seq.*

own father and mother." And so it is possible that the judgment passed upon it by the richest intellect and most profound mind among living Protestant theologians may prove to be prophetic—" The Protestant Church in Germany," he says, " has educated a theology" (I should reverse this relation), " which, in the course of time—and that by no accidental process, but by the necessity of its very existence —will be brought into the most complete hostility with the same Church, and enter on a course, of which the sole, inevitable result must be its complete dissolution."[1]

Theology in Germany has indeed again become believing, but much is wanting to its being a rightly believing one in the sense of the confessional writings. Even those theologians who boast particularly of their faithful devotion to the Lutheran system are not orthodox. " The fact is obvious to every one," says Julius Müller, " that among all the Lutheran theologians who have lately published any comprehensive works in the domain of doctrines of faith, there is not a single one who does not consider the Lutheran symbolic books as requiring modification in some point or other."[2] And here come into consideration definitions of profound importance. " For many years," said Ehrenberg, at the Berlin General Synod, " he had been looking for a man who agreed in all points with the symbolic books of his confession, but as yet he had never found one."[3] For a century it has been maintained that no theologian, whether from his professorial chair or in the pulpit, has been instructing his hearers in complete accordance, either as to form and substance, with the symbolical books.[4] And so imperiously does this position, especially in reference to the solemn confession of faith, bear upon the clergy, that they have found out a way by which they might make that which is the fact appear to be in accordance with what was required both by law and custom.

[1] ROTHE's " Theologische Ethik," iii. 1015.
[2] " Deutsche Zeitschrift," 1855, p. 107.
[3] " Verhandlungen der evang. Generalsynode zu Berlin," p. 301.
[4] " Monatschrift für die unirte evang. Kirche," 1847, ii. 84.

U

So long as German Protestants were in the habit of submitting to every ecclesiastical regulation made by their monarchical supreme bishops, they quieted their consciences with the reflection that the princes had prescribed an oath to be taken as to the symbolical books; and then, about the close of the last century, jurists gave expression to this opinion: that the views taken as to the accepted teaching in reference to the symbolical books was only to continue as long as the Protestant princes might desire they should be maintained.[1]   After a long dispute upon the point, as to whether a person had to swear as to the symbolical books, either "*because*," or "*in so far as*," they contained Scripture doctrine, there came the period of Rationalism, in which "light work" was made with both oath and creed, and each individual found a consolation for himself in the multitude around him who entertained the same views, and were placed in a like predicament with himself.   Ever since 1817, the Church authorities proved themselves to be ingenious in discovering devices for giving full scope to private judgment, and in constructing formulas peculiarly qualified to evade or to weaken the rigidity of Confessional declarations.   And so persons promised to teach " in the spirit," or "according to the principles," or " in so far as they were scriptural," or " with a certain regard to the declarations of creed:" and in Baden they went so far as in their " Confession" to maintain a free examination of the Scriptures.   In Saxony and in Baden, however, the old, strict, and unconditional " Declaration" was adhered to.

All propositions and discussions upon the same question have, up to this time, been attended with an unsatisfactory result.   The Churches of the Reformation are in this predicament—they cannot well subsist without a solemn Declaration from their clergy and a settled doctrine; and neither can they subsist if they have either the one or the other. On one side it is said: " What can a Church be from which every symbol has vanished—what can it be but a Babel?"[2]

---

[1] TÖLLNER's " Unterricht von symbolischen Büchern," p. 30.

[2] BRÜMEL, in the " Luth. Zeitschrift," 1855, p. 275.

On the other side it is replied, and with perfect justice too: "A rigid binding down to symbols, in the present state of theology, can only lead to hypocrisy and intolerable violence to conscience."[1] Thus it is indispensable to make the solemn Declaration very vague, in order that a *free* scope be afforded to the clergy as to the symbol. And hence it is only "according to its spirit" that they can be judged; and the signification to be given to "the spirit," and the weight to be attached to it, must in the end be left to the clergy themselves, unless there happens to be, as in Saxony, a living, active, acknowledged authority to interpret and determine what doctrine is to be taught.

At the foundation of the Evangelical Church Union at Wittenberg, in the year 1848, a considerable number of distinguished theologians for the first time declared that "they stood, as to their creed, upon the ground of the Reformed Confession." This very wide phrase, and at bottom binding to nothing those who made it, has since that time become a great favourite. Then in the year 1853 it was declared, at a meeting in Berlin, "that the Augsburg Confession should be regarded as the standard and expression of a common creed and doctrine." This was the strongest and greatest effort at effecting a submission to a certain formula which had yet been made. The matter, however, though seriously proposed, was not seriously meant, for even those who were present assenting to such a proposition were thoroughly well aware that amongst themselves, and in all Germany, there was not a single theologian who did, in point of fact, accept all the articles of the Augsburg Confession. How little the parties who passed such a resolution felt themselves bound in points of faith by it, was soon shown by some of those who had taken part in the proceedings of the meeting at which it was passed (Schenkel, for instance), publishing writings which were in distinct and strong contradiction to the Confession of 1530.

And then, where "the Union" is most firmly established, there the authority of the symbolical books is irremediably

---

[1] Thus speak Rothe, Petersen, and Marheineke.

ruined. At church assemblies and pastoral meetings it has recently been declared that in Prussia, according to the Tenth Article, a person is free to partake of the Lord's Supper in three different senses—in the Lutheran, or the Calvinistic, or in accordance with the Union signification; and there are others, also, who maintain there is nothing to prevent its being taken and understood in a fourth or a fifth sense![1] Besides this, there was the fact, which was not, and could not, be disputed, viz., that by the Solemn Declaration contained in the Ordination Formula, many were, in Prussia (as well as in Saxony and Hanover), forced by the law to lie—the fact is not to be palliated, but to be lamented—and the only way of quieting individuals so situated was with the reflection that there was a multitude of others who were telling lies, or had lied; and that such lying must be borne with, because numbers of their followers would be involved in an inextricable embarrassment if a serious construction were put upon the Solemn Obligation.[2]

If the Solemn Obligation were to be accepted as effectively binding, and really to be acted upon, then the theological-scientific education of the sacerdotal order must be abandoned, and persons in authority restrict themselves to the formation of establishments for clerical candidates similar to the Dissenters' academies in England. No theologian can, or will, any more seriously bind himself to the whole doctrine of the Augsburg Confession and Concordian formulas. The use which hitherto has been made of these by-gone rules of creed has been mainly polemical. Every one lays down the measure of the symbolical books upon that which he desires to denounce as heterodox; but every one, at the same time, denies that his own doctrine is, when he departs from such a standard, to be decided by it. No one who is clothed with an official professional position can venture to stand against the torrent of modern exegesis; and when, for example, Erlangen theologians vowed that there was no passage in the Bible could be expounded in a sense different from that

---

[1] "Deutsche Zeitschrift," 1854, p. 200.

[2] Brux's "Repertorium," viii. 134.

which was laid down in the symbolical books, then "the Scripture Evidence" of Professor von Hofmann was pointed at; and he then was, on all sides, accused of being a falsifier of the pure Lutheran doctrine of " Satisfaction," and "Justification"—and so did the same book serve to show that, at this time of day, neither the big nor the little flies will remain quiescently pendent in the spider's web of such Solemn Obligations.

All are agreed in this—that the main doctrine of the whole of the Confessional writings is that of "Justification;" that in that dogma Protestant antagonism to the Catholic system has its centre and its most pregnant expression. In it "the Reformation recognises its central point, its noblest jewel, its essential substance—it is that wherewith Evangelical Christianity, founded upon the Gospel, stands and falls."[1] "No one understands anything of *Christianity* who has not a clear and vivid comprehension *of this doctrine*. This doctrine is, however, in its innermost core, destroyed in the Romish Church."[2]   "In accordance therewith," says Hengstenberg's organ, "in every sermon must our banner be at least once unfurled."[3] "The doctrine of Justification," it is said in Erlangen, "is the permanent death that gnaws the bones of Catholics."[4]   "It is the standard by which the whole of the Gospel must be interpreted, and every obscure passage explained."[5]

If now one should say to a religious member of the German (and especially on account of this doctrine self-styled "Evangelical") Church: "This doctrine is abandoned by the scientific theologians of Germany; there is scarcely one theologian of any name who will stand up, in serious earnestness, and with a view to the inevitable consequence following from it, for this dogma of the Reformers and of the symbolical

[1] KLING, in HERZOG's "Encyklopädie," xii. 582.
[2] Thus writes F. W. KRUMMACHER in the "Halleschen Volksblatte," 1853, p. 203.
[3] "Evang. K.-Z.," vol. xlviii., pp. 415-416.
[4] "Zeitschr. für Protest.," vol. xxvi., p. 119.
[5] *Ibid.*, vol. xxix., p. 134.

books, and the Concordian formula in particular"—if these words were so spoken, they would only provoke an incredulous and compassionate smile. And yet such is absolutely the fact. Already had Tholuck's "Literary Advertiser" (litterarischer Anzeiger) directed general attention to the unheard-of levity with which the article on "Justification" was at the present time treated;[1] so that what the Reformers had (as in the case of Osiander and others) rejected, was now declared to be the orthodox doctrine. And then it has been shown by Schneckenburger[2] that the new Lutheran theologians have disowned both the doctrine of Luther and the symbolical books, and have abandoned the main article of "Justification," or they have given to it a signification the very opposite to that which the first Reformers had desired or intended. And so it has come to pass, as he remarks, that there is but one theological writer, who can at the present time be named, who remains true to the old Lutheran doctrine, and that is Petri.[3] Since Schneckenburger's death the contradiction between the dogmatic and exegetical deductions of theologians, and between a general appeal to the "Confession," the "pure Doctrine," and the article of "the standing and falling Church," has become more sharp, harsh, and dissonant. A few years ago Kahnis, too, declared, "he recognised in the direction of the 'Union' theology (Nitzsch, Lange, Müller, &c.) no theologians who stood on the basis of 'Justification through faith.'" Kahnis had, he said, to remark with respect to "Justification"—first, that he held with the Lutheran theologians—Martensen, Von Hofmann, Sartorius, and others; and, secondly, that he had found himself formerly in a position like to theirs.[4]

[1] "Jahrg," 1848, p. 248.

[2] "Vergleichende Darstellung des lutherischen und reformirten Lehrbegriffs," 1855, ii. 38-45.

[3] Although SCHNECKENBURGER is right, upon the whole, in his judgment of the Lutheran doctrine and theologians, still he has fallen into error when he ascribes to the Reformers an opposite doctrine, by hunting up a few theologians of the same confession, who held opinions opposite to the prevailing and adopted doctrine, and then putting those few forward as the real representatives of the Protestant Church doctrine.

[4] "Die Lehre vom heiligen Geiste." Halle, 1847, p. 82.

And here, if the author is not to be reproached with the introduction of what may be considered as superfluous, he would wish to cite the names of theologians, some living, and some dead, who were participators in the latest theological development, and who have abandoned the Protestant doctrine of " Justification," as it is set forth in the Concordian formula and the Heidelberg Catechism, and which was the prevailing doctrine until 1760.

These theologians are—Olshausen, Schleiermacher and his entire school, Heydenreich, Brandt, Nitzsch, Ullmann, Neander, Sartorius, Bähr, Schenkel, Martensen, Nägelsbach, J. T. Beck, Köllner, Schöberlein, Gerock, Hundeshagen, Richard Rothe, J. P. Lange, Ebrard, Von Hofmann, Julius Müller, Lipsius, Beneke, Rennecke, Sack, Dorner, Köstlin, Baumgarten, Düsterdiek, Kurtz, Ackermann, Krehl, Schmid, Weizsäcker, Kalchreuter, Krahner, Gess, Stier, Grüneisen, Hagenbach, and De Wette.[1] This list could, upon more diligent examination, be certainly considerably enlarged. It indisputably embraces the most gifted individuals, and who, as the most profound investigators in Biblical learning, have especially imparted a new impulse to theology. And, assuredly, many others might take their place by the side of those that have been named, if they had not preferred, upon such a subject as this, to content themselves with the hackneyed phrases of " Justification by Faith," &c., &c.; and at the same time carefully eschewed every close exposition and minute anatomization of the dogma.

It has, indeed, been for some time customary to make an open avowal as to an adherence to the material principle of the Reformation, and so to carry on a game with phrases, as if they

---

[1] Even the theologians, who pass in our days as the purest Lutherans, have not escaped the reproach of having fallen away from the Lutheran doctrine of " Justification." This has occurred with KLIEFOTH, (see " Zeitsch. für luth. Theol.," 1854. p. 84), and so with Thomasius, Harless, and Preger (see KLIEFOTH's " Kirchl. Zeitsch.," 1858, p. 404). Guerike, who has obtained, beyond all others, the praise of holding by the purest Lutheran orthodoxy, is shown in THOLUCK's " Theol. Anzeiger," 1848, p. 322, &c., to have had in his description of the " Justification" creed, in his " Symbolik" (2d Edit., 1846, p. 305), to have destroyed what was the leading idea of Luther and the Reformation.

were so many counters; whilst, as regards these phrases, no
fixed ideas are attached to them, or different ideas are
affixed to the same solemn words of "Justification by Faith."
"Of what avail is it," says a theologian, "to Evangelical
Christianity, if it confesses that it is only through faith that
righteousness and salvation are attainable, when it is at the
same time not agreed as to *wherefore* there is faith unto
salvation."[1] Upon this point Schenkel is a remarkable
example; for he, upon every opportunity, repudiates the
Reformer's doctrine of Justification as untenable; and then
again can speak exactly like one of the mob of preachers
upon the grand material principle of Protestantism! Thus,
too, Bunsen intimates that Justification alone through Faith
has been translated out of the Semitic tongue into the
Japhetic, and that it is "the principle of moral self-
responsibility."[2] And very recently, Rossman, in his
"Remarks upon the age of the Reformation," ("Betrachtung-
en über das Zeitalter der Reformation,") made the discovery
that every modern state is based upon the evangelical
principle of Justification through Faith!

It is indisputably one of the most suggestive and, at the
same time, widely comprehensive events in the later history
of religion, that the doctrine which was peculiarly the foundation of the whole edifice of Protestant teaching should be
scientifically prostrated completely to the earth. It is, in
sooth, still a standing reproach for one theologian to make to
another that it is sought to lead him into error, and to turn
him away from the "Gospel," when the attempt is made to
divert him from the pure doctrine of Justification by Faith.
But then, when a person is compelled to propound a scientific
exposition of the dogma, and when general phrases can no
longer be employed, then there regularly is brought into
view a doctrine which Reformers and the genuine followers
of Luther denounce as "Papistical" or "Arminian."

[1] Löwe in the "Göttinger Monatschrift für Theol. und Kirche," 1851,
p. 336. Also Hase, "Die Entwicklung des Protestantismus," 1855, p.
19, speaks openly upon the contradiction between the now widely extended notion of Justification through Faith and the orthodox doctrine.
[2] "Hippolytus," i. 339.

Exegetic theology in Germany has become so powerful, and distinguished expounders of the Bible have still so high a scientific reputation to maintain, that the repulsion of this theology to the expositions of the sixteenth and seventeenth centuries, is an impossibility. Not a few of the modern exegetists have, with the very best intentions, attempted to connect together the doctrines of the Reformers and the Bible. With such intentions they went to work; but their labour came to—naught! The staff is broken upon which they leant who sought to render the Confessional writings again available; and the toil has been vain of those who have sought to restore the old Protestant creed, and to re-animate the faith at one period placed in the symbolical books. Even the distinctive appellation of "Evangelical," has no longer its right signification; for what was meant at the time of the Reformation by that word was—the "Imputation" doctrine, with all its consequences.   .

And yet all things were attempted, and all, too, ventured, for the purpose of upholding this "article of a standing and falling Church!" It was for the sake of this that the Epistle of St. James was pronounced to be "an epistle of straw;" and it was for the sake of this that in the *Augsburg Confession*, laid before the Emperor and the Empire, the barefaced falsehood was promulgated, that this doctrine had previously been maintained by St. Augustine; and when Melancthon, out of sheer down-right shame, had omitted it from an edition of the Confession, still it was—despite of most earnest protests on the part of a few theologians—again (in 1576) foisted into the text of the Confession! For the sake also of this doctrine, had Luther deliberately and purposely given a mistranslation of several passages in the Bible, and especially of the Epistles of St. Paul; it was, too, to uphold this, his favourite dogma, that the great Reformer interpolated fanciful expressions of his own, that were foreign to, and altogether undiscoverable in, the original text.

The Reformers went further. For the purpose of being able to preserve and maintain an article of faith which was utterly unknown to all Christian antiquity, a breach was

made with all ecclesiastical tradition, and the authority
of the dogmatic testimony of the Church in every age
rejected. "This," says Julius Müller, "must be openly
admitted, by every unprejudiced historical investigation, that
not merely the ecclesiastical theology of the middle ages,
but even the Patristic theology of the fourth, fifth, and sixth
centuries, are, upon every point that is a matter of dispute
between Catholicism and Protestantism, more on the side of
the former than of the latter."[1]

If Müller intended to intimate that this important fact
lay concealed from the men of the Reformation, viz., that
their doctrine was at variance with that which was maintained in the first centuries of Christianity, he is partly right,
that is, he is so far right in this, that the fact was carefully
concealed from the people—that the laity did not know anything about it; but it was far otherwise in the narrow circle
of the Reformers, because there the circumstance was openly
adverted to. Melancthon declared in his letter to Brenz that
what he had maintained for the German Protestants in the
Augsburg Confession was an untruth. Luther had frequently and frankly avowed that his doctrine was quite different from any to be found in the most ancient Churches ;
and hence it was that he contemned the Fathers, as witnesses
to what was the Ancient Church doctrine. His labours to
lower, so far as he possibly could, in public estimation, the
authority of the Ancient Councils, were plainly in correspondence with the consciousness of their being adverse to
his doctrine. The same thing has been acknowledged by
Calvin, viz.—that the new doctrine of "Justification" was
neither to be found in tradition nor amongst the Fathers.
And when the United Theologians and preachers of Rostock,
in a written appeal to the preachers of the cities of Lübeck,
Hamburg, and Lüneburg, declare—"That as to the articles
of 'Free Will,' 'Grace,' and 'Justification,' the teaching of orthodox antiquity is in complete concordance with that mentioned by Catholic theologians"[2]—when such a circumstance,

[1] "Deutsche Zeitschrift," July, p. 214.

[2] See BERTRAM's "Evangel. Lüneburg," p. 271. They remark that
there are only a few passages in the later writings of Augustine and

we say, as this occurs, then it is plain that those who really are theologians indulge in no illusions upon these points. But then—when persons are speaking before the world—another, and quite a different, form of language is used.

A something, however, must be said upon this point, and what it is may be surmised from the view which Stahl takes of it, viz.—"Imputed righteousness is the mystery which contains the innermost essence of the Christian religion, and the fulness of Divine Light; and it is only through the Reformation that this Divine Light was shed upon the spirit of mankind."[1] And this doctrine it is which peculiarly qualifies

Prosper (upon the irresistible operation of Grace). They are an exception to the Catholic and Ancient Church doctrine.

[1] HENGSTENBERG's "K.-Z.," 1853, pp. 324-325. The theologians of modern times are in the habit of avoiding the use of the expression "imputed righteousness" as a distinction from true, interiorly affected "righteousness." The discourse is ever only of the righteousness by faith, justification through faith. This designation, however, in the mouth of a Protestant is so much the more inapplicable and deceptive, as it is the Catholic Church that has been peculiarly competent to show how faith, operating through love, has been found to be right in the sight of God; whilst, on the other hand, according to the old Protestant system, it is not faith, but the imputation of the sufferings of Christ, which makes man appear justified before God, or that the process of justification is therewith fulfilled, that God attributes to man the sufferings and the fulfilment of the law by Christ, as if man himself had yielded the same obedience, and that man, through faith, knows and becomes assured of this imputation. By such a mode of comprehending the subject, man is justified in a very vague manner—merely through the means of a very forced figure of speech; so that one can only be said to be justified through faith, as it might be affirmed "that he had eaten a full meal because he had handled a fork." But what service the imputation doctrine can confer upon individuals or the community may be inferred from the following words of VILMAR :—"Even in Luther, despite of all the boundless graces bestowed upon him, there is sin—and sin never to be justified But we see in him not sin, but to the sinner imputed righteousness through faith in the one Redeemer, Jesus Christ; and all have heard what He has said, that through this imputed righteousness is alone to be judged what may, in man's whole existence, happen, or apparently occur to him. Take away this imputed righteousness, let us not see it, and then nought remains of him but the weakest sinner, and in all his thoughts the wildest nonsense that the dreariest of madcaps ever devised."—"Zeitschr. für luth. Theol.," 1848, p. 284.

the Lutheran Church to hold a high position in the Catholicity of its doctrine—of that Catholicity which, as he says,
ever consists in God-appointed doctrine and ordinance, and
in being the bond of Christianity for all places and through
all times, and in opposition to human invented error, which
never has been *universally* accepted.[1]

In the author's judgment the importance of the subject
here mentioned can scarcely be too highly appreciated. Here
upon the one side stand Luther, Melancthon, Calvin, and
their disciples, the Protestant Confessional writings, and the
combined Lutheran and Calvinistic theology of the sixteenth
and seventeenth centuries. They all have professed to find
that doctrine which we for brevity sake name "the doctrine
of Imputation," laid down distinctly in the Bible. On the
other side is the newer and the latest theology, the whole
modern scientific exegesis, and it rejects the doctrine, it rejects the Reformation exposition of fragmentary Bible passages as false and untenable. But it is a supreme evangelical principle, that the Scripture is perfectly clear and sufficient on all fundamental points. How, then, is this fundamental difference to be cleared up? And thereby is concerned a doctrine which, as everyone admits, has an incalculable influence upon Christian consciousness and ecclesiastical
life—a doctrine (by the admission or confession of many
Protestant theologians), that had formerly been a source of
destruction to countless beings, and has caused a desolation of the Churches, of which persons formerly had no fore-
thought. The whole edifice of the Protestant Church and
theology reposes, therefore, on two principles—one material,
the other formal: the doctrine of Imputation, and the sufficiency of the Bible. But the material principle is given up
by exegesis and dogmatic theology; and as to the formal
principle, for the sufficiency of the Bible, or even for the
inspiration of the writings of the disciples of the Apostles,
not the shadow of a scriptural argument can be adduced.
The time will, it *must*, come when the whole vast importance
of this matter will excite universal attention. To such

[1] "Die lutherische Kirche," 1859, p. 452.

serious thought must the experience which has now been gone through force the attention of those who, in driving Rationalism out of the pulpit, and re-establishing a Protestant believing body of preachers, have found the experiment not correspond with their expectations. " For a long time," says Baumgarten,[1] "persons might entertain the notion that it was Rationalism made our churches empty, and our preaching unattended to. But now since Christ crucified is again preached, and yet no serious effect, upon the whole, is to be observed, it is necessary to abandon this mistake, and not to conceal from ourselves that preaching is unable to revive religious life." "The impotency of the present preaching," he continues, "is still more appalling, when it is generally known and confessed that those who could testify to the extreme depth of the degradation to which it has descended, refrain from telling the entire of its evil consequences."

Delitzsch has confirmed the testimony given by Baumgarten. " It is," he says, "indeed true that the nullity of results from preaching is one of the saddest circumstances of the day."[2] And there have of late been many Councils held as to the causes of this deplorable fact. The Berlin meeting of the Evangelical Alliance occupied itself a good deal with this theme. " Wherefore," it was asked, "has it come to pass that, despite of a restoration of theology to the Ecclesiastical Confessions, there should be exhibited so little of spiritual life amongst the congregations ?" Professor Krafft, who delivered a lecture on the subject, has recognised some of the causes of the evil. He has said, and that, too, plainly enough, that the doctrine of the symbolical books had, at a former period, effected " the downfall of all spiritual life ; and persons, therefore, must not be surprised, if its renewal at the present moment should bear similar fruit."[3] The preacher Beyschlag, of Carlsruhe, who, immediately after Krafft, addressed the meeting, has spoken still more clearly on the same theme,

[1] " Nachtgesichte des Sacharias," 1855, ii. 121, et seq.
[2] " Erlang. Zeitschr. für Protestantismus," 1858, p. 305.
[3] " Verhandlungen," p. 186.

which he referred to as "the most peculiarly pressing and urgent ecclesiastical question of the time."[1]   The whole calamity of the Protestant Church up to this very day was "its one-sided creed—confession"—the "dead orthodoxy," with its doctrine of " Sanctification."[2]   "Out of it Rationalism had naturally sprung; and the revival of this orthodoxy has become a chronic Church epidemic, seizing upon and carrying off great numbers of the clergy."

Naturally, these declarations, as to the phenomenon, were repudiated by many; but, then, as to the fact itself, all were unanimous.   And even at meetings of preachers (for instance, the Berliners, in 1858, and the Saxons, at Gnadau, in 1859), held consultations about it.   Lately, too, the tendency towards which the faithful were inclining was complained of even in a Palatinate ecclesiastical journal.[3]   " If," as it said, " one looks closely into the condition of individual congregations, to whom, for long years, the Gospel has been preached in its simplicity and purity, it will be found that the Word seems to have fallen on land covered with thorns, or upon a stony soil, or upon the hard-beaten highway ;" and in such a complaint is involved the strongest demand for subjecting the so-called " Evangelical Gospel " itself to a revision.

In logical connection with the Imputation doctrine stands the Reformation apprehension of " *the four last things.*"   The old Lutheran and Calvinistic doctrine was, that every man, upon his death, instantly either attained to the happiness of Heaven, or was thrust down into Hell.   An indispensable absolution and purification from sin was regarded as a species of physical process, and lay in death and the corruption of the body—so that, as a modern writer has remarked, "all that was wanting to Death was the name of a Sacrament, and to join it on to, and make it the completion of, the other two."[4]

[1] " Verhandlungen," p. 194.

[2] In the same manner in which the " justitia forensis" was branded by him, was the old essentially Protestant doctrine referred to.   See p. 195.

[3] " Evangelischer Reichsbote," 1859, " Neujahrswort."

[4] FRIES, in the " Jahrbüchern für deutsche Theol.," i. 304.   I do not understand how KLIEFOTH (" Liturg. Abhandlungen," i. 169) can make

At the time of the Reformation, and even up to the end of the last century, the people were very ready to accept this notion, which the lightness of faith, and Declaration Acts, made appear to them as alike suitable and consolatory. Truly, indeed, as Professor Neumann has complained, "has the doing away of every species of communion between the living and the dead mainly led the mass of Protestants to the very brink of doubt in everlasting life."[1] From it has arisen that general beatification, and that pestilent mischief of funeral sermons, which have, in no slight degree, contributed to a moral and religious torpor, and to the wide-spread frivolous delusion, as to man's ascension into Heaven being alike instantaneous and easy of accomplishment."[2]

Theologians have now recognised the sad defect of the old system; and even zealous Lutherans cannot venture to fall back upon this point to the views promulgated by the early Reformers. Hence, for some time back, the necessity has been perceived for adopting a half-way manner of explaining it—as has been done, for example, by Kern, Fries, Girgensohn, and others. And then, as to a question connected therewith —that is, "If prayer for the dead was permissible or advisable?"—that is put to rest as an undecided point. Every preacher has, concerning it, either his own settled opinion, or —none! That which, in some places, it is recommended to the laymen to do, is, in other places, exposed to a severe censure. The old Lutheran theologians consistently declared that prayers for the departed were altogether useless.[3] The Prussian Agenda has adopted the practice, whilst, at the same time, in accordance with the example given by the Anglican Church Liturgy, it assures the hearers of the salvation of the deceased, and that he is indubitably in the full possession of beatitude; and hence its prayers may be

Rationalism responsible for what had previously been the doctrine of the Reformers.

[1] " Zeitschrift für luth. Theologie," 1852, 282.

[2] See upon this point the recollections of MAYWAHLEN in the Preface to his book, " Der Tod." Berlin, 1854.

[3] KLIEFOTH'S " Liturg. Abhandlungen," i. 311.

regarded as an insignificant formula. Besides this, there are
to be found amongst clergymen, as in Würtemberg, no few
adherents to the doctrine of a restoration of all things—for
example, the prelate Kapff—and these persons, in their
innocence! do not perceive that they thus shatter to pieces
the old Protestant system, and do not leave one stone of it
resting upon another!

In *Divine Service*, the doctrine of a Church gives a form
to its religious aspect. If there is in a Church a sound
and harmonious relation between doctrine and life, between
the clergy and the laity, it manifests itself in the appro-
priateness of the Divine Service, and the participation of the
people.

There are not more, it may be said, than three possible
modes of a Christian form of worship. Either the sermon
constitutes the main portion and centre of the worship, so
that the remainder, hymn and prayer, are merely subservient
assistants. Or, the main act of worship is a Liturgy, in
which there is a reading aloud of passages of Scripture and
forms of prayer. Or, in the third, the worship is an actual
celebration of the whole work of Redemption—a Communion,
in which all who are present participate in the complete act
of the Lord's Supper, and in which each of the whole community offers himself up, with Christ, a victim to the Father
—as the most perfect form of adoration to the Almighty
God. The first form is indisputably the most suitable to the
old and true Protestantism; the second is that which has
been chosen by the English Established Church, and though
pleasing to the higher classes, is not so universally acceptable
to the populace; the third is the form of worship of the
ancient Church, and of the ecclesiastical communities which
have maintained their continuity, either without interruption
or essential change—such as the Catholic, the Greek, the
Russian, and the Monophysite Churches in Asia and Africa.
In Protestant Germany, the sermon has always had the
absolute masterdom. The Divine Service is a preachment
service, and its Church peculiarly and especially a lecture-

room, or a school. It became an accepted maxim with its
theologians, that without a sermon there could be no real
Divine Service. In the same measured progress in which
this opinion advanced, it was found that, without any pre-
concert, and without any visible influence of one national
Church upon another, the few liturgical pieces which had
been at the first used in Divine Service, began to disappear
from amongst the congregations in all parts of Germany.[1]
And this impoverishment of the Divine Service was thus
shewn to be a perfectly natural circumstance, for it was one
in complete correspondence with the Protestant mode of
thought and feeling.

The consequence of this practice was—first, that the congregations were, for their edification, in subjectivity to the
clergy; secondly, that the complete passivity of the people
in the Divine Service became the characteristic mark of
Protestant worship. Theologians themselves have admitted
"that at no period has there been found the same rank
deficiency of congregational energy amongst Catholics as in
the midst of Protestants."[2]   "The Evangelical Church,"
says another, "repudiates every semblance of the office and
order of priesthood, and yet transfers the whole of the
Divine Service into the hands of a preacher, and affords to
him a proportionately higher power, and a far more exclusive
representation of the whole congregation, than the Romish
Church has ever conceded to one of its priests."[3] Hence
the attendance on Divine Service is altogether dependent
upon the popularity of the preacher; and hence persons are
accustomed to say, "I no longer go to church to *him*." A
third points out the contradiction that arises between the
numerous discourses of a priesthood and the immobility of

[1] GRUNEISEN, "Die Evang. Gottesdienstordnung." Stuttgart, 1856,
p. 41. He shows how naturally it came to pass in Würtemberg since
the sixteenth century, until at length its Divine service had not its equal
for " poverty and partiality."

[2] BAHR, " Begründung einer Gottesdienstordnung." Karlsruhe, 1856,
p. 154.

[3] REES VON ESENBECK, " Der christl. Gottesdienst," 1854, p. 161.

the congregations, who never say even an " Amen" to the
prayers offered up for them, but merely let themselves be
talked at; and it is affirmed that the much lauded and often
praised simplicity of the Protestant Divine Service should
be most properly described as " poverty-stricken" and
" monotonous," and not only imparting an impression of
" dryness," but also as being characterized with "weakness,
weariness, and somnolency."[1]

And it has come to this, that, by the admission of the
clergy themselves, they have no longer congregations, but
merely a public audience, and that audience chooses the
preacher it prefers—fancying him for his voice, manners,
and attitudes—running after him who best suits its own
notions, and then forsaking him if he has exhausted his gifts as
an orator, or has ceased to be the fashionable.   And there
is also the declaration of a very calamitous fact—of visits to the
Church being barren of fruit, of being negligently paid, and
so the churches left empty.   "The community," says a
Prussian clergyman, "are sickened with sermons; and the
multitude has become tired, at last, of having always to go to
school !"[2]

In such circumstances, it is a remarkable symptom of the
present state of affairs—viz. the experiment at an intrusion
upon the territory of the Divine Service, such as had never
before been attempted.   For three hundred years there
never had been so much written upon the same topic as
within the last ten or twenty years.[3]   The first species of
aid that presented itself, naturally, was to increase the
number of hymns and prayers, such as has happened in
Prussia since the introduction of the liturgical element.

But then this fact has come out on all sides—namely, that
the churches are really only visited by the public for the
sake of the sermon.   The singing and the Divine service are
neglected, and it is only a short time previous to the delivery

[1] Schönerlein, " Ueber den liturgischen Ausbau," 1859, p. 83.
[2] Cunz, " Das geistliche Amt und der Pastorenstand," p. 60.
[3] Bahr, p. 1.

of the sermon that the churches begin to fill. Such is certainly the case in all Saxony.[1] And then wherever the "Agenda" is introduced, there is the same account to be given of the behaviour of the people. "In North and Middle Germany," says Zittel, "I have often had the opportunity of remarking how three fourths of the church visitors only began to enter the church when the liturgy was over, and that immediately after the sermon they again left it.[2] Even the General Superintendent Hofmann has remarked that in most cases congregations exhibit not the slightest participation in the Service during the Liturgy, or they are merely represented in the children's choir.[3]

There is an awful lack of the solemn festivals of the Catholic Church, in which each great festival is symbolically individualised, and adapts itself in a life-like manner to the popular sentiment and feeling. The Protestant Church, on the other hand, "which has an absolute horror of all symbolical significations in its Divine service," and therefore, as it is said by a clergyman of that church, "there is in our festivals something so monotonous, and in all their physiognomies something so similar, that they can neither be distinguished from one another, nor from the usual Sunday services."[4] And then, if an alteration be attempted, and a symbolical element introduced, the same fate overtakes it as befell the attempt to make the people kneel down during Divine service—that is, it is almost everywhere put an end to.[5] The preachers and the Consistories were perfectly willing again to introduce the practice; but the population refused with the declaration—"Kneeling is a Catholic practice." It was further desired that Protestant churches should be not merely stations for preaching, but also houses of prayer;[6] for they were in this respect in such a scandalous

[1] HENGSTENBERG's "K.-Z.," 1858, p. 1114.

[2] HUNDESHAGEN, "Der Badische Agendenstreit." Frankfort, 1859, p. 13.   [3] MESSNER's "Kirch.-Ztg.," 1860, p. 105.

[4] ZITTEL, "Zustände," &c., p. 236.

[5] SCHÖBERLEIN, "Ueber den liturg. Ausbau." Gotha, 1859, pp. 329, 330.

[6] "Erlang. Zeitsch.," vol. xxv., p. 185.

condition, that "one could not bring a heathen inside of
them without blushing for shame."[1] They seemed but to
be intended for a brief assembling together. The only use
to which they were applied was for a meeting of an hour or
two's duration every eight days. The people did nothing for
the adornment of their churches; they were nothing more,
in public estimation, than "the stone houses in which the
preacher made a speech on Sundays," and they were regarded
as quite good enough for that purpose. But here is a point
on which advice is of no use. If there were another service
in the course of the week, it would be only another sermon
over again, and the people (it was generally acknowledged)
had already had quite enough of preaching. And then—
there is the fact—that it is only within the last ten or twenty
years that there ever had been in many places Divine service
in the middle of the week.

But then there was another mode of proceeding—one,
however, that has not yet been introduced—and that will
not be attempted, because of the universal opposition it would
provoke, but that still in theory is recommendable—and that
is, in accordance with the custom in the old church, to make
the Holy Communion the main part and centre of the Divine
service, and therewith to recognise and exalt the character
of the Victim in this Holy Action. Such a course is now
recommended by the most illustrious of the theologians—by
Kliefoth, Hengstenberg, Höfling, Sartorius, Harnack, Löhe,
Kahnis, Bachmann, &c. And here is to be noted an essential
difference between Lutheranism and Calvinism—that the
Lutherans in their churches have an altar, and thereby at
least intimate the desire for a Sacrifice and its admissibility;
whilst the Calvinists have only a common table for their
celebration of the Lord's Supper.[2] This Sacrifice theory is,
however, an open repudiation of real Protestantism, for its
originators and promoters, when they proceed seriously with
the subject, are compelled to abandon the name of "Lutherans." And sharp reproaches have not failed to be made

---

[1] HENGSTENBERG'S "K.-Z.," 1857, p. 529.
[2] GÖBEL'S "Reform. K.-Z.," 1855, p. 167.

against such theologians for their " Mass-Sacrifice theory,"
and with respect to their "catholicising." [1]

There is a very pressing necessity felt as to the restoration
of the fitting celebration of Sunday devotion, and impressing
upon the people an attendance upon Divine service as a
sacred duty. But here again every struggle is impeded by
Protestant principles, which rise up in the way as insur-
mountable obstacles.

Kraussold,[2] Liebetrut, and others, have shown that the
principles of the Reformation have rendered it impossible to
found upon them an obligation to the solemn observance of
the Sabbath. The Sabbath has fallen with the Mosaic law;
the Sunday is not to be found commanded as a Holy
Day in the New Testament; the Church has no higher
authority to introduce such a Holy Day: to its commands,
therefore, there is as little obedience due (through Evangelical freedom) as to its Ordinances respecting Fasting,
Confession, and so forth. How, then, is it possible to make
a Protestant population comprehend that they are bound
to the observance of the Sunday as a Holy Day? The
numberless councils for the last thirty years that have been
held upon this question have, as a matter of course, only
served to establish the complete impossibility of solving it.
Already has a demand been made to change the Lutheran
translation of the Bible; but when the people seek there for
a passage upon the Sunday, and upon the obligation to
observe it holy, and can find no such thing, then the preacher
by his interposition will not be able to afford much help in
getting out of the difficulty.[3]

A similar difficulty manifests itself in the case of the Baptists,
who form a considerable and constantly increasing fraction of
Protestant Christianity. It is now admitted on all sides
that neither a command of Christ nor of the Apostles can be
cited in support of Infant Baptism. At the Church
Assembly at Frankfort, in the year 1854, space was afforded

[1] See " Studien und Kritiken," 1836, p. 472.
[2] " Drei Kapitel über die Sonntagsfeier." Erlangen, 1850.
[3] " Deutsche Zeitschrift," 1855, p. 273.

for the reception of the Baptists present, by the declaration
of the President, that "Infant Baptism was one of those
problems that had not yet been fully solved." And there
have been a few theologians, such as Ebrard, who would
much rather yield the point and abandon Infant Baptism, so
that the principle of the literal interpretation of the Bible
may be preserved, and persons not be compelled to recognise
the authority of the Church. For years persons have, in
Conferences and Church Assemblies, been labouring at the
double question of Infant Baptism and Baptism by effusion
or aspersion, without being able to make one step in
advance.

But this is not all: Even as regards Marriage and the
Nuptial Benediction there are now assertions set up, from
which, in point of fact, all that can be said or inferred is,
that those who make them would, if they could, support
them by Scriptural quotations. Thus, a short time ago, the
Lutheran Pastoral Conference at Ravensberg, amongst
others, adopted a resolution to the effect, " That the Church
cannot acknowledge any real marriage without Ecclesiastical
Benediction."[1] At the same time, it was declared to be the
determination of the Assembly to enter a Protest against all
civil marriages within the Church, and to excommunicate
everyone who entered into a civil marriage. It may easily
be guessed what answer these pastors would be able to give
if a layman had called upon them for Scriptural proofs in
sustainment of such propositions.

The utter helplessness of the clergy in their relations with
their congregations in general, as well as individual members
—the fact that at present the pulpit is the only place from
which, and the sole means through which, the preacher can
exercise any effective influence—all these things have
attracted the attention of many to the two most deeply felt
defects of ecclesiastical life : and these are a want in the care
of souls and of Church discipline. Upon the possibility and
the urgency of attempting a restoration of both, there has

[1] " Darmstädt K.-Ztg.," 1859, No. xxxiv.

been much both thought and written. Almost every assembly of preachers is occupied especially with the question of Church discipline, of which the last remnants have long since disappeared. And then it has been thoroughly recognised that "a cure of souls" can be only attainable when the souls show themselves as they really are to their clergyman—make themselves known to him—seek for and desire his advice and special guidance; and the only means by which such objects are attainable is through confession. "The Confessional," says Kliefoth, "is the place ordained for the cure of souls."[1] The practice of "Confession" has, however, disappeared from all parts of Germany. The preacher now announces a general absolution from the pulpit, without even the form of a confession of sins being gone through or acknowledged and admitted by an affirmation on the part of the congregation.

Every attempt to facilitate a revival of the practice of Confession instantly encounters a determined opposition on the part of the people.[2] "Private Confession," it is said, in the Protestation of the Augsburg Protestants against the Orders of the Upper Consistory, in the year 1856, "is, considering the position of Evangelical clergymen, and their connection with family life, an institution that would be absolutely intolerable." "The people," say the Erlangen Theolo-

[1] "Liturgische Abhandlungen," ii. 496.

[2] The following report from Riga shows what are the means employed to render it impossible for preachers to have a real "cure of souls":— "The office of the clergyman as a spiritual director—the cure of souls—is here, as with us elsewhere, fallen into desuetude. People have long since desisted from making the clergyman the confidential depository of their spiritual condition. The moment it is suggested, then there is a notion of 'auricular confession,' 'priestcraft,' 'tyrannizing over consciences,' &c., &c., &c. Many would, upon being noticed in making a nearer approach to the clergy, be warned, as if they were upon the point of abandoning the evangelical faith and becoming Catholics."—"Kirchliche Vierteljahrsschrift," Berlin, 1845, p. 166. Cunz and others had remarked that when a person in Protestant districts happened to ask a question as to "who was the *spiritual director* of the place?" he received as an answer, "There are no Catholics here, and the only clergyman here is—*a preacher*."

gians, "never have had confidence in their clergymen as
Father-Confessors."[1]   It is, then, no longer possible to re-
establish "Confession" in any form whatever—not even in
the old Lutheran fashion, whereby all that was done was to
recite to the preacher "a General Confession of Sins," which
was either got off by heart, or read out from a piece of paper
—even that, the easiest, most commodious, and most imperfect
form of Confession—one, too, of which conscientious clergymen in the seventeenth century had such a horror, that they
declared "the Lutheran mode of making confessions was the
plague of their Church"—well! even that can be never
more introduced and established.   Every attempt must be
wrecked upon the rock of that prime and darling doctrine of
"a universal priesthood," by means of which everyone is
made his own priest and teacher, and stands in need of no
intermediary, no witness, and no office, but can, with a clear,
unswerving conscience, absolve himself of his own sins!
So has it at all times been held in every Calvinistic Reformed
Church, and consequently there is nothing less thought of in
"the Union" than the revival of Confession.   "Of what
avail to me is mine own priesthood," says a Protestant layman, "if I must first be assured by a pastor, who knows
nothing of the state of my soul, that my sins have been forgiven me?"   The power of dispensing with every species of
priestly intercession—"the directness of a communication
with Christ"—is, as it has been in various modes already
expressed, that which, connected with the Imputation doctrine, makes (with many) the Protestant religion far prefer-
able to the Catholic.[2]

For the purpose of winning an assent to the possibility of
establishing a sacerdotal, sin-absolving office—and to induce
persons again to recognise-—(that which is alike strange and
foreign to the notions both of preachers and laymen in the
world of Protestantism)—an individual really having a cure
of souls—there has been devised a portrait of a universal
priesthood, which very closely resembles the Catholic view,

[1] " Zeitschr. für Protest.," vol. xxi., p. 52.
[2] See, for example, the "Deutsche Zeitschrift," 1857, p. 66.

and is the very opposite of that which Luther drew at the commencement of his career. This has been done by Hengstenberg,[1] amongst others. But all such theories have not the slightest influence in practical life.

And so, too, every hope and expectation must be abandoned, of ever seeing " Church discipline " in any form whatsoever introduced. As to " Confession," and " discipline " exercised through the practice of Confession, there cannot be as much as one word spoken. And so there finally remain —as means of enforcing discipline—" an exclusion from the Communion table, and the refusal of Christian burial." As to the first means, it is inapplicable, because of the indifference there is felt with respect to the Sacrament of the Altar ; and the general negligence in attending it is one of the crying evils of the Church at the present moment. From various quarters it is reported that the number of those partaking of the Lord's Supper is constantly declining more and more,[2] and that even the most of those well disposed towards the Church content themselves with Communion once in a year.[3] " Hundreds of thousands of Evangelical Christians," says Frühbuss,[4] " are self-excommunicated, and will have absolutely nothing to say or do with the Sacrament of the Altar." There are numberless others who, from a scruple of conscience, or from the Unionist mode of administering the Sacrament, will not participate in it. And so, it may be seen that there are, in the Church, vast numbers against whom " an exclusion from the Sacrament " could not be employed for the purpose of enforcing Church discipline. The matter, however, is still worse as regards " Christian burial." In the North, the custom is entirely abandoned of the clergymen accompanying the body of the deceased to the grave.[5] In Hamburg, for instance, interments take

[1] See his expressions in his " Kirchen-Zeitung," 1852, p. 19, and on the " Catechismus Romanus," pp. 2, 7, 22.

[2] BAUMGARTEN, " Der Kirkliche Nothstand in Mecklenburg," 1861, p. 41.

[3] HENGSTENBERG's " K.-Ztg.," 1858, p. 1115.

[4] " Ueber Wiederbelebung der Kirchenzucht." Breslau, 1859, p. 50.

[5] " Berlin Kirchenzeitung," 1844, No. lxiii.

place without any participation on the part of the ecclesiastical authorities.[1] "In town and country," says Frühbuss, "it is the rule not to have a religious burial, when one wishes to avoid payment of fees. The poor people, looking to a saving of expenses, pray for permission to have "a quiet funeral." From this practice has arisen a general notion that a quiet funeral—"a still burial," that is, one divested of ecclesiastical ceremonies—is much "more solemn;" and so it is regarded as the prerogative of persons distinguished for learning and science, and has become a privilege of many orders in society.[2] In Prussia, it has been moreover remarked that, if Church discipline were once again actively enforced, and that the most important canons of the Primitive Church were put into execution, the most of those who are now discharging the duties of educational professors, and three-fourths of the Pastors, would be put at once under a ban of excommunication.[3]

The Protestant Church in Germany has no room for a multiplicity of offices and vocations. Every one who enters into its service must be a preacher—must make that his main occupation; and he is, therefore, exposed to all the temptations and mischiefs which a constant call for public speaking must inevitably entail upon him. "He may, or he may not, have gifts for his office," says Karsten, "but still he must preach; and by that which he least understands will the measure of his capability be taken; whilst that which he really does thoroughly comprehend, in the existing condition of his office, he cannot make use of for the benefit of the congregation."[4] "And then, how very few, in fine, will be found to be the number of really good preachers! If we

---

[1] HENGSTENBERG's "K.-Z.," 1857, p. 60.

[2] KLIEFOTH's "Liturg. Abhandlungen," i. 201. FRÜHBUSS, p. 68, remarks, that in Berlin a few cigar-smokers are preferred to pastors as attendants upon the bodies of the deceased.

[3] FRÜHBUSS, p. 61.

[4] "Die protest. Kirche," p. 54.

reckon them up, we shall discover that not one-tenth part of the clergy are suited to be preachers."[1] Hence comes the prevalence of a conventional style of speaking, of traditional cues, hollow phrases, and theological inanities, upon which, if one attempts to lay hold, they are found to elude the grasp like a vaporous mist. The universal domination of mere phraseology has attained to an unexampled height amongst modern German homilists. "Shall we never have done," exclaims the preacher Hoyer, "with the awful chattering of contemporary theology, which, like a bewildering demon, has seized hold of our poor students, walks with them in their official duties, and talks with them in their sermons; and when it cannot render them unintelligible, is yet able to make them spiritless, tame, and disagreeable?"[2]

For a very long time, the wretched condition of *candidates for holy orders* has been discussed in writings, and debated in public conferences. "We are," say the complaints of candidates for the office of preachers, "after we have terminated our academical studies, for the best part of our lives (very generally for fifteen years) excluded from the service of the Church. We must become tutors in public schools or private families for many years, and when we, at last, and at a late period of life, attain the position of preacher, we then find that occupations 'not in accordance with our vocation' have estranged us from it.[3] "Without any immediate connection with the Church," so describes Schmieder their position, "without any cohesion amongst themselves, they wander about, isolated, homeless, often without any means of livelihood, a prey to want—utterly hopeless! The Church leaves them to their fate! How many candidates have been overwhelmed through this pressure of circumstances upon them, and have silently been destroyed by their misery!"[4] A person has only to compare the organization of the Protestant Church with the Catholic, where

---

[1] CUNZ, "Das geistliche Amt.," p. 51.
[2] "Zeitschrift für luth. Theologie," 1855, 295.
[3] LANDSCHREIBER, "Die Kirkliche Situation." Leipzig, 1860, p. 80.
[4] "Verhandlungen des Kirchentags zu Elberfeld," p. 57. .

every young man, the moment his preparatory studies are completed, finds his fitting employment in the service of the Church; a person has only to make this comparison, and he will at once discover where lies the root of the evil so generally complained of."

It is well known that every candidate, so soon as he has obtained a position affording the necessary means for the maintenance of a family, enters into the state of marriage. Then anxiety respecting his income, and care concerning his wife and children, become the main affairs of life; and what a state of dependence and slavishness is inextricably bound up with his domestic circumstances, is briefly and graphically portrayed by Schenkel.[1] "There arises," he justly observes, "a species of demoralization, which is an unavoidable concomitant of his condition, and compels him to be ever sufficiently prudent, so as not to give offence to personages of influence. This incompetent, inadequate, thought-smothering, unprotestant institution has had such a character-degrading effect in our German Protestant Church." The opinion thus expressed is not incorrect; but then, that the questionable institution is unprotestant, is an opinion so far from being correct, that it may, on the contrary, be affirmed that it is one of the consequences naturally developed by the Reformation.

Then there have been large districts and parishes of two, three, and four thousand souls, with two such parishes united in one, in order that a suitable maintenance might be provided for "the families" (of the clergymen). And yet the pressure of want is felt more and more by such "families" every year. Thus, the Schleswig Consistory, in an Appeal made in the year 1858, had complained that "there had lately been many parishes in which no one could venture to take upon himself the office of pastor, for the clergymen in them were in such constant anxiety to procure a sufficiency of daily bread *for their families*, that they had lost all satisfaction in the discharge of their parochial duties, and were

[1] "Die Erneuerung der deutschen evangelischen Kirche." Gotha, 1860, p. 55.

destitute of that ease of mind requisite for a proper performance of them."[1] On all sides the description becomes
still more gloomy of " the destitution of the parish clergy,"
of the increasing household expenditure of their "families,"
and of their incomes at the same time either remaining the
same, or diminishing. It has been the custom to bestow the
highest eulogies upon the prerogative of the clergy of the
Evangelical Confession, that they, as husbands and fathers of
families, were identified with laymen in their mode of life,
united with them in social intercourse, and therefore forming no particular order in society, and belonging not to a
distinct " caste," and so being, in fact, made to correspond
with, and carry out the doctrine of, " a common priesthood,"
which required that there should be the greatest possible
similarity of condition between laymen and preachers.
Meanwhile it is shown, and there are a thousand voices to
testify to the fact, that for three hundred years one constant
complaint has been made, as to the rank of a preacher being
universally despised, and their office so little prized, that
they have very seldom been able to win the love or confidence of the people; and that the general disfavour in which
they stood made itself painfully felt in the wretched income
and the poverty-stricken state of the majority of the body.
In the past century the contempt and degradation that had
fallen upon the order of preachers, were the motive to Ja-
blonsky for entering into a negotiation with England, and
this with the approval of the Prussian Court, for the purpose
of introducing the Episcopacy into Prussia.[2] In the year
1792, a preacher mentions that the best theologians of the
time were accustomed to lay upon Luther the responsibility

[1] KRAUSE's " Kirchenzeitung," 1858, p. 72. Compare with this the
complaint made in the " Göttinger Monatschrift," 1849, p. 325: " In the
smaller districts the preachers, *with their families,* cannot live without
the greatest economy. and even so find it very difficult ' to make both
ends meet' (kaum durch kommen)."

[2] " Christian Remembrancer," 1845, i. 120. See HENKE's " Magazin,"
v. 224, where will be found a vivid description of the prevailing contempt for clergymen.

of their condition having become so lamentable.[1] In our
own time the Prussian Government has desired to create a
respect for the preachers' class, by the bestowal of titles and
orders,[2] and has shown itself quite willing to regard the
clergy as a particle of its widely-extended, many-branched
bureaucratic officials, and to permit it to have some share in
the honours and prerogatives enjoyed by other government
employés. The Upper Consistory of Mark has, indeed,
complained that there is not the slightest prospect for
preachers attaining to independence through a marriage with a
wealthy wife, as few maidens with large dowries could ever be
induced to prefer a preacher to any other person for a husband![3]

To such lengths has an alienation between pastors and
people reached, that, according to the declaration made by
the preacher Kuntze at the meeting of "the Alliance" in
Berlin, "the people being now estranged from the Church,
look upon preachers, the Church, and Christianity itself, as
a species of mere governmental and police institution, and
exhibit in the plainest and most distinct manner their dislike
and contempt for the three together."[4] "So far," he says,
"as we are concerned, the Church has not the slightest influence upon the feelings or consciences of the population.
With such effect have persons laboured for the spiritualiza-
tion of the Church, that body and spirit are both very nearly
annihilated. In the estimation of the multitude, all that the
pastor now represents is—himself!"[5] "Amongst most congregations," says Moll, "there is a dislike and an avoidance
of any communication with the clergy; whilst a necessity
for their services is neither felt nor understood. No confidence is reposed in the clergyman; and the general exhortation made by the Agenda to congregations, to seek in their
spiritual necessities for the aid and counsel[6] of their pastors,

[1] STEINECK, "Nachricht von dem Leben des J. M. Götze." Hamburg, 1792, p. 19.
[2] HENGSTENBERG'S "K.-Ztg.," vol. xxx., p. 20.
[3] HENGSTENBERG, vol. xxx., p. 22.
[4] Ibid., p. 22.
[5] "Verhandlungen," p. 432.
[6] HENGSTENBERG'S "K. Z.," 1857, p. 690.

has scarcely been attended to by a single individual."[1] "There exists," said Jaspis, at the Church Assembly at Hamburg, in the year 1858, "a frightful partition between the people and their spiritual directors—so great is it, that in many places earnest clergymen give up all as lost, and do not venture to do anything."[2] A year earlier, Dean Rinck had spoken the following bitter words, at a Church Assembly held in Stuttgart:—" A universal complaint must be preferred against our modern clergy, that they have so completely abandoned the attempt to exercise an active personal influence upon the souls and families of those committed to their charge, as if it was their desire that the spiritual care of their flocks should be taken away from them."[3] A highly respectable theologian of Würtemberg said to Professor Schaff, "The people now regard us clergymen as nothing better than royal officials and black-coated policemen."[4]

So far have gone an absolute discouragement and complete despair as to the possibility of accomplishing any fruitful result with religion, that the question has been propounded, " Whether or not a person ought to remain in the service of the Church, or if it was not absolutely necessary to leave it?" Superintendent Thym refers to cases having occurred, within his own experience, as to how such a question assails and afflicts almost all pious souls who thoroughly comprehend the terrific perdition of the time, and who are also well aware how little they, with all their labours, can do to mitigate it.[5]

A Würtemberg clergyman remarks: " The Church has disappeared—even almost to its very name—both amongst the educated classes and with the multitude in Germany. Theologians, indeed, speak much of a Church—that is, of

[1] " Die gegenwärtige Noth der evang. Kirche Preussens," pp. 11, 26.

[2] " Verhandlungen, herausgeben v. Biernatzki," p. 8.

[3] " Verhandlungen," p. 140.

[4] " Germany, its Universities, Theology, and Religion." Edinburgh, 1857, p. 116.

[5] " Ist die evangeliche Kirche Babel, und der Austritt aus ihr daher unerlässliche Pflicht," Von SPENER, überarbeitet von THYM. Griefswalde, 1853.

the dignity, power, and revenues of a Church. The people, too, now and again go 'into the church;' but it is only as 'the public' they go there, and not as 'a congregation;' but that they themselves are a part of the Church—that they are the living stones wherewith are built up the edifice of an ecclesiastical community—that is a thing either not thought of, or it has never been brought home to their understanding. Cæsaro-Papism, and still more Bureaucraticism combined with Nationalism, have impaired the Church utterly, and given to it the appearance of being nothing better than a mere political association; whilst Pietism has abolished the last remnant of all right notions respecting a true Church community, by concentrating such notions upon its own little 'gatherings' (Gemeinschaften). In the place of an objective Church creed, there is everywhere to be met with the individual 'subjective stand-point'—the individual 'sovereign I,' and the spirit of 'individualism'—the spirit of these times, with its pass-words and talismans, which persons prefer bearing rather than submit themselves to the yoke of Christ and the creed of the Reformers."[1] Not less disheartening is the judgment pronounced by two Saxon clergymen : " The Church knows nothing of the necessities and spiritual wants of its members; it has for them neither eyes, hands, nor heart; it holds no relation with daily life; it is nothing more than a *Sunday institution,* and is unconscious of all that passes during the week. Preaching and baptism, surplice-fees and theological squabbles, are the sole visible signs by which its existence is made known to the bulk of mankind."[2]

When the present situation of the Protestant clergy in Germany is portrayed, the description, of course, includes an account of the *religious condition of the laity.* What is said of the one is, for the most part, applicable to the others. All tends to prove this lamentable fact—*the masses are non-Churchmen.* It would be both weakness and folly to waste

[1] SCHAFF's " Kirchenfreund," 1857, p. 416.
[2] Kirchen und Schulblatt," von TEUSCHER und HANSCHMANN. Weimar, 1852, p. 65.

time in useless lamentations over this circumstance. What is necessary to be done is to look the fact straight in the face.[1]   A broad and deep chasm lies between Theology and the Christian knowledge of the people : the one has ascended to the highest point of speculation, whilst the latter is still stumbling through the alphabet.[2]   The Erlangen theologians complain " that every one amongst the Protestant populations fancies he can make a religion for himself, and no one any longer rightly knows what he ought to believe and what he ought to maintain ; and with this confusion in their ideas, the people are also to be remarked for having lost their moral stability."[3]

But what might occur if a knowledge of the true state of affairs should penetrate amongst those who may be rightfully called " the people," and especially amongst the intellectual and educated classes? It may sound like a paradox, but still every one who thoroughly comprehends the subject will admit its truth—that the universal religious indifference of the educated classes at this moment is the chief security for the existence of the Protestant Church.   If there once awakens in those circles a living interest for religious matters ; if they take the Bible in their own hands for the purpose of testing their religion ; if they should desire to learn in what relation to each other stand the now existing theology and the doctrines taught from the pulpit, and how their preachers coincide in their opinions with those expressed in other states and countries—if they should do these things, there will come the day of discovery and of exposure ; and then, too, the confidence now reposed in the Church will be at an end. Then also will they perceive that Luther's Bible not merely abounds with gross faults and misapprehensions of the original text, but also that he frequently and intentionally, and for the purpose of upholding his doctrine, disguised the Apostolic words ; and that the Epistle of St. Paul in par-

[1] " Sächsisches Kirchenblatt."   Preface to 1860.
[2] *Ibid.*, 1860, No. vi.
[3] " Zeitschr. für Protestantismus," vol. xx., p. 371.

ticular was mishandled by him.[1]   They would learn, also,
that the grand "acquisition" of the Reformation, the Protestant "Justification" doctrine, is now abandoned by the
most distinguished theologians as "untenable," and by the
exegetists branded as "unbiblical."   Nitzsch, indeed, recommends to theologians silently to correct the symbol;[2] but
the time cannot be far distant when this silent correction
will become notorious to the multitude ; and the secret will
not long remain unspoken, viz., that not a single theologian of
any name or note binds himself down to the Confessional
writings.

The first prelate of the Saxon Church, Liebner, a short
time since, portrayed, in the darkest colours, the utter want
in Christian knowledge, "which was," he said, "actually
astounding, not only amongst the multitude attached to the
German Evangelical Church, but even amongst the great
body of the educated classes."[3]   The Churches of his Confession appeared to him to resemble a Manichæan world—a
kingdom of light, composed of German theology and its
guardians ; a kingdom of darkness, composed of laymen, for
the main part deeply immersed in negative and positive
ignorance ; and both the light and the darkness standing in
strong contrast opposed to one another.   That, beyond all
other things concerning which the great mass of laymen had
formed the most perverse notions, was first as to the Reformation, and then of Luther himself.   "The laymen," such is

---

[1] The only preacher of whom it is known that he, on this point, conducted himself with candour towards his congregation, was the Prussian
preacher, Ehrenström, who afterwards emigrated to America. He taught
Greek to members of his congregation, and then pointed out to them the
different passages that Luther had falsely translated. (WANGEMANN's
"Preuss. Kirchengeschichte," iii. 132). On the other hand, PALMER
("HOMILETIK," p. 303) emphatically warns all preachers never to say to
the people that this or that passage was falsely translated by Luther—
that the fact was to be as a mystery, on which they were to remain silent ;
or, at the utmost, all they ought to do should be to admit that the translation was obscure and indistinct.

[2] "Deutsche Zeitschrift," viii. 201.

[3] "Zur Kirchlichen Prinzipienfrage der Gegenwart ; Zeugnisse a. d
Sächsischen Kirchenregimente." Dresden, 1860, p. 19.

Liebner's opinion, "have pictured to themselves Luther as a man who was to be venerated as a grand deliverer, who had freed them not merely from the yoke of Popes, Bishops, and Councils, but also from the tutorship of Protestant theologians, and conferred upon each man the right to believe according to the extent of his faith, and to live according to the measure of his conscience. Such, however," he added, "is not the Luther of the theologians."

Laymen, on the other side, counterbalance these heavy complaints with severe replies. "When," it is said, "Liebner so loudly lauds the high pretensions of existing theology,[1] and that it has been in constant unity and continuity with the Scripture, and exhibiting itself as a progressive and internally developing Church, and, therefore, to be truly Catholic, then can intelligent laymen ask—'Have you yourselves not unfrequently said, and proved to us, that the Reformation was the deepest and most incurable breach that ever had been made in the unity and continuity of the Church? Is it not, too, an admitted fact that the main doctrine of the new Church was previously completely unknown, and that it was not a Continuation, but a Negation of doctrine hitherto taught? Is the destruction of the Primacy, the Episcopacy, and the entire Church Constitution, a perduration of Ecclesiastical Continuity? Is annihilation the same thing as development and perpetuation? You reproach us with wandering in the dark night of theological ignorance; but, before you repeat the reproach, place, if you can, in our hands an Ariadne thread, which will help to guide us in safety out of the labyrinth of doubt and uncertainty in which we are now straying. Give us a clear answer to this most urgent of all questions—*Who* is it that we are to believe? Is it the particular preacher beneath whose pulpit accident has placed us? Is it the Consistory of the country? Is it the

---

[1] *Ibid.*, p. 37. So had STAHL, in a preceding year, in a discourse upon ecclesiastical congregational order, spoken "of the faith of the Church being the same for centuries." Is it possible that Stahl fancied he could persuade the Berliners that what their forefathers believed in the year 1580 was that which had been believed by the people of Berlin in 1516?

theological Faculty of the National University? Is it the temporal Prince, who is also a Supreme Bishop? Is it the symbolical books, from which every theologian has emancipated himself? Is it our own private judgment upon particular passages of the Bible? We take up your latest commentators upon the Bible to help us on our way—and what do we discover? Ten different explanations of one and the same passage in the Scriptures, and each explanation backed up by the name of some celebrated theologian! How many are the confirmatory passages in Scripture cited in the symbolical books, to which a different interpretation is now attached from that there assigned to them? We have asked you for bread, and you have given us a stone. You have always on your lips the words Protestant Freedom, but it is an iron yoke which you lay upon us; it is a spiritual bondage that you would exact from laymen. Should we accept, with a blind faith, doctrine from a preacher who is bound by no higher authority than himself, and cannot prove that the doctrine he teaches is a common, general, and accepted doctrine? It has been said by one of yourselves: A community can never be more grossly tyrannized over than when it is compelled to place itself beneath the unrestrained will of any one individual—and when it must be guided in accordance with his peculiar notions.' "[1]

When Liebner maintains that his own and his colleagues' theology contains within its bosom all the saving means which the necessities of the time require, but that this is only a secret doctrine—so he allows all sorts of conjectures to be formed as to the meaning of his mystery; whilst a very different opinion is loudly expressed by others as to what have been the achievements of theology in the present day. A very short time has elapsed since Stahl made the declaration "that the theological science of Germany was at best but a double-edged sword, and as capable of inflicting a wound upon faith as infidelity."[2] So, too, Professor Krafft, of Bonn, and the preacher Beyschlag complained, at the

[1] KARSTEN, " Die protest. Kirche," p. 29.
[2] MESSNER's " K.-Ztg.," 1861, p. 377.

Berlin meeting of the Evangelical Alliance, that the modern orthodox theology, with its recoil upon the symbolical books, was the principal cause of the religious weakness of German Protestantism.[1]

The Bible Societies have for the last fifty years distributed in Germany, as in other places, millions of Bibles. Even the poorest person can now, with very little trouble, possess a German Bible. The effect, however, is, according to the assurance of a preacher, " that there is no book less studied than the Bible—that amongst a hundred Christian households there was scarcely one to be found in which the Holy Scriptures were still read." [2] " The people," says Güder, " nurture a secret distrust of the Scriptures." [3] " Even the best amongst the country people," observes another, " mostly read it only on Sundays and festival days."[4]

Nevertheless, it has lately happened that a Faculty altogether theological declared " that naught of *the doctrine of the Church* can now be referred to by the preachers in their addresses to the people ; because the main decisive question is—' Why and wherefore they should believe ?' And this misleads the people as to a false notion that, when they are taught to believe anything upon the mere human authority of the Evangelical Church, they should also be bound to accept an interpretation of the Scripture for doing so. And hence it is that no preacher can suggest to his congregation that they should simply receive his doctrine, but he must refer each to an examination of the Bible for himself—and it is the result of this self-study, and not the testimony of his own Church, that is to determine the acceptance of Christian doctrine. And with this state of circumstances, it is found that nineteen out of every twenty of the still churchgoing population must be declared to be creedless ; and if one should be able to carry into effect this theory upon the

[1] " Verhandlungen," pp. 187, 196.
[2] THOLUCK's " Liter. Anz.," 1845, p. 289.
[3] " Deutsche Zeitschrift," 1855, p. 151.
[4] HENGSTENBERG, " K.-Z.," 1852, p. 873.

creed preached from the pulpit, the churches would soon
become empty—a matter upon which the Faculty would
give themselves so much the less trouble, as they have here
a very weighty authority on their side—namely, the Evangelical Alliance, whose second Article has determined " that
it is the right and the *duty* of every Christian man to interpret the Scripture according to his own conviction of its
meaning." Theologians and preachers, who have attached
themselves in crowds to the Alliance, in Berlin, have accepted this Article without hesitation. It is not as yet
adopted in the Catechism. How many laymen, it may be
asked, are there in all Germany, who think of this " duty,"
and of fully performing it ?

There is a small number of Lutheran theologians, men of
very earnest views, and who in reality imagine that, woful
as may now be the appearance of the Lutheran Church in
Germany, still it bears within itself, and it alone does
so, every hope of a better state of Church affairs in the
future. Somewhat larger may be the number of those who
bind up their expectations with " the United Church," and
dream of a grand development for it at a near period.
A few thoughtful theologians, however, acknowledge that
neither " Lutheranism," nor " Calvinism," nor a commingling of both elements into a " Unionism," can have
either a long duration, or hold out the hope of a vigorous
development, and therefore they await a *Church of the future.*
This fact must, indeed, be admitted by every believing
Christian, that the present state of Church fragmentation
cannot possibly be a normal state, nor be of long continuance ; but, on the contrary, " that the Church's inborn
essence of Unity will yet overcome that disruption which has
been effected by the powers of this world." [1]

In this future Unity it is said that even the Catholic
Church will be included; and that it should, in essential
things, become Protestant, is what is naturally required ; as

---

[1] Thus do the Göttingen theologians express themselves in their Declaration, 1854, p. 66.

well as that its "reserved" organism should be destroyed. For this, it is hoped, events sooner or later will provide. Now, the right view to take of such a notion as this is—"that an amalgamation of the Catholic Church with the Protestant, so that the peculiarities of both may be transferred into one United Church, is—an impossibility." That which is essentially Catholic, and that which is essentially Protestant, are not like the two opposite sides of the same substantiality, which conjointly make it complete, and united together form a richer and more harmonious totality; but they stand in relation to each other as two repellents, for the one is a negative of the other.

A union of the two Churches, through amalgamation, could only be effected by the one of them ceasing to be what it is, and breaking off from its tradition—whether that tradition was Protestant or Catholic.

The acceptation of one single principle, upon the one side or the other, would be sufficient to attain this object. At the moment, for instance, in which German Protestantism should acknowledge that there is a Church, in the sense of one that is real, divine, with promises and power, and an established institution, then, in that moment, it would enter upon the process of being Catholicised; and so, too, would the Catholic Church be self-dissolved upon the day in which it would accept the Second Article of the Evangelical Alliance, and proclaim—"that no one must henceforth submit himself to religious authority, but must, on the contrary, found his faith, in the last instance, upon nothing else than his own interpretation of the Bible."

Fichte (if the author mistakes not) was the first who, in 1806, gave expression to the notion, "that there must, out of Peter's (the Catholic) and Paul's (the Protestant) Churches, be a third, which would be a transfiguration and amalgamation of the two, and which, by "the abolition of the peculiarities" of each, should be their successor— "a John's Church." Schelling, at a later period, in his lectures, expatiated on this idea, and it has, since then, been many times referred to with great applause. Thus, for

instance, Professor Piper, in the Church Assembly at Stutt-
gart, in 1857, consoled his auditors with the expectation of
their yet beholding a " John's Church."[1]   So also has
Merz presented his readers with a view of "a Church of
Humanity of the living John ;" and, with this John's
Church, the commencement of "a fourth revolution in the
Church."[2]

Ullman,[3] yielding to a like turn of thought, has discovered
three leading forms of Christianity, which found an outward
manifestation in the Greek, Roman, and Protestant Churches;
and then directs attention to a fourth, in which Christianity,
as a religion of the Divinity with humanity, will constitute
itself as a perfect absolute religion, and be " the Church of
the future."

Such a notion as this is doubtless at the present moment
very widely extended.   As to the comparison of the opposition between Catholicity and Protestantism, as a difference
between Peter and Paul, it is intrinsically untrue, and will
scarcely be regarded as permissible by any theologian ; whilst
there are doubtless many theologians who suppose that there
will yet be a new Church, in which there will be but one
shepherd and one flock, and that this Church will present
itself in a form very different from that which is now exhibited by Protestantism.

If one would describe, as does the Berlin " Deutsche
Zeitschrift," the existing Protestant Church as " a mere
outward form, a stranger alike to the sympathies and life of
the people, and as the mere ruin of times that have passed
away ;[4] or if the notion concerning it be that expressed by
Schenkel, Lange, and Rothe,[5] that " Protestantism has never
yet brought forth one real, substantial, operative Church,"

---

[1] " Verhandlungen," p. 48.
[2] " Armuth und Christenthum," p. 88.
[3] " Wesen des Christenthums."   Hamburg, 1849.
[4] " Jahrg.," 1851, p. 304.
[5] ROTHE's " Theol. Ethik," iii. 1012.   SCHENKEL, " Das Prinzip des
Protestantismus," p. 11.   LANGE, " Uber die Neugestaltung des Ver-
haltnisses zwischen Staat und Kirche," 1848, p. 89.

then indeed are persons justified in fixing their thoughts upon "a future" or "a John's Church;" or they must, like Hase, begin to prophesy of the downfall of Christianity itself, and of the birth and predominance of a completely new religion. As to the budding forth of a Church in the State, such as Rothe expects, it must be a future Church of a peculiar constitution—in fact, nothing less than a Universal State Church!

But when an attempt is made to impart a corporeal, substantial form to this shadow of a future Church, then are the ideologists found to evaporate in empty phrases, or they picture forth a modern millennium, and emit a cluster of hopes, and a swarm of wishes, bright, brilliant, fugacious and volatile as butterflies, "and in whose actuality the simple Christian will place as little faith as any other human being in his sober senses." [1]

In close connexion with these expectations of a new Church is to be found in all the Protestant portions of Europe a very general and longing desire for a new "descent of the Holy Ghost." In England there are some prayer societies established for that purpose. At the Church Assembly in Berlin, and in despite of the unanimous adhesion to an unchanged Augsburg Confession, the cry went forth "that there could be no salvation without a new descent of the Holy Ghost!" In the pulpits, as in pamphlets, a second Pentecost, without which it was said "the world could not much longer go on, was wished for, and therefore was to be expected." Even Delitzsch [2] himself says, "It is indispensable that there should be a descent of the Spirit from above." Such a repetition of the Festival of Pentecost is, however, neither promised in Scripture, nor in the eighteen

[1] Such is the proper remark of the "Zeitschrift für luth. Theol.," 1857, p. 311. "These churches of the future," says Rudelbach, in the same journal (1853, p. 90), "are the *scabies* of the day, and bear with them all the characteristics of that malady—they show that there is inwardly decay, and exteriorly, irritation."

[2] "Erlanger Zeitschrift für Protest.," 1858, p. 305.

hundred years of the duration of the Church has it ever been either desired or hoped for.[1]

Near to these hopeful expectants, who are looking forward to a new Church, and to a second Pentecost as the birth-day of their new Church, are those numerous individuals, more down-hearted or less aspiring in their anticipations, who announce the near approach of the ending of this world, and the return of Jesus Christ to judgment, or to the commencement of the millennium.

When an expectation of a millennium of an earthly kingdom of Christ shews itself (the Augsburg Confession notwithstanding) amongst the Lutherans,[2] it is to be regarded, as being based upon their despair of any improvement of their Church, as a perception of the inevitable dissolution of that Church; and to such sentiments must be attributed the origin of such an idea. Clergy and theologians who stand like incompetent physicians by the sick-bed of their Church are, it may be said, " born Chiliasts." By them it is said: " The discipline of faith has no hold any more either above or below—and even the simple but true preaching of the Gospel encounters manifold contradictions or multitudinous indifference."[3] Or they take the same view with Rudelbach, when he says, " Where one fortress of Lutheran orthodoxy tumbles down after another, and when at the head-quarters (of Lutheranism) there is such an awful chasm opened, then must it be plainly seen that the days in which we live are ripe for the great apostasy."[4]

Many, too, seek for salvation and consolation in new interpretations of the Apocalypse, and in a reference to the

---

[1] " If such a notion," says Hase, with respect to it, "is seriously entertained, then these persons place their hopes in the performance of a miracle, such as has not occurred since the times of the Apostles. In so doing they only openly declare their despair to conduct their religious affairs in accordance with that historical and natural development with which Christ has guided his Church through eighteen ~~hundred~~ centuries." —" Prot. K.-Z.," 1856, p. 1151.

[2] Recently by Lessing, Flörke, Karsten, &c.

[3] HENGSTENBERG'S " K.-Z.," 1859, p. 1181.

[4] " Zeitschrift für luth. Theologie," 1859, p. 255.

approaching millennium, when and where all that is now wanting to the Protestantism of to-day shall be supplied, and "the crooked ways be made straight." And then—there is Auberlen, who has recently discovered that the whole visible Church, including even the Protestant portion of it, has become part and parcel of "the harlot" in the Apocalypse, and, therefore, there is nothing left to mankind but to await the millennium ;[1] and another, Nägelsbach, is charmed with Auberlen's "consolation for all, who on the one side would willingly aid the Church, but on the other see no possible means of being able to render it effectual assistance"—so that, in fact, all that any one is able to do is—to wait ![2]

Others, like Baumgarten, admit that the existing Church is fundamentally perverted, but they console themselves with the prospect of a speedy conversion of the Jews. "The whole development of the Church hitherto," it is maintained by Baumgarten, is a gross erratic wandering of State-Churchdom—a degenerate Heathenish Church ; but that converted Israel is destined to become for all nations "the redeeming and sanctifying head,"[3] and will once more present a bleeding victim in the temple of Jerusalem! It is more positively announced by another that there will soon appear one who has been foretold by Christ as an earthly Consoler and Messias. We are now, it is said, in the year 5976 of the Redemption, and in the year 6000 will be the first resurrection and the millennium.[4]

Finally, the present Minister of Public Worship and Education in Prussia, Von Bethmann-Hollweg, shortly before his appointment to office, gave expression to his despair in Chiliastic aspirations.[5] "To the Apostles, Peter and

---

[1] "Der Prophet Daniel und die Offenbarung Johannis," 1854, p. 294.

[2] REUTER's " Repertor.," vol. xcii., p. 204, and again in vol. ciii., p. 85.

[3] HENGSTENBERG's " K.-Ztg.," 1859, p. 697.

[4] CHRISTIANUS, "Das Evangelium des Reiches ;" Leipzig, 1859. The author asserts that he has availed himself especially of the works of the Erlanger theologian, Von Hofmann.

[5] In GELZER's " Monatsblättern," 1858, vol. xi. p. 126.

Paul, who have each had their Churches, for a time must that of John succeed. In Church and State are alike exhibited the counteraction of every progressive step—there is dissolution both in State and in Church; there is the decay of organic forms, and there is an incapacity in the age to create new. Both Church and State must perish in their earthly forms, that the kingdom of Christ may be set up over all nations—that the bride of the Lamb, the perfect community, *the new Jerusalem, may descend from Heaven.*"

Not long before this was published, another Protestant Statesman had warned his Protestant readers to turn away from false prophets who announce the end of the world, because they have come to an end of their own wisdom.[1]

A description of the present state of ecclesiastical affairs makes it necessary to devote a few sentences to a description of the position which Protestantism in Germany maintains with regard to the Catholic Church. The adherents of both Confessions associate and intermingle daily more and more with each other. With equal steps they advance, and a contact of mind with mind becomes more frequent; and everywhere the Protestant churches and congregations place themselves close to the Catholics; and they do so as—adversaries. Even in the extremities of the North, as of the South, the toleration of a foreign faith can now only be a question of time. As to the situation which Catholics appear to occupy, it shall be referred to in another place. What is desired in this part of the work is to fix attention upon the course of conduct exhibited by the ecclesiastical leaders and orators of the Protestant Church towards the Catholic, and on the false position in which they place themselves.

This may, with truth, be said—that Catholic tendencies lie at the bottom of the whole movement that has been made towards a religious life and an ecclesiastical restoration in Protestantism. He who has watched this movement receives the same impression as if he saw a number of individuals

[1] BUNSEN, " Gott in der Geschichte," i. 133.

thrust into a narrow, stifling, dark, and loathsome cell; and
that those who were so packed together were attempting to
open now this door and then that, in order that they might
inhale fresh air and new strength; but that, with every such
attempt, there pealed forth in their ears a loud chorus of
clerical and lay voices, exclaiming—"Shut out the miasma;
keep away from you the foul grave-stench that arises from
old, mouldering tombs." It is with the reproach, "You are
becoming Catholic," that the opponents of the movement
have sought to check it. It is with the cry, "You want to
make Catholics of us," that the great masses of the population
have, for twenty years, repelled every earnest effort made
towards the enrichment and improvement of Protestantism
in dogma, in ecclesiastical life, and in the Divine service.
Who can deny that, consistently with the principles from
which the spirit of Protestantism has originated, such a
course of conduct—so marked with fear and caution—is not
perfectly natural? "The attitude of Protestantism," says
Stahl, "is ever that of the Borghese gladiator. It is a permanent assault, the uttermost tension of every sinew and
muscle, against Rome. Its whole energy is directed to this
point—never to let near it Catholic doctrine and discipline,
as the smallest manifestation in that direction excites far
more horror than would be caused by the grossest transgression in an opposite way, &c., &c., &c."[1]

In the years 1848-1851 there were many signs given, from
which might be inferred a closer approximation of the two
Confessions: it appeared as if both—the motives and doctrines which separated them not being brought prominently
forward—could, and did, cordially join hand in hand together
for the common protection and preservation of moral and
religious principles, both in political and social life. In the
Diet of some provinces such an association of believing Protestants and Catholics had been formed with very happy
results. It had so shewn itself that, in most of the affairs
then pending, the only alternative to choose between was,
"Christianity or Atheism"—and at such a crisis the causes

[1] " Die lutherische Kirche und die Union."   Berlin, 1859, p. 456.

for a separation of creeds had better be avoided as questions for discussion. But then came the Church Assembly in Bremen, which must have produced a deep and painful impression in all parts of Catholic Germany ; because there the great majority of an Assembly, composed of professors and clergymen, expressed themselves with such bitter and unrelenting hatred against a Church to which belonged the larger number of their own countrymen, as well as a preponderating number of all baptized Christians. A particular provocation on the part of the Catholics had not been given to afford an opportunity, or to supply a pretext, for any such explosion. And yet, at that Assembly, a resolution was *unanimously* passed : " That the expression of this confessional hatred should, in every German congregation, be adopted as a constituent portion of the Divine service, and that in every place should again be sung forth the words :

> ' As pious men, we pray and hope
> For sudden death to Turk and Pope.' " [1]

Rationalist times had made a change with regard to those words, which theologians and pastors, having now again become believers, deemed it to be an urgent task for them to restore to popularity, and again excite the people to their repetition ! An intimation as to the probable or necessary consequences of such circumstances as these, or what may be their signification as pathological symptoms, it does not belong to us here to notify; but we supply the place that might be otherwise occupied, by the expression of opinions formed by two individuals, who, from the high official positions formerly held by them, had the best opportunity of knowing the matters of which they spoke, and who were both the most determined political opponents of Catholic interests, and both zealous friends and supporters of the Evangelical Church. These two individuals are the President von Gerlach and the Privy-Councillor Eilers. The first of these says : " We daily see how small, in comparison with the power of the Catholic Church, is the influence which the Evangelical has

---

[1] " Und steur' des Papsts und Türken Mord !" " Verhandlungen," p. 152.

upon the enlightenment and sanctification of the mass of the population, and upon the majority of its own members. The cause for this is not far to seek."[1]

The second of these, Eilers, was well known as one of the most influential officials in the Eichhorn Administration, and who, in his day, held in his own hands the management of three newspapers, devoted to the purpose of opposing the Catholic Church; and which were, for that purpose, subsidized by the Government. These are his words: "I have made it my study to ascertain the connection that exists between what is the Christian life of the Catholic population, and its institutions and practices; and, *with an unwilling heart,* I am compelled to admit that, in general, a far more Christian-like life is led by those who belong to the Catholic than to the Evangelical Church. It is a well recognised fact that the Evangelical clergy, *in general,* are far—very far—behind the Catholic in their devotion and efficiency in the discharge of their pastoral duties."[2]

When two laymen express themselves in a manner so reasonable and conciliatory, may it not be hoped that the time is coming, and perhaps is already near, when preachers and theologians may give way to milder thoughts and gentler expressions—and that they may learn to think and believe that what, upon the whole, the Catholic Church in Germany has done is no more than it could not leave undone? All the reproaches and complaints made against the Church amount to this—that those—preferred under the name of a reformation and a breaking away from the past, have been refuted—that the Church has remained true to the commission entrusted to it: and thus adhering firmly to the principles on which it was established, it has regularly and consistently been developed; and, furthermore, that, rigidly abiding with unbroken steadiness to its ecclesiastical life, and in cohesion with other portions of the same Church, it has fulfilled—its mission.

[1] "Aktenstücke aus der Verwaltung des evangel. Oberkirchenraths." Berlin, 1856, iii. 423.

[2] EILERS, "Meine Wanderung durch's Leben." Leipzig, ii. p. 226.

THE POPE AND THE STATES OF THE CHURCH

TO THE TIME OF THE FRENCH REVOLUTION.

Down to the period of the fall of the Western Roman
Empire, the Popes were subjects of the Roman Emperors.
They stood, subsequently to the close of the fifth century, in
the same relation with respect to the Ostrogoth kings of
Italy; and one of the Pontiffs, John I., died in the prison
into which he had been thrown by King Theodoric. When
the Ostrogoths had been overthrown by the arms of the
Byzantines, the Popes then became subjects of the Eastern
Roman Emperors. The Popes, although grossly maltreated,
and placed in an embarrassing position, between Constantinople, the Exarchate, and the Longobards (ever craving for
the possession of Rome), still continued constantly to increase,
both in power and influence, in Italy. At the close of the
sixth century the Pope was already the richest landowner in
the Peninsula. Large patrimonies scattered over the whole
of the Peninsula, as well as in Sicily, Sardinia, Corsica, and
even France, belonged to the Pontiff; and these being attended
to by ecclesiastical managers, enabled the Pope to supply the
population of Rome with food, and to purchase peace from
the Longobards. Gregory the Great exercised upon his
numerous estates a certain jurisdiction, and superintended
the Imperial Government officers. And then, in the same

proportion in which the Eastern Roman sovereignty became
crippled, and that the Exarchate was scarcely able to maintain itself against the strength of the Longobards, the power
of the Pope naturally rose of itself, and the temporal
dominion of Rome fell to him—not as a possession to be
ambitiously sought for, but as a mere matter of necessity
and duty. The Popes were compelled to become war-leaders,
to build fortifications, to enlist soldiers, and to appoint
officers.

The iconoclast strife, combined with the harsh, provoking
Church-intermeddling and political despotism of the new
Byzantine Soldier-Emperors, led to a breach between Rome
and Constantinople, and this breach to the loss of the rich
Papal territories in Sicily and Lower Italy, which were taken
by violence away from the Papal See, by the Emperor Leo.
For this loss a rich recompense was soon afforded. The
Longobard king, Luitprand, with a generosity not common
to that prince, presented a portion of Southern Tuscany to
the Church of St. Peter; and the Frank king, Pepin, made
over, in the same way, the districts that he conquered—
Emilia, Flaminia, and the Pentapolis—that is, the land on
the sea coast, from the mouth of the Po to Ancona; and
eastward, from the ridge of the Apennines to the Reno.[1] The

[1] It will, we conceive, be useful to the general reader, before accompanying the author in his sketch of the history of the Papal States, to
know exactly what territories were comprised in them, previous to any
recent invasion from Piedmont. Upon the return of Pope Pius IX. to
Rome, he issued several edicts in the months of September, October, and
November, 1850, regulating various details as to institutions, and establishing the following organization, which makes known the names of the
various districts and provinces over which he ruled as Sovereign :—

"The whole of the State was distributed into five great divisions. One
of these was to bear the name of the District of Rome (' Circondario di
Roma'), and the other four were to be termed ' Legations.' The great
divisions were subdivided into provinces, the provinces again into
governments, and the governments into communes.

"In the district of Rome were included, besides Rome and the
Comarca, or country immediately about the city, three provinces—Viterbo,
Civita Vecchia, and Orvieto.

"The four Legations were—

z

Pope, on his side—although he and the Romans still acknowledged, in theory, the Byzantine authority—granted to the
Frankish king and his sons the Roman "Patriciate"—that is
to say, the office of "Protector of Rome, and of the Roman
See."

Although Pepin had laid the keys of the towns of the
Exarchate on the altar of St. Peter at Rome, still, the Pope
could exercise no real authority in them; on the contrary,
Sergius, and, after him, Leo, constituted themselves Archbishops of the richly-endowed Church of Ravenna, and
rulers over the Exarchate; and when, by the victories of
Charlemagne, the endowments were renewed, still the Papal
See did not obtain exclusive governmental power within the
district. The Frankish kings granted to the Church of
Rome the revenues of the lands, but retained for themselves
the supreme authority over them.[1] Charlemagne, indeed,
confirmed the endowments of his father, and in subsequent
years added to them new patrimonies and revenues, and gave
Tuscan cities to the Pope; and we see afterwards—that is,
after 780—the Pope in possession of the dominion of
Ravenna, but still acknowledging the supremacy of Charlemagne, by a steady execution of the imperial commands.[2] The
city of Rome belonged to the Pope; but he himself desired
to see the military and judicial authority in the hands of
Charlemagne, as "Patricius," and provided for the Roman
people taking an oath of obedience and fidelity to the
king.

By Charlemagne's taking upon himself the imperial dignity, and founding or re-establishing a Western Empire, the

"1. Romagna—comprising four provinces, Bologna, Ferrara, Forli,
and Ravenna.

"2. Le Marche—comprising six provinces, Urbino and Pesaro, Mace-
rata with Loreto, Ancona, Fermo, Ascoli, and Camerino.

"3. Umbria—comprising three provinces, Perugia, Spoleto, and Rieti.

"4. Marittima e Campagna—comprising three provinces, Velletri,
Frosinone, and Benevento."—"Despatches from Mr. Lyons respecting the
condition and administration of the Papal States." London, 1860, p. 11.

[1] VESI, "Storia di Romagna," i. 394.

[2] "Cod. Carol. 67, ap. Cenni Monum. 81," p. 439.

temporal power of the Pope became both more distinctly marked and more secure.

The shadow of a Byzantine supreme authority had now disappeared. Rome belonged to the Western Empire, and the Pope and the Romans took an oath of fealty to the Emperor. As the Emperor was to be, beyond all other things, the protector of the Church, and as the temporal possessions of the Pope now stood specially under the imperial guardianship, so were they also under the imperial authority. The limits between the Imperial and Papal authority were never very exactly drawn. The kingdom of Italy, which was held by Pepin, the son of Charles, was composed of the former Longobard territories in Northern and Middle Italy. In Rome and the Roman territories, the imperial supreme authority was exercised by envoys or messengers—"Missi." Since these formed a superior class of officers to those who were appointed by the Pope, the officers named by him in the towns under his rule were called "*duces*"—and as the imperial officers had superintendence over them, the Emperor Lothair, in the year 824, decreed that these "*missi*" should be nominated jointly by the Pope and the Emperor; and that every neglect of the Papal officers, the *duces* and *judices*, should in the first instance be reported to the Pope. Both powers, the Papal and the Imperial, mutually supported each other. The Pope let the Roman people swear fidelity to the Emperor; and the Emperor—as Lothair did—threatened everyone with his displeasure who should not in all things render obedience to the Pope. Official documents were dated according to the years of the Emperor's reign, and the Roman coins were impressed with his image. The election of the Pope, which was made by the great persons at Rome—ecclesiastics and laymen— was to be subjected to the confirmation of the Emperor: this was positively settled, and was in itself established as a guarantee for the freedom and regularity of the election—but the distance of the Emperor from Rome, the long delay, and the interests of the Roman parties, led to this arrangement being frequently unattended to.

The state of affairs, so regulated, and so favourable to the

Papal See, was not of long duration. The Carolingian house and its power went to destruction through internal discord, fratricidal wars, and constant territorial partitions, without there being any strong dynasty to fill its place. The splendour of the Empire grew pale, and in the person of Louis II. it was limited to Italy, whilst he no longer possessed the power of protecting Rome and the peninsula against the incursions of the Saracens from the South. And when, on the death of the childless Louis, the territorial empire came to an end, and the Popes, by the act of coronation, decided as to who was to be possessor of the Imperial dignity, without consideration as to the order of succession, an extremely important step was taken for the elevation of the Papal authority. Neither the Italians nor the Pope obtained any substantial benefit from enfeebled imperial shadows. The defenceless Pope could not prevent his cities being torn away from him and the Romish Church by Italian princes. And worse still were the proceedings adopted on the part of his Roman nobles, who, no longer restrained by the strong hand of an Emperor, took upon themselves the power of electing an occupant for the chair of St. Peter—and often filled it with their own tools, and made use of it for their own purposes.

Thus began, with the close of the ninth century, that dark anarchical age when the Papacy was degraded and maltreated by powerful laymen. The Roman clergy of the time were destitute of a firm organization, and proved utterly powerless when opposed to the nobles. The Popes succeeded each other rapidly. They were elevated by one faction, overthrown by another, imprisoned and murdered. The Romans did at that period all they possibly could utterly to destroy the Papacy, but the moral strength of the institution was invincible. Of the Papal States which had been created by preceding Popes and Emperors, there were now only fragments remaining. The towns of the Romagna were obliged, when the invasions of the Hungarians commenced, to do unaided all they could to defend themselves.

In Rome there ruled, after an intriguing woman, Marozia, her son Alberic, and he, through his family influence, his riches, and by holding possession of the castle of St. Angelo, exercised, as " Prince and Senator of all in Rome," unlimited power until the year 954. The Exarchate and Pentapolis were in the power of Berenger, King of Italy. Alberic must, however, himself have felt that a temporal Princedom of Rome could not be of long duration, and he therefore secured the election to the Papal dignity for his young son and heir, Octavius. Thus had Rome, in the person of Octavius, or John XII., a spiritual prince; but the Church a good-for-nothing Pope.

Then appeared—and invoked by the Pope himself—the German King, Otho the Saxon, who became the second restorer of a Western Empire, which empire was now transferred to the German nation. He from that time forth exercised, both in Rome and with regard to the Pope, his imperial rights to their widest extent. He caused John XII. to be deposed by a Synod, and Leo VIII. to be elected in his place; and when the Romans once more endeavoured to get possession of the Papal chair, by the election of Benedict V., he had him deposed and sent into exile in Germany. As to a real free election of a Pope, there was not a thought or talk about it, neither all this time nor during the whole of the following century. In Rome as well as out of Rome there was naught on which the Pope could rest for support. Without the Emperor he was a mere ball tossed about by the hands of the audacious nobility factions. Emperors, acting under the advice of their bishops and spiritual councillors, had given more worthy Popes to the Church than the Roman chiefs, for whose selection there was no motive beyond the gratification of their own ambition; and they sometimes preferred the most unworthy candidate, because they hoped to find in such a more pliant tool.

Immediately after the death of Otho I. the disorders of the factious nobles again burst forth. Two parties, the Sabini and the Tusculani, struggled for power; the Popes were elevated sometimes by the one, and sometimes by the other party; but, after a brief period of time, were deposed again, and ended their days in dungeons, or were murdered. It was not until Otho III. appointed his cousin, Bruno, and afterwards the celebrated Gerbert, as Popes, and protected them by an armed force, that the Papacy could once more obtain and exercise its influence and authority in ecclesiastical affairs.

After the early death of Gerbert, or Sylvester II., the House of the Tusculani, probably descendants from that Alberic who had formerly been the master and ruler of Rome, gained possession of power in the city, and also over the Papal See. A Pope of this house, Benedict VIII. (whose reign, although it only lasted for twelve years, had been the longest of any of the Popes for two centuries), could, when borne up by his family power, and strongly supported by the Emperor Henry II., command as master in Rome, and also exercise his power and authority in the affairs of the Universal Church. But his pontificate likewise served to secure power in his own family; for after his death there succeeded two Popes of the same house—his brother, John XIX., and his nephew, Benedict IX. But the crimes of the latter became intolerable. The evils of dissension were added to the disgrace and degradation of the Church, and then Germany at last came forward with thorough and enduring aid. The strong arm of Henry III., and the series of German Popes he gave to the Church, purified and elevated the stained and degraded Roman See. The reformation of the clergy, which had become a matter of urgent necessity, and for which the congregation of Clugny had been making a prefatory preparation, could only now be commenced.

The greater portion of the Papal States had, during the whole of this period (that is, from the year 800 until 1050 or 1060) fallen into the hands of laymen. Ravenna, and its territory, and the towns of the Pentapolis, had become the Emperor's. In Sabinum and Præneste there was a branch of the house of the Crescenti.[1] Southern Tuscany, with Spoleto and Camerino, was held by Ugo the Great, Duke of Etruria, but destined soon to fall into the grasp of the

---

[1] See GFRÖRER's "Papst. Gregorious VII.," v. 597.

Emperor.   The revenues of the Roman See consisted of rents paid by some holders of fiefs.

Some light is thrown upon the state of things at the end of the tenth century, by the Deed of Donation of Otho III., of the year 999.[1]   The Emperor animadverts in sharp terms upon the carelessness and fatuity of former Popes (for they, as the impotent creatures of the Albani and Crescenti, had been in the current century intruded upon the Church), who (as the Pope himself said, for tributes of a very small amount) had frittered away almost the whole possessions of the Church, both in and outside of the city, and had, to replace them, taken what was imperial property. He, therefore, bestowed, for the maintenance of the Papal dignity, certain fiefs belonging to him—the eight countyships of Pesaro, Fano, Sinigaglia, Ancona, Fossombrone, Cagli, Aesi, and Osimo.   In the following century these districts were again lost, and had again to be won back.

In the dispute with the Emperor, Henry III., Benevento was taken away from the Pope, Leo IX., who gained, however, for the Papal See, that which was far more valuable

---

[1] I entertain no doubt about the authenticity of this so much (and still in WILLMAN's "Jahrbücher des deutschen Reichs," ii. 2, pp. 233-43) disputed document (ap. PERTZ, "Mon.-Germ. IV.," B. 162).   I am of this opinion with Muratori, Pertz, Giesebrecht, Gfrörer, Gregorovius, who also have decided on its authenticity, against Baronius and Pagi. Pope Sylvester himself complains in the feofment-diploma of Terracina of the year 999, that the Papal property had been dissipated from the Roman See, "Cum lucris operam darent et sub parvissimo censu maximas res ecclesiæ perderent" ("Ap. CONTATORE Hist. Terrocin.," p. 41), and the real "Comitate" are mentioned in a letter of Otho's to the Pope as "qui sub lite sunt," ("GERBERTI Epistolae," p. 70).   He has, says the Emperor, delivered them to the Marquis Ugo of Etruria, who also possesses the Countships of Spoleto and Camerino, out of love to the Pope, in order that the people may have a ruler, and the Pope may, through the same person, receive from the "Comitate" fitting services and dues.   The Popes neither could nor should directly rule over the territories bestowed on them, but might enjoy the revenues in gold, or natural productions, and have military aid, in case of war.   Consequently the supreme imperial authority over the territories given to the Pope must be maintained.   The grounds, for upholding the authority of the documents which Giesebrecht and Gfrörer have cited, might be still further enlarged.

than the possession of that territory—and that was, the vassal-
ship of the Norman conqueror of Lower Italy. That which
Leo IX. had commenced with the brothers Humphrey and
Robert, was continued with Robert by Gregory VII., and
completed by Innocent II., in the year 1139, with King
Roger. For what was still withheld from them, and the
loss of which Nicholas I. continued to complain of (namely,
their rich patrimony in Lower Italy and Sicily), there was,
however, one compensation left to the Popes, viz.: that
they were recognised as the Suzerain lords of a mighty
kingdom—that the princes of this kingdom did homage
to them as vassals, and paid them tribute. Subsequently,
indeed, it was precisely this very vassal kingdom that
became the cause of the Pope's falling into a dependence
upon France, and that led to the episode at Avignon, and,
through it, to the great schism, the consequences whereof
remain to this day unfathomable.

In the long struggle concerning Investitures, the spiritual
power of the Papacy developed itself in all its greatness,
whilst the material basis of the temporal position upon which
the Popes were placed was weak and insecure. Gregory
VII. at first ruled in Rome with a firm hand; but after a
few years there sprang up an imperial party amongst the
populace, and its constantly increasing strength induced
Gregory to unite with the Normans in Lower Italy. The
same party drove his successor, Victor III., out of the city,
and compelled Urban II. to seek refuge for some time in
France. The districts lately bestowed upon the Church, as
a portion of its estates, were then, for the most part, in the
hands of imperial feudatories—of such persons as that
Werner, or Guarnieri, who describes himself, in writing, as
"By God's grace, Duke and Marquis of the Marche of
Ancona, and enlarged by the marquesates of Camerino and
Fermo."[1]

<hr/>

[1] PERUZZI, "Storia d'Ancona," i. 280. ["E perciocchè egli s' intitola,
ed è intitolato 'Guarnerius Dei gratia Dux et Marchio,' se ne può in-
ferire, che non la sola Marca d'Ancona, ma anche il Ducato di Spoleto,
fossero a lui sottoposti."—MURATORI, "Annali d'Italia," a. 1016.
Monaco, 1762, vol. vi., p. 350.]

Urban II., one of the most powerful Popes out of Rome, was, in Rome itself, absolutely powerless; and, being robbed of his revenues, was, for a long time, living upon alms. His successors, Paschalis II. and Gelasius II., were several times compelled to abandon Rome, on account of the predominant sway of the noble families. The two mightiest houses now in Rome were the families of the Frangipani, and of Peter Leoni; and it was only when these two factions were at variance that the Popes could, by adhering to one of them as a support, maintain anything like an independent position in Rome. One of these families—(it was by the elevation of a son of Peter Leoni's, under the name of Anacletus II.)—plunged the whole Church into a long and lasting schism. Some years afterwards, in 1143, the Roman people revolted, appointed from amongst themselves a senate, independent of the Pope, and a municipal chief, with the title of "Patricius;" and Lucius II., in the attempt to make himself master of the city, met with a violent death.[1]

The Emperor, Frederick I., forced the Romans, who then, under the influence of Arnold of Brescia, were dreaming of a restoration of the ancient republic, to deliver up all the regalia into the hands of Pope Eugenius III.; and he who did this was — of all the Emperors since Charles the Great—the most determined opponent and champion against an independent Papacy, as well as of ecclesiastical states, as a basis on which it might be maintained. And thus had the Popes, during the whole of the twelfth century, no fixed settled territory of their own in Italy. They were never able to maintain themselves in Rome, but for a short and transitory time; and outside of Rome there was not one town of importance on which they

---

[1] [The character of the Romans in the twelfth century is accurately described by Muratori in a few lines, when referring to an incident in the life of Gelasius II. "Egli (the Pope) non si potea fidar de' Romani, gente venale in que' tempi, e tante volte provati da' suoi predecessori e da lui stesso per poco fedeli."—"Annali d'Italia," a. 1118. Monaco, 1762, vol. vi., p. 390.]

could with security calculate; and hence it is that we see them so frequently turning towards France for a prolonged residence. After Urban II., this was done by Paschalis II., Gelasius II., Calistus II., Innocent II., Eugenius III., and Alexander III. After the death of the last-named Pope, Lucius III., and Urban III., preferred remaining in Verona, because the Romans would not submit to them. The gift of the illustrious Countess Matilda had afforded to the Popes a grand prospect of the secure possession of an extensive territory. Had the terms of this donation been literally complied with, the Popes would have at once become the greatest landed princes in Upper and Middle Italy. Liguria and Etruria, say contemporaries, were included in the donation; but as the imperial fief could not possibly be separated from the allodial property, the Emperor seized upon, and, under the pretext of relationship, laid claim to, and escheated the whole inheritance. The Popes were compelled to let this be done by Henry V. The Emperor Lothair, however, recognised their right so far as to submit, with Duke Henry of Bavaria, in the year 1133, to accept an endowment of the allodium of the Countess, from Innocent II.; in consequence of which, in the year 1135, a Marquis of Etruria, named Engelbert, having received a portion of this property from the Emperor, made an oath of fealty to the Pope, on account of the Matilda-endowment. The recurrence of the Estates to the Papal See, after the death of Henry, was, meanwhile, vainly sought and stipulated for. The Emperor, Frederick I., and his son, Henry VI., held fast by the inheritance, until Innocent III., at the proper moment of time, asserted, with his customary active vigilance, the right of his See; and thus, at last, the so-named "patrimony of St. Peter," namely, Southern Tuscany—out of the inheritance bequeathed by Matilda—really came into the possession of the See of Rome.

Innocent III. (1198—1216) was not so much the restorer, as he was, practically, the first actual founder of the Papal States; for, previous to him, no Pope can be named who actually reigned over a large territory. Previously, the

Popes had possessions from which they received taxes and feudal services, but not a single state that they governed. When he (Innocent), in the year 1198, entered into his Pontificate, all (belonging to the Church) was in the hands of strangers. The Swabian knight, Conrad, was Duke of Spoleto. In the Campagna, Henry VI. had distributed fiefs amongst his military followers. In Ravenna, the Marche and Romandiole, the Seneschal of the Empire, Markwald, was in command; and in the Exarchate and Pentapolis, the cities (once the great commercial movement had extended over the whole of Upper and Middle Italy) had developed themselves as municipal Republics. The cities had well understood how to turn to their own advantage the dispute between the Emperor and the Pope, and, as Macchiavelli says, had employed the imperial power against the Pope, and then made use of the latter to obtain freedom, self-government, the right of election, and the yearly change of their chief magistrates, consuls, or podestas.

Even in his first year Innocent had brought under submission the important cities of the Marquesates of Camerino and Fermo, and of the Duchy of Spoleto; and then Perugia, Montefiascone, Radicofani, and Aquapendente, along with the Countship of Benevento. The cities of the Romagna speedily recognised the supreme authority of the Church— an authority so mildly exercised that they could scarcely perceive it.[1] The freedom and full autonomy of the cities were granted. Thus Innocent, in 1198, declared Perugia to be a property of the Roman See; but he then also confirmed the constitution of the city, its government by consuls, and the free use of the laws which the citizens had made for themselves.[2] In this respect the Popes gave more than the Emperor. The cities had only to pay a small yearly tribute, and, in case of necessity, to furnish men-at-arms; and even this was not usual, for it was remarked of Viterbo, that,

---

[1] VESI, "Storia di Romagna," ii. 224.

[2] See introduction to the Chronicle of Perugia in "Archivio-Stor.," vol. xvi., I., p. xxii., and INNOCENTII, "Epistolæ," i. 375, 426.

before the fifteenth century, it had to pay nothing.[1]　It was
in Rome itself that the Pope had the toughest resistance
to overcome, and he was sometimes obliged to quit the city,
until at last he was able to induce the Romans to leave to
him the nomination of the Chief Captain of the municipality,
who was also now called "Senator."

In the desperate conflict with the too powerful Frederick
II. the most of that which had been won by the Popes was
again lost; and then, after the death of the Emperor and
the downfall of his son Manfred, its gradual restoration had
to be sought for.　An injurious effect of the quarrel between
the Emperor and Pope was the formation of the Guelph
and Ghibelline parties, which penetrated into all the cities,
and continued to abide in them.　The Church-friends, the
Guelphs, were everywhere the democratic party; whilst the interests of the nobles, as a class, in the success of the Imperialist
Ghibellines, won for them consideration and power.　Where
the latter gained the upper hand the supreme authority of
the Papal See could not be, even nominally, maintained;
and as to the Guelphs, they also, whenever they could,
wished themselves to govern, and to wage war and make
peace, according to their own will and 'pleasure.　The
Popes (with all the splendour of appearance which could be
afforded by the victories of the Guelphs in a great part of
Italy, and beyond the limits of the Church States), were still
in such a position that no city was really subject to them,
and they were often in embarrassment as to where they
should take up their abode.　Thus Clement IV., in one of
his writings of the year 1265, says that, after he had consecrated a church in Assissi, he would go again to Perugia,
since he could not procure a dwelling-place anywhere else;
because the other cities of his Patrimony were entangled in
feuds, or had not a sufficiency of provisions.[2]　If he wished
to make a city a permanent residence, he must have first
entered into an agreement with the municipality, by which
the Roman Court should retain a free, unhindered movement

[1] BUSSI, "Istoria di Viterbo," p. 47.
[2] "Bullarium Franciscanum," ed. Sbaralea, iv. 29.

within its own sphere of action; and it must also have been promised that the city would choose only for their consuls and podestas men who were faithful to the Roman See; and also that they would not impede the Papal Marshal in the exercise of his judicial office over the personality of the court.[1]

Thus nearly all supreme sovereign rights had passed away to cities, or to individual noble families—a part of them also became vested in bishops and monasteries; and the Papal authority in temporal affairs became little more than a supremacy of dignity over a number of municipal republics, and of noble and princely signories.[2] The sovereign authority of the Pope was restricted to the exercise of a judicial power, that was, upon the whole, very much limited to the disposal of the pecuniary means and troops which well-disposed cities and dynasties furnished, and to acts of arbitration. The wonted method by ban and interdict no longer operated with an unerring effect upon Guelph cities, and far less upon Ghibelline. Rome, where the Savellis, Orsinis, and Colonnas now preponderated, was, as usual, a restless city, always suspicious and on the watch against the strengthening of the Papal Government, and ever inclined towards the Imperialists and Ghibellines.[3] They were so, partly out of opposition to the Pope, and partly because of the theory then prevalent over all Italy: viz., that it was the people and the city who were the real heirs and possessors of the Imperial dignity and pre-eminence;[4] so that the Pope could only in

---

[1] Such are the terms of the treaty that was made in the year 1278, in the name of Nicholas III., with the town of Viterbo. See MARINI, " Degli Archiatri Pontificij." Rome, 1783, ii. 11.

[2] CANTU, " Storia degli Italiani," iv. 11; LEO's " Geschichte der italiänischen Staaten," iv. 423.

[3] " Populus urbis (Romæ), qui naturaliter imperialis existit."— SABA MALASPINA, Ap. Murator, S.S. Ital., vii. 842.

[4] This was not merely a Ghibelline notion, as Dante describes it in his " Monarchia," but it was also that of the Guelphs, as Matteo Villani represents it, lib. iv., c. 77, and lib. v., c. 1, prologo, when he says, amongst other things: " L' autorità del popolo Romano creava gli imperadori: e questo medesimo popolo, non da sè, ma la chiesa per lui, in

the name and by the authority of the Roman people transfer the election of an Emperor to the princes of Germany.

Rudolph of Hapsburg had in his interview with Pope Gregory X., at Lausanne, in 1274, solemnly granted and confirmed to him the full possession of the Papal State terri- tories, according to the then existing designation—the land of Radicofani to Ceperano, the Exarchate of Ravenna, the Pentapolis, the Marche of Ancona, the Duchy of Spoleto, the country of the Countess Matilda, and the Countship of Berti- noro. Even Corsica and Sardinia were included in this grant.[1] At the same time was abandoned the appointment of an Imperial Count, or Vicar of the Empire, who had hitherto, in the exercise of an imperialist jurisdiction, restricted very much the Papal power in the Romagna, the Pentapolis, the Marche, and Spoleto. In the year 1278, Rudolph actually sent a special envoy to Pope Nicholas III., for the purpose of having recalled and declared null and void the oath which his chancellors had caused to be sworn by the cities of Bologna, Imola, Faenza, Forli, Cesena, Ravenna, Rimini, and Urbino.[2]

The appointment and elevation of the House of Anjou to the Sicilian throne was a momentous turning-point in history; for by it was transformed the condition of Italy, the character of the Guelph party, and, beyond all other things, the position of the Papal See. The Guelphs ceased to be a national party, a party opposed to foreign domination; a party essentially devoted to the Church. They became Angiovini, accessible thereby to French influence, and subservient to French interests. The Popes lost the leadership of the Guelph party, which had passed over to the Anjous, and to other princes of the royal family of France;

certo sussidio de' fedeli cristiani, concedette l'elezione degli imperadori a sette principi della Magna." From this it further was concluded, " That the Tuscans were originally Latins, that is, Romans, and so were not subjected to the sway of the Emperor, and naturally still less to that of the Romans."—See " Storia Fiorentina di Pietro Boninsegni," p. 437.

[1] PERTZ, " Mon. Ger.," iv. 403, 404.

[2] RAYNALD, ad a. 1278, § 51.

and so arose that bastard Guelphdom which Dante so much
hated. Through it was the vast importance of the Empire
to Italy, to the Pope and the States of the Church, attacked
at its very roots, and by it was the imperial action in the
Peninsula crippled. French cardinals, French popes (Clement IV., Urban IV., and, chiefest, Martin IV.), did what they
could to strengthen the influence of their nation, and of its
two dynasties, the Capets and the Angiovines, in the Peninsula. Martin IV. appointed Frenchmen attached to the
suite of Charles of Anjou to be governors in provinces of
the Papal States; he subjugated, with the hired arms of
Frenchmen, the Ghibelline Forli;[1] and he nominated Charles
himself as "Senator of Rome." The latter placed there his
own officers, whilst the Popes seldom permitted themselves
to be seen in Rome; and so much more did they prefer
residing in Viterbo, Orvieto, or Anagni, that, when Innocent
V., in the year 1276, said mass in St. Peter's Church, he
observed that it was the first time a Pope had done so in the
same place for the space of thirty years.[2] The relations of
the Popes with the population of the Papal States, and
especially of those who were French Popes, became more harsh,
and more marked with rigid force. It became so particularly
whilst the authority over the provinces lay in the hands of
Charles of Anjou—far more than in those of the Pontiff.
Gregory X., the wisest and noblest of the Popes of that age,
had everywhere endeavoured to reconcile the Guelphs and
the Ghibellines, and to amalgamate the two parties; but his
successors, under the Anjou influence, turned away from the
path he had pursued. The Ghibellines were driven to
despair. Ban and interdict, employed as instruments of
government, had become, from too frequent use, ineffective.
The wars which the Popes had to carry on by means of
foreign "condottieri," and by giving high pay to foreign
hirelings, multiplied fiscal burdens on the people; whilst the
unproductiveness of the revenues derived from the States of
the Church compelled the Popes to maintain their wars with

[1] "Chron. Pipini," ap. MURAT, ix. 720.
[2] "Annal. Salisburg," ap. PERTZ, "Mon. G.," xi. 801.

the revenues of the Church, and by the imposition of new ecclesiastical tributes. In the first years of the fourteenth century there was already to be found some unknown statesman to make the following proposal—viz.: That the lands of the Pope should be given over to some powerful king in emphyteusis, under the obligation of leaving to the Pope the revenue derivable from them; and thus the Pope might become the organizer and protector of the public peace, and no longer have occasion to wage wars, or to accumulate treasures.[1]

The French Popes believed they had discovered the means whereby they might, for a long time, be able to bring the Pontificate into French hands exclusively, and that was by naming Frenchmen as cardinals until they should become the majority. For them Rome and Italy were foreign countries—they wished to live on their native soil; and so came the transference of the Court of Rome to Avignon, where it remained for seventy years. The States of the Church had now nigh lost all their importance. In Avignon they were treated and regarded as a distinct province, which need not be very closely looked after, and that might be governed through deputies. The influence of the Parisian Court was so powerful at Avignon, and in many cases it was so overwhelming, that the Pope did not appear to be master of one inch of ground in Italy.

With the commencement of the fourteenth century had arrived the period of decay for the free States of Italy. These, with few exceptions, had, through civil strife, been changed into Principalities. This was the case, beyond all others, with those in the Romagna and the Marche, where the Polentas in Ravenna, the Malatestas in Rimini, the Manfredis in Faenza, the Ordelaffis in Forli, the Montefeltros in Urbino, and the Baranos in Camerino, had arrogated all power to themselves. The whole of the Papal States was broken up into fragments. In Rome and in the Campagna reigned anarchy and wild club-law—so that, to use the words

---

[1] "De recuperatione terræ sanctæ," in the "Gesta Dei per Francos."
—BONGARS, ii. 324.

of Villani, "strangers and pilgrims were as lambs in the
midst of wolves, and everything became an object of plunder
and a booty." Then it was that the tribune, Cola Rienzo,
his thoughts filled with images of the ancient Roman
glories, succeeded in bringing back, for a short time, a transitory glimmer of a well-ordered republic, affording a guarantee
for legal freedom. The rights of the Pope, as their only
lawful lord, had, indeed, been constantly maintained by him.
But, then, he neither knew how to rule nor to fight; and,
although appointed Senator by the Pope, and sent back to
Rome after his fall, he was soon ruined through his own
vanity and indiscretion. Then it was that Cardinal Albornoz
(1353—1368), who had been sent from Avignon, showed that
he was equally great as a warrior and a statesman, and gradually freed the towns and territories of the Papal States
from their tyrants. At the same time, he became, through
"the Aegidian Constitutions," which subsisted down to the
latest time, the legislator and creator of public law in the
Romagna.

The arbitrary conduct and oppression of the French
Legates soon provoked a universal revolt. Within nine
days, in the year 1376, eighty towns and villages of the
Papal States, excited by the Florentines, who were imbittered
against Gregory XI., rose in insurrection, and either declared
themselves to be free, or called back amongst them the
tyrants who had been deposed by Albornoz. At that time,
too, revolted Perugia—a city which had long jealously preserved its freedom, even though its Guelph and well-disposed
inhabitants called themselves "the people of the Church."
The city had only submitted to the Pope since 1370. After
its revolt it was able to conclude a peace with the new Pope
on its own conditions.[1] At that time grass was growing in
the public streets of Rome, and the number of its inhabitants
was only 17,000.

The great revolt had enkindled a war which, according to
the manners of the times, was carried on by a profuse application of ecclesiastical censures, combined with the employ-

[1] MARIOTTI, "Memorie di Perugia," 1806, p. 81.

AA

ment of foreign, brutal, barbarous, and mercenary troops.
And then broke out, after the death of Gregory XI. (who
had lately come to Rome from Avignon), that momentous
schism in the Church, the consequences of which are incalculable, and the effects of which are felt to the present day.
"A Roman or an Italian at least will we have!" exclaimed
the people, before the windows of the Conclave. "We,
Frenchmen will not let escape from our grasp the prize of
the Pontificate, with all that depends upon it," thought in
silence the French Cardinals; and, in opposition to the Italian
Urban VI. elected that Cardinal Robert of Geneva, to whose
hands was still adhering the blood of the luckless inhabitants
of Cesena. With France, nationality was of more avail than
the right and weal of the Church. The anti-Pope was
recognised, and therewith the curse of schism was brought
down upon the whole of Europe. The entire of Christendom
and the Papal See, in their incapacity to help themselves
and the Church, felt now the consequences of the Empire
having dwindled into a shadow, and the office of "Protector
of the Church and the See of St. Peter" having become a
mere empty title!

The utter shattering of the Papal States into fragments
was then at its acmé: the old leaders again reappeared;
republics were formed, or new rulers sprung up in many
places; and then Urban's successor, the money - needing
Boniface IX., sold to the tyrants and republics, for immediate payment and a yearly tribute, the sovereign rights
of which they were already in possession.

When Martin V., at the termination of the schism, was
elected as sole Pope, in 1418, and appeared in Italy, he
found Rome and Benevento in the hands of the Neapolitans,
a republic in Bologna, and the Romagna, with the Marche, and
Umbria in the hands of different chiefs. Many places were
won back, and again lost through new insurrections; whilst
several of the Princes recognized the Pope. The election of
his successor, Eugenius IV., in the year 1431, was a decisive
event for the future of the Papal States. He confirmed by
oath a statute determined upon in Conclave—in accordance

with which all the Papal feudatories, vicars, and official persons in the Papal States should take the oath of fealty and allegiance, not to himself alone, but also to the College of Cardinals, to which, in cases of a Papal vacancy, the sovereign authority of the country belonged. At the same time he bound himself to leave to the Cardinals the half of all the revenues he received; and he obtained, by this means, the sympathy and co-operation of the College in the exercise of all the more important rights of his sovereignty.[1] This was a new constitutional law for the Papal States, and a very comprehensive limitation of the temporal power of the Pope was thereby created. It was, however, a matter that lasted but for a very short time.

When the Spaniard Alphonzo Borgia, with the name of Callistus III., mounted the Papal throne in the year 1455, he found eight families of princes in possession of their fiefs—the Manfredis in Faenza and Imola, the Ordelaffis in Forli, Alexander Sforza in Pesaro, Domenico Malatesta in Cesena, Sigismondo Malatesti in Rimini, and Frederick of Montefeltro in Urbino, the Baranos in Camerino, and the Estes in Ferrara. All the other chiefs had been previously set aside.[2] In Rome and the Campagna the Popes of this age, like their predecessors, were able to do very little. To the arbitrary power and mutual hostilities of the Barons, who still perpetuated a state of open, unbridled violence, and who had their relations and adherents amongst the Cardinals, the Popes had no armed power to control or oppose. And then came frequent and short Pontificates, whilst the constant interruptions of the Conclave would permit no thorough and permanent measure to be adopted.

A centrifugal impulse, a tendency to fragmentation, to the formation of many petty sovereignties, had been, for a century and a half, so predominant in Italy, that now—at the close of the fifteenth century—the Popes themselves were

---

[1] See RAYNALD, ad a. 1431.

[2] See RIGHI, "Annali di Faenza," 1840, ii. 204; "Compendio della Storia d'Imola," 1810, 241. UGOLINI, "Storia dei Conti e Duchi d'Urbino." Florence, 1859, i. 340, &c.

seized with it. First amongst them, Sixtus IV. made one of his nephews Lord of Imola and Forli, and another Prince of Sinigaglia and Mondovio. The statute of 1431, providing for the rights of the Cardinals, proved itself to be, in such cases, utterly inoperative. Then came Alexander VI., and his son Cæsar Borgia, to overturn all the principalities in the States of the Church, with the single exception of the Duchy of Montefeltro. Even the powerful barons of Rome and of the Campagna were expelled. Alexander wished to make his son prince over a considerable patrimony—in fact, of one that would comprise the greater part of the Papal States. It was not to be accomplished. Julius II. took away from Borgia all that had been bestowed upon him. The work of restitution so commenced was persevered in. The Pope forced the Venetians to yield up to him those portions of the territory of the Romagna they had won in war; he struck down the dominion of the Bentivogli in Bologna, and of the Fredduccini in Fermo; and thus became—after Innocent III. and Albornoz—the third founder and restorer of the Papal States. It was as a warrior and conqueror that the grey-haired Pope won back Parma, Piacenza, and Reggio. Not long before then, every puny chieftain with a couple of castles and a hamlet could set at defiance the temporal power of the Pope; whilst now it excited the greatest respect, even from the mightiest States.

A well-ordered and united government had never long existed in the territory of the Papal See; and now, as that which had been combined together, in consequence of the old disruptions, was only conjoined but loosely, or did not at all adhere, so there sprang up, as suddenly as if they started out of the earth, several little chiefs and small tyrants. This was the case especially in the Marches. With the exception of one or two, Leo X. drove out all these petty chiefs, or had them executed. He, being bent, above all things, upon the aggrandisement of his house—the Medici—took the Duchy of Urbino from its Duke, Francesco Maria della Rovere, in order that he might bestow it on his nephew, Lorenzo de

Medici. After Leo's death, however, Della Rovere again reconquered and regained his Duchy.

Ever since the close of the fifteenth century there was a transition going on all over Europe, from the manners and circumstances of the mediæval to those of modern times: the change was coming in some places with a slow, and in others at a speedy pace. And so too was it with the Papal States. There began now to be carried out two objects that were in accordance with the spirit of the age. The first was an endeavour to draw more closely together the political bands, so as to make the whole State more uniform; and next to extend and exalt the Papal authority, even to the degree of its becoming an unlimited power. This appeared so much the more necessary because the old, and now quite senseless, factions of the Guelphs and the Ghibellines were still maintained, especially amongst the country people, and led to the perpetration of numerous crimes and acts of violence. Leo X. had, for the most part, confided the government to Florentines, his countrymen, who, principally for the sake of getting money, practised the greatest oppressions. The cities sent ambassadors, one after another, to make complaints. They did so in vain. At Rome they were far more intent upon taking away the freedom which many towns still possessed; and such an intention was carried into full effect at Ancona, by Clement VII.,[1] when he, by a sudden invasion and military occupation, got possession of it in 1532. A similar purpose was accomplished by Paul III. in the year 1540, in Perugia, when the town, having revolted on account of the raising the price of salt, was then compelled to submit, and lost all its rights and liberties.[2] In a similar manner had Ravenna, Faenza, and Jesi been previously punished. Since the middle of the sixteenth century all had been completely subjected in the Papal States: cities and barons yielded an unconditional obedience. And yet the nepotism of some of the Popes led them, in harsh contrast to the prevailing tendency of the times towards a con-

---

[1] "Relazioni degli Ambasciatori Veneti," vii. 55.

[2] MARIOTTI, pp. 113-160.

solidation of the State, to its dismemberment. Thus Paul
III. made his son, Luigi Farnese, Duke of Parma and
Piacenza; and that territory has been lost irretrievably to
the Roman See. Paul IV. despoiled the Colonna family of
the Duchy of Palliano to bestow it upon his nephew, Caraffa,
who was, soon after the death of his uncle, subjected to legal
punishment by the late Pope's successor, Paul IV. And
herewith came to an end that species of nepotism which
aggrandised the kinsmen of a Pontiff at the expense of the
Papal States. After having lasted from the reign of Sixtus
IV. to that of Paul IV., then came Pius V., who prohibited,
in the most emphatic manner, every endowment of what was
a property belonging to the Roman Church, no matter under
what title or pretence soever it might be made;[1] and he
forewarned by excommunication all who should but advise
its being done : and the law forbidding these, as well as every
temporary alienation, he had subscribed by all the Cardinals.
From this time there occurred two important events in the
exterior history of the Papal States—the lapse of Ferrara,
by the death of Duke Alphonso II., in the year 1596, and of
the Duchy of Urbino, in the year 1631.

With the eighteenth century came times in which the
Popes had bitter experience of their weakness and helplessness, when opposed to foreign Courts—times in which the
States of the Church, so far from aiding to serve the Papal
independence, were, on the contrary, regarded and treated
as the very means by which a Pope could be forced to adopt
measures which otherwise he never would have assented to.
The Bourbon Courts imitated the example of Henry V.,
who, by laying waste the Roman territory, forced Pope
Paschalis II. to yield up to him the "Investiture," for the
maintenance of which the Papacy had been for thirty years
contending. One might have considered it as an impossibility
that a Pope would have laid a hand upon the destruction of
a Society, against which no substantial or proved accusation
existed, and with the downfall of which (apart from other
reasons) was involved the ruin of the mightiest and most

[1] Bulla " Admonet nos," 29. Mart., 1567.

flourishing missions amongst the heathens, and at the same time the Church itself rendered the poorer by so many thousands of souls. But the Bourbon Courts knew well how to obtain what was apparently impossible. They caught hold of the Roman See by the Papal States. They seized upon Avignon and Venaissin, Benevento and Pontecarro, and threatened at the same time to take Castro and Ronciglioni.[1] And when they had tormented to death the steadfast Clement XIII., they managed, through their adherents amongst the Cardinals, that the man who offered to be the accomplisher of their will should be placed in the chair of the Apostles. And when two Popes, one after the other, Pius VI. and Pius VII., calmly abiding in their own country, allowed themselves to be made prisoners by French authorities, to be dragged away to France, and to be thrown into prison, then, indeed, a comparison might well be instituted between times past and present. An Alexander III., or an Innocent IV., would have passed over into Sicily, and there, unattainable by Gallic tyrants, they would, under English protection, have continued to govern the Church. Not so the two Piuses. Both were excellent, conscientious men; but they regarded the quality of a territorial prince more highly than that of the head of the Church. They would not forsake their dominions and their people; they preferred, like the Roman senators of old, to await the Gauls, seated in their chairs, and—the world knows how they were treated!

At the close of the eighteenth century happened a circumstance, such as had not occurred during a thousand years. Pius VI., in the treaty of Tolentino, of 1797, had to resign to France not only Avignon and Venaissin, but also the three legations, Ravenna, Ferrara, and Romagna. For him remained Rome, the Patrimony, Umbria, and, he was permitted to hope, Ancona to be restored to him. It was, however, easy to foresee that the remainder would soon be taken out of his hands. But Pius had recognized, as a matter of fact, that there were cases in which the Pope, although

---

[1] THEINER's "Geschichte Clemens XIV.," i. 97.

not the proprietor, but merely the depository or trustee
of the Papal States, might nevertheless alienate a part of
them—that is, where the actual mission of the State can,
apart from the portion that has been alienated, be still carried on.

INTERNAL CONDITION OF THE PAPAL STATES PREVIOUS TO 1789.

Macchiavelli's remark, that " the Papal States stood in no
need of any defence against external foes, because they were
protected by religion," is an observation that has, at subsequent periods, been frequently repeated.   There appeared to
be a great advantage in the fact; for a country so situated
could require no standing army, and no costly expenditure
upon the maintenance of fortresses; whilst its inhabitants,
feeling themselves in full possession of undisturbed security,
might, free from peril, devote their lives to industrial pur-
suits.[1]   From the time that Paul IV. had compelled King
Philip of Spain formally to engage in a war, which was carried on with the greatest aversion by the latter, no portion of
the Papal States had ever been intruded upon by an enemy,
until Urban VIII., misled, like Paul IV., by his nephews,
brought on the unmeaning war of Castro, which, ending with
a dishonourable peace, became, through increased taxation,
by the accumulation of debts, by the impoverishment of the
country, and by the hateful employment of spiritual combined with temporal weapons, a long-enduring calamity for
the Papacy and the country.[2]
A distinction has been drawn between two periods of
nepotism—of what were called " the great" and " small "
nepotisms.   In the former, Popes wished to found large
principalities for their families ; in the latter, which began

[1] " Relaz. Venet.," vii. 407.

[2] Cardinel Sacchetti expresses himself in very strong terms upon these
results in a letter addressed to Alexander VII.   This document has been
frequently reprinted.   It is last published by MASSIMO D'AZEGLIO, " La
Politique et le droit Chrétien."   Paris, 1860, p. 165.

with Gregory XIII., and the bull of Innocent XII., but
ended with the death of Alexander VIII. (1691), the
exertion made was to raise the Papal families by means of
rich endowments, and by elevating them in rank to an
equality with the first and noblest houses of the land.   Thus
the Buoncompagnis, through Gregory XIII., the Perettis
through Sixtus V., the Aldobrandinis through Clement VIII.,
the Borgheses through Paul V., and the Ludovisis through
Gregory XV.; but the enrichment of the Barberinis, through
Urban VIII., surpassed everything that had previously occurred.   At the same time it frequently happened that a kinsman
was, as " Cardinal Padrone," entrusted with the supreme reins
of government.   For a considerable time it was thought that
a Cardinal's nephew could not possibly be wanting in the
Papal Courts.   If a successor to the See called the nephews
of the antecedent Government to account, and prosecuted
them, the memory of the preceding Pope would become dis-
honoured, and a wound inflicted upon the authority of the
Pontificate.   The Popes of the eighteenth and nineteenth
century have, on the whole, kept themselves clear of these
faults and gross abuses.   Pius VI., with his Braschis, forms
the only exception.   Nepotism on the part of the Popes is
now extinguished, and lives only in history.   But it is otherwise with the nepotism of Cardinals and the " Prelati."

Had the Statute of Eugenius IV. remained in force the
College of Cardinals would have constituted a beneficial
restraint in the affairs of the Government.   Nepotism could
not have become so injurious; whilst favoritism, and such
deeds as those of a Camillo Astalli, Mascambruni, Don
Mario, and a Coscia would have been prevented, or would
have been rendered less pernicious.   The country and its
interests would also have had in the Cardinals authorised
advocates and representatives.   But that Statute had speedily
become a mere dead letter.   The Popes felt themselves to be,
and acted as, completely absolute rulers.   And even when
Paul IV. announced to the Cardinals his spoliation of the
Colonnas for the benefit of his nephew, and the war in which
he had engaged against Spain and the Emperor, they listened

to him with downcast eyes, but did not venture to say a word in opposition to his proposed policy. Since then the College has remained completely passive as a corporation. It serves merely to listen to Allocutions upon momentous events, and to be witnesses to the publication of treaties and important arrangements, to undertake the election of the Popes, and to represent the supreme power during the vacancies of the Papal chair. The newly elected Pope enters at the instant into the full enjoyment of a sovereignty, the boundlessness of which has not its like in all Europe. Paruta describes, in the year 1595, the relations between the Pope and the Cardinals: "Since Pius II.," he says, "the authority of the Cardinals has been so depressed, that the Popes have attracted all to themselves. At present particular affairs are laid before the College only in the form of a promulgation, and not to ask its advice; and if, in rare cases, the Pope should ever desire their counsel, or rather appear to desire it, they confine themselves merely to the laudation of whatever has been proposed by the Pope."[1]

In the beginning of the sixteenth century, and under Julius II. especially, the cities enjoyed great freedom. The Pope was desirous, says Guicciardini, of acting in such a manner as to inspire the people with an attachment to churchmen; so that at Bologna, when taking the oath of allegiance, upon its passing over to the Papal Government, it was regarded as a transition from the servitude which hitherto had existed (under the Bentivoglios), into a state of freedom, in which the citizens, in the peaceful possession of their native land, would be allowed to take part in its government as well as in its revenues.[2] And a contemporary of Julius, Macchiavelli, describes it as a peculiarity of the Papal States, that the sovereign was not required either to defend or rule over his subjects; whilst they, on their side, had no desire to be ruled, yet never thought of separating from him.[3]

In the course of the sixteenth century there was first

---

[1] "Relaz. Ven.," x. 413.

[2] Lib. vii., c. 1; lib. ix., c. 5.   [3] "Il Principe," c. 11.

formed an actual government of the State by ecclesiastics; and at the same time the administration was centralized in Rome. Before 1550 there were laymen acting as chiefs in the administration. This at least very frequently happened in the Romagna. But it is remarkable that the cities themselves often preferred "Prelati" as temporal governors, and expressly desired to have them. Fermo, until the year 1676, maintained its right to have a relative of the Popes for its governor; and afterwards in his place came a congregation of Prelati merely for this district. Bologna maintained many privileges, and especially that of having a President of its own in Rome, who sometimes offered an active and persevering resistance. Upon the whole, however, there was (at least since the end of the sixteenth century) no more of corporate or individual independence either in the cities or amongst the noble vassals. Of the city of Rome, it is said, by Cardinal de Luca, that it presented merely the shadow of a municipal government.[1] It is, however, admitted that some of the large cities were allowed to govern themselves in a tolerably independent manner, and that the lords of the soil had also, within their own territories, full power of action.[2]

Sixtus V., who has been regarded as the chief founder of the modern system of the Papal Government, established the institution of Standing Congregations, which was well calculated for that time, when it was an object to raise a barrier against nepotism and favoritism, and to have an Institution which would possess both uniformity and stability in the management of the public business, and be able to restrain the worst excesses of arbitrary authority. In connexion with this institution was developed "the Prelature"—the formation of a class of a

---

[1] "Dottor Volgare," lib. xv., c. 34.

[2] The Venetian Relation of 1615 ("Cod. Ital.," p. 358) remarks that in Rome there still remained the form of an independent municipal administration; but that all these were things "che servono piuttosto per apparenza, che per assistenza di governo." Its regulations were altogether dependent upon the will of the Pope.

superior or higher order of officials in the Papal State. The
commencement of this class is placed in the time of Gregory
XIII. In the former periods ecclesiastical officials were
named "Curiales." In a closer view of this body, the
"Prelature" might be regarded as "a noviciate"—a preliminary state of preparation, and a nursery for the occupation of the higher offices in the State. Those who entered
it had to prove they were possessed of an income of 1,500
scudi—and thus all persons without means were excluded
from this class, and the career which it opened to its
members.

A serious burden upon the country was the great number
of Roman officials, whose places some of the Popes, when
they found themselves in financial difficulties, had created
merely for the purpose of selling them. The duties they had
to discharge were insignificant, and some of them were
merely titles without any office whatsoever. The purchasers
paid either a yearly contribution or a lump sum at once, and
could also sell their appointments again. There was no fixed
salary attached to these appointments; but the occupiers
received the profits and fees of their offices. In the year
1470 there were already 650 purchasable places. Afterwards
Sixtus IV. created a whole College, merely to sell the
places; and at a later period succeeding Popes, and Leo X.
in particular, imitated this example, There were under
Paul IV. so many as 3,500 such places. With reference to
this matter persons tranquillised their conscience with the
consideration that by such means were obviated the necessity of burdening the people with new taxes. It was, in
fact, a system of disguised loans in the form of annuities.
The consequences made themselves chiefly felt in matters
affecting ecclesiastical jurisdiction, for the purchases had
main reference to the produce of Departments interested in
Benefices and Dispensations. And in the administration of
the Papal States its effects were also felt, for the Government
situations were also sometimes sold;[1] and the mere exist-

---

[1] SARACINI, "Notizie storiche della città d'Ancona," p. 335, mentions
that the Governorship of Ancona was sold to Benedetto Accolti, for the
yearly payment of 20,000 scudi.

ence of a numerous class of officials who had purchased their appointments, and regarded them as articles of trade, could not but introduce at last a grovelling, griping spirit into the whole administration.[1] It was one of the merits of the excellent Innocent XII., that, in the year 1693, he abolished the selling of places, by restoring the purchase-money to the buyers.[2] But, assuredly, he could not do away with the consequences of a custom that had existed for more than two hundred years, and the results of which have been felt down to the most recent times.

The ecclesiastics formed at Rome, in many different ways, a superior and privileged order, and such as cannot be found in any other country in the world. As clergy and laity were thus separated by a broad and deep chasm from one another, the laity were filled with jealousy against the clerical order, thus placed in a position so superior to their own, and defended on all sides by inviolable privileges; and the consequence was that the feeling of jealousy often became one of decided aversion. On the one side, it was frequently maintained in the sixteenth century that there prevailed amongst the people a decided dislike to a government by priests;[3] and on the other side it was remarked by the celebrated statesman and historian, Paolo Paruta (a seriously religious man), in the year 1595, that the preservation of the rights and immunities of the clergy was regarded as the first and most important of all affairs. He had, he says, frequently observed, and not without wonder and vexation, that even "Prelati," leading very unspiritual lives, were highly esteemed and rewarded, if they but defended the privileges of the ecclesiastical order against the laity; and that it was sometimes made a matter of reproach to a "Prelato"

---

[1] MURATORI, "Annali," a. 1693, xvi. p. 237. Ed. Milan.

[2] " Per la qual cosa si viene a riempire la corte d' uomini mercenarii e mercanti . . . non avendo detti mercenarii d'offici involto l'animo che in cose meccaniche e basse. . . . si che tolta l'economia esteriore ogni altra cosa si reduce a deterioramento." Thus writes the Venetian ambassador Grimani, under Clement IX.—"Tesori della corte Rom.," p. 426.

[3] " Governo dei preti," an expression since then frequently made use of.

that he favoured the laity too much. It seemed, he says, as
if the clergy and laity did not belong to one and the same
flock, and were not included in the one Church.[1]

It was further noticed that Popes were no longer taken
from the regular clergy—(from Sixtus V., who died 1590,
Benedict XIII., in 1724, was the first monk who sat in the
Papal chair)—and that since government by nepotism had
become customary, the regular clergy were seldom promoted
or employed. All was in the hands of the secular clergy,
and especially of those who did that which the regulars
could not do—serve "the nephews"—or who appeared better
adapted for office by their juridical studies.[2]

A very striking contrast was presented between the spiritual and temporal government of the Popes. The first
bore throughout the stamp of dignified stability, resting upon
fixed rules and ancient traditions; whilst the government of
the country was, on the contrary, a prey to continual changes
of men, manners, and systems.[3] In comparison with the
reigns of worldly princes, the pontificates were short. On
the average, the reign of a Pope did not last more than nine
years.[4] It seldom happened that a new Pope continued in

---

[1] " Relazioni Venete," x. 375.

[2] Grimani, who describes these circumstances, maintains, " Nelle con-
correnze un pretuccio ignorante e vizioso otterrà il premio sopra il religioso
dotto e dabbene," and ascribes, amongst the injurious consequences of the
system, the great want then felt of men of talent to occupy official positions in the Papal States. With the cessation of nepotism (since Innocent XII.) circumstances in this respect must have improved.

[3] The Relation (" Cod. Ital.," p. 358), "della qualità e abusi della
Corte di Roma," f. 127, remarks, " The constant changes in the Government astonish every one that comes to Rome, so much so, that some suppose the cause of it is to be found in the air, the climate, or the town
itself." The fact, however, is universally remarked. Thus it is spoken
of in an instruction to the Spanish Ambassador at Rome in the seventeenth century, and which is annexed to the work, " La monarchia di
Spagna crescente e calante," 1699, p. 7. " Questa corte (the Roman
Court) è variabilissima, e così bisogna, come il buon piloto, mutar le vele
conforme al vento che soffia," &c. See also CANTU, " Storia degli
Italiani," v. 660.

[4] Thus, for example, in two centuries (from 1589-1789) there were in

temporal affairs the system of his predecessors. He came to power under a lively impression of the discontents that had been aroused by certain evils of the previous administration, and was therefore so much the more inclined to produce a favourable impression for his own government by the adoption of opposite proceedings. Thus it has been remarked, with respect to the cultivation of the Roman Campagna, that every Pope followed a different system; and the consequence has been that in that which was the main point to be achieved nothing has been done.

Beyond all other things to be remarked upon is the fact that persons were changed under every new Pope, which led to the most influential offices never remaining long in the same hands—and thus were men gifted to be statesmen, and with an aptitude for business, either prevented from having time to acquire due knowledge and experience, or if they had acquired both, then they were not afforded the opportunity of turning them to practical account. Paruta alludes to the great disadvantage which this custom brought along with it. The new Popes were usually distinguished for their piety or learning; but they were unpractised in affairs of State,[1] and therefore needed so much the more old and experienced ministers, and a firm, permanent council. Instead of this, there appeared to be nothing more pressing for the new Popes to do than to fill the principal offices with their nephews, favourites, and fellow-countrymen.[2] Clement IX.

France five Kings, in Germany nine Emperors, in Spain seven Kings; but in Rome, twenty-three Popes.

[1] It is remarkable that the recent practice should be so different on this point from what prevailed in the Middle Ages, and when the Papal election was free from foreign influences. In the eleventh, twelfth, and thirteenth centuries, persons were constantly elected as Popes who had already filled, under one or two preceding Popes, the most important offices in the Roman Church. On this ground were elected Gregory VII., Urban II., Gelasius II., Lucius II., Alexander III., Gregory VIII., Gregory IX., Alexander IV. The Cardinal-State-Secretary is now peculiarly " the Government," and yet it is regarded as a regular rule that he is never to attain to the Papal dignity.

[2] " Relazioni Venete," x. 420.

was the first who, to the great vexation of his countrymen at Pistoja. departed from this custom ; and, with the exception of a few high offices, retained in their position all those who had been appointed by his predecessor.[1]

The management of the finances of the Popes, since the beginning of the sixteenth century, appears in an unfavour. able light, if we consider the figures and the expedients resorted to. Despite of the multiplied taxes, which were so much the more oppressive, as the prosperity of the population was by no means on the increase,[2] the National Debt was continually increasing, whilst Popes, by the erection of the " Monti," as well as by the sale of offices, were adding to an alienation of the revenue. It was remarked that since Sixtus V. the Popes left nothing to their successors but debts.[3] They had amounted, under Clement VIII., to 12,242,620 scudi, or 17,751,799 rix dollars—that is, three-fourths of the entire revenues of the State were required for the payment of interest. Innocent X., in 1685, left a debt of 48,000,000 scudi. The motive for such a heavy burden on the State (apart from the two useless Italian wars, and what was squandered in nepotism and favouritism) was one well calculated to increase the renown of the Popes. They could not withdraw themselves from the obligation of supporting the Catholic powers in the religious struggles of the sixteenth and seventeenth centuries, and especially from furnishing contributions in money, troops, and ships for the wars against the Turks. They had the task in Italy, in common with the Venetians, of serving as the bulwark of Christianity—a task that had been transmitted to them from their predecessors—and to maintain it against its hereditary

---

[1] GRIMANI, " Relaz. in den Tesori," p. 417.

[2] Of Clement IX. it is remarked by MURATORI (xvi. 92), " He was continually thinking of the means whereby he might relieve his people of many of the taxes imposed upon them by his predecessors. He instituted a congregation for that purpose, but it was found, on account of the State debts, to be an undertaking impossible to bring to a successful issue."

[3] GRIMANI, " Relazione," in the " Tesori della Corte Romana," 1672, p. 429.

enemy in the East. France, and the Poles, especially Hungarians, the Imperial Court, and most frequently of all the Venetians, sought for and received large sums of money. All who were persecuted and despoiled in the south-eastern countries turned first to the Popes for aid, and regularly obtained from them generous assistance.[1] The burdens which the population had at that time to bear were imposed upon them as victims to the general weal of Christendom. But their sacrifices brought with them two evils. First, there was in the country no species of industrial pursuit in a thriving condition, and the cities, with few exceptions, remained small and poor: next, everything that was used came from abroad,[2] and thus the land, despite of the excellence of its natural productiveness, became constantly poorer. The administration of finances was, as a matter of course, managed in secret, for there was not even a word said of a publication of the accounts; and as none but a Cardinal could be a Treasurer, he, by reason of the privileges of his position, was above all responsibility! The people felt the pressure of increasing taxation, and were continually becoming more dissatisfied with a "Priest Government." Their discontent must, in Paruta's time (about the year 1595), have assumed a very serious aspect.[3] The evil became still greater in the following cen-

---

[1] RANKE ("Die römische Päpste," i. 422) says: "The Popes wished to govern their principality as if it was a large property, from which a portion of the rents should be applied for the benefit of their own families; but the main part be especially allocated to the necessities of the Church." What he says with reference to a care for their own families can only be applied to Pontiffs before 1691, and, even then, is not applicable to them all. It is particularly not so to Clement IX., who might be called "admirable," if he had not been somewhat indolent and apathetic.

[2] This is particularly dwelt upon in the Venetian Relation of the year 1615 (in "Cod. Ital.," f. 45, of the Munich library), "Quasi tutte le cose, che si usano, sono portate da paesi forastieri," &c.

[3] "Relaz. Ven.," x. 396. Of the "gravezza quasi insopportabile dell' imposizion," Tiepolo had already spoken about the year 1570; see RANKE, i. 421. In the year 1664, Cardinal Sacchetti again complains of "il numero innumerabile delle gabelle," &c. We learn from Pallavicini that the people ascribed the pressure of taxation to nepotism, the dotation

tury; and, even though we should regard as an exaggeration
the assertion of Cardinal Sacchetti, that in the year 1664
the population had been diminished by one-half, still it is
positively true that numbers, to escape the burden of taxation,
had emigrated.

In the year 1670, the debt had increased to 52 million
scudi, and absorbed even the *dataria* rent, which otherwise
should, as usual, have been appropriated to the necessities of
the Papal Court. Under Clement XII., the deficit was
120,000 scudi. It was better at the time of the death of
Benedict XIV., in the year 1758. The deficit had then
been reduced by more than one-half, but the interest on the
public debt swallowed up the half of the income. After
this, the storm of the French Revolution burst over the
Papal States; and then there was a Roman Republic, which,
after the capture of Pius VI., dragged on for a few years a
miserable existence; and with it came a state bankruptcy,
which set aside the paper money created by Pius VI.[1]

In the seventeenth and eighteenth centuries, the condition
of the country is usually described in gloomy colours. The
foreign ambassadors believed " that, if a temporal monarch
had the government of the Papal States, they might be
raised to a high degree of prosperity, and even of wealth;"[2]
as all the conditions for attaining both were to be found in
the soil and the population. The causes assigned, in explanation of the general decay, are very various. Above all
things was, as a matter of course, the constantly disordered
state of the finances, which was now, indeed, not merely
ascribed to nepotism and favoritism, but the grounds for which
were found to lie much broader and deeper. To the drainage
of money occasioned by the absence of domestic manufactures, there was to be added that which passed away into
foreign countries, as payments upon the interest of the debt,

and enrichment of Papal families—" Populus, qui præ multis vectigalibus
humeris sibi ferre videbatur recentiores pontificias domos tot opibus
onustas," &c. In the MS. Life of Alexander VII.

[1] Coppi, " Annali d'Italia." iii. 219.
[2] So says the " Venet. Relation" of 1615.

as the chief creditors were Genoese and Florentines. According to the remark of the President de Brosse,[1] payments to the Church in Rome, that came from foreign countries, were never sent in cash, but in bills upon bankers, who immediately met with them the demands of the foreign creditors of the state.

The laws concerning trade were so inconceivably perverse, that the suspicion was expressed that they had been purposely calculated for the suppression of skill, and the destruction of industry. As to the absurd duties levied in the interior of the country, they operated in the same direction.

To these must be added the arbitrary proceedings with respect to the corn-trade, (the institute of the "*Annona*,") and the introduction of monopolies in the most important necessaries of life : matters concerning which there had been long and frequent complaints.[2] There was, too, a

[1] "Le President de Brosse en Italie, lettres," &c. Paris, 1858, ii. 452, *et seq.* These letters were written in 1739 and 1740.

[2] The author, in a subsequent passage, again refers to the baleful effects of the Roman "Annona," or Corn Law. Mr. Lyons, in a letter addressed to the Marquis of Normanby, from Rome, July 30, 1856, makes some remarks on the same subject : "I have," says Mr. Lyons, "the honour to transmit to your Lordship two printed copies and a translation of an Edict published yesterday, by which the exportation, from these States, of corn of all kinds, is suspended until further orders. The second paragraph of the Edict, declaring that the circulation of corn within the State remains perfectly free, is supposed to have been occasioned by an absurd and mischievous Notification, issued, on the 22nd instant, on his own authority, by Monsignor Amici, the lately appointed Extraordinary Papal Commissioner for the four Legations, and Pro-Legate of Bologna. This Notification is couched in language more calculated to excite and to justify than to allay the popular irritation, and contains a number of minute and vexatious regulations, intended for the prevention or punishment of the imaginary offence of 'engrossing,' or buying up large quantities of corn. The prejudices and ignorance of the mass of the people in these States on the subject of the corn trade may, perhaps, require to be treated with a gentle hand ; but it might have been expected that the acts of a public functionary, in the high situation occupied by Monsignor Amici, would have been directed rather towards correcting them than towards fostering and sanctioning them. The Government at Rome has

complete absence of all representation of the interests of the people. An individual city might make its wishes and complaints known in Rome; but then anything analogous to a provincial representation in the Papal States, much more a representation of the whole country, was never even thought of.[1]

The President de Brosse considered that the administration of the Papal States (about the year 1740) was the most defective of any in all Europe, but, at the same time, the mildest. The mildness degenerated into weakness and negligence, and so contributed to the impoverishment of the country, by permitting all things to go to decay, in the hands of aged and infirm sovereigns. He likewise thought that the Pope would be one of the richest monarchs in Europe, if he raised as much money from his subjects as other sovereigns, and if his finances were tolerably well managed.[2] Such was the opinion also entertained in Italy, with reference to the defective character of the Papal government. Becattini, in his eulogistic biography of Pius VI., confesses: "That, with the exception of Turkey, the country beyond all others the worst governed was that of the Papal States. The baleful

disapproved Monsignor Amici's Notification; but his proceeding does not afford a favourable specimen of the enlightenment, or of the administrative capacity of the ecclesiastics selected for high civil employment. . . . The practice adopted by the Papal Government of regulating the corn trade by successive temporary Edicts, issued according to the circumstances of the moment, has, in addition to its inherent evils, the great disadvantage, in these States, of giving rise to all kinds of suspicion against those in power. Every change is popularly attributed to direct corruption, or to a desire to favour the speculations of particular persons, supposed to be connected by ties of family or interest with men high in office. Whether these accusations are, in truth, founded or unfounded, there can be no doubt that they are believed in to an extent which materially injures the reputation and authority of the Government."— "Despatches from Mr. Lyons respecting the Condition and Administration of the Papal States." London, 1860, pp. 26, 27.

[1] "Gegenwärtiger Zustand des päpstlichen Staats." Helmstadt, 1792, p. 217. See the "Riflessioni" of Cardinal Buoncompagni, in the year 1780, partly translated in Le Bret's "Magazin," ix. 452-527.

[2] "Lettres familières," ii. 452, 465.

annona, or corn-law, the tormenting and demoralising "victualling tribunals," the want of manufactures, the increase of smuggling caused by the high duties on imports; the enrichment of state-farmers (farmers-general), to the great injury of the public treasury; and the number of homicides: such were the circumstances pointed at as characteristics of the condition of the Papal States.[1] And one is, in fact, in considering them, strongly reminded of the expressions of the old chancellor, Clarendon.[2] The mildness of the Papal government has also been lately remarked upon by an Englishman very familiar with Italian history.[3]

Strangers who have been in the country, and who have taken the trouble to acquire a knowledge of the manner in which its government has been carried on, have most generally been at first astonished at the absence of all restraints upon, and then the omnipotence of, the sovereign. Thus speaks Grosley, who visited the Papal States about the year 1760,[4] "The Papal is the most absolute of all the governments in Europe. Of all the restrictions that are to be found in monarchical states, such as—fundamental laws of the realm, a coronation oath, regulations made by predecessors, national or provincial assemblies, powerful corporations—of all these there is to be found not one in the Papal States." One looks with wonder at an institution like to that of " the *Uditore Santissimo,*" which, in the name of the Pope, can interfere arbitrarily in the administration of justice, in every department, and can withdraw both suits and suitors from the jurisdiction of the regular judges! Upon a closer examination it is, however, found that this absolute power is much modified by custom—by that, above

[1] CANTU, " Storia degli Ital.," vi. 126.

[2] " He observes, that of all mankind none form so bad an estimate of human affairs as churchmen."—HALLAM's " Constitutional History of England," iii. 330.

[3] " Whatever objection there may be to the Papal sway, it cannot, in fairness, be regarded as otherwise than mild."—DENNISTOUN's " Memoirs of the Dukes of Urbino," 1851, iii. 233.

[4] " Observations sur l'Italie." Paris, 1774, ii. 329.

which a Pope never, or scarcely ever places himself—that it is also modified by many considerations, and by the utmost possible forbearance towards persons; a forbearance that has become a principle of government—so that, in truth, this mild despotism is found to exist more in appearance, and in theory, than in fact, or practical life.

THE PAPAL STATES FROM 1814 TO 1846.

When Napoleon I. despoiled Pope Pius VII. of the Papal States, his primary and principal motive for so doing was not because he desired to have possession of the country, but because he would not allow the Pope to be in that position of independence which the government of those states secured to His Holiness; and because the Emperor wanted to make of the Pope an instrument wherewith nations might be subjected to the imperial sway. Napoleon has acknowledged this. "I did not despair," he says, "of obtaining by some means or other the guidance of the Pope for myself, and then—what an influence it would have been!"[1] He wished to establish the Papal Court at Paris—to make it a French and Imperial Institution, and by these means to get possession of the Papal influence over all Catholic populations—and so be a ruler over their souls as well as their persons.[2] He did not succeed in this; for the Pope, although a captive, and, according to the captor's own expressions, "gentle as a lamb, and an angel in goodness," would neither be led, nor allow himself to be made use of. The momentary weakness which the tortured, enslaved, and outwitted Pius had manifested in his signature to the Concordat of Fontainebleau, in the year 1813, with an implicit renunciation of his temporal powers, was very speedily repaired; and at the end of a few months he was able, as a steadfast sufferer, and

[1] "Mémorial de Ste. Hélène," v. 326.

[2] "S'en servir comme un moyen social pour réprimer l'anarchie, consolider sa domination en Europe, accroître la considération de la France et l'influence de Paris, objet de toutes ses pensées."—" Mémorial de Ste. Hélène," l. c.

now peaceful victor, to return, and pass through the provinces of his restored dominions to his capital, amid the most sincere expressions of joy from the whole people—and from those, too, of the Romagnole, that had been so long separated from him. His return was a grand triumphal procession.

The whole of the Papal States, such as he had never before possessed them, were transferred to him by the Treaty of Vienna; and, in the person of Consalvi, he had at his command a statesman of rare endowments, to aid him in solving the difficult problem of re-establishing in part the traditional mode of Papal administration, instead of the French hitherto existing.

That the form of the solution should have entangled the State and the Papacy in new and insoluble difficulties, or such difficulties as up to the present time never have been solved, was a fact that could only be subsequently learned by experience.

In the preliminary observations to the " Motu Proprio" of 6th July, 1816, by which was regulated the government of the Papal States, Consalvi declared— " That formerly an aggregate of various customs, laws, and privileges had existed in the State; and that it was an advantage and a Divine dispensation, that—by the interruption of the papal reign, and during that interregnum—all those inequalities should be removed, and unity with uniformity introduced. For," as he said, "a government was so much the more perfect the more it approached to a system of unity."

This statesman did not take into consideration that an absolute government can only be rendered endurable, and can alone be saved from sinking under the burden of its enormous responsibility, when it not merely tolerates and acknowledges a variously organized life, protected by custom and precedent, but also permits it to move freely within its subordinate sphere. His lauded unity and uniformity were destructive, and he also had to acquire by experience a knowledge of the fact that it is far easier to destroy than it is to construct or to create, in the management of public affairs, the spirit, strength, and vigour of a healthy existence.

Thus, there was not a single one of the old municipal and provincial institutions re-established. The *Gonfaloniere* and the *Anziani* of the Communes, retained no more their independent positions; and even Rome and Bologna had but a shadow of municipal government. The local laws and statutes which, in sooth, granted very various, and, for the purposes of justice, very inconvenient privileges, as well as all the rights of the Communes, with exemptions and immunities, were abolished. Consalvi entered, therefore, willingly upon the inheritance which the Revolution had left to him as an incarnate Napoleonised government; and he was thankful to the latter, because it had prepared the way so energetically and unsparingly for his administration, and so completely smoothened a path for him—and yet, he in one respect departed completely from the French system, by again placing power in the hands of "ecclesiastics." The Papal States were to be an absolute government by officials, in accordance with the French pattern, but then the highest orders of officialism were reserved for the "*Prelature.*" This form of a clerical, omnipotent, bureaucratic, administering, governmental officialism, was essentially a novelty, far and away different from the state of affairs in the olden time, and, above all, absolutely different from what existed during the Middle Ages. Now, the whole of the kingdom was divided into seventeen Delegations, or Legations, where a cardinal was placed at the head of affairs. The *Delegati*, corresponding in position with the French Prefects, must be members of the Prelature. They had to decide upon everything; and to assist them, they had merely a deliberative council, the members of which were nominated at Rome. To these *Delegati* belonged the appointment of the magistrates who carried on the government of the Communes, and amongst whom sat clergymen, who took precedence of the lay members. Below the *Delegati* were persons named *Governatori*, but having an inferior jurisdiction. In Rome, the old supreme authorities were again re-established—the *Congregazione della Consulta, del buon Governo, economica, dell' Acque, degli Studii;* and then the *Camera Apostolica,* endowed with the most heterogeneous at-

tributes, and divided into twenty-one subordinate departments, or Circles, with a *Cardinal Camerlingo* (chamberlain)
and *Tesoriere,* or treasurer.   To these were to be added fifteen different courts of judicature.   At the head of the Government, both spiritual and temporal, was placed the Cardinal State-Secretary.   The nursery-school from which the
Government took its officials was from that class of Roman
Abbátes, who, with insufficient judicial and without any political economic knowledge, were better taught than educated,
and might more fitly be entrusted with the arrangement of
ecclesiastical ceremonies than with the management and interests of everyday life; but who, relying upon the favour
and patronage of a Cardinal or "Monsignore," could win for
themselves even in Rome but very little respect, and in the
provinces were, for the most part, objects of the smallest love
and regard.   Of all the systems of government established
in Europe, the Roman was indisputably the most complicated
—so much so, that in some cases a circumlocutory and time-
wasting correspondence must be carried on preliminary to
the ascertainment of the simple fact as to which one of the
several authorities a matter should be submitted for its settlement.   And by some of these authorities, meanwhile,
would it be observed that it was only in accordance with its
name and title that they could take any cognizance of it.

And yet, some of the institutions of Consalvi proved
themselves to be both judicious and beneficial; as, for instance, the *Delegati* placed by the side of the permanent governing *Congregazioni,* an imitation of the French Prefectoral
Council.   It was also generally recognized that the Tribunal
of the *Sacra Ruota* was an admirable court of judicature,
with an exemplary mode of legal procedure.

In the German Ecclesiastical States the spiritual was
separated from the temporal government; but in the Papal
States they were intermingled with each other.   This was
declared to be an indispensable necessity.   It was maintained
that the double position of the Supreme Head must be repeated and imitated amongst those of inferior rank.[1]   There

---

[1] RANKE, in his "Historisch-politischen Zeitschrift," i. 682.

is as little of propriety in the fact, as there is of justice in the assertion. Because a king is at the head of the military defences of a country, as its commander-in-chief, and at the same time the head of the civil government, must it also necessarily follow that there should be the same combination of military and civil life amongst all the subordinates of his government? On the contrary, it is well known that in every properly-regulated State, the most complete separation of the civil from the military administration is maintained without the slightest difficulty. And so also *could* it be in the Papal States—the spiritual could be dissevered from the political, the ecclesiastical divided from the civil; and, despite the union of both in the one Head, they might very well be distributed amongst different members of the same nation.

Financial affairs were found by Consalvi to be in a state of the most absolute ruin. They had been so of old; and their condition was to be traced to transactions in preceding centuries, to the robberies of the French, and the urgent necessities of the Napoleonic domination. In 1846, the deficit amounted to 1,200,000 scudi, or 1,740,000 rix dollars. At the same time the revenue had, in consequence of the French system of government, been nearly trebled. It was a matter of course that the taxes imposed by the French must be substantially maintained.

The whole body of the French system of administering justice, in all its branches, with its modes of procedure, was put an end to by the Papal Delegate Rivarola, previous to the Pope's arrival at Rome; and, at the same time, all provincial statutes and peculiar municipal privileges of cities were abolished. The vacancy thus created was filled up by the Canon Law and Papal constitutions of the olden time— making altogether an incomprehensible, confused, and partly self-contradictory conglomeration of enactments. A calamitous confusion in all branches of the administration of justice was the immediate consequences of this change. And this confusion was increased by the rivalry of the Episcopal Courts, which drew before their bar every matter in which a clergyman was concerned. Then, too, were re-established the old tribunals of the *Fabbrica di San Pietro* for all religious legacies, and the *Cherici di Camera* for all matters connected with the domain lands. Then new codes were promised. Upon the whole, the power of ecclesiastics in temporal matters became infinitely greater than it ever had been before. So many barriers to it had been struck down; and, in addition, everything connected with education, and a very rigid censorship, (the last being most reluctantly endured by the higher classes,) were vested in the hands of ecclesiastics!

And yet, notwithstanding all this, Consalvi was regarded by the numerous and powerful party of the *Zelanti* (the zealots), to which the majority of the Cardinals belonged, as a dangerous innovator!—so much so, that Cardinal Mattei, Dean of the College, and Prince of Velletri, caused a proclamation of the State-Secretary's to be torn down in Velletri by his own bailiffs!

Italy was treated like Poland at the Congress of Vienna: it was regarded as "a geographical expression." Nations, their wishes and their wants, were not there taken into consideration. Austria then dominated not only where her own interests and sympathies were involved, but her word of command influenced and controlled the other Italian States. Nought was to be conceded to the people, in the form of rights and institutions, but what appeared to be conformable to the interests of the Austrian Bureaucracy—as those interests were then comprehended at Vienna. The consequence was that in the course of a few years Italy was covered over with a net of secret societies. The cherished desire of the higher classes was to shake off the yoke of Austria. The French had, when in Spain, been able to win a party for themselves—the "Afrancesados;" but Austria could never once gain for herself a similar party in Italy. The occupiers of lands in the Lombardo-Venetian kingdom might rejoice at living in security under a well-regulated government; but in the cities all were Anti-Austrian, and all for "national independence." The youths studying in the Universities were soon drawn into the whirlpool of a secret

and mighty movement. And then came literature, with its
irresistible weight, to impart its influence. Every prohibition
of a book produced a greater sale for it; and persons were
more eager to read an author, and reposed more confidence
in what he wrote, once he had become an object of political
persecution. The secret societies—the Carbonaris, Adelfis,
Guelphs, Sublime Masters—those, who had formerly made
themselves partly known by their anti-Napoleon tendencies,
now rendered their existence from time to time remarkable
by a political assassination—or by an assassination to which
a political colouring was given. Consalvi, hated by two
opposite parties—by those resolved upon a political revolution, and by the Zelanti—must be overthrown, and a Spanish
Cortes Constitution, or something like it, proclaimed. The
flame was, however, then opportunely smothered by the
speedy suppression of the insurrection in Naples and Piedmont.

With the death of Pius VII., and the elevation of Leo
XII., came to an end the ministry of Consalvi—a virulently-
vituperated individual.[1] Under the new Pope, Leo XII.
(the elect of the Zelanti), an opposite system to that which
had hitherto prevailed came into operation. Leo had been
chosen partly on account of his opinions, and partly also because he was sickly, frail, and had the appearance of one
likely to die very soon.[2] He made Cardinal della Somaglia
his minister—a man eighty years of age, and not of active
habits. And so, at a most difficult and perilous period, when
there was much required to be done, to be regulated, to be
created, the destiny of the country was placed in the hands
of two grey-haired valetudinarians, weary of life, and just
dropping into the grave! The Pope had been pressed, at

[1] For an opinion of the Romans respecting him, see COPPI, "Annali,"
vii 334. He is there reproached as having been "corteggiatore degli
stranieri potenti ed imperioso sui sudditi pontificj."
[2] This is said by the French Consul in his despatch in ARTAUD,
"Hist. de Leo XII.," i. 130, and by Chateaubriand himself in his
"Memoires," viii. 215, ed. de Berlin. Della Genga was, in fact, not
elected until after Austria had interposed its veto upon Cardinal Severoli.

the commencement of his reign, to nominate a Congregation of Cardinals for affairs of State; and they, it was thought, would be able substantially to carry on the government; but Leo soon put an end to this expectation by the declaration that he only intended to summon them occasionally, and then merely for the purposes of consultation.

The weak, sickly Pope toiled on incessantly. The tendency of his measures, opposed to those of Consalvi, was in accordance with the wishes of the Zelanti. The Provincial Councils, one of Consalvi's best institutions, were again abolished; and not only was the Inquisition re-established, but there was also introduced an extensive spy-system, both for the supervision of the conduct of officials, as well as the morals of the population.[1] It was the firm belief of Leo that safety alone was to be found in the restoration, so far as it was possible, of ancient institutions and manners. Therefore was everything connected with instruction more absolutely than before transferred to the clergy; "inoculation" was put an end to, and the immediate result was a greater number of deaths. Even the Latin language was again introduced into the proceedings of some of the courts; and Leo's Government became the most unpopular that there had been in Rome for a century; and the people made him feel this, by the cessation of the usual plaudits that are given to a Pope when he appears in public.

And yet Leo was animated with the very best intentions. He felt the untenableness of the new circumstances and institutions; but he fell into an error as to the proper remedy to be applied, and in making the attempt to breathe fresh life into that which was dead and gone by for ever. He recognized clearly enough that the whole system of officialism was rankling and rotting with a grievous defect, and that in such a circumstance lay a serious danger for the existing order of things. He had long before then remarked that a clerical official organism must be destitute of a rigid

[1] COPPI, "Annali," vii. 337. I may here remark that Coppi, so often referred to by me, is an esteemed Roman clergyman, who has often been consulted upon affairs of State, as he himself mentions, vii. 146.

and settled discipline, mainly because its members are priests, and, therefore, endowed with the privileges of their order; that there is no law and no means by which they could be kept in check; and that they were alone to be operated upon by a hope of promotion.

"Rome," says the French Ambassador, in a dispatch of the year 1823,[1] "is a republic in which every one is a lord in his δικαστήριον. Consalvi had tried to change this; but upon the first rumour of his downfall, all these little authorities instantly re-established themselves." In a Government so constituted as that in which ecclesiastics hold all the higher appointments and offices of honour, and in which to laymen alone is permitted the retention of a number of small situations, inferior places, and lower pay, there must ever be wanting that moral motive power, without which modern bureaucracy cannot exist: it combines a feeling of official honour, with the influence of a corporative spirit—things through which the multitude, who may not be actuated by high religious feelings, will yet be impelled strictly to adhere to the path of duty, and faithfully to discharge all the requirements of their respective positions. Thus the lay government officer (and the Italians are but too well-inclined so to act) has regarded his situation as a maintenance, as a benefice for himself, and of which he ought, for the advantage of himself and his family, to make out as much pay and profits as he possibly could. Leo sought a remedy against such an abuse, in the establishment of a "Congregazione di Vigilanza,"[2] whose duty it was to receive and examine into all accusations that might be preferred against the Government

---

[1] In ARTAUD, "Hist. de Léon XII.," i. 134.

[2] "Bisogna far per la famiglia," is a common saying amongst the lay officials. I was told, by a distinguished individual in Bologna, that it is their excuse for every act of corruption and embezzlement. There, too, is to be heard another common saying, characteristic of a glaring want in administrative discipline, "Da noi, l'una metà commanda e l'altra non ubbidisce." This naturally may be said in a State where the ecclesiastics, as formerly in some lands, and still, for example, in Hungary, the nobility, regard themselves as a privileged, and therefore as the governing class.

officers, and which the Pope declared, to his great grief, he had found to be both numerous and well founded. Its only result, as Coppi remarks, was, that the spy system, with its deleterious consequences, was much increased.[1]

The newly-elected Pope, in 1829, nearly resembled his predecessor. The pure and pious Castiglioni, or Pius VIII., was a sickly, tottering old man, who had but a few months to live. Still, he instantly suppressed the " *Congregazione di Vigilanza*," and the spy system, which his predecessor had organized. He earned praise by having done so little, when Leo had done so much. The secret societies had meanwhile threatened to make an attack on the Papal States. In the Romagna several political assassinations were perpetrated; and the Cardinal Rivarola, having been, on that account, dispatched thither, had 508 persons capitally convicted, amongst whom were 30 nobles, 156 occupiers of land, or shopkeepers, 74 *employés*, and 38 soldiers; but on none of these was the punishment of death inflicted. And yet, all that had been so accomplished was but to crush a single head of the hydra, and then soon to see others and new rise up in its place !

The mischief of secret societies, which, for nearly the last fifty years, has been the greatest national plague of Italy, is generally regarded as being an Italian, and peculiarly a Southern Italian, malady. But, first, it is to be observed that, in a country where there is a complete subjugation of the press, and where a suspicious police dominates over a people dissatisfied with their condition, the formation of secret societies is as much in accordance with natural circumstances, as that there must, in the human body, if ('εξανθήματα) pustules upon the skin be violently driven in from the surface, interior sores inevitably produced. Secondly, the formation of a secret society is the natural production of that impulse towards social activity, which an intellectual and lively population feels, when placed in a position where the necessaries of life are easily, and with little trouble, attainable. Now, when the Italians found that

[1] COPPI, vii. 374.

they were excluded from the regular gratification of this impulse, through their exclusion from a participation in public affairs, and cut off from all opportunity of discussion, through the operations of the censorship, so they sought to indemnify themselves through the occupation and personal importance which the membership in a secret lodge conferred upon them. It must, however, in truth, be said that these combinations, in which even morally professing individuals eagerly entered, became but too often so many *cloacas* of the worst corruption, and a curse to the entire country. This system of secret associations rendered the present time intolerable, and the future hopeless; whilst it forced those in authority to have recourse to measures of rude violence, in the place of carrying on a peacable and well-ordered government. The Papal authorities, in the difficult position in which they found themselves placed, had recourse to a very hazardous remedy: they promoted the establishment of the *Sanfedisti*, a voluntary, but, at the same time, a non-legal association, composed mainly of the poorest and lowest classes, which soon got beyond their control, and, in some districts, became, in fact, master over the Government.

The successor, at the close of the year 1830, of the deceased Pius was a Carmelite monk, Mauro Capellari, who was made a Cardinal in 1826, and who, up to the time of his election as Pope, had lived a total stranger to state affairs. Gregory XVI., a monk, a scholar, and an author, was, to the end of his days, devotedly attached to literature; but his knowledge of ecclesiastical affairs was as solid as his comprehension of worldly matters was slight. And so reigned over the Papal States a series of Popes, who, in all that related to the Church and its concerns, were not merely faultless, but pre-eminently excellent; and yet, as temporal princes, possessed naught beyond their just intentions.

The Revolution of July in Paris acted as a signal for popular insurrections; and in the course of a few weeks the greater part of the Papal States, as well as Modena and Parma, were in a flame. The outbreak took place whilst the Conclave was still sitting. The people were won over to the

cause of the insurrection by the removal of the imposts upon
salt and flour; and the insurgents, confident that France
would not permit any intervention on the part of Austria,
hastily gathered together a Congress of popular representatives, by whom it was declared " that the Pope was deprived
of his temporal sovereignty."   Rome remained loyal; but
outside of Rome the Papal officials in most places abandoned
their posts hastily and recreantly—a proof in itself how
insecure is the basis upon which rests a State destitute of all
popular institutions.   The revolution was as short-lived as a
child's game.   The bloodless advance of the Austrians replaced, with very little trouble, the old government, upon
the condition of a general amnesty, with the exception of
thirty of the insurgent leaders.

A Conference of the Great Powers, in which Prussia,
Russia, and England participated, presented to the Pope, on
the 31st May, 1831, the celebrated Memorandum upon
which a great portion of the history of the Papal States has
ever since then turned.   That Memorandum recommended, in
the first place—that improvements should be introduced, not
only into the provinces that had revolted, but also into those
that had remained loyal, as well as into the capital itself;
secondly, that the laity should be admitted into all offices
connected with the Government and the administration of
justice.   Further, that there should be an independent local
administration of the communes, through Elected Councils,
a restoration of the Provincial Councils; and, finally,
" internal security against the changes incident to an elective
sovereignty."[1]

Coppi, who was charged to draw up a plan of reform in
correspondence to these requirements, states that Gregory
and the majority of the Cardinals rejected every important
change; that they were for maintaining the old monarchical
and ecclesiastical principles, and for conceding nothing to the
popular or lay party—" because if anything were voluntarily
conceded there would be no right afterwards to recall it."[2]

[1] See " Mémoires de Guizot," 1859, ii. 432. COPPI, viii. 143.
[2] COPPI, viii. 148.

Two things in particular were absolutely not to be assented to : there was to be no election of Communal and Provincial Councils, and there was to be no lay Council of State by the side of the Cardinal College.

The Cardinal Secretary of State, Bernetti, who had, at first, spoken of "a new era commencing with the existing Pontificate," addressed a despatch to the French Ambassador, in which was announced that which, in the general expectation of many, was about to be accomplished, without, however, specifically binding himself as to any fixed institutions or positive changes. But still there was promised "the new establishment of a government, with complete publicity as to its acts; such an improvement in the administration of the finances as no longer to afford an opportunity for suspicion as to their allocation; and the introduction of conservative institutions."[1] The Government was afterwards bitterly reproached, both at home and abroad—that, although fifteen years of the Pontificate had passed away since these promises had been made, yet not one of them had been fulfilled.

An attempt was, on one occasion, made to sustain the Government by the enlistment of 5,000 Swiss, since reliance could no longer be placed on the native soldiers; but the English plenipotentiary, Seymour, now declared, "That the financial condition of the Roman Government did not capacitate it to take into its pay so many foreigners, whose services could be required solely for the purpose of keeping down a whole discontented population : and since his government could no longer entertain the hope that any good could be effected through it in Rome, he had received instructions at once to leave the city."[2]

And yet there can be no question as to the fact that Gregory candidly acknowledged the necessity for comprehensive reforms. I. Bernardi has recently declared that, to his astonishment, he heard, in the year 1843, the following words come from the lips of the Pope himself :—"The civil administration of the Roman States stands in need of great

[1] GUALTERIO, "Documenti," i. 94.
[2] *Ibid.*, i. 102.

reform. I was too old when I was elected to be Pope. I did not expect to live so long, and had not the courage to begin the undertaking. For whoever begins it must carry it through thoroughly. I have now only a few years to live — perhaps only a few days. After me they will choose a young Pope, whose mission it will be to perform those acts without which it is impossible to go on."[1]

But in such matters as these, even the most resolute will of a Pope, when he has only a few by his side, and in the different departments of the public service, entertaining his own views, he can neither do much, nor can what he does be maintained for any length of time. Up to this period it had been inexpressibly difficult to carry out certain reforms in the Papal States. A Pope, with the purest intentions and most resolute will, must be baffled when he had arrayed against him the still, dogged, combined opposition of those who found their advantage in the maintenance of the old and settled state of things. The Pope must fail when the right men for carrying out reforms are not at hand to assist him. And so formerly had Adrian VI. and Clement VII., notwithstanding their thorough good-will to effect an improvement in ecclesiastical affairs, been able to effect nothing. It happened in Rome, as it was wont to occur in Arragon, whenever the King gave a command that was displeasing to the people: the Arragonese expressed, in a settled form of words, their allegiance to the sovereign and their resolution not to obey him.[2]

The measures of reform sanctioned by Gregory, and which were brought forward in the months of July, October, and November, 1831, were looked to as being something more than one could expect, after the Pope had refused to enter into any fixed engagement. That which was particularly

---

[1] "Rivista Contemporanea," 1860, Febr., p. 97. The same things were told to me by a celebrated Roman scholar some time before they were printed in the "Rivista". I have thus not the slightest doubt as to the authenticity of the fact.

[2] "Se obedezca, pero no se cumpla." Let the order be attended to, but not acted upon.

sought for was an improvement in the administration of
justice.   There was, for instance, that monstrous institute of
the *Uditore Santissimo*, the mere existence of which was
regarded by every statesman and lawyer as a scandal to the
Papal See.   It was in 1831 completely put an end to.[1]

As to the population, they, indeed, who had been expect-
ing and anxious for other matters quite different from this,
were not appeased by these edicts; and Count Pellegrino
Rossi, afterwards the minister of Pius IX., wrote, with
reference to what was then passing, in the following manner,
to Guizot: "We must yield to no delusion on this subject.
A revolutionary spirit, in the sense that the present system
of the Roman Government is utterly intolerable to the population, has penetrated to the very heart of the country.   It
is only when there has been a complete and comprehensive
change in the manner of dispensing law, and that a reform in
the entire mode of making laws has been effected, that any
hope can be entertained of reconciling the people to the Papal
Government."[2]

Scarcely, however, had the Austrians withdrawn their
troops, when the uproar broke out anew.   The moderate
party would have been content to see the Memorandum
acted upon; but they, as it ever happens in revolutions,
were speedily overborne by the Radicals; and the afflicted
population welcomed with shouts of joy the Austrians, upon
returning amongst them.   Then speedily arrived the French,
and took possession of Ancona, so that the field should not
be left to the Germans alone.   The edicts, which had been
but a short time before promulgated, were now recalled in
Rome, or they were permitted to remain inoperative.   This
naturally produced general discontent; and from that time
forward the position of affairs every year became worse.
The " Papal Volunteers," enlisted out of the lowest classes,
exercised a gross terrorism; political assassinations, commenced by the revolutionary party, became more frequent;
the Government was, in consequence, rendered more sus-

---

[1] See with respect to it Guizot, " Mémoires," ii. 436-442.
[2] Guizot, l. c., p. 449.

picious and persecuting; and its whole support was thus
placed on the fourfold weapons of the Austrian, French,
Swiss, and its own troops, on the Sanfedisti and the Volunteers. Espionage—doubly detestable and dangerous under a
priestly government, because the people become thereby suspicious of the misuse of a religious medium—was now generally resorted to. The opponents of the Government had
meanwhile, and mainly through the influence of Mazzini,
divided themselves into "Liberals" and "Radicals"—
(the Young Italy party.) The latter were peculiarly and
exclusively "the destructives," who wished to annihilate
all governments, as well as the Church, and to change the
entire of Italy into a single Republic, in accordance with
the pattern of 1793. In Middle Italy they were, however,
still without influence; and after fifteen years, although they
had seduced a number of students, still, upon the population
itself, the real people, they had, according to their own confession, made no impression.[1]

In the year 1838, the French withdrew from Ancona,
and the Austrians from the Legations. The Swiss troops
were gradually increased. The number of 17,000 men, which
I find given, must either be an exaggeration, or it must comprise the whole of the military force. Certain it is that
these foreign soldiers were a heavy burden upon a failing
exchequer, with a yearly deficit of a million of scudi.

Gregory XVI., old and sickly, became inaccessible to
strangers, and those who were about him endeavoured to
conceal from his knowledge whatever might be disagreeable
for him to hear. His understanding failed him for the comprehension of state affairs; and thus all came into the hands
of the Secretary of State, Lambruschini, and of the "Mon-
signori," who were acting as Legates and Delegates in the
provinces. A standing Military Commission, which decided
upon complaints of political transgressions in an arbitrary

---

[1] In the "Archivio triennale delle cose d'Italia" (Capolago, 1850, i.
191) a Mazzinianer thus writes: "Noi dovevamo confessare che, in
quindici anni, non eravamo riusciti che a propagare nella gioventù studiosa
la passione politica, ma nel vero popolo mai."

manner, maintained, with the help of Swiss regiments, public order: and so contributed, with the deeds of violence committed by the Sanfedisti, to nurture the general discontent. The Government seemed to be unconscious what bitterness of feeling was produced by the conviction that the country was compelled to bear a heavy burden of taxation, in order that pay might be given to foreign soldiers employed for the purpose of keeping the people down, and at the same time of enabling those in authority to refuse compliance with what were the wishes of the nation.[1]

There were at that time two main causes for the spirit of discontent that prevailed, and the desire to shake off Papal domination. The one lay in the hatred against Austrian rule, and the policy of Vienna, which oppressed the whole of the Peninsula, and overpowered the nation. It was believed that the Papal Government was totally devoted to Austrian influence; and that it was only through means of Austria it could itself be maintained. The other cause lay in internal circumstances, which existed not only from 1824 to 1846, but still are again partly to be met with, from the time of the restoration of Pius IX. These circumstances, such as they were and are since 1850, require to be looked at somewhat closely.

It must, first of all, be remarked that the Papal States, as well as Italy generally, suffer from one great evil—and that is a want in the requisite orders of society. There is to be found there no self-independent peasant-proprietor class; and there is no landed aristocracy. There is but a citizen class in the towns, and patricians; and these latter, for the most part, incompetent, degenerate, and demoralized individuals. Leo XII. recognized this evil, and intended to elevate a nobility class, by his concession to it of certain rights; but the attempt failed, as it could not but fail, where there was an ecclesiastical body who, with their prerogatives, overshadowed the social position of every one else. By the side

---

[1] The Italians have an energetic proverb, which was, at this period, to be often heard in the mouths of the people: "Pagare il boja che ci frusti."

of them an independent nobility could not possibly be elevated.

And yet the people in the Papal States are not, judging of them by those endowments which they possess in common with other Italians, difficult to govern. A German, writing from the Campagna of Rome, in the year 1857,[1] says: " Amongst all those thousands that passed me by, and of all the processions that I came up with after the completion of the festival, I never could observe even the slightest trait of rudeness in their conduct. In fact, the purity of manners of the country people in this district, and especially as regards sobriety, and propriety of behaviour towards women, might well excite the envy of more thoughtful nations. There, for instance, they have not the slightest notion of that doleful practice which is the curse of Ireland, namely, that a land-lord can, whenever he pleases, drive a farmer out of his holding."[2] The rural population was by no means so hostile to the Papal Government as were the townsfolk.[3] Complaints were made, not only as to the incapacity and negligence of the Government for not affording sufficient protection to the dwellers in the country around from bands of robbers, but also as to the high and oppressive fees persons were compelled to pay to the ecclesiastical autho-rities, and especially in the Episcopal Courts. This state of feeling was in complete accordance with that of the town populations, who were, in general, indisposed to "priests' government;" and who, too, had also to endure a number of grievances and annoyances. Beyond all other afflictions, that, however, which was felt to be the most galling was the exclusion of laymen from the higher offices of state; for all such were absolutely reserved for the " Prelati." The offices in the public service were so distributed between clergymen

<hr>

[1] " Allg. Zeitung," 5th Jan., p. 75.

[2] HELFFERICH, " Briefe aus Italien," ii. 57.

[3] Cardinal Massimo. in his report from Imola in 1845, says, that there was there " una parte ben piccola della classe agricola, non ancor guasta del tutto nelle campagne," devoted to the Government.—" Documenti sul Gov. pontif.," i. 66.

and laymen, that the former were the rulers, and the latter
the mere instruments by whose means the administration
was carried on.   The Secretaryship of State, the Sacra
Consulta, the Camera Apostolica, the Buono Governo, the
Congregazione Economica, the Police, the Treasury, the War
Ministry,[1] the Legations and Delegations, the management
of judicial affairs, and of instruction—all! all were in the
hands of Cardinals and *Prelati*.   Every lay official was thus
made aware that his progress in life was hemmed in by
certain barriers he never could pass over ; that, no matter
what number of years he had been in office, or how useful and faithful had been his services, still he could not
obtain promotion to the highest position in his department ;
that an ecclesiastic, no matter how inferior in competency,
would still be preferred to him!   Human nature in the
Papal States is not different from what it is in all other
parts of the world ; and so the whole of the lay *employés*
were utterly discontented, and perfectly ready, as recent
circumstances have shown, to give in their adhesion to any
other form of government.   But the very mode in which
appointments to public offices were made constituted in
itself a subject of grave complaint.   The system that prevails in other states, where there are long preparatory studies,
and repeated examinations, to secure the just distribution of
public offices, was unknown at Rome.   A layman, to arrive
even at the lowest situation, must belong to a religious con-
fraternity, or be the *protégé* of a " *Prelato*," or a Cardinal, or of
some order of friars.   Thus the official laymen were frequently
the compulsory and, but too often, the needy clients of
" *Prelati*."   The consequence of all this was that the best,
the most intellectual, the most independent, and those who

---

[1] " Das Kriegsministerium," DÖLLINGER, p. 572.   This statement is
not in accordance with the report of Mr. Lyons, who says : " All the
Ministers, except the Minister of War (or of Arms, as he is called), are
ecclesiastics."   And again : " All the ministers, except the Minister of
Arms, are prelates."—" Despatches from Mr. Lyons respecting the Condition and Administration of the Papal States."   London, 1660, pp. 5
and 8.—Note by TRANSLATOR.

had a fitting respect for their own reputation turned away
from the service, and, by so doing, condemned themselves to
a life of torpor and idleness—and so, too, added to the masses
of malcontents, and, when the opportunity arrived, of—
conspirators !

In a letter to the author, from a German nobleman, whose
fame is European, as a keen and profound observer of the
condition of foreign nations, and who lived a considerable
time in the Roman States, it is observed : " There is a deep
depravity of the middle and higher classes, and of the
employés who spring from such classes, and whom the Papal
Government has done so much to degrade.   The negligence
and venality of these persons can only be compared to what
prevails amongst Russian officials.   Amid 5000 officials
there are to be found between two and three hundred ecclesiastics.   These latter are far better than the others — they
are almost never corruptible, for the sake of money ; but they
are inefficient, without energy, and slothful.   And then, as to
the lay officials, they are undoubtedly, almost without a single
exception, corruptible."

To these circumstances was to be added the feeling that,
from the want of inviolable ordinances, the freedom, property,
and honor of individuals were at the mercy of persons armed
with power; for the laws afforded no security, as they could,
in particular cases, be set aside by the supreme authorities.
Bailiffs, or constables (*sbirri*), required no special warrant to
break into a dwelling, whether they chose to do so by night
or by day.[1]   The three main causes of discontent with the
administration of justice in the Papal States were, the civil
jurisdiction of the Bishops ; the privileged exemption of
clergymen as to the courts that should have jurisdiction over
them, as well as to the dissimilarity of punishments inflicted

---

[1] AGUIRRE, " L'Italie après Villafranca," 1859, p. 10.   The author is,
or was, an inhabitant of the Roman States.   He is one of those who
wish to maintain the temporal sovereignty of the Pope, and who believe in the curability of existing evils.   The picture, however, that
he presents of the system of Government hitherto prevailing is a very sad
one.

upon them; and, lastly, by the tribunal of the Inquisition.[1] The Bishops, who had their own prisons, decided upon and inflicted pains and penalties in all questions affecting the persons and property of ecclesiastics, in matters concerning relations between the two sexes;[2] and in cases of blasphemy, and the transgression of the laws respecting fast and festival days.

The Cardinal and Bishop of Sinigaglia, in the year 1844, issued an ordinance forbidding young men and maidens from sending presents to each other; and if a father should be found not complying with this order, then it was directed, in cases of transgression, that the father and son, or father and daughter, should be imprisoned for fifteen days.[3] The Bishops, at the Provincial Synod of Fermo, in the year 1850, threatened with punishment every innkeeper who supplied their guests with flesh meat on fast-days, unless they could produce two witnesses, one of whom must be a physician, and the other a curate.[4]

A new and peculiar sort of punishment was devised, and by it 229 persons in the Romagna were, at one and the same moment, made to suffer. This was the *"Precetto Politico"* of the first class. The person upon whom this punishment was imposed was compelled to reside in his birth-place; he must be in his own house by a certain hour in the morning; every fourteen days he must present himself before the police-inspector; and every month go to confession, and he must shew, by witnesses, that the priest, with whom he had been at confession, was a Father-confessor approved of by *the police!*—and, then, every year, he must make a Spiritual retreat of three days, in a monastery appointed for him by a Bishop! Neglect of any one of these regulations became punishable with three years of compulsory labour! In Italy there were many who opined—"There are few countries in

---

[1] MONTANELLI, "Memorie sull' Italia," ii. 79.

[2] Cause di stupro e di illegitima pregnanza.

[3] This document is printed by GENNARELLI, "I lutti dello stato Romano." Florence, 1860, p. 160.

[4] "Documenti sul Governo pontificio," ii. 299.

Europe where such a commingling of the police officer with religion would be patiently submitted to."

The Bishops and the *Prelati*-police have hitherto penetrated too deeply into domestic and family-life; and yet there was superadded to both the judicial jurisdiction of the Inquisition! This was, notwithstanding the mildness for which it was famed,[1] still detested and dreaded, because the principle upon which it was based was this: that every one who knew of a misdemeanour being committed was liable to punishment, if he did not denounce it; and, then, he who became the denunciator was shrouded in mystery, whilst the accused was never permitted to know the names either of his accuser, or of the witnesses against him.[2]

In the year 1841, the Inquisitor at Pesaro, Fra Filippo Bertolotti, issued an Edict, by which he required, under a threat of various punishments, excommunication amongst the rest, that every one should give information of all ecclesiastical offences coming to his knowledge; such, for instance, as that of a person, who had not received permission to do so, eating flesh or using milk upon fast-days![3] Foreigners dwelling in the Papal States have, in amazement, asked: "If the servant-men and maid-servants employed in the kitchens of the '*Sant' Uffizio*' would make it a matter of conscience, if they had chanced to cook any meat for their masters on a fast-day, to denounce them, and involve them in legal proceedings?"

---

[1] If I am not mistaken, there never was, in the Papal States, since the end of the sixteenth century, a single capital execution enforced through the instrumentality of the Inquisition, or on account of a religious transgression.

[2] As a proof of the bitter feeling of the people against the Inquisition, see the letter of the Chevalier Tommaso Poggi of Cesena to the French Ambassador in Rome, Saint-Aulaire, printed by GUALTERIO, "Documenti," i. 274. Amongst other things, it is there said, "The innermost secrets of our conscience, and of our families, form the subject-matter of their hateful prosecutions and dark sentences. So little is there a thought in Rome of the Government reconciling itself with the population and public opinion "

[3] "Documenti," i. 303.

A clergyman, when he is armed with a double power, the judicial and the adminstrative, must always find the effort exceedingly difficult to reconcile his personal opinion and his subjective judgment upon individuals, and to prevent his tenderness and his inclination from winning an influence over him in the discharge of his official duties. As a priest, he is the servant of all, and the herald of grace, of pardon, of the remission of punishment; and he therefore too readily forgets that in human concerns the law is "deaf and inexorable," and that tampering with a law to favour one person is an injury to another, or it may be to many others, or it may be to the whole frame of society; and that he who may thus begin with the best intentions, gradually will find himself placing his own will above what is the strict law. As it is, Italians are but too little disposed either to comprehend or to practise the impartial, passionless administration of the law, without consideration as to its consequences. The path of descent being once trodden, leads him, who has entered upon it, unavoidably to a precipice. For then come the subaltern lay employés of the Courts, who for the most part are indebted for their appointments to favour and ecclesiastical patronage, and who, receiving a scanty salary, have wives and children to maintain, and before their eyes the example of their superiors, who have been dealing with the law according to their will and pleasure. Hence follows corruption and arbitrary conduct in law proceedings, which Cantu has declared to have been the characteristics of all legal processes under Gregory XVI.[1]

But still more critical and perilous is the exercise by priests of the powers of a police. Here is an employment which requires things to be done that in a Christian point of view had better be avoided. The police, in an absolute government, is armed with a power that is essentially omnipotent, and in its contact with others, in the struggle of everyday life, and in a time of political excitement, and nu-

[1] "La giustizia era corruttibile non solo, ma esposta agli arbitrij de' superiori, e alle interminabili restituzioni in intero."—"Storia degi Italiani," vi. 684.

merous conspiracies, makes a cruel use of its omnipotence. It leaves unpunished things which, judged of according to the Gospel, are mortal sins; and it punishes others in which a Christian can discern nought that is sinful. Is it then to be wondered at that the people find it impossible to discover what can be a justification for this contradiction between the priestly character and the police-officer's active vigilance?

In strong and dark contrast with what was a characteristic of the Papal Government, with that mildness for which it was justly praised—has been the arbitrary power of imprisonment, filling the gaols with captives for whom no one—as in other countries—would be permitted to go bail. Cardinal Morichini, in his Finance Report, expatiated upon the wretched state of the prisons, and the unavoidable demoralization of persons confined in them.[1] Even in this matter financial difficulties rendered it impossible to effect a comprehensive reform. In the doleful times that have passed since 1848, there grew up a system of incarcerating masses of persons in unhealthy gaols, and from that system sprang still greater rancour against the authorities. The "Governatore" of Faenza, Luigi Maraviglia, made, in the year 1853, this representation of facts: "A great number of persons have, without a hearing, without process, perhaps, even, without the suspicion of crime—but merely from precaution— been dragged to prisons, where they now are, for a full year, still remaining! More that 450 processes are already pending for four or five years. By such modes of proceeding can no love for princes be implanted in the hearts of the people."[2] It is to be understood that such circumstances as these occurred without the slightest knowledge on the part of the Pope. Had he been made acquainted with them, his own goodness of heart and love of justice would, most assuredly, have impelled him to oppose and put an end to them.

For full thirty years misfortune after misfortune has fallen upon the Papal Government in the States of the Church; but of all these calamities the most lamentable assuredly is,

[1] "Documenti sul Gov. pontif.," f. i. 578.
[2] "Documenti," i. 42.

that it should be deemed necessary to transfer to ecclesiastics
the judicial condemnation and punishment of political offences.
When, as it has often happened, the opinions and sentiments
of an individual, admitted by the rulers themselves to be
those universally prevailing, were brought forward as subsidiary proofs, and used as grounds for inflicting the severest
punishment upon a man, against whom there were not otherwise sufficient proofs for a conviction—where these things
could be done, there indeed must the breach between the
people and the clergy be still further widened.[1]

The exceptional and privileged position of a very numerous
priesthood gave rise to another complaint. The Cardinal de
Luca had laid down the principle that the enactments and
laws of the Pope, as a temporal prince for the clergy, were
not binding, if it was not expressly said, or was not to be
presumed from the contents, that he had issued the ordinance
as Head of the Church.[2] The clergy also had their privileged
"forum," so that, if a priest and a layman were participators
in the same crime, they must be tried by two different courts
of justice. Even the punishments inflicted upon them were
different. Priests convicted of crime had still the privilege
of being subjected to a milder punishment than if they were
laymen.[3] "An inverse proportion of punishment would be
the more righteous," was the opinion expressed by Massimo
d'Azeglio.

A highly critical case of this sort, and one that was hailed
by the English journals and periodicals with a malicious joy,
whilst it excited a painful surprise in all Europe, was brought
prominently before the public in the year 1852. In the law
proceedings in London, instituted by the Roman Dominican
monk, *Achilli*, who had become a Protestant, it appeared

---

[1] See in the second volume of the " Documenti sul Governo pontificio,"
the printed acts of the prosecutions and sentences, *passim*.

[2] "Dottor volgare," lib. xv., c. 1.

[3] Thus runs the definition of the law: "Ove pero possa aver luogo la
pena stabilita pei laici, si accorda loro (ai cherici) nei delitti communi
un grado di minorazione di pena." And "Se la pena stabilita della legge
è l'opera o la galera, trasmettono il condannato al luogo ove trasmetterebbe
il Tribunale Ecclesiastico."

that he was a man who had been charged with shameful crimes, such as in Germany would have assigned him to an infamous punishment in a convict prison, but that, having been arraigned before the ecclesiastical courts in Rome, he was there treated with an indulgence such as it would be impossible to meet with in any other country; and it also appeared that, despite of the condemnation upon him by the Provincial of his Order, he had been taken as an associate and attendant in visitations, and that he was afterwards made a Professor in the College of Minerva, at Rome, and then sent as a preacher to Capua![1]

And here a passing remark may be permitted to the author. Surprise has frequently been felt with respect to the complete change that has taken place in the policy of England, with reference to the Papal States in particular. England had energetically co-operated in the restoration of those States to Pius VII. For a long time, the Roman Government regarded the English as a kindly disposed and friendly power. Gregory XVI. declared to Lord Normanby, in the year 1844, that it was his ardent desire England should enter into direct diplomatic correspondence with the Roman See, and send an ambassador to Rome. In the month of April, 1847, the Papal Nuncio, in Paris,

[1] It was in the "Dublin Review," of June 1850—a Catholic periodical, published under the patronage of Cardinal Wiseman—that these facts were first brought to light. Then followed the celebrated prosecution of "Achilli," *versus* Dr. Newman, by means of which the testimonies of the witnesses to these facts became more widely known. The subject filled for weeks the English journals. The costs of the prosecution against Dr. Newman were defrayed by a general subscription in Catholic countries. The report of the case, published by Mr. Finlason, passed through several editions in a very short space of time. What conclusions were drawn from this case on the side of the Protestants, and what reproaches against the Papal See were grounded upon it, may be surmised from one article (amongst numberless others) published in the "Christian Remembrancer," vol. xxiv., pp. 401-424. Neither in England nor in Rome was an answer attempted to be given to the scathing, and, under the circumstances, naturally severe reproaches of the "Times."

Fornari, said to the same Lord Normanby, that it was the constant wish of the Roman Government that England might, through such means, afford a more active and energetic support, and thereby also promote an improvement in the social condition of Italy.[1] Lord Palmerston, who was then Foreign Minister, sent Lord Minto to Rome, with instructions to promise to the Pope the most determined support of England in carrying into effect the Memorandum of the Powers in 1831. At that time, the statesmen of England had no thought of doing anything calculated to hasten the overthrow of the temporal sovereignty of the Pope. But all that is now, in sooth, very much changed.[2] Since 1851, the English Government has become the open adversary of the Papal States, and has thrown all the weight of its influence into the scale of Piedmont. It does so under the pressure of public opinion in England—a power to which every cabinet there must submit. Even a Tory ministry would be compelled to pay attention to the potency of this popular feeling in its Italian policy. The public opinion now prevailing there has been formed, fashioned and moved by the statements of English individuals residing in the Papal States, which statements have appeared in the daily papers; as well as by the work of Farini, which has been translated into English by Mr. Gladstone, the Chancellor of the Exchequer.[3] And now the will of the entire nation, and the policy of its government, are alike arrayed in a most hostile manner against the maintenance of the Papal State. With a portion of the population—and it is only a portion—the Protestant hatred against the Papal See has been sharpened into still stronger animosity, on account of the rage excited by two recent measures of Rome—first,

[1] See the Blue-book, " Correspondence respecting the affairs of Italy," 1846-47. London, 1849, pp. 36, 38.

[2] See Lord Minto's report of his interview with the Pope, January, 1848. " Correspondence," Part ii., 1848, p. 44.

[3] " Lo stato Romano, dall' a. 1815, all' a. 1850," 4 vols. Farini's work has been noticed in Rome itself for its preciseness in matters of fact, and trustworthiness. Coppi has made considerable use of it.

the establishment of an Episcopacy in England, and, secondly,
by the rejection of the Queen's Colleges, with their mixed
education in Ireland.   The policy of the English Cabinet is
also influenced by a wish to see a powerful Italy formed—
a power capable of maintaining itself upon a firm basis—and
which, under the guidance of England, may serve as a coun-
terpoise to the threatening ascendancy of France.

As to the state and social condition of the clergy, it has
called for a deeply penetrating reformation.   That the clergy
have been, on the whole, morally blameless, is universally
admitted;[1] but the conditions for entering upon the priesthood have been placed upon too low a scale.   A person,
notwithstanding his thorough want of knowledge, and mean
capacity, easily becomes a priest; and then there have been
for those persons such a number of benefices, affording neither sufficient occupation nor a becoming subsistence.   The
consequence has been that an immense multitude of idle
ecclesiastics were to be seen wasting their days in coffee-
houses, and loitering in the street, passing their time in an
unpriestly manner, so that a reverence for the entire order
had very much diminished amongst the population.[2]   In the
country parts, a great number of the pastors were in a state
of lamentable poverty,[3] and for this reason, therefore, as
well as from innate dulness, they left the people without instruction.[4]   The higher orders of the laity wish that the pres-

[1] FARINI, i. 164. See also "Appendice al libro d'Azeglio," 1846, p.
57. AGUIRRE, p. 112.

[2] Those who have been in Rome well know what is meant by the expression, "preti di piazza." Something like the same thing is to be seen
in Russia.

[3] "I curati che sono generalmente poverissimi, ed hanno il peso de'
poveri," says Cardinal Morichini, in his Report, p. 575.

[4] "Appendice al libro d'Azeglio," p. 56. The author, a Romagnese,
says: "Il clero pontificio è il più ignorante di tutto il clero cattolico
salvo poche eccezioni." In other parts of Italy it is, in fact, not one
whit better, as bishops grant ordination with a facility of which no one
in Germany can have an idea. See what is said upon the incredible
ignorance of the Piedmontese clergy, by the distinguished teacher, Professor DOMENICO BERTI, "Rivista Italiana," 1850, i. 123, 124.

sure of the censorship was either put an end to, or mitigated.
"The state to which we are brought," say intellectually
gifted persons in the Papal States, "is this—that in the
finest, and, mentally, most richly endowed part of Italy, we
are absolutely without any literature—nothing now appears
but a few volumes on archæological subjects, and local
histories—not a line of the slightest importance upon
science and general literature." In fact, Leo XII. had,
through the Dominican monks, rendered still more severe the
existing preventive censorship; and his timidity compelled
him to do this, as his aim was that no publication containing an expression calculated to excite the displeasure of
foreign powers, or to give rise to important disputes, should
be allowed to be printed, except with the direct sanction of
the Secretary of State.[1]   People felt themselves cribbed and
hemmed in upon all sides.   The inhabitants of Forli wished
to establish an Agricultural Association.   After a long
delay, they at last obtained permission to do so, from the
"Congregazione degli studi," but it was upon the condition
that all the members should first be approved of by the
president of the Government; that they should assemble
together for no other purpose than to speak upon agricultural affairs; and, furthermore, that at each of the meetings
there should be read a lecture, which had previously received
the approval of the Censorship.[2]   The whole project was, of
course, on the instant, abandoned.   The Government suffered
much, too, in public respect, and in the confidence of the
people, through the utterly disordered state of its finances.
Loans were contracted upon the most unfavourable conditions—upon one occasion, a bargain was made with Roth-
schild, at $62\frac{1}{2}$ per cent. upon the nominal value.   There was
a yearly deficit of more than two million of guilders, and, at
the same time, gross confusion and disorder prevailed in the
palace expenditure.   There was scarcely a country in Europe
in which there was to be found so fathomless an arbitrary
power in financial matters.   The treasurer, Tosti, was
regarded as a pattern of the worst finance minister that could

[1] Coppi, ix. 76.   [2] "Documenti," i. 540.

by any possibility be ever discovered. When Galli entered into this department of the ministry, in the year 1848, he declared in an official report: " that, as to the past, he could not undertake even the smallest share of responsibility— there were so many accounts unsettled, and there were so many vouchers wanting; and then the authorizations for ex- penditure were partly not to be found, or those that were discoverable were so overladen with charges, additions, and deductions, as to render the authentication of them impracticable." [1]

In addition to all this, it was made a matter of reproach to the Papal Government, in every part of Italy, that it, by means of the lottery, at which priests felt no scruple in taking an active part, had nurtured and incited a vice—the rage for gambling—to which the common race of Italians are already but too much addicted. Alexander VII. and Benedict XIII. had formerly forbidden lotteries, under pain of ex- communication. Cardinal Morichini, in his report upon the state of the finances, declared it to be urgently advisable to sacrifice the income derived from the lottery, " as a victim to public morality." [2] And joyfully would the Pope have as- sented to this; but the deficit and the new calamities that befell the country rendered it impossible for him to do so. [3]

The temper of the provinces became still more gloomy and embittered. The cities addressed strongly-worded petitions to the College of the Cardinals. These petitions state: " The intervention of the Great Powers has been of no avail to us. Of their proposals not one has been carried into effect; whilst the concessions that had been made have been recalled. The people are never, even once, permitted to lay their wishes before the Government. [4] About two thousand individuals have had sentences of condemnation passed upon

---

[1] Aguirre, p. 141.

[2] See what is said upon this point by Azeglio, " Raccolta degli scritti politici," 1850, p. 67. Tommaseo, " Roma e il mondo," 1851, p. 243, and almost all who have written on the circumstances then occurring.

[3] Documenti sul Governo pontif., i. 577.

[4] Gualterio, " Documenti," p. 184.

them; and of these some are now in prison, or, as outlaws, wander in foreign lands. And in what description of prisons are the incarcerated? In pestiferous dungeons, where the convicted are huddled up with the unconvicted—those charged with political offences with those who have deprived others of property or of life.[1] In our legislation there is neither unity nor harmony. No one can know whether an obsolete or a new law, a 'Motuproprio' or an Edict, will, in any given case, be brought forward against him or for him.[2] In our Penal Code all is vague, uncertain, and contradictory. A lawless police pushes its arbitrary power to the extremest point, and meddles in everything.[3] Appointments and promotions in the public service are dependent upon the favour and dislike of a few in power; knowledge, science, experience, and substantial services are of no use to the possessors.[4] We will not be allowed to have railroads; whilst trade is struck down under an oppressive system of prohibitions. We are exhausted by means of monopolies and tax-farming, which enhance the prices of the indispensable necessaries of life, enrich a few at the cost of the State and the people, demoralise one part of the population, and bring down upon the Government the hatred of many thousands.[5] Through the operation of an absurd system of excise, our country has become the classic land of smugglers and contrabandists; and as to our native industry, it is not permitted, either by law or circumstances, to develop itself.[6] And we are on the road to universal pauperism by the enormous disproportion between our imports and exports.[7]

[1] "Appendice al libro d'Azeglio," p. 51.

[2] AGUIRRE, p. 134.

[3] "Un capo di polizia appunto perchè non vi è un codice, può far tutto," &c.—"Appendice," p. 47.

[4] What is here expressed in mild terms is represented in very dark colours by the Italians—for instance, in the "Appendice," p. 79, by AGUIRRE, AZEGLIO, and others.

[5] "Appendice," p. 68.

[6] "L'industria rimasta in culla fra noi nel mezzo del progresso di tutta l'Europa," says Cardinal Morichini, in his Report, p. 377.

[7] Imports, 92,000,000 francs; exports, only 31,000,000 francs.— ZELLER, "Histoire de l'Italie," 1853, p. 558.

We are, forsooth, told that we pay fewer taxes than other populations; but this does not disprove the fact that we are far more poor than others, and that we are compelled to bear oppressive communal tolls, and such other burdens."

The Military Commissions, and the conduct pursued by them in the Romagna in 1843 and 1844, increased the feelings of animosity and discontent. A party of insurgents took, without opposition, possession of the town of Rimini, and then made their escape into Tuscany. In the year 1845 there was published a Manifesto, addressed to the sovereigns and people of Europe, in which the following concessions were required:—"1st, An amnesty. 2nd, The promulgation of civil and criminal codes in conformity with those in force amongst other civilized nations, and including publicity in the proceedings, in the hearing of witnesses, and in the abolition of confiscation of property and punishment of death for political offences. 3rd, The releasing of laymen from the jurisdiction of the Inquisition and of the Ecclesiastical Courts; and, further, the free election of Municipal Councils; the institution of a Council of State at Rome; the bestowal of all civil, military, and judicial offices upon laymen; an amelioration of the censorship; the dismissal of foreign troops; the management of education by laymen; and the establishment of a National Guard." Farini was the author of this Manifesto; but, at a later period, even he seemed to regard some of the demands made in it as unreasonable, or as going somewhat too far.

The Papal Government declared, in an official reply,[1] that it rejected all these demands. The exclusion of laymen from the higher offices in the State was, it maintained, considerably ameliorated by the fact that a person could be a "Prelato" without being a priest—as all that was required was wearing the dress of an ecclesiastic and keeping the vow of celibacy.[2] Then, as to the Inquisition—its proceed-

[1] The document will be found in MARGOTTI, "Le Vittorie della Chiesa." Milano, 1857, pp. 490-507.

[2] Few persons could feel satisfied with this reference to the part assigned to the "Prelati," whose only participation in the sacerdotal

ings were conducted with great mildness and tenderness ;
but still it would not be fair to confine its jurisdiction to
clergymen, and to leave laymen free from its operations.   As
to the Universities and literature—they were in a prosperous
condition (but it must be owned that all Europe maintained
the very opposite of this assertion).   Such was the opinion
then put forward by the Secretary of State : it affirmed that
the averments as to existing evils in the Papal States, and a
necessity for reforming them, were nothing more than the
wicked invention of some malcontent and uneasy spirits.

In the whole of Italy a conviction the very opposite to
this prevailed.   Men whose words had the greatest weight
with the nation spoke out distinctly, "that affairs could not
remain as they were in the Papal States."   A great sensation was caused by the writings of Massimo d'Azeglio.   Even
Cesare Balbo, an ardent Guelph, and the historical venerator
of the Papacy,[1] rejoiced that the publications of Azeglio and
Galeotti had appeared, because they exposed the defects and
malpractices in the Government of the Papal States ; and it
was his opinion that the literary work of Azeglio had not
been without influence upon the Conclave by whom Pius IX.
was elected as Pope.[2]

The Marquis Gino Capponi—a man honored and respected
beyond all others in Italy—thus expressed his opinion :[3] "In
the Papal States there never will be peace, unless the government be taken out of the hands of priests and transferred to

character was, that they wore the habit of a priest, and took a vow of
celibacy, and were thus made to appear as laymen concealed under a
priest's mask. It is comprehensible how such a double character should
have given rise to the suspicion that an amphibious position like this was
only assumed from ambition or avarice, and that those occupying it
should not stand very high in public opinion ; whilst the married lay
employés, who saw those half-priests promoted over their heads, could
not but feel still more bitterly against them on account of their own
advancement being prevented.

[1] "Io son gran papolino, al solito," was his own expression respecting
himself in the year 1848.   Ricotti, "Vita di Balbo," 1856, p. 265.

[2] "Lettere di politica e letteratura," 1855, p. 356.

[3] Anonymously in the "Gazzetta Italiana." See, with reference to it,
Montanelli, "Memorie," i. 84.

laymen; and that it bears in mind how, in the Middle Ages, the Papal sovereignty reposed upon the power of an idea, and the prestige of a name, whilst it was on all sides controlled by the conflicting jurisdictions of the people and the nobility. The existing mode of government—this sacerdotal, all-intermeddling, tax-imposing, catch-poll system of administration, is a novelty of modern times. The Pope must bring back his sovereignty to what it formerly had been, and gradually constitute a different description of Ministers, different institutions and laws; or else—the Tiara will be stained with blood, and at last rolled in the mire."

Difficulties, abortive efforts, humiliations, and defeats befell the Government, and daily overwhelmed it. There was no end to the incongruities, inextricable embarrassments, and collisions in which the governing "Prelati" and priesthood found themselves involved between their ecclesiastical status and the fitting discharge of their official duties. These grew upon them, as polypi are generated out of one another. The instruments of government broke to pieces in its hands. The Papal soldiery became such objects of contempt that the people would not enlist in their ranks; and when a few were, by the temptation of high pay, brought together, they soon again were disbanded, and it was necessary to call in the Austrians to protect the Papal troops from the scorn and assaults of the population.

In the year 1843 the Government received a report from Ferrara, " That the whole of the population of the Romagna was inimically disposed towards the Government."[1] From Imola the Cardinal-Legate, Massimo, reported, on the 12th August, 1845: " The pride of the population makes a priests' government intolerable to it. From the patricians down to the lowest shop-boys, they are all sworn to protect every one who is prosecuted, and to save him from punishment. Many of the officials and clergy are inclined to be on a good understanding with the innovators. The whole of the pre-

[1] " I pochissimi amici del Governo non hanno voce in queste provincie, perchè appunto sono pochi e l'Universale è nemico."—" Documenti," i. 70.

sent generation, from the age of eighteen and upwards, must
be regarded as lost ; for they are completely inimical to the
Government, and always to be found in an attitude of hostility against it."[1] The Governor of Rome, Marini, in his
answer, says : " From many other places the reports are to
the same effect ; but the main-spring of all this evil is to be
found in the fact—compulsory idleness, a want of contented
industry ; and both of these are concomitants of the present
system of government."[2]

Many of the ecclesiastics, such as Cardinal Massimo, were
disposed to trace the main cause of the melancholy state of
things and aversion to the Papal Government, to the seeds
of indifferentism and infidelity which had been spread amongst
the people by the French troops when in occupation of the
country.[3] But laymen, like Aguirre, Tommaseo, and Azeglio, replied : " It is the gross faults and abuses of the civil
government which make the people falter in their faith, and
shake their confidence in the Papal guidance of the Church.
The unfavourable opinion fostered by the condition to which
the priests' government of the Papal States has reduced
them, opens a path for erroneous doctrines in religion."[4]

Pius IX.—1846-1861.

Out of a Conclave—one that had only lasted three days,
and was the briefest that had occurred for nearly three hundred years—came forth Pius IX. The arrival of foreign
Cardinals had manifestly not been expected. What was particularly aimed at was to guard against Austrian influence,
and the Austrian negation. Cardinal Mastai, that Gregory
himself had desired to have as his successor,[5] and who was

---

[1] " Documenti," i. 66. At the same time the Cardinal admits the defective mode of administering the law : " Si rende formolaria ed ineffi-
cace."

[2] "L'ozio e il niun sfogo che hanno gli amor proprii eccitati dall'
esempio degli esteri," l. c., p. 67.

[3] "Documenti sul Gov. pontif.," i. 66.

[4] AGUIRRE, p. 174 ; TOMMASEO, " Roma e il mondo," p. 73 ;
D'AZEGLIO, " La Politique et le droit chrétien," p. 115.

[5] So says SILVIO PELLICO, " Epistolario," 1856, p. 324.

then but fifty years of age, appeared to be the fitting man.
As Nuncio in Chile, he had looked upon the world outside of
the Papal States, and he had made a comparison between
the condition of other lands and his own.   To continue to
govern in the spirit of his predecessors, and especially of
Lambruschini, was simply an impossibility; but Pius had
not the slightest inclination to do so.   He saw a greater
amount of disorder than he could cure; but he brought the
purest motives, the most unbiassed will, and the most unconditional self-devotion with his summons to the throne; and
he avowed his mission to be that of a reformer in the government of the country, and a pacificator between the ruler
and the ruled.   In the firm belief that love alone can beget
love, and beneficence gratitude, Pius commenced his reign
with a comprehensive Amnesty.   By so doing he freed himself, in the most decided manner, from the mode and policy
of administration hitherto pursued; but he also, at the same
time, and by the same act, as Prince Metternich said, "threw
open the door of his house to the professional robbers"—he
permitted the Radical Conspirators who had, until then,
carried on their plots in foreign countries to make his own
land the seat and centre of their manœuvres.   In the purity,
and in the moral nobility of his own disposition, Pius never
hesitated, although he was not unaware as to the consequences of what he had done.   He held it to be his duty to
grant the Amnesty, not only as a political act of conciliation,
but also as a reparation for wrong that had been inflicted.
The Prussian ambassador, Herr von Usedom, quotes the
words spoken by the Pope on this topic: "To grant an
Amnesty was not only a political necessity, but it was likewise my duty.   The hatred which the old system had produced against the Papacy must be assuaged; and in a word,
the old must be retrieved by the new, and amends made for
the past."[1]

Pius conceived himself forced at last to carry into effect
the promises that had been made in 1831.   On the 23rd
April, 1848, he declared in an Allocution to the Cardinals:

[1] "Politische Briefe und Characteristiken," 1849, p. 254.

" That in the latter years of Pius VII. the Great Powers of Europe had represented to the Papal See that it could, in its civil government, create institutions which would be more in correspondence with the wishes of the laity." At the same time, he supported himself altogether upon the Memorandum of the Powers in 1831, which had declared the introduction of Provincial Councils, and the admission of laymen to administrative and judicial offices, as *vital questions* for the Papal Government. His predecessors had done a few things in that direction, and had promised others; but their ordinances had neither corresponded with the desires of the Great Powers, nor had they given satisfaction, nor secured the public weal and tranquillity of the State.[1]

Commissions were then established for an examination into the whole system of government, for an improvement in legislation, and for a more suitable classification of the various branches of the executive. The selection of Gizzi as Secretary of State met with general approval. The laying down of railroads, which had been refused during the reign of Gregory, was now sanctioned. The Government permitted that in the same place where only a few months previously every word relating to political affairs must be suppressed, a political journal might be established, and that the wants and circumstances of the Papal Kingdom, as well as of all Italy, might be discussed. A Censorship-edict, declaring the establishment of a Censorship College, was an improvement in the antecedent state of affairs, where everything had been left to the arbitrary judgment of a few monks. Now discussion upon scientific matters, contemporary chronicles, and questions upon agriculture and trade, were left free.[2]

The greatest joy was excited by a Decree of the 19th April, 1847, which announced a convocation of notables from the provinces to a State Consultation. A council of ministers was formed; Rome had a communal representation; several other reforming decrees appeared, and the

---

[1] " Documenti," i. 405.   [2] COPPI, ix. 78.

State Consultative Assembly met, and propounded moderate propositions.

In a few weeks Pius became the idol of all Italians; and every voice gave utterance to the same language respecting him. His name was then a talisman! Nought was rightly done, but what was done by him! All hopes were centred in him, and he was hailed as the national hero of Italy! He was as their "Priest King" to break the chains of the nation, and other governments would be forced to act in imitation of his example! "Then," says Montanelli, "was the prestige of the Pope the sole defensive bulwark between us and the arms of Austria."[1]

Laymen and priests vied with each other in tendering their homage to the reforming Pope. "Pius," says Count Balbo,[2] "is only now reigning for six weeks, and in that brief span of time has become the most active reformer in this eventful century. The great majority of ecclesiastics in the Papal States are thoroughly aware that it is only by such a course as this that the hatred of the town population against their entire order can be put an end to. It is hoped that the time has now for ever passed away, in which tribunals could be seen composed exclusively of priests condemning to death or the galleys persons accused of political offences—and doing that, too, without affording to them the means of defending themselves.[3]

That which was the feeling of all intelligent and religious Italians at the time, was no more than truly expressed by Count Cesare Balbo, when he addressed these noble lines to Pius :—

> "Tu non ci maledici! Tu sei figlio
> Di nostra età, e l'intendi e la secondi :
> Perdura e avanza ! a te bramando mirano
> Ormai due mondi.

*   *   *   *

[1] "Memorie sull' Italia," ii. 180.   [2] "Lettere," p. 366.

[3] Compare the letter of Poggi to Saint-Aulaire, in GUALTERIO, "Documenti," p. 273.

> " Tu principe, tu padre, tu pontifice,
>   Ogni via già t' apristi, ogni speranza ;
>   Ora dal volgo di color che dubbiano
>   Ti scerni e avanza."[1]

And not only in Italy, but in the whole Catholic world, there was universal joy, and Pius became the " Amor et deliciæ generis humani." The clergy in all countries, the religious Catholics, each and all were rejoiced that at last the reconciliation of the Roman See with the ideas of freedom amongst modern nations could be announced and ratified ; and that the stain could be wiped away which had been brought upon the whole order of the priesthood by the misdeeds and unpopularity of a clerocracy in the States of the Church.[2]

It is well-known that, contemporaneous with the commencement of the reign of Pius IX., the demand for national independence, and for a free Italy, arose from one end of the Peninsula to the other. " We will," it was said, " be a nation; we shall possess the strength and dignity of a nation —our weight shall be felt in the scale of nations, and our importance in the world's history; we will no longer be enchained by the external interests of Transalpine powers." The movement was no longer confined to the lodges of the secret societies—it prevailed over all Italy—it was felt by all the educated classes of society—it was participated in by all the higher and the middle ranks. All desired national independence—the overthrow of Austrian rule in Upper Italy— the abolition of Austrian supremacy in the whole peninsula : all longed for political freedom.

Even in Rome those who were then about the Pope did not recoil from that universal spirit which then exhibited itself for shaking off the yoke of foreigners, as well as for the establishment of an Italian Kingdom ; and it is even reported

---

[1] Thou cursest us not! Thou art a son of our own age, and thou dost understand it, and thou helpest us. Hold fast, and—Onward ! Two worlds now look with longing love upon thee. Thou Prince, thou Father, thou Pontiff—every path is open before thee, all hope is in thee. From the common crowd of doubters separate thyself, and—Onward !

[2] The applause bestowed upon the reforming Pope, especially by the French bishops, is worth remembering.

that Pius himself had given expression to these words: "If victory should favour the army of Charles Albert, then was he himself ready with his own hand to crown him King of Upper Italy.[1] One of Rosmini's plans for the organization of an Italian Confederation met with the approval of the Pope. A Diet of all the Italian States in Rome should consult together, and determine upon war and peace, tolls, treaties of commerce, and other matters of common interest to them all. Rome would thus become the Frankfort of the Italian Confederation of States.

But then came Rome to be oppressed by the disastrous machinations of political clubs (the Circolo Romano), and of a civic guard, which soon proved itself to be here, as everywhere else, inefficient, useless, and evil-disposed, when its services were required for the maintenance of order, and a protection to the Government. Radical demagogues inflamed and fanaticised the populace with endless street demonstrations, and the Government could no longer count in Rome upon obedience to its orders.[2] Under the mask of public demonstration of respect and gratitude, the attempt was made to degrade the Pope into a tool of Mazzini, and to force him into a war against Austria. Pius was to be compelled, not merely to take a part in the war, but, as the first, the foremost herald of hostilities, to place himself at its head.[3] The ministries, for the most part composed of laymen, rapidly succeeded each other in office. At the beginning of the year 1848, and when revolutions had already taken place in France and Sicily, appeared the "Statuto Fondamentale" —a constitution, in the preamble to which Pius declared: "he would not less prize his people, nor show less confidence in them than had been done in neighbouring states, where the population had been regarded as sufficiently sagacious to be entrusted, not merely with a representation having the capacity to consult together, but also with power to resolve, and to have their decrees carried into effect. Such preroga-

---

[1] GIOBERTI, "Rinnovamento civile d'Italia," i. 210. COPPI, x. 368.

[2] RANALLI, "Del riordinamento d'Italia," 1859, p. 298.

[3] RANALLI, "Del riordinamento d'Italia," p. 298.

tives he would confide to two Chambers—one to be named by himself, and the other to be elected. As to those points not specified in this Statute, and in matters affecting religion and morals, he reserved for himself and his successors the full exercise of their sovereign authority.[1]

There was an essential difference between the "Statuto" and any one of the modern constructed constitutional forms of Government. For there was still left the College of Cardinals, as a wholly independent corporation—one, too, in some measure participating in the sovereignty; and it was to remain not only by the side of, but above both the Chambers. Thus there were, in effect, three deliberative assemblies. It was natural; perhaps, it was unavoidable, that the "Statuto" should be assented to by Pius. Still, as the result has shown, and as, indeed, it might easily have been recognised and foreseen, the people had been but insufficiently prepared or educated for a right use of the political functions bestowed upon them by the "Statuto." What was beyond all things needed, and was indispensable for them to possess, was more of civil freedom in their dealings with officials—less subjection to the arbitrary conduct and vexatious proceedings of the police—more practice and experience in municipal and provincial self-government. The preliminary conditions to normal constitutional life were altogether wanting. Beyond all things, there was required an absolute separation between lay and ecclesiastical powers and attributes. When, for instance, the Cardinal Vicar, who supplied the place of the Pope in his character of Bishop of Rome, had his police of morals, and when he, with his episcopal authority, exercised a civil jurisdiction, with his own tribunal and his own agents, it is not easy to perceive how such an institution could be maintained along with a representative government. However much the representation of the people and their rights might be limited, and the powers of the government strengthened, it is still inevitable that the mere existence of an Assembly, the creation of the free choice of the people, must give to the lay element a vast preponderance in the State,

---

[1] COPPI, x. 183.

over the clerical.   And then this occurring when there was
in the administration an inverse order of things prevailing—
when the lay members were doomed to be stationary, were
absolutely excluded from the higher offices, and made depen-
dents upon clerical superiors—when such an absurdity as this
was persisted in, a peaceful solution of all these difficulties
was neither to be looked for nor expected, nor even thought
of.   At almost every Elected Assembly it was determined to
withdraw from the clerical jurisdiction the powers exercised
by it—to seek and find the means for the abolition of the
Inquisition, of the civil jurisdiction of the Bishops, and the
legalised immunities and privileges of the clergy.   And yet
it was a commission of the " Prelati"—a commission from
which all laymen were excluded—that devised the "Statuto;"
and that same " Statuto" the College of Cardinals had, as it
is known, upon the assurance of Pope Pius himself, unanimously approved of.[1]   Had the inevitable consequences of
the " Statuto" been then foreseen ?—or was it determined to
let a gradual change take place, when the declaration might
be made that it had proved in operation to be absolutely
objectionable ?   No one now can answer these questions.
Soon afterwards the Censorship was made more stringent
upon writings touching on theology and religion.   Meanwhile Rome had become the central point of the Mazzinists
and Revolutionists; whilst it is to be remembered that the
movements of 1831, 1843, and 1845, had left a burning
flame beneath their ashes.[2]   The resistance of the Pope
against a participation in the war against Austria was made
use of to despoil him of all power, and to force upon him the
revolutionary ministry of Mamiani.   Then it was that the
Pope's new Minister, Pellegrino Rossi, formerly the French
Ambassador, seized, with a strong hand, the reigns of government; and it seemed as if order would be restored, and the
fast-advancing steps of revolution checked, when the heads

[1] " L'intero sagro Collegio vi ha convenuto di buon grado ed unani-
mamente," were the words of the Pope to the Roman municipality.—
FARINI, ii. 5.
[2] RANALLI, " Istorie Ital.," i. 36.

of the anarchical party, Sterbini, Ciceruacchio, and others, resolved upon, and carried into effect, the assassination of the man who was the most formidable opponent of Unionism, and of a "one and indivisible Italian Republic." Then followed the storm of the Quirinal, and the flight of the Pope to Gaeta. And this time, too, despite of the personal respect, and of the veneration for Pius IX., the Papal power in the whole country was easily overthrown. The utter incapacity of a population, of whom ninety-nine in every hundred had never, either before or after the Revolution, taken a book or newspaper in their hands, made the task attempted to be performed by the Triumvirate and their adherents much more easy of accomplishment.

During the sixty-nine days of the Republic created by the Garibaldists and Mazzinists, the inhabitants of the Papal States must have drained to the very dregs the intoxicating cup of revolution. The birds of prey quickly gathered round the fallen body of the State, and the people were, under the name of a Democratic Republic, composed of the anarchists of every country, tyrannised over and despoiled by a plundering faction. Of "democratic speech-makers," and of empty-headed chatterers, there was a superfluity ; but of all things else—a deficiency.

When the French appeared, for the purpose of restoring the Pope, General Oudinot mentions what he then found to be the prevailing spirit amongst the population : " There is for Pius IX. a personal affection entertained ; but everyone is afraid of a clerical government."[1] He transferred the conquered city to the commissioners appointed by the Pope —Cardinals Dalla Genga, Vanicelli, and Altieri—on 1st August, 1849. It was not until the 4th April, 1850, Pius IX. made his entry into Rome.

In the Allocution of the 20th April, 1849, Pius declared that it never had been in his thoughts to change the nature and character of his government; that he had distinctly

---

[1] That a vast majority of the population in Rome wished for the return of the Pope is a fact attested by an eye-witness, HELFFERICH, in his " Briefen aus Italien," ii. 56.

pointed to the fact of the "Statuto," with its representative constitution, as perfectly compatible with the character of the Papal sovereignty.   But now came into the possession of power those who regarded the salvation of the State to consist in the speedy restoration of all that had been previously overthrown.   Even the Inquisition was revived; a "moderate" party, such as there was in 1847, and on which the Pope might now, as then, rely for support, was declared to be no longer procurable.   All who were around the Pope desired that the institutions and concessions of 1847 and 1848 should be put an end to.   Cardinal Antonelli go verned in this sense, as Secretary of State, and became the sole leader of the administration, whilst the other five ministers were but the first official servants of government.   Count Balbo had been sent to Gaeta, for the purpose of impressing, in the name of the Piedmontese Government, upon the Pope and his minister, the wisdom of holding fast by the "Statuto;" but his appeal proved to be of no avail.[1]   Pius was convinced that the incorrigible would only make use of every concession that was granted to them to carry on their plots as enemies to all social order and positive religion.   A restricted amnesty, with but a few, and these unavoidable, exceptions, was granted. By the institution of the "*Staats Consulta,*" laymen had the right of giving an opinion upon domestic concerns; but the decision upon them was reserved for the "*Prelati,*" in whose hands were again placed all the higher offices.   The municipalities, however, were promised a certain sort of independence.   The Communal Councils were to be chosen out of electoral bodies of Council men, sixfold in number to those nominated; and the Pope reserved to himself the nomination of the first.

For ten years (1849—1859) did the Government of the Papal States, supported by the Austrian occupation in the Romagna, and by the French in Rome and Civita Vecchia, pursue, upon the whole, a peaceful and equable course. Seldom, indeed, has a government begun and ended its wearisome day-work under such disheartening circumstances

---

[1] Ricotti, "Vita del Balbo," p. 273.

—surrounded on all sides by bitter, malignant, self-seeking, and skulking foes, and nowhere having a firm support, and in no one a cordial, steady, and reliable friend.

The Report of the French Ambassador, Count Rayneval, in the year 1856, defended, in most points, the Government of the Papal States, under the present Pope and Cardinal Antonelli, against the reproaches of the Italians, and the wide-spread opinion in England and France regarding them. The Report certifies that dissatisfaction and discontent continue to prevail amongst the population; but the cause for this state of things "is to be sought," it says, "not in the faults of the system of government, but in the defects of the national character," and especially in the then existing situation and temper of the Italians. The English Envoy, Mr. Lyons, who was in Rome at the same time, has, in his Report, made frequent reference to Rayneval's Memorial, which he maintains was drawn up in agreement with, and according to, the data supplied by the Papal Government, for the purpose of influencing the Paris Cabinet to favour the continuance of the French Protectorate, and to shew that the Pope ought not to be pressed to make changes in his mode of government. He disputes, in many points, the correctness of M. Rayneval's representation. And, yet, both the one and the other, Rayneval and Lyons, coincide in some main points. Both give the assurance that no blame should be cast upon the existing Government for the general discontent and desire of the population for a change in the supreme authority over them. There are, as Mr. Lyons affirms, but two descriptions of men in the country; the first are unflinching, active, and irreconcileable enemies of the Government, whose watchword is, "No more government by priests!" These can never be won by reforms in particular matters; all they would do with every concession made to them would be to employ it as a weapon against the Government. It is not reform, but the overthrow of the Government, that they aim at. The others are indifferent, tepid, unreliable, and, in a moment of danger, the Government would not find in them the slightest support. They would not lift a finger in aid of the assailed ruler. The supposition thus made by the English Envoy was, in the year 1859, but too accurately verified, and too fully justified. Even the lower classes of the Papal *employés* were, as Mr. Lyons declares, notoriously disaffected to the Papal sovereignty,[1] and they were also described by him as being lazy and corrupt.

There are two matters which must not be overlooked by any one who would pass a sound judgment upon the condition of the Papal States. The first is the reflection that those who are rulers are, essentially, of the population, and participate in the popular virtues as well as popular defects. A want of energy and activity cannot reasonably be made a matter of reproach against a Government, when in it is discernible a national trait. Secondly : when once the fitting relations between a people and their Government become disturbed, then mutual confidence between them disappears, and a malcontent population is disposed to make their rulers responsible for all the wrongs and crimes of which they are themselves guilty, and which, whether they be sins of commission or omission, are characteristic of them, as a nation. In what an extreme degree this is the case in the Papal States, has been remarked upon by Count Rayneval. The inhabitants of the Papal States are, in some respects, like to the Mexicans, of whom it has been said by a keen observer, lately arrived from that country, that "they blame the Government if their coat is torn !" This mode of reasoning in the Papal States, it must, however, in candour, be admitted, is the natural consequence of the tutorship system of government, which restricts both a discussion upon, and a participation in, public business. Hence, too, flows a fatal distrust. "They dream," says the French Ambassador, "of naught else than dishonesty and extortion. They complain that the State does not engage in carrying out great undertakings, which, if it did, they would at once make those undertakings an object for their attacks."[2]

[1] Despatches from Mr. Lyons respecting the Condition and Administration of the Papal States." London, 1860, p. 53.

[2] "Allg. Zeitg.," 1857, p. 1666.

EE 2

The first and most pressing problem of all, is that affecting the relation of the ecclesiastical and lay holders of government situations; or, in other words, the question of "the secularization of public offices." Many hold this as being the most difficult to determine—as actually insoluble. It involves not merely the point that almost all the higher offices are in the hands of ecclesiastics, and that such offices are so regulated as to be inaccessible to laymen; but the Government says,[1] "That the Pope is an ecclesiastic, and that under the Pope, as sovereign, the direction of the administration must be essentially ecclesiastical. Besides that, we have only a very small number of laymen from whom we could make a selection, and the cities themselves (for instance, Orvieto and Camerino a short time previously) had desired to have ecclesiastics for their governors." To this it was replied by laymen, and the ambassadors of foreign powers: "The Government should be secularized, so that laymen of talent, honour, and ambition may have opened to them a path, and a hope of promotion, to the higher offices; and that it may thus plainly be made worth their while earnestly and seriously to prepare themselves for admission to the public service. So long as this is not the case, capable laymen will hold themselves aloof; laymen and ecclesiastics will be separated into hostile classes—and the former being constantly discontented, will wish for, and conspire to effect a change in, the form of the government. Moreover, situated as things now are, an accomplished and independent-minded layman would find himself, upon all occasions, compelled to sacrifice his judgment to that of his ecclesiastical superiors—that which would be done by very few, and these not the most competent or reliable persons." To these objections was to be added another, "that," as a shrewd French observer remarked,[2] "the priests stand like sentinels, at the opening of every

[1] Cardinal Antonelli, in an interview with Mr. Lyons, "Despatches," p. 17.
[2] H. v. METZ-NOBLAT, in his "Varia, Morale, Politique, Littérature." Paris, 1861, p. 433.

public career, to examine the candidate's testimonials of piety, and fulfilment of ecclesiastic duties ; for without these no one is permitted to enter the Government service."

" We will have," declared an Italian, lately, "along with the wished-for secularization in the Papal States, not merely the exclusion of priests from government offices, but also the cessation of a *caste*-government, and the establishment of equality in the temporal hierarchy, as well as a participation in the government of the country and the management of its affairs."[1]

Count Rayneval coincided in the view of the Government, for he directs attention to the fact "that the people exhibit towards the lay employés of the Government no marks of respect, and are much less tolerant of their superiority over them[2] in rank and position, than they are as regards ecclesiastics. And such feeling is so much the more plainly recognisable in the fact that many more violent personal assaults have been made upon lay than upon ecclesiastical officials." But he remarks, at the same time, that "the cry for a complete secularization of the Government is applauded by the people."

What we then see is this : a condition of circumstances in which they who are in reality "the people" are accustomed to find the ecclesiastical officers both more capable and less avaricious than the lay official subordinates ; and then, even though they may be, in general, dissatisfied with the administration, still they are unwilling to speak against the "Priest-Government." On the other hand, the higher orders, that is, all those who believe that they themselves, or their kinsmen, have a claim to participate in the service of the State are discontented ; they feel that they are excluded from office, and, therefore, demand that all situations and offices should be occupied by laymen. If this be laid down as a principle to be rigidly enforced, it is, in fact, an opening to the speedy secularization of the Papacy itself. On the other side, it is clear that if things remain as they now are,

---

[1] " Rivista Contemp.," viii. 470.

[2] " Denkschrift, Allg. Ztg.," 1857, 17th April.

a reconciliation of the two classes, and consequently a peaceful and beneficent maintenance of the Papal States, is scarcely to be hoped for. The disproportion lies, however, not so much in the number as in the outrageous contrast of social positions—the disparity complained of makes the clerical a governing, and the lay a subordinate class; it appears in public and private personal conflicts between a layman and an ecclesiastic, for it places every advantage within the reach of the latter, and renders the defeat of the former almost a matter of certainty. In other countries, we see ecclesiastics and laymen in the same description of employment standing well and amicably, as well as working harmoniously together; as, for instance, in Universities and Gymnasia, and as employés of the Government. Such a state of things would also be attainable in the Papal States, if the conditions were: "Equality of rights and of duties, free competition—accessibility to official life—the capability and suitableness of the individual, but not the paramount privileges of the class in society to which he may belong."

There is another difficulty to be found in the want of a rigid conformity to law. From the reports received on all sides, a person must feel convinced that one of the greatest defects in the condition of the Papal States is to be found in the want of conformity to law. There is unknown there the peaceful, firm, and, for rulers and for ruled alike, the equal—binding and unapproachable sanctity of law. There is too much confided to the power, and too much is made dependent upon the wilfulness, of particular officials. It is remarked by Mr. Lyons, "that the Court of Rome . . . . shows an extraordinary disregard to laws and forms in its dealings with its subjects, and seems almost always to assume an arbitrary power to act in each matter according to the circumstances of the moment."[1] There is an instance of a governor declaring "that, for want of proofs, the accused could not be convicted, but still he should be punished with imprisonment for eight days, upon bread and water."[2] And then there was

1 "Despatches," p. 61. See AGUIRRE, p. 124.
2 "Documenti, sul Gov. pontif.," ii. 580.

Cardinal Bernetti, the Secretary of State, who declared, with respect to an individual against whom there were not sufficient proofs, "that upon his first transgression he should receive, in addition to whatever might be the legal punishment of his offence, five years hard labour."[1] This exercise of an arbitrary power, this licentiousness on the part of the Administration and the authorities, who, on every occasion, are prepared to evade the law, has been branded by Count Rayneval, when he declares, "L' interprétation de la loi l'emporte sur la loi elle-même." The mischief is, that a sound political life can scarcely be developed when a government is carried on in this manner. The example of those in power renders it impossible for a people who live under the constant impression of arbitrary proceedings to have a due respect and reverence for the objective power, the law; on the contrary, the idea will gain ground with them that men in such a country are not the subjects of the law, but of the individual caprice of a certain number of persons, whose conduct is influenced by their passions and the interests of their order.[2]

It is perfectly manifest that "constitutionalism," as it is ordinarily understood and acted upon, could not be applied to the States of the Church. It would not be tolerated that a warlike faction could, by refusing the supplies, force the Pope, "the supreme shepherd of nations," to go to war with a Christian power, as they sought to compel him to declare war against Austria. The Pope must be in possession of a real and not a nominal sovereignty, so that he may be seen, as well as seem to be, in his ecclesiastical power and actions, fully and completely free. It can be a matter of not the slightest import, if he is under coercion, whether that coercion be exercised by a foreign power, or by a haughty and despotic parliamentary majority. But such a sovereignty, and a clerical-bureaucratic omnipotence tutoring everybody, and intermeddling with and managing everything, are two conditions of government as wide asunder from each other as the two poles. The autocratic sovereignty of the Pope is compatible with a participation of the people in legislation,

<hr/>

[1] "Documenti," ii. 595.   [2] Marsuzi de Aguirre, p. 166.

the autonomy of corporations, a moderate freedom of the press, and the separation of religion from the police. Formerly, it was Austria and the different Governments in Italy that were subjected to the guidance of Austria, that had, under the pretence that the principle of popular elections was irreconcileable with due order in their States, opposed the adoption of elective Provincial and Municipal Councils.[1] In accordance with the *Motu Proprio* of 1850, these elections were to take place, and the French defenders of the Papal See, Montalembert and De Corcelle, have appealed to the fact. The Italians reply: "That the Electoral system of Municipal and Provincial Councils is good in theory, but that Cardinal Antonelli had, in a circular of 29th April, 1854, ordered the Electoral Colleges not to be called together.[2] The Government could cite in its justification the remark of the English diplomatist, that it must conduct itself in accordance with the law of self-preservation; for, as he remarks, "the natural unwillingness of the Government to allow its own enemies a place in them" (the Communal Councils) "is unfortunately sufficient to exclude in many districts the men otherwise best qualified."[3] In fact, the number is far too great, as the British diplomatist says, of those in whose eyes "the standard of value for a scheme of reform is the means it would supply for throwing off the yoke of the Holy See." These are the persons who "would be sorry to have fewer causes of complaint—sorry for anything which would diminish the extent or the intenseness of disaffection."[4]

Another circumstance, and one of far too common occurrence, has contributed to the contempt into which the Government has fallen with its own subjects, by increasing the conviction that they live under a pure despotism; and that circumstance is the promulgation of laws which are afterwards permitted to remain a dead letter."[5]

[1] GALEOTTI, "Della sovranità dei Papi," 1846, p. 339. See remarks of H. v. ECKSTEIN, "Allg. Zeitung," April, 1860, p. 1803.

[2] FARINI, in the "Rivista Contempor.," 1857, ix. 19.

[3] LYONS, "Despatches," p. 19.   [4] LYONS, "Despatches," p. 20.

[5] Particular attention has been attracted towards this point by the

The Pope himself has long since admitted that an intellectually-gifted and extremely energetic people like the Italians could not endure the suppression of all public discussion, and an exclusion from all active participation in public life; that their impulsive activity required that there should be beds and channels into which it might be poured, and then, within due and prescribed limits, it might flow on beneficially. That by the side of public deliberative assemblies there should be a rigid preventive censorship prohibiting all discussions, as well as that there should be maintained certain institutions and privileges which have long since disappeared out of every other part of the world—that the duration of these contradictions could be prolonged is an impossibility. And hence concessions are refused by those who are for perpetuating the old systems, and who, as it has often been repeated, labour their very utmost to prevent the establishment of elective and consultative colleges, although in so doing they are acting contrary to the wish of the Pontiff, and inflicting pain upon him.[1] They who act thus well know that the chimney cannot be left stopped up once a fire is kindled on the hearth.

In the year 1856, the Inquisitor, Airaldi, issued a long Edict, in which, under a threat of the severest censures, he called for the denunciation of every ecclesiastical and religious offence that might be known by anyone to have been committed by others—he declared it to be the bounden duty of such to make certain sins known; as, for instance, a maidservant incurred excommunication and became liable to punishment, if she neglected to inform the Inquisition of anyone in the house in which she lived having eaten meat on a Friday or a Saturday evening! All the newspapers[2]—the

anonymous Italian author of "Mémoires du Comte Aldini," in the "Revista Contemp.," viii. 469.

[1] The author of an article in the "Rivista Contemp.," 1856, viii. 470, maintained, upon what he said was the best authority, that Pius himself complained of the conduct of the Government then existing.

[2] It was first brought to notice in the "Correspondance Italienne lithographiée," 19th October, 1856.

"Siecle" leading the van—instantly got possession of this document, and it was printed in full. What commentaries
were made upon it in France, England, and Italy !—what
inferences were drawn from it as to the character of the
Papal Government, and what little hope of reform to be
looked for from it ! Of all this it is not now necessary to
say a word. The numberless enemies of the Papal See could
scarcely be tendered a more welcome gift. The hope, however, was entertained that something might be done to
remove the impression caused by this circumstance. One
journal brought the intelligence that Airaldi had been removed from his office, but the " Ecclesiastical Journal," published in Rome, instantly contradicted that statement, and
declared that " Airaldi had only done his duty ! "[1]

It would seem, in point of fact, as if persons in the narrow
circles at Rome had either no precise notion, or some idea
far removed from the truth, as to the gigantic powers of
" journalism," and of that " public opinion " which is formed
through or reflected by journalism. Every one who is acquainted with the present condition of Europe, and the relations between existing powers, is well aware that three such
events as the case of Achilli, the Edict of Airaldi (and others
antecedent to and like it), and the affair of Mortara, have
weighed more in the balance, on the question of the Papal
States, than a battle lost or won. The question here is, not
how each of these circumstances should be judged of by its
intrinsic merits, but in what manner they contributed to influence an irresistible public opinion in Europe. At present,
all are living in glass houses, and it is not sufficient to treat
with governments, for behind them are the peoples upon
whose fixed opinions depend the resolutions of those in authority. How unfavourable in Italy, in England, in the
greatest part of France, Germany, etc., is public opinion, for
the continuation of the temporal sovereignty of the Pope,
every one, who will only make use of his own eyes, can but
too plainly discern.

It cannot appear to be a matter much to be wondered at,

[1] The " Civiltà Cattolica," in its number of 20th December, 1856.

that, wherever the co-operation of laymen is needed in Rome, all should go wrong, and that the Government (as all the foreign diplomatists testify) should nowhere find a support in the population. At great cost, and with inexpressible difficulty, there was incorporated anew, in 1850, a small Papal native army; but the events of 1859 shattered into pieces this instrument, and destroyed this hope. The facts proved that these troops were completely untrustworthy, and recourse was unavoidably had to foreign soldiers.

Prelati and Delegati were constantly sending in reports of the systematically hostile spirit of the population—of their dogged repugnance to enlist in the Papal military service—of their refusal to undertake any communal office which would bring them in contact with the Government, and render it necessary for them to carry out its orders. The Delegato Folicaldi wrote from Ferrara, in the year 1849 : " The Liberals say, ' The Austrian rather than the Papal,' only for the purpose of expressing their hatred against the Papal Government." [1] From Bologna, the Prelato Bedini wrote to say that he could only discover a few persons who would undertake the office of " Censor." It was the same at Ravenna and Ferrara. At Faenza, no one would accept of any kind of office ; and the Delegato Lasagna, writing from Cesena, 1858, says: " In this district there are only a few persons well disposed towards the Government." [2]

Nevertheless, the administration of Pius IX. is wise, benevolent, indulgent, thrifty, attentive to useful institutions and improvements. All that proceeds from Pius IX., personally, is worthy of the Head of the Church—it is elevated and liberal in the best sense of the term. No sovereign spends less on his Court, and his own private wants. If all thought and acted as he does, his would be a model State. Both the French and the English envoys affirm that the financial administration had improved, that the value of land was increasing, agriculture flourishing, and that many symptoms of progress might be observed. [3]

[1] " Documenti," i. 57.   [2] " Documenti," i. 210.
[3] LYONS, " Despatches," p. 54.

Whatever can be expected of a monarch full of affection for his people, and seeking his sole recreation in works of beneficence, Pius abundantly performs. " *Pertransiit bene-faciendo.*" These words have been spoken of One, far, far higher, and yet, when applied to Pius, they are but the simple truth. In him, we can clearly perceive how the Papacy, even as a temporal State, might, so far as the character of the Prince is concerned, through judicious elections, be the most admirable of human institutions. A man in the prime of life, after an irreproachable youth, and a conscientious discharge of episcopal duties, is elevated to the highest dignity and sovereign power. He knows nothing of expensive amusements, he has no other passion than that of doing good, no other ambition than to be beloved by his subjects. His day is divided between prayer and the labours of government; his relaxation is a walk in the garden, a visit to a church, a prison, or a charitable institution. Free from personal desires and from terrestial bonds, he has no relations and no favourites to provide for. For all, there is the like claim, and the like access to him. For him, the rights and powers of his office exist only for the sake of its duties. His abstinent and thrifty palace-expenditure affords to him abundant means to relieve want and mitigate suffering on all sides. He, too, like most of the Popes, has had buildings erected; yet his are not splendid palaces, but works of general utility. Grievously outraged, maltreated, repaid with ingratitude, he has never harboured a thought of revenge, never committed an act of severity, but ever forgiven and ever pardoned. The cup of sweetness and of bitterness, the cup of men's favour and disfavour, he has not merely tasted, but drained to its very dregs; he has heard, too, the cry of " Hosanna!" and he has heard it soon followed by the cry of " Crucify him!" The man of his confidence, yea! the first great mind of his nation, had fallen beneath the dagger of the assassin; and the bullet of an insurgent struck down the friend by his side. And yet no feeling of hatred, no breath of anger, could ever obscure, even for a moment, the spotless mirror of his soul. Untouched by human folly, unmoved by human malice, he proceeds with a firm and regular pace on his way, like to the stars in heaven.

Such I have seen the action of this Pope in Rome—such it has been described to me by all, whether near him or afar; and if he now seems to be appointed to pass through all the painful and discouraging experience that can befall a monarch, and to continue, to the end, the course of a prolonged martyr-dom, he resembles in this—as in so many other things—the Sixteenth Louis; or rather, to ascend still higher, he knows that the disciple is not above the Master, and that the pastor of a Church, whose Lord and Founder died upon the Cross, cannot marvel and cannot refuse—that the Cross should be laid upon him also.

At present, the utmost efforts are made, in Italy and France especially, to mislead public opinion. One Italian after another comes forward to show that the Papal See is, according to the principles on which it is based, not in a condition to comply with the demands which the genius of the age, and the prevailing tendencies in social and political life, make upon those who are in authority. The same has been maintained by the English Minister, Gladstone, in the British Parliament, in the year 1856, and ever since then.[1] The Pope, it is said, is, as a Sovereign of the Church States, bound by the Canon Law, and, therefore, fettered down to the conditions and legal customs of the Middle Ages. Hence, it is said that, as there has been a complete change effected in all the relations of civil life, it is manifestly im-possible that a people of the nineteenth century can be ruled by the principles of the thirteenth; and so the temporal sovereignty of the Pope is a contradiction in itself—a perma-nent state of war, that can only be maintained by force of arms; and hence it is doomed—whether sooner or later—to die! All the friends of the Church, and of the Papal See,

[1] See the work of MONTANELLI, "L'Impero, il Papato, e la demo-crazia," Florence, 1859. The essays of MINGHELLI, VAINI, and of an anonymous writer, "Patrizio Romano," in the "Rivista Contemporanea," 1861; the treatise of GENNARELLI, "I Lutti dello Stato Romano," 1860, and several others.

are called upon to oppose such an opinion; for it is only that which, according to the Catholic doctrine, is of Divine Institution, and what is essential for all times and unchangeable, to which the Pope is bound.

Happily, the sovereignty of the Pope is of a very elastic nature, and it has already gone through many different forms. If a comparison be instituted between the use which the Popes made of their sovereignty in the thirteenth or fifteenth century and the form of government which Consalvi introduced, it will be seen that few things could exhibit a stronger contrast with one another. There is no reason, therefore, to doubt that it will now, after a violent interruption, assume the form best adapted to the character of the age and the requirements of the Italian people. Let it be but seen that the Papal Government possesses a vast advantage over all other forms of sovereignty; and instantly the people will willingly again place themselves under the dominion of the Papacy. What is there to prevent us from thinking that a state of circumstances may arise in which, when elections to the Papal dignity occur, the persons chosen shall no longer be decrepit, aged individuals, but men in the prime of their years and their strength—a period, too, in which the people shall be reconciled to their government by free institutions, and share in the conduct of their own concerns—whilst the upper classes are satisfied by the opening of a suitable career in public affairs? In such a condition of circumstances, the public and speedy administration of justice would win the confidence of the people; an honourable *esprit du corps*, a feeling of self-respect, and a pride in their integrity, and in the dignity of the class to which they belonged, would animate the Government *employés*; the hostile separation between ecclesiastics and laity would be put an end to, by an equality in their privileges and their duties; the police would no longer prop themselves up by religious means, and religion would no longer hobble like a cripple, and rely for support upon the crutches of a policeman. The Pope and his territory could then be placed under the protection of the Catholic Powers—the same Powers that have guaranteed the neutrality of Belgium and Switzerland. The Great Powers that have become security for the integrity of the wretched, self-collapsing empire of the Turk, could also shield the dominions of the Pope. Defended by such a buckler, and the ruler over a peaceful, contented people, the Pope's hands would be completely free. The barriers to material and intellectual intercourse which have until now maintained, by an unnatural separation, different portions and districts of Italy apart from each other, would then be thrown down. International affinities and certain free admissibilities, such as are enjoyed by University professors in Germany, might leave open to the ambitious in their own land a career for employment in the civil and military service in other parts of Italy. The Pope would have no enemies to fear, either at home or abroad; his subjects would be released from the detested conscription; the State-budget would be without the burden of army estimates, and for the maintenance of public security all that would be required would be a few brigades of a Gendarmerie. For the execution of works of general necessity sufficient funds would not be wanting.

And this is no vain, empty fancy-sketch. Abstracting those misfortunes and faults which every one of good will, and right intentions, and unprejudiced feeling will admit to be curable, and supposing that peace and order prevail in Italy, then might the Government of the Papal States be a model Government—a pattern worthy of imitation by all other States and administrative authorities. That it should be such a pattern for others has not only been declared by Tommaseo, but also by the Bishop of Orleans, whose work has been declared by the Pope himself to be the best of all that have appeared in defence of the sovereignty of the Papacy. Even he (the Bishop of Orleans) marks it as a rightful requisition, that the lands of the Church should be more prosperous and better governed than others, and that their people should be more contented with their lot than any other population.[1] Monseigneur Düpanloup likewise an-

[1] " Si la perfection doit se rencontrer sur la terre quelque part, ce doit

nounces that *those who,* "*under the pretence of dogmas, main-tain that the Pope cannot put his Government in harmony with modern times and the legitimate wishes of the people, are persons who thereby declare the destruction of the Papal power to be unavoidable.*" Let it now be considered what high authoritative approval the book has received in Rome which contains these words, and there will then be found that they are full of hope and of cheering promise.

There are persons now in Italy who urge, as regards the temporal sovereignty of the Pope, a pressing difficulty, and which they declare to be insoluble. It is a perfect freedom of religious worship.[1] They say: Religious freedom in a double sense—freedom for all religion, and freedom to choose, and openly profess and practise a form of religion different from that which is the predominant faith as well as the creed of the majority of the nation. This is a requirement from which no state in Europe will dissent. The principle has been introduced into other parts of Italy; but the Pope will never permit it.

I regard this assumed difficulty as insignificant—that is, that it has already practically been solved, or is still in process of solution. Life, that concrete actuality, with its unavoidable demands, is accustomed to cut through those knots which to many have seemed inextricably involved. Attempts have already been made in the States of the Church, as in so many other places, by gold and eloquence, to win proselytes to Protestantism. Hitherto, these efforts have proved fruitless.[2] But admitting it had been otherwise, and that in reality several conversions had taken place, would it then have been in the power of those in authority to employ any means of punishing the converts, and, above all, to maintain a last-

être dans les états de l'Eglise.   J'admets cette exigence comme un hom-mage involontaire qui nous honore, et avec lequel nous devons compter."—" La Souveraineté Pontificale," 1860, p. 570.

[1] MONTANELLI, " L'Impero, il Papato, e la Democrazia in Italia," 1859, p. 29.

[2] See on this subject, ODDO, " L'Independenza, il Cattolicismo, e l'Italia," 1859, p. 34.

ing coercion as regarded them? We all know thoroughly well to what a high state of perfection the art is carried now-a-days of putting a pressure upon an unpopular government—how it works through the medium of diplomacy, or by agitation, or by open attacks in the press, and by speeches in Parliament—until its power may at last be compared to that of an armed intervention, and its final success is inevitable. It is notorious that the case of the Jew boy Mortara has been to the enemies of the Church and of the Roman See one of the most welcome circumstances that could have occurred, and they have known how to make a large capital out of it. But if the event were now to occur that an Italian, having become a convert to Protestantism, were to be denounced to the Inquisition, and imprisoned by that tribunal, &c.—what would be the consequence? A cry of indignation would be raised from Norway to Sicily—newspapers, popular meetings, Parliaments and Chambers, would occupy themselves with the affair—a powerful agitation, such as we have witnessed with respect to the Florentine Madiais, would be renewed and brought before the world in still more huge dimensions; and certain Powers, which it is needless for us to name, would seize with delight upon the pretext thus afforded them to rob the Pope of all that still remains to him of his temporal sovereignty. And where are the hands that in such a circumstance would be raised in defence of the Pope? There is now much talk of the introduction of Protestantism into Italy. Should this talk become a reality, and Protestantism gain a strong position, and have an influence upon ideas and feelings in Italy, then would most assuredly the situation of the Papal See be, in an incalculable manner, embarrassed, and the reconciliation of the Pope with the popular spirit be rendered, perhaps, an impossibility. But nothing practical will ever come of such a movement. Even in the century when Protestant ideas possessed their greatest strength, and had attained their mightiest powers of attraction—and when they were in the north of Europe truly popular, and dominated over the minds and hearts of all—even then Protestantism in Italy was only

FF

thought of by a few scholars and ecclesiastics; whilst the people were never seriously affected by it. The peculiar Protestant spiritual testimony of Italians, and the contingent which they, on behalf of Italy, gave to the religious movement of the sixteenth century was—Socinianism! It is not to be expected that the ideas which three hundred years ago, in all their youthful freshness, had such mighty attractions for mankind, and yet whose ardent power was wholly lost upon the Italians, will, at this period of the world's history, be able to make any considerable impression upon the people of Italy —even though they come recommended by the influence of the Piedmontese Government and the enticements of English coin. "The Italians," said to me a man of whom all Tuscany is proud, a few years since in Florence, "can never be made believing Calvinists or Lutherans. All that these English and German labours will, or can, ever be able to effect is this—that a number of persons will be estranged from all religions, and plunged into infidelity. With us, Protestantism can never be anything more than a power of destructiveness, and the founder of social disorders and dissensions.[1]

So has the English preacher, S. W. King, who visited Italy in the year 1858, likewise admitted that the labours (which had been richly supported by English money) of the Waldenses, and other preachers of Protestantism in Italy, had for the most part proved to be ineffective; that in Piedmont, where there had been the greatest exertions, Protestantism had made but little progress; and that outside the Valleys of the Waldenses there were not 1,000 Protestants in the whole kingdom.[2] It astonished him to find the opponents of the Church able to quote quite glibly passages from

[1] "In the same spirit speaks."—GIURIA, "Silvio Pellico e il suo tempo," 1854, p. 81.

[2] "The Italian Vallies of the Pennine Alps;" London, 1858. See GIAC, ODDO, "L'Indèpendenza, il Cattolicismo e l'Italia," 1859, p. 40. He holds that the notion, that Protestantism can ever become a power in Italy, is absolutely groundless and absurd. Such, too, is the opinion of MASSIMO D'AZEGLIO.

the Bible against the Catholic religion, whilst they showed
that they themselves had no faith in the Bible, nor in the
passages they cited!—a circumstance that is quite intelligible
to those well acquainted with Italian affairs.   Recently, too,
at a meeting of "the Protestant Alliance," at Geneva, the
paid agents of "the Alliance," the Messrs. Bert, Valette,
and Mazarella, felt it necessary to let down, in a very
modest, moderate style, the high hopes that had been entertained of the glorious consequence to follow from "the
Gospel in Italy," and to admit to an audience hungering for
far different tidings, that, as yet—there had, in reality, very
little been done!

The French Government has proposed, over and over again,
to the Papal Administration, both general and particular
reforms.   Even Austria, in the year 1859, declared herself
ready again to take up the negotiations with the Papal
Government for reforms, which had been entered upon, in
1857, by France, and subsequently abandoned,[1] or to make
new representations on the same subject at Rome.   The
Roman Cabinet has, upon its part, never absolutely rejected
these reforms.   On the contrary, in the year 1860, it stated
"that the Holy See regarded the question of reforms as one
that was in principle conceded, but maintained its right to
postpone the announcement of them until it was again put
in possession of those provinces belonging to it which had
been annexed by Sardinia."[2]   At an early period, the Pope
had declared that he was ready to introduce the reforms proposed by the Great Powers, but under the stipulation (as well
as an unavoidable condition) that the integrity of the Papal
States should be guaranteed.   This was refused in Paris;
and by that refusal may be measured the candour, sincerity,
and fair-dealing involved in the proposed demand made for
reforms.   With this, also, is combined another matter, made
known by Lord John Russell's declaration in Parliament, and
the knowledge of which will astonish no one—namely, "that

[1] "Malmesbury Correspondence," p. 155.

[2] Report of the Duke of Grammont, 14th April, 1860. "Allg. Ztg.,"
1861, p. 718.

the Courts of Vienna and Madrid had tendered a proposal in Paris, that the affairs of the Papal States should be made the subject of a united consultation and decision; but, in Paris, this proposal had been declined, under the pretence that, in the arrangements of the Vienna Peace, with respect to the Papal States, England, Prussia, and Sweden had been participators "[1]—an expression that sounds very like a mockery, considering all the circumstances that have occurred of late years; and what things have been contrived between Paris and Turin, in which, most assuredly, the opinion of Prussia or of Sweden was never asked for. And then, almost at the very time that those events became known, the Pope was compelled to have solicitations made at Paris, "that France should not hasten the withdrawal of the troops in occupation of Rome."[2] In regarding a situation so very lamentable as this, one feels sorely tempted to wish that a crisis might come—even though it be in the form of a catastrophe—but still one that might, at least, put a stop to the continuation of such ceaseless sorrows, combined with such deep humiliations.

From the facts of the immediate past can probabilities as to fast-coming events be clearly surmised. The Romagna, which, in 1846, desired to be annexed to Tuscany, wished, in 1859, upon the withdrawal of the Austrian gar-

---

[1] "Weekly Register;" London, June 22, 1861. [The precise words used by Lord John Russell are thus reported in "Hansard": "I have received a communication from the French Ambassador in London, informing me that a proposal has been made to the French Government by the Austrian and Spanish Ambassadors in Paris, in general terms, that the Roman Catholic Powers should act in concert with regard to the temporal power of the Pope. There was no mention of armies, or of protecting by arms the temporalities of the Pope. It was a general proposal, and to that proposal an absolute negative was given by the Government of France. I may, perhaps, state that the ground on which the proposition was refused was, that the general arrangements with regard to the temporalities of the Pope were settled at Vienna by Great Britain, Prussia, and Sweden, as well as by the Roman Catholic powers."—Hansard's "Parliamentary Debates" (third series), vol. clxiii., pp. 1327, 1328. June 20, 1861.]

[2] "Allg. Ztg.," 1861, 25th June, p. 2872.

rison, to become Piedmontese; and 121 Deputies—one half
of them consisting of nobles—voted unanimously for annexation to Piedmont. The French Emperor, too, wrote to the
Pope :[1] "That the Legations could now only be retained in
obedience to the Papal See by means of a prolonged military
occupation; and that this could give rise only to a continual
state of rancour, discontent, and fear. The Pope, therefore,
would, for the sake of the peace of Europe, make a sacrifice
in the loss of those Provinces." The same motive can be
made equally available, whenever the moment may come,
when the Pope will be required to renounce his sovereignty
over the remainder of his territories. "There is," said
Napoleon III., in another letter to the Pope, "an inexorable
logic in facts."

Shortly afterwards appeared in Paris the well-known
pamphlet, "The Pope and the Congress," of which it was
said by Lord John Russell, "that it had stripped the Pope
of more than the half of his dominions." It proposed "to leave
to the Head of the Church the city of Rome and a garden."
At the same time, however, Cavour said in his Parliament,
at Turin, that *this* was the demand of Italy—viz. : "Rome
is precisely the very thing that we want; and Rome we
must have, as the capital of our kingdom."

The conduct pursued was utterly unprecedented. The
Pope was required to disarm his own troops, at the very
moment that his territories were overrun with foreigners, and
his subjects called upon by them to take up arms. Without any
Declaration of War against him, his dominions were invaded,
an Ultimatum was presented to him, his little band of soldiers
was overwhelmed with an army ten times their own in number;
and at the same time furious proclamations were issued, threatening with death and extermination "the Papal hordes"—
and then! Cavour declared (11th October, 1860), in Parliament, "that all these memorable circumstances are
the necessary results of *our* policy for the last twelve
years!!!"

What are to be the guarantees for this (Sardinian) Go-

[1] The letter is published in the "Moniteur," 11th January, 1860.

vernment? Would it not itself deride the credulity of those
who placed faith in its promises? It will remain consistent
with its character. It unites the shameless tyranny of a
Convention, and the impudent sophistry of a Government
of advocates, with the ruthless brutality of a military despotism.
Far more secure could Pius feel upon the Turkish soil, and
in his dealings with the Sultan, than in the neighbourhood
of the Piedmontese beast of prey, or in the power of a
Ricasoli, or a Ratazzi, or, above all, of those lawyers and
literati, those land-plagues that, with trumpery, pompous
rhetoric, and hollow-sounding phrases, are now—and mayhap
for some little time longer—may be permitted to swim upon
the surface of society. (Rather than trust to these) Pius
may imitate the example of the great Popes of the twelfth
century. They, confiding in the spiritual power of the
Papacy, have sought for and found, on the other side of the
Alps, that freedom and independence which were denied to
them in Italy. Germany, Belgium, Spain, the Ionian Islands,
Catholic Switzerland—he can select any one of these he
chooses, certain that his arrival will be greeted by a joyful
and reverential population, in the midst of whom he will find
full freedom of action.

If Piedmont, with the connivance of France, should
wrest from the Papacy Rome, and the remainder of the
Papal States, then will the rightful possession of them by
the Pope be interrupted, but not abolished. The Papacy has
seen many monarchies created, and then dissolved into atoms.
The See of St. Peter will outlive the Kingdom of Italy, and
many other sovereignties. It can, with patience, wait:
patiens quia aeternus. "The strength of the Papacy," writes
Lord Cowley, the British Ambassador at Rome, on the 19th
January, 1859, "lies in his weakness, and we may well ask
—what can you do with a man who, the moment that pressure is put upon him, exclaims, 'Do with me what you will
—drive me from Rome; but, remember, I am as much the
Pope, whether seated on a barren rock, or on the throne of
St. Peter?'"[1]

---

[1] "Official Correspondence on the Italian question, by the Earl of
Malmesbury." London, 1859, p. 22.

Let this fact also be borne in mind, that Rome (as it has been already remarked by the Marquis Gino Capponi,) stands much more in need of the Pope, than the Pope does of Rome; and that, with a continuous absence of the Pope from Rome, the decay of that city inevitably begins. "In Rome," says Cernuschi, one of the Roman Revolutionists of 1849, but whose opinions have changed since then—"in Rome, above the Catacombs, in the midst of the Basilicas, and by the side of the Vatican, there is no room, space, nor place for a democratic tribune, much less for a king." Rome may yet have to learn, whether it is for its greater advantage to be the domicile of Victor Emmanuel, the titular capital of a kingdom in which the centrifugal tendency is much stronger than the centripetal; and whether the preference so given to it is a compensation for the rank and importance it had previously enjoyed as the metropolis of all Catholic Christendom—as the first religious city of the entire world. We shall see what was seen in the fourteenth century. Roman envoys will seek out the Pope, and earnestly entreat him to return to "his faithful city."

There is one fact to which persons cannot now close their eyes, and that is, that the Pope and the whole "curia" are at this moment dependent upon the French Government. The mere threat to withdraw the French garrison, and to yield up to their fate the Pope, and the remnant of the Papal States still left to him, must force Rome to yield to the threatener everything that it would not be a sin to concede. And the demand might fairly be submitted to, when with it would be involved the duty of self-preservation. But such a state of circumstances, it is plain, must be in the highest degree alarming for other nations. But for the absolute confidence which every one has in the exalted conscientiousness and pure truthfulness of the present Pope, and the lucky circumstance that there is now no ecclesiastical complication which the Parisian Court could use for its own selfish ends—only that these things are perfectly plain, the existing relations between France and Rome could not be patiently endured by the Catholic world. But then these

relations may suddenly change, and as, sooner or later, they
are sure to change, so can no one seriously desire their much
longer continuance.   No Catholic could or would find such
relations to be tolerable, if they became permanent.   The
French garrison is not in Rome, having for its main object
the defence of the city against an attack on the part of
Piedmont—a word of command sent by the telegraph from
Paris to Rome would be of sufficient potency to effect that
purpose.   The French are in Rome to protect the Pope
against his own subjects, and the Garibaldian free corps.

Already has the French Government, in principle, abandoned
the maintenance of the dismembered Papal States.   It had
declared itself in favour of a Confederation, as the best form of
political existence for the peninsula; and in so doing, had given
a guarantee for the preservation of the temporal sovereignty of
the Pope.   But on the 25th of June, 1861, France recognised the new kingdom of Italy; and a few days afterwards,
the Piedmontese Government publicly announced: "That
persons should not let themselves be deceived by appearances—
that Piedmont would, *at the fitting time*, and with the assent
of France, make its entrance into Rome, constitute Rome to
be the residence of the King, and incorporate the remnant
of the Papal States with the new kingdom."

For the present, it is the interest of the French Government to see the Pope so weak that he cannot dispense with
the support of France, and that whatever may be desired
from him should be rendered impossible of refusal, by the
threat that the Pope would be left as a defenceless prey to
his Italian enemies.   If the withdrawal of the French
garrison were to have the effect of removing the Pope and
Court into France, then would the French sooner give up
to-day than to-morrow the city of Rome, and all that remain
of the Papal States, to the Piedmontese.   That the Pope
should become a dependent upon Piedmont, is one of those
plans which does not lie within the contemplated policy of
the Emperor.   But if the transference of the Court of Rome
to France could be effected, thus would the greatest triumph
of Cæsarism be accomplished.   The nephew, the heir and

executor of the ideas and plans of "the uncle," would then, by "pacific" means, and the avoidance of direct force, attain what the first Napoleon was never once able, even with the stress of imprisonment, to extort.

There is now in Europe no Power which either will or can afford to the Pope effective aid in the preservation of the territories that are still left to him.

Three mighty races, three great complex nationalities, are now struggling for dominion over the world; and all three are seized with the fearful travail—throes of new formations. These are the Roman world, under a French ἡγεμών, as leader—the Sclavonic, with a Russian primacy—and the Germanic, with England's preponderance. In the last of these the Protestant interest is, through England and Prussia, the most predominant. The consequence is, that England shows itself to be hostile to the continuance of the Papal States, and for the last two years has taken an active part aiding in their destruction; whilst in Prussia the majority are moved towards the same view from a double interest—first there is the religious notion, to which the weakness and depression of the Roman See is agreeable; and then there is the political feeling, that regards with complacency the principle of annexation effected by a vote of the plebiscity, and which it is considered desirable to have imported into Germany. At such cost are persons quite prepared to sacrifice the common interest of all sovereigns, and contentedly to look on until the overthrow of the principle of legitimacy and of all public law in Europe is completed. The Sclavonic world stands partly under the influence of Russia, but partly also distinct from it, and contemplates every question with a view to see how it may affect the great interests of nationality—and so doing, shows itself disposed to sympathise with Italian nationality against an isolated Church sovereignty over a distinct state. As to Catholic Germany, it is, by reason of the weakness of Austria, completely destitute of any political centre, and of all influence beyond the borders of Germany—it is upon this question powerless, and must confine itself to addresses, and innocuous announcements of the notions that it entertains.

France, in the year 1849, as a Republic, restored by force of arms the Pope who had been despoiled and driven away by the Revolution. At that time a great majority of the French nation was favourable to the cause of the Pope. His liberal government affording a willing hand to every just demand of his subjects, and his exertions to introduce re- forms, had won for him the applause of all Europe, and made him the most popular of princes. But when he was rein- stated by French arms, and that event was followed by a complete re-establishment of an ecclesiastical adminis- tration, and when the Statuto, and, with it, self-government and popular representation, were abolished, and a con- dition of circumstances was renewed which it was supposed had been for ever got rid of, then it was that the feelings of the French with respect to the Papal Government were changed. The daily journals—those newspapers that are the most read—have now had for ten years time opportunity and unrestrained freedom to depict in the darkest colours the condition of the Papal States, and to portray the clerical government as an irremediable mass of corruption. The great amount of good that has been effected, or is in process of accomplishment, they have never mentioned; they have carefully suppressed all notice of it, or they have misrepresented it, whilst they have, at the same time, given an exaggerated description of every abuse. And so it has come to pass that episcopal pastorals and the most eloquent writings of the first men in France have in these latter years been able to produce no favourable influence upon national feeling in support of the maintenance of the Papal States; and, consequently, if the Emperor were to withdraw his troops, there would be apparent no very strong movement in France, and none at all of a character threatening danger to its Government.[1]

---

[1] A correspondent of the "N. Preussischen Zeitung" (26th Sept., 1861), who has shown himself to be generally well informed, says: "The *Catholic* population (of France) are absolutely incapable of understand- ing how it can be necessary for the Head of the Church to be also a Sovereign; and the French episcopacy have contributed to the adoption of

The feelings of the people in those portions of his territory still remaining in possession of the Pope are in favour of their being incorporated with the new Italian kingdom.[1] In consequence of directions received from Turin, all there remains tranquil; but when the two governments of Paris and Turin have made up their minds, and they consider that the time for action has arrived, then we may be sure there will be an insurrection of the inhabitants and a *plebiscite* to give to the attack of the Piedmontese the appearance of being nothing more than a compliance with, and a fulfilment of, the popular will.

And so, then, we at last come to this, that it is the Italian nation—the nation to which also the Pope, as well as the "Prelati" of the Curia belong—that has to decide upon the fate of the Papacy; and this it is which is truly tragic in the present situation of affairs—that here Italians stand opposed to Italians. And herewith is the Papacy in a far different position than it was in former times; for now the active majority of the nation seems determined on no longer enduring a Papal Government in the midst of the Peninsula. It is, they say, with its past antecedents, become a strange and antipathetical institution to the rest of Italy; and it is, in its dependence upon foreign protection, and guarded, in consequence of its own cravings, by foreign arms, a horrifying excrescence, a breath-smothering wen, and an ever-threatening danger to the body politic of Italy.

such a notion, because they have—whether forced to do so or not, is an historical question we do not here enter into—shown themselves to be well content with a government allowance—that which was given to the Church by the State for the loss of the property of which it was despoiled—such property being, in fact, *their* temporal power. Add to this feeling the overwhelming influence of the anti-religious newspapers, and it is impossible not to entertain the conviction that the temporal power of the Pope has nothing favourable to expect from the verdict of public opinion in France. It is the Emperor alone who can give, by a favourable vote, a fitting solution to the difficulty."

[1] "Allg. Zeitung," 26th May, 1861. See also "Neue Preuss. Ztg.," 8th August, 1861. "The whole population of that district (Subiaco) is pervaded but by one thought, and that is to see themselves included amongst the Piedmontese."

When the Popes were, in former times, either threatened or attacked, the Italians either stood by their side or remained passive. But now almost the whole Italian literature preaches the same opinion, and the whole of the periodical press—with the exception of the "Armonia" in Turin and the "Civiltà" in Rome—inculcate the pet doctrine of the day; viz., that the Pope must, for the sake of the welfare of Italy, be stripped of his temporal sovereignty; and this, it is said, must be done under the pretence either that the greatness and unity of Italy require such a sacrifice, or that the defects of the Papal Government are held to be irremediable. A powerful Italy is wished for, because the example of a single united powerful France has worked upon the minds of the higher classes in Italy, who have for a long time been imbued with French literature. To obtain this commanding position, it is affirmed that Italy can alone reach it by absorbing those States which are in their nature neutral, and by means of which the country is separated into two distinct halves.[1] Besides this, it is added, as a point about which there can be no dispute, that there is an utter impossibility a Roman priest-government can ever reform itself, or adapt itself to the wants, ideas, and wishes of modern times. Such are the notions that Cavour has spread abroad. When, in the spring of the present year, Mr. Pope Hennessey spoke in the British Parliament in favour of the rights of the Papacy, Mr. Layard called upon him to name a single man of any intellectual importance in Italy, who, on the question of the Papal States, was on the side of the Papal Government; and Mr. Hennessey could only name one, and that one was—the Jesuit—Secchi. In point of fact, two individuals conspicuous for their talents amongst the clergy have very openly declared as their opinion—that the Papal States, at least in their present condition, must either cease altogether or be completely altered. The two men who have given this opinion are Passaglia and Tosti.[2]

[1] See the memorial of Count Rayneval, in "Allg. Ztg.," 1857, 15th April.

[2] The letter of the latter, dated from Montecassino, 15th June, is

And yet the time will assuredly come when the Italian
nation will be again reconciled with the Papacy and its
dominion in the midst of the people.   That unhappy, hateful
pressure which Austria imposed upon the entire Peninsula,
was in reality the main cause why the value of the Papal
See as a moral bulwark to all Italy became so very much
obscured in the eyes of the nation.   The Roman Government itself groaned under this pressure, and yet was forced
to strengthen and confirm it, by calling in the Austrian
troops of occupation, and by the political helplessness that
forced it to follow, in temporal and political affairs, the will
of the Cabinet of Vienna.[1]

For fifteen hundred years the Papal See was the pivot upon
which turned the destiny of the Italians.   The greatest and
the mightiest institution of the Peninsula is this See ; and
upon its possession rested the weight of Europe, and the
world-renowned importance of Italy.   Every thoughtful
Italian must acknowledge that, if the Papal See be lost
to Italy, then the sun has disappeared from its firmament.
The partition between the nation and the whole course of
Italian history on the one side, and of the Papacy on the
other, could alone be put an end to, when Italy should
become that which might make her united—that is, her conversion into a purely military state, living in a constant state
of war, and maintaining herself by conquests.   This, however, is a state of circumstances so totally repugnant to the
nature and disposition of the present race of Italians, that

printed in the "Edinburgh Review," July, 1861, p. 277. In that letter
he prays of the Pope to cast away the burden of the Papal States,
"Perchè oggi i popoli non si lasciano più portare addosso, come una
volta, ma vogliono andare co' piedi loro," &c. Tosti's treatise, "S.
Benedetto al Parlamento nazionale" (Naples, 1861), in which a request is
made for leaving Montecassino untouched, takes its stand upon the propriety of having a united Italian kingdom, and by implication abandons
the maintenance of the Neapolitan Kingdom, as well as of the Papal
States.

[1] "Che è egli (the Pope) in realtà se non un suddito dell' Austria ?"
said Torrelli, in the year 1846, in his "Pensieri sull' Italia," p. 83.
That was, until 1859, the opinion generally entertained in Italy.

the military enthusiasm that now prevails, and yet has left the greater portion of the population unmoved, is certain in a very short space of time totally to subside.

A remarkable expression of Sismondi's is well worthy of notice, viz., that the contumely with which Alexander VI., during his government, had covered the Church of Rome, annihilated that religious respect which had previously protected all Italy, and so rendered it an easier spoil for hostile attempts to be made against it. Thus it was since Leo I. —for fourteen hundred years—every enfeeblement and depression of the Papacy was at the same time a downfall for Italy. In the grandeur and the majesty of the See of St. Peter, the Italians participated. And when Italians turned their arms against this See, and when, with the spoliation of this See, they enriched themselves, and when they hoped with the princely robes they had torn from the Pontiff to cover their nakedness, then were they ultimately compelled to feel that they had been guilty of " *felo de se*," had laid suicidal hands on their own body, and vented their blind rage on its noblest organ. This is a fact which has been recognized by all persons, in modern times, thoroughly well acquainted with Italian history. Balbo, Troya, Cantù, Galeotti, Gino Capponi have not spoken otherwise respecting it. And even Ferrari would admit it, but that he is restrained by his cheerless, unchristian fatalism.

But the predominant party now in Italy is not only for an incorporation of the whole of the Papal States in the new United Kingdom, but they would also make use of the spiritual power of the Papacy for their political objects—for objects which are still incalculable. They would have the Pope, not a world-Pope, but a Pope for the Italians, to do their will, and to prop up their kingdom; and much, indeed, would they be amazed and embarrassed to find the Pope making preparations to pass beyond the Alps. There might be an attempt to create a schism—an essay at establishing an anti-Pope—but such, in sooth, would be but a harmless experiment; and its only end would be "reading a lesson" to the Italians, that an institution like the Papacy can never be made use of for selfish purposes, and that those who so seek to pervert it will, at last, only bring down upon themselves both loss and shame.

For centuries long, in Italy, the people hoped in the fulfilment of a prophecy respecting "an Angelic Pope" (Papa Angelico), who was yet to come, and to bring order out of disorder, peace out of disunion, piety out of irreligion, and who also was to be the renovator and the benefactor of Italy.[1] That which is a Barbarossa sleeping in a cavern under a mountain, for the Germans, is the "Papa Angelico" for Italians. In the saga is expressed the feeling, that the destiny of Italy is determined by the Papacy, that both have become united together, and that it is the mission of the Papal See to be the guardian genius of the nation, to abide with it, and to watch over it.

Although the understanding of Italians may be, for one moment, darkened, yet it will again be able clearly to discern that the Papacy is an exalted deposit and pledge, entrusted to them by God, and that, as a nation, they will be held responsible for the use or misuse that they make of it. The greatest men amongst the Italians in modern times have avowed that a monarchical unity was antagonistic both to the character and the past history of the population, and did violence to the Italian municipal spirit. Balbo, Gioberti, Rosmini, Galeotti, were all in favour of a Confederation, as being most in accordance with the Italian tradition and the popular sentiment, and therefore they regarded a united Italian kingdom as an impossibility. And even now there are many deep-thinking Italians who see in this attempt at creating a United-Kingdom edifice, nothing more than an effort to put the roof on a building which has

---

[1] In CAMBI ("Storie Fiorentine," iii. 60), it is said that in the year 1514 a monk, Theodore, had cajoled the people with the assurance, "avergli un angelo rivelato, come egli sarebbe quel Papa Angelico, che i popoli italiani aspettavano." Savonarola was also accused that his ambitious intention had been "farsi Papa Angelico." See "Scritti vari del P. VINC. MARCHESE." Florence, 1855, p. 294.

neither side walls nor a solid foundation.[1] The road to what
is possible will yet be discovered, out of the by-path of that
which, by experience, is found to be impossible. The party
which struggles for unity and centralization, after the
French pattern, has now the upper hand; but it will not
be able to retain it, and the adherents of a federative unity
will be then its successors in power and influence.[2] Not many
weeks since, one of the early leaders of the Italian Revolution, Cernuschi, demonstrated the impracticability of a
United Italy, and prophesied a speedy dissolution to the new
kingdom.[3] A Confederation of Italian States, with the Pope
as Moderator at their head: such was the hope of Pius IX.,
and the object for which he struggled.[4] And the establishment of such is still attainable, and presents itself as a plan
the most suitable for the popular genius; and as such it will
be regarded when the existing Piedmontese annexation
unity has fallen into fragments, when the Italians are
wearied of Piedmontese officials, and when their shoulders
have been galled and bruised from the heavy yoke of a Piedmontese administration. Men cannot, when they please,
improvise united nationalities. To form a united nation,
there must be the still, silent process of spontaneity; and to
complete it, the slow, gradual working of centuries. Piedmont has neither the vocation nor the capability, in any one
respect, to effect a fusion of the scattered parts of Italy,
differing from each other in manners, tastes, and customs.
Neither will the other parts of Italy ever really become
Piedmontese, nor will Piedmont become Italian. Beyond
the military spirit which certainly is to be found in Piedmont, though wanting in the remainder of Italy, the population of Piedmont possesses none of those peculiar gifts, as

[1] See the remarks of the Marquess Bourbon del Monte in " Correspondant," 1859, xii. 472.

[2] A proper distinction is there made between the two parties by MON-
TANELLI, " Memorie," i. 33.

[3] " Neue Preuss. Ztg.," 16th July, 1861. " Ami de la religion," 18th
July.

[4] " Un Papato moderatore della lega degli Stati Italiani."—FARINI,
ii. 69.

a distinct race, which fit it for the intellectual or political leadership of a whole united Italian nationality.

What the Government in Turin can offer to the Pope; what it formerly, under Cavour and through Passaglia, has offered; and what it, under Ricasoli, does offer, or thinks of again offering, is a subject with respect to which there is no mystery.[1] The matter is one partly affecting the position of the Pope, and partly the freedom of the Church in Italy. With reference to the latter, Cavour, on the 26th March, 1861, made the declaration in Parliament, "That Italy will emancipate the Church from the State, and secure its liberty on the amplest foundations." With respect to the Pope and Court of Rome, it was announced, "That there was every readiness to concede to the Pope and the Cardinals, as Princes and Privy-Councillors of the Church, all the privileges of a sovereign's immunities both for his own person and the members of the Sacred College." It was added "that an establishment of a free fixed landed property—an endowment from the State—would not be refused;" for it was perceived, even in Turin, that the Pope could not well be placed in the position of a government-pensioner. And yet, with these two conditions united together—sovereignty and an independent landed property—there would be nothing more effected than the new commencement of another Papal state! But now Piedmont is prepared to rob the Pope of that which is his own, in order that he may be endowed with the property of strangers—and when that has been done, there is something more to be thought of: namely, what reliable securities can the Turin politicians or the future Roman Government tender to the Pope and the whole Catholic world? Who is there to guarantee the faithful performance of what they promise? Or who is there to go bail for the guarantees? Who is to be guarantee for the guarantors?

Is a Government that prides itself in its perfidy, and respects neither the rights of nations, nor the faith of treaties, nor the legitimate possession of property—that has no regard

[1] See as to this matter the "Edinburgh Review," 1861, July, pp. 260-9.

GG

but for brute force, and the power of the stronger, and the authority of accomplished facts; is a Government that, in one of its decrees, declared the memory of a murderer to be holy and sanctified; is a Government that is restrained neither by the bonds of law, morality, nor religion, to be the Government that is to secure to the Church its freedom, and to the Pope his inviolability and independence? Let the question be asked in Turin of the Brofferios and the Gallengas, who regard the Church as a useless log, from which anyone can, like the Horatian carpenter, chop out, as he fancies, either a stool or an idol,[1] and they will tell you what would be the lot assigned to it. Their "freedom of the Church" would begin by "freeing" it from the burden of its earthly possessions. And when they had done that, then they might deal with the Mendicant as their whims, their caprice, or their innate despotism might dispose them to act. Their doings with religious communities, their oppression and spoliation of monasteries and convents, their banishment and maltreatment of bishops, are now before the world, as the superabounding first-fruits of the new era of "religious freedom" inaugurated by them.

That the Papal See could be, in a kingdom like the Piedmontese, really free, is an absolute impossibility. Even if the present and future statesmen of that kingdom had the sincere intention not to violate the freedom of the Papal See, still circumstances would overmaster them. The daily press would be untiring in its mischievous meddling and incitements—it would to-day be describing the Pope and all about him as secret conspirators, and then to-morrow denouncing them as popular demagogues; and so there would be put in force, and in a very short space of time, too, the whole apparatus of the police, with political measures of restraint and coercion. As opposed to the powers and influences that now prevail in Piedmont, and will for a time reign over it, every compact and assurance would be but as a

---

[1] [" Olim truncus eram ficulnus, inutile lignum;
  Cum faber, incertus scamnum faceret—ne Priapum,
  Maluit esse deum."—" Hor.," lib. i., serm. 8.]

drag-chain made of paper to restrain the downward career of a fast-running carriage. Upstart advocates and journalists would, upon the very first opportunity, sweep down, with the besom of brutal violence, the whole cobweb of solemn stipulations. Italian Barères would surpass their predecessors, in the Paris Convention, in the utterance of sonorous phrases, in palliation of every infringement of right that might be practised, and every deed of violence that might be perpetrated. Then, too, they would be acting upon the apothegm: "Il faut aviler et puis détruire." And as "the monarchy" was treated in France, so the posthumous posterity of the Convention in Italy are already preparing to follow out a similar series of events, and to complete them all with a final, fatal verdict against "the Papacy." According to statements made in the public journals, "There are at this time in Rome nine of the Cardinals disposed to enter into terms with Piedmont." This is scarcely credible. They must be indeed blindfolded, if they could think of so acting; or do they imagine that the time has, even now, come when the Mazzini Wolf will lie down meekly, gently, and tenderly by the side of the Church Lamb?

Should the hour arrive when the Pope has to make his choice between the condition of being "a subject" or "an exile," then will he, as we confidently hope, adopt the better alternative; for the Pope is—in the whole Catholic world—at home.[1] It is only amongst the professors of another creed he would be a stranger. To whatever side he then may turn, he will everywhere meet with his children, and everywhere will be venerated as a father. "Thou art mine, and we are thine"—such is the salutation with which he will be in all places greeted.

Rome, too, may then remember with what shouts of joy in the time of the seventh Pius the appearance of the Pope, released from his French prison, and returning to his native land, was hailed in Italy. The circumstance, too, of the

---

[1] Petrarch, in his letter to Pope Urban V. in the year 1366, says, " Ubicunque ille (Pontifex) sibi moram eligit, illic sponsa, illic sedes propria sua est."—Ap. RAYNALD, ad. a. 1366, § 22.

Pope's absence would have this beneficial result—that it would make, in a tangible manner, clear to the religious portion of the nation certain facts, and they might thus then say: "It is our Unity-advocates who have imposed upon us the triple yoke of a Conscription, Exorbitant Taxes, and Foreign Government-Officers—and now, in addition to all these, they have driven away from us the Pope, and forced him to become an exile on the other side of the Alps." There would, it must be admitted, in such a temporary separation of husband and wife, in the departure of the Pope from Rome, be many inconveniences experienced. It could not occur without great and manifold disturbance and interruptions to the ecclesiastical department, to the members of the Court, to the many and numerous religious congregations which would have to be transported *en masse* to a foreign land. In former times, the machinery of the Government of the Church was much more simple; and when the Pope (as it often happened) had to take up his abode in another city than Rome, or to travel across the Alps, the whole members of the Court that followed him could find sufficient room in a single French abbey. It is now far otherwise. There are, too, some Powers that may suppose it will be easier for them to gain what they desire from a Court suffering from oppression, and forced away from its native soil. Thus it will be seen that, if there is a necessity for quitting Rome, it will not fail to be accompanied by difficulties and painful circumstances. But, then, that which is the less of two evils must be chosen; and there can be no doubt that the temporary embarrassment of the Papal See is a far less evil in comparison with that which would involve the renunciation of a principle, that, once abandoned, would prove to be lost irretrievably.

The removal of the Papal See to France would, under existing circumstances, be regarded as tantamount to the formal challenge to a schism; or it would, at the least, afford a welcome pretext to all who wish to curtail the Papal rights, or to interrupt the communication between the Pope and the several Churches; and it would put arms into the hands of governments that wish to impede the action of the Papal authority upon the churches and populations in their respective states.

And, then, what humiliations await both Pope and Cardinals, and what a yoke would be imposed upon them, if they were once but to be on French soil, and within the power of those individuals on the banks of the Seine who are already boasting that they can count upon a number of votes at the next Conclave! When Spain had become acquainted with the designs of Piedmont upon Umbria and the Marches, she was prepared to send an army into Middle Italy, for the defence of the Papal territory, and invited the French Government to strengthen its garrison in Rome, for the same purpose. To that invitation, a reply in the negative was given, "because England did not wish it." And it has come to this—the French people, who, in the year 1849, had purchased, with the blood of their warriors, the restoration of the Pope, are now, twelve years later, compelled to abandon the Pope, because—England so wills it!

If the Court of Rome should reside for a time in Germany, the Roman "*Prelati*" will, doubtless, be agreeably surprised to discover that our people are able to remain Catholic and religious without the leading-strings of a police; and that their religious sentiments are a better protection to the Church than Episcopal prisons, which, thank God! do not exist. They will learn that the Church in Germany is able to maintain herself without the Holy Office; that our Bishops, although, or because, they use no physical compulsion, are reverenced, as if they were princes, by the people; that they are received with triumphal arches, and that their arrival in a place is a festival for the inhabitants. They will see how the Church with us rests on the broad, strong, and healthy basis of a well-organised system of pastoral administration, and of popular religious instruction. They will perceive that we Catholics have maintained for years, straightforwardly, and without reservation, a struggle for the deliverance of the Church from the bonds of bureaucracy; that we cannot en-

tertain the idea of denying to Italians what we have
claimed for ourselves; and that, therefore, we are far from
thinking that it is anywhere an advantage to fortify the
Church with the authority of the police, and with the power
of the secular arm. Throughout Germany we have been
taught by experience the truth of Fénélon's saying, "That
the spiritual power must be kept carefully separate from the
civil, because their union is pernicious." They will find,
further, that the whole of the German clergy is prepared to
bless the day, when it shall learn that the free sovereignty
of the Pope is assured—without sentence of death being still
pronounced by ecclesiastics; without priests continuing to
discharge the functions of treasury-clerks, or police-direc-
tors, or to conduct the business of the lottery ; and, finally,
the Prelati will convince themselves that all the Catholics
of Germany will stand up, as one man, for the independence
of the Holy See, and the legitimate rights of the Pope ; but
that they are no admirers of a form of government of very
recent date, which is, in fact, nothing else than the product
of the mechanical polity of Napoleon combined with a clerical
administration. And this information will bear good fruit,
when the hour shall strike for their return home, and when
restitution has been made. Another thing will also occur—
whether the Italian Kingdom can establish itself, or—what is
certainly far more probable—fall again into pieces. The time
will come when the people of Italy will desire to make peace
with the Papacy; and then they will recognize how truly
had one of their most exalted men of genius—Tommaseo—
spoken, when he uttered these words : "It would be a folly
in Italy to cast away from itself, to any other nation, the
Papacy, which is its sword and its shield."[1] And Tommaseo
also intimates that it might be well if the Papacy were
removed for a short time out of Italy; for so would the
present race of Italians best learn what a treasure to them
had been its possession.

Meanwhile, Pius and the men of his Council will " ponder
over the days of old, and the years of the past."[2] They will

---

[1] " Roma e il mondo," p. 349.   [2] Psalm lxxvi. 6.

read the future in the earlier history of the Papacy, which has already seen many an exile and many a restoration. The example of the resolute, courageous Popes of the Middle Ages will be as a guiding light to them. There is no question now as to suffering martyrdom, or of clinging to the tombs of the Apostles, or of descending into the cata-combs—but here is the matter to be thought of—to quit a land of slavery, in order to exclaim, upon a free soil : "The bonds are snapped asunder, and we are emancipated!" For the rest, God will provide ; and the unceasing gifts and pure sympathies of the Catholic world will provide. And the parties, too, in Italy, will provide for the consequences. When these parties have torn and exhausted the land of which they have made a battle-field ; and when the sobered and saddened people, tired of the rule of lawyers and of soldiers, have understood the worth of a moral and spiritual authority—then will the time have come to think of returning to the Eternal City. In the interval, the things will have disappeared for whose preservation such pains had been taken; and then there will be better reason than Consalvi had, in the preface to the "*Motu Proprio*," of the 6th July, 1816, to say: "Divine Providence, which so conducts human affairs, that, out of the greatest calamity, innumerable bene-fits proceed, seems to have intended that THE INTERRUPTION OF THE PAPAL GOVERNMENT *should prepare the way for* IT IN A MORE PERFECT FORM."

APPENDIX.

TWO LECTURES DELIVERED IN MUNICH,

5TH AND 6TH APRIL, 1861.

I.

WILL the Papal State maintain itself or vanish? Will the Head of the Church remain as sovereign prince, or is the time arrived when the temporal power of the Pope must be separated from the spiritual?

A large portion of territory is already torn from him, the remainder is threatened—the seizure even of his capital is prepared for. Should this take place, what will be the consequences to the Christian world? What is to become of the Papal See when the ground beneath its feet is taken away? And will it be possible to fulfil its high mission when it is, so to speak, suspended in the air, or placed in dependence on a foreign power intent on its own objects? These questions keep every man in breathless suspense. No human foresight, no power of imagination, is capable of measuring all the consequences, operative through ages to come, bound up inevitably in their decision.

Of the good right of the Pope, which rests upon the strongest and most legitimate titles of acquisition and possession, acknowledged by mankind, there can be no doubt. As little can exist of the faithless Macchiavellism, and the revolting injustice of the policy pursued towards the Roman See. On this point we all think alike. It may, however, be as well to mention a fact generally ignored, at least in Italy, that Pius is an electoral prince, that he has to administer a property only entrusted to him for life, and that he is bound by oath to preserve the States of the Church intact.

Unquestionably, the Papacy is older than the States of the Church; the Roman bishops have been from all time Chief Shepherds of the Church; but in latter ages only have they become Temporal Princes. The Roman See subsisted seven centuries without possessing in sovereignty a single village. And even after the large donations of the Frankish kings, and that the Emperor had laid the foundation for a State of the Church, centuries had still to pass away before the Pope came into quiet possession and actual administration of the land in its subsequent extent. In Rome itself the Popes' power was long disputed; they were frequently and for a long time compelled to leave their city, and to prefer having their residence in Viterbo, Anagni, Orvieto, or they were necessitated to pass the Alps and seek elsewhere an asylum— most frequently in France. In the fourteenth century there came no Pope to Italy for nearly seventy years. The Court (Curia) resided in Avignon. In fact, it was not till the time of Leo X., about 350 years ago, that the Popes held quiet possession of the State, with its three million of inhabitants.

It is also true that the electoral form, excellent for the Church, has, politically considered, serious disadvantages. The many and frequent changes of rulers, and, with them, systems of government—the formerly prevailing efforts of the elected to elevate and enrich their kindred—the want of a native-born dynasty, which should become, through the attachment of the people, at once a pledge and a bulwark of steadfastness and duration—all this shows that the form of an electoral monarchy, with many advantages, has also its dark side; and history teaches that electoral states, being exposed to stronger convulsions, are more easily subverted than hereditary principalities. In Rome, however, till very lately, this danger was warded off by the universally recognised inviolability of the Papacy, by the religious reverence that environed and protected the chair of the Apostolic princes.

The heroes of Church science have not however considered this union of the highest ecclesiastical power and dignity with a temporal kingdom as an advantage or a perfection, but rather as a something urgently commanded by the necessity of the times. "It would be better in itself," says Cardinal Bellarmine, "if the Popes concerned themselves only with spiritual affairs, the Kings with temporal; but, on account of the wickedness of the times, Divine Providence has seen fit to bestow temporal principalities on the Pope and other bishops. It has been with the Church as with the Jews, amongst whom the kingly dignity and the pontifical were first united in the time of the Maccabees. In the earlier ages the Church did not need princely authority for the support of her majesty—now it seems to be a necessity."[1]

This necessity indisputably exists in our time as strongly as ever. And yet there has arisen, even in the Catholic world, numerous voices—some even of theological importance—which speak of a time for the separation of these hitherto united powers—which announce that the time is come when the secularization of the Church State is both called for and unavoidable. The causes of this striking manifestation are to be sought for in the condition of Italy, the internal circumstances of the Papal States, the sentiments of the Italian peoples, and more particularly of the Pope's subjects.

The Papal Government has the reputation of being one of the mildest and most moderate in all Europe. And yet it is true, that for nearly forty years deep discontent and dissatisfaction have reigned in the States of the Church, but most

[1] "De Rom. Pontifice, Disputationes," vol. i., p. 1104. Ed. Ingolstadt, 1596.

strongly in the towns; and in a land where no independent yeomanry exists, it is the population of the towns in a yet higher degree than elsewhere that decides on everything. In these chief places of the nation secret political societies, conspiracies, and attempts at insurrection have grown rank and numerous; hundreds live compromised or banished—they pass their days as fugitives in foreign lands.

The weakness of the Papal Government increases from year to year. Pius IX. attempted in vain by concessions, and by granting a Constitution, to effect a reconciliation. He began his reign with a most complete amnesty, which recalled the accused and culpable of four insurrections. This measure brought back to the country the irreconcileable opponents of its Government, and placed them in a position to make war upon it.

The catastrophes that followed in quick succession are well known. As before, so since 1849, two foreign powers, Austria and France, have been obliged to garrison the country with their troops.

The Papal See, which in its ecclesiastical position and its spiritual rights found in the whole Catholic world the most complete recognition and the readiest obedience, more, perhaps, than had ever been the case in like degree in any former time; yet on its temporal, political side has presented the melancholy spectacle of the weakest, most helpless Government in all Europe; and one, too, only able to maintain itself by the double prop of foreign Powers and their bayonets.

And yet no government could labour more to remove notorious abuses of administration, to introduce improvements, to take into consideration the reasonable wishes of the people, so far as the interests and principles of self-maintenance or of the existing system of a government administered by ecclesiastics, were not brought in question. For twelve years the history of the present Pope's reign was one continuous chain of useful and beneficent reforms. But all these improvements were and are insufficient to remove the deep discontent and aversion of the people.

Every government which is not supported merely by the bayonets of its soldiers, must—even if there be a class of discontented—be able to depend upon the majority of the population, through their attachment to the dynasty, their conservative feelings, or, at least, through an interest in self-maintenance and fear of revolutions—and thus be in union with the nation.

All this is wanting in the States of the Church : there is no dynasty, all attempts to form a native army have failed utterly, the dislike to the Papal military service is universal, and foreign mercenaries only embitter it. Foreign diplomatists remark in their reports : "The impotence of the Papal Government is glaringly evident—it can rely on no one class of the population—in the moment of an attack upon it not one would raise a hand in its defence, and no one make a sacrifice for its support." Hence it comes that the temporal dominion of the Papal See has numerous enemies, not only among its own subjects, but throughout Italy. The public opinion of Italy is against it. It is looked upon as the great obstacle to the realisation of the Italian ideal—the development of one grand nationality, one powerful Italian State, which should take its place among the "Great Powers" of Europe. Count Rayneval says justly, "The displeasure and discontent of the population arise chiefly from this : that Italy does not play such a part in the world as she has dreamed of. In all times when this feeling of national ambition is awakened, the temporal power of the Pope will be looked upon by it as a hindrance."[1]

It is further not to be denied that for a hundred years a tendency to secularisation has passed through the whole of Europe. The union of spiritual dignities with temporal officialism has, henceforward, no sympathy to reckon on from the nations of Europe. Even the German spiritual principalities, in which, unlike the Papal States, the administration was chiefly in lay hands, have been destroyed, not merely by revolution, but by public opinion, which saw in them something foreign to the age; unnatural—a ruin of the past; and

[1] "Allg. Ztg.," 15th April, 1857.

since 1814 not a single voice has been raised for their restoration. In our time, therefore, a union of temporal
functions and action with the ecclesiastical is no longer an
element of strength, but of weakness. Nothing gives rise to
more bitter feelings than the application of secular governmental measures, or even of the power and chastisements of
the police to effect religious purposes, or the reverse, the
application of religious means to political objects.

This repugnance to the admixture of the spiritual and
temporal, or to the exercise of political power and police
office functions by ecclesiastics, is not the operation of weakened religious feeling, but the consequences of altered views
and a change in circumstances. The Spaniards present a
striking example of this. With the Spaniards there was
a kind of necessity for that which appeared elsewhere intolerable. They desired to listen to the Church even in
temporal matters; and if the State wanted taxes the intervention of the Church was requisite—an ecclesiastical form
must be given to the impost; and then only did the nation pay
it willingly. Thus the Spanish Inquisition was a kind of State
and Police institution, that was acceptable to the people only
under such a form. All this is now changed even in Spain.
And with us, in Germany, it would stir up the most vehe-
ment opposition if a prelate were to become minister, or a
bishop the president of an administration.

Formerly there was little governmental action in the territories of the Pope. The municipal form existed throughout,
and administered its own affairs; whilst the State contented
itself with the supreme direction without much interference
in details. It is now altogether different, in consequence of
the system established by means of the French Napoleonic
administration, to whose inheritance Cardinal Consalvi succeeded. Since then it has been an *ecclesiastical* government,
and such it is at present; and although in the year 1848
there were 5,059 lay employés to 109 ecclesiastics, still it
has been felt as an intolerable burden, and as such to be
shaken off; and—as it is generally considered—"the sooner
the better."

The judicial power, also, mostly exercised by ecclesiastics in the Papal States, has given occasion to manifold complaints. And it may be a subject of consideration whether in our times an ecclesiastic, by his condition, his mental cultivation, and his pastoral far more than forensic modes of thought, is adapted for a judge; and whether the temptation would not be too strong for him to give to a frequently milder, but, in the end, purely despotic procedure, the preference over an objective and severely legal judgment and decision.

Hence the condition of the Papal States, apart from all foreign intrigues, incitements, and acts of violence, has been for years lamentable and discouraging.

The Government, necessarily rendered distrustful by the aversion of a large portion of the population, thinks less freedom must be granted in the interests of its own self-preservation; and no assemblies for discussion can be permitted, because its enemies would speedily become masters of them. On all sides the Government must act obstructively, and for that very reason it loses more and more the support of public opinion; and hence the striking contrast between times past and the present! When, in 1809, Pius VII. answered the decree of deposition launched against him by Napoleon I., by excommunicating the French Emperor, the act awakened the enthusiasm of the people; all Romans who were in the French service threw up their employments; and, in short, the whole nation made its resolution plainly manifest, to rule itself exactly according to the Bull of Excommunication. Some years later, the return of Pius from his French imprisonment was a real triumphal procession throughout the whole land. How changed is all this now!

Cardinal Pacca relates that at the period of the Napoleonic dominion he had, after a year's meditation, reconciled himself to the thought that the extinction of the temporal sovereignty of the Papal See would be coupled with many and no small advantages for the Church—that the jealousy and dislike to the Roman See would be removed, or at least diminished. Pacca was of opinion that Europe was advancing towards a great universal monarchy, in which the Pope, without prejudice to his spiritual dignity, might again become a subject, as under the Roman Empire. In this, however, he greatly deceived himself. A universal monarchy in Europe is, happily, not to be thought of, and the Pope cannot become a subject; he cannot belong exclusively to any one kingdom—he must exercise his high office freely and independently, as the common father of all. As Cæsar said that Cæsar's wife must not be even suspected, so the merest suspicion of dependence would be fatal to the Papal See. The most unconditional, unreserved confidence is the breath of life to spiritual authority. If there were the appearance, the conjecture, that the Papal See, in matters spiritual, acted under the influence, or for the interest, of a political power, it would operate as a deadly poison on the Church. From this consideration a change in the position of the Papal See is becoming more and more an urgent necessity. So long as two foreign Powers, Austria and France, held garrisons in the Church States, it might seem that the Pope, between the two neutralising each other, enjoyed freedom. But when, in consequence of the late war, the Austrian occupation ceased, and the French must be looked upon as the only support of the Papacy, a condition of things has existed which is only bearable as being provisional and transitory. Placed as it now is, the possession of a Church State would be productive of results the very opposite to what it ought to produce, and whereby alone it can be justified. Instead of acting independently as the highest guide of the Church and assuring its freedom, it will sink continually in public opinion, as an institution which cannot dispense with the prop of foreign soldiers; and the Pope, like all who ask and need foreign help, must become a dependent on his Protector—or, what is nearly as bad, he will appear to be so, for that Protector can at any time disquiet or coerce him, by the threat of withdrawing his troops.

II.

In my first Lecture I spoke of the difficult position of the Ecclesiastical States, which has its foundation rather in false relations within, than in the hostile and rapacious advances of foreign powers, as the enemy has made, and continues to make, the discontent of the people the pretext for and fulcrum of their operations.

The thought here forces itself upon me, that the Church State had its beginning with the German Empire; and it may well be affirmed that the fall of that Empire inflicted a wound on the Roman State from which it is still bleeding. The Emperor was the armed "Protector" of the Papal See—on him lay the duty of wielding the sword, and when the Popes took this on themselves, it was either a mistake, or an act of the direst necessity. And although the Empire had long presented only the shadow of the old idea and purpose, yet was it to the last the prop and centre of the ancient political order of Europe, and covered with its majesty the Papal See, as a member engrafted upon the United Roman Empire. If with the Empire an outward stay has fallen, inwardly the State is sickening under the false relations in which "an ecclesiastical administration" necessarily stands to a modern system of statesmanship. It is difficult to reject the opinion that lay hands are better suited to direct the action of state and police, with their manifold increasing material wants and cares—they are better suited than those of priests for a police and administrative omnipotence, a care for lotteries, theatres, gaming-houses, and houses of public entertainment, for managing passports and manufactories. It is, indeed, frequently asserted that the Pope, as an ecclesiastical prince, *must* commit the administration to "ecclesiastical" officers. This necessity, however, is not very evident. At least, the ecclesiastical sovereignties of Germany, to which Bellarmine appealed in justification of the Pope's temporal dignity, afford no parallel. The prince-bishops and ecclesiastical electors never hesitated to govern their countries through the instrumentality of lay ministers, chancellors, councillors, employés and judges.

The government of Francis Louis, of Erthal, Prince-bishop of Würzburg and Bamberg, was a model government, one blessed throughout the land; I have in my youth—(my grandfather was in the Bishop's service)—heard old men speak of it with enthusiasm. It was, however, conducted by lay administrators.

Pius himself had acknowledged the want of thorough reformation in this respect—his lamented minister Rossi had presented a plan to the government which the Great Powers, in the Memorandum of 1831, had previously recommended. It is known how the dagger of a Mazzinist cut off, with this distinguished man, the many hopes bound up with him. And after his restoration, Pius thought himself obliged to make no concessions, which, as the English envoy, Mr. Lyons, said, "might be used as weapons in the hands of enemies to the government, to contend against it."

"What will all this end in?" That is the question every man proposes to himself—every man tries to answer, or would like to hear answered. In the complicated relations and unnatural tension under which Europe now labours, positive conclusions are naturally excluded; we can only speak of possibilities and probabilities.

The first *possibility* is, that a new war breaking out, a victory of the Austrian arms should restore Austrian preponderance and the Papal dominion over the whole extent of the States of the Church. Whether such a turn of affairs is hoped for by many, I do not know; but what I do know is, that it is not wished by any intelligent friend of the Papal See. A permanent occupation of the country by Austrian troops, which would then become necessary, would render the Pope's situation worse, and his temporal sovereignty more unmaintainable. New insurrections and political convulsions with Mazzini views would inevitably follow.

A second *possibility* is, the transplanting the Papal See to France. Such, it is well known, was the plan of the first

Napoleon, which was frustrated by the firmness of Pius VII.
The Emperor has left no doubt on this point; for, subsequently, at St. Helena, he spoke with complaisance of the
plan, and of the splendid results that would have been consequent on its realisation. That the nephew has entered on
the inheritance of the ideas and plans of his uncle is well
known. The carrying through of these projects, or the
fulfilment of these hopes, would certainly produce incalculable
mischiefs. A Gallicised Papacy would become a formidable
source of confusion and discord; and one of our best read
journals has openly expressed the expectation that a schism
in the Catholic Church would be the result.[1]

I confess that I entertain no fear for the one or the other—
not of a schism in the Church; it is now four hundred years
since even an attempt at a division has been made. Division and Catholicism are two things so diametrically opposed,
that nothing but some extraordinary complication, a dispute
on principles, on ideas, could again lead to such a result.
I am convinced that no materials, and no disposition to such
a malady exists, in the whole compass of the Catholic Church.
The universal feeling of the religious in all Catholic countries
would reject such an attempt with abhorrence, and the irreligious would at the utmost be able only to perform a second
act of the Ronge-May-festival night of 1846.

It will not, however, come to a repetition of the fourteenth century—we shall see no second Avignon with French
cardinals and a French Pope. The episcopacy, the clergy,
all the Catholic faithful of France, would protest against a
Papal Court wholly in the power of the Emperor; a will-
less instrument of his policy. The whole collective Catholic
states and people of the universe would cast their weighty
" No " into the scale against such a project.

Of the three parties into which the French may be divided
when such a question is in agitation, the devout minded, the
Radicals and the Bonapartists, only the latter, numerically
the weakest, would, provided their master so willed it, be
favourable to such a measure; the other two, i.e., the great

[1] " Allg. Ztg.," April 2, 1861.

majority of the nation, would be averse to, and strive against it. The Catholics, because they would see, in the attempt to make the Papacy an instrument of political interests, a degradation of it, to be warded off at any cost; the irreligious because they would on no account have the highest spiritual authority in close proximity to themselves, and in their own land; because they dread the mighty influence which it would exercise over the whole body of the clergy and the believing part of the nation.

Third Possibility.—That the French Emperor should bring the question of the temporal sovereignty of the Pope to the decision of a Congress of the Catholic Powers—evidently, in the present position of affairs, the justest, most rational, and the only method whereby the Emperor can turn aside the reproach made against him in the very heart of his own nation, viz., that he has humbled himself to be the instrument of English hatred to Rome, and thereby placed the French nation in a position as false politically as it is morally unworthy. These Powers would be, France, Austria, Spain, Portugal, Belgium, and, it is to be hoped, Bavaria. Piedmont has, indeed, openly declared that she no longer acknowledges any national rights; yet, in the present relation, as she alone is in a condition to represent Italy, she must be admitted. What such a Congress would resolve may be predicted with some probability.

The majority of voices would press for the maintenance of the remaining possessions of the Papal See, and for the restitution of at least some portion of what has been violently taken away. It will also desire, as the only means of satisfying the people, municipal self-government, participation of the laity in the government, representation for (the purposes) of finance and legislation—in short, they would demand the introduction of those institutions which now prevail throughout Europe, with the exception of Russia and Turkey, and which were substantially demanded by the Five Great Powers in the year 1831, and without which none can see how a reconciliation between the Government and the

HH 2

people, and permanent order, are to be maintained, otherwise than by permanent occupation by foreign troops.

Fourth Possibility.—That the Pope should be obliged to quit Rome, and take up his abode for a time in some other Catholic country. Rome, and the remainder of the States of the Church, would be, forthwith, incorporated with the new Piedmontese kingdom. It is self-evident that all those arrangements which the Papal Government thinks it cannot grant would be immediately introduced—the secularisation would be complete. The whole present order of things would be passed over as with a sponge; the clergy, as in all other parts of Europe, with the abolition of all privileges burdensome and offensive to other classes, would, like other citizens, be placed under the common law; and, herewith, the main source of the dislike of the people to the priesthood be put an end to. Then, when the germ of decay which the new Italian kingdom bears in its bosom develops itself, and the return of the Pope to Rome, and the resurrection of the whole State of the Church, or a part of it, takes place, the Pope will find "accomplished facts;" he will enter upon an entirely altered position; he will be the head of an administration entirely, or in great part, secular in its members, and whose precedent condition, or the forcing back into forms now dead, it would be as unwise as difficult, if not impossible, to accomplish.

Fifth Possibility.—That the States of the Church should be irreparably lost to the Papal See. Even this eventuality must be looked in the face. It is conceivable that it is already resolved on in the councils of Providence. The Church has truly the promise that the gates of Hell shall not prevail against her, but she has no promise that the successor of St. Peter should always remain monarch of a temporal kingdom. If Italy, or Europe, be destined to become the theatre of new revolutions, the position of the Head of the Church is indisputably better and more dignified if it be not welded to the ponderous, helpless burden of a secular kingdom, which he could neither maintain nor protect against ever-recurring insurrection, and against the thronging billows of revolution. Should, however, a permanent and well-ordered State establish itself in Italy, public opinion, or rather the public conscience of Catholic Europe, will be strong and powerful enough to create and make firm a position through which the freedom of the Papal See, and the sovereign dignity and inviolability of the Head of the Church, would be protected and secured.

In Germany a small, feeble State, surrounded by stronger neighbours, like Frankfort, can subsist free and independent. And shall, in Italy—well ordered, and recovered from the revolutionary fever—the Pope not be able to maintain his smaller or greater territory and capital intact? Will not Rome itself—this out-and-out papal and ecclesiastical Rome, which but for the chair of St. Peter and the tombs of the Apostles would long since have sunk to a little provincial city or market-town—prefer to be a world-city, the metropolis of a spiritual kingdom of two hundred millions, than the seat of a kingdom of twenty millions? The reconciliation of the people to the Papal dominion is here presupposed; for who can be blind to the fact that, since 1831, this dominion—over three millions of people—has been a source of weakness, dependence, anxiety, and care for the Papal See; that this task of keeping down a discontented population longing for the institutions of other countries has been as a leaden weight attached to the foot of the successor of the Apostles? And who will maintain that it is the Divine Will that this lamentable, unnatural state of things should drag on for an indefinite time—that the alternation of revolt, political trials, dungeoning, banishment, and foreign occupation should prolong itself indefinitely, as was contemplated by Count Rayneval?

We cannot conceal from ourselves that the situation is, in the highest degree, *tragical*. The Pope is bound, by the most sacred pledges, to surrender nothing of that which has been entrusted to his keeping; he must continually protest against the spoliation of his territory. The Papal Government can find few among the laity who have the necessary instruction for higher employments, and on whose fidelity he can rely.   As I said before, the Pope believes himself bound, by the duty of self-preservation, by the right of self-defence, to maintain the old system of ecclesiastical government, without serious change of form.   And yet, as things now are, it is not to be hoped for that the people will be ever frankly reconciled to this form of clerical administration, and will renounce the rights and institutions subsisting in other parts of Italy.   The difficulty of the position is heightened by the painful collisions in which the bishops, and, more or less, the whole body of the clergy throughout Italy are entangled.

Let us not, however, forget that history is, before all things, God's judgment; and that to this Judgment every human will and purpose must submit.   We can only say, *"Laissez passer la justice de Dieu."*   It is the beautiful privilege of God, that He, when men will to do evil, can turn that evil to good.   The position of the Pope between the two allied Powers, who are throwing the dice over him, reminds us of the Lear of Shakespeare between his daughters, Goneril and Regan, and where no Cordelia is to be found.   But Lear will not die; Goneril and Regan will reap what they have sown—the Church will say at last, " My loss is a gain."

Who will pronounce on the immediate future?   Do we know what is coming in Germany?   Are we in Central Europe not approaching some mighty convulsion?   Is not the Mazzini party lurking behind Piedmont to hurl Italy into the throes and tortures of a social and antichristian revolution?   Who can say how much in Italy and elsewhere will meet destruction?   One thing, however, is certain. Amidst all wrecks, one Institution will remain erect, will constantly emerge from the flood of revolution—for it is indestructible, immortal—it is the Chair of St. Peter.   If I am asked, whence I draw this assurance, I may point to the Bible as my answer — " Thou art the Rock," &c. But I will give another answer, derived from the very nature of the thing itself: The Papal See will not be destroyed, because it is reachable by no human power; because no one on earth is strong and powerful enough to destroy it.   If all the Powers of Europe were to unite for its destruction, they could not effect it. All that human power can do is to compel it to make a pilgrimage; and, for a longer or shorter time, to keep its seat away from Rome. And, lastly, this Chair will not be destroyed, because it is indispensable and irreplaceable, for it forms the keystone of the whole building of the Church. " *On ne détruit que ce qu'on remplace.*" That the Papacy can ever be replaced by anything else, no one will seriously maintain. It is the keystone that holds the whole edifice of the Church together, that makes the Church what it is, and what it ought to be: a world-Church —the only society that has in earnest fulfilled the given purpose of God—that is, to embrace all humanity, and find room for all nations.

Should this all-keeping, all-sustaining keystone be taken away, the whole will fall asunder, the Church will be split according to monarchies and nationalities; from the Christian religion will be rent that noble jewel bestowed by her founders; that privilege that stands alone in history—the privilege and the strength to unite all nations in one great whole, yet without injury to them as nations. The faithful throughout the world desire not to belong to a French or a Spanish, a Bavarian or an Austrian Church; they desire to belong to ONE church, THE Church, the only Catholic Church —in other words, all will be subject to the Pope, and will, in community with him, feel and acknowledge themselves as members of "the Catholic Church."

The Papacy, then, will continue, because God wills it, because every Catholic believes it, because two hundred millions of men in all parts of the world desire it, because everyone who knows the condition of the world acknowledges it. There are enemies—many enemies—of the Temporal Power of the Papacy; but, within the Catholic world, there lives no enemy of the Pope's Spiritual Power, or only such as are at the same time the enemies of the Christian religion. I am not afraid to maintain that, even outside the pale of the Catholic Church, in the Protestant world, so far as it is really Christian, reflecting believers, especially among the laity, do not object to the Papal power *in itself*. They ask themselves: "Is there not something beautiful, something good, something willed of God, that the different Christian nations and countries should be united in one Church—one world-embracing community of faith and love—that the common affairs of the entire be conducted by one hand;" and the answer from all is—"Yes." If it be further asked: "Shall this centre of church unity, this bearer of the highest authority of the Church, be a temporal monarch?" the answer will be—"No—that is impossible; he must be no Emperor, no King, no President of a Republic; he must be a Pope—that is, he must be a Spiritual Father." So soon, how-ever, as the observation is made, "This real, living, concrete Pope is already there; he dwells in Rome, and at present bears the name of Pius; and the larger part of assembled Christen-dom obeys him willingly and gladly—will you accept him?" Then there is heard an angry protest, a many-voiced cry of "No; him by no manner of means." "And why not?" "Because he does not teach as we teach." "And what, then, shall he teach?" And a voice from one corner of Germany cries out: "He shall teach what is agreeable to the German nation—that nation of thinkers and inquirers. He shall teach, therefore, as Wittenberg taught from 1520 to 1546. Then and there the true Christian doctrine, in completest purity, first saw the light." Forthwith a different cry is heard from another corner of Germany: "That is an obso-lete resting-place; in latter times the German people have made the grandest progress; they stand now on the summit of intelligence and theological penetration. In three centuries we have learned much, and unlearned more. The Pope must teach now, as they think and teach in the chief seats of German science, in Berlin, and, perhaps, in Leipzig or Göttingen. Then we would accept him." "Not so," says a voice from the west; "neither Wittenberg nor Berlin, but Geneva is the birth-place of true Christianity; if the Pope were converted to Calvin—if he teaches as the French Reformer taught—he may be something for us." "Let him take heed how he does that," is the cry from the other side of the Channel, from England. "Neither Wittenberg nor Geneva has discovered

genuine Christianity. That precious jewel has been decreed
of Heaven to the Anglo-Saxon race. The true Church is
that of which Queen Elizabeth was the mother: it is the
English-episcopal Church. This Church alone maintains the
true medium between the extremes of Continental Protestantism and Catholicism. Let the Pope become Anglican,
and we will then let him talk to us." "You are all in error,
sheep without a shepherd," the North exclaims. "The true
Church, the beloved of God among churches, is that only
which the shepherd chosen of God, the Czar in St. Petersburg and his Holy Directing Synod, leads in the pastures of
the Divine Word. Russia is, as the Emperor Nicholas has
often called it, '*Holy Russia*,' and the Russian people are
'God's chosen in these present times.' Let the Pope acknowledge this and act accordingly, and we will willingly concede
him the first rank amongst the five orthodox patriarchs."
And, lastly, a new and strongly represented party, particularly in Germany and in England, claims to be heard—the
men of "The Church of the Future." "You all," say they,
"demean yourselves as if the true Church really existed
anywhere, but that is a monstrous delusion. All existing
church communities are but fragments, or the stones and
building materials from which God will in nearer or remoter
times construct the true church, responsive to all wants.
Until that time, we have only provisional churches, and a
provisional doctrine, and the Pope had better prepare himself
for this Church, lying yet unborn in the lap of the future, and
in the mean time put a note of interrogation to the doctrines
hitherto prevalent in the Church."

So far these parties; and now, on the other side, the two
hundred millions, Europeans, Asiatics, Americans, these
world-churches, to whose community belong at least a fragment of every considerable people on the whole earth. These
say unanimously, "Our Christianity shall have no national
supplementary flavour; it shall be no especial German, or
Italian, or French, or English, or Russian Christianity—it
shall not tickle the palate of this or that people, like a fiery
artificially-prepared potation; our doctrine, our religious

practice, shall be and is a pure, clear stream of running water, colourless and odourless, the universal, wholesome drink for all, to-day as yesterday, to-morrow as a thousand years gone by. The Pope cannot, dare not teach otherwise than as those two hundred millions believe, and have long believed. And these millions will, must have a Pope; will not allow him to be taken from them, will not suffer him to fall. They prove that they are ready to make any sacrifice for his preservation; for his freedom. German, Irish, and French blood has flowed in his defence, and for a just and noble cause. We will also in the coming time, and before all the clergy in Europe as in America, willingly, joyfully, abundantly bring our tribute to alleviate the situation of our common Head and Father, and to furnish him with the means of free and vigorous action in his high office. But we will not cling to that which is transitory and accidental; we will not desire that any people shall be constrained to accept what we ourselves would not bear; we will not stand up for a system of government which is in point of fact not more than forty-five years old, and the deficiencies of which the Pope himself has acknowledged, and which, in the course of that time, has generated nothing but discontent and revolt amongst the majority of the people. He who will support himself on such a staff, when the staff has already become rotten, must run the risk of falling to the ground.

The Greek myth says: When a new god, Apollo, was to be born, the island of Delos rose from the sea to be the birth-place of a deity. We will in all confidence expect that a Delos shall not be wanting to the Chair of St. Peter, should it even have to arise from the depths of the sea!

THE END.

R. BORN, PRINTER, GLOUCESTER STREET, REGENT'S PARK.

MESSRS. HURST AND BLACKETT'S

LIST OF NEW WORKS,

PUBLISHED AND IN PREPARATION.

THE LIFE OF J. M. W. TURNER, R.A. FROM

Original Letters and Papers furnished by his Friends and Fellow Academicians. By WALTER THORNBURY. 2 vols, 8vo. with Portrait and other Illustrations. 30s. (Now ready.)

THE LIFE AND CORRESPONDENCE OF ADMIRAL

SIR CHARLES NAPIER, K.C.B. From his Private Papers and Official Documents. By Major-General ELERS NAPIER. 2 vols. 8vo. with Portrait and Charts 30s. (Now ready.)

FRENCH WOMEN OF LETTERS. By JULIA

KAVANAGH. Author of "NATHALIE," "ADELE," &c. 2 vols. post 8vo. 21s. (Ready in November.)

THE PRIVATE DIARY OF RICHARD DUKE OF

BUCKINGHAM AND CHANDOS, K.G. 3 vols. with Portrait. (In the Press.)

THE LIFE OF THE REV. EDWARD IRVING. WITH

Selections from his Correspondence. By Mrs. OLIPHANT. 2 vols. with Portrait. (In the Press.)

THE COURT AND SOCIETY FROM ELIZABETH TO

ANNE. Illustrated from the Papers at Kimbolton. Edited by the DUKE OF MANCHESTER. 2 vols. 8vo. with Illustrations. (In Preparation.)

TWENTY-FIVE YEARS' MUSICAL RECOLLEC-

TIONS. By HENRY F. CHORLEY. 2 vols. post 8vo. (In the Press.)

MEMOIRS OF QUEEN HORTENSE, MOTHER OF

NAPOLEON III. Edited by LASCELLES WRAXALL. 2 vols. post 8vo. 21s. (Just ready.)

MEMOIRS OF THE COURTS AND CABINETS OF

WILLIAM IV. AND VICTORIA. From Original Family Documents. By the late DUKE OF BUCKINGHAM AND CHANDOS,
K.G. 2 vols. 8vo. with Portraits. 30s.

Among the principal interesting subjects of these volumes will be fonnd :—
The Re-establishment of the Royal Household—The Sailor King and his Court
—The Duke of Wellington In, and Out of, Office—The Reform Cabinet and the
Conservative Opposition—Career of Sir Robert Peel—Civil List Expenditure—
Vicissitudes of Louis Philippe—Attacks on the Duke of Wellington—Corona-
tions of William IV. and Queen Victoria—Rise and Fall of O'Connell—Lord Mel-
bourne and his Ministry—Proceedings of the Kings of Hanover and Belgium—Pri-
vate Negotiations at Apsley House—Secret History of Court Arrangements. &c.

"These volumes bring to a conclusion the interesting series of memoirs which have been,
published under the auspices of the Duke of Buckingham during the last few years.
Founded on the traditions of a family whose members have long possessed the *entrée* into
the charmed circle of courtiers and politicians, and enriched by the private and confidential
letters of the great men of the time, these works possess a peculiar interest which is not
always the attribute of state memoirs. They lift the veil of mystery with which the agents
of court influence and cabinet intrigues shroud their actions from the eyes of the public
and show us the motives which actuated our statesmen, and the degree in which the private
expressions of their views coincided with the public declaration of their sentiments. The
number of original documents in the present volumes invests the work with a fresh and
authentic interest. As forming the conclusion of a valuable and important series, these
memoirs should find a place on the shelves of every library."—*Sun.*

"This work itself, and the original documents which it contains, form a valuable contribution to the history of a most interesting and critical period. The narrative is everywhere enlivened and illustrated by private letters, chiefly addressed to the Duke of
Buckingham, from the Duke of Wellington, Sir Robert Peel, the Duke of Cumberland, the
Marquis of Londonderry, Lord Grenville, and other statesmen; and in addition to the
narration of the fluctuation of parties, many interesting particulars are given respecting
personages who acted chief parts on the political stage. The Duke of Wellington's letters
occupy a considerable space in the volumes, and are all worth perusal."—*Post.*

MEMOIRS OF THE COURT OF GEORGE IV. FROM

Original Family Documents. By the late DUKE OF BUCKING-
HAM AND CHANDOS, K.G. 2 vols. 8vo. with Portraits. 30s.

"The country is very much indebted to the Duke of Buckingham for the publication of
these volumes—to our thinking the most valuable of the contributions to recent history
which he has yet compiled from his family papers. Besides the King, the Duke of
Buckingham's canvass is full of the leading men of the day—Castlereagh, Liverpool, Canning, Wellington, Peel, and their compeers. We are sure that no reader, whether he seeks
for gossip, or for more sterling information, will be disappointed by the book. There are
several most characteristic letters of the Duke of Wellington."—*John Bull.*

MEMOIRS OF THE COURT OF THE REGENCY.

From Original Family Documents. By the late DUKE OF BUCK-
INGHAM AND CHANDOS, K.G. 2 vols. 8vo., with Portraits, 30s.

"Here are two goodly volumes on the English Court; volumes full of new
sayings, pictures, anecdotes, and scenes. The Duke of Buckingham travels over nine years
of English history. But what years those were, from 1811 to 1820! What events at home
and abroad they bore to the great bourne!—from the accession of the Regent to power to
the death of George III.—including the fall of Perceval; the invasion of Russia, and the
war in Spain; the battles of Salamanca and Borodino; the fire of Moscow; the retreat of
Napoleon; the conquest of Spain; the surrender of Napoleon; the return from Elba; the
Congress of Vienna; the Hundred Days; the crowning carnage of Waterloo; the exile to
St. Helena; the return of the Bourbons; the settlement of Europe; the public scandals at
the English Court; the popular discontent, and the massacre of Peterloo! On many parts
of this story the documents published by the Duke of Buckingham cast new jets of light,
clearing up much secret history. Old stories are confirmed—new traits of character are
brought out. In short, many new and pleasant additions are made to our knowledge of
those times."—*Athenæum.*

WORKS BY MISS FREER.

HISTORY OF THE REIGN OF HENRY IV. KING OF
FRANCE AND NAVARRE. From numerous Original Sources. By MARTHA WALKER FREER. 2 vols. with Portraits, 21s.

" Various circumstances combine to make us regard the Life of Henry IV. as one of the most attractive in the wide range of biography. The chequered nature of his career from childhood to manhood, the perils that environed him in a Court hostile to his religion and race, his unfortunate marriage, his personal bravery, his skill as a commander—these and many other characteristics that will suggest themselves to our readers, cause us to hail Miss Freer's new work as a welcome addition to our stock of books. It is a well-known feature in Miss Freer's works, that not content with the ordinary sources of information to which popular writers have recourse, she investigates for herself the MS. documents of the period under review, and is thus enabled to supply us with new facts, and to bring us face to face with the persons whose actions are recorded. This, which constitutes one of the great charms of M. Michelet, as a historian, is likewise a marked characteristic of Miss Freer, and confers a great additional value upon her historical portraits."—*Critic.*

"To become the chronicler of such a reign as that of Henry IV. is no mean task, and Miss Freer has accomplished it with singular good taste, good sense, and vigour. The story never flags. Our authoress is always faithful, accurate, and intelligent. Her style is good, and her subject abounds with interest for every student of history."—*Herald.*

"We know no works of this kind, with the exception, perhaps, of Macaulay's history, which are more pleasant reading than the histories of Miss Freer. The charm of the style and manner, and the accuracy of the details, combine to render her works a valuable addition to our literary treasures."—*John Bull.*

"In telling the reign of Henry IV., Miss Freer has one of the most interesting portions of French history for her story. She has told it from first to last with taste, using a clear, vigorous style."—*Examiner.*

HENRY IV. AND MARIE DE MEDICI. FORMING
Part II. of " The History of the Reign of Henry IV. King of France and Navarre." By MISS FREER. 2 vols. with Portraits. 21s.

" Miss Freer's ability and research have raised her to a conspicuous position among our historical writers. Among the most prominent of her qualities is a rare spirit of moderation and impartiality. Important and eventful as the reign of Henry IV. was, its details are little known by general readers among us, and therefore in presenting so complete and interesting a narrative Miss Freer has done good service to the public, besides enhancing her own well-earned reputation."—*Sun.*

"In these volumes we have the second part of a work the greatest to which Miss Freer has dedicated her powers. She draws her materials from sources mostly original, and she has selected for illustration a period the interest of which can scarcely be said to be second to any in modern times. There was romance in Henry the Fourth's character and in his career, and events of importance were grouped around his life. Miss Freer writes only after the most conscientious research, and with a mastery of the subject which will of itself go far towards explaining the vitality and animation which so distinguish her productions. Where a style of such supreme attractiveness is combined with such accuracy in detail, it is impossible not to give the work a high place in the literature of the day."—*Sunday Times.*

HENRY III. KING OF FRANCE AND POLAND;
HIS COURT AND TIMES. From numerous unpublished sources. By MISS FREER, 3 vols. post 8vo. with portraits, 31s. 6d.

" Miss Freer having won for herself the reputation of a most painstaking and trust-worthy historian not less than an accomplished writer, by her previous memoirs of sovereigns of the houses of Valois and Navarre, will not fail to meet with a most cordial and hearty welcome for her present admirable history of Henry III., the last of the French kings of the house of Valois. We refer our readers to the volumes themselves for the interesting details of the life and reign of Henry III., his residence in Poland, his marriage with Louise de Lorraine, his cruelties, his hypocrisies, his penances, his assassination by the hands of the monk Jaques Clément, &c. Upon these points, as well as with reference to other persons who occupied a prominent position during this period, abundant information is afforded by Miss Freer; and the public will feel with us that a deep debt of gratitude is due to that lady for the faithful and admirable manner in which she has pourtrayed the Court and Times of Henry the Third."—*Chronicle.*

ELIZABETH DE VALOIS, QUEEN OF SPAIN, AND

THE COURT OF PHILIP II. From numerous unpublished sources in the Archives of France, Italy, and Spain. By MISS FREER. 2 vols post 8vo. with fine Portraits by HEATH, 21s.

"It is not attributing too much to Miss Freer to say that herself and Mr. Prescott are probably the best samples of our modern biographers. The present volumes will be a boon to posterity for which it will be grateful. Equally suitable for instruction and amusement, they portray one of the most interesting characters and periods of history."—*John Bull.*

THE LIFE OF MARGUERITE D'ANGOULEME,

QUEEN of NAVARRE, SISTER of FRANCIS I. By MISS FREER. Second Edition, 2 vols. with fine Portraits, 21s.

"This is a very useful and amusing book. It is a good work, very well done. The authoress is quite equal in power and grace to Miss Strickland. She must have spent great time and labour in collecting the information, which she imparts in an easy and agreeable manner. It is difficult to lay down her book after having once begun it.."—*Standard.*

THE LIFE OF JEANNE D'ALBERT, QUEEN OF

NAVARRE. By MISS FREER. Cheap Edition, 1 vol. 5s. with Portrait.

"This book reflects the highest credit on the industry and ability of Miss Freer. Nothing can be more interesting than her story of the life of Jeanne D'Albret, and the narrative is as trustworthy as it is attractive."—*Post.*

THE SECRET HISTORY OF THE COURT OF

FRANCE UNDER LOUIS XV. Edited, from Rare and Unpublished Documents, by Dr. CHALLICE. 2 vols. with fine Portraits. 21s.

"We recommend these volumes to our readers as amusing, interesting, and instructive."—*Critic.*

"A valuable and interesting work. It unites the fascination of a romance with the integrity of history."—*Chronicle.*

"The interest of this work will be readily acknowledged. Every page contains a contribution to the general chronicle of the times, while anecdotes and sketches of character abound."—*Illustrated News.*

MEMORIALS OF ADMIRAL LORD GAMBIER, G.C.B.

with Original Letters from LORDS CHATHAM, NELSON, CASTLEREAGH, MULGRAVE, HOLLAND, Mr. CANNING, &c, Edited, from Family Papers, by LADY CHATTERTON, SECOND EDITION, 2 vols. 8vo, 28s.

"These volumes are an important addition to our naval literature; but they are also valuable for the light they throw on the domestic history of the time. The correspondence is particularly rich in anecdotes, glimpses of society and manners, and traits of character."—*U. S. Magazine.*

A BOOK ABOUT DOCTORS. BY J. C. JEAFFRESON,

Esq., New, Revised and Cheaper Edition, 1 vol., 10s. 6d.

"This is a rare book; a compliment to the medical profession and an acquisition to its members; a book to be read and re-read; fit for the study and the consulting-room, as well as the drawing-room table and the circulating library. Mr. Jeaffreson takes a comprehensive view of the social history of the profession, and illustrates its course by a series of biographic and domestic sketches, from the feudal era down to the present day. The chapters on the Doctor as a bon-vivant, the generosity and parsimony, the quarrels and loves of physicians, are rich with anecdotes of medical celebrities. But Mr. Jeaffreson does not merely amuse. The pages he devotes to the exposure and history of charlatanry are of scarcely less value to the student of medicine than the student of manners. We thank Mr. Jeaffreson most heartily for the mirth and solid information of his work. All the members of our profession will be sure to read it."—*Lancet.*

"A pleasant book. Out of hundreds of volumes, Mr. Jeaffreson has collected thousands of good things, adding much that appears in print for the first time, and which of course gives increased value to this very readable book."—*Athenæum.*

LODGE'S PEERAGE AND BARONETAGE. Under

THE ESPECIAL PATRONAGE OF HER MAJESTY AND H.R.H. THE PRINCE CONSORT. Corrected throughout by the Nobility. THIRTIETH EDITION, in 1 vol. royal 8vo., with the Arms beautifully engraved, handsomely bound, with gilt edges, price 31s. 6d.

LODGE'S PEERAGE AND BARONETAGE is acknowledged to be the most complete, as well as the most elegant, work of the kind. As an established and authentic authority on all questions respecting the family histories, honours, and connections of the titled aristocracy, no work has ever stood so high. It is published under the especial patronage of Her Majesty, and His Royal Highness the Prince Consort, and is annually corrected throughout, from the personal communications of the Nobility. It is the only work of its class, in which, *the type being kept constantly standing*, every correction is made in its proper place to the date of publication, an advantage which gives it supremacy over all its competitors. Independently of its full and authentic information respecting the existing Peers and Baronets of the realm, the most sedulous attention is given in its pages to the collateral branches of the various noble families, and the names of many thousand individuals are introduced, which do not appear in other records of the titled classes. For its authority, correctness, and facility of arrangement, and the beauty of its typography and binding, the work is justly entitled to the high place it occupies on the tables of Her Majesty and the Nobility.

" Lodge's Peerage must supersede all other works of the kind, for two reasons ; first, it is on a better plan ; and, secondly, it is better executed. We can safely pronounce it to be the readiest, the most useful, and exactest of modern works on the subject."—*Spectator.*

"A work which corrects all errors of former works. It is the production of a herald, we had almost said, by birth, but certainly by profession and studies, Mr. Lodge, the Norroy King of Arms. It is a most useful publication."—*Times.*

"As perfect a Peerage of the British Empire as we are ever likely to see published. Great pains have been taken to make it as complete and accurate as possible. The work is patronised by Her Majesty and the Prince Consort; and it is worthy of a place in every gentleman's library, as well as in every public institution."—*Herald.*

"As a work of contemporaneous history, this volume is of great value—the materials having been derived from the most authentic sources and in the majority of cases emanating from the noble families themselves. It contains all the needful information respecting the nobility of the Empire."—*Post.*

" This work should form a portion of every gentleman's library. At all times, the information which it contains, derived from official sources exclusively at the command of the author, is of importance to most classes of the community ; to the antiquary it must be invaluable, for implicit reliance may be placed on its contents."—*Globe.*

" This work derives great value from the high authority of Mr. Lodge. The plan is excellent."—*Literary Gazette.*

"When any book has run through so many editions, its reputation is so indelibly stamped, that it requires neither criticism nor praise. It is but just, however, to say, that ' Lodge's Peerage and Baronetage ' is the most elegant and accurate, and the best of its class. The chief point of excellence attaching to this Peerage consists neither in its elegance of type nor its completeness of illustration, but in its authenticity, which is insured by the letter-press being always kept standing, and by immediate alteration being made whenever any change takes place, either by death or otherwise, amongst the nobility of the United Kingdom. The work has obtained the special patronage of Her Most Gracious Majesty, and of His Royal Highness the Prince Consort, which patronage has never been better or more worthily bestowed."—*Messenger.*

" ' Lodge's Peerage and Baronetage' has become, as it were, an 'institution' of this country ; in other words, it is indispensable, and cannot be done without, by any person having business in the great world. The authenticity of this valuable work, as regards the several topics to which it refers, has never been exceeded, and, consequently, it must be received as one of the most important contributions to social and domestic history extant. As a book of reference—indispensible in most cases, useful in all—it should be in the hands of every one having connections in, or transactions with, the aristocracy."—*Observer.*

LODGE'S GENEALOGY OF THE PEERAGE AND

BARONETAGE OF THE BRITISH EMPIRE. A NEW AND REVISED EDITION. Uniform with "THE PEERAGE" Volume, with the arms beautifully engraved, handsomely bound with gilt edges, price 31s. 6d.

The desire very generally manifested for a republication of this volume has dictated the present entire revision of its contents. The Armorial Bearings prefixed to the History of each Noble Family, render the work complete in itself and uniform with the Volume of THE PEERAGE, which it is intended to accompany and illustrate. The object of the whole Work, in its two distinct yet combined characters, has been useful and correct information; and the careful attention devoted to this object throughout will, it is hoped, render the Work worthy of the August Patronage with which it is honoured and of the liberal assistance accorded by its Noble Correspondents, and will secure from them and from the Public, the same cordial reception it has hitherto experienced. The great advantage of "The Genealogy" being thus given in a separate volume, Mr. Lodge has himself explained in the Preface to "The Peerage."

THE BOOK OF ORDERS OF KNIGHTHOOD, AND

DECORATIONS OF HONOUR OF ALL NATIONS; COMPRISING AN HISTORICAL ACCOUNT OF EACH ORDER, MILITARY, NAVAL AND CIVIL; with Lists of the Knights and Companions of each British Order. EMBELLISHED WITH FIVE HUNDRED FAC-SIMILE COLOURED ILLUSTRATIONS OF THE INSIGNIA OF THE VARIOUS ORDERS. Edited by SIR BERNARD BURKE, Ulster King of Arms. 1 vol. royal 8vo., handsomely bound, with gilt edges, price £2. 2s.

"This is indeed a splendid book. It is an uncommon combination of a library book of reference and a book for a boudoir, undoubtedly uniting beauty and utility. It will soon find its place in every library and drawing-room."—*Globe*.

THE LIFE AND TIMES OF GEORGE VILLIERS,

DUKE OF BUCKINGHAM. By MRS. THOMSON. 3 vols.

"These volumes will increase the well-earned reputation of their clever and popular author. The story of the royal favourite's career is told by Mrs. Thomson very honestly, and is enriched abundantly with curious and entertaining details—of which a full publication is now made for the first time."—*Examiner*.

BRITISH ARTISTS, from HOGARTH to TURNER;

A SERIES OF BIOGRAPHICAL SKETCHES. By WALTER THORNBURY. 2 v

"The interest of Mr. Thornbury's pictures is undeniable—a result partly due to the talent of the painter, partly to his subjects; for next to the lives of actors those of artists are among the most interesting to read. Especially so are those of our English artists of the last century—lives abounding in contrasted and often dark hues, interwoven with the history of men still remarkable in letters and politics. Capital subjects for a biographer with a turn for dramatic and picturesque realisation are such men as the bright, mercurial Gainsborough; the moody, neglected Wilson; Reynolds, the bland and self-possessed; Barry, the fierce and squalid; shrewd, miserly Nollekins; the foppish, visionary Conway; the spendthrift Sherwin; the stormy Fuseli; Morland, the reprobate; Lawrence, the courtly. The chapters devoted to these heroes of the English schools are not so much condensed biographies as dramatic glimpses of the men and their environments. Certain striking scenes and circumstances in their lives are vividly and picturesquely painted—made to re-live before our eyes with all the vraisemblance of the novelist."—*Critic*.

MEMOIRS OF ROYAL LADIES. BY EMILY S.

HOLT. 2 volumes post 8vo. with Illustrations. 21s.

"These attractive 'Memoirs of Royal Ladies,' accounts of whose lives have never before appeared in our language, are full of entertaining matter, while they display abundant evidence that they are the result of much research and careful study."—*Press*.

TRAVELS IN THE REGIONS OF THE AMOOR,

AND THE RUSSIAN ACQUISITIONS ON THE CONFINES OF INDIA AND CHINA; WITH ADVENTURES AMONG THE MOUNTAIN KIRGHIS, AND THE MANJOURS, MANYARGS, TOUNGOUZ, TOUZEMTZ, GOLDI, AND GELYAKS. By T. W. ATKINSON, F G.S., F.R.G.S., Author of " Oriental and Western Siberia." Dedicated by permission, to HER MAJESTY. SECOND EDITION. Royal 8vo., with Map and 83 Illustrations. £2 2s., elegantly bound

" Our readers have not now to learn for the first time the quality of Mr. Atkinson as an explorer and a writer. The comments we made on, and the extracts we selected from, his ' Oriental and Western Siberia' will have sufficed to show that in the former character he takes rank with the most daring of the class, and that in the latter he is scarcely to be surpassed for the lucidity, picturesqueness, and power, with which he pourtrays the scenes through which he has travelled, and the perils or the pleasures which encountered him on the way. The present volume is not inferior to its predecessor. It deals with civilization, semi-civilization, and barbarous life. It takes us through localities, some of which are little, others not at all, known to even the best read men in the literature of travel. The entire volume is admirable for its spirit, unexaggerated tone, and the mass of fresh materials by which this really new world is made accessible to us. The followers, too, of all the ' ologies will meet with something in these graphic pages of peculiar interest to them. It is a noble work."—*Athenæum.*

" We must refer to Mr. Atkinson as one of the most intelligent and successful of the civilized travellers of our own day. By far the most important contribution to the history of these regions is to be found in Mr. Atkinson's recent publication on the Amoor—a work which derives equal interest from his well-stored portfolio and his pen."—*Edinburgh Review.*

" This is in every respect an *aureus liber.* Its magnificent apparel not inaptly symbolises its magnificent contents. Mr. Atkinson has here given us a narrative which could be told by no other living Englishman. The intrinsic interest of that narrative is enhanced by Mr. Atkinson's gift of vigorous and graceful description. Thanks to the power of his pen, and the still more remarkable power of his pencil we follow his travels with eager interest and anxiety. He himself is the chief object of interest, from his thirst for adventure and daring exploits, and the countless shapes of terror and death that he encounters. The work is a magnificent contribution to the literature of travel. More useful and pleasant reading can nowhere be found."—*Literary Gazette.*

" Mr. Atkinson has here presented the reading world with another valuable book of travels. It is as interesting, as entertaining, and as well written as his previous work. It is a volume which will not only afford intellectual entertainment of the highest order, but fitted to instruct both the philosopher and the statesman. The vast territorial acquisitions lately made by Russia in the Northern parts of Central Asia along the whole frontier of China, is described by an eye witness well qualified to estimate their real value and political advantages. Our readers, we feel sure, will peruse this interesting book of travels for themselves. It contains something for every taste."—*Daily News*

" The success of Mr. Atkinson's ' Oriental and Western Siberia' has happily induced him to write and publish another volume, and written with the same unflagging interest. A more pleasing as well as more novel book of travels it would be difficult to find. The illustrations are admirably executed, and they add ten fold to the value of a volume already possessing intrinsic merits of the highest kind. Independently of the deep interest it excites as a traveller's tale, the work presents peculiar geographical and ethnological information, and points out a boundless field of commerce to English enterprise. It marks with a decided pen the gradual advances of Russia towards British India, and the sweeping rush of her conquering energy from Siberia to the Pacific. Thus Mr. Atkinson's book has not only a literary, but a political and commercial importance. There is food for all readers and interest for all."—*Globe.*

" This is noble and fascinating book, belonging in right both of subject and treatment to the choicest class of travel literature. The vast panorama unfolded is one of the most marvellous in the world, and has hitherto been among the least known to the nations of the west. It is now set before them with requisite clearness and force of expression by one who has the highest claims to confidence as an observer and delineator."—*Spectator.*

" A really magnificent volume, which for many years to come must be a standard authority upon the country of which it treats. It is very interesting and abounds in incident and anecdote both personal and local."—*Chronicle.*

ORIENTAL AND WESTERN SIBERIA; A NAR-

RATIVE OF SEVEN YEARS' EXPLORATIONS AND ADVENTURES IN SIBERIA, MONGOLIA, THE KIRGHIS STEPPES, CHINESE TARTARY, AND CENTRAL ASIA. By THOMAS WITLAM ATKINSON. In one large volume, royal 8vo., Price £2. 2s., elegantly bound. Embellished with upwards of 50 Illustrations, including numerous beautifully coloured plates, from drawings by the Author, and a map.

"By virtue alike of its text and its pictures, we place this book of travel in the first rank among those illustrated gift books now so much sought by the public. Mr. Atkinson's book is most readable. The geographer finds in it notice of ground heretofore left undescribed, the ethnologist, geologist, and botanist, find notes and pictures, too, of which they know the value, the sportsman's taste is gratified by chronicles of sport, the lover of adventure will find a number of perils and escapes to hang over, and the lover of a frank good-humoured way of speech will find the book a pleasant one in every page. Seven years of wandering, thirty-nine thousand five hundred miles of moving to and fro in a wild and almost unknown country, should yield a book worth reading, and they do."—*Examiner*.

"A book of travels which in value and sterling interest must take rank as a landmark in geographical literature. Its coloured illustrations and wood engravings are of a high order, and add a great charm to the narrative. Mr. Atkinson has travelled where it is believed no European has been before. He has seen nature in the wildest, sublimest, and also the most beautiful aspects the old world can present. These he has depicted by pen and pencil. He has done both well. Many a fireside will rejoice in the determination which converted the artist into an author. Mr. Atkinson is a thorough Englishman, brave and accomplished, a lover of adventure and sport of every kind. He knows enough of mineralogy, geology, and botany to impart a scientific interest to his descriptions and drawings; possessing a keen sense of humour, he tells many a racy story. The sportsman and the lover of adventure, whether by flood or field, will find ample stores in the stirring tales of his interesting travels."—*Daily News*.

"An animated and intelligent narrative, appreciably enriching the literature of English travel. Mr. Atkinson's sketches were made by express permission of the late Emperor of Russia. Perhaps no English artist was ever before admitted into this enchanted land of history, or provided with the talisman and amulet of a general passport; and well has Mr. Atkinson availed himself of the privilege. Our extracts will have served to illustrate the originality and variety of Mr. Atkinson's observations and adventures during his protracted wanderings of nearly forty thousand miles. Mr. Atkinson's pencil was never idle, and he has certainly brought home with him the forms, and colours, and other characteristics of a most extraordinary diversity of groups and scenes. As a sportsman Mr. Atkinson enjoyed a plenitude of excitement. His narrative is well stored with incidents of adventure. His ascent of the Bielouka is a chapter of the most vivid romance of travel, yet it is less attractive than his relations of wanderings across the Desert of Gobi and up the Taognou Chain."—*Athenæum*.

"We predict that Mr. Atkinson's 'Siberia' will very often assume the shape of a Christmas Present or New Year's Gift, as it possesses, in an eminent degree, four very precious and suitable qualities for that purpose,—namely, usefulness, elegance, instruction and novelty. It is a work of great value, not merely on account of its splendid illustrations, but for the amount it contains of authentic and highly interesting intelligence concerning regions which, in all probability, has never, previous to Mr. Atkinson's explorations, been visited by an European. Mr. Atkinson's adventures are told in a manly style. The valuable and interesting information the book contains, gathered at a vast expense, is lucidly arranged, and altogether the work is one that the author-artist may well be proud of, and with which those who study it cannot fail to be delighted."—*John Bull*.

"To the geographer, the geologist, the ethnographer, the sportsman, and to those who read only for amusement, this will be an acceptable volume. Mr. Atkinson is not only an adventurous traveller, but a correct and amusing writer."—*Literary Gazette*.

THE OKAVANGO RIVER; A NARRATIVE OF

Travel, Exploration and Adventure. By CHARLES JOHN ANDERSSON. Author of " Lake Ngami." 1 vol. 8vo. with Portrait of the Author, and numerous Illustrations. 21s. bound.

"Mr. Andersson's book, from the number of well-told adventures, its unpretending style, its rich fund of information, and spirited illustrations, will command a wide circle of readers, and become a favourite with all those who can appreciate daring perseverance, and a buoyant spirit under overwhelming difficulties. The interest of his story never flags for a moment."—*Athenæum.*

"Mr. Andersson is one of those whom the world and the Geographical Society delight to honour. Not for adventures only, but for science's sake does he betake himself to the wilds, in which he has all the delights attractive to the true sportsman, but in which he fearlessly encounters all perils that he may discover a river, depict a new people, or bring to light a fresh species. His 'Lake Ngami' was deservedly popular; and, on behalf of the reading world, we are glad to welcome its successor, 'The Okavango River.' The volume, which is profusely and splendidly illustrated, will take a high place among works of adventure and exploration. There can be no question of the great service Mr. Andersson has rendered to geographical science."—*Herald.*

"This book illustrated with many animated pictures of adventures connected with the wild sports of the journey it describes, is one that will be popular as a budget of trust-worthy travellers' tales, besides being valued for the information it gives to geographers. Many adventures and perils from men as well as from lions, give interest to the account of Mr. Andersson's journey from the Okavango; and when all is told we have in the four closing chapters an excellent account of the west coast of Southern Africa, a region which this traveller has more than once explored."—*Examiner.*

"Mr. Andersson's adventures stamp him as an one of the most enterprising travellers of modern times, and well worthy to take rank by the side of Livingstone and others, who have attempted to penetrate the interior of the great African continent. Every page of his present work is full of interest."—*Observer.*

"Mr. Andersson's narrative of his discovery of the Okavango River is very interesting. The book is one which will please alike the traveller, the sportsman, and the student of natural history. It abounds in startling adventures."—*Morning Post.*

"Mr. Andersson's new work is full of startling accounts of encounters with all kinds of wild beasts—the elephant, the rhinoceros, the hippopotamus, the lion, the giraffe, &c.—all of which will be read with delight by the sportsman; while the traveller and the student of geography or ethnology will find plenty of food for the mind in the other parts of the book. It is profusely and beautifully illustrated, and cannot but become one of the favourite works of the season."—*Bell's Life.*

LAKE NGAMI; OR EXPLORATIONS AND DIS-

coveries during Four Years' Wanderings in the Wilds of South-Western Africa. By CHARLES JOHN ANDERSSON. Second Edition.1 vol. royal 8vo., with Map and upwards of 50 Illustrations, representing Sporting Adventures, Subjects of Natural History, &c.

"This narrative of African explorations and discoveries is one of the most important geographical works that have lately appeared. It contains the account of two journeys made between the years 1850 and 1854, in the first of which the countries of the Damaras and the Ovambo, previously scarcely known in Europe, were explored; and in the second the newly-discovered Lake Ngami was reached by a route that had been deemed impracticable, but which proves to be the shortest and the best. The work contains much scientific and accurate information as to the geology, the scenery, products, and resources of the regions explored, with notices of the religion, manners, and customs of the native tribes. The continual sporting adventures, and other remarkable occurrences, intermingled with the narrative of travel, make the book as interesting to read as a romance, as, indeed, a good book of travels ought always to be. The illustrations by Wolf are admirably designed, and most of them represent scenes as striking as any witnessed by Jules Gérard or Gordon Cumming."—*Literary Gazette.*

TRAVELS IN THE HOLY LAND. By FREDRIKA

BREMER. Translated by MARY HOWITT. 2 vols. (Just ready.)

TWO YEARS IN SWITZERLAND AND ITALY.

By FREDRIKA BREMER. Translated by MARY HOWITT. 2 vols.

"This is certainly one of the best works Miss Bremer has ever yet produced. We can scarcely find words adequately to express our admiration of the manner in which she has told all she saw and felt during the two years she passed in the loveliest parts of Europe. The book is the best that ever was written on such themes."—*Messenger.*

SIX YEARS OF A TRAVELLER'S LIFE IN

WESTERN AFRICA. By FRANCISCO VALDEZ, Arbitrator at Loanda, and the Cape of Good Hope. 2 vols. with Illustrations.

"A book of value and importance."—*Messenger.*

TEN YEARS' WANDERINGS AMONG THE ETHIO-

PIANS; with Sketches of the Manners and Customs of the Civilised and Uncivilised Tribes from Senegal to Gaboon. By T. J. HUTCHINSON, F.R.G.S., Consul for Fernando Po. 8vo. with Illustrations. 14s.

"A work of very considerable interest, that cannot fail to be highly valued by the merchant and the trader, as well as by the philantrophist, the ethnologist, the geographical explorer, and the man of science."—*Observer.*

THE MEDICAL MISSIONARY IN CHINA: A NAR-

RATIVE OF TWENTY YEARS' EXPERIENCE. By WILLIAM LOCK-HART, F.R.C.S. F.R.G.S, of the London Missionary Society. Second Edition, 1 vol. 8vo.

"We heartily commend this work to our readers. It contains more information upon the social life of the teeming millions of Chinese than any book it has been our fortune to meet."—*Baptist Magazine.*

TRAVELS IN EASTERN AFRICA, WITH THE

NARRATIVE OF A RESIDENCE IN MOZAMBIQUE: 1856 to 1859. By LYONS McLEOD, Esq. F.R.G.S.. &c. Late British Consul in Mozambique. 2 vols. With Map and Illustrations.

A RESIDENCE AT THE COURT OF MEER ALI

MOORAD; WITH WILD SPORTS IN THE VALLEY OF THE INDUS. By CAPT. LANGLEY, late Madras Cavalry. 2 vols. 8vo. with Illustrations. 30s.

SIXTEEN YEARS OF AN ARTIST'S LIFE IN

MOROCCO, SPAIN, AND THE CANARY ISLANDS. By MRS. ELIZABETH MURRAY. 2 vols. 8vo. with Coloured Illustrations.

"Mrs. Murray's book is like her painting, luminous, rich and fresh. We welcome it (as the public will also do) with sincere pleasure."—*Athenæum.*

A SUMMER RAMBLE in the HIMALAYAS; with

SPORTING ADVENTURES IN THE VALE OF CASHMERE. Edited by MOUNTAINEER. 8vo. with Illustrations. 15s.

"This volume is altogether a pleasant one. It is written with zest and edited with care. The incidents and adventures of the journey are most fascinating to a sportsman and very interesting to a traveller."—*Athenæum*

THE ENGLISH SPORTSMAN IN THE WESTERN
PRAIRIES. By the Hon. GRANTLEY BERKELEY. Royal 8vo. with numerous Illustrations.

" This is a splendid volume, full of adventure and anecdote. One of the most skilful and ardent of our sportsmen, Mr. Grantley Berkeley is at the same time an excellent writer upon sporting matters. This is a very rare combination of qualities, for, generally speaking, the men who understand sport are unable to write, whilst those who can write are profoundly ignorant of sport. Now Mr. Grantley Berkeley not only understands his topics thoroughly, but is able to write with ease, freshness, and vigour about them. There is a zest in his descriptions which only a true sportsman can feel. There is a breath of the woods, an echo of the hunting-horn in his writings. We can see the exciting picture which his words would present."—Critic.

" We heartily commend this handsome book to the gentlemen of England. Its author is the present Cæsar of sport, who unites to his feats of hunting the ability of recording them."—Herald.

ESSAYS FROM THE QUARTERLY. BY JAMES
HANNAY. 1 vol. 8vo. 14s.

" A very agreeable and valuable addition to our literature. As a writer Mr. Hannay possesses very remarkable merit indeed. He is eminently readable, he has a vast deal of shrewd common sense, and a brilliancy of illustrative comparison quite unparalleled by any author of the present day. We could not point to any series of articles, not even excepting those of Macaulay, which are easier reading."—Spectator.

DOMESTIC SKETCHES IN RUSSIA. By LADY
CHARLOTTE PEPYS. 2 vols. post 8vo. 21s.

" This very agreeable book presents a photograph of Russian home life, the simplicity of which is as charming as the manner of relating it is attractive."—Messenger.

LIGHTS AND SHADOWS OF FRENCH MILITARY
LIFE. By the Author of " FLEMISH INTERIORS," &c. 3 vols. with Illustrations. (Just ready.)

REALITIES OF PARIS LIFE. BY THE AUTHOR
of " FLEMISH INTERIORS," &c. 3 vols. with Illustrations. 31s. 6d.

" ' Realities of Paris Life' is a good addition to Paris books, and important as affording true and sober pictures of the Paris poor."—Athenæum.

DOMESTIC MEMOIRS OF THE ROYAL FAMILY,
and the COURT OF ENGLAND, chiefly at SHENE and RICHMOND. By FOLKESTONE WILLIAMS, F.G.S., 3 vols. with Portraits.

" In the prosecution of his labours, the author has consulted antiquaries and archæologists, and examined contemporary authorities. The result is, a work, pleasant and instructive, abundant in anecdote, and agreeably gossipping. It, moreover, evinces considerable research, and a generally sound historical judgment."—Spectator.

THE RIDES AND REVERIES OF MR. ÆSOP SMITH.
By MARTIN F. TUPPER, D.C.L., F.R.S., Author of " Proverbial Philosophy," " Stephen Langton," &c., 1 vol. post 8vo. 5s.

STUDIES FROM LIFE. BY THE AUTHOR OF

" JOHN HALIFAX, GENTLEMAN," "A WOMAN'S THOUGHTS ABOUT WOMEN," &c. 1 vol. 10s. 6d. elegantly bound.

"Studies from Life is altogether a charming volume, one which all women and most men, would be proud to possess."—*Chronicle*.

"Without being in the same degree elaborate, either in purpose or plot, as 'John Halifax,' these 'Studies from Life' may be pronounced to be equally as clever in construction and narration. It is one of the most charming features of Miss Muloch's works that they invariably tend to a practical and useful end. Her object is to improve the taste, refine the intellect, and touch the heart, and so to act upon all classes of her readers as to make them rise from the consideration of her books both wiser and better than they were before they began to read them. The 'Studies from Life' will add considerably to the author's well earned reputation."—*Messenger*.

POEMS. BY THE AUTHOR OF "JOHN HALIFAX,

GENTLEMAN," "A WOMAN'S THOUGHTS ABOUT WOMEN," &c.
1 vol. with Illustrations by BIRKET FOSTER.

"A volume of poems which will assuredly take its place with those of Goldsmith, Gray, and Cowper, on the favourite shelf of every Englishman's library. We discover in these poems all the firmness, vigour, and delicacy of touch which characterise the author's prose works, and in addition, an ineffable tenderness and grace, such as we find in few poetical compositions besides those of Tennyson."—*Illustrated News of the World*.

"We are well pleased with these poems by our popular novelist. They are the expression of genuine thoughts, feelings, and aspirations, and the expression is almost always graceful, musical and well-coloured. A high, pure tone of morality pervades each set of verses, and each strikes the reader as inspired by some real event, or condition of mind, and not by some idle fancy or fleeting sentiment."—*Spectator*.

A SAUNTER THROUGH THE WEST END. BY

LEIGH HUNT. 1 vol. 10s. 6d.

"The title of this work is unexceptionable, it is happily and appropriately chosen to denote the gossiping contents of the book ; light, chatty, and amusing. The author quietly puts his arm in that of his reader, and as he passes on from Hyde Park Corner down Piccadilly or Pall Mall to the Haymarket and Soho, points out the anecdotes connected with each locality. Touches of quiet, genial, humour, playful interruptions, and amusing stories told in a quaint, unaffected style contribute to the attractive conversational tone adopted, as he saunters along with his friend of the hour. The reader will find himself agreeably carried on from the first to the last of 'The Saunter' by its cheerful tone and entertaining gossip."—*Literary Gazette*.

"This book is ever fresh. Few men felt, as Leigh Hunt did, the human poetry of the memories that crowd upon the lettered and thoughtful rambler about London streets. His gentle, genial humour shines in a book like this—worthy companion to his 'Town' and 'Old Court Suburb'—with light that will not become dim with lapse of time."—*Exam*.

"If any of our readers are in want of a genial, gossiping volume, full of pleasant historical allusions, and written by one who was deservedly a great favourite in the world of letters, we can recommend them Leigh Hunt's very pleasant 'Saunter.' It will suit town or country readers equally well."—*Critic*.

RECOLLECTIONS OF A FOX-HUNTER. BY SCRU-

TATOR. 1 vol.

"'This is Scrutator's best book. It is a sort of memoir of the hearty and accomplished writer, including pleasant notices of sporting celebrities, such as Assheton Smith, &c., but the burden of the volume consists of experience in the hunting-field—real truths conveying excellent lessons as to horse and hound, and ensuring for the volume an honoured place in every sportsman's library."—*Era*.

THE AUTOBIOGRAPHY OF A STAGE-COACHMAN.

By THOMAS CROSS. Dedicated to Henry Villebois, Esq., Master of the Norfolk Hounds. 3 vols. with Illustrations.

"The autobiography of Mr. Cross is a faithful chronicle of a by-gone form of civilization. It is one of Mr. Cross's chief merits that he tells many a good anecdote in his own characteristic way."—*Examiner*.

THE LAST OF THE MORTIMERS.

By the Author of "MARGARET MAITLAND," &c. 3 vols.

WHITE AND BLACK.

A TALE OF THE SOUTHERN STATES. 3 v.

THE HOME AT ROSEFIELD.

By EDWARD COPPING. 3 vols.

NOTICE TO QUIT.

By W. G. WILLS. 3 vols.

"A novel of remarkable power. The luterest never flags. There is real genius in this writer."—*Spectator.*

EAST AND WEST.

By J. FRAZER CORKRAN. 3 vols.

"A good novel. The author has knowledge in abundance."—*Daily News.*

SIR RICHARD HAMILTON.

2 vols.

COUNTY SOCIETY.

3 vols.

"An admirably written and entertaining novel."—*Observer*

A HERO IN SPITE OF HIMSELF.

By CAPTAIN MAYNE REID. From the French of Luis de Bellemare. 3 vols.

ALONE IN THE WORLD.

By the Author of "COUSIN GEOFFREY," &c. v.

PAUL FOSTER'S DAUGHTER.

By DUTTON COOK. 3 vols.

UNDER THE SPELL.

By the Author of "GRANDMOTHER'S MONEY," "WILDFLOWER," &c. 3 vols.

"The best story hitherto written by a very pleasant novelist."—*Examiner.*

A FAMILY HISTORY.

By the Author of "THE QUEEN'S PARDON." 3 vols.

NO CHURCH.

By the Author of "HIGH CHURCH." Third Edition. 3 vols.

"We advise all who have the opportunity to read this book. It is worth the study. It is a book to make us feel what may be accomplished by each and all of us who choose to set about it in a simple, earnest spirit, unprejudiced by sectarian or party feeling, only having a lively faith in God's mercy, and a fervent charity towards our fellow men. As a love story, the book is interesting, and well put together."—*Athenæum.*

MY SHARE OF THE WORLD.

By FRANCES BROWNE. 3 vols.

KATHERINE AND HER SISTERS.

By the Author of "THE DISCIPLINE OF LIFE," &c., 3 vols.

ICE-BOUND.

By WALTER THORNBURY. 3 vols.

"In 'Ice-Bound' Mr. Thornbury has put forth all his powers, and has produced one of the best books of fiction he has ever written."—*Messenger.*

THE HOUSE ON THE MOOR.

By the Author of "MARGARET MAITLAND," 3 v.

"This story is very interesting and the interest deepens as the story proceeds."—*Athenæum.*

HOMELESS; or, A POET'S INNER LIFE.

By M. GOLDSCHMIDT. Author of "JACOB BENDIXEN." 3 v.

THE WORLD'S VERDICT.

By the Author of "MORALS OF MAY FAIR," 'CREEDS,' &c. 3 vols.

WHEEL WITHIN WHEEL.

By the Author of "ALICE WENTWORTH," "THE LEES OF BLENDON HALL." &c. 3v.

"A good novel."—*Athenæum.*

THINKING AND ACTING.

By A CLERGYMAN'S DAUGHTER. Author of "HELEN LINDSAY," OUR "HOMELESS POOR," &c. 2 vols.

NOW IN COURSE OF PUBLICATION.

HURST AND BLACKETT'S STANDARD LIBRARY

OF CHEAP EDITIONS OF

POPULAR MODERN WORKS

ILLUSTRATED EY MILLAIS, LEECH, BIRKET FOSTER, &c.

Each in a single volume, elegantly printed, bound, and illustrated, price 5s.
A volume to appear every two months. The following are now ready.

VOL. I.—SAM SLICK'S NATURE AND HUMAN NATURE.

" The first volume of Messrs. Hurst and Blackett's Standard Library of Cheap Editions of Popular Modern Works forms a very good beginning to what will doubtless be a very successful undertaking. ' Nature and Human Nature' is one of the best of Sam Slick's witty and humorous productions, and well entitled to the large circulation which it cannot fail to obtain in its present convenient and cheap shape. The volume combines with the great recommendations of a clear, bold type, and good paper, the lesser, but still attractive merits, of being well illustrated and elegantly bound."—*Morning Post.*

"This new and cheap edition of Sam Slick's popular work will be an acquisition to all lovers of wit and humour. Mr. Justice Haliburton's writings are so well known to the English public that no commendation is needed. The volume is very handsomely bound and illustrated, and the paper and type are excellent. It is in every way suited for a library edition, and as the names of Messrs. Hurst and Blackett, warrant the character of the works to be produced in their Standard Library, we have no doubt the project will be eminently successful."—*Sun.*

VOL. II.—JOHN HALIFAX, GENTLEMAN.

" This is a very good and a very interesting work. It is designed to trace the career from boyhood to age of a perfect man—a Christian gentleman, and it abounds in incident both well and highly wrought. Throughout it is conceived in a high spirit, and written with great ability, better than any former work, we think, of its deservedly successful author. This cheap and handsome new edition is worthy to pass freely from hand to hand, as a gift book in many households."—*Examiner.*

"The new and cheaper edition of this interesting work will doubtless meet with great success. John Halifax, the hero of this most beautiful story, is no ordinary hero, and this, his history, is no ordinary book. It is a full-length portrait of a true gentleman, one of nature's own nobility. It is also the history of a home and a thoroughly English one. The work abounds in incident, and many of the scenes are full of graphic power and true pathos. It is a book that few will read without becoming wiser and better."—*Scotsman*

VOL. III.—THE CRESCENT AND THE CROSS.

BY ELIOT WARBURTON.

"Independent of its value as an original narrative, and its useful and interesting information, this work is remarkable for the colouring power and play of fancy with which its descriptions are enlivened. Among its greatest and most lasting charms is its reverent and serious spirit."—*Quarterly Review*

"A book calculated to prove more practically useful was never penned than ' The Crescent and the Cross'—a work which surpasses all others in its homage for the sublime and its love for the beautiful in those famous regions consecrated to everlasting immortality in the annals of the prophets, and which no other writer has ever depicted with a pencil at once so reverent and so picturesque."—*Sun.*

VOL. IV.—NATHALIE. BY JULIA KAVANAGH.

"' Nathalie ' is Miss Kavanagh's best imaginative effort. Its manner is gracious and attractive. Its matter is good. A sentiment, a tenderness, are commanded by her which are as individual as they are elegant. We should not soon come to an end were we to specify all the delicate touches and attractive pictures which place ' Nathalie' high among books of its class."—*Athenæum.*

VOL. V.—A WOMAN'S THOUGHTS ABOUT WOMEN.

BY THE AUTHOR OF "JOHN HALIFAX, GENTLEMAN."

" A book of sound counsel. It is one of the most sensible works of its kind, well-written, true-hearted, and altogether practical. Whoever wishes to give advice to a young lady may thank the author for means of doing so."—*Examiner.*

HURST AND BLACKETT'S STANDARD LIBRARY
OF CHEAP EDITIONS.

Each in a single volume, elegantly printed, bound, and illustrated, price 5s.

VOL. VI.—ADAM GRAEME, OF MOSSGRAY.
BY THE AUTHOR OF "MRS. MARGARET MAITLAND."

"'Adam Graeme' is a story awakening genuine emotions of interest and delight by its admirable pictures of Scottish life and scenery. The eloquent author sets before us the essential attributes of Christian virtue, their deep and silent workings in the heart, and their beautiful manifestations in the life, with a delicacy, a power, and a truth which can hardly be surpassed."—*Morning Post.*

VOL. VII.—SAM SLICK'S WISE SAWS
AND MODERN INSTANCES.

"The humour of Sam Slick is inexhaustible. He is ever and everywhere a welcome visitor; smiles greet his approach, and wit and wisdom hang upon his tongue. The present production is remarkable alike for its racy humour, its sound philosophy, the felicity of its illustrations, and the delicacy of its satire."—*Post.*

VOL. VIII.—CARDINAL WISEMAN'S RECOLLECTIONS
OF THE LAST FOUR POPES.

"A picturesque book on Rome and its ecclesiastical sovereigns, by an eloquent Roman Catholic. Cardinal Wiseman has here treated a special subject with so much generality and geniality, that his recollections will excite no ill-feeling in those who are most conscientiously opposed to every idea of human infallibity represented in Papal domination."—*Athenæum.*

VOL. IX.—A LIFE FOR A LIFE.
BY THE AUTHOR OF "JOHN HALIFAX, GENTLEMAN."

"We are always glad to welcome Miss Muloch. She writes from her own convictions, and she has the power not only to conceive clearly what it is that she wishes to say, but to express it in language effective and vigorous. In 'A Life for a Life' she is fortunate in a good subject, and she has produced a work of strong effect. The reader having read the book through for the story, will be apt (if he be of our persuasion) to return and read again many pages and passages with greater pleasure than on a first perusal. The whole book in replete with a graceful, tender delicacy; and in addition to its other merits, it is written in good careful English."—*Athenæum.*

VOL. X.—THE OLD COURT SUBURB. BY LEIGH HUNT.

"A delightful book, of which the charm begins at the first line on the first page, for full of quaint and pleasant memories is the phrase that is its title, 'The Old Court Suburb.' Very full too, both of quaint and pleasant memories is the line that designates the author. It is the name of the most cheerful of chroniclers, the best of remembrancers of good things, the most polished and entertaining of educated gossips 'The Old Court Suburb' is a work that will be welcome to all readers, and most welcome to those who have a love for the best kinds of reading."—*Examiner.*

VOL. XI.—MARGARET AND HER BRIDESMAIDS.

"We may save ourselves the trouble of giving any lengthened review of this work, for we recommend all who are in search of a fascinating novel to read it for themselves. They will find it well worth their while. There are a freshness and originality about it quite charming, and there is a certain nobleness in the treatment both of sentiment and incident which is not often found."—*Athenæum.*

VOL. XII.—THE OLD JUDGE. BY SAM SLICK.

"These popular sketches, in which the Author of 'Sam Slick' paints Nova Scotian life, form the 12th Volume of Messrs Hurst and Blackett's Standard Library of Modern Works. The publications included in this Library have all been of good quality; many give information while they entertain, and of that class the book before us is a specimen. The manner in which the Cheap Editions forming the series is produced deserves especial mention. The paper and print are unexceptional; there is a steel engraving in each volume, and the outsides of them will satisfy the purchaser who likes to see a regiment of books in handsome uniform."—*Examiner.*

2490

HURST AND BLACKETT'S STANDARD LIBRARY
OF CHEAP EDITIONS.

Each in a single volume, elegantly printed, bound, and illustrated, price 5s.

VOL. XIII.—DARIEN. BY ELIOT WARBURTON.

"This last production, from the pen of the author of 'The Crescent and the Cross,' has the same elements of a very wide popularity. It will please its thousands."—*Globe.*
"We have seldom met with any work in which the realities of history and the poetry of fiction were more happily interwoven."—*Illustrated News.*

VOL. XIV.—FAMILY ROMANCE; OR, DOMESTIC ANNALS OF THE ARISTOCRACY.
BY SIR BERNARD BURKE, ULSTER KING OF ARMS.

"It were impossible to praise too highly as a work of amusement this most interesting book, whether we should have regard to its excellent plan or its not less excellent execution. It ought to be found on every drawing-room table. Here you have nearly fifty captivating romances with the pith of all their interest preserved in undiminished poignancy, and any one may be read in half an hour. It is not the least of their merits that the romances are founded on fact—or what, at least, has been handed down for truth by long tradition—and the romance of reality far exceeds the romance of fiction."—*Standard.*

VOL. XV.—THE LAIRD OF NORLAW.
BY THE AUTHOR OF "MARGARET MAITLAND."

"In this delightful work Scottish life and character, in connection with the fortunes of the house of Norlaw, are delineated with truly artistic skill. The plot of the tale is simple, but the incidents with which it is interwoven are highly wrought and dramatic in their effect, and altogether there is a fascination about the work which holds the attention spell-bound from the first page to the last."—*Herald.*

VOL. XVI.—THE ENGLISHWOMAN IN ITALY.
BY MRS. G. GRETTON.

"Mrs. Gretton had opportunities which rarely fall to the lot of strangers of becoming acquainted with the inner life and habits of a part of the Italian peninsula which is the very centre of the national crisis. We can praise her performance as interesting, unexaggerated, and full of opportune instruction."—*The Times.*

VOL. XVII.—NOTHING NEW.
BY THE AUTHOR OF "JOHN HALIFAX, GENTLEMAN."

"We cordially commend this book. The same graphic power, deep pathos, healthful sentiment, and masterly execution, which place that beautiful work 'John Halifax,' among the English Classics, are everywhere displayed."—*Chronicle.*

VOL XVIII.—THE LIFE OF JEANNE D'ALBRET.
BY MISS FREER.

"We have read this book with great pleasure, and have no hesitation in recommending it to general perusal. It reflects the highest credit on the industry and ability of Miss Freer. Nothing can be more interesting than her story of the life of Jeanne D'Albret, and the narrative is as trustworthy as it is attractive."—*Post.*

VOL. XIX.—THE VALLEY OF A HUNDRED FIRES.
BY THE AUTHOR OF "MARGARET AND HER BRIDESMAIDS."

"We know no novel of the last three or four years to equal this latest production of the popular authoress of 'Margaret and her Bridesmaids.' If asked to classify it, we should give it a place between 'John Halifax' and 'The Caxtons.'"—*Herald.*

VOL. XX.—THE ROMANCE OF THE FORUM.
BY PETER BURKE, SERJEANT AT LAW. (January 1862.)

"This attractive work will be read with much interest. It contains a great variety o singular and highly romantic stories."—*John Bull.*